COUNTRIES AT
THE CROSSROADS

COUNTRIES AT THE CROSSROADS

A Survey of Democratic Governance

Sanja Kelly

Christopher Walker

Jake Dizard

EDITORS

FREEDOM HOUSE

NEW YORK • WASHINGTON, D.C.

ROWMAN & LITTLEFIELD PUBLISHERS, INC.

LANHAM • BOULDER • NEW YORK • TORONTO • PLYMOUTH, UK

ROWMAN & LITTLEFIELD PUBLISHERS, INC.

Published in the United States of America
by Rowman & Littlefield Publishers, Inc.
A wholly owned subsidary of The Rowman & Littlefield Publishing Group, Inc.
4501 Forbes Boulevard, Suite 200, Lanham, Maryland 20706
www.rowmanlittlefield.com

Estover Road, Plymouth PL6 7PY, United Kingdom

Library of Congress Cataloging-in-Publication Data

Countries at the crossroads : a survey of democratic governance / Sanha Kelly,
    Christopher Walker, Jake Dizard, editors.
        p. cm. — (Countries at the crossroads)
    ISBN-13: 978-0-7425-5898-4 (cloth : alk. paper)
    ISBN-10: 0-7425-5898-3 (cloth : alk. paper)
    ISBN-13: 978-0-7425-5899-1 (pbk. : alk. paper)
    ISBN-10: 0-7425-5899-1 (pbk. : alk. paper)
    1. Democracy—Case studies. 2. Representative government and representation—
Case studies. I. Kelly, Sanha. II. Walker, Christopher, 1964– III. Dizard, Jake.
JC423.C7196 2008
321.8—dc22

                                                                    2007046022

Printed in the United States of America

∞™ The paper used in this publication meets the minimum requirements of American
National Standard for Information Sciences—Permanence of Paper for Printed Library
Materials, ANSI/NISO Z39.48-1992.

CONTENTS

COUNTRIES AT THE CROSSROADS
2006–2007

2006 COUNTRIES	2007 COUNTRIES
Armenia	Algeria
Azerbaijan	Angola
Bahrain	Bangladesh
Cambodia	Bhutan
East Timor	Bolivia
Georgia	Burkina Faso
Guatemala	China
Guyana	Colombia
Indonesia	Ecuador
Jordan	Egypt
Kazakhstan	Eritrea
Kenya	Ethiopia
Kyrgyzstan	Honduras
Malawi	Iran
Malaysia	Laos
Morocco	Libya
Nepal	Mauritania
Nicaragua	Mozambique
Nigeria	Paraguay
Pakistan	Peru
Sierra Leone	Philippines
South Africa	Russia
Sri Lanka	Rwanda
Tanzania	Swaziland
Uganda	Syria
Ukraine	Tajikistan
Venezuela	Thailand
Vietnam	Tunisia
Yemen	Turkey
Zimbabwe	Zambia

ACKNOWLEDGMENTS

Countries at the Crossroads is the product of the collective contributions of numerous Freedom House staff members and consultants. This study was also made possible by the generous support of the Bureau of Democracy, Human Rights, and Labor at the U.S. Department of State, and the U.S. Agency for International Development.

Country report authors made an outstanding contribution to this effort, working to produce thirty clear, informed analyses of a highly diverse group of countries. The report authors are: Jennie E. Burnet, Dan Connell, John Daniel, Bradford Dillman, Jake Dizard, Stephen Fairbanks, Thomas Gold, Paul Hutchcroft, Cédric Jourde, Edmond Keller, Michael Kevane, Stephen King, Harvey Kline, Peter Lambert, David Lesch, Robert Lloyd, Lawrence Markowitz, Duncan McCargo, Andrés Mejía Acosta, Alison Pargeter, Imogen Parsons, Orlando J. Pérez, Fahim Quadir, Sarah Repucci, David Simon, Kathryn Stoner-Weiss, Martin Stuart-Fox, Denis Sullivan, Donna Lee Van Cott, and Richard Whitecross.

A group of distinguished regional experts served on the advisory committee, providing valuable input on the narratives and scores. They are: Morton Abramowitz, Lisa Anderson, Joel Barkan, Linda Beck, Daniel Brumberg, John Carey, John Entelis, Nina Khrushcheva, Rene Lamarchand, Tom Lansner, Terrence Lyons, Carrie Manning, Amit Pandya, Michael Shifter, Peter Sinnott, Bridget Welsh, Elizabeth Wishnick, and Coletta Youngers.

The *Countries at the Crossroads* methodology was originally developed with the expert contribution of a group of senior advisers, including Larry Diamond, Hoover Institution; Paul Martin, Columbia University; Rick Messick, World Bank; Ted Piccone, Open Society Institute; Louise Shelley, American University; and Ruth Wedgwood, Johns Hopkins University. Jay Verkuilen of the University of Illinois, Urbana-Champaign, provided invaluable guidance, in addition to his participation in the methodology committee.

Freedom House staff devoted extensive time and energy to launch this year's edition. Sanja Kelly was the managing editor of the study. Christopher Walker, director of studies, and Thomas Melia, deputy executive director of Freedom House, provided overall guidance and support for the project, in addition to serving on the survey's internal review committee. Research Analyst and Assistant Editor Jake Dizard and Editorial and Research Assistant Tyler Roylance supplied important research, editorial, and administrative support, as did staff members Elizabeth Floyd, Astrid Larson, Katrina Neubauer, and Thomas Webb, and interns Ilana Abrahams, Rose Grogan, Douglas Horn, and Amy Rossnagel. Colleagues in the Washington, D.C. and other Freedom House offices supplied important feedback on the reports. Nancy van Itallie copyedited the volume. Ida Walker was the proofreader, and Beverly Butterfield designed and typeset the volume.

EXPERT ADVISORY COMMITTEE

RULING BY LAW:
AMBITIONS AND LIMITS OF THE
TWENTY-FIRST CENTURY AUTHORITARIAN MODEL

Christopher Walker and Sanja Kelly

"There's no quick fix." These shrewd words were spoken by a senior World Health Organization official commenting on the food and product safety scandals that broke in 2007 and drew the world's attention to two of China's several emerging crises.[1] A steady stream of news reports chronicled the thousands of products requiring recall, ranging from tainted pet food to lead-laced children's toys. But the observation on the absence of quick fixes for complex problems has far wider implications for Chinese society, which now faces development challenges on a range of fronts.

Explosive growth, for example, has brought with it catastrophic environmental damage, apparently costing hundreds of thousands of Chinese lives each year. The tens of thousands of local protests bubbling up across China, an expression of increasing expectations and frustrations, are testing officials' capacity to respond with better governance. Meanwhile, Chinese officials are under pressure from other quarters for improved performance. International nongovernmental organizations have seized on China's hosting of the Olympic Games in Beijing in 2008 as an opportunity to shine a bright light on the less desirable aspects of the Chinese system, including dreadful records on civil liberties and political rights.

This intensive and, for China's leaders, unwelcome scrutiny has moved the leadership from its comfort zone—delivering economic growth—and is slowly putting pressure on the government to focus not only on growth but on dealing with its by-products. This includes mounting demands for government responsiveness to ordinary citizens' needs.

Christopher Walker is Director of Studies at Freedom House. **Sanja Kelly** is Managing Editor of *Countries at the Crossroads*, Freedom House's annual survey of democratic governance.

1

To date, the Chinese authorities have executed a finely calibrated balancing act, seeking to offset emerging calls for political accountability with continued economic expansion. Recent events, however, suggest that this task is becoming increasingly difficult. The relatively incremental and often cosmetic reforms the Chinese have pursued so far appear inadequate for meeting the unyielding demands that accompany integration in the global economic system, the ever more probing attention of international watchdogs, and most important, the inclinations of ordinary Chinese citizens, who no longer seem quite as ready to accept the corrupt and substandard governance that the Chinese Communist Party has offered to date.

The stakes are exceptionally high in this endeavor. Stewardship of the country's natural environment has emerged as a potential Achilles' heel. The environment is, however, only one of a number of significant and growing challenges. The Chinese government is being scrutinized for its management of the country's fraying social safety net; the fallout from major, periodic public health crises; and its response to the massive demographic dislocations that have accompanied booming economic growth.

The piecemeal, clumsy, and sometimes brutal manner in which the authorities have dealt with these issues calls into serious doubt whether a system that is economically dynamic but whose political leadership is unaccountable to public opinion can survive over the long haul. The ability of China's leaders to pass this formidable test will determine not only the survival of China's authoritarian-capitalist project; it will also signal whether this system remains an attractive model for other developing countries to emulate.

The Russian Model

The emergence of a twenty-first-century authoritarian-capitalist model is not limited to China. Russia, another regional power with ambitions on the global stage, is developing a model of governance that denies basic political rights for its citizens and shuns democratic accountability, while charting an economic course that is capitalist, albeit with deep state involvement in economic affairs. President Vladimir Putin's Kremlin presents what it calls "sovereign democracy" as its paradigm for governance. This concept, which in practice contains little in the way of genuine democratic governance, is also held out as an example for hybrid regimes and autocracies on the Russian Federation's periphery.

Russia, too, is facing a number of daunting societal challenges: a looming HIV/AIDS scourge, a withering demographic crisis manifested by a rapidly shrinking population, and runaway corruption that touches virtually every sector and gnaws at society's fabric. In Russia, as in China, a system whose leadership operates by hoarding power and strictly controlling politics, policy, and information finds itself at a severe disadvantage when managing simmering societal grievances.

In order to acquire a deeper understanding of the forces at work in leading powers such as China and Russia, along with a set of other strategically important states, Freedom House examines their governments' performance in *Countries at the Crossroads*, its annual survey of democratic governance.

Countries at the Crossroads provides detailed written analysis and comparative data on sixty critical, policy-relevant countries. The polities evaluated represent a range of systems: traditional or constitutional monarchies, one-party states or outright dictatorships, oil-rich petrostates, and states where democratic reforms have stalled. A new edition of *Crossroads* is published each year, with one set of thirty countries analyzed in odd-numbered years and the other thirty in even-numbered years. In this way, *Crossroads* covers an extensive range of countries while offering readers useful time-series data, as well as comprehensive narrative evaluation of the progress and backsliding in each country.

Crossroads' methodology examines in fine detail issues that illuminate the degree to which government authorities are meeting basic standards of democratic accountability. The survey examines four core dimensions of governance: accountability and public voice, civil liberties, the rule of law, and anticorruption and transparency. Within these main thematic areas, eighteen specific subareas are evaluated.

Corruption in the Absence of Democratically Accountable Institutions

The deficiencies the *Crossroads* analysis identifies in the Chinese and Russian systems do not by themselves suggest that either regime is in imminent danger of breakdown or implosion. Strong economic growth in both countries provides a considerable cushion for the state in the near to medium term. Russian and Chinese leaders are also quite adept at using the levers of state power to repress independent voices and institutions—with lethal brutality when deemed necessary.

However, the reports do suggest that the inability of critical institutions to play a meaningful and independent role in these societies raises fundamental questions about whether genuine and enduring reform can be achieved, particularly in combating deeply entrenched corruption. Self-policing or reform by decree hold dim prospects for success in the absence of a well-functioning, independent judiciary, civil society, or news media, all of which are currently sidelined as independent actors in China and Russia.

The 2007 *Crossroads* report on China notes that over the past three decades, "the Chinese Communist Party (CCP) has been reshaping the PRC into a market-based and globally integrated economy, society, and culture. It labels this project 'socialism with Chinese characteristics.'" The report further observes that "while producing gross domestic product (GDP) growth rates that are among the world's highest, the party's strategy has led to the sort of severe inequality, weak social-welfare system, worker exploitation, job insecurity, and environmental degradation that is associated with capitalism at its worst."

The Russian authorities' current governance experiment is also built on soft sand. The *Crossroads* report on Russia observes that "by 2005, having endured significant rollbacks of electoral rights, Russia could no longer be considered a democracy at all according to most metrics," and that "the country has come to resemble the autocratic regimes of Central Asia more than the consolidated democracies of Eastern Europe that have recently joined the European Union."

One of the stubborn threads that run through the Chinese and Russian systems is the hard line the authorities consistently take toward news media. The precise methods for controlling politically consequential media content differ somewhat in the two systems, although the effects are quite similar. The ability of news organizations to report independently on the performance of officials and other powerful interests, scrutinize policies, and cover public health and other critical issues is severely limited.

Control of information and politically consequential discourse is a dominant feature of both systems. In Russia, "the media remain tightly controlled by the presidential administration, and over the last seven years Russia has been one of the three most dangerous places in the world to be a journalist (behind Iraq and Colombia)." Under President Putin's leadership, the news media, especially television, have been brought under the sway of the authorities in some ways reminiscent of the Soviet era.

In China, "the CCP views the media as an instrument to articulate and support its policies; to mobilize, unite, and divert the people; and to manage the impressions it gives to its own citizens and the outside world."

With the Chinese and Russian economies deeply integrating into the global system, it is not enough to control domestic media. International reputation matters, too. Both China and Russia have enlisted the help of high-powered Western public relations firms for image management purposes and, in certain cases, to deal with looming crises. China in particular has sought Western consultancies to help manage the scrutiny that accompanies the hosting of the 2008 Olympics. The recent consumer-product scandals' threat to the "Made in China" brand has also caused Chinese officials to enlist the help of outside image managers. PR management alone, however, is unlikely to ameliorate the deep structural challenges these two systems confront.

The limits of cosmetic approaches to reform are visible in the pervasive corruption that has defied reform edicts and state-directed media campaigns in China and Russia. Not surprisingly, official corruption is one of the greatest burdens on the two systems—and one of the greatest threats to the leadership in these countries.

Corruption is often a symptom of other systemic pathologies. As dominant power holders wield effectively unchecked authority, existing mechanisms tend not to be sufficient for addressing corrupt practices. *Crossroads* findings note the glaring inadequacy in the efforts to combat corruption at all levels, especially the grand corruption that finds its way into the countries' most lucrative strategic sectors. The judiciary, which should be one of the frontline defenses against corruption, is kept on a short leash. The *Crossroads* China report notes that the country's "judiciary remains a tool of the CCP, and it rarely shows signs of independence or autonomy. The courts, including the Supreme People's Court, are answerable to the National People's Congress."

Russia's judicial system has been subjected to an increasingly harsh campaign of manipulation and control in which executive branch interference in politically or economically consequential cases is a regular occurrence. President Putin's "dictatorship of law" has not made headway against the corruption and bribery that pervade the judicial process and drain sound judgment and impartiality from court rulings. As a result, average Russians have little faith in the system and see little reason to address grievances through the courts. This lack of faith has prompted many Russian citizens to seek justice beyond Russia's borders—in the European Court of Human Rights—where by mid-2007, 22,700 of the pending 99,600 cases, or 22.8 percent, were Russian, a 400 percent increase over figures from 2000.

Authoritarian Projection of Influence Abroad

China and Russia are also actively exerting influence abroad. China, for example, provides material and political support to odious regimes in Sudan, Burma, North Korea, and Zimbabwe. Russia, for its part, works to undermine nascent democratic reform in neighboring countries such as Georgia and Ukraine.

Energy plays a pivotal role in these countries' international approaches. Russia, rich in crude oil and natural gas, exerts influence in neighboring former Soviet states by using its energy resources to subsidize politically friendly, autocratic countries and pressure states that display disloyalty to the Kremlin. Energy-hungry Beijing, on the other hand, is scouring the globe in pursuit of oil and gas to fuel its economy and is willing to do whatever it takes to enter into energy deals with some of the world's worst governments. There is little to suggest that the government in either one of these countries is yet prepared to act consistently as a responsible stakeholder on the international stage.

At the same time, both China and Russia crave the cachet of membership in Western and international organizations. The China report notes that China "sought to export revolution in the 1960s [but] now revels in its prestige as a prominent member of the UN Security Council and the World Trade Organization (WTO), its hosting of the 2008 Summer Olympics and the 2010 World Expo in Shanghai." Russia, for its part, in 2006 held the presidency of the Group of Eight (G8) industrialized nations and the chairmanship of the Council of Europe, whose mandate is to promote human rights and democracy and uphold the rule of law in Europe. The country was recently selected to host the Winter Olympics in Sochi in 2014.

The Chinese and Russian models are being viewed carefully by leaders in a host of developing countries. Leaders in China and Russia have looked at each other's experience, as well, and drawn certain conclusions about how most effectively to pursue their development and bolster regime security.

The challenges that China and Russia confront are complex and daunting. The authorities in these countries do their societies no favors by denying ordinary citizens and critical domestic institutions the opportunity to play a meaningful and sorely needed role in their countries' political life. The governance of these countries is relevant not only to their citizens, however. In an integrated world, no country or person is entirely immune from the problems of its neighbors. In China's case, public health pandemics, such as SARS and HIV/AIDS, do not respect national borders. The fallout from China's polluted environment wafts over neighboring countries in Asia and as far as the west coast of the United States. The international community therefore does not have the luxury of remaining a passive observer on the fundamental issues of democratic governance in these two critical and strategically important countries.

REGIONAL REVIEW OF SELECT COUNTRIES FROM *CROSSROADS* 2007

Middle East and North Africa

In **Iran**, President Ahmadinejad was elected on the promise of bringing Iran's oil wealth to the "dinner table" of ordinary Iranians. Instead, unemployment has risen along with inflation, and Iran's small refining capacity—the country imports 40 percent of its gasoline, at US$4 billion each year—has forced an easing of long-standing subsidies at the pump. Rationing implemented in 2007 now limits cars to less than a gallon a day. Meanwhile, Iran is in the throes of the harshest crackdown since the 1979 Islamist revolution, with women and student activists, media, and Iranian-American scholars and aid workers in the crosshairs. The *Crossroads* 2007 evaluation of Iran noted the ongoing problem of interference in the democratic process by unelected bodies. The dominance of the Supreme Leader and the Council of Guardians was evident in the vetting process of candidates. The report found erosion in several areas from what were already weak scores. Rule of law registered a decrease on the basis of heightened political interference by the executive branch and especially harassment and detention of lawyers for political activists or people charged with offenses supposedly endangering national security. Iran's civil liberties record also deteriorated. National security is used as grounds for political arrests or surveillance. In 2007, four Iranian-American dual citizens were arbitrarily detained in cases that attracted worldwide attention.

Egypt saw declines across a number of sectors. This was reflected in not-so-subtle manipulations of the electoral process in both the presidential and parliamentary elections of 2005. The country also suffered a decline in effective and accountable government due to extralegal pressure and a constitutional change that resulted in the limiting of the power of judges to monitor the executive (especially during elections). A repressive 2006 media law that sets forth thirty-five offenses punishable by prison, as well as restrictions on internet reporting, reduced Egypt's media freedom score. A decline in freedom of association was registered, the result of the heavy-handed tactics of security forces during and after the 2005 elections. These included imprisonment of Muslim Brotherhood members and particularly aggressive suppression of protests, with reported sexual battery of female protesters.

Sub-Saharan Africa

In **Ethiopia**, the past two years have featured a mix of advances and setbacks. Prior to the 2005 elections, Ethiopia saw a dramatic increase in civil society and media activity. Despite accusations from the opposition of fraud, intimidation, and disappearances, the run-up to the elections was more open than in previous instances, resulting in a small rise in the accountability and public voice score. The aftermath, however, sent the country back toward repression. Opposition-led protests concerning electoral grievances resulted in nearly 200 deaths by late 2005, along with mass detentions and the arrest of journalists, activists, and opposition members on allegations including treason and genocide. Since April 2007, many of these people have been released, acquitted, or pardoned. Nonetheless, the press, civil society, and would-be opposition supporters are still feeling repercussions. Media freedom remains highly restricted, and most outlets now exercise self-restraint to avoid attention from the government. Meanwhile, corruption has been on the rise, as weak checks on the actions of public officials, conflicts of interest between the private and public sectors, and a lack of transparency impede progress in reducing graft.

Mauritania enjoyed the most significant positive change among the thirty countries examined in the survey. The country's bloodless coup in August 2005, which ousted Colonel Maaouya Sid Ahmed Taya, initiated a transition to democracy that has the potential to alter the political system fundamentally. Since the coup, the conduct of elections and press freedoms have improved, and a liberalized political environment accounts for significant rises in all of the country's scores. Whether liberalization will be sustained or advanced remains uncertain, however. Mauritania still confronts a legacy of weak civilian control of the military, pervasive clientelism, and the marginalization of the country's non-Arabic speaking communities. The most significant improvement appeared in the accountability and public voice section, where preelection reforms, including a new electoral commission and census, as well as new rules for voting by the military, enhanced the process. Moreover, the state relaxed restrictions on civil society organizations beginning in 2005. Media freedom improved based on a 2006 media law that eliminated some of the harshest previous forms of censorship and state control.

Asia-Pacific

Bangladesh underwent a sharp drop in the accountability and public voice category as a result of the stalemate over parliamentary elections that developed in late 2006 and culminated in the military takeover of January 2007. Further erosion resulted from the weakening of effective separation of powers during the coverage period. This included a concerted effort by political parties to increase their influence over judicial appointments and processes. Civil liberties also declineed as a result of increased party beatings and mass arrests combined with decreased effectiveness in citizens' means of redress.

In the **Philippines**, despite competitive elections over the past decade and a half, several features of the political system tarnish the quality of freedom, including rising concerns about the integrity of electoral institutions, civilian killings, and military unrest. These negative trends account for the declines the Philippines suffered over the *Crossroads* coverage period. Pressure on the media is among the challenges the country confronts. Although the Philippine media are free of official state censorship, journalists have faced increases in harassment by local politicians and powerful business interests. Killings of civilian activists, leftists, and church personnel continued in 2005 and 2006.

Democratic advances achieved in **Thailand** since the end of military rule in 1992 were abruptly reversed in September 2006 when a military junta, calling itself the Council for National Security (CNS) ousted the country's divisive prime minister Thaksin Shinawatra. The CNS selected a former army commander, Surayudh Chulanont, as prime minister, abrogated the 1997 constitution, and established an unelected Parliament. Although the coup leaders initially enjoyed popular support, promising a new constitution and elections, the country remains in crisis as Thaksin's allies persist in their protests, and the new government has not yet followed through on reestablishing democracy. Thailand underwent a significant drop on the *Crossroads* elections indicator due in large part to the coup but also to the progressive enfeeblement of democratic institutions earlier under the Thaksin regime, including the dominance of the Thai Rak Thai party and the dissolution of Parliament in 2006. Between 2005 and 2007, political violence continued in Thailand's southern border provinces, where the majority of citizens are ethnic Malay Muslims; by early 2007, more than 2,000 people had been killed by either security forces or Islamist extremists.

Latin America

In **Peru,** institutional weakness continued as a primary factor inhibiting more rapid development. The 2006 election did not result in substantially better political party dynamics. Although the justice system began to show signs of improvement—reflected in a small boost in the rule of law category—Peruvians' faith in such institutions as the police and judiciary remained very low. Anticorruption enforcement, although vastly reformed from the 1990 to 2000 regime of Alberto Fujimori, was not strong enough to act as a credible deterrent to corruption. Impunity also remained the norm for human rights violations that occurred during the internal conflict of 1980 to 2000. Despite the complexity of institutional reform, Peruvian GDP continued to climb rapidly, reaching 8 percent in 2006, and as of March 2007, President Alan Garcia's approval ratings remained high.

In **Colombia**, President Alvaro Uribe's 2006 reelection victory, which followed a constitutional change in 2005 allowing him to run for a second term, was approved by international observers as free and fair. However, later in 2006 information emerged that seemed to provide proof of long-rumored links between paramilitaries and government officials. Subsequent investigations discovered paramilitary influence in the Congress, the national prosecutor's office, the military, and the judiciary, highlighting the threats to the rule of law stemming from Colombia's ongoing battle with rebel groups. These discoveries detracted from Uribe's otherwise notable efforts to improve security and contain paramilitary factions and caused Colombia's scores to decline somewhat. In order to deal with its internal conflict, the government initiated talks with the National Liberation Army guerrillas and completed the demobilization of 30,000 members of the paramilitary known as the United Self-Defense Forces of Colombia. The demobilization occurred under the terms of the 2006 Justice and Peace Law, which offered reduced sentences for former paramilitaries in return for the surrender of weapons and ill-gotten assets. Nonetheless, serious questions remained about the legislation's perceived leniency and whether prosecutors were given enough time and resources to conduct adequate investigations.

NOTE

[1] Henk Bekedam, the World Health Organization's top representative in China, quoted in David Barboza, "China Moves to Change Damaged Global Image," *New York Times*, 29 July 2007.

COMPARATIVE COUNTRY SCORES:
ACCOUNTABILITY AND PUBLIC VOICE

Country	Electoral Laws and Elections	Effective and Accountable Government	Civic Engagement	Media Independence
Algeria	3.00	2.75	2.67	3.00
Angola	1.75	1.75	3.33	3.00
Bangladesh	2.50	2.00	5.00	4.25
Bhutan	1.75	4.00	3.00	4.50
Bolivia	4.75	3.50	5.00	5.00
Burkina Faso	2.50	3.25	4.33	4.00
China	0.25	1.75	1.67	1.00
Colombia	4.50	4.25	5.00	4.50
Ecuador	4.25	2.75	5.00	4.50
Egypt	1.25	2.50	2.00	1.75
Eritrea	0.00	1.25	0.00	0.50
Ethiopia	1.25	3.25	1.67	1.25
Honduras	4.75	2.75	4.00	4.38
Iran	1.75	1.75	2.00	1.00
Laos	0.50	1.75	1.00	1.38
Libya	0.25	1.00	0.33	1.13
Mauritania	3.50	2.75	4.00	4.00
Mozambique	3.75	3.75	5.33	4.25
Paraguay	3.75	3.25	5.67	4.50
Peru	5.50	3.50	3.33	4.88
Philippines	3.25	3.25	6.00	4.13
Russia	2.00	3.00	2.00	2.50
Rwanda	1.25	1.75	1.33	1.38
Swaziland	0.25	1.75	3.00	2.50
Syria	1.25	2.00	1.00	1.38
Tajikistan	1.25	1.50	1.67	1.63
Thailand	2.25	2.75	4.33	2.63
Tunisia	1.25	3.00	1.33	1.38
Turkey	5.25	4.00	4.33	4.00
Zambia	4.25	4.00	4.33	3.75

COMPARATIVE COUNTRY SCORES:
CIVIL LIBERTIES

Country	Protection from State Terror/ Torture	Gender Equity	Minority Rights	Freedom of Belief	Freedom of Association
Algeria	2.43	3.75	3.75	2.00	3.40
Angola	2.14	3.25	2.75	3.00	3.00
Bangladesh	2.29	4.00	4.00	5.33	4.20
Bhutan	5.00	4.00	2.25	4.33	3.00
Bolivia	3.00	3.25	3.75	6.00	4.80
Burkina Faso	3.00	3.75	4.50	6.00	3.80
China	1.57	3.50	2.50	1.33	1.80
Colombia	2.86	4.00	3.25	5.67	4.00
Ecuador	2.43	4.25	3.75	6.00	4.20
Egypt	1.14	2.25	2.75	2.33	1.80
Eritrea	0.29	3.50	0.75	0.00	0.20
Ethiopia	2.00	3.25	3.00	4.00	2.00
Honduras	2.71	3.25	2.75	6.00	4.00
Iran	1.14	1.75	2.00	2.00	1.80
Laos	1.14	3.25	2.75	3.00	1.80
Libya	1.29	3.00	1.00	1.67	0.80
Mauritania	2.86	2.75	2.25	2.67	4.20
Mozambique	2.86	3.75	4.00	6.33	5.00
Paraguay	2.57	4.00	3.00	6.00	4.60
Peru	3.71	3.75	3.50	6.00	5.20
Philippines	2.00	4.00	3.50	5.33	4.40
Russia	2.57	4.00	3.00	4.00	3.00
Rwanda	1.14	2.75	2.00	2.00	1.40
Swaziland	2.57	2.50	2.75	5.67	2.40
Syria	1.43	2.75	2.00	3.00	1.60
Tajikistan	1.71	3.75	2.50	2.00	2.60
Thailand	3.00	3.75	3.50	4.00	4.00
Tunisia	2.43	4.25	4.00	2.67	2.20
Turkey	3.71	3.75	3.75	3.67	4.20
Zambia	4.00	3.50	4.75	6.00	5.00

COMPARATIVE COUNTRY SCORES:
RULE OF LAW

Country	Independent Judiciary	Civil/Criminal Proceedings	Accountability of Security Forces	Property Rights	Equal Rights
Algeria	2.20	2.67	1.50	4.00	3.33
Angola	2.20	2.50	2.75	2.00	3.67
Bangladesh	2.80	2.17	1.25	4.00	3.33
Bhutan	5.00	5.00	5.25	3.67	4.00
Bolivia	2.80	3.50	4.25	3.33	4.00
Burkina Faso	3.40	3.33	2.50	4.00	4.00
China	1.80	1.17	2.50	2.67	3.00
Colombia	5.00	3.83	2.75	4.00	3.33
Ecuador	2.40	3.00	3.00	4.33	3.33
Egypt	3.40	2.17	1.00	4.33	2.33
Eritrea	1.20	0.00	0.00	1.33	1.00
Ethiopia	2.00	2.17	2.25	1.67	3.67
Honduras	3.20	3.33	3.25	4.00	4.00
Iran	2.20	1.83	1.50	3.67	1.67
Laos	1.80	1.17	1.00	3.00	3.00
Libya	1.00	2.00	0.25	3.00	3.00
Mauritania	3.20	2.33	2.00	2.00	3.00
Mozambique	3.60	3.50	4.50	3.33	4.67
Paraguay	3.00	3.67	3.25	3.67	3.00
Peru	4.00	4.00	4.00	4.33	4.00
Philippines	3.80	3.00	2.00	4.33	3.33
Russia	3.20	3.00	2.50	3.33	3.67
Rwanda	1.20	0.50	1.50	1.33	1.67
Swaziland	2.00	2.17	1.00	2.33	3.00
Syria	1.80	2.83	1.00	3.00	2.33
Tajikistan	1.80	2.67	2.75	3.00	3.67
Thailand	4.60	4.67	2.00	4.33	3.33
Tunisia	2.20	2.67	1.75	4.00	4.00
Turkey	3.60	3.83	3.75	4.33	4.33
Zambia	5.00	3.33	4.75	3.33	4.33

COMPARATIVE COUNTRY SCORES:
ANTICORRUPTION AND TRANSPARENCY

Country	Environment Against Corruption	Anticorruption Standards	Anticorruption Enforcement	Governmental Transparency
Algeria	2.20	2.75	2.50	3.14
Angola	1.60	2.25	2.25	2.29
Bangladesh	1.80	2.25	2.75	3.00
Bhutan	3.60	5.00	4.75	3.14
Bolivia	2.40	3.00	3.50	3.43
Burkina Faso	3.00	3.25	3.25	3.71
China	2.80	2.50	2.50	2.14
Colombia	4.00	3.75	3.50	3.71
Ecuador	3.00	3.00	2.50	3.71
Egypt	1.60	1.25	1.75	2.29
Eritrea	1.00	1.50	0.50	0.43
Ethiopia	2.40	3.00	1.75	2.29
Honduras	3.20	3.25	3.25	2.86
Iran	1.40	2.50	1.50	2.00
Laos	1.80	1.75	1.00	2.00
Libya	0.80	0.75	0.50	0.57
Mauritania	2.80	3.00	2.75	2.14
Mozambique	2.80	3.00	3.25	3.86
Paraguay	2.80	3.75	3.50	3.29
Peru	3.40	3.25	3.75	3.57
Philippines	3.00	3.00	3.50	4.00
Russia	2.40	3.00	2.25	3.14
Rwanda	2.80	2.75	2.50	1.86
Swaziland	1.80	2.75	1.50	2.14
Syria	1.20	2.50	2.00	2.00
Tajikistan	1.60	1.25	1.50	2.14
Thailand	3.00	4.00	3.00	3.71
Tunisia	3.20	4.00	2.25	2.86
Turkey	3.20	4.00	3.50	3.86
Zambia	3.20	3.75	3.75	3.14

INTRODUCTION TO COUNTRY REPORTS

The *Countries at the Crossroads 2007* survey contains reports on thirty countries. Each report begins with a section containing basic political and economic data arranged in the following categories: **capital, population**, and gross national income (**GNI**) **per capita.** In addition, numerical ratings are provided for **Accountability and Public Voice, Civil Liberties, Rule of Law,** and **Anticorruption and Transparency.**

The **capital** was obtained from the CIA *World Factbook 2006.* Population data were obtained from the Population Reference Bureau's *2007 World Population Data Sheet.* Data on **GNI per capita** were obtained from the World Bank World Development Indicators database (www.worldbank.org).

The **Accountability and Public Voice, Civil Liberties, Rule of Law,** and **Anticorruption and Transparency** categories contain numerical ratings between 0 and 7 for each country, with 0 representing the weakest performance and 7 representing the strongest performance. For a full description of the methods used to determine the survey's ratings, please see the chapter "Survey Methodology."

Following the political and economic data, each country report is divided into five parts: an introduction, and analyses of **Accountability and Public Voice, Civil Liberties, Rule of Law,** and **Anticorruption and Transparency.** The introduction provides a brief historical background and a description of major events. The **Accountability and Public Voice, Civil Liberties, Rule of Law,** and **Anticorruption and Transparency** sections summarize each government's degree of respect for the rights and liberties covered in the *Countries at the Crossroads* survey. Each section contains a set of recommendations highlighting the specific areas of most immediate concern for the government to address.

ALGERIA

CAPITAL: Algiers
POPULATION: 34.1 million
GNI PER CAPITA: $3,030

SCORES	2005	2007
ACCOUNTABILITY AND PUBLIC VOICE:	2.90	2.85
CIVIL LIBERTIES:	2.90	3.07
RULE OF LAW:	2.49	2.74
ANTICORRUPTION AND TRANSPARENCY:	2.55	2.65

(scores are based on a scale of 0 to 7, with 0 representing weakest and 7 representing strongest performance)

Bradford Dillman

INTRODUCTION

Since Abdelaziz Bouteflika was elected president in 1999, Algeria has made considerable progress toward reducing internal violence, improving economic conditions, and reforming some public institutions. However, the government continues to deal with the aftermath of a violent struggle in the 1990s between the military and Islamist groups that left between 150,000 and 200,000 people dead. The conflict left a legacy of major human rights violations by government security forces, unfair multiparty elections, a state of emergency that limits free expression and association, and a widespread breakdown in the rule of law.

Between the end of 2004 and the beginning of 2007 the Algerian government instituted a process of "national reconciliation" designed to end residual violence by Islamists, offer amnesty to government and Islamist forces that had committed atrocities since the war's start in 1992, and provide compensation to some victims. The most important

Bradford L. Dillman is Associate Professor of International Political Economy at the University of Puget Sound. He is the author of numerous publications on Algeria and the political economy of the Middle East, including *State and Private Sector in Algeria: The Politics of Rent-seeking and Failed Development* (Boulder: Westview Press, 2000).

step in this process was a referendum in September 2005, in which voters overwhelmingly approved the Draft Charter for Peace and National Reconciliation, a document issued by Bouteflika in August 2005 that established a set of principles for laying to rest the crimes of the 1990s.

The charter called for granting amnesty to most insurgents, except for those who had committed massacres, rapes, and bombings. It also called for the end of legal proceedings against most insurgents and the release from jail of those already convicted. It offered compensation to the family members of those who had disappeared after arrest by security forces and held out the prospect of financial assistance to families of insurgents. It also praised, however, the actions of the army, security forces, and members of government-supported local militias called Patriots, and explicitly rejected the notion that the state (as distinct from individual agents of the state) was responsible for a deliberate policy of disappearances. It excluded from future political life anyone who had committed acts of terrorism or "instrumentalized" Islam.

The charter revealed that the formula Bouteflika is relying on to move the nation forward is "amnesty and amnesia" as opposed to "truth and reconciliation." In February 2006, Bouteflika issued several decrees that formally implemented the charter. His government offers immunity from prosecution to almost all of those who committed abuses during the war, an end to investigations of responsibility for human rights abuses, and an end to public discussion about atrocities.

Helped by dramatically higher oil and gas revenues, the state has lowered the unemployment rate and increased social spending and capital investment. Reports of human rights violations have declined sharply. Despite instances of attacks by armed groups, the government in recent years has significantly reduced threats to citizens' personal safety and property. Recent legal reforms give greater rights to women in the workplace and family.

Bouteflika has been unwilling, however, to spend his political capital on democratizing the political system and moving toward a market-propelled economy. His authoritarian and anti–private sector proclivities are evident in his resistance to political reforms, his crackdown on journalists, and his commitment to a substantially larger role for the state in the economy. Although he certainly faces opposition to some reforms from the military, his own party, and labor unions, his efforts to make public officials accountable, respect civil liberties, and strengthen the judiciary are inadequate and often half-hearted.

ACCOUNTABILITY AND PUBLIC VOICE

FREE AND FAIR ELECTORAL LAWS AND ELECTIONS:	3.00
EFFECTIVE AND ACCOUNTABLE GOVERNMENT:	2.75
CIVIC ENGAGEMENT AND CIVIC MONITORING:	2.67
MEDIA INDEPENDENCE AND FREEDOM OF EXPRESSION:	3.00
CATEGORY AVERAGE:	**2.85**

Algeria's elections in the last five years have had varying degrees of fairness and honesty. Turnout for the parliamentary elections in May 2002 was officially only 47 percent, and opposition parties complained of many instances of fraud. The National Liberation Front (FLN) gained 199 of 389 seats and has dominated the National Assembly in alliance with the National Democratic Rally (RND) and the Islamist-leaning Movement of Society of Peace (MSP). According to official figures, which opposition political parties claimed were inflated, 97 percent of voters approved the peace charter and turnout was 80 percent, despite a boycott by the two leading Berber parties.

Current electoral laws create a proportional representation system in which voters choose candidate lists in multimember districts. There is little evidence that campaign spending limits are enforced. Some political parties suggested potential revisions to the electoral code in advance of the May 2007 legislative elections, including quotas for female candidates on each party list and an open-list system whereby each voter could rank the names on the list that they vote for. However, in January 2007, Prime Minister Abdelaziz Belkhadem advocated changes to the electoral code that would likely reduce the competitiveness of elections, proposing that polling for local assemblies be switched to a winner-take-all system. He also suggested that the state cut off financial assistance to political parties that have very little support.[1] Moreover, the government failed to make revisions to the electoral code that would reduce the kinds of fraud and unfairness that characterized past elections.

By the end of March 2007, the Front of Socialist Forces (FFS) and the El-Islah party (the faction loyal to Islamist politician Abdallah Djaballah) called for a boycott of the May 2007 legislative elections.

Two-thirds of the seats in the upper house of parliament, the National Council, are filled through indirect elections by local assembly members within each of the country's forty-eight provinces (*wilayas*), and one-third are filled by presidential appointees. In the most recent (partial) elections in December 2006—in which half of the council's elected seats were up for grabs—the FLN won the majority of the seats. No party except the FLN and the RND—already governing allies—gained more than a handful of seats, revealing once again that the chronically lackluster indirect elections are heavily stacked in favor of the parties that dominate the local assemblies.

In the last presidential election in 2004, the government hampered the ability of Bouteflika's rivals to campaign effectively and gain press coverage. Two potentially strong candidates were prevented from running. Four losing candidates claimed, without offering specific evidence, that there was fraud and falsification of election results. In July 2006, Bouteflika announced his intention to revise the constitution, although his timetable for a referendum on constitutional revisions has been pushed back to sometime in 2007. Press reports indicate that he intends to amend the constitution so that he can stand for a third five-year term beginning in 2009. He is also expected to create the position of vice president and reinforce the powers of the president relative to the parliament. He has no apparent interest in letting political parties and civic groups participate in writing amendments.

The president's bid for more power, which contradicts his commitments to democratization of the political system, comes at a time when his health is in question. In November 2005, Bouteflika flew to France for extended treatment of an initially undisclosed medical condition. For more than three weeks the Algerian public did not know what their president was being treated for or how serious his illness was. Only belatedly did officials reveal that he had undergone surgery for a bleeding stomach ulcer. Even more troubling, Bouteflika disappeared from public view for seven weeks in the summer of 2006 with no explanation. This secrecy about his health and whereabouts is symptomatic of the broader lack of transparency in government.

The legislature and judiciary act more like rubber-stamp bodies than effective overseers of the executive branch. For example, Bouteflika presented his 2007 budget to the parliament in September 2006, and lawmakers passed it in November with only minor amendments. In January 2007, MSP leader Abou Djerra Soltani criticized the two legislative chambers for failing to exercise their basic responsibility as lawmakers. While the legislature does compel testimony of high-ranking officials and submit written questions to ministries, the impact on policies is limited. Parliamentary commissions of inquiry do not make their reports public. Most important draft laws are written by the executive. The president in recent years has made a habit of utilizing his constitutional prerogative to issue ordinances when the parliament is not in session. When it reconvenes, parliament must approve or reject the legislation, but there is little debate and no opportunity to introduce amendments. Legislation by decree also severely limits public involvement in policymaking.

The 1996 revised constitution forbids political parties from being formed on the basis of religion, ethnicity, gender, or regionalism. In order to gain legal status—and thus the rights to participate in elections, rent space, and create bank accounts—political parties need approval from the minister of the interior. The government has refused to authorize a number of parties in recent years. More significantly, the government refuses to permit any legal political role for former leading members of the defunct Islamic Salvation Front (FIS), an Islamist party whose victory in the first round of parliamentary elections in 1991 was overturned by a military coup in January 1992. The FIS was formally banned in 1992, and its members engaged in a violent struggle against the government until 1997, when its armed wing signed a truce with the government. Former FIS leaders Ali Benhadj and Abassi Madani were released from prison in June 2003 after ten years of incarceration, but Benhadj was re-arrested and imprisoned in the summer of 2005 for comments he made to Al-Jazeera television regarding the Iraqi insurgency. He was released in March 2006. The Interior Ministry has refused to authorize a new party—the Movement for Freedom and Social Justice—proposed in January 2007 by Anouar Haddam, a former FIS official who has lived in the United States for more than a decade. In effect, the government has frozen the political party landscape, hindering any effective challenge to the dominance of the FLN-RND-MSP coalition.

Selection, promotion, and dismissal in Algeria's civil service is often not based on open competition and merit. In July 2006, the government issued a new ordinance to govern work conditions in the civil service, but implementing legislation had yet to be issued by early 2007. The Algerian press has reported on the poor qualifications of many civil servants and frequent irregularities in civil-service exams.

Algeria's vocal civic associations and business organizations have a limited influence on legislation. The Interior Ministry refuses formal authorization to a number of nongovernmental organizations (NGOs) that are critical of government policies. The government consults on an ad hoc basis with associations representing private business owners (*le patronat*) and organized labor. Most domestic human rights NGOs have faced harassment, and it is illegal for them to receive funding from abroad. In September 2006, Amine Sidhoum Abderrahmane and Hassiba Boumerdassi, two human rights lawyers representing families of the disappeared, were charged with introducing unauthorized objects into a prison and were scheduled to be tried in February 2007. Similar forms of harassment of lawyers have occurred in the last three years.

Algeria has a vibrant written press that, nevertheless, is very circumspect when reporting on the military, security operations, and terrorism. The 1990 information code states that freedom of speech must respect "individual dignity, the imperatives of foreign policy, and the national defense." The penal code, amended in 2001, mandates large fines and prison terms of up to two years for journalists found guilty of insulting or libeling the president, the National Assembly, the National Popular Army, or other state institutions. The penal code criminalizes some forms of speech by defining terrorism in very broad terms to include "interfering with public freedoms" and "impeding public authorities and institutions."

The government continues to systematically harass journalists who criticize public officials. In the last three years a large number of journalists have been brought to court, fined, or imprisoned for alleged violations of the information code and other laws. In December 2004, a court sentenced three reporters and the director of publication at *Le Soir D'Algerie* to one year in prison for defaming the president. According to Reporters Without Borders, 114 journalists were prosecuted in 2005 for libel and a variety of press law violations. At least 18 journalists in 2005 were sentenced to prison for defamation, and many others faced heavy fines. Among those facing prosecution were the former editor of *Liberte*, the editor of *Le Soir d'Algerie*, and journalists from *Le Matin*.

In June 2006, the director of *Le Matin*, Mohamed Benchicou, was released from prison after two years, but several defamation charges are still pending against him. In July 2006, Bouteflika issued a pardon to all journalists convicted of defamation and insulting state institutions. However, authorities soon began harassing reporters again. In December 2006, a court in Jijel imposed a fine and three-month prison sentence on the editor of *El Watan*, Omar Belhoucet, and one of his reporters for libeling a local official.[2]

ANEP, a public company that monopolizes all print and broadcast advertising for public companies and the administration, often penalizes outspoken newspapers by withholding advertising. The government owns five main printing companies, but some private newspaper publishers now own their own printing presses. The government appears to have no interest in allowing the formation of privately owned Algerian stations that could undermine the state's monopoly on television and radio broadcasting. Although internet penetration is low and access is too expensive for many families, the government allows private providers and refrains from imposing controls or filters on content.[3] Satellite television is readily available to most households without restrictions.[4]

The government allows a broad range of cultural expression, despite some limitations designed to placate Islamist sensibilities and restrictions on political cartoonists. In the last five years, the government has not imposed significant restrictions on *rai* music or Berber audiovisual material. Algerian cinema and theater have suffered from lack of public funding, and self-censorship remains a significant constraint in many cultural arenas.

Recommendations

- The government and the National Assembly should amend the Charter for Peace and National Reconciliation to allow for open, legal discussion of responsibility for past crimes, prosecution of public agents who have committed serious human rights abuses, and mechanisms for citizens to compel public institutions to release evidence about the fate of their family members.

- The Parliament should work to strengthen its administrative capacity and increase public awareness of and participation in the legislative process.
- The government should cease its campaign of harassment against the private media, eliminate criminal sanctions for defamation, and revise legislation to define much more narrowly what constitutes libel and defamation.
- The government should privatize ANEP and printing companies and actively promote the development of private television and radio stations.
- The government should eliminate restrictions on political activities by former members of the FIS and desist from refusing to authorize new political parties.

CIVIL LIBERTIES

PROTECTION FROM STATE TERROR, UNJUSTIFIED IMPRISONMENT, AND TORTURE:	2.43
GENDER EQUITY:	3.75
RIGHTS OF ETHNIC, RELIGIOUS, AND OTHER DISTINCT GROUPS:	3.75
FREEDOM OF CONSCIENCE AND BELIEF:	2.00
FREEDOM OF ASSOCIATION AND ASSEMBLY:	3.40
CATEGORY AVERAGE:	**3.07**

In recent years, reports of torture or abuses committed by the gendarmerie and the police have declined, indicating some progress in observance of human rights standards in these two institutions.[5] However, there is no evidence that police officers or gendarmes investigated for human rights abuses have been prosecuted under more stringent anti-torture provisions in the penal code. In normal criminal cases, the police and gendarmerie generally adhere to the code of penal procedure, which allows them to hold a suspect in pretrial detention (*garde a vue*) for up to forty-eight hours before the suspect must be either released or arraigned by an examining magistrate. In theory, arrested individuals have the right to demand a medical examination at the end of their detention. They are also supposed to be given the opportunity to communicate with family members while in detention, but in practice this access is often denied. Poor conditions prevail in Algeria's grossly overcrowded prisons. Recognizing this fact, the minister of justice in October 2006 announced plans to build eighty-one new prisons by 2009, provide financial aid to poor prisoners upon their release, and recruit more doctors to treat the prison population.[6]

The Defense Ministry's Department of Information and Security (DRS), also known as Military Security, continues to commit serious human rights abuses. This intelligence agency, responsible for anti-terrorism activities, often holds people in secret detention for longer than the twelve days permitted in cases of suspected terrorism or subversion, subjecting many to torture and other forms of ill-treatment with apparent impunity. Civilian authorities do not appear to exercise any control over the DRS, according to Amnesty International, and complaints of DRS abuse reported to prosecutors are not investigated.[7] Public prosecutors apparently do not exercise their right to inspect detention facilities under the control of the DRS. While in pretrial detention, detainees do not have a legal right to access to a lawyer.

Reports of severe human rights abuses have decreased markedly since 2004, but violence by both state and nonstate actors remains significant. The local press periodically reports on antiterrorism operations involving the deaths of suspected terrorists, security forces, and civilians. Much of the information is relayed from official sources without independent verification. Insurgents—many of whom supposedly belong to the Salafist Group for Preaching and Combat (GSPC), a group that since 2006 has claimed affiliation with al-Qaeda—engage in episodic attacks in different parts of the country, but the number of attacks is low compared with levels during the 1992–2000 civil conflict.

Government officials have asserted that only several hundred armed insurgents remain. However, press reports since 2004 have indicated that annual deaths from armed violence by Islamists and government forces still number in the hundreds. Algerian papers reported 400 terrorism-related deaths in 2005 and 140 such deaths in the first four months of 2006. Other attacks followed later in 2006. Bombings of several Algiers police stations in October killed three people. According to an Agence France-Presse review of official reports and press stories, fifty people—including twenty-six members of the security forces—died in clashes between the government and Islamists in a five-week period starting in November.[8] The GSPC claimed responsibility for an attack in December 2006 on a convoy of Western oil contractors in Algiers. In February 2007, the GSPC carried out a series of bombings of police stations.

The Charter for Peace and National Reconciliation makes almost impossible any investigation of human rights abuses since 1992, whether those abuses were committed by agents of the state, government-backed militias, or Islamists. A government-controlled National Consultative Commission for the Promotion and Protection of Human Rights (CNCPPDH) stated in March 2005 that 6,146 people who disappeared after being arrested by security forces between 1992 and 2000 still remain unaccounted for. Human rights groups believe that more than 10,000 have disappeared, although the lack of any investigations means an authoritative accounting of the disappeared will likely never occur. A handful of Islamists in exile have voluntarily returned to Algeria or announced their intention to return. These cases suggest that the fear of prosecution or harassment among former FIS members and regime opponents has significantly subsided. In December 2006, Bouteflika issued a decree renewing the mandate of CNCPPDH, after a year during which its operations had ceased. Attorney Farouk Ksentini was renamed as head of the organization, which includes forty-three other appointed members. CNCPPDH, which has a contentious relationship with Algeria's independent human rights groups, has not made any of its reports available to the public.

Although the government has taken significant steps in the past two years to strengthen the legal and civil rights of women, numerous discriminatory laws and practices remain in force. In March 2005, the parliament approved a decree previously issued by Bouteflika that amended the 1984 family code. The revisions represented a positive change, but fell short of what many women's associations had hoped for. Under the revisions, a woman no longer has a legal obligation to obey her husband, a woman's consent is required for marriage, the legal age of marriage for men and women is equalized at nineteen years, and it is slightly easier than before for women to initiate divorce proceedings. After divorce, a former husband is required to provide a place for his ex-wife to live and to pay alimony, and women have equal rights to custody of their children. When ex-husbands fail to pay alimony, the state is supposed to pay ex-wives out of a special fund, which has not yet been established. Women's groups complain that civil servants and judges have yet to uniformly adhere to and enforce these stronger rights for women.[9]

Polygamy is still legal, although subject to more restrictions. Minors and adult women are still subject to male guardianship, and a man can still repudiate his wife through a form of unilateral divorce. On a more positive note, Muslim Algerian women are now permitted to marry non-Muslim male foreigners as long as the foreigners commit to conversion to Islam. In addition, changes to the nationality code in February 2005 allow Algerians to hold dual citizenship. For the first time, Algerian women married to non-Algerian men have the right to pass on Algerian citizenship to their children.

Autonomous women's groups—many of which have not been granted official status by the Interior Ministry—argue that the government has done little to counter widespread domestic violence and sexual harassment in the workplace, despite the passage of a law in November 2004 that makes sexual harassment a crime punishable by up to two years in prison. Between 2004 and 2005, complaints of domestic violence rose 25 percent.[10] SOS Women in Trouble, a local NGO, believes that local law enforcement officials are now better trained to understand and respond to complaints of violence against women. Algerian officials asserted in 2005 that the government had recently conducted a groundbreaking national survey on domestic violence with the aim of introducing new legislation.[11]

According to the National Statistical Office, women constituted only 17 percent of the overall workforce in 2006, although women have significant employment opportunities as schoolteachers and lawyers, and nearly 60 percent of workers in the health field are women. A survey of nearly 14,000 women conducted in early 2006 by a national research center on behalf of the government found that only 19 percent of adult women held jobs. Of those, 58 percent worked in the public sector, 19 percent in the private sector, and 21 percent in the informal sector. None of the presidents of local communal assemblies (APCs) are women, and women constitute less than 7 percent of the members of the upper and lower houses of the national legislature. Trafficking in Algerian women is not a significant public policy problem, but the UN Committee on the Rights of the Child in October 2005 noted "deep concern" about the rise in child prostitution in Algeria.[12] The country is an important point of transit for trafficked persons from sub-Saharan Africa.

Algeria passed legislation in 2002 to protect the rights of persons with disabilities. Approximately 500,000 Algerians are officially registered as disabled, granting them access to some social assistance and disability payments. However, many public buildings and government services are not easily accessible to people with disabilities, and more than 35,000 children with disabilities are still unable to benefit from the special-education schools and services that the government operates.[13]

The Ministry of Religious Affairs exercises significant control over religious personnel, institutions, and practices. It appoints imams to mosques, pays their salaries, and exercises disciplinary oversight. The government monitors Friday sermons, vigorously tries to restrict political activity within mosques, and sets the educational curriculum and hiring standards for Koranic schools. Imams can be imprisoned for three to five years for engaging in any activity that is contrary to the mission of the mosque or that undermines national cohesion. Religious organizations must register with the government.

In February 2006, Bouteflika issued an ordinance (later adopted by parliament with only one dissenting vote) that regulates conditions for the religious practice of non-Muslim groups. Although there is little evidence to date suggesting that the government has prevented non-Muslims from exercising their faith, the new law discriminates against non-Muslims, who were not consulted when it was drafted. It enhances the government's ability to regulate religious fundraising, to prevent the formation of autonomous religious groups, and to limit how non-Muslims can discuss their faith with Muslims. Non-Muslim religious associations must be approved by a newly created National Commission of Religious Worship. The ordinance—which went into effect in September 2006—requires non-Muslim worship services to be open to the public, to occur in registered buildings, and to take place at previously declared times. The ordinance essentially criminalizes proselytizing by non-Muslims. It provides for imprisonment of up to five years for individuals who engage in activities "tending to convert a Muslim to another religion" or who distribute documents designed to "shake the faith of a Muslim." The law also imposes criminal sanctions on anyone who organizes unauthorized religious gatherings or preaches in a house of worship without prior approval from Algerian authorities.

While many Berbers, who form Algeria's largest ethnic minority, express social and political grievances, they do not face significant discrimination on the basis of their ethnicity. Many have demanded that Tamazight be recognized as an official language that can be used in public administration. Following riots in 2001, the national gendarmerie withdrew from many parts of Kabylia. Because the gendarmerie does not have an effective presence in the region, there has been an increase in petty and organized crime. In July 2005, Bouteflika dissolved most of the municipal and local councils in the Kabylia region and ordered new, partial elections in November 2005—a decision that grew out of government negotiations with Berber leaders. Although turnout was only 30 percent, all of the Berber-based political parties participated, and the opposition parties FFS and Rally for Culture and Democracy (RCD) won most of the contested seats.

The constitution guarantees the right of workers to form and join labor unions. Since 1990, civil servants and public sector workers have formed dozens of autonomous unions, but the Ministry of Labor has in most cases refused to authorize them formally, even though they meet legal criteria. By law, unions may not affiliate with political parties or receive funding from foreign sources. Important autonomous unions include the National Autonomous Syndicate of Public Administration Personnel (SNAPAP) and the National Teachers Council (CNES), which represents professors. Grievances over salaries and work conditions are common in these independent unions, which regularly stage work stoppages and strikes that the government considers illegal. The autonomous unions report that public officials often subject union members to administrative sanctions, firing, police intimidation, and judicial proceedings.[14]

The General Union of Algerian Workers (UGTA) is Algeria's only large, authorized union. It has close ties to the government. Officials regularly consult with the UGTA, which in 2006 engaged in collective bargaining with the government and employers' associations to produce a multiyear "economic and social pact." Autonomous unions were not allowed to participate in these negotiations.

The state of emergency, in effect since the 1992 coup, requires political parties and organizations to seek formal authorization to assemble and to stage demonstrations. Authorities regularly refuse to permit demonstrations or meetings, often without offering justification. For example, in December 2004 and January 2005, authorities refused to approve a request by the human rights group LADDH (Algerian League for the Defense of Human Rights) to hold a conference in Tizi Ouzou. In December 2006, the Interior Ministry and local authorities refused to authorize a congress of the Democratic and Social Movement (MDS), an ex-Communist party experiencing internal divisions. In February 2007, police blocked five associations that represented families of the disappeared from holding an international conference at an Algiers hotel.

Local public disturbances such as spontaneous protest gatherings, roadblocks, sit-ins, and unauthorized marches are relatively common occurrences, often sparked by grievances against the quality of public services and the administration of public institutions. The police reported a significant increase in the number of disturbances to which they responded in 2006.[15] Protests over housing conditions, lack of public transport, and university policies, among many other things, reflect anger over a lack of transparency in public institutions and the lack of public involvement in local governance. Protesters frequently accuse the police of harassment and excessive use of force.

Recommendations
- The state of emergency declared in 1992 should be officially repealed.
- The government should revise legislation and exercise more effective oversight over the police and gendarmerie to ensure that individuals held in custody and/or charged with crimes are always guaranteed access to a lawyer during detention, interrogation, appearance before an examining judge, and throughout all judicial proceedings.
- The government must subject the DRS to civilian oversight and strip it of law enforcement powers and the ability to run detention centers.
- The judiciary should compel the Interior Ministry to respond in a timely fashion to requests for legal authorization by unions and civic organizations. In cases of denial of authorization, the ministry should provide explicit reasons that those organizations can fairly challenge in a court of law.
- The penal code should be amended to make spousal abuse a crime, and the government should invest significantly more money in offering assistance to victims of domestic violence.

RULE OF LAW

INDEPENDENT JUDICIARY:	2.20
PRIMACY OF RULE OF LAW IN CIVIL AND CRIMINAL MATTERS:	2.67
ACCOUNTABILITY OF SECURITY FORCES AND MILITARY TO CIVILIAN AUTHORITIES:	1.50
PROTECTION OF PROPERTY RIGHTS:	4.00
EQUAL TREATMENT UNDER THE LAW:	3.33
CATEGORY AVERAGE:	**2.74**

Algeria's judiciary is not independent from the executive branch. The lack of impartiality and independence of judicial authorities is widely criticized, even by the government itself. The Supreme Judicial Council (CSM), which is constitutionally responsible for assigning, promoting, and transferring judges, is headed by the president of the republic, who has undue influence over the composition of the judiciary. Judges, prosecutors, and magistrates are averse to making judicial decisions contrary to government expectations.

The CSM meets on a regular basis to impose sanctions on individual judicial officials who abuse their power. In an early 2005 crackdown, the government removed more than thirty judges who were accused of corruption. The Statute of the Magistrate does not guarantee the independence of judges, whose promotions are subject to background checks by the security services. As noted by the minister of justice, magistrates in Algeria still lack adequate training, including in areas such as organized crime, intellectual property rights, and financial affairs.[16]

Article 45 of the 2006 ordinance implementing the Charter for Peace and National Reconciliation compels judicial authorities to dismiss complaints or accusations of human rights abuses against security forces. Article 46 provides for imprisonment of up to five years for anyone publicly criticizing the conduct of the forces. Together these provisions prevent the judiciary from exercising authority over the security forces. Instead, they turn the judiciary into an instrument to suppress free speech about human rights violations.

The public perception of corruption and bribery in the judicial system is widespread. In a speech to magistrates in September 2006,

Bouteflika condemned the "harmful" practices and "excesses" of some judges and lawyers.[17] Magistrates typically overlook procedural irregularities, such as summary investigations or suspects' statements made under duress.

The presumption of innocence until proven guilty is recognized by the constitution. Suspects are supposed to have the right to a lawyer in penal matters, but defendants often lack representation at their first appearance before an examining judge, and examining judges usually fail to inform them of their right to be represented by a lawyer. Detainees suspected of serious crimes are sometimes denied access to a lawyer and held incommunicado, in violation of the penal code. The right to a fair trial is frequently undermined by the use of coerced confessions. While in DRS custody, detainees are often forced to sign interrogation reports they have not read before they appear before a magistrate. There is little evidence that judges order investigations when defendants complain of torture or ill-treatment. However, according to Algerian lawyers who have communicated with Amnesty International, the police and the gendarmerie have made improvements in their adherence to the law, more frequently informing arrested suspects of their rights and permitting many of those in custody to communicate with their families.[18]

In November 2006, the Council of Ministers approved a draft law that would revise the codes of civil and administrative procedure. A new code would strengthen the ability of judges to speed up judicial proceedings and limit supposedly specious appeals and delaying tactics by defendants. It would encourage greater use of arbitration and mediation. The impetus of this effort seems to be a desire to weaken the rights of defendants in the courts. The changes in administrative procedures would grant greater powers to judges to temporarily suspend some decisions of government agencies, suspend government contracts and purchases that do not follow prescribed legal procedures, and issue injunctions against administrative agencies.[19] The requirements of the new code would probably not take effect until a year after its enactment, so the impact on the rule of law will not be immediately measurable.

Senior officers in the armed forces (including retired officers)—often referred to as *le pouvoir*—continue to play an important role in Algerian politics. Although Bouteflika has for several years tried to assert more civilian control over the military, the army and security services have relatively free rein in antiterrorism operations and internal security issues. In July 2006, Bouteflika promoted Ahmed Gaid Salah, Benabbes Ghaieziel, and Mohamed Mediene to the rank of lieutenant general; all three had helped organize the 1992 coup and are powerful figures with ties to prominent retired generals. The DRS has since 1990 remained under the control of Mediene, a powerful, autonomous officer. The former head of the LADDH, Ali-Yahia Abdennour, contends that the DRS has considerable influence over seven government ministers and maintains surveillance of all ministries and their personnel.[20]

The Algerian constitution guarantees the right to own private property. In recent years the government has made efforts to provide families with access to credits that allow them to purchase their existing, government-owned apartments or finance the purchase of new apartments. However, the right to own private property is limited by the government's unwillingness for many years to definitively sell off significant amounts of public land and property. Instead, the government has sought to retain de jure ownership of land and property while granting legal use of it to private actors through long-term concessions and other arrangements.

Poorly defined land-ownership statutes make it difficult for many citizens to enforce their property rights and to gain access to property. The private sector's access to state-owned land for investments in industry and tourism is still limited. The most valuable land in Algeria is considered property of the state, which has controlled it since its abandonment by French colonists during the independence movement. Farmers now have long-term leases on publicly owned land, but they are technically barred from selling their leases or diverting use of land from agricultural purposes. In practice, farmers have been selling their lease rights to buyers who often use agricultural land to build illegal lodgings or set up unauthorized commercial facilities. The gendarmerie announced in January 2007 that—on the instructions of judicial officials—it had questioned more than 16,000 people over an eighteen-month period about misuse of rural property for nonagricultural purposes.[21]

In January 2007, Finance Minister Mourad Medelci said that a long-term survey of land boundaries, ownership, and values (completed in 64 percent of rural territory and only 33 percent of urban areas) found that 33 percent of properties lack certificates of ownership.[22] The government has yet to resolve the problem of access to industrial real estate, despite years of complaints from investors who find it difficult to buy or lease land for their projects. Although indications are few that the government is taking effective steps to reform this system, in February 2007 the government announced plans to establish a new agency to regulate state-owned real estate and make more industrial real estate available to private companies by ceding property to investors or establishing land-use concessions.[23]

Recommendations
- Magistrates, judges, and public prosecutors must be empowered to sanction security forces and public officials for violations of the law.
- The government should take steps to grant full property rights—via complete privatization of significant segments of public land and property instead of leases and concessions—to farmers, private investors, and inhabitants of public housing.
- The government should create a more independent Supreme Judicial Council (CSM), a majority of whose members are not appointed by or subject to oversight by the executive. The CSM must be empowered to conduct autonomous investigations of judicial officials, publish results of disciplinary proceedings against judicial officials, and monitor the judiciary's professional standards without executive interference.
- Public institutions should implement an extensive public relations campaign to inform women of their legal rights under new laws relating to family relations, nationality, and harassment in the workplace.

ANTICORRUPTION AND TRANSPARENCY

ENVIRONMENT TO PROTECT AGAINST CORRUPTION:	2.20
EXISTENCE OF LAWS AND ETHICAL STANDARDS BETWEEN PRIVATE AND PUBLIC SECTORS:	2.75
ENFORCEMENT OF ANTICORRUPTION LAWS:	2.50
GOVERNMENTAL TRANSPARENCY:	3.14
CATEGORY AVERAGE:	**2.65**

Despite passage of an anticorruption law in February 2006 that establishes a code of conduct for public workers and protects whistle-blowers, corruption remains pervasive in Algeria. Implementing legislation for the anticorruption measures was not issued until November 2006, so their practical effects have yet to be seen. Algeria's score in Transparency International's 2006 Corruption Perceptions Index was 3.1 out of 10, placing the country among the six worst performers in the Middle East and North Africa.[24]

The February law requires public agents—defined as officials in legislative, executive, administrative, and judicial bodies—to make asset declarations at the time they start their jobs and when they leave, expanding on rudimentary asset-declaration requirements set out in a 1997 presidential decree. The asset declarations of high-ranking officials, including the president, members of parliament, and ministers, are to be published in the *Journal Officiel.* Moreover, asset declarations of local elected officials are to be posted for one month at the headquarters of communal and regional legislative bodies. There are no provisions for public disclosure of the asset declarations of other public agents. In October 2006, the Algerian press reported that a majority of public officials, including legislators, did not issue the legally mandated asset declarations, and that none had faced punishment for failing to do so. There was no mechanism to determine whether asset declarations that were turned in by public officials were accurate or complete.[25]

Article 8 of the February 2006 anticorruption legislation obliges public agents to inform their superiors if they have a conflict of interest that may affect their public duties. The law also holds public institutions responsible for establishing procedures to make information publicly available on decision making within those institutions, simplifying administrative procedures, and responding to citizens' complaints. Transparency International reports, however, that government agencies usually deny the public and press access to information.[26]

The decrees implementing the Charter for Peace and National Reconciliation established the National Commission for Prevention of and Struggle against Corruption, composed of seven presidential appointees who are charged with gathering information on suspected public corruption (which they are to forward to the Ministry of Justice) and issuing an annual report on anticorruption activities to the president.

In February 2007, the Council of Ministers approved a draft ordinance that, if enacted, would discourage government workers from accruing private gains from their public positions. The ordinance would prevent civil servants and public-sector managers from having any direct or indirect interest in companies that they regulated or contracted with. Moreover, for two years after leaving their jobs, public administrators would be barred from working or consulting for any private company they had previously regulated. This ordinance is an important step in preventing conflicts of interest among public officials and barring former officials from exploiting their ties to government institutions once in the private sector.[27]

The Algerian Association to Fight Corruption (AACC), an affiliate of Transparency International, has criticized the new anticorruption law for a number of weaknesses: high-ranking military officers are not required to submit asset declarations; the anticorruption commission is subject to presidential influence; and protections for whistle-blowers are insufficient.[28] AACC reports on a recent case in which an official in the National Group for Aerial Navigation (ENNA) who made public allegations of embezzlement and bad management against high-ranking members of ENNA was arrested and brought before a military court—which eventually dismissed charges against him.[29]

Since 2005, the government has begun to revive its moribund privatization program, but the pace of sell-offs of state-owned enterprises and businesses is very slow. The most noticeable advance has been in preparations to sell a 51 percent stake in Credit Populaire d'Algerie—one of the biggest state-owned banks—to a group of private foreign investors. All partial or wholesale privatizations must be approved by the Conseil de Participation de l'Etat, an institution that generally does not release detailed information to the public about the conditions under which privatization occurs. State oil company Sonatrach, Air Algerie, and some other public companies are considered strategic assets that are exempt from privatization.

In cooperation with the World Bank, Algeria in 2006 completed a Public Expenditure Review for the first time in ten years; the results have not yet been made public. The World Bank, the International Monetary Fund, and the AACC are concerned that current massive capital expenditures may be leading to poor-quality public investments and insufficient oversight of projects. Auditing and accounting practices for state enterprises are generally poor and nontransparent.

The Algerian media regularly report on alleged corruption. For example, the local press reported in early 2006 that a crackdown on corruption in the customs office led to the firing of at least one hundred agents, some of whom were high-ranking customs officials. Prefects in Oran and Blida were targets of a government corruption probe that led to their removal from office in 2005.

Since 2004, the government has shown some dynamism in investigating two of the worst financial scandals in Algerian history. In January 2007, a criminal tribunal in Blida began proceedings in the Khalifa Bank scandal, in which more than one hundred people have been implicated, including senior bank management and a former central bank governor, Abdelwahab Keramane. At the same time, a trial opened in Oran in a scandal involving another private bank, the Banque Commerciale et Industrielle d'Algerie (BCIA), whose directors are accused of embezzling funds. Both of these high-profile cases include accusations that public bank officials and overseers were complicit in financial crimes or negligent in their oversight of the banking system. The local press has given extensive coverage to testimony in the Khalifa trial.

Public access to government information is limited, and there are no effective mechanisms for citizens to compel government agencies to release information about government operations and legal proceedings. The executive branch formulates the annual budget with little involvement from civic groups. Although the National Assembly does make amendments to the annual budget law, it does not effectively oversee executive spending.

The government does not publish audits of state enterprises. An audit court (Cours de Comptes) is supposed to send an annual report to the president on the finances of the state and the public services. In August 2005, some officers of the Cours de Comptes held a press conference to criticize restrictions on their ability to conduct audits.[30] The court has made public only two annual reports since 1995. Sonatrach, the most important state enterprise, does not publish detailed accounting data.

A Law on Public Tenders specifies procedures that government agencies must follow when they procure goods and services, but in practice these procedures are not always adhered to. State-owned enterprises are not obliged to issue tenders when they purchase goods and services. The AACC has strongly condemned the trend in public procurement procedures toward private agreements between government agencies and private contractors.

Recommendations

- The government should accelerate privatization, including of all state banks and many public enterprises, with full public disclosure of terms and conditions of sale by the National Investment Council.
- The government should enact a comprehensive freedom of information law that defines the obligations of public institutions to release information and that provides strong legal mechanisms by which citizens can compel public agencies to release information that is necessary for the exercise of citizens' rights and public oversight.
- The legislature must dramatically strengthen the protections for whistleblowers and establish public agencies with the power to investigate the asset declarations of public officials and refer suspected violations to the courts.
- The government should significantly increase cooperation with nongovernmental organizations, such as the AACC, that are committed to fighting corruption and expanding government transparency.

NOTES

1 "Belkhadem veut remanier son gouvernement," *Le Quotidien d'Oran*, 6 January 2007.
2 "Media Sustainability Index—Middle East and North Africa" (IREX, 2006), http://www.irex.org.
3 Ibid.
4 Ibid.
5 "Unrestrained Powers: Torture by Algeria's Military Security" (London: Amnesty International [AI], July 2006), http://web.amnesty.org/library/pdf/MDE280042006ENGLISH /$File/MDE2800406.pdf.
6 Farouk Djouadi, "Les prisons toujours surpeuplees," *L'Expression*, 28 October 2006.
7 Ibid.
8 "Algeria Bus Bomb Attack Leaves One Dead," AFP, 10 December 2006.
9 Samia Lokmane, "Code de la famille: constat d'echec," *Liberte*, 7 March 2006.
10 "Violence against women—scourge still plaguing Algeria," AFP, 8 December 2006.
11 "Summary record of the 667th meeting" (New York: United Nations, Committee on the Elimination of Discrimination against Women, 19 May 2005), http://www.bayefsky .com/summary/algeria_cedaw_c_sr_667_2005.pdf.

12 United Nations, Convention on the Rights of the Child, Committee on the Rights of the Child, CRC/C/15/Add.269 (15 October 2005).

13 "Bouteflika calls on Arab League for disabled rights strategy," AFP, 4 December 2006.

14 "Declaration pour la defense des libertes syndicales" (Algeria-Watch, 2006), http:// www.algeria-watch.org/fr/article/pol/syndicat/declaration_syndicats.htm.

15 Nissa Hammadi, "Troubles a l'ordre public Alger en tete de liste," *Liberte*, 20 January 2007.

16 "Belaïz: "Les Anglais nous accordent l'aide nécessaire" *Liberte*, 28 March 2007, accessed at http://www.presse-dz.com/fr/article-presse-algerie-2903.html

17 "Pas de prolongation des delais de la Charte," *El Watan*, 26 September 2006.

18 "Unrestrained Powers" (AI).

19 "Communique du Conseil des Ministres du dimanche 26 Novembre 2006" (Algeria), http://www.el-mouradia.dz/francais/Communiques/2006/Com-261106.htm.

20 Lahouari Addi, "En Algerie, du conflit arme a la violence sociale," *Le Monde Diplomatique* (Paris), April 2006.

21 *Le Quotidien d'Oran*, 18 January 2007.

22 Badreddine Kris, "Le tiers des proprietes foncieres sans acte de propriete," *Liberte*, 30 January 2007.

23 "Les texts sur le foncier industriel adoptes," *La Nouvelle Republique*, 3 February 2007.

24 "Corruption Perceptions Index" (Berlin: Transparency International [TI], 2006).

25 Nissa Hammadi, "80% des responsables ne declarent pas leur patrimoine," *Liberte*, 5 October 2006.

26 *Global Corruption Report 2006* (TI, 2006), 124.

27 "Communique du Conseil des Ministres du mardi 13 fevrier 2007" (Algiers, Presidency) http://www.el-mouradia.dz/francais/Communiques/2007/Com-130207.htm.

28 Djilali Hadjadja, "Etat de droit, garde-fous et contre-pouvoirs," *Le Soir d'Algerie*, 29 January 2007, 10.

29 "Algeria Chapter focused on protecting whistleblowers and the victims of corruption" (TI, 9 December 2006).

30 Beirut: UNDP-POGAR: Programme on Governance in the Arab Region, http://www .undp-pogar.org/countries/anticorruption.asp

ANGOLA

CAPITAL: Luanda
POPULATION: 16.3 million
GNI PER CAPITA: $1,980

SCORES	2005	2007
ACCOUNTABILITY AND PUBLIC VOICE:	1.79	2.46
CIVIL LIBERTIES:	2.81	2.83
RULE OF LAW:	2.22	2.62
ANTICORRUPTION AND TRANSPARENCY:	2.10	2.10

(scores are based on a scale of 0 to 7, with 0 representing weakest and 7 representing strongest performance)

Imogen Parsons

INTRODUCTION

Angola's twenty-seven-year civil war, which began with the country's independence from Portugal in 1975, ended in 2002 when Jonas Savimbi, leader of the armed rebel movement National Union for the Total Independence of Angola (UNITA), was killed by government forces. In 2006, peace also spread to Angola's oil-rich Cabinda province thanks to a peace agreement with the Front for the Liberation of the Enclave of Cabinda (FLEC), a separatist rebel group.

Peace has created an opportunity for the government to complete its transition to multiparty democracy and a free-market economy, which began in the late 1980s and led to the signature of the Bicesse Accord, an abortive peace deal, in 1991. The process had stalled after the first—and last—multiparty elections the following year. UNITA rejected the Popular Movement for the Liberation of Angola (MPLA) victory in

---

Dr. Imogen Parsons recently completed her doctoral thesis on Angola at the London School of Economics, and has published a number of articles focusing on postconflict reconstruction, demobilization, and reintegration of ex-combatants. She lived and worked in Angola from 2002 to 2004.

the parliamentary elections, claimed fraud, and returned the country to civil war. Although economic reforms were executed, including liberalization and privatization, in practice the main beneficiaries were the existing political elites, and the power of the president and ruling party were consolidated as a result. Space for alternative political actors or civil society groups to emerge was heavily restricted and remained so throughout the war.

The government's reliance on the international community's assistance has further decreased due to rising oil prices, the discovery of new and substantial oil reserves, and the willingness of donors such as China to make large loans free of political conditions. However, the Angolan government has also shown a desire for international legitimacy, which has translated into a willingness to work with international institutions to improve transparency and accountability. Notable progress has been made since a low point in 2003, when an International Monetary Fund (IMF) document suggesting that billions of dollars had gone missing from government coffers was leaked to the international media.

Substantial revenues have yet to bring widespread economic and social development. Angola's ranking in the 2006 UN Development Programme Human Development Index, although improved since 2004, stands at 161 out of 177.[1] The government still fails to provide even basic services to the majority of the Angolan people. Profits from the oil industry are concentrated in the oil sector, which is largely offshore, employs a small proportion of the population (some 10,000 people), and offers only limited benefits to the country as a whole.

Finally, political accountability remains limited. Instead of disintegrating or losing power, as some predicted, the ruling MPLA has further consolidated its power, while UNITA has failed to reconstitute itself as an effective political opposition. Elections have been repeatedly delayed despite increasing domestic pressure, and although voter registration is under way, a firm date has yet to be set. That said, there have also been positive developments: greater official accountability has emerged through the work of civil society and independent media, and the government has become increasingly willing to consult with, and listen to, outside voices.

ACCOUNTABILITY AND PUBLIC VOICE

FREE AND FAIR ELECTORAL LAWS AND ELECTIONS:	1.75
EFFECTIVE AND ACCOUNTABLE GOVERNMENT:	1.75
CIVIC ENGAGEMENT AND CIVIC MONITORING:	3.33
MEDIA INDEPENDENCE AND FREEDOM OF EXPRESSION:	3.00
CATEGORY AVERAGE:	**2.46**

Angola continues to await repeatedly deferred presidential and parliamentary elections, the first and last of which were held in 1992 when the MPLA was returned to power—a position it had held since independence from Portugal in 1975. The international community considered the elections generally free and fair, although UNITA protested supposed electoral fraud and returned the country to civil war as a result. Elections have, since the end of the war in 2002, been repeatedly promised "in two years." Although an electoral timetable approved in 2004 anticipated elections in 2006, the government stated in early 2007 that legislative elections will be held in 2008, with presidential elections following in 2009.[2]

Progress is slowly being made toward new elections. A new package of electoral laws was passed in 2006 following consultation with opposition parties, and, although slowed by technical difficulties, voter registration began in late 2006. Following the recommendation of the National Electoral Commission, opposition parties are taking part in and monitoring the process, and have been promised equal access to media coverage for campaigning purposes, including in state-operated media. Political tensions have been relatively minor so far. UNITA has complained of an increase in political interference and violence since the start of the registration process, even including an alleged assassination attempt against party leader Isaias Samakuva; although troubling, these reports do not yet represent a picture of widespread or systematic abuses.[3]

Centralization of power around the president during the 1990s, led many to believe that MPLA member power was a weakened force. However, MPLA membership has increased since the end of the war, particularly in the central highlands and former UNITA-supporting areas, as

people have been encouraged to join by financial and material inducements. At the end of 2004, membership stood around 2 million, more
than double the number in 1992. Party membership is viewed by some
as enhancing—if not as a prerequisite for—educational progress and
promotion to senior levels of the state sector,[4] and MPLA youth organizations have historically played an important role in providing opportunities for young people by effectively integrating them into patronage
networks. Nonetheless, the MPLA has made moves to become more
open by introducing competition into the selection process for members of parliament (MPs), insisting that more than one candidate be put
forward for each post.

Government and parliamentary posts are allocated according to the
terms of the Government of National Unity (GURN), which was
formed in 1997 and based on the 1992 election results. As a result, both
are MPLA dominated, and while UNITA and smaller parties are represented in both, they have little power. Although UNITA holds a number of ministerial posts and provincial governorships, even in these cases
the MPLA deputy is frequently the more powerful official. This form of
power sharing was almost certainly a positive factor in bringing peace,
but observers have asked whether—five years on from the end of the
war—this does not diminish UNITA's status as an opposition that represents a real alternative.

Certainly one result of this system is a feeble and MPLA-dominated
parliament, with a weak mandate and powers frequently limited to "consultation" on matters such as government appointments and legislation.
Indeed, around 90 percent of legislation is estimated to originate from
the executive,[5] while parliament is relegated to a rubber-stamp role. The
MPLA holds 200 seats and UNITA 70, while the 10 smaller parties, with
20 seats between them, are even less well represented. MPs are prohibited from also holding cabinet and other positions in government, meaning there is no overlap but also little consultation. Moreover, MPs and
committees frequently lack the technical capacity to exercise oversight
functions effectively, and the civil service is highly politicized.

Government accountability is further limited by the lack of directly
elected representatives: parliamentary elections take place on a closed
party list basis, provincial governors are centrally appointed, and there
are no local elections. The government reportedly intends to launch a
limited decentralization trial after the elections,[6] but there seems to be

little appetite for comprehensive structural reform of the overall system. The draft new constitution—repeatedly delayed and now likely to be approved only after parliamentary, and possibly presidential, elections have taken place—does not envisage any substantial changes.

UNITA has failed to reorganize as an effective opposition, exhibiting few policy differences from the MPLA.[7] Despite the fact that there are some 128 registered political parties, only the MPLA and UNITA enjoy national representation and support. To compensate for this, opposition parties have formed coalitions and have been active both in campaigning for new elections and in promoting other issues, but they have not effectively exerted pressure. Political parties are entitled to state funding, but this is proportional to the size of their representation, meaning the myriad of small parties receive relatively little support. Few observers believe that anybody except the MPLA will win the next elections.

The constitution provides for the separation of powers, but the judiciary and parliament are weak and unable to hold the executive accountable. Power remains heavily centralized, concentrated in the presidential office and the MPLA, which is headed by President Dos Santos. The president is effectively head of government as well as state; he presides over the council of ministers, can appoint and dismiss the prime minister and other ministers and vice ministers, and also appoints the attorney general and some members of the judiciary, including Supreme Court judges. Provincial governors are also directly appointed by the president. In addition, Dos Santos enjoys a considerable personal power base, including a range of charitable activities administered by his personal foundation. He continues to marginalize rivals, as seen in early 2006, when Fernando Miala, head of the external intelligence services, was dismissed. Miala apparently enjoyed a significant support base, including a private charity foundation, and was believed to harbor political ambitions.[8]

The government retains the ability to exercise some control over civil society. All groups are required to undertake potentially onerous registration processes and those engaging in political activities can be denied registration; the government seldom uses this power outside of Cabinda. Mpalabanda, a Cabinda-based human rights organization created in July 2003, was banned by the authorities in July 2006 for its involvement in politics. Nonetheless, the postwar period has seen a growing government willingness to consult with nongovernmental organizations (NGOs) and civic groups on policy and legislation. Although changes made as a result of public consultation processes have to date been somewhat under-whelming, examples such as the 2004 Land Law and the media and electoral laws in 2006 represent progress.

Independent media continue to provide an effective outlet for crit-icism of government policy, albeit still generally only in the capital, Luanda, where a number of independent newspapers regularly publish articles critical of the government. Self-censorship is said to be common, but reports of actual harassment and arbitrary detention have declined since 2004; one journalist was held in 2005, but there were no reported detentions in 2006. No new cases of defamation have been brought, and although a number of accusations are still outstanding, the accused jour-nalists have not been prosecuted and continue to work. Additionally, the defamation conviction obtained against the editor of independent newspaper Angolense was overturned in early 2005.

Access to independent media remains rare outside the capital, and state media continue to be heavily influenced by the MPLA. Indepen-dent newspapers are rarely seen outside Luanda; only a small number of independent radio stations operate, and in any case these are rarely expressly critical of the government. The often critical Catholic radio station Radio Ecclesia continues to broadcast in Luanda, but—despite having been officially given permission to operate nationwide and hav-ing invested (with international donor support) in provincial infra-structure—its attempts to broadcast outside the capital have been blocked by the government. Although internet access is not restricted, lack of infrastructure, low literacy rates and high cost mean that in prac-tice it is only accessible to a small proportion of the population.

A new media law passed on February 2, 2006, represents an im-provement on previous legislation. It brings an end to the state monop-oly on broadcasting, creates public TV and radio that will be governed by the principles of public interest, and removes provisions allowing prosecution of journalists for defamation of the president even where the facts reported are true. Opposition groups were consulted in the drafting of this law, although a UNITA proposal that a new body be cre-ated as a guarantor of press freedom was not included in the final ver-sion. Concerns remain, however: licensing procedures for private broadcasters are still under government control, and the potential exists for excessive penalization of poorly defined criminal conduct.[9] It is thus likely that the state will retain some ability to influence the media, and that many media outlets will remain politicized.

Broader freedom of expression is not prohibited but in practice is limited; this is partly a legacy of the war, but cases such as the car washer killed by members of the presidential guard for singing lyrics from an antigovernment rap song may weigh heavily on the minds of Angolan citizens.

Recommendations

- Elections should be held as soon as possible, with equal campaigning time given to parties in state-run media. NGOs and civil society organizations should be engaged to ensure appropriate civic education is undertaken early and on a nationwide basis.
- Decentralization pilot programs should be initiated at the earliest opportunity, with a view toward instituting locally elected government as anticipated in the new draft constitution.
- Independent media, including Radio Ecclesia, should be allowed to broadcast nationwide, and public broadcasters must be allowed to operate without political interference, particularly in the run-up to elections.
- Parliament should be fully consulted by the executive, including during the development of legislation and the selection of high-ranking officials. Adequate resources and training must be available to MPs and national assembly staff to enable them to carry out their role effectively.

CIVIL LIBERTIES

PROTECTION FROM STATE TERROR, UNJUSTIFIED IMPRISONMENT, AND TORTURE:	2.14
GENDER EQUITY:	3.25
RIGHTS OF ETHNIC, RELIGIOUS, AND OTHER DISTINCT GROUPS:	2.75
FREEDOM OF CONSCIENCE AND BELIEF:	3.00
FREEDOM OF ASSOCIATION AND ASSEMBLY:	3.00
CATEGORY AVERAGE:	**2.83**

The Angolan constitution provides comprehensive guarantees of social and economic rights, although they are not necessarily codified into national law and are not always respected in practice.

State security services—the army and police—have been accused of a number of human rights abuses in recent years, including torture, extrajudicial killings of members of criminal gangs (see Rule of Law), and beatings and shootings during forced evictions. Violence has also been directed at foreign diamond miners and other illegal workers, who have been forcibly repatriated in a series of operations. In 2003, a thirty-page report accused the Angolan army of a catalogue of disappearances and deaths in Cabinda.[10] Further alleged abuses occurred in 2004 and 2005, although the human rights situation has improved as military operations have decreased. Rebel group FLEC has also been accused of atrocities, including attacks on people suspected of collaborating with the Angolan army, although, again, to a lesser extent since 2004 as FLEC capacity and activity levels have decreased. The army has taken some steps to address these issues, including transferring units away from Cabinda. In at least one case military legal proceedings have been initiated against members of the armed forces, although many cases remain unsatisfactorily investigated.[11]

Sporadic accusations of harassment of former UNITA combatants and party members by the MPLA and members of the Civil Defense Force (ODC) also persisted into 2005 and 2006. For instance, in March 2005, UNITA's thirty-ninth birthday, clashes between UNITA and MPLA members in Cuando Cubango resulted in twenty-eight injuries. In April 2005, UNITA accused the MPLA of destroying its Moxico Headquarters, apparently in response to the discovery of a land mine on a local airstrip. The government has also been accused of denying identity papers and pensions to demobilized UNITA soldiers.[12] Overall tensions have decreased since 2004, and cases of actual violence are rare; nevertheless, the start of election campaigning could result in renewed hostilities.

The state's ability to protect citizens from abuse and crime is hampered by the lack of capacity in the justice system, as is the ability of citizens to seek redress should their rights be violated by the state. Progress has been made, however, through the recent appointment of an ombudsman, a new post provided for under the constitution but unfilled until now, whose role is to defend citizens' rights and provide a means of seeking redress from the state. Paulo Tjipilica, the appointee, is a trained lawyer, former minister of justice, and former senior member of

UNITA. His power extends only to the ability to make recommendations, however, so the change should not be overstated.

Lengthy periods of pretrial detention are common, and conditions in Angolan prisons remain basic, with chronic overcrowding and reports of sexual abuse of female prisoners and juveniles. However, although illegal detentions continue to take place, in recent years NGOs have reported better access to judicial information. Furthermore, local and international human rights observers have been allowed to visit prison facilities and work is under way on a new prison facility for women. One local NGO, the Association for Justice, Peace, and Democracy (AJPD) has been allowed access to prisoners and has succeeded in securing the release of some.

Women enjoy relatively high status compared with those in many other postconflict and developing countries; they are at least somewhat represented in government (comprising 16 percent of the national assembly, although numbers in local government are lower) and are well protected under the constitution. However, lack of access to formal justice means their rights are often ignored in practice, and societal attitudes, particularly in rural areas, are often retrograde. Domestic violence—which is not in itself a crime as no specific legislation criminalizing it exists—is common, and women still face discrimination in the workplace.

Trafficking in women is not believed to be common. Although Angola is one of the few Southern African countries not to have acceded to the UN Protocol to Prevent, Suppress and Punish Trafficking in Persons, the government has, since 2004, steadily increased its efforts to prevent trafficking in children. No specific antitrafficking laws exist, but laws prohibiting forced labor and kidnapping may be applied, and a new statute requires documentation for international travel by unaccompanied minors. The National Commission to Combat Child Labor and Trafficking in Minors has met monthly, there have been national awareness campaigns, and in 2005 and 2006 police officers and border officials received training in how to deal with child trafficking.

Individual ethnic groups are not specifically discriminated against, though tensions do occasionally exist due to political affiliations that correspond to ethnicity; for instance, UNITA remains primarily Ovimbundu-based. Various NGOs and other interested parties have devoted considerable effort since 2002 to working with the San (bushmen) people, whose traditional way of life was under threat as a result of the war.[13]

The San have also benefited from new land legislation that enables communities to register land ownership (see Rule of Law). Of greater concern is the increasing tide of xenophobia, which government officials and security services may be exacerbating through the stigmatization and forced removal of illegal diamond workers, most of whom migrate from the Democratic Republic of Congo. This campaign is particularly dangerous as it revives memories of violence directed at Bakongo returnees from the Congo in 1992, when little more than having the wrong accent could result in beatings or even death.

Angola's social service provision is weak, and people with disabilities—of whom there are many due to the long history of war and the high number of land mines—are largely reliant on family members and, where it is available, on charity. Disabled people and their interests have no apparent representation in government, which has not made their protection a high priority, although relevant government bodies do exist. Another group of concern is HIV/AIDS sufferers, who are frequently socially ostracized and for whom little protection exists. This group, currently believed to make up around 3-4% of the population, is believed to have grown rapidly since the end of the war due to the opening up of internal and regional transport and, in particular, the high rate of returning refugees.

Religious freedom is generally respected, although public and government attitudes toward the small number of Muslims in Angola have become considerably more negative since 2004. The colonial law banning non-Christian churches is still in force, but it has not been brought to bear against Muslims or other non-Christian groups. However, three mosques were closed in early 2006 for disrupting public order by impeding traffic flows, and only one has since been reopened.

Christian churches continue to play a strong role in society, often providing services such as health and education, as well as social safety nets for groups such as widows and disabled people. Since the colonial period, churches have taken an active role in mobilizing civil society and even in criticizing government policy, a stance that continues to be tolerated. The Angolan government even co-hosted a conference on peace and reconciliation with the Inter-Church Committee for Peace in Angola (COIEPA) in mid-2005. In Cabinda, however, efforts have been made—including by the Vatican—to depoliticize the church and break the links between religious and insurgent groups.

Apart from Cabinda, where freedom of expression remains limited, political parties, civil society groups, and others have been relatively free to organize and protest in recent years, this represents an improvement over the 2002–2004 period. Notification and authorization are still required for demonstrations and in most cases have been granted. Where unauthorized demonstrations have occurred, human rights organizations have reported detentions of protesters. For example, some twenty-seven members of the opposition party Party for Democratic Support and Progress of Angola (PADEPA) were detained on their way to protest against corruption in November 2006 and held for a week.[14] An unauthorized PADEPA demonstration in 2005 also resulted in detention of a senior party member. Trade unions are active, although those not linked to the MPLA are weak.

Recommendations

- The government must refrain from detaining opposition party members, civil society activists, and antigovernment protesters arbitrarily and for excessive periods of time.
- The government should make clear to both MPLA and opposition party supporters that violence directed at opposition party members is unacceptable, take clear steps to investigate allegations, and, where appropriate, prosecute perpetrators.
- The new ombudsman must be given the resources necessary to accomplish his job, and the government must ensure that his recommendations are transmitted to the highest levels of government and subsequently acted upon.
- The government should step up efforts to strengthen civil liberties within the judicial system by improving conditions within prisons and reducing the length of pretrial detention.

RULE OF LAW

INDEPENDENT JUDICIARY:	2.20
PRIMACY OF RULE OF LAW IN CIVIL AND CRIMINAL MATTERS:	2.50
ACCOUNTABILITY OF SECURITY FORCES AND MILITARY TO CIVILIAN AUTHORITIES:	2.75
PROTECTION OF PROPERTY RIGHTS:	2.00
EQUAL TREATMENT UNDER THE LAW:	3.67
CATEGORY AVERAGE:	**2.62**

Overall, the judiciary in Angola does not act as an effective check on executive power. The president retains the authority to appoint and dismiss many members of the judiciary, including the power to appoint Supreme Court justices without National Assembly approval. Senior members of the judiciary are often MPLA members, and the party has been accused of seeking to influence both judges and prosecutors. However, no specific cases have been proven, and in the past courts have ruled against the Angolan government on issues related to media freedom and political freedom of expression.[15] A constitutional court, although provided for in the constitution, has still not been created; its functions are currently exercised by the Supreme Court instead.

The majority of the Angolan people do not have access to formal justice systems, blocked by lack of physical infrastructure and personnel, financial constraints, and corruption, as well as illiteracy and an inadequate awareness of rights. In 2003, only 23 of 168 municipal courts were functioning, and there is a serious shortage of trained lawyers and judges. Free legal aid exists in principle, but in practice it is largely limited to the capital due to the scarcity of lawyers outside Luanda. Access is further restricted by bureaucratic hurdles that poor and illiterate Angolans struggle to overcome. Although Angolans are technically innocent until proven guilty, lengthy pretrial delays are common. Corruption is widespread, encouraged by the fact that judges and court officials are poorly paid. It is often necessary to hand over a significant amount of money even to bring a case to court, let alone to have it acted upon.[16]

Attempts are under way to address these problems. A plan of action developed in 2005 encompasses structural and legislative reforms aimed at strengthening the justice system nationwide. The government has made efforts to rebuild courts and train new magistrates and prosecutors, including at the municipal level. Radio and television have been used to spread knowledge of citizens' and human rights, including the right to free legal aid, and innovations such as a new court filing system are helping to combat corruption. In addition, some prosecutions of corrupt officials for drug trafficking and human rights abuses have taken place in recent years, although not on the scale common in 2003 and 2004 (see Anticorruption and Transparency). Illiteracy and poverty will remain barriers to justice, however, and it is likely that traditional systems will continue to be relied on, with corresponding disadvantages for women in particular.

Civilian control over the police, military, and internal security forces is effective, although the presidential guard and intelligence services report directly to the president rather than through a ministerial hierarchy. The previous climate of impunity has been increasingly challenged in both the armed forces and police. Allegations of abuses by the Angolan armed forces in Cabinda have resulted in disciplinary actions and the initiation of legal proceedings, although reports of abuses persist elsewhere (see Civil Liberties). Both police and military have received human rights training in recent years, and some police officers have been expelled from the force for beatings and misuse of firearms. In August 2006, a police officer was sentenced to seventeen years' imprisonment for unlawfully killing a homeless sixteen-year-old boy, an unprecedented judgment that human rights organizations welcomed.[17]

Property rights in Angola remains highly problematic. New land laws passed in late 2004 have met with a mixed reception. Provisions endowing individuals and communities with the right to legally register ownership of previously informally occupied land have often been positively received in rural areas.[18] NGOs and civil society groups, however, have expressed concern that the supporting regulations and bylaws are not entirely clear and that the three-year time limits placed on the registration process may undermine security of tenure, particularly in urban and periurban areas where evictions are already common.

Many civil society groups were concerned by the imprisonment of the director of the NGO SOS Habitat following protests against the uncompensated eviction of thousands of residents of Luanda's informal urban settlements. These evictions, which have been ongoing since 2003 and frequently accompanied by reports of beatings and abuses by security forces, have attracted considerable international criticism, including from the UN Special Rapporteur on adequate housing, to little avail.[19] There are also fears that farmers will be subject to land expropriation, particularly in fertile areas where large-scale plantations are being created. A number of NGOs are supporting individuals, families, and communities in registering their land, and as a result of one NGO-supported project in Luanda and Huambo, 500 land titles had already been presented by mid-2006.

Recommendations

- All Angolans must be made aware of their right to free legal aid and educated in how to gain access to it. Access to legal aid must be extended throughout the country.
- The Angolan National Army and Police must ensure that allegations of human rights abuses are investigated, with transparent legal proceedings instituted when appropriate. Human rights training of security forces must be continued.
- In order to address the current climate of impunity, allegations of corruption among government officials and security forces at all levels, particularly among medium- to high-ranking officials, should be investigated and punished.
- The government should ensure that individuals and communities are provided with sufficient information and support to enable them to register land deeds in line with the new land law.
- Forced and uncompensated evictions of residents of informal settlements must cease. Where resettlement does take place, or has already taken place, the government should provide adequate compensation.

ANTICORRUPTION AND TRANSPARENCY

ENVIRONMENT TO PROTECT AGAINST CORRUPTION:	1.60
EXISTENCE OF LAWS AND ETHICAL STANDARDS BETWEEN PRIVATE AND PUBLIC SECTORS:	2.25
ENFORCEMENT OF ANTICORRUPTION LAWS:	2.25
GOVERNMENTAL TRANSPARENCY:	2.29
CATEGORY AVERAGE:	**2.10**

Corruption in Angola remains an impediment to good governance at all levels. As in previous years, the major focus of increased transparency efforts has been on oil, which contributes between 40 percent and 50 percent of GDP and almost 90 percent of government revenues. High oil prices and new finds have swelled government coffers, pushing economic growth above 20 percent in recent years. Substantial progress has been made since 2003–2004, when accusations of graft and financial predation were rife and international organizations alleged that billions had disappeared from government accounts.[20] However, Angola still scored just 2.2 out of 10 in Transparency International's 2006 Corruption Perceptions Index (an improvement on previous years, as it scored 2.0 in 2004 and 1.7 in 2002), ranking 142 out of 163 countries surveyed.[21]

Government officials commonly maintain private business interests alongside, and even overlapping with, their official posts. Some legal provisions exist to prevent such conflicts of interest—for instance, National Assembly members cannot be employed by foreign or international businesses—but these are insufficient and ineffective. High-ranking officials are drawn in by lucrative opportunities, while civil servants outside Luanda may feel obligated to conduct private business activities due to the low government salaries, which are frequently paid months in arrears.

Low-level corruption remains endemic, partly due to the low salaries paid to public servants and a weak institutional and regulatory framework. Bribes are frequently required even for basic services, including education and justice, while small payments are often demanded by police at checkpoints. Officials boost their incomes by levying additional charges for administrative services such as identity card applications, registration of businesses, or release of imported goods. The situation is worsened by the many layers of bureaucracy businesses must negotiate; according to World Bank data, Angola is ranked last out of 155 countries surveyed regarding ease of doing business.[22]

Institutional mechanisms to monitor government activities exist in the form of the Tribunal de Contas (the Accounts Court) and the attorney general, although the latter's degree of political independence is questionable. Following a number of high-profile prosecutions in 2003 and 2004, including those of a UNITA member of parliament and the Angolan ambassador to South Africa, little activity has been evident over the past several years.

Independent media and civil society organizations frequently highlight and criticize corruption and lack of transparency. For instance, the Coalition for Reconciliation, Transparency, and Citizenship launched an anticorruption campaign in March 2005, while opposition party PADEPA has organized a number of demonstrations on this issue, not without personal risk. Many cases of detention and prosecution of journalists and activists have been related to corruption accusations, particularly when directed at high-ranking government individuals, who still benefit from considerable legal advantage derived from the status of their office. State media are highly unlikely to report upon such stories. The recent filling of the ombudsman post may help to address these problems. Discouragingly, however, an anti-corruption researcher and campaigner was arrested in early 2007 in Cabinda and now faces charges relating to crimes against state security

Access to government information has improved but is still poor, partly due to lack of popular access to information more widely within Angola (communications infrastructure is lacking and literacy is low), but also due to a general climate of secrecy, dating from the colonial period and consolidated throughout the war, which still prevails. The internet is used by the government to disseminate official documentation and information, but the majority of the population does not have internet access.

Although still not formally participating in the Extractive Industries Transparency Initiative (EITI), Angola has, since 2004, taken a number of steps in line with EITI and attends its conferences as an observer. In 2004, the government took the unprecedented step of publishing details of an oil signature bonus, a one-off payment to the state normally worth around $1 billion that is made on the award of exploration rights and previously would have been highly secret. The government now publishes company payments by month and by block on the Ministry of Finance website (albeit with around a six-month time lag), and in 2005–2006 state oil company Sonangol made public details of an oil licensing competition for several blocks. International audits of Sonangol have taken place, although the results have not been published at time of writing. The government has also accepted a package of World Bank technical assistance to improve transparency and reduce off-budget expenditures, including through implementation of a new integrated financial management system.

Angola has also signed on to a number of regional and international initiatives, including the African Union's Peer Review Mechanism in mid-2004. Since then, the government has ratified the United Nations Convention Against Corruption (UNCAC) and approved accession to African Union Convention Against Corruption.

The IMF has, however, warned that a number of the issues identified in the KPMG "Oil Diagnostic Report" published in May 2004 have yet to be addressed, including the elimination of conflicts of interest through separation of Sonangol's regulatory functions from its commercial interests.[23] Furthermore, attention has so far been focused on the oil sector; similar efforts to reform the diamond sector and to prevent conflicts of interest within the state diamond company, Endiama, are also needed.[24] Access to high oil revenues and commercial loans—particularly from China, which lent $2 billion in 2004—mean the international community lacks leverage to push the Angolan government to carry out such reforms, and progress toward an agreement with the IMF has largely stalled. The relatively low proportion of government revenue generated by internal taxation also reduces the scope for internal accountability pressure.

Transparency is also weak in budgetary processes and in the allocation of concessions and contracts, which are highly centralized and frequently dependent on informal patronage networks. Foreign humanitarian assistance and support to vulnerable populations has at times been used to garner political support, and transparency in the allocation of subcontracts is limited. In some cases mechanisms have been created to address this, including a financial management and procurement unit established to oversee disbursement of World Bank support focused on reintegration of ex-combatants.

Recommendations
- Institutional reform should be carried out to address potential conflicts of interest caused by Sonangol's and Endiama's dual roles as regulator and commercial business.
- The government should adhere to EITI and continue to publish full details of oil revenue, as well as reduce the time lag between payments and publishing.
- Government officials' private business affairs should be registered, with details made public. Moreover, provisions prohibiting conflicts of interest among public officials should be strengthened and more resources devoted to their enforcement.
- The government should take clear steps to promote greater transparency in policy and decision making, committing to disseminate information by means of the internet, media, and other publicly accessible sources.

NOTES

1 *Human Development Report 2006* (New York: United Nations Development Programme, 2006).

2 "Angola: Elections continue to elude hopeful Angolans," IRIN, 14 February 2007; "ANGOLA: Organising the opposition," IRIN, 27 March 2007.

3 Ibid.; "'Difficult' to hold Angolan vote in 2007: President," AFP, 20 December 2006; "Angola: Political climate heats up in countdown to elections," IRIN, 8 March 2007.

4 *Angola: Drivers of Change, Position Paper 2: Politics* (London: Chatham House, April 2005).

5 See Inge Amundsen, Cesaltina Abreu, and Laurinda Hoygaard, "Accountability on the Move: The Parliament of Angola" (Bergen: Christian Michelson Institute [CMI], CMI Working Paper 2005:11, 2005).

6 See *Angola: Drivers of change* (Chatham House, April 2005).

7 "Observations and Recommendations on a Visit to Angola" (London: All Party Parliamentary Group on Angola, September 2006).

8 *FAST Update Angola: Semi-annual risk assessment January–July 2006* (Bern: Swisspeace Foundation, 2006)

9 See "Still Not Fully Protected: Rights to Expression and Information under Angola's New Press Law" (New York: Human Rights Watch [HRW], Vol. 18, No. 11 (A), November 2006).

10 "A Year of Pain" (Cabinda: Ad-hoc Commission for Human Rights in Cabinda, 3 November 2003)

11 See "Angola: Between War and Peace in Cabinda" (HRW, 23 December 2005).

12 *FAST Update Angola: Semi-annual risk assessment Dec 2004 to May 2005* (Bern: Swisspeace Foundation, 2005)

13 *Where the First are Last – San Communities Fighting for Survival in Southern Angola* (Maynooth, Ireland: Trocaire, 2003), http://trocaire.org.

14 "Angola: New OPEC Member Should Tackle Corruption Not Critics" (HRW, December 15, 2006).

15 Elin Skaar and José Octávio Serra Van-Dúnem, "Courts under Construction in Angola: What can they do for the poor?" (CMI, CMI Working Paper 2006:20, 2006); *Angola: Promoting Justice Post-conflict* (London: International Bar Association [IBA], July 2003.

16 Skaar and Serra Van-Dúnem, "Courts under construction in Angola" (CMI, 2006).

17 "Angola: A step towards ending police impunity" (London: Amnesty International [AI], 15 August 2006).

18 "ANGOLA: Resettlement, land reform boost agricultural production," IRIN, 18 January 2006.

19 See "Angola: Lives in ruins, forced evictions continue" (AI, 17 January 2007); see also "ANGOLA: Poor shut out of 'New Life,'" IRIN, 24 April 2006; "Christian Aid fears Mugabe-style slum clearances in Angola over Christmas," 20 December 2006, at http://www.christian-aid.org.uk/news/stories/061222s.htm.

20 Justin Pearce, "IMF: Angola's 'missing millions,'" BBC News, 18 October 2002, referring to "Angola: Staff Report for the 2002 Article IV Consultation" (Washington, DC:
International Monetary Fund [IMF], 18 March 2002); "Angola: Selected Issues and Statistical Appendix" (IMF, 11 July 2003); see also, *Some Transparency, No Accountability:
The Use of Oil Revenue in Angola and Its Impact on Human Rights* (HRW, A1601, 13 January 2004).

21 "Corruption Perceptions Index" (Berlin: Transparency International, 2006).

22 *Doing Business 2006* (Washington, D.C.: World Bank, 2006).

23 "Article IV Consultations, Preliminary Conclusions of the IMF Mission" (IMF, 29
March 2006); "IMF Executive Board Concludes 2006 Article IV Consultation with
Angola" (IMF, Public Information Notice [PIN] No. 06/133, 15 November 2006).

24 "IMF Executive . . ." (IMF, 15 November 2006).

BANGLADESH

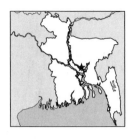

CAPITAL: Dhaka
POPULATION: 149.0 million
GNI PER CAPITA: $480

SCORES	2005	2007
ACCOUNTABILITY AND PUBLIC VOICE:	3.63	3.44
CIVIL LIBERTIES:	4.05	3.96
RULE OF LAW:	3.42	2.71
ANTICORRUPTION AND TRANSPARENCY:	2.64	2.45

(scores are based on a scale of 0 to 7, with 0 representing weakest and 7 representing strongest performance)

Fahimul Quadir

INTRODUCTION

Democracy seemed likely to take root when Bangladesh emerged from a long period of military authoritarianism in December 1990, especially after a new constitution in 1991 replaced autocratic presidential rule with a parliamentary system. Since then, however, Bangladesh has been struggling to foster a democratic political culture amid frequent disputes over the rules of the game. Despite widespread initial optimism, the constitutional provision for organizing national elections under a nonpartisan caretaker government proved to be a major stumbling block in the country's efforts to consolidate democracy.

Increased tension between the two main political alliances, rampant corruption, the emergence of a neopatrimonial state, and the deterioration of law and order have contributed to the creation of a volatile and unpredictable political environment in the country. Mainstream opposition parties have turned to extraconstitutional tactics, including *hartals* (general strikes) and violent protests, and the ruling parties have engaged in their own undemocratic practices. The leadership on both

Fahimul Quadir is Associate Professor of the Division of Social Science and the Director of the Graduate Program in Development Studies at York University, Toronto.

sides have failed to use democratic institutions to reconcile their differences. In late 2006, Bangladesh plunged into a major political crisis when the coalition government, dominated by the Bangladesh Nationalist Party (BNP), failed to reach an agreement with the fourteen-party opposition Grand Alliance, led by the Awami League (AL), over the formation of a caretaker government (CG) to oversee parliamentary elections in January 2007.

In October 2006, President Iajuddin Ahmed stepped in to lead the CG himself. It was tasked with reorganizing the Election Commission (EC) and updating the voter list in order to pave the way for credible balloting. The opposition decided to take to the streets to pressure Ahmed's government, leading in December 2006 to an anarchic situation marked by widespread rioting and killings by rival groups.

The country narrowly escaped a total breakdown when the military quietly seized power on January 11, 2007, by instructing President Ahmed to declare a state of emergency and appoint a new, technocratic CG headed by former World Bank executive Fakhruddin Ahmed. Although the promulgation of the emergency measure has restored relative peace and stability, Bangladesh is now confronting the challenge of putting itself back on the path of democracy. Fakhruddin Ahmed's military-backed government has focused on the restoration of law and order, cracking down on top criminals and corrupt politicians and renewing public trust in key state institutions. These activities seem to have taken precedence over setting a date for the next general elections and reinstating basic human rights. Given that the CG currently enjoys widespread support from ordinary citizens,[1] Western governments, and donor agencies, it is uncertain whether power will be transferred to a democratically elected government in the near future.

ACCOUNTABILITY AND PUBLIC VOICE

FREE AND FAIR ELECTORAL LAWS AND ELECTIONS:	2.50
EFFECTIVE AND ACCOUNTABLE GOVERNMENT:	2.00
CIVIC ENGAGEMENT AND CIVIC MONITORING:	5.00
MEDIA INDEPENDENCE AND FREEDOM OF EXPRESSION:	4.25
CATEGORY AVERAGE:	**3.44**

Bangladesh's constitution, which was adopted in 1972 and last amended in 2004, provides the framework for the operation of government and the conduct of elections. Bangladesh is a parliamentary democracy, with a president who serves as chief of state, a prime minister who serves as the head of government, and a unicameral, 345-member Parliament. Members of Parliament elect the president to a maximum of two five-year terms. The president is responsible for appointing the prime minister, who must command the support of a legislative majority. Despite the president's power to appoint the prime minister, the constitution mandates that the president must act in accordance with the prime minister's advice.[2] Bangladesh's Parliament is composed of members elected by simple majority in single-member districts to five-year terms.[3] In 2004, a constitutional amendment added 45 seats to the 300-seat legislature; these are reserved for women and distributed among political parties in proportion to their legislative strength.[4]

Political turmoil and violence have marred Bangladesh's elections since independence, with both presidents and prime ministers assassinated or forced into early elections by civil unrest. Since 1990, the Bangladeshi political environment has been dominated by deep-seated enmity between the country's two most powerful *begums* (female notables), namely Sheikh Hasina, of the left-of-center coalition led by the AL, and Khaleda Zia, of the center-right alliance headed by the BNP. Zia is the widow of a former military ruler, and Hasina is the daughter of the country's first prime minister. Neither of the begums has shown any interest in reconciling their personal or political differences through existing political institutions, including the Parliament, in recent years. Each in turn has used electoral victory to prevent the other from playing a constructive role in government. Furthermore, both leaders exercise autocratic rule within their respective parties, making it impossible for internal dissenters to challenge party policy.

The dispute over the formation of a preelection CG in late 2006 escalated into the worst political deadlock in Bangladesh's thirty-five-year history. The problem began in mid-2005, when opposition parties, especially the AL, demanded an immediate restructuring of the constitutional provision for forming CGs and a reorganization of the Election Commission (EC). Much of the controversy revolved around the fourteenth constitutional amendment, passed on May 14, 2004, which raised the retirement age of judges by two years. The AL claimed that the provision was designed to allow former chief justice K. M. Hasan to become the chief adviser of the caretaker government (CCG). Critics of Zia's government alleged that Hasan was once a BNP activist and thus was not fit to lead a nonpartisan caretaker government or oversee a credible election.[5]

Since the major political parties could not agree on a CCG, President Iajuddin Ahmed decided to assume the post himself on October 29, 2006, in order to avert a constitutional crisis. As CCG, he was tasked with organizing parliamentary elections within 90 days. Although the AL-led alliance vehemently opposed the president's move, it gave him four days to prove his political neutrality. The alliance also presented an eleven-point list of demands, which included the removal of three election commissioners and correction of the voter list. The alliance made it clear that if its demands were not met, it would not hesitate to return to the streets.

The CCG's reluctance to meet the demands of the Grand Alliance immediately brought renewed pessimism to the political landscape, and the alliance decided to mount a new campaign of general strikes and roadblocks. Ahmed responded by deploying the army on December 10, further alienating the opposition. In addition to making the scheduled January 22 parliamentary elections uncertain, the president's unilateral decision to call in the army caused serious divisions among his key advisers, most of whom would not endorse the move.

The Grand Alliance announced its refusal to participate in the impending elections and added President Ahmed's resignation as CCG to their growing list of demands, alleging that his goal was a BNP victory and describing him as the "key obstacle" to free, fair, and neutral elections.[6] They launched a nationwide, seventy-two-hour transportation blockade on January 7, and even after the voter list was corrected and updated, the opposition continued to press for the announcement of a new election date, the immediate restructuring of the EC, and the depoliticization of the civil administration. On January 10, Sheikh Hasina announced fresh agitation programs, including a four-day, nationwide blockade of rail, bus, and air services and multiple two-day hartals.[7] The alliance also announced a countrywide demonstration for January 11 to protest police atrocities against Grand Alliance leaders and workers that had taken place during the January 7–9 blockade.

The future of the January 22 elections became even more uncertain when leading foreign diplomats openly voiced their concern over President Ahmed's handling of the situation and the failure of the major political parties to achieve a consensus on an electoral process. Most of them questioned the CG's legitimacy as an organizer of credible elections and made it clear that the international community would not accept the results of voting that was boycotted and resisted by major political parties. The U.S. government urged both the CG and the EC to take immediate steps to ensure a congenial atmosphere so that all parliamentary parties could participate in the upcoming balloting;[8] the European Commission and the United Nations made similar statements.[9] Pressure began to mount for Ahmed's resignation as CCG, and international election observers refused to come to Bangladesh to monitor the scheduled voting.

Events took a dramatic turn when the military ordered President Ahmed to declare a state of emergency on January 11.[10] He resigned as CCG and postponed the elections. Nine other advisers to the CG also resigned to pave the way for the formation of a new, more acceptable caretaker government capable of holding a credible election within the "shortest possible time." Meanwhile, the emergency proclamation automatically suspended numerous constitutional protections, including such basic human rights as the freedom of movement, freedom of association, freedom of thought and conscience, freedom of speech, freedom of profession or occupation, and property rights. Critically, the validity of the state of emergency and the suspension of fundamental rights cannot be challenged in court.[11]

On January 12, former World Bank executive Fakhruddin Ahmed was appointed chief adviser of a technocratic CG. The military-backed CG immediately suspended all political activities, indefinitely postponed the elections, took effective measures to reorganize the EC, instructed it to update the voter list, and promised to crack down on "corrupt politicians and godfathers of criminals." It announced the creation of a joint force including the army, the police, and the Rapid Action Battalion (RAB) to curb criminal activities. Within hours of the declaration of the state of emergency, the army began to arrest key political leaders and businesspeople, including influential former ministers and noted entrepreneurs, on charges of corruption and irregularities. The CG also

put a number of political leaders of both the BNP and the AL under surveillance. In addition to the arrest of high-profile politicians, the military rounded up more than 40,000 alleged criminals and thugs.

Despite uncertainties over the date of the upcoming parliamentary
elections, the CG's effort to bring order and stability seemed to draw
widespread support from ordinary citizens, mainstream civil society
groups, some influential political parties, and important external actors,
namely the U.S. and British governments. The U.S. government considered the emergency declaration an inevitable outcome of the political parties' failure to "resolve their differences through dialogue."[12]

Although Bangladesh has witnessed the rotation of political power
among the two key political parties since the restoration of democracy
in 1991, elections have often failed to give all parties an equal opportunity due to the absence of an effective campaign finance law. The current legal mechanism requires all candidates to submit a detailed report
of their campaign financing. It also bars candidates from spending more
than 500,000 taka (US$8,000) on their election campaigns. It is no
secret, however, that most candidates, particularly the winners, spend far
more than the limit and use illegal sources to raise money. The current
mechanism fails both to ensure the accuracy of candidates' financial statements and to penalize those who overspend. This has created ideal conditions for corrupt politicians to capture state power and has further
strengthened the culture of corruption, favoritism, and nepotism.[13]

Since the return to democracy in 1991, successive regimes have not
yet been able to use parliamentary surveillance bodies or government
watchdog agencies such as the Anticorruption Commission to make the
system responsive, transparent, and accountable. The absence of effective legislative monitoring of the executive has made the situation even
worse. Most parliamentary oversight committees—including the Public Estimates Committee, the Public Accounts Committee, and the
Public Undertakings Committee—have so far failed to improve accountability and transparency, although they now seem to have the formal power to investigate irregularities and the misuse of state power and
public resources. Moreover, the judiciary is politicized and therefore unable
to stand as an institutional counterweight to the powerful executive.

Bangladeshi citizens are increasingly losing confidence in the country's administrative institutions, which are viewed as lacking integrity

and efficiency.[14] This is partly due to the politicization of the civil bureaucracy. Instead of maintaining autonomy vis-à-vis political parties, a large number of civil servants, especially those at the senior level, are becoming ever more involved in partisan politics. Analysts worry that this partisanship often begins at the recruitment stage, which is supposed to be managed by a politically neutral agency called the Public Service Commission (PSC). The media and opposition parties have brought a series of allegations against the PSC in recent years, including the charge that it was allowing the ruling BNP's political interests to influence important decisions regarding recruitment and promotion.[15]

Despite Bangladesh's dysfunctional system, in recent years the country has seen an expansion of the democratic space necessary for civil society groups to play an important role in protecting and promoting basic human rights. In addition to pursuing an agenda for democracy and human development, these groups, which include think tanks, development groups, advocacy groups, and the media, have succeeded in monitoring and checking the arbitrary exercise of power by ruling elites.

In recent years, development and advocacy groups have also enjoyed a great deal of autonomy vis-à-vis the state. Despite a cumbersome bureaucratic process of registration and funding approval, nongovernmental organizations (NGOs) have been able to carry out their routine activities largely without state interference. The government has shown serious interest in building partnerships with NGOs to deliver key services to citizens.[16] The NGO sector has also continued to enjoy widespread financial and political support from external organizations. Key donor organizations have worked closely with the country's renowned voluntary sector, which has continued to represent the interests of various marginalized communities, including women and the rural poor.[17]

While most NGOs are able to implement their programs without any serious political interference, the relationship between the state and a few groups, including the development NGO Proshika and Transparency International Bangladesh (TIB), remains very tense. The BNP government maintained that Proshika is a partisan, antigovernment group, and the caretaker regime of Fakhruddin Ahmed has not altered that stance. In early February 2007, the NGO Affairs Bureau refused to release 1.98 billion taka (US$29 million) in foreign grants to Proshika on the grounds that it was engaged in antigovernment activities.[18] Separately, the BNP-led coalition government in 2006 refused to accept the findings of TIB's national corruption survey, claiming that the report was methodologically flawed and politically biased.[19]

Bangladesh's lively media operate in what the Committee to Protect Journalists (CPJ) calls relative freedom from direct government control and censorship. Protected by the constitutional guarantee of freedom of the press, both the print and electronic media seem to enjoy a great deal of latitude in reporting virtually any event of sociopolitical importance. However, the hostility of the civil bureaucracy, various regulatory laws, and Article 39 of the constitution—which provides exceptions to the press freedom guarantee in matters of state security, defamation, and incitement—often limit the ability of the press to report evidence of governmental failures, question state policies, and scrutinize key leaders. Although the government has not used much of its regulatory authority to control the media in the past two years, it still has absolute power over issuing or revoking operating licenses. The independence of the country's media is also threatened by the editorial bias of outlet owners. A number of popular dailies and television stations are now owned by business or political leaders who are primarily interested in advancing their personal and partisan interests.[20] Some media conglomerates appear to have become active agents of partisan politics in recent years.

Given the frequent use of criminal defamation laws by influential members of the ruling coalition, the relationship between the government and the mainstream media has become more confrontational in the past two years. A case filed by Public Works Minister Mirza Abbas against the publisher and the editor of the daily *Prothom Alo* drew attention from both national and international human rights activists, who viewed it as an attempt to restrict press freedom. Similar legal actions by government officials against journalists in different parts of the country also cast profound doubts on the ability of the press to perform its duties freely.[21] Threats of violence against news correspondents by political groups also increased in the past two years. In its 2006 annual report, Reporters Without Borders stated that seventy journalists were forced to flee their homes because of the fear of physical violence in 2005. Some of them reportedly received death threats from political groups and militant organizations, and a Maoist armed group killed two reporters that year.[22]

Although no journalists were murdered in 2006, a number of news correspondents were physically assaulted by political activists, police, and gang members. Between March and May 2006, some thirty-six journalists were attacked by supporters of the ruling BNP. In April 2006, police attacked and injured twenty journalists in the port city of Chittagong during a cricket match between Bangladesh and Australia. The journalists were protesting the ruthless beating of a photojournalist by the police earlier that day. Attacks on journalists suddenly increased just after the establishment of President Ahmed's caretaker government in October 2006, but then dramatically decreased after the entry of the new CG in January 2007. However, an unfavorable media environment remains as the Emergency Power Act of 2007 has severely restricted freedom of the press. The government now has the ability to impose a ban on any political news coverage that it considers provocative or harmful. The emergency act has given the government sweeping power to seize printed materials, hinder access to the internet, confiscate broadcast equipment and printing presses, and censor news items. Violators can be jailed for up to five years.

Recommendations

- The caretaker government should immediately rescind the state of emergency and make necessary arrangements for holding free and fair elections before the end of 2007.
- The role of caretaker governments should be limited to assisting the Election Commission in organizing credible general elections, making sure that the administration does not get involved in promoting a particular group or party.
- The Election Commission should be reformed to ensure that it is completely free from government interference. It should enjoy full financial and administrative autonomy so that it can perform all of its duties, including the appointment of election officers and updating the voter list, in an impartial and technocratic fashion. Moreover, the commission should be empowered to amend current campaign finance laws and regulations, and to strictly enforce them to prevent candidates' use of illicit "black money."
- The appointment of election commissioners should be confirmed only after consensus is developed through open dialogue with political parties and key civil society groups.

- The government should increase the resources devoted to investigating attacks against the press, paying particular attention to violence committed by thugs associated with political parties.

CIVIL LIBERTIES

PROTECTION FROM STATE TERROR, UNJUSTIFIED IMPRISONMENT, AND TORTURE:	2.29
GENDER EQUITY:	4.00
RIGHTS OF ETHNIC, RELIGIOUS, AND OTHER DISTINCT GROUPS:	4.00
FREEDOM OF CONSCIENCE AND BELIEF:	5.33
FREEDOM OF ASSOCIATION AND ASSEMBLY:	4.20
CATEGORY AVERAGE:	**3.96**

Bangladesh's constitution guarantees the protection of basic human rights, including freedom of assembly and expression. The country has ratified all the major international treaties that recognize the inherent dignity of all citizens regardless of their gender, class, ethnicity, and religion, as well as those that promote freedom, justice, and security. However, gross violations of human rights have continued in recent years, and the government has failed to make a dent in the climate of impunity that has long pervaded Bangladesh.

The BNP-led coalition government aimed to curb growing crime and terrorism through the creation in 2004 of a new security force popularly known as the Rapid Action Battalion (RAB). This force, composed of personnel from the army and the police, has actually worsened the country's human rights record. Although the battalion has enjoyed widespread public support,[23] partly because of its apparent success in cracking down on hitherto untouchable gangsters, thugs, and criminals, it has been accused of torturing innocent people and killing alleged criminals in what it calls crossfire.

According to recent official statistics, as of March 7, 2007, the RAB had arrested 17,332 people on various charges and killed 397 people in "exchanges of fire." Of the arrested individuals, 2 were described as top terrorists, 685 others were also called terrorists, 83 were listed criminals, and 305 were suspected members of the banned militant Islamist organization Jamaat-ul-Mujahideen Bangladesh (JMB).[24] Both donor agencies and human rights activists have expressed deep concern over the RAB's use of undemocratic means to curb crime in Bangladesh. Many claim that the RAB has routinely engaged in extrajudicial and unlawful killings,[25] arbitrarily arrested and tortured people on unfounded criminal charges, and denied the fundamental right of arrested individuals to be tried in a court of law.[26]

The police forces, which remain institutionally weak and corrupt, have also been accused of routinely making arbitrary arrests, attacking opposition rallies, and torturing arrested individuals to obtain confessions. Police have allegedly used Section 54 of the criminal procedure code to arrest people without a warrant and detain them for twenty-four hours without allowing access to lawyers and family members.[27] The police arbitrarily arrested a large number of opposition supporters during the political rallies, blockades, and hartals in 2005 and 2006. In most cases, those arrested were detained for weeks without a trial. Deaths in police custody remain a major concern for human rights activists in Bangladesh. Some fifty-one prisoners, of whom thirty-two were standing trial, were reported to have died in 2006 alone. The brutality of prison guards, violent actions by fellow inmates, and the denial of prompt medical treatment are cited as major causes of the deaths of these prisoners.[28]

In spite of some recent initiatives, Zia's government was not able to significantly reduce Bangladesh's historically rooted political violence. In one incident on January 27, 2005, a grenade attack at an AL rally in Habiganj killed five opposition supporters, including former finance minister S. M. S. Kibria. After carrying out an investigation, the police charged a handful of suspects, including local BNP leaders. The government did not meet demands for a public inquiry into the attack.

In 2005, the country also witnessed an escalation in violent political attacks by the JMB. The group claimed responsibility for some 400 coordinated bomb attacks on August 17, 2005, that targeted government offices and buildings in sixty-three of the country's sixty-four districts, killing two people and injuring hundreds. The JMB was also allegedly responsible for Bangladesh's first suicide bombing, in November 2005, which killed dozens of people and injured several hundred.

Responding to growing criticism over its failure to address political extremism, the BNP-led coalition government acted quickly to launch investigations and bring the perpetrators to justice. Between December 2005 and October 2006, the authorities arrested more than 300 alleged militants, including the six leaders of JMB; filed 241 cases; and sentenced twenty-nine people to either death or life in prison. The government also banned all activities of four extremist groups, including the JMB.[29] On November 28, 2006, the Supreme Court rejected the appeals of six of the seven militants sentenced to death, allowing their executions to proceed on March 30, 2007.[30]

Although the constitution declares equal rights for men and women in all spheres of public life, civil and criminal laws often discriminate against women. However, evidence suggests that NGO programs, government initiatives, and tougher laws have contributed to the improvement of women's status in recent years. According to a 2005 report by the International Labor Organization, women's participation in the Bangladeshi labor market has increased in recent decades, and women are now represented in a variety of economic sectors.[31] They now hold important public offices, serve as private sector professionals, and lead social movements that seek to place women at the forefront of political change. This progress has been bolstered by the fourteenth constitutional amendment, which reserves 45 of Parliament's 345 seats for women. Nonetheless, women still face discrimination, receive lower wages than male workers, and are less well represented in the formal sector.

These positive changes have apparently failed to reduce violence against women. While the absence of reliable data makes it difficult to determine whether gender-based violence has increased or decreased in the last few years, recent news reports confirm that it is still widespread. According to Amnesty International, in the first quarter of 2005 "more than 1,900 women were allegedly subjected to violence, over 200 were killed allegedly following rape, over 300 women were allegedly abused for not meeting their husband's dowry demands, and over 100 were trafficked."[32] The same report states that 138 women were the victims of acid attacks in the first nine months of 2005. A large number of crimes against women go unreported, particularly in rural areas, where social stigma coupled with the indifference or hostility of the police often forces female victims to keep their traditional silence.[33] Furthermore, most of these victims lack the social and financial support necessary to seek justice.

Despite constitutional guarantees against both religious discrimination and the exploitation of religion for political purposes, ethnic and religious minorities continue to experience discrimination and violence. Yielding to both national and international pressure, the government in recent years has taken some important steps to curb violence against minorities, including Hindus, Ahmadis, and different ethnic groups in the Chittagong Hill Tracts (CHT). For example, it has attempted to protect Hindus, who account for roughly 16 percent of the population, during their major festivals and in times of sociopolitical crisis. However, the Hindu minority remains vulnerable, and the authorities have failed to adequately investigate and punish previous attacks.

Similarly, the government's efforts to prevent organized persecution of the Ahmadi community have proven inadequate. The sect, which has some 100,000 members in the country, is seen as heretical by many Muslims. Although most human rights activists hailed a December 2004 Supreme Court order suspending the ban on Ahmadi publications and welcomed recent government action to prevent anti-Ahmadi groups from entering Ahmadi mosques, agitation against the community continues to threaten members' physical safety.

The political climate in the CHT has generally improved in the past several years, but the government has not been able to increase security for the region's various tribal groups, in part because of its failure to fully implement a 1997 peace accord designed to end a tribal insurgency. A recent Amnesty International report asserts that "tribal people continue to be the targets of mass attacks by Bengali settlers apparently aided by army personnel acting with impunity. The government has apparently failed to prevent these abuses or to bring those perpetrating them to justice."[34]

Despite Bangladesh's strong tradition of trade unionism, some two million workers in the garment sector, which accounts for more than US$6 billion in cumulative investments and US$8 billion in annual exports,[35] are reportedly denied the right to fair and humane treatment. Factors including government inaction, factory owners' intransigence, and the absence of an effective pay-equity law have resulted in appalling and unsafe working conditions for the garment industry's largely female workforce. Most of the workers face overt wage discrimination based on gender and social class. Following a series of deadly fires in garment factories over the past few years, workers have begun to organize themselves into effective unions, campaigning for a minimum wage, safe working environments, paid maternity leave, and overtime pay. However, they are often subjected to physical attacks and dismissal threats by management. In May and June 2006, the striking workers of several knitwear factories in Gazipur and Savar were assaulted by police and gangs reportedly hired by the factory owners. Although a tripartite Minimum Wage Board recommended an increase in the minimum wage, most of the workers' demands were not even addressed by the government or the owners.[36]

Permits for public protests are not legally required, but freedom of assembly is limited in practice. According to a recent report by Amnesty International, opposition supporters were often subjected to police brutality during protest meetings in 2006. Opposition rallies were also attacked by members of the ruling BNP and its coalition partners, who injured a large number of AL supporters in both 2005 and 2006.[37] In addition, the police used excessive force in dealing with spontaneous protests, including those arising from a 2006 electricity crisis. Amnesty International reported that in April 2006 at least a dozen people protesting the shortages in the northern town of Kansat were killed when police opened fire on them. The government has not brought anyone responsible for these killings to justice.[38]

Recommendations
- The government should immediately set up an independent national human rights commission to closely monitor human rights. This comission should be able to conduct thorough investigations of complaints of discrimination and harassment based on religion, ethnicity, gender, and class. Existing laws need to be changed or enforced to ensure equal treatment regardless of religion, race, and ethnicity.
- The government should intervene to protect people facing discrimination in employment based on membership in professional associations and trade unions.
- Top leaders of political parties should be held responsible for violence perpetrated by partisan thugs during public protests.
- In consultation with the proposed human rights commission and civil society groups, the government should undertake extensive programs of public education to make people aware of their basic human rights.

RULE OF LAW

INDEPENDENT JUDICIARY:	2.80
PRIMACY OF RULE OF LAW IN CIVIL AND CRIMINAL MATTERS:	2.17
ACCOUNTABILITY OF SECURITY FORCES AND MILITARY TO CIVILIAN AUTHORITIES:	1.25
PROTECTION OF PROPERTY RIGHTS:	4.00
EQUAL TREATMENT UNDER THE LAW:	3.33
CATEGORY AVERAGE:	**2.71**

Bangladesh's ability to develop a rules-based, transparent, and predictable system of governance is severely constrained by its legal system, which is considered outdated and understaffed. The current system lacks efficiency, effectiveness, and accountability, causing long and in most cases unnecessary delays in the delivery of justice. Increasing politicization of the judiciary, a deeply flawed police force,[39] and growing corruption have seriously undermined the rule of law.

Although Section 22 of the constitution calls for an independent judiciary, the lower courts operate under the political control of the executive branch. Various government ministries, often acting under the orders of the ruling party, make all important decisions regarding appointments, transfers, and promotions of lower-court judges and magistrates. It has become a tradition for ruling parties to use government departments to influence the enforcement of law. In addition to protecting ruling party members from prosecution, successive governments have used the lower judiciary to harass opposition activists and dissident voices. The political appointment of prosecutors also negatively affects the rule of law. Prosecutors often lose their jobs before the completion of their tenure if they fail to satisfy ruling elites.[40]

The situation is deteriorating for higher courts, including the High Court and the Supreme Court (SC), whose judges are appointed by the president based primarily on their loyalty to the ruling party. Because the constitution stipulates that the most recent former chief justice is appointed as CCG prior to elections, Zia's BNP-led government was particularly interested in finding a suitable candidate for the post. Mainstream opposition parties claim that the BNP-backed constitutional amendment of 2004 was specifically designed to allow Chief Justice K. M. Hasan to become the CCG and conduct the January 2007 elections.

Although a 1999 SC decision called for the effective separation of the judiciary from the executive branch, successive governments have found ways to delay implementing rules that would free the courts from political control. When the CCG of 2001 launched a plan to liberate the judiciary from the executive, both the AL and the BNP asked the government to wait. After coming to power later that year, the BNP-led coalition government continued to appeal to the SC to extend the deadline.[41] On October 20, 2005, the SC rejected the government's twenty-first appeal on the subject, expressing its grave concern over the government's reluctance to implement the court's 1999 decision. On January 5, 2006, the SC struck down yet another government request for an extension, making clear that it would not entertain any such appeals in the future, and two contempt-of-court cases were opened against the government for its failure to implement the 1999 SC order.

On January 16, 2007, the new CG made the decision to end the saga by publishing official notifications of key rules on judicial independence. The measures provide recruitment guidelines for lower-court judges; recommend judicial salaries, allowances, and other benefits; and lay out the organization and disciplinary system of the judicial service. Collectively, these rules ensure that the lower courts and magistrates, previously under the control of government departments, will be brought under the authority of the SC.

Bangladesh has no program to safeguard victims and witnesses against intimidation by the accused, and the government does not take responsibility for compensating or rehabilitating victims. The inefficiency of all levels of bureaucracy makes the pursuit of complaints even more difficult. A number of recent studies have shown that the poor, including women and other marginalized groups, do not have access to the same legal opportunities and benefits as more privileged segments of the population, and that current laws and legal institutions routinely fail to protect them from arbitrary and unfair treatment by powerful sociopolitical actors.[42] In addition, the country also lacks a well-functioning alternative dispute-resolution mechanism, such as mediation.

While the legal system assumes that individuals charged with criminal acts are innocent until proven guilty, there is no guaranteed access to essential financial or legal assistance. A number of advocacy groups—including Ain O Shalish Kendra (ASK), Bangladesh Legal Aid Services (BLAST), Bangladesh National Women's Lawyers Association (BNWLA)—and some development NGOs have recently stepped up their efforts to help the poor gain access to justice. However, resource constraints, coupled with the programs' relatively recent launches, prevent them from offering services to all communities in need. It is virtually impossible for such voluntary legal clinics to make up for the absence of publicly funded legal aid.

The Bangladeshi constitution guarantees the property rights of both individuals and private firms, and the current legal system generally allows citizens to utilize, sell, and invest in properties without undue interference. However, weak enforcement, high levels of corruption, governmental inability to protect the rights of marginalized communities (including ethnic and religious minorities), and the highly flawed property registration process often deny people full access to land and other key properties. Bangladesh's poor record was clearly reflected in the 2007 International Property Rights Index (IPRI), which ranked the country as the worst performer of the seventy countries evaluated. Bangladesh proved disappointing in nearly every sector of the index, including legal and political environment, physical property rights, and intellectual property rights. Compared with fourteen other countries in the region, however, Bangladesh did well in gender equality regarding such issues as access to land, access to bank loans, and inheritance.[43]

Until the indirect seizure of power by the military in early January 2007, all security forces—including the national police force, the paramilitary force known as the Bangladesh Rifles (BDR), and the regular military—were operating under the control of the civilian government. Both the police force and BDR are controlled by the Ministry of Home Affairs, while the military is managed by the Ministry of Defense. None of these security services had made any direct effort to take control of the government for many years, but the military played a major role in political affairs prior to the 1990s, and it has since remained an important political force. Successive governments have occasionally called in the military to crack down on criminals, restore law and order, and deal with other emergency situations. The BNP-led coalition government first used the military in 2002 during its four-month-long

Operation Clean Heart campaign, in which forty-four people were reportedly killed in army custody and a large number of people were rounded up without specific charges. The army has also played an important role in the RAB's anticrime drives since the unit's formation in 2004.

After the January 2007 emergency declaration, the army's desire for veto power over Bangladesh's political system first became evident in early March, when Fakhruddin Ahmed's CG announced the creation of a National Security Council. The council will include the chiefs of the army, air force, and navy. Although the CCG will be the head of the council, it gives "the army a formal mechanism for bossing the administration it installed in January."[44] The formation of the council was "in effect an admission by the army's top brass that it has become impossible to govern the country behind the curtain any longer."[45]

The armed forces now seem to be at the forefront of Fakhruddin Ahmed's ambitious plan to free the country from the control of corrupt and immensely powerful politicians within the shortest possible time. While this effort has drawn widespread support from ordinary citizens, the authorities have failed to ensure basic human rights during their crackdowns on alleged criminals, and there is no independent mechanism, such as a national ombudsman, to investigate complaints against the armed forces or the police.

Recommendations
- The country should set up an ombudsman to receive and investigate complaints about the actions of various government entities, including the justice system, the police and the armed forces.
- A new, efficient system of property registration should be enacted that does not discriminate based on gender or ethnicity.
- The current CG's plan for separating the judiciary from the executive branch should be implemented without any further delay.
- The government should work with civil society groups to implement a national system of legal aid with sufficient organization and resources to broaden vastly the degree of legal aid available in the country.

ANTICORRUPTION AND TRANSPARENCY

ENVIRONMENT TO PROTECT AGAINST CORRUPTION:	1.80
EXISTENCE OF LAWS AND ETHICAL STANDARDS BETWEEN	
PRIVATE AND PUBLIC SECTORS:	2.25
ENFORCEMENT OF ANTICORRUPTION LAWS:	2.75
GOVERNMENTAL TRANSPARENCY:	3.00
CATEGORY AVERAGE:	**2.45**

Recent studies conducted by major donor agencies, including the World Bank, the Canadian International Development Agency (CIDA), and the Asian Development Bank (ADB), suggest that Bangladesh's latest achievements in macroeconomic management and private sector development have been impressive when compared with many other Asian countries.[46] The economy grew at a strong rate of 5.6 and 6.7 percent in 2005 and 2006, respectively, despite challenges including devastating floods in 2004 that affected some 40 percent of the country, shocks resulting from the depreciation of the U.S. dollar, higher oil prices, and increased political unrest and violence.[47] The government's reform programs have continued to reduce the role of the state in the national economy, kept the fiscal and current account imbalances at a manageable level, and maintained low inflation rates.

However, Bangladesh's bureaucracy, which lacks accountability, transparency, and predictability, has remained a major source of frustration for both investors and ordinary citizens. Excessive centralization in decision-making processes, coupled with the growing problem of weak contract enforcement, have significantly increased the cost of doing business and set the stage for institutionalized forms of corruption. Increased alignment between big business and ruling party elites has made it even easier for policymakers to use public office to advance personal goals, and the growing presence of businesspeople in government has eroded the state's ability to enforce contracts impartially. Businesspeople accounted for more than 60 percent of the members of Parliament elected in 2001, and were represented in both the BNP and the AL. Many of these entrepreneur-lawmakers reportedly have used their newfound political power to "secure control over disbursement of public resources and influence public procurements."[48] Although public officials are legally required to submit financial statements, most either do not bother to disclose their finances or submit statements containing false information. Furthermore, unlike in most democracies, it is not mandatory in Bangladesh for senior bureaucrats to disclose their expenses, and powerful public figures are rarely investigated or prosecuted for corruption.

Corruption has become so endemic in recent years that most people regard it as a fact of life. According to a recent survey conducted by the Bangladesh Unnayan Parishad, a Dhaka-based think tank, Bangladeshis believe that the government agencies tasked with enforcing the law are themselves the source of all kinds of corruption. Some 95 percent of respondents stated that the police were the most corrupt department, followed closely by customs, other arms of the executive branch, and the judiciary.[49] Transparency International's 2006 Global Corruption Report concurs with these findings, asserting that corruption is rampant in both the police and customs departments. Traders routinely bribe customs officials to get their shipments through the port of Chittagong, which accounts for 75 percent of the country's exports and imports.[50] High levels of corruption also exist at the National Board of Revenue (NBR), which is responsible for collecting taxes from individuals and businesses. Considering the scale of the graft, it is no surprise that the country has only 1.4 million registered taxpayers and just 300,000 businesses registered to pay the valued added tax (VAT) collected from consumers. NBR officials allegedly help both individuals and businessmen to avoid taxes in exchange for bribes.

The BNP government decided to set up a tax ombudsman's office in December 2004 to deal with tax-related malpractice and injustice. The relevant legislation was enacted by the Parliament in July 2005. However, the government waited another year before it appointed the first tax ombudsman in July 2006, and the office was not able to launch its operations formally until that December. Since its inception, it has received only thirty complaints against NBR officials. The tax ombudsman recently expressed his dissatisfaction with the response to his office's efforts. Most taxpayer complaints apparently did not provide any details about the accused officials' alleged misdeeds.[51]

Progress was also very slow in launching the Anticorruption Commission (ACC), which was first set up in February 2004 under tremendous pressure from the donor community. Serious questions arose about the body's independence, as the government reportedly appointed the commissioners on a partisan basis. The ACC's lack of financial autonomy and its inability to develop an acceptable staff-recruitment policy have also seriously undermined its credibility. It remained fairly inactive until the formation of Fakhruddin Ahmed's CG in January 2007. Since then, the ACC has aggressively pursued its mission.

Continued political pressure makes the Office of the Comptroller and Auditor General (CAG) largely ineffective in auditing government operations and providing the Parliament with independent information and advice on the stewardship of public funds. Given the lack of a comprehensive procurement policy, the CAG often fails to conduct appropriate audits of state purchases or enforce strict financial discipline through annual departmental reviews. Political pressures reduce the scope for the auditors to prepare financial statements based on actual facts, and in most cases auditors are not empowered to include opinions on the legality of the examined transactions. The CAG generally does not bring gross irregularities to the attention of the public or Parliament.

Despite the politicization of universities in Bangladesh, most educational institutions have managed to maintain their academic integrity. With a few exceptions, students' academic performance determines their progress. The admissions process is usually based on an open competition for the places available, and the majority of those admitted have scores substantially above the minimums set by the respective universities.

Lack of transparency has long been a feature of Bangladesh's political system. Citizens are often unaware of how key policies are formulated, important decisions are made, and public resources are distributed. Successive governments have promoted a culture of secrecy that pervades almost all areas of decision making. The lack of public scrutiny and participation enables corruption, cronyism, and nepotism on the part of public officials. The BNP-led coalition government made no concrete effort to reverse this frustrating situation, though it took the minor step of revamping the websites of most government departments, which now provide information on rules, regulations, and requirements for government services.

Budget making remains a fairly top-down process in which various powerful actors use their political heft to steer allocations toward their agencies, but do not follow an overall strategic vision. The absence of computerized accounting and reporting and the shortcomings in procurement policy also make the financial management system ineffective. In recent years, however, the government has made efforts to introduce strategic budgeting and improve the coordination of capital and recurring budgets. Yielding to donor pressures, the government also introduced reform programs to computerize the financial management system and strengthen the role of the CAG in auditing public expenditures. Although the BNP-led government adopted a more effective legal framework for procurement that ensures open bidding and fair competition among all parties, it did not fully implement it.[52] The government, through the activities of the Economic Relations Division, has generally been responsive to the demands of the donor community regarding the proper administration and allocation of foreign aid.

Recommendations

- The Anticorruption Commission should emerge as an independent agency capable of confronting rampant extortion and bribery. It should be legally autonomous and have the power to subpoena information from officials.
- The government should introduce a reform program aimed at improving transparency. All government officials should be required to submit an annual statement of personal assets, and senior officials should also disclose their annual travel and hospitality expenses.
- The Office of Comptroller and Auditor General should be given the power and authority to carry out routine performance audits and studies of all government departments and agencies, without interference from the political leadership.
- The country should set up a new service program designed to give citizens easy, one-stop access to necessary information on all government policies, programs, and actions. This service should also give dissatisfied individuals the ability to complain and hold government officials personally accountable for their actions.

NOTES

[1] Recent media reports suggest that the return of relative stability to Bangladesh's chaotic political environment has created some optimism among ordinary citizens.

[2] The Constitution of the People's Republic of Bangladesh, Part IV (Government of the People's Republic of Bangladesh, 2004), http://www.cao.gov.bd/constitution/index.htm.

[3] "Election Profile: Bangladesh," *IFES Election Guide* (IFES, 2004), http://www.election guide.org/country.php?ID=19.

[4] "Background Note: Bangladesh," (United States Department of State, Bureau of South and Central Asian Affairs, May 2007), http://www.state.gov/r/pa/ei/bgn/3452.htm.

[5] Abdul Hannan, "Has the Government Lost Touch with People?" *Daily Star* (Dhaka), 7 November 2005.

[6] "Iajuddin 'Key Obstacle' to Fair Polls: AL, LDP Tell EU Observer," *Daily Star*, 21 December 2006.

[7] "Hasina Declares Tougher Actions," *Daily Star*, 11 January 2007.

[8] "Pressure on CA Mounts to Ensure All-Party Poll: Burns Calls Iajuddin," *Daily Star*, 9 January 2007.

[9] "Int'l Community Puts Immense Pressure on Iajuddin," *Daily Star*, 12 January 2007.

[10] Various reports now suggest that the military quietly seized power without making it public. See Sengupta Somini, "Bangladesh Military Government Holds 40 in Graft Sweep," *New York Times*, 14 March 2007; "Bangladesh: Everybody but the Politicians Is Happy," *Economist* 382, no. 8515 (10 February 2007): 64.

[11] Shakhawat Liton, "Emergency Declared: Iajuddin Quits as Chief Adviser," *Daily Star*, 12 January 2007.

[12] "US, UK Reaction to Emergency," *Daily Star*, 13 January 2007.

[13] World Bank, *Bangladesh Country Assessment Strategy: 2006–2009* (Washington D.C.: World Bank, 2006), 17.

[14] World Bank, *Bangladesh PRSP Forum Economic Update: Recent Developments and Future Perspectives* (Dhaka: World Bank, November 2005).

[15] Bangladesh Rural Advancement Committee (BRAC) University Center for Government Studies (CGS), *The State of Governance in Bangladesh, 2006* (Dhaka: BRAC University, CGS, 2007).

[16] World Bank, *Bangladesh Country Assessment Strategy: 2006–2009*, 16.

[17] The donors are now channeling more than 25 percent of their total aid through the voluntary sector. See ibid.

[18] Rashidul Hassan, "NGO Bureau Yet to Release Tk 198 Cr to Proshika," *Daily Star*, 23 February 2007.

[19] CGS, *The State of Governance in Bangladesh, 2006*, 119.

[20] Ibid., 126.

[21] Bob Dietz, "Bangladesh," in *Attacks on the Press in 2006* (New York: Committee to Protect Journalists [CPJ], 2006).

[22] Reporters Without Borders (RSF), "Bangladesh," in *Annual Report 2006* (Paris: RSF, 2006), http://www.rsf.org/article.php3?id_article=17344.

23 CGS, *The State of Governance in Bangladesh, 2006*, 86.

24 This information was collected from RAB's official website, http://www.rab.gov.bd
    /arrestnother.html.

25 See European Commission (EC), "The EU's Relations with Bangladesh," EC, April
    2007, http://www.ec.europa.eu/comm/external_relations/bangladesh/intro/index.htm.

26 Aasha Mehreen Amin and Kajalie Shehreen Islam, "A Successful Police State," *Star Week-end Magazine* 5, no. 118 (3 November 2006): 13.

27 Ibid.

28 Human Rights Watch (HRW), *World Report 2007* (New York: HRW, 2007), http://
    hrw.org/englishwr2k7/docs/2007/01/11/bangla14864.htm.

29 Ibid.

30 Julfikar Ali Manik, "Only Presidential Mercy Can Now Save JMB Leaders," *Daily Star*,
    29 November 2006.

31 Rushidan Islam Rahman and Naoko Otobe, "The Dynamics of the Labor Market and
    Employment in Bangladesh: A Focus on Gender Dimensions," *Employment Strategy
    Papers* (Geneva: International Labor Organization, 2005), http://www.ilo.org/public
    /english/employment/strat/download/esp2005-13.pdf

32 Ibid., 9.

33 CGS, *The State of Governance in Bangladesh, 2006*, 80.

34 Amnesty International (AI), *Bangladesh: Briefing to Political Parties for a Human Rights
    Agenda* (Dhaka: AI, October 2006), 7.

35 Asian Development Bank (ADB), *Bangladesh: Quarterly Economic Update* (ADB, December 2006), 3.

36 HRW, *World Report 2007*.

37 AI, op. cit., 8.

38 Ibid., 10.

39 Recent studies suggest that the people have little or no confidence in the police force,
    which lacks responsiveness, accountability, and professionalism. The police are also seen
    to be the most corrupt organization in Bangladesh. See Manzoor Hasan, *Corruption in
    Bangladesh Surveys: An Overview* (Dhaka: Transparency International Bangladesh [TIB],
    2002).

40 Asian Human Rights Commission (AHRC), "Bangladesh: Lawless Law-Enforcement
    and the Parody of Judiciary," news release, 24 August 2006, http://www.ahrchk.net
    /statements/mainfile.php/2006statements/702/.

41 M. Shah Alam, *Independence and Accountability of Judiciary: A Critical Review* (Dhaka:
    Centre for Rights and Governance, 2004).

42 World Bank, *Poverty in Bangladesh: Building on Progress* (World Bank, South Asia Region,
    2002); U.S. Department of State, *Country Commercial Guide for Bangladesh* (Washington D.C.: U.S. Department of State, 2003).

43 International Property Rights Index (IPRI), 2007 Report (Washington, D.C.: IPRI,
    2007), http://internationalpropertyrightsindex.org/index.php?content=cdata&country
    =Bangladesh.

44 "Bangladesh: One Begum Down," *Economist* 382, no. 8519 (10 March 2007): 69.

45 Ibid.

46 World Bank, *Bangladesh Country Assessment Strategy: 2006–2009*, 11–16.

47 ADB, Bangladesh: *Quarterly Economic Update*, 6–14.

48 "Clean Finance for Competent Candidates, Credible Elections," *New Age* (Dhaka), 4 September 2006.

49 Cited in Almas Zakiuddin, "Corruption in Bangladesh: An Analytical and Sociological Study," TIB, www.ti-bangladesh.org/docs/research/CorBang1.htm.

50 Transparency International, *Global Corruption Report 2006* (London: Pluto Press, 2006), 128.

51 "Complaints of Tax Harassment Will Be Taken Seriously: Tax Ombudsman," *Independent* (Dhaka), 13 March 2007.

52 World Bank, *Bangladesh Country Assessment Strategy: 2006–2009*, 18–20.

BHUTAN

CAPITAL: Thimphu

POPULATION: 0.9 million

GNI PER CAPITA: $1,410

SCORES	2005	2007
ACCOUNTABILITY AND PUBLIC VOICE:	2.40	3.31
CIVIL LIBERTIES:	3.36	3.72
RULE OF LAW:	4.23	4.58
ANTICORRUPTION AND TRANSPARENCY:	3.34	4.12

(scores are based on a scale of 0 to 7, with 0 representing weakest and 7 representing strongest performance)

INTRODUCTION

Between November 2004 and March 2007, Bhutan underwent major, peaceful political changes. On December 14, 2006, King Jigme Singye Wangchuck summoned the Cabinet of Ministers and, before a stunned assembly, informed them that he was abdicating the throne in favor of his eldest son, the *Trongsa Penlop*, Jigme Khesar Namgyal Wangchuck, who became the fifth king of the Wangchuck dynasty.[1]

Although the king had earlier indicated that he would abdicate before the centennial celebration of the monarchy's establishment in 1907, the announcement was greeted with widespread disbelief and sadness. The fourth king had provided the main impetus for political reform in Bhutan, and under his guidance the country has shown potential to eventually transition to democracy. The role of the monarchy has been transformed since direct royal rule ended and an elected cabinet of ministers took over responsibility for government in 1998. The changes initiated starting that year have been consolidated over the last few years and made possible a smooth transition to the new king, who will preside over the inauguration of the first written constitution of Bhutan in 2008.

On March 26, 2005, the draft constitution was publicly launched after a three-year period of drafting and revision. The drafting committee submitted an original draft to the former king in October 2002; it was thereafter refined in a process of consultation with the cabinet of ministers and external advisers. Since its public launch, which included a dedicated website with both English and Dzongkha versions available, a second draft was issued in August 2005 incorporating amendments based on the initial reactions of the Bhutanese public. In addition, the draft constitution has been formally presented by members of the royal family and the cabinet at meetings held throughout Bhutan. At the time of writing, a final version is being prepared for formal presentation to the National Assembly. The adoption of the draft constitution will pave the way for the first democratic parliamentary elections in 2008.

Since 2005, the government has focused on establishing the necessary framework for the new institutions outlined in the draft constitution. Legislation addressing central issues is being drafted and gradually presented to the National Assembly. In January 2007, a Judiciary Service Act was passed that, for the first time, clearly establishes the separation of the judiciary from the executive. The Anticorruption Commission has been actively developing its role in Bhutan, and an Election Commission was established in 2005.

In February 2007, the government announced that the terms of the 1949 Indo-Bhutan Treaty had been officially revised and a new Friendship Treaty signed between India and Bhutan. Under Article 2 of the 1949 treaty, Bhutan had been "guided by the advice of the Government of India in regard to its external relations." This requirement has now been removed. The renegotiation of the 1949 treaty reflects both the commitment of the Bhutanese authorities to establishing a stable constitutional democracy in Bhutan and the 1998 bilateral agreement reached between China and Bhutan regarding the border between Bhutan and Tibet.[2] It marks a maturing of relations between India and Bhutan, and a recognition of the major political transformation taking place in Bhutan.

While respect for human rights in Bhutan does appear to have improved, the Lhotshampa refugee problem remains unresolved. The issue arose in the mid-1980s, when changes to the Citizenship Act made it difficult for Bhutanese of Nepalese descent to acquire Bhutanese citizenship. Tensions between the government and the Lhotshampa community escalated when violent protests broke out in 1990 and 1991.

Following harsh repression of the protests, a significant number of Lhotshampas fled Bhutan and now reside in a series of refugee camps in eastern Nepal. The Joint Verification Process, established between the Bhutanese and Nepalese authorities, was interrupted by attacks on Bhutanese officials at the Khudunbari camp in December 2003 but has since resumed at the ministerial level. A group of nongovernmental organizations (NGOs), including Amnesty International and Human Rights Watch, issued a letter addressed to the delegates attending the ninth Bhutan Donors roundtable talks in Geneva in February 2006. They expressed concern that Bhutan's nationwide census undertaken in 2005 "may be categorising a significant number of Lhotshampas still living in Bhutan as non-nationals."[3] In 2006, the United States and Canada proposed accepting over half of the 108,000 Lhotshampa refugees living in camps in southeastern Nepal. It remains unclear how the plan will be implemented and what impact it will have on the politically organized refugees.

ACCOUNTABILITY AND PUBLIC VOICE

FREE AND FAIR ELECTORAL LAWS AND ELECTIONS:	1.75
EFFECTIVE AND ACCOUNTABLE GOVERNMENT:	4.00
CIVIC ENGAGEMENT AND CIVIC MONITORING:	3.00
MEDIA INDEPENDENCE AND FREEDOM OF EXPRESSION:	4.50
CATEGORY AVERAGE:	**3.31**

The Bhutanese public participated in an extensive series of consultations with the government related to the draft constitution. In each district, people had the opportunity to attend public meetings and express their views on the draft constitution and the changes that it would bring to the political structure of the kingdom. Two sets of mock elections have been held to educate the still mainly rural population about the process of voting and choosing between different political parties for the first time. For the ordinary Bhutanese man or woman, the changes are cause for anxiety. The neighboring states of Nepal, Bangladesh, and even India have not presented particularly good role models for parliamentary democracy.

The draft constitution's thirty-four articles formally recognize a wide range of human rights and civic responsibilities for Bhutanese citizens. The document proposes a bicameral system of government in which the majority party forms the government and the party with the second-largest number of votes forms the opposition.[4] In July 2006, a draft alternative constitution was launched by political exiles, notably human rights dissident Tek Nath Rizal, under an umbrella organization called the National Front for Democracy in Bhutan; for the most part it mirrors the official draft, but it contains key differences, notably in relation to the roles of the state-sponsored *Dratshang Lhentshog* (Central Monk Body) and the royal family.

Although the current cabinet has been subject to elections by the National Assembly, it cannot be viewed as based directly on the will of the people as expressed by regular, free elections. However, the chairperson of the cabinet, who acts as the prime minister, does rotate annually, and the system ensures that all ministers are able to participate fully in government. To date only one direct universal election has been held—the election of *gups* (heads of local government) in November 2002. Each adult over the age of twenty-one was eligible to vote. Article 23 of the draft constitution states that those who can "evidence by a Citizenship Card or certificate issued under law" that they are age eighteen and are registered in the census of "that constituency for not less than one year, prior to the date of election; and not otherwise disqualified from voting under any law in force in Bhutan" may vote "through secret ballot at an election."[5]

Until March 2007, political parties were not permitted in Bhutan. However, under the terms of the constitution, political parties are to be permitted for the first time and may now be formed. In an address to the *Lhengye Zhungtsho* (Cabinet of Ministers) in December 2006, the former king advised that "political parties need to be established at least six months before the elections to be held in 2008." Formal registration will be in July 2007, and the Election Commission is publishing the Political Party Rules and Notification.[6] The current focus on developing a democratic system is further emphasized by making governance the primary focus of the tenth Five Year Plan, scheduled for July 2008. The draft constitution seeks to prohibit the emergence of political parties based on ethnicity, language, or religion. This reflects a concern over the potential for conflict in a small country where there are nineteen languages, three large minority ethnic groups (Ngalong, Sharchop, and Lhotshampa) and two main religions, Mahayana Buddhism and Hinduism, as well as a small number of Christian converts (mainly among the Lhotshampa community). The perception that sectarian parties contributed to instability in neighboring Nepal led Bhutan to incorporate this prohibition. At present, regional differences have been contained, though it is unclear whether or not they will emerge once political parties begin to form.

The first election commissioner, Dasho Kunzang Wangdi, formerly the auditor general, was appointed on December 31, 2005, and is responsible for drawing up the new constituency boundaries and organizing voting sessions once the constitution is in place and the first elections called. The Election Commission of Bhutan was inaugurated in January 2006. It is responsible for the preparation of electoral rolls and the conduct of elections for local government and the new Parliament. The commission's other functions include voter education and the formulation of a fair and widely publicized system for dealing with complaints. Recognizing the importance of training election staff officers to ensure that the 2008 elections are a success, the Election Commission introduced trainers' workshops in order to prepare various stakeholders. A Delimitation Commission was established to delineate the new electoral boundaries.[7] This required the commission to scrutinize the current *gewog* (the smallest administrative unit in Bhutan, comprising several villages) and *dzongkhag* (administrative district) boundaries in an attempt to ensure that all the electoral constituencies have equal weight and representation in the future Parliament.

Around 400,000 voters are eligible to participate in the 2008 parliamentary elections. However, the Department of Civil Registration and Census reported in December 2006 that only 180,897 people had registered. Officials also noted that 48 percent of those who had registered had filled out the voter registration form incorrectly.[8] The Election Commission is considering conducting a further round of voter registration to ensure, for example, that people from outlying districts working in Thimphu are registered.[9]

The problems experienced during the 2002 gup elections appear to have been scrutinized and steps taken to ensure that the ballot boxes are standardized and that the visual and verbal instructions are clear. Recent mock elections to familiarize the electorate with the voting process highlighted the need for ongoing education of the rural population.[10] It remains to be seen if adjustments to the locations of polling stations, which were a problem in the 2002 elections, will ensure a higher turnout in the 2008 contest.[11]

Bhutan also recognizes the need to increase the participation of local people in decision making processes, especially in rural areas. Article 22 of the draft constitution enshrines the concept of democratic local governance, and amendments to the dzongkhag and gewog development committee acts set out the legal basis for the assignment of powers, functions, and finances at these levels. The *zomdu* (local village councils) have historically made all decisions affecting the local community, with the participation of all households. The gups and *chimi* (representatives in the legislature) who are elected receive salaries from the government. According to a report on decentralization in Bhutan, although local-level administrative autonomy has been enhanced, it still remains incomplete.[12]

The civil service is a central part of the administration of Bhutan. It has, until recently, been the main employer of young, educated Bhutanese. Many of those selected have received further education outside Bhutan, mainly in India but increasingly in countries including Australia, Canada, Singapore, the UK, and the United States. These graduates have ensured that the quality of the civil service has steadily improved.

The civil service is often commented on by Bhutanese, and under Royal Civil Service Commission Secretary Dasho Bap Kesang, a review and broad reforms are underway. In March 2007, the first 45 civil servants in specialist and executive categories and a further 235 permanent civil servants were promoted under the new position classification system. These promotions indicate major changes and improvements in civil service appointments.[13]

The state-sponsored Central Monk Body currently has representatives in the National Assembly and on the Royal Advisory Council. Their presence reflects the transformation of Bhutan from a theocracy established by the founder of Bhutan, the *Zhabdrung*, Ngawang Namgyal, to a monarchy in the early twentieth century. They have not sought to influence government policies directly but were active in promoting the abolition of the death penalty. Under the terms of the draft constitution, the current representation of the Central Monk Body in the legislature will cease, indicating a clear attempt to separate religion from politics in Bhutan. Indeed, the constitution refers to Buddhism as the "spiritual heritage of Bhutan" but does not declare it the official state religion. According to the draft constitution, all religions will be respected; this is an important issue, given past tensions with the Hindu minority. After initial concerns were raised in the consultation process, the people appear to have accepted that Buddhism will not be declared the official state religion.

According to a report issued by a Bhutanese newspaper, it appears that under the proposed rules, 9,287 monks and nuns registered with the Central Monk Body will not be eligible to vote, which will slightly reduce the eligible voting population.[14] This appears to be a strict interpretation of Article 3(3), which declares that "religious institutions and personalities shall remain above politics." However, according to other sources there is a fear that if this rule is more widely applied many lay *gomchen* (ritual practitioners) will also be ineligible to vote, which would be particularly problematic in central and eastern Bhutan.

Civil society in Bhutan is gradually developing. The main civil society organizations focus on children, women, and the environment, and these organizations work closely with the government to improve delivery of state services. Such organizations, notably the Bhutan Chamber of Commerce and Industry, exert varying degrees of influence on the development of government policies and legislation. An act governing nongovernmental organizations that would clarify their legal status has been planned for at least three years. Existing organizations are generally free from state pressures; however, they do attempt to balance any criticism, direct or implied, of the government with a close working relationship in order to ensure that the government takes their views into account.

Bhutan has substantially increased its Reporters Without Borders press freedom rating, moving from 157th in 2003 to 142nd in 2005 and to 98th in 2006, when it scored 25.00 out of 100.[15] This probably reflects the establishment of two additional newspapers in Bhutan, which tripled the number of newspapers from the previous one (*Kuensel*). The state has encouraged the development of media and private printing houses in the country, and the presence of an increasingly articulate and educated middle class is creating the demand for stronger media. The Media Act of 2005, however, provoked an outcry from a range of media representatives, especially those in the nascent film industry, as it was considered to be creating obstacles to the emerging film industry through overregulation. In May 2007, proposed controls over advertising received similarly unfavorable comment in newspaper editorials. Nevertheless, the state does not use the laws to fine or imprison those who scrutinize officials or policies. There are provisions for defamation in Bhutanese law but they are seldom invoked.

External comments on the draft constitution submitted through websites have been acknowledged by the government and appear to have influenced revisions to the draft constitution. There remains a sense that Bhutanese seek to maintain consensus in public but are increasingly willing to voice their concerns and frustrations through the new media, activity which the government has not sought to curb or prevent. Therefore, as a result of growing market competition and the public discussions surrounding the draft constitution, the willingness to report critically and reflect on the wider implications of new legislation and government policies has grown.

The Ministry for Information and Technology does not interfere with the media, with the exception of banning certain satellite television channels that are viewed as having a deleterious effect on young Bhutanese and Bhutanese social values, and the state does not hinder access to the internet. The state supports the Royal Academy of Performing Arts in Thimphu to promote Bhutanese culture. Smaller, privately run organizations seek to preserve and promote Bhutanese cultural forms—notably dances and songs from throughout the country. The small and gradually developing film industry is free to evolve without government interference.

Recommendations
- The government should publish and circulate the rules governing political parties and eligibility to vote, as well as engage in ongoing public education to ensure both voter registration and participation in national and local elections.
- The act governing nongovernmental organizations should be drafted and promulgated in order to strengthen the legal basis of such organizations.

- To ensure greater local participation and accountability, local level administrative autonomy should be enhanced, and local elected officials held accountable for their actions.
- The government should strengthen electoral management bodies and promote transparent management of the election process by disseminating pamphlets explaining the process and holding meetings in which the political process is explained in minority languages.

CIVIL LIBERTIES

PROTECTION FROM STATE TERROR, UNJUSTIFIED IMPRISONMENT, AND TORTURE:	5.00
GENDER EQUITY:	4.00
RIGHTS OF ETHNIC, RELIGIOUS, AND OTHER DISTINCT GROUPS:	2.25
FREEDOM OF CONSCIENCE AND BELIEF:	4.33
FREEDOM OF ASSOCIATION AND ASSEMBLY:	3.00
CATEGORY AVERAGE:	**3.72**

Although ordinary Bhutanese are gradually being educated about their rights and duties as citizens, the concept of civil liberties is comparatively new to Bhutan, and Bhutanese society is inherently conservative. Older generations retain a worldview shaped by their experience of a hierarchical, closed society. However, young Bhutanese educated in modern schools are adapting to new ideas and values. At present, people are apprehensive about the transition to a parliamentary democracy. The formation of the first political parties later in 2007 will undoubtedly make Bhutanese more conscious of their rights under the constitution and will affect the development of civil society.

The draft constitution sets out the fundamental rights of all Bhutanese citizens. In essence, it enumerates the civil liberties to be granted to Bhutanese, including equality before the law, freedoms of assembly and religion, and freedom from torture or cruel punishments. The death penalty was abolished in March 2004, and torture is officially prohibited. There have been no recent verified reports of torture being used in Bhutan.

Until the March 2007 announcement that political parties could be formed, all parties, including the National Front for Democracy in Bhutan, were typically located outside the country, mainly in Nepal or in West Bengal in India. In July 2006, the group presented an alternative draft of the constitution closely based on the official version at a ceremony on the Nepal–India border. It is unclear whether or not these activists will be able to return to Bhutan or participate in the political life of the country once the constitution is enacted. There have been no reports of political arrests in recent years, although the November 2006 arrest of a Lhotshampa suspected of being a Maoist does suggest that the government remains vigilant. Bhutanese authorities responded to criticisms expressed over prison conditions in the early 1990s and have actively worked with donors to improve prison conditions.

The civil and criminal procedure code of 2001 continues to ensure that detainees are brought before the courts as swiftly as possible. The High Court has stressed the importance of ensuring that cases are heard without undue delay (see Rule of Law). The state exercises control throughout the country through the police, and seeks to ensure that its citizens are not subject to abuse by private or nonstate actors, especially following the removal of the ULFA/Bodo guerrillas. These insurgents, who came from India's northeastern states to oppose the federal government and promote claims for independence, sought shelter in the dense jungles and rugged terrain of southern Bhutan and may have links with Maoists in Nepal. The guerrillas were forcibly expelled after a brief military campaign in November and December 2003. It remains unclear how closely, if at all, ULFA/Bodo forces have worked with Bhutanese opponents of the government. A December 2006 bomb blast in Phuentsholing, a reminder of the bombings in the marketplace in Gelephu in September 2004, served to highlight the possibility that repercussions may still follow the military campaign against the insurgents. A suspected Maoist was also arrested by Bhutanese authorities, raising the specter of ongoing terrorism from among the refugee population.

Currently, Bhutanese citizens have the right of petition and appeal through the formal courts up to the king, although it is necessary to exhaust all formal avenues before appealing to the king. The draft constitution provides for a Supreme Court, which will add a further tier to the existing Bhutanese judiciary. At present, it is too early to comment on how effective the Supreme Court will be as a venue for providing redress against violations by state authorities.

The National Commission for Women and Children (NCWC) was established in 2004 and since its inception has consistently worked to promote gender equality and other issues. In general, Bhutanese women enjoy greater personal freedom and equality with men than elsewhere in South Asia. The ratio of girls to boys at primary and secondary education is now at par.[16] There remain concerns, however, over maternal mortality and gender equality in employment. Women's participation in the labor force, particularly in the modern sector of the economy, remains modest. Lower levels of education and fewer skills result in women being "less employable," particularly in urban centers. About 19 percent of civil servants are women, and the number of women holding administrative and managerial positions is comparatively small. Female representation in the National Assembly, district development committees, and block development committees, although improving, is still low. The majority of the women's labor force today—up to 90 percent of rural women—is still involved in agriculture. Although some urban women have achieved prominence as the heads of successful businesses, in all sectors of paid employment, public or private, men significantly outnumber women.

The gap between male and female literacy is gradually being reduced; however, it remains one of the main barriers to female political participation, as suggested by the absence of any women candidates in the gup elections of 2002. RENEW, an NGO, is working to raise public awareness of issues affecting women. Additionally, the government has sought to work with various donors to promote awareness of remaining gender inequality and other minority issues, but it currently lacks the resources to intervene actively.

In December 2005, NCWC formulated a National Plan of Action for Women in collaboration with RENEW and other agencies. With the support of UN agencies, several workshops and events to raise awareness of gender issues were held in 2005 and 2006. In March 2006, the National Consultation on Women and Child Friendly Judicial Procedures, which targeted judicial and police personnel, was held by the Royal Court of Justice and NCWC. The executive director of the NCWC, Dr. Rinchen Chophel, noted that although existing laws provide an adequate umbrella to protect the rights of women and children, there was a pressing need "to strengthen the implementation and support mechanism to ensure that the rights are exercised and deliberated."[17]

The draft constitution recognizes the freedom of religion and conscience of Bhutanese citizens. It does not declare Buddhism to be the official religion of Bhutan; instead, it acknowledges it as the spiritual heritage of the country while respecting all other faiths. Proselytizing remains prohibited in Bhutan. No recent claims of religious discrimination have arisen from the Christian minority, and certain Hindu festivals are national holidays in Bhutan. The state does not involve itself in the appointment or internal organization of the various faiths, and the selection of religious figures in the Central Monk Body is entirely controlled by the monks themselves.

The state views the ethnic and linguistic diversity of Bhutan as important. However, in the mid-1990s, members of an eastern minority group, the Sharchop, did challenge the state with the creation of the Druk National Congress Party. Amnesty International reported a clampdown by the state in the east in 1997. Since then, the state has sought to address the grievances voiced by those living in the east and there is no longer resistance toward the government. No discrimination based on ethnicity or language is permitted in Bhutan.

Tensions arose between the Bhutanese government and the Lhotshampa community during the 1980s. The Citizenship Act of 1985 amended the basis for claiming Bhutanese citizenship, and a census conducted in 1988 further exacerbated tensions. In 1989, a royal *kasho* (decree) reintroduced the code of traditional dress known as *driglam namzha* and the requirement to wear the traditional *gho* and *kira* when visiting government offices and monasteries, while also emphasizing the use of Dzongkha as the national language. This was viewed as an attack on Lhotshampa cultural identity and in 1991 violence broke out, with the Bhutanese state adopting a hard-line policy against the unrest. As a result, a large number of Lhotshampa fled their homes in southern Bhutan and are now living in refugee camps in eastern Nepal.

Various international NGOs, among them Amnesty International, have argued in an open letter to donors that elements of the draft constitution concerning citizenship "tend to confirm our doubts about the possibility of Lhotshampas retaining or reacquiring their citizenship."[18]

Among the eight recommendations proposed by the NGOs is the repatriation of those refugees in Khudunbari camp verified by the Joint Verification Team as Bhutanese and the introduction of measures "to eliminate discrimination against Lhotshampas who remained in Bhutan and to ensure the protection of their fundamental human rights . . . to participate as full citizens." There are concerns that the draft constitution, which defines citizenship in terms of the 1985 Citizenship Act, will continue to restrict the granting of full citizenship to Bhutanese of Nepalese descent.

In a recent survey on human rights in South Asia published by the Asian Centre for Human Rights, Bhutan was held to have the worst human rights record, based mainly on the unresolved Lhotshampa issue.[19] The report notes that Bhutan has failed to withdraw the rule introduced in 1990 under which all Nepali-speaking citizens must obtain one of a series of certificates from the police stating that none of their relatives took part in the antigovernment protests of 1990 and 1991 in order to gain admission to schools or sit for examinations. Under this rule, the children of Nepali-speaking community, especially those whose relatives were living in refugee camps in Nepal, are denied access to education. It should be noted, however, that all Bhutanese, irrespective of ethnicity, are required to obtain these certificates. In September 2006, during a visit to Bhutan by a U.S. Congressional delegation, it was announced that the United States had agreed to take up to 70,000 people from the refugee camps. Australia and Canada also agreed to take smaller numbers of refugees.[20]

From a Bhutanese perspective, expressed by Karma Phuntsho, a young Bhutanese intellectual, "the negotiations and the process of verification seems to have been obstructed more by Nepal's political instability than by Bhutan's reluctance. Doubts are being cast over whether Nepal is genuinely committed to ending the crisis."[21] Nepalese authorities have faced a range of major issues, notably a bloody civil war, that have made it difficult to fully address the refugee situation. Following a series of meetings commencing in September 2005, the Nepalese government advised the Bhutanese that it does not consider the refugee issue to directly involve the government of Nepal; rather the problem is one for the Bhutanese to resolve directly with the refugees.

The Joint Verification Process agreed between Bhutan and Nepal represented the main breakthrough in recent years. During the National

Assembly session in December 2006, the foreign minister gave a briefing on the current status of Bhutan–Nepal bilateral talks, which have
resumed at the ministerial level after a lull following the events at the
Khudunbari camp, where Bhutanese officials were attacked by refugees
in December 2003. Bhutanese authorities advised their Nepalese counterparts that Bhutan would be willing to repatriate all refugees who were
categorized as Bhutanese citizens, although those who had "voluntarily
migrated" would be forced to reapply for citizenship, while those categorized as criminals would have to stand trial upon their return. Bhutan's
use of these categories is viewed by human rights groups as a violation
of the state's obligations under international law.[22]

Although the constitution provides for the freedom of association
and assembly, during the period of this report, there remained restrictions on these freedoms. At present, and reflecting the mainly agricultural nature of Bhutan's economy, there are no trade unions. As the labor
market develops it is possible that trade unions will emerge. There are
no organizations or associations that Bhutanese are required to join.
Demonstrations and public protests are unlawful in Bhutan, though this
may change once the constitution is brought into force.

Recommendations
- The government should invest greater efforts to promote civic awareness among citizens, especially rural populations, women, and minority groups by disseminating pamphlets explaining the process and
  holding meetings in which the draft constitution and the political
  process are explained in minority languages.
- The government should create a task force to evaluate the problem of
  female illiteracy and seek out international donors to contribute resources to tackle the problem.
- The Bhutanese government should acknowledge the rights of Lhotshampa citizens and amend the Citizenship Act in order to make the
  process of gaining citizenship more transparent, starting with elimination of the No Objection Certificates, Police Clearance Certificates,
  and Security Clearance Certificates.
- Rules for choosing representatives for both houses of the legislature
  must facilitate adequate representation of politically underrepresented
  regions and demographic groups by setting a quota for female and
  minority candidates within each party.

RULE OF LAW

INDEPENDENT JUDICIARY:	5.00
PRIMACY OF RULE OF LAW IN CIVIL AND CRIMINAL MATTERS:	5.00
ACCOUNTABILITY OF SECURITY FORCES AND MILITARY TO CIVILIAN AUTHORITIES:	5.25
PROTECTION OF PROPERTY RIGHTS:	3.67
EQUAL TREATMENT UNDER THE LAW:	4.00
CATEGORY AVERAGE:	**4.58**

The Bhutanese judiciary has been active in strengthening the legal system and promoting wider access to justice. As ordinary Bhutanese learn more about the modern legal system and an increasingly well-educated cadre of judges and lawyers emerges, reservations about the impartiality and fairness of the courts have significantly diminished. In January 2007, The Judiciary Service Act was passed by the National Assembly.[23] For the past decade, the judiciary has sought to ensure its autonomy, and the new law will enable the High Court to firmly establish its independence from the executive and legislature. In addition, the court structure in Bhutan has been augmented by the creation of a Supreme Court above the High Court, which will oversee the interpretation and application of the constitution. The new law establishes a Judicial Service Council to administer the judiciary, replacing the Royal Civil Service Commission. The chief justice, addressing the National Assembly, noted that the act seeks to ensure that the "delivery of justice and legal process is not compromised" by removing the possibility of "influential people telephoning judges." Another important aspect of the act is to enhance public confidence in the judiciary and enable ordinary citizens to raise complaints regarding judicial behavior. Broadly, the act gives the judiciary, through the new Judicial Service Council, complete administrative and financial independence over appointments, training, and promotion and the right to create or abolish posts in the judiciary in response to changing requirements and circumstances.

According to a recent report by the High Court of Justice, the importance and legitimacy of the judiciary is increasing. In 2006, 173 cases were appealed, up from 118 in 2005. This steady increase is less reflective of a growing litigiousness than a growing awareness of the modern legal system and the increasing professionalism of the judiciary.[24] Legal education continues for judges at all levels, and judges and lawyers continue to educate the wider public about the laws and the role of the judiciary. A recent report released by the High Court emphasized that of the 170 *drangpon* (judges), approximately 50 percent hold either bachelor's or master's degrees in law and have been trained in Bhutanese law at the Royal Institute of Management. However, there is an emerging problem facing the judiciary and the nascent legal profession in Bhutan: 95 percent of all those who have received formal legal training are employed by the government. As a result, lawyers available for the public to consult are in short supply. Moreover, although the Jabmi Act of 2003 provided for the creation of the *Jabmi Tshogde* (Bar Council) and a Bar Association of Bhutan, neither has as yet been formally constituted. Caseload pressure on the courts is increasing, and dissatisfaction is mounting with the delays caused as a result.[25] However, the Office of the Attorney General has indicated that it understands that there is a need for more lawyers and it has requested increased staff to cope with the increasing workload.[26]

In October 2006, the Royal Civil Service Commission (RCSC) announced that all fourteen of the dungkhags will have their own separate courts by 2008. This move reflects the ongoing reform and rationalization of the judicial infrastructure in Bhutan. Until recently, cases raised in dungkhag courts, with the exception of Phuentsholing, Wamrong, and Gelephu, were heard by *dungpas* (local officials) who lack legal training and were not subject to monitoring by the High Court.[27] Accordingly, they fell under the executive branch of the government, and the move by the RCSC and High Court will help ensure that the separation of the judiciary from the executive is thoroughly established.

The civil and criminal procedure code established that Bhutanese charged with a criminal offense are presumed innocent until proven guilty. The Office of Legal Affairs acts as the state prosecutor and is independent of the executive and legislature. Criminal trials are public and heard before an independent and impartial court. Under the Jabmi Act of 2003, the right to representation was established for criminal cases, including state provision of counsel when the defendant cannot afford to pay. The right to representation is upheld by the courts and representation is provided as a matter of course. Nonetheless, people generally have a very limited understanding of the legal process or the grounds for legal decisions, and a great deal of work remains to be done to improve the transparency of the legal process. This has been partially addressed by the recent move to publish court decisions on the official website of the High Court.[28]

The military has not interfered with government in Bhutan, and it is unlikely to do so. It remains numerically small, although it should be noted that following the brief military campaign against the ULFA/Bodo guerrilla forces, the use of militias has been reintroduced, ensuring that the wider population will be able to assist in the defense of the country if required. The police also do not interfere in the existing political process. Senior officers of the Royal Army and police force work closely with the government to maintain law and order.

The ordinary Bhutanese citizen may own property alone or in association with others. However, to own property or land in Bhutan an individual must be a full citizen. This can cause problems for those individuals who have permission to reside but are not recognized as Bhutanese citizens, especially Lhotshampas who are unable to meet the qualification requirements set out in the 1985 Citizenship Act. Non-Bhutanese are prohibited from owning land, which is registered on a cadastral system, with registration required for all land transactions. By law, the maximum landholding is fixed at twenty-five acres and the minimum at five acres. In general, the state protects and upholds the right of private citizens to hold property. However, in 2006, the state did repossess land around Dechencholing that had been illegally occupied. Compensation was provided by the state for those who were dispossessed. This eviction was an unusual step by the state and was necessitated by the growing shortage of land in and around the capital, Thimphu.

Recommendations

- The government should make all court cases, as well as the police investigations and allegations of misconduct, available in writing to the public.
- The government should increase funding and continue legal training programs to fill the critical need for qualified judges and lawyers.
- The government should encourage the creation of the Jabmi Tshogde and Bar Association to increase the quality and accountability of lawyers and access to them.

ANTICORRUPTION AND TRANSPARENCY

ENVIRONMENT TO PROTECT AGAINST CORRUPTION:	3.60
EXISTENCE OF LAWS AND ETHICAL STANDARDS BETWEEN	
PRIVATE AND PUBLIC SECTORS:	5.00
ENFORCEMENT OF ANTICORRUPTION LAWS:	4.75
GOVERNMENTAL TRANSPARENCY:	3.14
CATEGORY AVERAGE:	**4.12**

Bhutan's Anticorruption Commission (ACC) was established in January 2006. The first chairperson of the commission is Neten Zangmo, who is assisted by two commissioners. Below the secretariat, there is a legal and planning division and an administrative section. The commission has eight investigators, a prevention division, and a public education and advocacy unit. Critically, the ACC is an independent organization with wide powers that it can and does exercise. During 2006, the commission worked hard to raise awareness of corruption and educate the public. A dedicated website enables citizens to report instances of corruption and emphasizes the importance of confidentiality. The complementary Anticorruption Act was passed by the eighty-fifth session of the National Assembly in the summer of 2006. The act defines corruption, vests power in the ACC, and emphasizes the duty of Bhutanese citizens to act against corruption. Importantly, the act clearly states that it will be an offense of obstruction if any individual or entity refuses to comply with any demand for access or information made by the ACC.

For a young organization, the ACC has made major progress and is working closely with a range of government agencies, the private sector, and the media. It is undertaking systematic studies of land transactions, forestry services, and the issuing and renewal of driving licenses. The ACC is also tackling problems in construction, procurement, printing, and customs.[29] In 2006, the ACC conducted a major corruption perceptions survey, the results of which suggest that people are very concerned about corruption and perceive it as an institutionalized phenomenon that affects all sectors. Furthermore, in a move to prevent corruption by public officials, the ACC announced that all public officials from the prime minister on down should declare their assets by December 31, 2006.

This deadline was extended, however, due to a "poor response," to February 15, 2007.[30]

The ACC is ensuring greater transparency in the awarding of government contracts and is investigating allegations of corruption. Foreign assistance to Bhutan from its major donors is carefully accounted for, and the government ensures that it is fairly and correctly utilized for the purposes for which it is provided. Donors perceive Bhutan to be less corrupt than other South Asian states and more transparent in its use of external assistance.

The ACC has demonstrated its strength and vigor by passing two corruption cases involving a former district governor and a former judge, as well as local leaders in the first case and a former district engineer in the second, to the Attorney General's Office for prosecution. By December 31, 2006, the ACC had received 283 complaints, with complaints about civil servants relating mainly to the misuse of resources. Abuse of position, discrimination (for example, based on gender or ethnicity) and the misuse of resources appear to be the main complaints against corporate managers.[31] As the result of a three-month investigation by the ACC, almost two-thirds of the employees of the Royal Insurance Corporation of Bhutan Ltd. were found guilty of "misusing entitlement claims." The report revealed that seventy-one employees, including senior managers, had claimed in excess of 2.437 million Nu (approximately US$56,000) on medical bills and hotel rooms from their company.[32]

There is no freedom of information act in Bhutan. The focus of the past two years has been on creating the new framework and legislative basis for the introduction of the constitution. The provision of information about government services is improving steadily; currently, the main drawback is the considerable length of time taken to publish documents. However, there is no provision for information about government services and decisions in formats and settings accessible to people with disabilities. This may be addressed in the future, when the necessary infrastructure is in place, but is not currently feasible for the government.

Bhutanese do complain about the regulations and registration requirements that present barriers to establishing new commercial enterprises. However, these requirements are not especially onerous and the state is attempting to simplify registration requirements to promote private sector development. There are a few large private companies in Bhutan; however, the state did control the economy and used its resources to fund the major program of development. There has been a shift, reflecting the need to encourage greater individual self-reliance, towards the promotion of private enterprise.

There is limited information available on the administration of the tax regime or the conduct of internal audits. In December 2005, it was reported that the Public Accounts Committee established by the National Assembly Committees Act of 2004 had not met once since it was established. This committee supposedly has oversight of government accounts, but it was noted that no agency, including the Royal Audit Authority, had submitted any report to the Assembly. This caused a review and it was agreed that a report by the RAA would be submitted to the National Assembly in order to promote greater transparency in state expenditures.[33]

Corruption is discussed by Bhutanese, though it can be difficult to gauge the real extent of actual corruption as opposed to dissatisfaction caused by not being successful in securing official tenders. Rumors of corruption must therefore be treated with caution.

The media increasingly report on cases of corruption brought to the courts and have been instrumental in highlighting the work of the ACC. The establishment of the ACC has created the first independent body that can investigate cases based on reports by whistle-blowers and other anticorruption activists. The ACC website provides a form for individuals to submit anonymous reports of corruption, which will be investigated by the ACC. This will create a more secure environment for individuals to report cases of bribery and corruption.

Recommendations
- A bill should be introduced to strengthen, regulate, and protect in practice and under law the right to information, as a basic tool to strengthen democracy.
- The Public Accounts Committee must be more proactive and have the ability to request a report from any government agency. All government agencies should be required to submit annual reports before the Committee within a clearly specified time period.
- New laws specifically protecting whistle-blowers should be enacted to protect both public and private employees from reprisals for bearing witness against waste, fraud, and other abuses of power.

NOTES

1   "Breaking News: Royal Kasho (the Letter from His Majesty to the People of Bhutan),"
    Kuensel Online (Bhutan), 14 December 2006, accessed 15 December 2006. For reactions
    and reflections on the abdication, see "A Nation, a King, a Shared Mandate," *Kuensel,*
    21 December 2006, http://www.Kuenselonline.com/modules.php?name=News&Files
    =article&sid=7856; "A Monarch: Editorial," *Kuensel,* 21 December 2006, http://www
    .Kuenselonline.com/modules.php?name=News&Files=articlet&sid=7855. For an Indian
    perspective on the abdication of the king, see "Bhutan Abdication," *Statesman* (Kolkata),
    21 December 2006, accessed 23 December 2007.

2   "Rewriting History, India to Unshackle Bhutan," *Kuensel,* 9 January 2007.

3   Human Rights Watch (HRW), "Joint NGO Letter to the Delegates of the Bhutan
    Donors Round Table Meeting," HRW, 9 February 2006, http://hrw.org/english/docs
    /2006/02/09/bhutan12647_txt.htm.

4   For more details on the draft constitution and the current draft, see http://www
    .constitution.bt. Unfortunately, there is no website with the alternative draft constitu-
    tion launched by the National Front for Democracy in Bhutan.

5   Draft Constitution of Bhutan, available at http://satp.org/satporgtp/countries/bhutan
    /document/actandordinances/constitution.htm

6   "Notification" (Motithang: Election Commission of Bhutan, 19 March 2007), http://
    www.election-bhutan.org.bt/Docs/fppe/pdf.

7   "Draft Delimitation Plan By March," *Kuensel,* 7 February 2007, http://www.Kuensel
    online.com/modules.php?name=News&file=article&sid=8069.

8   "75% of Votes Registered," *Kuensel,* 29 November 2006, http://www.Kuenselonline.com
    /modules.php?name=Names&file=article&sid=7786, accessed 28 February 2007.

9   "Mitsi and Gung Transfer Still Open," *Kuensel,* 13 January 2007, http://www.Kuensel
    online.com/modules.php?name=New&file=articles&sid=7956, accessed 15 January
    2007.

10 "Whom Are You Going To Vote For?" *Kuensel,* 1 December 2006, http://www.Kuensel
    online.com/modules.php?name=Newsfiles=articles&sid.7791, accessed 15 January 2007.

11 A major problem for locating polling stations is the terrain and the remoteness of many
    communities. It is an issue which will require monitoring and more resources, which at
    present the government does not have.

12 Tashi Wangchuk, "Increasing Rural People's Participation in Local Decision Making,"
    Development Newsletter 1, no. 1 (Autumn 2006): 4–5.

13 "RCSC Promotes 235 Civil Servants Under the PCS," Bhutan Broadcasting Service,
    15 March 2007.

14 "Lay Monks Can Vote," *Bhutan Observer,* 2 February 2007.

15 Reporters Without Borders (RSF), *World Press Freedom Index 2006* (Paris: RSF, 2006).

16 Ministry of Finance (Bhutan), *Millennium Development Goals: Progress Report 2005*
    (Thimphu: Ministry of Finance, Department of Planning, December 2005), 37.

17 "Women and Children Friendly Legal Procedures," *Kuensel,* 4 April 2006, http://www
    .Kuenselonline.com/modules.php?name=News&file=article&sid=6753.

18 HRW, "Joint NGO Letter . . . "

19 Asian Centre for Human Rights (ACHR) SAARC Human Rights Report 2006 (New Delhi: ACHR, 2006), http://www.achrweb.org/reports/saarcar2006/main.htm.

20 Dharma Adhikari, "Bhutan's Democratic Puzzle," openDemocracy (Manchester, U.K.), 30 June 2006, http://www.openDemocracy.net. A reply to this article appeared in "US Congressional Delegation Visits Bhutan," Kuensel, 2 September 2006, http://www.Kuenselonline.com/modules.php?name=News & file=print&sid=7398.

21 Karma Phuntsho, "Bhutan Reforms, Nepalese Criticism," openDemocracy, 13 October 2006, http://www.opendemocracy.net/democracy-protest/bhutan_nepal_3996.jsp.

22 HRW, Last Hope: The Need for Durable Solutions for Bhutanese Refugees in Nepal and India (New York: HRW, May 2007).

23 "Act Empowers Judiciary, People," Kuensel, 13 January 2007, http://www.Kuensel online.com/.

24 "Appeal Cases Increase," Kuensel, 6 January 2007, http://www.Kuenselonline.com/modules.php?name=News&file=article7sid=7922, accessed 7 January 2007.

25 "More Lawyers Required, Says Attorney General," Bhutan Times, 18 March 2007.

26 "OAG: Short of Lawyer," Kuensel, 7 May 2007, http://www.Kuenselonline.com/modules.php?name=News&file=article&sid=8432, accessed 2 June 2007.

27 "Dungkhag Courts by 2008," Kuensel, 11 October 2006, http://www.Kuensel online.com/modules.php?name=Names&file=article&sid=7571, accessed 12 March 2007.

28 "Judgments Will Be Posted on the Web," Kuensel, 7 May 2007, http://www.Kuensel online.com/modules.php?name=New&file=article&sid=8414, accessed 8 May 2007.

29 United Nations Development Programme (UNDP), "Fighting Corruption Is A Collective Responsibility," UNDP Development Newsletter (Autumn 2006).

30 "Disclosing Wealth," Kuensel, 21 January 2007, http://www.Kuenselonline.com/modules.php?name=New&file=print&sid=7988, accessed 12 March 2007.

31 "Illegal Land Transfer," Kuensel, 10 January 2007, http://www.Kuenselonline.com/modules.php?name=News&file+article&sid.=7940, accessed 12 January 2007.

32 "71 Insurance Employees Could Face Prosecution," Kuensel, 10 January 2007, http://www.Kuenselonine.com/modules.php?name=News&file+article&sid=7941, accessed 12 January 2007.

33 "No Work of Public Accounts Committee," Kuensel, 3 December 2005, http://www.Kuenselonline.com/modules.php?name=New&file=article&sid=6286, accessed 31 May 2007.

BOLIVIA

CAPITAL: La Paz
POPULATION: 9.8 million
GNI PER CAPITA: $1,100

SCORES	2005	2007
ACCOUNTABILITY AND PUBLIC VOICE:	3.54	4.56
CIVIL LIBERTIES:	4.12	4.16
RULE OF LAW:	3.52	3.58
ANTICORRUPTION AND TRANSPARENCY:	3.12	3.08

(scores are based on a scale of 0 to 7, with 0 representing weakest
and 7 representing strongest performance)

Donna Lee Van Cott

INTRODUCTION

Bolivia has experienced significant political instability over the last five years, a trend that continued between November 2004 and March 2007. With a constituent assembly now engaged in the task of rewriting the Bolivian charter, fundamental questions of state structure—as well as what it means to be Bolivian—are under consideration, with high stakes for all citizens.

In June 2005, President Carlos Mesa was forced to resign following three weeks of nationwide social protest, the second president in three years to do so. Mesa was unable to achieve consensus on vital issues, including nationalization of the oil and gas industry, demands for autonomy from lowland elites, and the convocation of elections for a constituent assembly. The leftist opposition and the general public rejected the next two figures in the line of succession—the leaders of the Senate and Chamber of Deputies—because they were perceived to represent the corrupt and discredited elite. After pressure from Mesa, the Catholic

Donna Lee Van Cott is Associate Professor of political science at the University of Connecticut. She is writing a book about municipal government innovation by indigenous political parties in the Andes.

Church, and regional and international leaders, both stepped aside in favor of the politically independent chief of the Supreme Court, Eduardo Rodriguez, who was constitutionally required to hold new elections. During this period, the police and the military demonstrated admirable restraint in the face of provocations from protesters; this moderation stood in stark contrast to the harsh repression of protesters by security forces that played a major role in the ouster of former president Gonzalo Sanchez de Lozada in October 2003.

The election of coca growers leader Evo Morales and the Movement toward Socialism (MAS) party on December 18, 2005, with an absolute majority (54 percent) of the vote, provided a moment of catharsis and euphoria for the disenfranchised and frustrated indigenous majority. The large margin of victory allowed Bolivia to avoid a power struggle in the postelectoral period and marked the collapse of the old political party system and the tradition of pact making and patronage distribution that had sustained it. Top leaders in the military and Morales's main challenger, Jorge Quiroga, discouraged confrontation by pledging to respect the results.[1]

President Morales's inauguration on January 22, 2006, temporarily ended large-scale social mobilizations, although sectoral protests continued on a smaller scale. Political instability continues, however, owing to Morales's twin determinations to disregard his opponents and to utilize social movements to build support in the streets. Until late 2006, government supporters and opponents employed largely nonviolent tactics, with the exception of some incidents concerning land and natural resources issues. However, at the end of the year and into 2007, violent attacks increased as indigenous and poor peoples' organizations and their supporters clashed with mestizo and white individuals and groups threatened by the former's increasing political hegemony.[2]

By January 2007, serious fissures had developed within the diverse MAS coalition owing to ideological discrepancies and the struggle among rising political leaders for control over state jobs. On the one-year anniversary of his presidency, Morales replaced seven of sixteen cabinet ministers, including several controversial figures, with individuals having more technical expertise and stronger links to the MAS's labor-union base than to its indigenous supporters.[3]

A generally positive economic climate and assistance from foreign donors has helped Morales fulfill some of his promises. Robust earnings from gas exports produced GDP growth of over 4 percent in 2006. Tax income increased 46 percent to US$1.71 billion due to increased hydrocarbon tax revenues. Additional revenues from gas are expected to bring the government approximately US$1 billion annually after 2007, which will enable it to invest in a number of poverty alleviation, health, and education programs.[4] This relative economic prosperity may help account for the government's 70 percent approval rating in a February 7, 2007, poll of major cities.[5]

Several hurdles identified in the 2005 *Countries at the Crossroads* report have been overcome: hydrocarbon taxes and royalties have been renegotiated with investors on terms favorable to the government, and a constituent assembly has been elected and convened. Other hurdles remain: confrontation between lowland economic elites and highland, indigenous social movement organizations over departmental autonomy and land reform have strong racial overtones and are increasingly resulting in violence.[6] Additionally, the Constituent Assembly, already charged with tackling highly sensitive issues, saw its work delayed by squabbling over procedural issues.

ACCOUNTABILITY AND PUBLIC VOICE

FREE AND FAIR ELECTORAL LAWS AND ELECTIONS:	4.75
EFFECTIVE AND ACCOUNTABLE GOVERNMENT:	3.50
CIVIC ENGAGEMENT AND CIVIC MONITORING:	5.00
MEDIA INDEPENDENCE AND FREEDOM OF EXPRESSION:	5.00
CATEGORY AVERAGE:	**4.56**

The openness of Bolivia's democratic regime is exemplified by the rise of the MAS from regional upstart in the 1995 municipal elections to decisive victor in the 2005 presidential contest. The public's ability to express its preferences increased in December 2004 with the incorporation of citizens running on behalf of "citizens' groups" and "indigenous peoples" into the electoral system. Moreover, the December 2005 presidential and congressional elections witnessed 84.5 percent electoral turnout, the highest since the transition from military rule.[7] Although there were reports of a large number of voters being purged from the rolls for failing to participate in previous elections, polling was generally considered free and fair, as demonstrated by the considerable success of candidates opposing the status quo. While there are still no effective campaign finance limits, parties with representation in office received public funding in proportion to their representation.[8]

The results of the election demonstrate significant reconfiguration within a political party system that had been in flux since 2002. The traditional leading parties—the Leftist Revolutionary Movement (MIR), Nationalist Revolutionary Movement (MNR), and Nationalist Democratic Action (ADN)—nearly disappeared, with only MNR winning any congressional seats. Overall, the MAS coalition won 72 out of 130 seats in the Chamber of Deputies, to only 43 for the main opposition party, Social and Democratic Power (PODEMOS). In the Senate, however, PODEMOS gained 13 of the 27 seats to 12 for the MAS; as opposition candidates also won the other two seats, the upper house was expected to provide a check on MAS power (see below). Concurrent elections for departmental prefects—the first time these figures had been directly elected—resulted in victory for four PODEMOS candidates and two other opposition members, while the MAS won just three of the nine prefectures.

On July 2, 2006, 85 percent of registered voters participated in elections to select delegates for the Constituent Assembly. The MAS elected 137 out of the 255 delegates to the assembly. Collectively, the main opposition parties won eighty-six seats in a largely fair environment. The majority of the delegates are political newcomers representing labor unions and rural peasant groups. The assembly opened on August 6, 2006, with a symbolic march of indigenous people, who were joined by soldiers in a show of national unity.[9] The session started without prior consensus on important issues such as regional autonomy, land reform, resource exploitation, and the role of traditional indigenous social and legal structures under the new charter. For the first six months of the assembly's mandate, however, the assembly was unable to perform its role because MAS delegates used their absolute majority to overturn the stipulation in the law convoking the assembly that required a two-thirds vote of approval for each article in the new constitution. Tension over the issue built throughout the year, and by December opposition delegates and thousands of supporters throughout the country had launched hunger strikes and protests. Some MAS militants threatened and attacked strikers, without rebuke from the president.

On February 14, 2007, a fragile accord on the voting issue was reached that allowed substantive discussions to begin on February 26. Under the agreement, the first draft constitution is to be approved by an absolute majority of the assembly delegates, with specific articles approved by a two-thirds vote until July 2. Thereafter, remaining and contentious articles are to be forwarded to a reconciliation commission composed of party leaders and commission presidents. The assembly must approve the final draft by a two-thirds vote. Issues on which no consensus can be reached will be put to a national referendum. The accord also incorporated language promising to respect the results of the July 2006 autonomy referendum.[10] By law, the assembly must be dissolved on August 6, 2007, although the date could be extended.

Achieving an effective separation of powers has been a consistent problem in Bolivia. Since January 2006, legislative stagnation has resulted from polarization between the MAS majority and a weakened and reconfigured opposition. The executive branch persistently attempts to work around the Senate (where it lacks a majority), uses its majority in the lower house to stifle opposition, refuses to negotiate with opponents, and convokes protests to suppress constitutional opposition and avoid negotiation.[11] President Morales refuses to negotiate in good faith with most opponents. As moderate members of the MAS coalition in congress and the Constituent Assembly have tried to find common ground with the opposition in order to move forward on pressing policy issues, Morales increasingly has expelled or penalized dissident voices within the governing coalition. This refusal to negotiate is exemplified by actions with respect to exploitation of the land redistribution and regional autonomy issues.

President Morales achieved passage of a far-reaching land distribution law on November 28, 2006, in the face of strong Senate opposition: with twelve of twenty-seven members boycotting the session, the law passed in a 15–0 vote. Critics noted that the law passed in the Senate only after "alternates" for two opposition-party senators were induced to vote in favor of the bill, a practice that violates the constitutional role of alternates. The new law and the tactics with which it was passed provoked landowners, who launched strikes and road closures and increasingly are resorting to private security forces to protect themselves from land invasions.[12]

A referendum on the tense issue of regional autonomy was held concurrently with the Constituent Assembly elections. The balloting resulted in passage of the referendum in four of Bolivia's nine departments, all in the eastern lowland part of the country, and all of which have felt threatened by the political and economic program of the highland residents and lower classes that currently comprise the MAS' base. However, given that the referendum left ambiguous the specific form of autonomy, and that a majority of the population as a whole rejected the measure, the degree of regional self-government remains an open question that the Constituent Assembly is supposed to address.

Morales has resisted his legal obligation—and prior promise—to implement the affirmative response to the Regional Autonomy Referendum in the four departments in which it was approved. Morales's refusal to negotiate on this issue, and his provocative threats to the autonomy achieved thus far in the form of elected departmental prefects, impairs the possibility of agreement on any polarizing policy issue and of progress on institutional reforms. This inflexibility is also provoking violence between government and opposition supporters and between the departmental and national levels of government.[13] For example, on January 8, 2007, approximately 5,000 MAS-affiliated coca growers and peasants clashed with supporters of departmental prefect Manfred Reyes Villa after Reyes called for a new autonomy referendum in Cochabamba department. Two persons died and several hundred were wounded in the following days of civil unrest.[14] Tensions over the failure of the national government to defend departmental governments increased further after Morales named a key leader of the Cochabamba attacks to the position of Justice Minister on January 23.

Civil society is a highly active force in Bolivia. Numerous community groups, unions, business federations, and nongovernmental organizations (NGOs) mobilize citizens on behalf of a wide variety of causes while attempting to fill the many gaps left by the weakness of the state. NGOs with external funding often are able to influence policy because the government relies on international agencies for funding and technical support on many social policy issues. However, the high levels of poverty and illiteracy in Bolivia inhibit the ability of some groups to effectively structure themselves and coordinate their efforts.[15] Furthermore, a vicious circle obtains with respect to government weakness: its failings exacerbate complaints, leading to street protests to which the government cannot effectively respond, thereby weakening the government further. Finally, though politicization of civil society groups is not new, increased regional polarization has resulted in increasing tensions between civil society groups, and the offices of some NGOs and other groups were attacked during the unrest in December 2006 and January 2007.

The Bolivian press freedom environment is relatively strong. The government neither censors the media nor hinders internet access, and while libel remains criminalized, there are no recent reports of jail sentences being issued.

However, polarization within the media has increased along with polarization in the country as a whole. In late 2006, as opposition to the Morales government became more organized, attacks on both pro-government and pro-opposition media increased, with more than two dozen reported assaults on journalists in Cochabamba and Santa Cruz during the protests in December 2006 and January 2007. In addition, both state-run and opposition-aligned television stations were attacked on several occasions in 2006. The government has done little to protect journalists and media outlets from violent attacks. Morales has, on several occasions, characterized the media as an enemy. A survey of opinions expressed in the nation's six major dailies undertaken by a well-known journalist at the end of 2006 revealed a bias against the government and its social base of support, which is not surprising considering that white-mestizo elites own most major media companies.

Recommendations

- The Constituent Assembly should address urgent pending issues, including compromise on the issue of departmental autonomy and the creation of political institutions that incorporate indigenous authorities and values.
- The automatic purging from the voter rolls of citizens who did not vote in the previous election should be halted and all qualified citizens should be allowed to register to vote. Citizens who claim to have been wrongly purged should be able to cast a provisional vote.
- The government should refrain from attacking the press and make clear to its supporters, both rhetorically and, when necessary, through prosecution, that threats and intimidation directed against journalists are unacceptable.
- The Bolivian government should implement regional autonomy rights in the departments approving the referendum and desist from attacking such rights, rhetorically or legislatively.

CIVIL LIBERTIES

PROTECTION FROM STATE TERROR, UNJUSTIFIED IMPRISONMENT, AND TORTURE:	3.00
GENDER EQUITY:	3.25
RIGHTS OF ETHNIC, RELIGIOUS, AND OTHER DISTINCT GROUPS:	3.75
FREEDOM OF CONSCIENCE AND BELIEF:	6.00
FREEDOM OF ASSOCIATION AND ASSEMBLY:	4.80
CATEGORY AVERAGE:	**4.16**

Bolivia has ratified the major UN human rights conventions. Since November 2004, Bolivia has also ratified multiple regional and global treaties and conventions related to the prevention of torture, genocide, and forced labor, among other civil liberties issues. The 1967 constitution, revised in 1995, 2002, and 2004, protects a wide range of civil and political rights, including freedom of religion, freedom of expression, and freedom of association.

Reports of human rights violations have declined since 2004. The Mesa, Rodriguez, and Morales governments exercised more restraint toward protesters and relaxed the strict coca eradication policy that had been a source of confrontations between police and civilians. Nevertheless, the nongovernmental Bolivian Permanent Assembly for Human Rights (APDHB) concluded in its 2006 report that the "state has systematically violated human rights." The APDHB reported 4,115 cases of human rights violations by state authorities in 2005. The group received 430 charges concerning physical mistreatment by the police, while in 252 cases the Ministry of Justice was accused of retardation of justice, abuse of authority, and corruption.[16]

Bolivian prisons suffer from a litany of problems ranging from violence to lack of adherence to dietary standards. In 2005, state penitentiaries were blamed for 240 cases of abuse of authority, illegal detention, and mistreatment. Prisoners, as democratically elected unions or as criminal gangs, continue to run most prisons. More than 1,300 children live with their parents in jail. In September and October 2005, a breakdown in order at the main penitentiary in Santa Cruz allowed the escape of twenty-seven dangerous criminals, causing a major scandal. Indeed, the

Santa Cruz prison is notorious as a center for criminal networks. Despite improvements in the processing of criminal cases, a main problem in keeping order is overcrowding: the national system was built to hold 2,895 inmates, but by 2003 the prison population exceeded 6,500 prisoners. Overcrowding occurs in part due to the slow processing of people who have been charged and are awaiting trial; 75 percent of the prison population has not been sentenced.[17]

The increased partisan violence in late 2006 and early 2007 resulted in increased international attention to human rights violations. In February 2007, the UN High Commissioner for Human Rights visited Bolivia to prepare to open a permanent office. In early March 2007, an Amnesty International mission exhorted the government to investigate the January clashes in Cochabamba as well as other reports of human rights abuses and impunity.[18]

Human rights monitors and activists are frequently threatened and harassed by state and private actors during the conduct of their duties.[19] On January 24, 2007, the Observatory for the Protection of Defenders of Human Rights demanded protection for Bolivian activists in the department of Santa Cruz who had received threats in the course of their work.[20] Critics claim the Morales government has unjustly incarcerated and held, without due process, senior officials from previous governments for political reasons. For example, beginning in July 2006 Central Bank general manager Marcela Nogales was incarcerated and held for at least six weeks without being charged, in violation of Bolivian law.[21]

Violent and property crime have increased in recent years, including a marked swell in armed robberies against financial institutions. The failure of law enforcement to address the increase has led to a rise in vigilantism. Mob justice is rarely investigated or punished because police and prosecutors fear retribution and communities protect the perpetrators.

Many Bolivian women are unaware of their constitutional rights and suffer discrimination and abuse. Both the Mesa and the Morales governments, however, have worked to increase women's legal protections. One area of increased attention is domestic violence. Although the Panamerican Health Organization noted in 2005 that more than 50 percent of Bolivian women report suffering from domestic violence, this represents a decline relative to 1999. The Mesa government revised the Family and Domestic Violence Act to provide additional legal mechanisms to punish perpetrators of domestic violence, provide treatment for victims, and facilitate coordination among the government agencies responsible for implementation. In December 2006, the government introduced the Bill to Strengthen Human Security and Reproductive Sexuality, which contains components to protect women from domestic violence, as well as improve reproductive health by focusing on the provision of services in municipalities.

Employers are required by law to provide family leave benefits for women with young children and to make other special provisions for pregnant women and new mothers. Access to health benefits increased further on April 5, 2006, when the Constitutional Tribunal ruled that female workers have the right to share their health benefits with male partners.[22] Still, owing to the greater expense of providing benefits for women, employers often discriminate when hiring.

Women's economic advancement is also impeded by their unequal access to property rights. The Mesa government recognized the problem in 2005 and the Morales government promised to give priority attention to women's need for land under the 2006 agrarian reform law. Under current law men can sell their land without their wives' consent; moreover, a widow may be obligated to leave the land and return to her community of origin upon the death of her husband.[23]

As in the Mesa government, four of sixteen ministers appointed at the start of the Morales administration were female, including the high-profile ministers of justice and government. Nevertheless, women's participation is far below the gender parity that Morales had promised. Despite new quota laws designed to increase representation, women lost ground in the 2005 national elections: thirty women were elected to congress in 2002 (out of 157 seats), but only twenty-two were elected in 2005. None of the nine newly elected departmental prefects are female. The law convoking elections for the 2006 Constituent Assembly required that male and female candidates be alternated on participating lists. As a result, 40 percent of candidates were female, but no participating political party or civic association made women's rights or issues an important component of its platform. As of 2005, women comprised approximately 20 percent of judges and prosecutors.[24]

The U.S. State Department classifies Bolivia as "a source country" for adults and children "trafficked for labor and sexual exploitation." In recognition of recent efforts—passage in July 2005 of a new Law Against Trafficking of Children and Adolescents, the establishment of new anti-trafficking police units, a modest increase in protection of victims, the establishment by President Rodriguez of an interministerial commission to work on anti-trafficking issues and policies, and an increase in the number of prosecutions—Bolivia was upgraded from tier 3 to tier 2 in the 2006 Trafficking in Persons report.[25] Nevertheless, the government does not undertake significant efforts to enforce the laws and resources are insufficient to do so.

According to the 2001 census, indigenous peoples comprise approximately 62 percent of the population. Bolivia codified a limited array of rights for indigenous peoples in the 1994–1995 constitutional reform, including recognition of the legal standing of indigenous communities as public collective actors, the right to bilingual education, and the right of indigenous authorities to exercise administrative functions and to resolve internal conflicts. Violence between indigenous peoples and landowners in the east increased in 2006 in response to mobilization surrounding the new land law. Representatives of indigenous peoples argue that much of this violence is racially motivated. The Permanent Assembly reported at least 132 cases of violations of indigenous peoples' rights in 2005, including usurpation of lands, discrimination, and abuse of authority.[26]

Bolivia is meeting its reporting requirements under the UN Convention on the Elimination of Racial Discrimination. Indigenous organizations are now widely consulted on government policy issues, and many leaders of indigenous organizations are serving in high-profile positions. This advance is attributable to the rapid rise of the MAS, which draws many of its candidates and government appointees from affiliated indigenous organizations. On January 21, 2006, the day before his official inauguration ceremony, Morales participated in a rite at the ceremonial city of Tiahuanacu, where traditional indigenous authorities gave their blessing. However, the small Afro-Bolivian community continues to be marginalized politically and economically, and has not benefited from the increased attention to indigenous peoples' needs.

Bolivians with disabilities are protected under the 1995 Persons with Disabilities Act. Enforcement agencies, however, are inactive in many parts of the country, and no penalties exist for noncompliance with nondiscrimination and accommodation laws. Most government and private buildings lack wheelchair access and, according to the Permanent Assembly, "in general special services and infrastructure to facilitate the circulation of disabled persons do not exist. The lack of adequate re-sources impedes the full implementation of this law."[27] The official ombudsman known as the People's Defender reported progress in pro-viding access to state schools for students with physical and hearing dis-abilities; previously, only the blind were taken into account. In addition, in 2005 the government issued a decree requiring that government agen-cies register disabled persons in order to provide better health services.[28]

The Bolivian constitution recognizes Roman Catholicism as the offi-cial national religion but guarantees religious freedom to all other groups. Non-Catholic religious groups must register with the government in order to engage in political or proselytizing activity, but no such regis-trations have been denied since the 1980s. The Catholic Church receives some monetary support from the state, and the Bolivian Bishops' Con-ference has some influence over Bolivian political life. The Church's greatest area of influence is in education, exemplified by its ability to change the content of the government's proposed education law, which would have explicitly instituted secular education in deference to indige-nous peoples who reject Catholicism.[29] Minister of Education Felix Patzi, who proposed the controversial measure, was replaced during the Jan-uary cabinet shuffle.

The constitution and the General Labor Law protect the right to form trade unions for lawful purposes, and both employers and employ-ees are guaranteed freedom of association. The reaction of the state toward labor mobilization has varied in recent years, depending on the administration in office and the sector of the labor force protesting. Pres-ident Morales has been more restrained than his predecessors in repress-ing this important part of his political base. Indeed, the government received criticism for its hands-off approach in dealing with an October 2006 clash between rival miners' groups that left sixteen people dead in the town of Huanuni.

The large segment of the population working in the informal econ-omy is unprotected. Forced labor is exploited widely in the timber in-dustry in the Amazon, and the majority of victims are indigenous. Workers are paid in scrip or food and are routinely beaten and whipped for disobedience. Approximately 70,000 people work in conditions of slavery collecting nuts in the Amazon and are subjected to corporal punishment. In addition, an estimated 14,000 Guarani indigenous people live in slavery on plantations in three lowland departments, where they are forced to work for below-subsistence salaries and are frequently beaten.[30]

Freedom of assembly is widely respected in Bolivia, and the volume of protests attests to a significant mobilizational capacity by civil society groups. The large number of dead in the 2003 crisis leading up to President Sanchez de Lozada's ouster resulted in a more cautious attitude with respect to the use of force to break up protests. Nonetheless, the increasing militancy and violence in the protests associated with regional rivalries have challenged the government's ability to balance free assembly against potential chaos.

Recommendations

- The government should construct new prison facilities and work to decrease the number of pretrial detainees in order to promote a more efficient, rehabilitative model of punishment.
- The new constitution should address weaknesses with respect to the treatment of gender, particularly with respect to labor and health rights, and provide full constitutional protection of gender equality.
- The government should strengthen efforts to train judicial and police personnel regarding gender rights in order to increase sensitivity to crimes against women and reduce patriarchal attitudes that hinder the application of nondiscrimination and anti–domestic violence laws.
- The government must combat conditions of forced labor by investigating abuses and punishing landlords who engage in the practice.

RULE OF LAW

INDEPENDENT JUDICIARY:	2.80
PRIMACY OF RULE OF LAW IN CIVIL AND CRIMINAL MATTERS:	3.50
ACCOUNTABILITY OF SECURITY FORCES AND MILITARY TO CIVILIAN AUTHORITIES:	4.25
PROTECTION OF PROPERTY RIGHTS:	3.33
EQUAL TREATMENT UNDER THE LAW:	4.00
CATEGORY AVERAGE:	**3.58**

Bolivia's justice system is characterized by underpaid, poorly trained judges and administrative officials who are susceptible to financial and political pressure. Only 180 of the country's 327 municipalities have judges; just 76 have prosecutors.[31] Inefficiency generates long delays and violations of defendants' rights. User fees, transportation costs, and the necessity of bribery to ensure prompt attention and favorable outcomes place civil proceedings beyond the reach of most Bolivians.

The independence of Bolivia's judiciary from the executive branch is questionable. Owing to the failure of the Congress to act on judicial appointments, in December 2006 President Morales appointed four interim Supreme Court justices to fill vacancies. Preceding governments made interim appointments in 2004 and 2005 for the same reason. Opposition congressional leaders complained that this was a political move intended to achieve control of the judicial system during the congressional recess. During 2006, the government made progress in institutionalizing and professionalizing administrative judicial appointments through competitive application procedures, including a series of examinations. Moreover, a new judicial discipline regime went into effect in January 2007. The Morales government reports advances in administration of justice, pointing in particular to the Constitutional Tribunal, where 100 percent of cases brought were resolved in 2006. Bolivia also demonstrated progress in 2005 and 2006 in speeding up criminal proceedings: average times were reduced from approximately two to six years to approximately six to twelve months (depending on the study cited), a decline of 75 to 90 percent.[32] However, further progress with respect to judicial reform is delayed by the primacy of other urgent institutional and policy issues and by a lack of political will.

There are no effective legal procedures or independent agencies equipped to investigate and rectify problems in the justice system. Bolivians are presumed innocent until proven guilty, but public defenders are poorly trained, underpaid, and stretched too thin. There are only fifty-six public defenders, or 0.8 defenders for each 100,000 Bolivians, and they are only available in eleven municipalities. This represents an increase of 18 percent over 2002, but the budget for public defense has since been reduced by 28 percent.[33]

The Morales government intends to expand the operation and increase the legitimacy of indigenous community justice systems, which are less expensive, more accessible, and more culturally sensitive than ordinary courts. The constitution recognizes the legitimacy of these institutions, and the government has submitted to congress a law that would grant community justice the same rank in the legal hierarchy as ordinary law. Critics contend that indigenous law offers neither provisions for defense of the accused nor an appeals process or higher authority to remedy abuses, and often employs sanctions such as corporal punishment and even execution.

The 2004 creation of neighborhood integrated justice centers, which provide free legal services to the indigent, increased access to justice for the poor majority. The centers have resolved more than 1,100 cases in conflict-prone regions. A January 2006 reform institutionalized and rationalized the new justice centers and created a system of elected justices of the peace for rural areas. As of January 2007, the reform awaited implementing rules.[34]

As crime has increased in recent years, pressure from the public and prosecutors has increased on the government to revise the 2001 Code of Criminal Procedure due to the perception that it has resulted in an overly quick release of suspects awaiting trial. The current code benefits the innocent but leads to increased recidivism. A persistent problem is the lack of stability in the Ministry of Government, which has experienced frequent changes in leadership. Financial resources for effective law enforcement also are lacking. Nevertheless, the People's Defender insisted in its 2006 report that judicial officials repeatedly used lack of resources to justify "any lack, delay, or irregularity" in the administration of justice, problems that were due instead to "corruption, incompetence, and negligence." It reported 356 complaints against justice system officials in 2005 relating to failure to provide due process.[35]

Civilian executives have exerted greater control over the military since 2004. This is attributable to a loss of prestige and autonomy caused by what most Bolivians consider to be the excessive use of force against civilians during the 2003 crisis that forced President Sanchez de Lozada from office, as well as a scandal involving complicity in the dismantling of antiquated Chinese missiles at the behest of the United States.

In August 2005, in advance of the national elections, the armed forces high command announced that any member of the armed forces would face "drastic sanctions" if they were found to have violated the constitution by being directly involved in political parties or the new citizens' groupings. Since some were already involved as party founders and militants, the controversy led to the resignation of the vice-minister of defense. One week prior to the election, armed forces leaders announced that they would obey the new president's orders to the letter and called on the new congress to choose Morales as president even if he won a plurality rather than an absolute majority.

In December 2005, the Rodriguez government issued a warrant for the arrest of the commander of the Bolivian Air Force after he failed to appear at a hearing in connection with the investigation of the 2003 massacre. Less than a week after taking office, Morales removed the entire high command of the armed forces in order to achieve closer control over it and its political activities. Critics charge that he is politicizing the institution.[36]

Impunity for human rights abuses committed by the military and the civilian leaders who issue orders has long been the norm. However, on December 18, 2006, the public ministry brought formal charges of murder, torture, crimes against press freedom, genocide, and other serious crimes against former president Sanchez de Lozada and two of his ministers in relation to state repression of protests that occurred in September and October of 2003. All members of Sanchez de Lozada's cabinet have been charged with crimes, as have the former commanders of the armed forces.[37]

Legal protection of private property in Bolivia is enshrined in the constitution but is weak. Extensive corruption in the judicial system renders it difficult for Bolivians to enforce contracts. In addition, Morales's rapid move to address land claims by the poor has led landowners to criticize the government for failing to negotiate with them in good faith and for failing to prosecute squatters who seize their property. The Morales government also has failed to defend the property rights of foreign investors and to honor written contracts. On the other hand, since Morales has taken office indigenous communities' property rights have been less threatened by private actors, although clashes continue in rural areas over land claims.[38]

On May 1, 2006, Morales issued a decree that required foreign investors in the hydrocarbons sector to yield to the Bolivian state's "control and direction" of their operations in Bolivia and to negotiate new tax and royalties terms. The government achieved significant increases in the amounts that hydrocarbon companies pay: from US$460 million in 2005 to an estimated US$700 million in 2007, and more than US$1 billion annually thereafter.[39] In February 2007, Morales began to fulfill his promise to nationalize the mining sector by seizing the Swiss-owned Vinto tin smelter in Oruro. The government plans to continue nationalizing other mines that once belonged to Sanchez de Lozada.[40]

Coca eradication efforts have declined under the Morales government, which destroyed just over 5,000 hectares in 2006, the minimum permitted under an agreement with the United States. Morales has resisted undertaking an independent European Union–financed study to assess domestic demand for coca leaf for traditional social and cultural uses, and has instead suggested allowing peasant communities to use their own "social control" mechanisms to self-police production levels. This strategy is likely to increase the production of coca leaf for international drug markets, as coca remains more profitable to produce than alternative crops.[41]

Recommendations

- Efforts should continue to provide resources and initiate programs that make justice more accessible to underserved geographic areas and social groups.
- Efforts should continue to professionalize judicial and investigative offices through competitive examinations, technical training, and efforts to improve relations with citizens.
- Military leaders must submit to civilian jurisdiction in the investigation of human rights abuses.
- The postponed European Union–financed study of traditional coca leaf use should be undertaken immediately in order to determine the percentage of coca leaf production that can be considered legitimate to supply domestic demand versus the percentage that is likely diverted to the narcotics trade. Legal coca production should be reduced in line with the results.

ANTICORRUPTION AND TRANSPARENCY

ENVIRONMENT TO PROTECT AGAINST CORRUPTION:	2.40
EXISTENCE OF LAWS AND ETHICAL STANDARDS BETWEEN	
PRIVATE AND PUBLIC SECTORS:	3.00
ENFORCEMENT OF ANTICORRUPTION LAWS:	3.50
GOVERNMENTAL TRANSPARENCY:	3.43
CATEGORY AVERAGE:	**3.08**

Bolivia is one of the more corrupt countries in a region not known for its probity. In 2006 it received 2.7 out of a total of 10 possible points on Transparency International's Corruption Perceptions Index, placing it 105th out of the 168 countries ranked.

Firms are forced to navigate a complex bureaucratic system in order to do business. Payments to public officials to speed up bureaucratic procedures are common, and enforcement of laws and mechanisms regulating the bidding process is inadequate. A national survey found that 13 percent of interactions between individuals and public institutions require bribes, with an estimated cost of US$115 million in 2005; nearly half of Bolivian households reported making an illicit payment to state actors in 2005.[42] Most small-scale bribes end up in the hands of the police, customs officials, or judicial officials.[43]

In June 2005, President Rodriguez created a new cabinet position, Presidential Delegate for Transparency and Public Integrity, charged with overseeing governmental corruption investigations. Rodriguez also introduced a requirement that all public auditors within the public ministry take examinations. Of 230 auditors who completed the exam in 2005, 173 passed; of the 57 who failed, 39 were fired.[44] Several laws designed to combat corruption were passed in 2005, including the Financial Administration and Control (SAFCO) Law, the State Employees Statute Act, and the Sworn Declaration of Property and Income Law.

Morales made the fight against corruption a key campaign issue in the 2005 election. After assuming the presidency, he submitted to congress a bill aiming to establish a legal framework to investigate public officials and strengthen principles on ethics, transparency, and access to information.[45] Discussion of the bill began on December 8 and was continuing in March 2007. Critics complain that the law presumes the guilt of those investigated. Morales also downgraded the office for transparency and public integrity, which was seen as ineffective, to a vice ministry within the justice ministry.

Graft is widespread within the government. Financial disclosure procedures are inadequate and do not prevent officials from abusing their public positions for personal enrichment. It has become commonplace in recent years for public sector employees to move into private sector jobs in the same area of work, or vice-versa. According to a 2006 Transparency International report, "the use of privileged information and contacts by people switching between public and private sector posts in the same area of work has undermined the credibility of both sectors."[46] There have been numerous cases in which municipal officials have been found to be misusing public funds for personal benefit.[47]

Tax collection and administration is also a complex, bureaucratic process, susceptible to corruption and graft. Tax returns are often challenged by officials; more than half of Bolivian companies have reported that tax officials have requested a "special payment" in return for reversing unfavorable decisions.[48]

Several corruption cases have received attention in the media in the past year. Among others, five former presidents, an ex–Supreme Court chief, and a former Central Bank president have been accused of graft or negligent incompetence.[49] The lack of concrete evidence in many of the cases, and the tendency for those accused to be associated with the pre-Morales political elite, have led to accusations that the cases are part of an government effort to intimidate the opposition and consolidate power.[50] Morales, however, also dismissed several members of his own party in 2006, including deputy communications minister Jorge Estrello and MAS congressional leader Gustavo Torrico.[51]

In general, the media actively report on corruption cases. Morales's credibility on the issue of anticorruption declined in February 2007 after reports emerged in the press that between June and August 2006 thirty-six employees of state hydrocarbon company YPFB (Yacimientos Petroliferos Fiscales Bolivianos)—whose jobs were supposed to be filled according to technical criteria—had been appointed through nepotism, as political favors, or in exchange for money. The scandal exposed at YPFB unleashed a wave of investigations into politically motivated hiring practices throughout the administration. President Morales promised a complete investigation and punishment of those who bought or sold jobs. In addition to the YPFB scandal, journalists identified a wider network of corruption penetrating virtually every government agency.[52]

A weak judiciary, at times complicit in corruption, makes the pursuit of justice in corruption cases difficult. No law allows authorities to probe assets of public officials, and government officials are entitled to broad immunity against prosecution. Political pressure is often applied in the courts and cases are often drawn out and costly, discouraging individuals from taking their complaints to court.[53] There are few protections for witnesses and whistle-blowers who participate in anti-corruption cases, and the persistence of libel and defamation laws discourages citizens from coming forward. Business interests are particularly concerned about the politicization of YPFB, where technocrats have been replaced by inexperienced political appointees.[54] In August 2006, President Morales dismissed Superintendent Jorge Sainz after he acted as a whistle-blower in a corruption case against the head of YPFB.[55]

A 2001 law established "the right of civil society organizations and institutions to be informed of, oversee, and evaluate the results and impact of public policies and participative decision-making processes."[56] Since 1994, vigilance committees comprised of civil society representatives from each municipality have had the right to supervise the implementation of social projects and the procurement of goods and services. Committees must approve the municipal councils' annual financial reports, operating plan, and budget. In practice, however, vigilance committees do not play a robust role in planning or oversight.[57]

On the national level transparency remains poor, despite a law passed in January 2004 covering access to information and transparency. A report published by the Open Budget Initiative in 2006 found that the Bolivian government provides citizens with "scant or no information on the central government's budget and financial activities."[58] The government does not regularly publish reports detailing spending, releasing only a yearly executive budget proposal, which itself provides only minimal information to the public.

Recommendations

- In order to encourage citizens to come forward, laws punishing slander or insult of public officials should be decriminalized and norms should be created to protect whistleblowers and witnesses involved in cases of public corruption.

- The anticorruption and transparency portfolio should be returned to the cabinet level and an experienced, politically independent minister should be named to lead it.
- The transparency of government decision making, particularly with respect to economic policy, should be improved by involving a wider array of civil society representatives in policy making above the municipal level. The vigilance committee model should be expanded from municipal governments to other areas and levels of government.
- National level officials should hold discussions with civil society groups to formulate and implement specific transparency measures, such as stricter asset reporting guidelines for municipal officials, more frequent reporting of government expenditures, and stricter and better enforced conflict of interest regulations.

NOTES

[1] International Crisis Group (ICG), *Bolivia's Rocky Road to Reforms* (Bogota/Brussels: ICG, 3 July 2006), 3.

[2] ICG, *Bolivia's Reforms: The Danger of New Conflict* (Bogota/Brussels: ICG, 8 January 2007).

[3] "Morales cambia a siete de sus ministros cuestionados," *Los Tiempos*, 24 January 2007; "Morales refuerza el perfil izquierdista de su gabinete para su segundo año," *Los Tiempos*, 24 January 2007.

[4] "Standard & Poor's mantiene la perspectiva negativa a largo plazo para Bolivia," *La Razon*, 22 December 2006, http://www.la-razon.com; ICG, *Bolivia's Rocky Road*, 8; ICG, *Bolivia's Reforms*, 12; "Evo afina plan economico y social del 2007," *La Razon*, 18 December 2006; "Gas Boost for Morales," *Latin American Regional Report–Andean Group* (November 2006): 15.

[5] "Encuesta: el sistema político tiene signos vitales positivos," *Los Tiempos*, 12 March 2007.

[6] "La violencia aqueja al este cruceño; se busca una tregua," *La Razon*, 18 December 2006

[7] ICG, *Bolivia's Rocky Road*, 2.

[8] Only one of the six major parties mentioned in the 2005 report competed in the last elections, and it won less than 7 percent of the vote. See electoral data at http://www.cne.gov.bo; World Bank, "Worldwide Governance Indicators Country Snapshot," World Bank, http://info.worldbank.org/governance/kkz2005/sc_chart.asp, accessed 17 December 2006.

[9] ICG, *Bolivia's Rocky Road*, 16–17; S. Ramiro Ramirez, "Recuperar la soberania plena es vital para la Constituyente," Agencia Boliviana de Informacion (ABI), Direccion Nacional de Comunicacion Social, http://abi.bo, accessed 3 January 2007.

[10] "Entre aplausos, Asamblea aprueba formula mixta," *Los Tiempos*, 15 February 2007.

11 Dan Keane, "Bolivia Divided over Morales' Reforms," *Times Picayune* (New Orleans), 24 November 2006, http://www.nola.com; "El MAS excluye a Podemos y busca acuerdas con otros," *La Razon*, 6 December 2006.

12 President Morales distributed approximately 8,500 square miles of publicly owned land in 2006; under the new law the government expects to distribute 77,000 square miles of government land, mainly in the east of the country. Associated Press, "Land Redistribution Plan Passes in Bolivia," CNN.com, 29 November 2006; Fiona Smith, "State Property in Bolivia Turned over to Indians," *Times Picayune*, 4 June 2006.

13 Although the referendum failed nationwide (57.6 percent to 42.4 percent), legally it must be implemented for the departments where it passed. Corte Nacional Electoral, *Resultados Referendum Nacional* (La Paz: Republic of Bolivia, Corte Nacional Electoral, 2006), http://www.cne.org.bo; ICG, Bolivia's Reforms, 9–10.

14 "Bolivia Succumbs to Social Conflict as Morales Loses Control," *Latin American Weekly Report*, 18 January 2007.

15 CIVICUS, *Civil Society in Bolivia: From Mobilization to Impact* (Johannesburg: CIVICUS, 2006), 3, http://www.civicus.org/new/media/CSI_bolivia_executive_summary.pdf.

16 Asamblea Permanente de Derechos Humanos de Bolivia (APDHB), *Analisis de situacion de los derechos humanos en Bolivia el 2005* (La Paz: APDHB, 15 May 2006), 5.

17 APDHB, Analisis de situacion, 4–5; Defensor del Pueblo (Republica de Bolivia), *VIII Informe Anual del Defensor del Pueblo* (La Paz: Defensor del Pueblo, 2006), 33; Amnesty International (AI), "Bolivia: Human Rights Concerns," http://www.amnestyusa.org/countries/bolivia, accessed 17 December 2006; Centro de Estudios Judiciales del las Americas (CEJA), *Report on Judicial Systems in the Americas 2004–2005* (Santiago, Chile: CEJA, n.d.), 98, http://www.cejamericas.org/report.

18 "Arbour abrira oficina de DDHH en Bolivia," *Los Tiempos*, 14 February 2007; "Amnistia evalua DDHH en Bolivia y habla de impunidad," *Los Tiempos*, 5 March 2007.

19 APDHB, *Analisis de situacion*, 5.

20 "Piden seguridad para los defensores de los derechos humanos en Bolivia," *Los Tiempos*, 24 January 2007.

21 Mary Anastasia O'Grady, "Bolivian Witch Hunts," *Wall Street Journal*, 1 September 2006; ICG, *Bolivia's Rocky Road*, 6–7; Associated Press, "Ex-Bolivian Leader Blames US in Missile Scandal," CNN.com, 18 August 2006.

22 "Victory for Women," Inter Press Service, 25 May 2006.

23 United Nations Committee on the Elimination of Discrimination against Women (CEDAW), *Consideration of Reports Submitted by States Parties Under Article 18 of the Convention on the Elimination of All Forms of Discrimination against Women—Bolivia* (New York: CEDAW, 27 March 2006), 3, 7, 43; Martin Garat, "Women Gear Up to Break Their Silence," *Latinamerica Press* 39, no. 23 (13 December 2006); available at http://www.latinamericapress.org.

24 ICG, *Bolivia's Rocky Road*, 19; ICG, Bolivia's Reforms, 8; based on an examination of first names from the data compiled by the Political Database of the Americas (Washington, D.C.: Georgetown University, 2005), http://www.georgetown.edu/pdba/elecdata/bolivia/dic05.html; CEDAW, *Consideration of Reports—Bolivia*, 29; author interviews in Bolivia, August 2005.

25 U.S. Department of State, *Trafficking in Persons Report 2006* (Washington, D.C.: U.S. Deptartment of State, 2006), http://www.state.gov/g/tip/rls/tiprpt/2006/65988.htm.

26 "Sectores dicen que los ataques fueron raciales," *La Razon*, 19 December 2006; Defensor del Pueblo, *VIII Informe*, 14–15; APDHB, *Analisis de situacion*, 9–10; AI, "Bolivia: Human Rights Concerns."

27 APDHB, *Analisis de situacion*, 10.

28 Defensor del Pueblo, *VIII Informe*, 59.

29 David Ovando, "Gobierno se acerca a la Iglesia y garantiza materia de religion," *Los Tiempos*, 19 February 2007.

30 "Indigenas amazonicos son sometidos a la esclavitud," *La Razon*, 31 October 2005; APDHB, *Analisis de situacion*, 11; AI, "Bolivia: Human Rights Concerns.".

31 "Los jueces solo estan en 180 de 327 municipios," *La Razon*, 14 January 2007

32 "Designaciones interinas en la Corte Suprema son legales y reduciran la retardacion de justicia," ABI, 2 January 2007; ABI, "Presidente de la Suprema propone cumbre democratica para mejorar administracion de Justicia," ABI, 2 January 2007; CEJA, *Report on Judicial Systems*, 98.

33 CEJA, *Report on Judicial Systems*, 95.

34 U.S. Agency for International Development, "Democracy Strategic Objective," http://www.usaidbolivia.org.bo/US/1Dem.htm; "En la justicia comunitaria no existe defensa," *La Razon*, 14 January 2007.

35 Defensor del Pueblo, *VIII Informe*, 14, 34; "Vecinos esperaban a la fiscal mientras el linchado moria," *La Razon*, 17 January 2007.

36 ICG, *Bolivia's Rocky Road*, 5; "La postergacion de la orden de destinos molesta a los militares," *La Razon*, 23 December 2005; "Los militares revelan fisuras y se meten en la campaña electoral," *La Razon*, 14 December 2005; "La FFAA deliberan y piden repetar la primera mayoria," *La Razon*, 13 December 2005; AI, "Bolivia: Human Rights Concerns."

37 "El Fiscal acusa a Goni y a 2 ex ministros por otros 10 delitos," *La Razon*, 19 December 2006.

38 ICG, *Bolivia's Rocky Road*, 13, 31; ICG, *Bolivia's Reforms*, 5.

39 ICG, Bolivia's Reforms, 12; ICG, *Bolivia's Rocky Road*, i; Simon Romero and Juan Forero, "Bolivia's Energy Takeover: Populism Rules in the Andes," *New York Times*, 3 May 2006.

40 "Suiza pide a Morales que respete los acuerdos entre ambos paises," *Los Tiempos*, 10 February 2007.

41 ICG, *Bolivia's Reforms*, 13.

42 Business Anti-Corruption Portal, "Bolivia Country Profile," Global Advice Network, http://www.business-anti-corruption.com/normal.asp?pageid=164.

43 Transparency International (TI), Global Corruption Report 2006 (Berlin: TI, 2006), 130–132.

44 "La Fiscalia se deshace de los reprobados," *La Razon*, 16 September 2005.

45 "Bolivian Anti-Corruption Law May Become Retroactive," *Daily Granma*, 11 February 2007, http://www.granma.cubaweb.cu/english/news/art27.html.

46 TI, *Global Corruption Report 2006*, 130–132.

47 Ibid.

48 Ibid.

49 "Evidence Scant in High-Profile Bolivia Prosecutions," *International Herald Tribune*, 5 September 2006.

50 Ibid.

51 "La Fiscalia se deshace de los reprobados," *La Razon*, 16 September 2005; "El MAS y la oposicion abren discusion sobre polemica ley," *La Razon*, 18 December 2006.

52 "Avales: Evo pide carcel para cobrador y pagador," *Los Tiempos*, 12 March 2007; "Hubo trafico de avales del MAS en la gestion Alvarado en YPFB," *Los Tiempos*, 6 March 2007; "YPFB: reconocen que hay 30 recomendados, pero investigan," *Los Tiempos*, 14 March 2007.

53 Ibid.

54 "Morales radicalises YPFB," *Latin American Weekly Report*, 1 February 2007, 4.

55 "Bid to Speed Up 'Nationalization' Backfires in Bolivia," *Latin American Weekly Report*, 19 September 2006.

56 "Latin-America: The Use, and Abuse, of Developmental Aid," Inter Press Service, 12 October 2006.

57 Ibid.

58 International Budget Project, *Open Budget Index 2006* (Washington, D.C.: Center on Budget and Policy Priorities, 18 October 2006), http://www.openbudgetindex.org /CountrySummaryBolivia.pdf.

BURKINA FASO

CAPITAL: Ouagadougou
POPULATION: 14.8 million
GNI PER CAPITA: $460

SCORES	2005	2007
ACCOUNTABILITY AND PUBLIC VOICE:	3.44	3.52
CIVIL LIBERTIES:	3.88	4.21
RULE OF LAW:	3.32	3.45
ANTICORRUPTION AND TRANSPARENCY:	3.12	3.30

(scores are based on a scale of 0 to 7, with 0 representing weakest and 7 representing strongest performance)

Michael Kevane

INTRODUCTION

Burkina Faso's rich civic institutions are rooted in the history of the pre-colonial Mossi kingdoms, the traditions of stateless societies in the southwest, the Islamic brotherhoods that structure the lives of Muslims, the hundred-year presence of the Roman Catholic Church and Protestant missionary societies, and popular struggles for representation during the colonial and postindependence periods. This heritage is a constant feature of contemporary political discourse, with critics accusing the current regime of betraying the country's political traditions. The regime's defenders emphasize its continuity with the past and its efforts to restore civic life after the excesses of the revolutionary period of the 1980s.

Michael Kevane teaches at the Leavey School of Business at Santa Clara University and conducts research on economic institutions and growth in poor countries, with a focus on Africa, and Burkina Faso and Sudan in particular. He is the author of *Women and Development in Africa: How Gender Works* (Lynne Rienner, 2004), as well as articles in journals including *World Development, Review of Development Economics, Sudan Notes and Records, American Journal of Agricultural Economics*, and *Africa*.

In recent years, the government has taken a number of important steps in the process of deepening participation in governance and the protection of civil liberties. These have included peaceful and relatively free presidential elections, municipal elections, the decentralization of local governance through mayoral and council elections in rural communes, and continued expansion of civil society institutions. The positive developments, however, have been accompanied by allegations of widespread corruption, clashes between police and the army in Ouagadougou, and the July 2006 dismissal of the criminal case against a member of the Presidential Guard who was accused of killing a prominent journalist in 1998.

Freedom and democracy in Burkina Faso have often been overshadowed by the personal rule of President Blaise Compaore. He and other members of a revolutionary council seized control of the country in 1983, ending a succession of short-lived military governments that had followed the 1980 ouster of longtime ruler General Sangoule Lamizana. In the council, Compaore, Jean-Baptiste Lingani, and Henri Zongo shared power with Captain Thomas Sankara, the extremely popular and charismatic young president. Sankara soon consolidated his leadership position, adopted a more strident and Marxist rhetoric for the regime, and became heavily involved in foreign affairs as a "revolutionary" leader of the Third World. In 1987, Compaore launched his own coup, during which Sankara was assassinated. Lingani and Zongo were summarily executed in 1989, allegedly for plotting against Compaore.

Compaore in 1991 began fresh efforts to legitimize his rule. Through a new constitution, he institutionalized a process of gradual political liberalization. Later that year, he won a seven-year term as president in an election that was boycotted by opposition forces. The opposition had called for a truly representative constituent assembly to draw up the new constitution. Compaore was sworn in for a second term in 1998, after an election that was again largely boycotted by the opposition. In the period between 2000 and 2002, the constitution was amended to limit the presidency to two five-year terms, an independent electoral commission was created, and judicial reforms clarified the powers of the various appellate courts. The government was explicit in hoping for a strong showing by opposition parties in the 2002 legislative elections, and indeed, the combined opposition gained a substantial number of parliamentary seats. Compaore ran for the presidency again in 2005, following the expiration of his second seven-year term, arguing that the constitutional term limits did not apply retroactively. Opposition forces mounted and lost a legal challenge but decided not to boycott the election. Compaore received 80 percent of the vote, and the process was generally viewed as free, but not entirely fair due to the resource advantage held by the incumbent.

While the past decade has seen gains in the construction of the formal apparatus of freedom and democracy, they must be viewed through the prism of the still-unresolved killing of journalist Norbert Zongo and three traveling companions in 1998.[1] Zongo, as editor of the newspaper *L'Independent*, was a fierce critic of the government. His investigation into a convoluted corruption, torture, and murder case that allegedly involved the younger brother of the president, François Compaore, was proving to be extremely damaging to the legitimacy of the regime. Zongo's death prompted opposition parties and human rights activists to coalesce into what became known as the Collective Against Impunity, a loose umbrella group led by magistrate and human rights advocate Halidou Ouedraogo.[2] The Collective has organized peaceful demonstrations every year to mark the anniversary of the murders, and its actions were probably largely responsible for the constitutional and executive branch reforms of 2000–2002.

The Collective also maintained pressure on the government to pursue a judicial inquiry into the Zongo murders. In 2001, Compaore organized a National Day of Pardon for all illegal acts committed by his own and earlier military regimes. Since 1998, security forces have by all appearances been careful not repeat such crimes. Nevertheless, the unresolved murders of Zongo and his companions—combined with other unpunished and undocumented extrajudicial killings, disappearances, and alleged assassinations in the first decade of Compaore's rule—have raised concerns that many members of the president's inner circle are above the law and public accountability, and that the country's democratic institutions and civil liberties are merely tools of convenience for the leadership.

ACCOUNTABILITY AND PUBLIC VOICE

FREE AND FAIR ELECTORAL LAWS AND ELECTIONS:	2.50
EFFECTIVE AND ACCOUNTABLE GOVERNMENT:	3.25
CIVIC ENGAGEMENT AND CIVIC MONITORING:	4.33
MEDIA INDEPENDENCE AND FREEDOM OF EXPRESSION:	4.00
CATEGORY AVERAGE:	**3.52**

Electoral politics in Burkina Faso appear to be at the cusp of the divide between demoracy and authoritarianism. Suffrage is universal, and no special interest groups have formally disproportionate representation in government. Electoral reforms in 2002 led to a substantial opposition presence in the National Assembly, 54 out of 111 seats. The introduction of a single-ballot format reduced the opportunities for buying votes, and significant attention has been paid to regularizing the electoral rolls. In addition, public financing for political parties has undoubtedly provided incentives for more political newcomers to enter the ring in presidential and legislative elections.

Presidential elections in November 2005, municipal and communal elections in April 2006, and other special elections during the 2004 to 2006 period were held in a largely competitive and peaceful environment. The presidential poll resulted in a landslide victory for Compaore, who obtained slightly more than 80 percent of the vote. The remainder was divided among twelve other candidates, none of whom received more than 5 percent of the vote. A number of international observers issued favorable reports about the election, but noted some irregularities and possible fraudulent activities, particularly the manipulation of electoral rolls.[3]

Compaore has yet to indicate convincingly that he is willing to step aside in a peaceful transition, dissuading potentially viable candidates from entering the fray. He appears unlikely to surrender power without some provision of immunity for himself and other senior officials with respect to the violence committed by security forces since the 1983 coup.

The municipal and communal vote, which had been delayed twice due to organizational difficulties, produced a low turnout of 49 percent of the electorate.[4] The president's party, the Congress for Democracy and Progress (CDP), won approximately 73 percent of the seats in communal councils and close to 90 percent of mayoral posts across the country. While the outcome of the local elections was never in doubt, the act of finally decentralizing political authority after years of discussion and delay was a very positive development for Burkinabe democracy. In special elections for the municipal council of Po, held in February 2007 after the previous council was dissolved by the Ministry of Territorial Administration and Decentralization, the ruling party and the opposition each accused the other of buying votes with cash distributions.[5]

The CDP continues to dominate the political playing field. Many Burkinabe perceive that it has become a powerful electoral machine, much like the single-party systems of the 1970s, but now with the illusion of multiparty competition. In much of the country, the well-financed CDP is able to dominate elections without recourse to overt fraud. The party enjoys multiple benefits of incumbency, including the ability to attract considerable campaign donations and greater media attention than its competitors. Opposition politicians believe themselves to be generally threatened with violence should they come too close to defeating the ruling party. A number of politicians issued a public statement in 2005 asserting that they had been threatened by an unidentified Sierra Leonean.[6] The opposition also refers to the case of lawmaker Hermann Yameogo, the son of Burkina Faso's first president, Maurice Yameogo, who was detained at the Ouagadougou airport in September 2004 and accused of working with hostile foreign governments.

Support for the opposition weakened even further after several of its candidates were accused of accepting funding from the president and the CDP to organize parties that would help create the illusion of competition. During the presidential campaign of 2005, Laurent Bado, candidate of the Opposition Burkinabe Unifiee (OBU), publicly admitted having received thirty million CFA francs (US$62,300) from the president.[7]

Given the dominance of the CDP, opposition parties remain a last recourse for aspiring public servants and often attract CDP members who have lost favor within their own party. For example, in Bobo-Dioulasso, the second-largest city and potentially a major base for any electoral challenge to the president,[8] then-incumbent mayor Celestin Koussoube was unceremoniously dropped from the CDP list as rumors circulated that he was a potential threat to the leadership in Ouagadougou. He promptly switched parties, joining the Alliance for Democracy and the Federation, African Democratic Assembly (ADF-RDA), and was added to the list for the district of Konsa in the municipal elections of 2005. The high-profile switch prompted a rash of lower-level defections to and from each side, although Koussoube lost his bid for mayor when the new municipal council voted, 114 to 35, for Salia Sanou, a CDP stalwart and deputy in the National Assembly.[9]

Unlike national elections, communal elections seem to have genuine competition and accountability, both within the CDP and among political parties.[10] In Boromo, in the province of Bales, for example, local residents rejected CDP candidates selected by national party structures if they were deemed unresponsive to local needs, insisting instead on better-known and more responsible local candidates. Factional splits in the ruling party also allowed opposition candidates to be elected to the Boromo council. In Gourcy, center of the province of Zondoma, sharp rivalries within the CDP led to simultaneous party meetings held in different parts of the town, each seeking recognition from a delegation of CDP leaders who came from Ouagadougou to resolve the problem.[11]

The Independent National Electoral Commission (CENI) organizes and oversees elections. Appointments to the fifteen-member governing board are divided, with five representatives chosen by the executive branch, five by opposition parties, and five by civil society (one person from each of three major religious communities, one from the institutions of traditional chieftaincy, and one from the human rights community). The method of selection is opaque, and the rushed and irregular "election" of the human rights organizations' representative in August 2006 drew much protest.[12] Political parties are partially financed by the state.[13] The larger parties such as the CDP and ADF-RDA receive amounts based on their electoral returns, and smaller parties have been given equal shares of a remaining allocation. Annual grants to all parties together have been approximately 200 million CFA francs (US$415,000). There is little regulation of private financing of political parties.

A very small degree of rotation of power takes place within the elite of the ruling party. The prime minister since 2000, Ernest Paramanga Yonli, is among the longer-serving premiers of the Fourth Republic, as the regime of President Compaore is known. While a large number of ministers and the head of the CDP are longtime stalwarts of the regime, others are relative newcomers and technocrats.

Constitutionally, the National Assembly can hold the executive accountable through votes of censure and no confidence, but in practice it asserts little oversight and rarely questions government actions. In particular, the National Assembly has failed to establish commissions of inquiry to investigate any controversial government moves. Given the dominance of the executive and legislature by one political party, the independence of the judiciary is a matter of utmost importance. Reforms resulting from the Norbert Zongo crisis began the process of establishing a stronger judiciary, but there is still little pretense of judicial independence.

The government seems to actively promote and empower minority or historically disadvantaged social groups. For example, the government annually organizes the Journee Nationale du Paysan (National Day of the Farmer), an all-day affair at which government officials listen and respond to the concerns of rural community leaders. The government is also a strong promoter of artistic and cultural events. There are no apparent restrictions on cultural expression, whether in traditional forms (such as dance, masks, and oral poetry) or in new media of expression (including print and recorded music and video).

Sankara's rule in the 1980s created high popular expectations of effective and reasonably accountable governance, and the Compaore regime has generally sought to meet those expectations. Meetings and minutes of the Council of Ministers are regularly reported on and debated in the press. Civil service positions are usually allocated by national, competitive examinations, though allegations of irregular hiring and promotion are a staple of daily newspapers. Technocrats are well represented in the upper echelons of government. By and large, civic associations are allowed to flourish. Those that seek formal status may register with the government, and registration requirements are not viewed as onerous.

International nongovernmental organizations (NGOs) operate throughout the country, and the activities of international human rights groups and other civil liberties groups are not subject to any reported impediments. The International Organization for Francophonie (OIF), for example, organized a conference in September 2005 on sustainable development, including themes of governance and human rights, that drew more than sixty international NGOs and local civil society organizations. In October 2006, the UN Development Programme (UNDP) created a consultative committee to represent more than one hundred civil society organizations interested in working with the agency. There are few barriers to the establishment of domestic NGOs, particularly for development and associational activities. Farmer organizations, such as the Cotton Producers Group (GPC) in the cotton areas, and the village organizations known as Associations Naam–Six-S in the northwest, are active in associational life. Many villages have development NGOs.

Political associations are also in evidence. An association of several political parties called the Coordination for the Transparency of Elections (COTE) was formed in August 2005 to monitor the presidential election.[14] The Center for Democratic Governance regularly hosts conferences and workshops and organizes research on the political institutions of the country.

Article 8 of the constitution guarantees freedom of the press. The country's media outlets regularly report on the activities of the executive branch, and open criticism of government action or inaction is common. Several dozen newspapers are published regularly, including the sharply satirical *Journal de Jeudi*. The government-funded official newspaper, *Sidwaya*, has been reasonably neutral in tone and coverage, including during campaign seasons. The private sector has increased its presence in television and radio, with three television stations and numerous private radio stations broadcasting. The government television station, TNB, has accepted funding from a number of major private enterprises and individuals, including the wealthy entrepreneurs Alizeta Ouedraogo (thirty million CFA francs or US$62,300) and Oumarou Kanazoe (seventy million CFA francs or US$145,500), for the remodeling of the station headquarters, but denied that this would influence news coverage.[15]

The media are free of overt censorship, and several newspapers are openly antigovernment. However, the unpunished and unresolved murders of newspaper editor Norbert Zongo and his companions in 1998 have been considered by many to be a deliberate warning to journalists to exercise self-censorship. A number of libel cases have further underscored the ambiguity of the government's position regarding critical journalism. One case heard in January 2007 involved the bimonthly newspaper *L'Evenement*, which published accusations made by the international organization Reporters Without Borders that the president's brother had ordered Zongo's killing.[16] The defendants argued unsuccessfully that they were reporting the public accusations rather than the facts of the matter; they were sentenced to two-month jail terms and fines of 300,000 CFA francs (US$623). Libel is considered a criminal offense punishable by imprisonment rather than payment of monetary damages, and there seems to be little interest in the CDP to change that status.[17]

Internet access is widely available in the two major cities of Ouagadougou and Bobo-Dioulasso through an extensive array of private internet cafes. The costs are affordable to middle-class users. A number of websites (lefaso.net, for example) collate and archive articles from all of the major newspapers.

Recommendations

- The selection process for the governing board of the Independent National Electoral Commission (CENI) should be reformed to improve transparency and ensure that the outcome reflects the consensus of the National Assembly.
- Compaore should complete the transition away from personal rule by initiating an open discussion in the National Assembly on a grant of immunity for acts of violence committed by security forces prior to 2000, and by organizing a process to select a new CDP leader who could stand in the 2010 presidential election.
- Legislation should be enacted to regulate the financing of electoral campaigns, with reporting requirements for party contributions as well as provisions governing nonparty political campaigning.
- Penalties for libel should be reduced.

CIVIL LIBERTIES

PROTECTION FROM STATE TERROR, UNJUSTIFIED IMPRISONMENT, AND TORTURE:	3.00
GENDER EQUITY:	3.75
RIGHTS OF ETHNIC, RELIGIOUS, AND OTHER DISTINCT GROUPS:	4.50
FREEDOM OF CONSCIENCE AND BELIEF:	6.00
FREEDOM OF ASSOCIATION AND ASSEMBLY:	3.80
CATEGORY AVERAGE:	**4.21**

Overcrowded prisons and instances of arbitrary detention characterize the justice system in Burkina Faso. One survey found that city and town prisons were filled to double or even triple their intended capacity; an estimated one-quarter of the inmates were awaiting trial.[18] Burkinabe citizens often note the prevalence of arbitrary arrest and the ease of undocumented temporary detention despite laws providing formal protection against such abuses. Moreover, the popular opinion is that police routinely beat and torture criminal suspects, although no reliable or authoritative reports on the issue are currently available. The government supports a citizen's ombudsman, the Mediateur du Faso, whose office works to facilitate the process of seeking redress for arbitrary detention and other abuses against civil liberties.

There were no reports of torture or extrajudicial killings of political opponents between November 2004 and March 2007. Noel Yameogo, an official in the National Union for Democracy and Development (UNDD) party, was arrested at Ouagadougou airport in September 2004—along with his cousin, Hermann Yameogo—and held for six months without trial before he was released in February 2005.

Extrajudicial killings by police in rural areas continue to be a serious problem. The killing of Djolgou Yaarga, a gold merchant, and his two employees near the town of Piela in October 2006 illustrated the lack of accountability among rural police services. Despite scant evidence, the two employees were detained under suspicion of highway robbery while traveling on a work assignment. Yaarga, learning of the arrest, went to the jail to clarify the situation, but was also imprisoned. All three men were executed the following day without a hearing or trial.

The government continued its effort to institutionalize a formal apparatus for the protection of civil liberties. In 2002, it established the Ministry for the Promotion of Human Rights and subsequently named and continued to support Monique Ilboudo—a renowned lawyer, journalist, and defender of human rights—as human rights minister. The government continued to honor its commitment, made during the National Day of Pardon, to indemnify the families of victims of political violence. By the end of 2006, the families of 449 victims had received compensation, and the total amount disbursed had reached 4.7 billion CFA francs (US$9.7 million).

A number of nongovernmental human rights organizations, including the prominent Burkinabe Movement for Human Rights (MBDHP), continue to be active. The president of MBDHP, Halidou Ouedraogo, suffered a heart attack in 2006 and was medically evacuated to France for recovery and rehabilitation. In an interview after his return, he noted that numerous government officials had assisted him in his recovery.[19]

The Burkinabe state has expressed considerable interest in protecting the rights of minors, women, and socially distinct groups. Ilboudo, the human rights minister, has been able to bring about the ratification of a number of international protocols of high relevance to West Africa, including the Optional Protocol to the Convention on the Rights of the Child on the involvement of children in armed conflict, the Optional Protocol of the Convention Eliminating Discrimination Against Women, and the Optional Protocol on the rights of women of the Charter of the African Union.[20] However, implementation of many of the provisions of the protocols has been slow. In July 2005, a multilateral cooperation agreement on child trafficking was adopted by a number of West African states, including Burkina Faso. The signings and ratifications were accompanied by the establishment of programs to make citizens and local authorities more aware of the problem and encourage them to seek solutions, and the government has promised reforms of the relevant national laws.[21]

Women have enjoyed increasing freedom from discrimination as the customs and traditions of rural society erode. The government has strongly backed efforts to improve the low rates of female school attendance. Messages of empowerment, in newspapers, soap operas, radio programs, and other formats, are encouraged, and the CDP tried in the municipal elections of 2006 to increase gender equality in the party lists, with the goal of a 25 percent female quota in urban areas and a 50 percent quota of women candidates in rural areas. In early 2007, the government announced that it would support a 30 percent quota of women in decision-making positions in the executive branch.

The state supports the livelihoods of people with disabilities by encouraging civil society organizations devoted to improving their well-being. However, the circumstances of extreme poverty in Burkina Faso make state support for the rights of the disabled more rhetorical than effective. There has been little effort to make public buildings accessible to those with special needs, and the private sector is not held to any measure of accountability for discrimination or physical accommodation. The government hosted the Pan-African Disabled Games in July 2005.

Religious and ethnic tolerance has long been a hallmark of Burkin-abe society and state policy, and this continued through the survey period.[22] The constitution proscribes the formation of political parties on the basis of religious affiliation or ethnic identity. Political advertising designed to appeal to narrow religious or ethnic interests is prohibited. There is little evidence of employment discrimination based on religion and ethnicity.

The government and civil society organizations value the Burkinabe tradition of *parente a plaisanterie* (joking relationships) among ethnic groups as a cultural mechanism for defusing possible ethnic tensions. The government holds an annual Week of Culture festival and makes every effort to include all the ethnic groups of the country. Religious organizations abound in Burkina Faso, and there is considerable prosely-tizing and conversion among Christian and Muslim groups, as well as a substantial adherence to traditional religious practices. The govern-ment in general does not interfere with religious practices.

Freedom of association is increasingly respected, and there were few reported cases of police interruption of peaceful rallies or denial of demon-stration permits during the survey period. Trade unions and civic associ-ations are active in Burkina Faso. During much of 2005, the major unions organized short national strikes as they negotiated with the government over salaries and benefits. There has been little recent government inter-ference in their activities. The long process of privatization begun in the 1990s has resulted in a much-smaller parastatal sector, and this has reduced the ability of organized labor to effect government change.

Recommendations
- The National Assembly should hold hearings and work with the Ministry for the Promotion of Human Rights to submit and make public a report to the secretariat for the Convention Against Torture, indicating the specific steps that have been taken to enforce the pro-visions of the convention.
- The government should cease holding citizens in detention without charge for longer than the prescribed seventy-two hours.
- Cases of extrajudicial killing, especially by police in rural areas where there are few witnesses or checks on police power, should be exam-ined by an independent prosecutor.

- The National Assembly should organize public hearings and site visits to assess prison conditions throughout the country.

RULE OF LAW

INDEPENDENT JUDICIARY:	3.40
PRIMACY OF RULE OF LAW IN CIVIL AND CRIMINAL MATTERS:	3.33
ACCOUNTABILITY OF SECURITY FORCES AND MILITARY TO CIVILIAN AUTHORITIES:	2.50
PROTECTION OF PROPERTY RIGHTS:	4.00
EQUAL TREATMENT UNDER THE LAW:	4.00
CATEGORY AVERAGE:	**3.45**

A prosecuting judge's July 2006 decision to dismiss the case against the sole suspect in the Norbert Zongo murders presented a serious setback to the popular perception of judicial independence. The case documents seemed to indicate very strong evidence of the guilt of defendant Marcel Kafando, a member of the Presidential Guard, causing widespread public dissatisfaction when the case was dismissed. The prosecuting judge indicated that he had been unable to secure testimony from many members of the Presidential Guard and that a key witness against Kafando had recanted his testimony. However, many opposition figures argued that the evidence was more than sufficient had the prosecutor wanted to pursue the case vigorously.

Reforms resulting from the Zongo crisis began the process of establishing an independent judiciary, but there is still little pretense of judicial independence. According to the constitution, the judiciary is regulated by the High Council of Magistrates (CSM); the president of the CSM is the president of the republic. The reelection of President Compaore in 2005 was made possible in part by the preelection decision of the Constitutional Council, created in 2000, to reject the petition of four opposition presidential candidates who argued that Compaore had already served the maximum number of terms. The council found that the 2000 amendment limiting the presidency to two five-year terms was not retroactive. Of the ten members of the Constitutional

Council, the president appoints seven (including the body's president and three magistrates nominated by the justice minister) and the head of the National Assembly names three. All but the council's president serve nine-year terms, with one-third of the members subject to renewal every three years.

The judicial reforms of 2000 led to the creation of a Supreme Court with jurisdiction over the president in cases of treason, violation of the constitution, or misappropriation of public funds. The Supreme Court can hear an accusation only if it is referred with a vote by four-fifths of the members of the National Assembly, which is extremely unlikely. The members of the Supreme Court are selected from the National Assembly and the Appeals Court, and as long as the CDP remains in control of the executive and legislative branches, the Supreme Court will consist of CDP and presidential loyalists.

The evolution of a truly independent judiciary made slow progress between 2004 and 2007. Judicial independence was a central plank of the government's National Policy for Good Governance (PNBG), originally adopted by the Council of Ministers in 1998 and renewed in May 2006. The action plan for the PNBG document went through a participatory formulation process after being drafted initially by the High Authority for Coordination of the Fight against Corruption (HACLC), the government anticorruption unit. For example, a two-day workshop in Ouahigouya to discuss the document drew several hundred government and civil society participants and generated open discussion and suggestions for amendment.[23] Nonetheless, corruption remains one of the main problems in the Burkinabe judicial system. A 2005 report by the CSM found numerous instances of corruption in the national courts of Ouagadougou and Bobo-Dioulasso.

Judges in Burkina Faso are, given the circumstances, reasonably well-trained to administer justice. Under a judicial reform program that commenced in 2002, the number and training of magistrates has been increasing rapidly, and the government has embarked on a program to build and equip the infrastructure of appeals courts and Courts of First Instance (TGI).

Defendants are informally presumed guilty, despite legal provisions guaranteeing the opposite, and often do not have access to legal representation.

It is very difficult to gauge the effectiveness of civilian control over the military and police in Burkina Faso. A serious test of effective civilian control occurred in December 2006, in what became known as *l'affaire militaire-policier*. The incident began when an army recruit was shot dead by a police officer following an altercation. Infuriated, the recruit's army comrades raided a camp armory and proceeded to mount attacks against police positions throughout central Ouagadougou. The police responded with some small-arms fire but generally fled and removed their uniforms. Military personnel set up roadblocks and, according to some accounts, proceeded to confiscate the personal property of civilians who entered the downtown area the next morning. Authority over the military was not fully restored until the following afternoon. The civilian defense minister appeared in public with the security minister, who was in charge of the police, and reassured the public that the unrest was under control. The government officially announced that the violence had caused six deaths.

Rumors that the events were really an attempted coup d'etat circulated widely, as did assertions that the soldiers had attacked the main prison of Ouagadougou and either deliberately or accidentally allowed prisoners to escape. Moreover, it seemed that once soldiers saw that discipline was breaking down, they used the disorder as an opportunity to vent dissatisfaction with living conditions and pay. In the days following the violence, soldiers presented a list of demands to the authorities. On the evening of December 31, troops opened fire in other major towns in an apparent display of solidarity with the Ouagadougou soldiers. Prison guards attempted a mass strike in early January, claiming the right to indemnification for losses suffered during the two days of violence, as well as improvements in working conditions.[24]

The events point to ineffective mechanisms for communication and response to grievances within the security forces, and suggest that there is not yet full respect for the rule of law among younger recruits. Only a full public analysis of the violence can help ensure that soldiers remain in their barracks and police do not act with impunity. As of March 2007, neither the National Assembly nor the executive had indicated any commitment to such an inquiry.

The reaction to the army-police clashes contrasted with the spirit of open investigation and disclosure that animated a military tribunal convened in April 2004 to try a group of military officers and enlisted men who had been charged in October 2003 with involvement in an alleged coup plot.[25] The defendants were accused of taking money to carry out the coup and recruiting comrades within the military to support them. The trial was billed by the government as an example of the institutionalization of the rule of law and a divergence from the summary executions of coup plotters both in neighboring countries and in Burkina Faso in the past. Some of the accused were acquitted, and others were found guilty and sentenced to prison terms. President Compaore subsequently freed some of the imprisoned officers as part of the National Day of Pardon. Nevertheless, when two of the freed men, Bayoulou Bouledie and Bassama Bassole, sought out members of the press in April 2006, claiming that they were being followed and feared for their lives, they were detained for two days and then released without charge.[26] Commander Bernardin Pooda, another of the officers tried in 2004, was brought before a military tribunal again in early 2007 on charges of embezzling public funds while serving in the military.[27]

Individual and corporate ownership of private property is increasingly well respected. Contracts are generally enforced as part of the normal routine of governance. Labor contracts in particular are subject to considerable scrutiny and enforcement by the Work Inspectorate, a government agency. The most significant public taking of private property for redevelopment efforts, the Projet ZACA in central Ouagadougou, proved in early 2007 to be less poorly managed than public perception had hitherto held, as infrastructural improvements and land titling began in the project area. Decentralization policies have sped up the process of formal surveying, subdivision, and titling of residential parcels in larger villages and small towns. Agricultural, pastoral, and forested areas held as traditional, communal, or common property continue gradually to come under the umbrella of regularized and formal land-use rules as part of the National Program for the Management of Rural Lands (PNGT). The establishment of rural communes is likely to strengthen this process further. Generally, compensation is rendered for government takings.

Recommendations

- The High Council of Magistrates and the Constitutional Council should be made completely independent of the executive, and the voting margins for referring cases of presidential malfeasance to the Supreme Court should be lowered.

- A public parliamentary inquiry into the *l'affaire militaire-policier* should be conducted, and reforms—such as a regular monthly dialogue and joint activities among the various security services—should be implemented to ensure that the events are not repeated.
- The government should regularly publish the salaries and supplemental pay scales of magistrates as one in a series of steps to reinforce public confidence in the integrity of the judiciary.

ANTICORRUPTION AND TRANSPARENCY

ENVIRONMENT TO PROTECT AGAINST CORRUPTION:	3.00
EXISTENCE OF LAWS AND ETHICAL STANDARDS BETWEEN PRIVATE AND PUBLIC SECTORS:	3.25
ENFORCEMENT OF ANTICORRUPTION LAWS:	3.25
GOVERNMENTAL TRANSPARENCY:	3.71
CATEGORY AVERAGE:	**3.30**

Anticorruption rhetoric has been an important element of Burkinabe political discourse since the Sankara period, when public integrity in word and deed were given great salience. Burkinabe are quick to note that when Sankara was killed in 1987, a public inquest into his assets revealed only a guitar, his aging Renault, and a sizable book collection. The long-serving military ruler Sangoule Lamizana was also revealed to have benefited little from his presidency; an inquest held under the revolutionary Sankara regime found his accounting of presidential funds to be adequate.

However, there are few checks on corruption at the apex of public power in Burkina Faso. The listings of assets of the president and other members of government, as prescribed by Article 77 of the constitution, appear to be irrelevant, as the Constitutional Council does not make these listings available to the public. The prohibition on government officials benefiting from or participating in transactions involving the public domain is commonly evaded in practice, due in part to the extended family relationships of the Burkinabe elite. Little positive or negative evidence of these practices is available to the public, however. In recent years, President Compaore and other high officials have repeatedly been accused of violating the tradition of modesty and integrity, but his appetite for large-scale corruption is either well concealed or well moderated.[28]

On numerous occasions over the period between 2004 and 2007, the president and prime minister have publicly proclaimed the importance of integrity in public administration. The government ratified the African Union Convention against Corruption in 2005 and the UN Convention on Corruption in 2006. The Compaore regime has since 1991 followed an economic model of liberalization and privatization, which often has the effect of reducing the scope for corrupt practices by bureaucrats. The government does a fair job of making budget discussions, bidding for publicly financed projects, and the allocation of public expenditures transparent.

Nevertheless, corruption remains a significant though not insurmountable problem. Burkina Faso's score on Transparency International's Corruption Perceptions Index was low in comparison with those of many other African countries. The range of scores for 2005 (the first year the country was given a score in the index) was 2.7 to 3.9, with an average of 3.4, ranking the country 70 out of 158 countries, in the company of Ghana, Mexico, and Egypt. For 2006, the country scores ranged from 2.8 to 3.6, and the average score ranked Burkina Faso 79 out of 163 countries, flanked by Senegal and Lesotho.

The respected anticorruption NGO National Anticorruption Network (REN-LAC), which has regularly surveyed government and private-sector employees on the issues of corruption, has found that the urban elite perceives corruption as a serious problem, with only minor changes from year to year.[29] Typically, about half of the respondents indicate that corruption is widespread, about three-quarters say that the problem is worsening rather than improving, and one-third to one-half report that they have personally had experiences with corruption. Corruption is believed to be especially widespread in the customs and police services. Education and the media are consistently viewed as the least corrupt professional sectors.

The media report widely on cases of corruption, and the REN-LAC reports contain summaries of the content of newspaper articles dealing with corruption. One observation REN-LAC makes is that a large number of articles are unsigned; the nature of corruption is such that hard evidence is difficult to obtain and the actors involved are often powerful public figures. Nevertheless, a number of journalists (Michel Zoungrana, Lierme Some, and San Evariste Barro) and independent newspapers (*L'Observateur Paalga*, *L'Independent*, and *Le Pays*) have strong reputations for regularly reporting on corruption.

Possibly the most significant action against corruption in 2005 was the dismissal of Mathieu Ouedraogo, the minister of primary education (Ministere de l'Enseignement de Base et de l'Alphabetisation), following accusations that he had embezzled 700 million CFA francs (US$1.45 million). There was no official comment on his removal from office, and he was subsequently named ambassador to South Africa. The lack of follow-through in the form of a public inquiry or judicial process suggested to many that the government was not serious about punishing major corruption. Most observers continue to believe that government officials at the highest levels will not be investigated or prosecuted for alleged corruption. The government insists that corruption is taken seriously and that no officials are above the law.

Important corruption cases or accusations have implicated public officials in major cities such as Ouagadougou, Bobo-Dioulasso, Koudougou, and Ouahigouya. In two of these cities, mayors were removed following administrative findings of malfeasance or negligence in administration; in others, lower-level officials were removed from office or high-ranking officials were induced to respond more forthrightly to public accusations of corruption.

A smaller but typical case reported by REN-LAC concerned the secondary school of the small town of Zorgho, where a French donor city had agreed to build a science laboratory.[30] The school official in charge, François Kabore, was found to have embezzled a large fraction of the donated funds and never completed the laboratory. After his election as mayor, however, he was arrested and found guilty of fraud in the allocation of residential parcels following the surveying of the town, and was sentenced to prison. The Council of Ministers removed him from office in January 2005. Other public officials have been implicated in similar fraudulent sales of residential parcels allocated by the government in newly surveyed zones.[31]

Major corruption makes front-page news, but petty corruption in government bureaucracies—by the semipublic cotton marketing companies, in schools, by customs agents, and at the revenue service—is also viewed in the Burkinabe newspapers and in ordinary discourse as a troubling low-level threat to the social fabric. Cotton farmers see the semipublic cotton companies as major venues of corruption. In an attempt to increase competition and reduce corruption in the sector, the monopoly company SOFITEX was partially broken apart into regional public-private entities in 2004. But the companies retain their local monopolies over the sale of fertilizer and pesticides, and over the grading of cotton quality and subsequent purchases from farmers. At numerous points in the supply and marketing chain, cotton company employees have opportunities to extract bribes from farmers.[32]

Another area of concern is brand fraud, in which low-quality goods are sold with the tag of a high-quality product attached. This type of fraud has been found in consumer durables such as the ubiquitous *mobilette* (moped) that the majority of the urban population uses for motorized transport, as well as in pesticides and construction materials. In 2005, the National Assembly undertook an inquiry into the quality of mass-produced foodstuffs, and the resulting report identified numerous irregularities. This was one of the few instances in which the legislature took up the corruption issue.

Over the past decade the government has been steadily privatizing many areas of the economy, including health and education, leading to the rapid growth of private clinics and schools. The overall incidence of abuse of public office may be declining as the private sector provides more services to the public.

Several entities in the executive branch are responsible for combating corruption. There are inspection services tasked with auditing public accounts and investigating corruption and fraud. Revenue-collection and human-resource divisions of government are particularly prone to corruption, and the leadership has devoted considerable resources to improving the auditing and control capacities of these services, but such capacities remain limited.

Three higher-level entities—the National Ethics Committee (CNE), the High Authority for Coordination of the Fight against Corruption (HACLC), and the Public Accounts Court—were established with much fanfare in the aftermath of the Norbert Zongo crisis. They have, however, been allowed to lapse into a low level of effectiveness. The resources allocated for their activities have remained limited, and they are seen essentially as reporting and coordinating bodies; that is, they are considered a part of the government rather than outside or independent entities.

The nine-member CNE, the government ethics watchdog, was supposed to be the highest-profile entity created. However, the committee has had a rather limited impact. Only two annual reports (for 2002 and 2003) have been delivered to the prime minister, and although they were made available to the public, little effort or resources were directed to printing and distributing copies. The first report severely criticized and called for reform of the inspection services. One recommendation was for the government to publicize the services' reports. The government's response, cited in the second CNE report, was that releasing inspection-service reports would violate the separation of powers, according to which the judicial system is responsible for prosecuting corrupt actions by public officials. There is always a balance in any system of governance between the public release of information in advance of a judicial process and the presumption of innocence for individuals who might be named in a government report. However, the government's position, that the results of all inquiries should be withheld, essentially tipped the balance entirely to one side.

Reports and recommendations were also produced by the HACLC, a government anticorruption body that began functioning in 2003. It acts as a coordination unit within the government for public information and administrative action, and manages a hotline service for citizens to report corruption and request assistance. In presenting the agency's 2004 annual report, Honore Tougouri, then the president of the HACLC, observed that it had not received a response to the recommendations in the 2003 report. During HACLC workshops in December 2004 and December 2005, attendees made proposals to give the entity some independent prosecutorial powers. Presenting the 2005 report in March 2006, Tougouri repeated calls for greater coordination and investigatory authority. He stepped down in 2006, and new HACLC members were sworn in. They had not yet announced a report for 2006 as of early 2007, nor had any of the reports been made fully public. The government did adopt in May 2006 a National Plan of Action against Corruption, as recommended by the HACLC, and Compaore gave the agency his support in his campaign statement for the 2005 election.[33] The plan of action called for a number of reforms, but the government has not yet passed legislation to adopt the proposed changes.

Finally, the Public Accounts Court (Cour des Comptes) was tasked in the judicial reforms of 2000 to 2002 with oversight of public finances, enhancing the normal investigations of the inspection services. Through 2005, the court had not yet issued any formal public reports on its investigations. The press indicated that the court had distributed reports to members of the National Assembly, but no details were published on the content of those reports. In October 2006, the Council of Ministers adopted new rules that gave the court more autonomy and strengthened the career paths of the magistrates.

The plethora of bureaucratic anticorruption structures has led observers in the opposition and civil society to suggest that the grand strategy of the regime is to buy off critics and incorporate them into public service. These critics are promised much authority and independence but then receive small budgets and have their reports ignored.

The right of citizens to obtain information about government operations in a timely and reasonable manner remains limited, and the government has not adopted freedom of information legislation. The government made an initial investment in e-governance, creating websites for many of the major ministries, but the sites have not been maintained, and access to documents and reports is limited. The government does not make analyses of annual expenditures and receipts widely available. Information for people with disabilities is very limited, although government investment in radio and television services increasingly provides visually impaired persons with access to information.

Recommendations

- Article 77 of the constitution should be revised to include public access to the listings of assets submitted by members of the government.
- Reports and inquiries of the National Ethics Committee, the High Authority for Coordination of the Fight against Corruption, the Inspector General's Office, and the Public Accounts Court should, as a matter of policy, be made available to the public, either without delay or after some fixed period following their finalization or presentation to the Council of Ministers.

- A special prosecuting unit should be established to handle cases of corruption by high government officials, and it should make public at the end of every year a summary of investigations under way and prosecutions brought against government officials.

NOTES

1 See Jean Ouedraogo, "Burkina-Faso: Autour de l'affaire Zongo," *Politique Africaine* 74 (2006): 163–172; "Burkina Faso: Un An Apres et Toujours Pas de Justice," *Article 19*, No. 54 (December 1999), www.article19.org/pdfs/publications/burkina-faso-un-an-apres-french.pdf; M. Hilgers and J. Mazzocchetti, "L'Apres Zongo: entre ouverture politique et fermeture des possibles," *Politique Africaine*, No. 101, 2006.

2 Sayouba Ouedraogo, "Collectif des organisations democratiques de masse et de partis politiques contre l'impunite au Burkina Faso" (Quebec: Cahiers du CRISES—Collection Mouvements sociaux—No. MS0601, 2006).

3 See "Declaration de la RADDHO sur L'election Presidentielle du 13 Novembre 2005" (Ouagadougou: Rencontre Africaine pour la Defense des Droits de l'Homme, 16 November 2005); "Communique de la mission francophone d'observation de l'election presidentielle du 13 novembre 2005, au Burkina Faso" (Ouagadougou: Organisation Internationale de la Francophonie, 15 November 2005).

4 See Jean-Pierre Jacob, "Un Unanimisme Politique Presque Parfait: Les Elections Municipales du 23 Avril 2006 dans Trois Communes de la Province des Bale (Centre-Ouest, Burkina Faso)," (Ouagadougou: Laboratoire de recherche RECIT, Etude Recit No. 14, 2006).

5 Ali Traore, "Les populations prennent d'assaut les bureaux de vote," *Sidwaya*, 19 February 2006, 2.

6 Alternance 2005, "Rumeurs Persistantes de Menaces de Mort Contre les Responsables de l'Opposition," *L'Observateur Paalga*, 5 July 2005, http://www.lobservateur.bf/Oarticlearchive.php3?id_article=3101; Mathieu N'Do, "Bassolet Verse dans la Delinquance Caracterisee," *L'Observateur Paalga*, 25 July 2005, http://www.lobservateur.bf/Oarticlearchive.php3?id_article=3227.

7 Seni Dabo, "Laurent Bado: 'Nous avons reçu 30 millions du CDP,'" *Le Pays*, lefaso.net, 4 July 2005.

8 See Adaman Drabo, "Bobo: Des Militants Quittent l'ADF-RDA pour le CDP," 10 February 2006, http://www.lefaso.net/impression.php3?id_article=12308&id_rubrique=; Djibril Toure, "Rivalites entre le CDP et l'ADF/RDA a Bobo-Dioulasso: Attention au Retour des Vieux Demons!" *L'hebdomadaire* No. 358, 24 February to 2 March 2006, http://www.hebdo.bf/actualite2/hebdo358/focus_rivalites358.htm.

9 Paul-Miki Roamba, "Commune De Bobo Dioulasso: Salia Sanou nouveau maire," *Sidwaya*, 6 June 2006, http://www.lefaso.net/article.php3?id_article=14304.

10 Jacob, "Un Unanimisme Politique . . ." (Ouagadougou: Laboratoire de recherche RECIT, Etude Recit No. 14, 2006).

[11] Cyr Payim Ouedraogo, "CDP/Zondoma: 1 parti, 2 meetings," lefaso.net, 13 December 2004.

[12] Herve D'Africk, "Renouvellement des commissaires de la CENI: Moussa Michel Tapsoba elu sous haute tension," lefaso.net, 14 August 2006, www.lefaso.net/impression .php3?id_article=15709&id_rubrique=.

[13] Abdouramane Boly and Salifou Sampi, "Le Mode de Financement des Partis Politiques au Burkina Faso," *ACCPUF—Bulletin* No. 6 (November 2006): 89–90.

[14] Adama Ouedrogo Damiss, "Resultats provisoires de la CENI: Le fair-play de la CO.T.E.," *L'Observateur Paalga*, 21 November 2005, 8.

[15] Issa Sanogo, "Yacouba Traore (TNB): 'Le mecenat d'OK et de TAN-Aliz ne va pas changer notre maniere de voir les choses,'" *L'Opinion*, 12 October 2006, www.lefaso.net /impression.php3?id_article=16902&id_rubrique=.

[16] See San Evariste Barro, "Proces 'L'Evenement'—Qui perd gagne," *L'Observateur Paalga*, January 25, 2007; Committee to Protect Journalists, "Murder unsolved, but Burkinabe journalists convicted of defamation," news release, 23 January 2007, www.cpj.org/news /2007/africa/burkina23jan07na.html.

[17] "Conseil Superieur de la Communication: les rapports 2004 et 2005" (Ouagadougou: Office of the President of Burkina Faso, 9 September 2006), www.lefaso.net/impression .php3?id_article=16214&id_rubrique=.

[18] Grupo Abele, "Dossie sulle prigioni in Burkina Faso," Rome, 2004, http://www.gruppo abele.org/images/file/dossier%20prigioni.pdf.

[19] Boureima Diallo and Agnan Kayorgo, "Me Halidou Ouedraogo: 'Non, je ne suis pas passe a l'ennemi,'" *L'Observateur Paalga*, 13 December 2006, www.lefaso.net/impression .article.php3?id_article=17870&id_rubrique.

[20] "Promotion de la femme: Les Projets de Gisele Guigma," *L'Observateur Paalga*, 2 August 2005, 24.

[21] "Lutte Contre le Trafic et les Pires formes de Travail des Enfants," *L'Observateur Paalga*, 5 July 2005, 26; "Lutte Contre la Traite des Enfants," *L'Observateur Paalga*, 5 July 2005, 2.

[22] "Ecole Nationale de Police: Pratiques Religieuses et Ordre Politique," *L'Observateur Paalga*, 19 July 2005.

[23] *Rapport de Synthese de l'Atelier National de Validation de la Politique Nationale de Bonne Gouvernance* (Ouahigouya: Ministere de la Fonction Publique et de la Reforme de l'Etat, 14 May 2005).

[24] Alassane Neya, "Soulevement des gardes de la securite penitentiaire: Le ministre de la Justice desamorce la 'bombe,'" *Sidwaya*, 6 January 2007, www.lefaso.net/impression .php3?id_article=18364&id_rubrique=.

[25] Vincent Ouattara, *Proces des Putschistes a Ouagadougou* (Ouagadougou: Imprimerie du Progres, 2005).

[26] Committee to Protect Journalists, "Antoine Bationo, *Le Pays*, and Boureima Jeremie Sigue, *Le Pays*, Harassed," 20 April 2006, www.cpj.org/cases06/africa_cases_06/burkina 20apr06ca.html.

27 H. Marie Ouedraogo, "Affaire commdant Pooda: Renvoyee a la demande de la defense," *L'Observateur Paalga,* 22 February 2007, www.lefaso.net/impression.php3?id_article =19390&id_rubrique=4.

28 Vincent Ouattara, "L'ere Compaore: Crimes de sang et crimes economiques."

29 See *Etat de la Corruption au Burkina Faso* (Ouagadougou: REN-LAC, Imprimerie FGZ Trading, 2004, 2005).

30 *Etat de la Corruption au Burkina Faso* (Ouagadougou: REN-LAC, Imprimerie FGZ Trading, 2005), 79–80.

31 "Mairie de Koudougou: Les Jours de Marcelin sont-ils Comptes?" *L'Observateur Paalga,* 26 July 2005, 5.

32 Thomas Bassett, *Price Formation and Power Relations in the Cotton Value Chains of Mali, Burkina Faso, and Côte d'Ivoire* (New York: Oxfam, 2006).

33 Blaise Compaore, *Le Progres Continu pour une Societe d'Esperance,* (Ouagadougou: Congres pour la Democratie et le Progres, October 2005), 72.

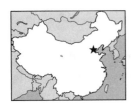

CHINA

CAPITAL: Beijing
POPULATION: 1,318 million
GNI PER CAPITA: $2,010

SCORES	2005	2007
ACCOUNTABILITY AND PUBLIC VOICE:	1.08	1.17
CIVIL LIBERTIES:	1.61	2.14
RULE OF LAW:	1.76	2.23
ANTICORRUPTION AND TRANSPARENCY:	2.18	2.49

(scores are based on a scale of 0 to 7, with 0 representing weakest and 7 representing strongest performance)

Thomas Gold

INTRODUCTION

The People's Republic of China (PRC) currently operates with a number of political and economic contradictions at its core. After nearly three decades of government-initiated market reforms, it formally remains a centralized, hierarchical, one-party state led by a Communist Party that is explicitly committed to building socialism as the forerunner of an ideal Communist society. But in practice, the central authorities in Beijing have a very difficult time compelling lower levels of the party and state to implement national policies, obey official rules, and provide accurate reports.

China is not a monolith by any stretch of the imagination. Geographically large and diverse, it has a population comprising fifty-six nationalities of widely divergent traditions, practices, and standards of living. Its history since the middle of the nineteenth century has been

Thomas Gold is Associate Dean of International and Area Studies and Associate Professor of Sociology at the University of California, Berkeley, where he also directs the Berkeley China Initiative. His current research examines international environmental NGOs in China, private enterprise in China, and social-political transformation in Taiwan. Rongbin Han provided research assistance for this chapter.

full of lurches, starts, and stops. Entire birth cohorts of people trained in a particular set of skills, values, and expectations have seen these discarded in favor of a new model, leading to enormous differences between generations, even among those brought up since the establishment of the PRC in 1949.

Since the end of 1978, the Chinese Communist Party (CCP) has been reshaping the PRC into a market-based and globally integrated economy, society, and culture. It labels this project "socialism with Chinese characteristics." While producing gross domestic product (GDP) growth rates that are among the world's highest, the party's strategy has led to the sort of severe inequality, weak social-welfare system, worker exploitation, job insecurity, and environmental degradation that is associated with capitalism at its worst.

In place of the Marxist call for the proletariat to rise up and struggle against the bourgeoisie, the CCP has invited China's new entrepreneurs to join the party, giving this class political legitimacy as an advanced social force. It has also passed a law protecting private property, and currently promotes the Confucian concept of building a harmonious society. Although the reforms have lifted tens of millions of rural and urban Chinese out of poverty, many people—especially those workers who have experienced a dizzying decline from their once-vaunted status as "masters of the country"—have greeted the changes with little enthusiasm.

Through the 1970s, the CCP tried to micromanage all aspects of Chinese life according to a blueprint for building socialism. By contrast, in the reform era that followed PRC founder Mao Zedong's death in 1976, it has adopted a policy of "crossing the river by feeling for the stones," improvising as fast as it can to keep the economy growing and material living standards rising. In this way, it hopes to buy off discontent stemming from the many contradictions noted above. The CCP's willingness to experiment represents an astounding leap of faith for a Leninist party once committed to total control. It has retreated significantly from that goal, opening up space for individuals to make their own decisions regarding career, education, residence, marriage, taste, and belief.

A country that sought to export revolution in the 1960s now revels in its prestige as a prominent member of the UN Security Council and the World Trade Organization (WTO), its hosting of the 2008

Summer Olympics and the 2010 World Expo, as well as its self-styled "peaceful rise" and affirmation in September 2005 by the United States as a "responsible stakeholder" in global affairs. While China's worldwide quest for natural resources to fuel its economy has attracted criticism for bolstering pariah regimes in countries including Sudan, Burma, and Zimbabwe, Beijing has also made concerted efforts to fulfill the responsible stakeholder role by helping to mediate the North Korean nuclear crisis and, after much prodding, agreeing to UN troop deployments aimed at stanching genocidal bloodshed in Sudan's Darfur region.

The state constitution and laws provide for numerous rights and freedoms. While ensuring their implementation remains very problematic, it is also difficult to quantify the dynamism and change sweeping China, including in the realm of political practice. China is vibrant, undisciplined, and rollicking, yet simultaneously arbitrary, polluted, and oppressive. It is carving out a path of its own, one not traveled by other developing countries or states in transition from socialism. Its leaders and citizens are grappling with a relentless onslaught of unprecedented challenges, while also trying to construct and consolidate institutions to manage the new order.

Although the CCP no longer advocates revolutionary transformation, the past quarter-century of evolutionary reform has arguably brought about a more profound metamorphosis than any of Mao's mass-mobilization campaigns. But the overlapping legacies of the imperial, nationalist, and Maoist periods still weigh heavily on Chinese society. This was quite clear in the summer of 2007. While touching off the one-year countdown to the Summer Olympics with a spectacular display of national pride and fireworks, Chinese leaders were dealing with a number of potentially explosive crises. Those include behind-the-scenes struggles over the selection of delegates and formulation of policies for the 17th Party Congress scheduled for the fall; concerns over the safety of Chinese food, toys, pharmaceuticals, and other products for both the global and domestic markets; mounting evidence of severe environmental degradation at home and its spread abroad; tightened restrictions on press freedom as media workers from around the world began to converge on China for the Olympics; and the cover-up of yet another public health threat.

ACCOUNTABILITY AND PUBLIC VOICE

FREE AND FAIR ELECTORAL LAWS AND ELECTIONS:	0.25
EFFECTIVE AND ACCOUNTABLE GOVERNMENT:	1.75
CIVIC ENGAGEMENT AND CIVIC MONITORING:	1.67
MEDIA INDEPENDENCE AND FREEDOM OF EXPRESSION:	1.00
CATEGORY AVERAGE:	**1.17**

China's booming economy has become increasingly privatized and market driven, and its urban and rural citizens have gained a significant measure of control over their economic, social, and cultural lives, but formal political life remains highly repressive and almost entirely monopolized by the CCP. There is no pretense of currently holding, nor does the regime plan to hold, regular, free, or fair elections above the village level. At a news conference on March 16, 2007, marking the conclusion of the Fifth Session of the National People's Congress (NPC), Premier Wen Jiabao reiterated that although "we must guarantee the people's rights to democratic election," the nation's priorities are "to develop our social productive forces . . . [and] promote social fairness and justice."[1] In an article published on February 27, 2007, Wen estimated that the "intitial stage of socialism" said to lead to "socialist democracy" would take 100 years, and asserted that it required leadership by the CCP.[2]

As with other Marxist-Leninist parties, the CCP legitimizes its exclusive rule by claiming to be the vanguard of the leading forces in society. Previously this referred to the proletariat and poor peasants, but under the CCP's current formula of "The Three Represents," attributed to former general secretary Jiang Zemin, the party represents the interests of the most advanced forces in society, advanced culture, and the interests of the whole people (as determined by the party, of course). "Advanced forces" is seen as code for the new entrepreneurial elite. Entrepreneurs, the former targets of the dictatorship, are now being recruited into party, and legislative and consultative bodies at all levels. However, the entry of capitalists per se into the party and state should not be seen as an inevitable step toward a multiparty system or democracy. Scholarly researchers have found no evidence that China's new elite has any commitment to or desire for democracy.[3] Indeed, many local entrepreneurs are dependent on the largely unchecked power of local chiefs, with whom relationships based on crony capitalism are forged.

Except at the level of the village (which is not a unit of the formal government) and in urban neighborhoods, there are no elections for public office.[4] The nomination of candidates for village chief remains a tightly controlled process, and even when non-CCP members win, they are often aggressively recruited into the party or subverted in carrying out their duties. Even then, the division of labor between the elected village head—often focused on economic development—and the appointed party boss has not been clarified, and relations can be hostile. Fraud, violence, and corruption have marred many of the elections.

There are eight "democratic parties" in China, mostly left over from the pre-PRC era. In the 1980s, they began to recruit new members. The main function of the parties is to "mutually supervise" the CCP, and they do not contest the limited elections that are held. Many of the parties' members are appointed to the Chinese People's Political Consultative Conference (CPPCC) at several levels, up to the national, where they conduct investigations and comment on pending legislation and other matters. The CPPCC meets at the same time as the People's Congress. It has no power and serves primarily to co-opt well-known individuals from various sectors of society.[5]

There are closely managed elections for delegates to People's Congresses at the local level,[6] and some non-CCP members have stood and won, with victories reported in the media. These delegates select representatives to the next higher level of the Congress, all the way to the NPC, which is elected for a five-year term and has approximately 3,000 members. Common citizens thus have little influence over the selection of their government leaders. The process is managed in secret within the CCP, and there is no opportunity for the rotation of power among parties.

The only parts of China with a competitive multiparty system are the special administrative regions of Hong Kong and Macao, which Britain and Portugal returned to China under special arrangements on July 1, 1997, and December 20, 1999, respectively. On March 25, 2007, Hong Kong's incumbent chief executive (CE), Donald Tsang, was reelected by an 800-member election committee whose members represent a range of professional and business communities, religious groups, and the local and national legislatures. He had originally been chosen in 2005 to replace the first CE, Tung Chee-hwa, who resigned before the end of his second term. Unlike his predecessor, Tsang faced an opponent in 2007, meaning at least 100 of the electors had nominated his rival. Though the outcome was never in doubt, there was an actual campaign and public debates. According to its Basic Law, Hong Kong is supposed to be moving toward universal suffrage for the election of its leaders, but Beijing has so far delayed any major expansion of voting rights.[7]

The executive, legislative, and judicial branches of the PRC government do not oversee one another. Key figures are all appointed by, and accountable to, the CCP, where ultimate power lies. The political system is designed to ensure that the CCP remains in power by holding the top positions in all organizations of state, economy, and society, or through party structures parallel to and within these organizations. The party's Central Discipline Committee investigates and punishes wrongdoers among the membership, but these cases do not always make it to the formal legal system. Party branches monopolize the formulation of policy and appointment of personnel. That said, party control waxes and wanes, and dissent periodically emerges during meetings of the NPC. One instance of dissent arose during the recent passage of a Property Law.[8] A draft was prepared in 2004, after years of discussion, and the law was expected to pass in 2006. But strong opposition from several corners delayed passage until March 2007. Opponents of the measure, who included intellectuals and party members, saw it, not without reason, as a stunning betrayal of the ideals they thought the CCP stood for, and argued that it sanctioned corruption and inequality. Ultimately, it passed with 97 percent of the vote, a less-than-perfect endorsement that indicated at least some ongoing disapproval.

The criteria for selection of civil servants have shifted along with the party's priorities. When the leadership's concerns were primarily political, demonstrated loyalty was the paramount qualification. With the change of focus to the Four Modernizations (agriculture, industry, science and technology, and national defense) since 1978, the party has sought out more technically skilled experts to join the party and staff state bureaucracies. The civil service exam was reestablished in 1994.[9] Heads of ministries and subsidiary bureaus are almost universally CCP members, and their main commitment is to the party, or often to powerful patrons and factions within it. A major early achievement of the reforms was the introduction of a retirement system for party and state officials. This was illustrated by the requirement that Jiang Zemin retire as CCP general secretary, state president, and chairman of the Central Military Commission between 2002 and 2004, although many members of his Shanghai faction remained in their jobs for several more years.

One of the most noticeable trends in China in recent years has been the growth of the nongovernmental organization (NGO) sector, and with it the makings of civil society, despite government efforts to restrict both. The state is of two minds about NGOs and civil society more broadly. NGOs are more likely to be welcomed when they supplement the work of the state, for instance by opening orphanages, delivering care to the elderly or disabled, or providing education and other forms of welfare to the rural poor, especially girls.[10] But groups face suspicion when they adopt a more investigatory and critical stance or attempt to press their cases publicly, as have NGOs dealing with HIV/AIDS, environmental crises, and migrant workers.[11] Many of these groups and causes attract foreign support, heightening their sensitivity.

The government's policies toward NGOs pass through alternating periods of restriction and loosening, and the shifts are often unpredictable. In recognition of the significance of the emerging NGO sector, Beijing's prestigious Tsinghua University in 1998 established an NGO Research Center to investigate the topic, propose related legislation, and make policy recommendations to the government.[12] The restrictions on NGOs are clearly motivated by the CCP's concerns that groups in China, including foreign ones, might play the same sort of role as those in Georgia, Ukraine, and Kyrgyzstan in fomenting Color Revolutions. Nonetheless, numerous NGOs, especially in the environmental field, operate very actively in China. Although there are no established channels by which civic organizations can participate in the policy process, they comment quite forcefully on affairs of the day through their websites and blogs. They have had some successes, such as delaying (but apparently not canceling) dam building on the Nu River in the southwest and on a sacred Tibetan lake.[13]

The exact number of NGOs is not known because registration requirements are onerous and many groups prefer to avoid contact with the authorities. The Ministry of Civil Affairs reported 346,000 registered NGOs by the end of 2006, an 8 percent increase over the previous year.[14] The All-China Environmental Federation, a GONGO (government-organized NGO), acknowledged that only 23.3 percent of environmental organizations were formally registered.[15]

The CCP views the media as an instrument to articulate and support its policies; to mobilize, unite, and divert the people; and to manage the impressions it gives to its own citizens and the outside world.[16] Although the constitution's Article 35 guarantees free speech and freedom of the press, Article 51 warns that these cannot infringe on the "interests of the state." This deliberately vague guideline is an obvious impediment to media freedom. The party and the state own all media in whole or in part, and they are closely regulated by the authorities. However, with the advent of market-based reforms, even state-owned outlets must compete for audience and advertisers. This is done through sensationalized stories, articles about celebrities, and some degree of investigative reporting, but not through the free presentation of alternative viewpoints.

The party and state use a variety of tactics to control the media. In many cases they rely on "prior restraints," severely restricting the outlets that are allowed to operate and expecting journalists to practice self-censorship.[17] The line between what is permitted and what is forbidden is never clear or fixed, but when the media are perceived to have crossed it, the authorities turn to various forms of overt intimidation and punishment. This may involve the use of the courts, police, or thugs; financial pressure; the closure of outlets; or the firing of individuals. For example, when Chinese reporters, including those from CCP mouthpiece *People's Daily*, were interviewing relatives of people killed in a bridge collapse, they were set upon and beaten by local toughs. Foreign journalists have likewise been detained and manhandled.[18]

There is general agreement that the situation for journalists in China has deteriorated in recent years.[19] In one well-known case in September 2004, Zhao Yan, a crusading journalist for the rights of farmers and a researcher for the *New York Times*, was detained for "providing state secrets to foreigners" by revealing before the official announcement that Jiang Zemin would retire.[20] He was exonerated of this but was subsequently sentenced to three years' imprisonment on a fraud charge. Both of his trials were closed to the public.

Later that year, Shi Tao, an editor with the *Dangdai Shang Bao* (*Contemporary Business News*) of Changsha, Hunan, was arrested for divulging state secrets—namely, instructions from the Propaganda Department to his paper.[21] In April 2005, Shi received a ten-year prison sentence. An additional disturbing aspect of his case was the revelation that Yahoo!

Holdings (Hong Kong), a division of the U.S.-based internet company Yahoo!, had provided information about his internet protocol (IP) address to the authorities.[22] Subsequently, U.S.-based internet giant Google also admitted that it had modified its Chinese search engine to block sensitive topics including the 1989 Tiananmen Square massacre and the banned Falun Gong spiritual movement.[23] Ching Cheong, a Hong Kong citizen working for the Singapore-based *Straits Times*, was arrested as a spy in April 2005. As of December 2005, China had thirty-two journalists in jail, more than any other country.[24]

The rapid growth of the internet in China, coupled with the extensive restrictions imposed on it by the authorities, is a revealing example of the contradictions currently permeating the country.[25] By the end of 2006, China had an estimated 144 million internet users, 23.4 percent more than the year before.[26] Although a visit to a typical internet café would indicate that a number of people (especially young men) use the medium primarily to play games, many Chinese surf the web in search of information about world or domestic affairs that they cannot get from official sources. They also use it to express their own opinions, with researchers at Tsinghua University predicting a total of 100 million Chinese bloggers in 2007.[27] The "blogosphere" may come to serve as a healthy safety valve for public debate as well as an important means of communication between the people and the state. However, the state continues its efforts to monitor, filter, and control the internet, erecting what foreigners call "The Great Firewall of China."[28] Arrayed against the state's surveillance are numerous "hacktivists," who seek out or create ways to circumvent government controls.[29] In one recent example of the state's influence, on August 22, 2007, the Internet Society of China, an offshoot of the Information Ministry, convinced at least twenty leading blog service providers to sign a "self-discipline pact," encouraging them to register users under their real names and contact information. Reporters Without Borders condemned the pact, which Yahoo.cn and MSN.cn (a division of U.S.-based Microsoft) signed, though many bloggers did not appear to be terribly intimidated.[30]

China's journalists have actively protested acts of repression. For instance, in 2005 hundreds of reporters and staff at the outspoken *Beijing News* publicly demonstrated "against an editorial takeover by one of its parent publications, party mouthpiece *Guangming Daily*."[31] In February

2006, the top editors of *Freezing Point*, a weekly investigative supplement to the *China Youth Daily*, were removed after an article by historian Yuan Weishi criticized China's textbooks, though the paper had skirted the limits of what was permissible since its inception in 1995. A group of retired officials and intellectuals issued a public statement protesting the paper's closure, and a dismissed editor, Li Datong, went public with his criticisms.[32] The shocking revelations of kidnapping and slavery at brick kilns in Shanxi province in the spring of 2007 prompted reflection on the responsibilities and shortcomings of the media by one of the more daring papers, *Southern Metropolis Daily*. Even *China Daily*, the official English-language paper, published a signed opinion piece stressing the need for investigative reporting.[33]

Sensitive to global public opinion in the run-up to the 2008 Summer Olympics in Beijing, the Foreign Ministry in December 2006 announced new regulations permitting foreign journalists to conduct interviews anywhere in the country without prior permission from local officials. The rules were to expire on October 17, 2008.[34] International human rights groups including Human Rights Watch, Amnesty International, the Committee to Protect Journalists, and Reporters Without Borders have begun to test the limits of this policy, and their disconcerting findings indicate that it has not been successfully implemented.

Many official media outlets, concerned with public opinion and frustration regarding corruption, conduct hard-hitting investigations of wrongdoing at the local level. Here again, the authorities have not clearly defined the limits of what can be revealed, the proper selection of targets, and the autonomy of reporters to pursue their own stories rather than be used by officials to expose and bring down other officials.

Limits are similarly vague for other types of artistic expression, but control has softened considerably with the advent of market-based competition.[35] Television now offers a wide variety of program choices, and entertainment provides a way to divert the public's attention from politics and other sensitive topics. One television show that drew a great deal of scrutiny in 2005 was the *Super Girl* contest, a satellite broadcast out of Hunan that used the same format as *American Idol*. It became a matter of official concern not only because of the winner's androgyny, but because millions of fans nationwide voted by cellular telephone, clearly indicating that they were willing to express their opinions in a democratic contest.

Recommendations

- China's leaders should continue to expand and perfect village elections and experiment with township and urban elections. Institutions for positive working relations between elected officials and local party chiefs should be built.
- The leadership should continue to raise the quality of civil servants at all levels. Higher officials should regularly spend time at local levels to better understand the situation on the ground and in order to close the gap between the leadership and the people.
- Registration for civil society groups should be made easier, and the government should work to build channels for such groups to engage in public discourse with the party and state on important issues, such as the environment, corruption, and welfare. Moreover, the leadership should invite representatives of NGOs to testify before congresses or publicize their opinions in the media.
- The government should recognize the diminishing returns of its attempts to monitor the internet and encourage party and state officials to engage in competition and debate with bloggers and other internet users. Officials should not fear the expression of public opinion and diverse views.

CIVIL LIBERTIES

PROTECTION FROM STATE TERROR, UNJUSTIFIED IMPRISONMENT, AND TORTURE:	1.57
GENDER EQUITY:	3.50
RIGHTS OF ETHNIC, RELIGIOUS, AND OTHER DISTINCT GROUPS:	2.50
FREEDOM OF CONSCIENCE AND BELIEF:	1.33
FREEDOM OF ASSOCIATION AND ASSEMBLY:	1.80
CATEGORY AVERAGE:	**2.14**

Even though political institutions in China have not undergone major change, the degree to which Chinese can manage their own lives has increased substantially in the reform era. This is a very significant development, but it should be emphasized that not all Chinese are pleased with the reforms, which have also produced great economic inequality and made the fulfillment of basic needs less secure. And, as with so many things in China, the boundaries of what is permissible are arbitrary and constantly shifting.

It is worth noting that the 1982 constitution (amended several times) stresses the fundamental agency of the state rather than the individual, and the rights of citizens are listed along with their numerous duties and obligations. Article 33 was amended in 2004 to proclaim that "the state respects and preserves human rights." However, the preponderance of the evidence, much of it from Chinese official sources, clearly indicates that these rights are commonly ignored in practice. Citizens have begun to demand that the organs of authority respect and enforce their constitutional rights. This includes not only the sophisticated urban middle class but, even more significantly, vast numbers of farmers. The call for the enforcement of rights already on the books, rather than any demand for electoral democracy, constitutes the core of popular political struggle in China.

In spite of obstructions, restrictions, surveillance, and intimidation, the UN Commission on Human Rights Special Rapporteur on torture and other cruel, inhuman, or degrading treatment or punishment effectively corroborated long-standing allegations of these practices during a visit to China in late 2005.[36] A number of international organizations regularly publish information about the brutal treatment of detainees and deplorable prison conditions in China. Even internationally known activists, such as the lawyers Gao Zhisheng and Chen Guancheng (who is blind), have been beaten.[37] Central authorities have also recognized some of these practices and announced measures to curb them. These include prohibiting the use of evidence obtained through coerced confessions, punishing officials who use or sanction torture, and passing laws on criminal procedure.[38] In 1998, China signed—but has yet to ratify—the International Covenant on Civil and Political Rights (ICCPR). It did ratify the UN Convention Against Torture in 1988. The absence of an independent judiciary is one major obstacle to implementing these covenants, as is the general problem of local authorities ignoring orders from the center, misreporting the situation in their jurisdictions, and receiving protection from patrons at higher levels.

In 2005, officials acknowledged an upsurge in protests of various kinds, some of which attracted the attention of the domestic and international media. One traditional form of protest that remains popular is the petition, by which individuals bring complaints against local officials to higher levels in the administrative hierarchy in a bid to resolve grievances such as corruption, forced resettlement, land grabs, and miscarriage of justice.[39] This use of the law by petitioners is referred to as "rightful resistance."[40] Petitioners believe that higher-level officials, including the top leaders in Beijing, will support them and punish miscreant subordinates once their misdeeds are exposed. In reality, petitioners are commonly sent back home, where humiliated and furious local officials exact revenge both through the formal legal system and the use of thugs.[41]

Other protests are defined as "mass incidents," which include "riots, protests, demonstrations, and mass petitions."[42] The Ministry of Public Security stated that there were 58,000 such incidents in 2003, 74,000 in 2004, and 87,000 in 2005, with a decline in 2006, although the criteria for categorizing various types of disturbance remain confusing.[43] One major protest took place in early December 2005 in Dongzhou, a farming and fishing town in Guangdong, 125 miles northeast of Hong Kong. The proximate cause was inadequate compensation for land confiscated to build a power plant; villagers had failed in their efforts to utilize the petition system. Ordinary police and members of the paramilitary People's Armed Police (PAP) suppressed them violently, killing between ten and twenty.[44] The use of police, the PAP, and hired thugs to deal with such protests reveals a distinct lack of respect for the civil liberties of the participants, who generally begin their pursuit of justice with nonviolent petitions. The crackdowns result in arbitrary arrests, torture, and an atmosphere of terror.

The regime in 2007 missed a chance to dismantle the reeducation through labor (RTL) system (*laojiao*), adopted in 1957. The system permits police to sentence people to a maximum of four years' incarceration for petty crimes, although it originally targeted counterrevolutionaries. A Chinese legal expert acknowledged in early 2007 that the practice violated the state constitution, the Criminal Procedure Law, and the International Covenant on Civil and Political Rights.[45] Sentences under RTL may be stiffer than those under the criminal law, and detainees in RTL facilities face torture and harsh conditions. Although a proposal to abolish RTL was on the agenda for the 2007 meeting of the National People's Congress, it did not pass, largely due to opposition from the Ministry of Public Security.[46]

The CCP made the liberation of Chinese women a top priority from its earliest days, and it achieved a great deal, particularly in freeing many women from arranged marriages and getting them into the wage-earning workforce. Nearly all girls receive some primary education. Article 48 of the constitution grants women "equal rights with men in all spheres of life," and they are supposed to receive "equal pay for equal work," but as in most societies, gender inequality in China is entrenched and very resistant to change.[47]

Since the late 1970s, the state has implemented a draconian family-planning policy, generally limiting urban families to one child and rural families to two. Given China's traditional preference for males, which no legislation can eradicate, an unintended consequence of the single-child policy has been the selective abortion of female fetuses and even the revival of female infanticide. Ninety-nine cities have more than 125 boys for every 100 girls, and there are already "18 million more men than women of marriageable age."[48] Ironically, this has in turn resulted in an upsurge in trafficking in women to supply the market for brides and female labor, including sex work. NGOs have been active in addressing this problem, and the government has severely punished traffickers, tried to reunite victims with their families, and cooperated on the issue with other countries in the region.[49]

The Chinese government is a latecomer in paying attention to the special needs of people with disabilities, estimated at eighty-three million in the country. China still lacks many facilities and programs to ensure their full participation in society, and poverty and unemployment rates among the disabled are high,[50] despite increased activity by NGOs.

The constitution declares that "all nationalities in the People's Republic of China are equal" and protects their "lawful rights and interests." There are officially fifty-five minority nationalities, with populations ranging from 15.5 million (Zhuang) to 2,300 (Lhoba) people. Some maintain distinct cultures, including folk religions, while others have assimilated to the culture of the majority Han, who make up 92 percent of the population. Minorities are exempt from the single-child family policy in their regions, which has bred resentment among some Han.

The minority nationalities that have attracted the most foreign attention are the Tibetans and the Uyghurs; the latter, along with several other Muslim peoples, populate the far western region of Xinjiang. The

Tibetans and Uyghurs both have elaborate religion-based cultures that are quite distinct from the Han culture. The state in recent decades has rebuilt temples and mosques, many of which were destroyed under Mao, though such restorations stem from a desire to co-opt the people and earn tourist income as much as from any respect for the cultures themselves.

The state is most concerned with Tibetan and Uyghur separatist movements, which receive various forms of support from abroad. The authorities take a rigid and punitive position on these movements, vilifying Tibet's exiled leader, the Dalai Lama, and characterizing dissident Uyghurs as Islamist terrorists. The Dalai Lama has in fact renounced independence as a goal for Tibet, saying he seeks only to broker more autonomy for the people who still venerate him. Within his movement, however, there are restless members who do advocate a more extreme, even violent approach.

Under a policy of developing the western regions of the country, Han Chinese are flooding into Tibet, Xinjiang, and Inner Mongolia, where they now dominate the economy as well as political and cultural life. Some foreign critics have condemned this as a thinly veiled form of cultural genocide. The opening of the last link of the Beijing–Lhasa railway in mid-2006 has been both hailed as a pipeline for the development of the Tibetan region and condemned as a funnel for outside influence.[51]

The state operates affirmative-action programs for minorities, recruiting many to top schools so that they can return to their home regions as loyal officials. Communist Party members cannot be religious believers, as communist ideology regards religion as nonscientific and a tool of the old exploiting classes and foreign imperialists. However, many CCP members do practice religions, mainly Buddhism, and some were open followers of Falun Gong until it was suppressed in 1999. Open believers cannot rise to the top of the political system, although they occupy important lower posts in the bureaucracy.

One disadvantaged group that has drawn attention in recent years is the so-called migrant or floating population. Until the 1990s, Chinese without official urban residence permits (*hukou*), typically farmers, could not live in the cities. Movement from city to city was also quite difficult. With the dismantling of collective agriculture and the rise of the market economy, rural people began migrating to cities to seek employment. However, the migrants, estimated to number over 130 million, still live in a sort of legal limbo. They are regularly cheated out of their wages, and have little recourse to claim them. Many work in very difficult and dangerous fields, such as construction, suffering high accident rates without insurance. They often live in appalling conditions, and if their families join them, the children are not eligible for schooling.[52] The recent brick-kiln enslavement scandal in Shanxi province—and the collusion of local officials and police in this brutality—focused attention at least briefly on the exploitation of migrant labor. The case also revealed the weakness of the legal system.[53]

Article 36 of the constitution protects "freedom of religious belief." There are five officially recognized religions: Daoism (Taoism), Buddhism, Islam, nondenominational Christianity, and Catholicism. Each has a state-run association to manage and monitor its affairs. According to the constitution, the state cannot "compel citizens to believe in, or not to believe in, any religion" and cannot discriminate against believers. The state protects "normal religious activities," which it defines and manages through the Religious Affairs Bureau. In March 2005, the government passed regulations on religious affairs; the official goal was to better protect religious freedom, but critics claim that the vagueness and arbitrariness of the term "normal," as well as strictures against using religion to "disrupt public order," give the authorities wide scope to suppress any behavior that raises their suspicions.[54]

Officials have fueled resentment by demolishing so-called house churches, buildings where Catholics and other Christians choose to worship outside the state-managed congregations for various reasons. Some Catholics remain loyal to the pope instead of the Chinese Catholic Patriotic Association, provoking government friction with the Vatican, which insists it has ultimate authority over doctrine and the appointment of church officials (and which maintains diplomatic relations with Taiwan). The state sees this as interference in China's internal affairs. In truth, many foreign religious groups do support Catholic and other Christian "underground" congregations. Their activities sometimes go beyond the defense of human rights and civil liberties and aim at religious conversion. Many Chinese outside the government resent this and associate missionary work with past imperialist aggression against China.

In February 2006, Pope Benedict XVI provocatively made Bishop Joseph Zen of Hong Kong a cardinal. Zen, a Shanghai native, has frequently criticized the CCP. But in July 2007, the pope issued a letter to Chinese Catholics trying to reconcile the official and underground churches, without relinquishing the Vatican's right to appoint bishops. As older bishops die off, this may become a greater source of conflict.[55]

While Buddhism as a whole is not terribly problematic from the regime's point of view, Tibetan Buddhism is extremely sensitive. A particularly contentious case of state involvement in the appointment of religious leaders involves the Panchen Lama, Tibet's second-highest ranking religious figure. The tenth Panchen Lama died in 1989, and a competition began between the CCP and independent believers to find his reincarnation. In May 1995, the Dalai Lama recognized a six-year-old boy as the reincarnation, but in November the state named another. The first boy disappeared, and his whereabouts remain unknown.[56] In 2006, the state-approved Panchen Lama made his first major public appearance at an international Buddhist convocation in China.[57] In August 2007, in a patently bizarre move analogous to the policy on naming Catholic bishops, the atheistic state's Religious Affairs Bureau issued a set of fourteen regulations requiring that all reincarnated lamas receive government approval through the official Chinese Buddhist Association. Beijing is clearly positioning itself to assert authority over Tibetan Buddhism as the Dalai Lama ages.[58]

While Christianity is associated with imperialist aggression and Tibetan Buddhism with separatism, China's leaders link Islam to both separatism and terrorism. As noted above, the state has built new mosques and restored older ones that had been confiscated and used for other purposes. There is state-sponsored and private Islamic education, and many Chinese Muslims study abroad in such countries as Egypt, Syria, Pakistan, Iran, and Saudi Arabia, sometimes bringing back intolerance toward local practices. Nonetheless, women play an active role in Islamic education in China.[59]

The numbers of religious believers have increased steadily, although reliable figures are hard to come by. This is true of Christians in particular. Officially, there are about 5 million Catholics and 15 million other Christians, but some estimates suggest 10 million Catholics and anywhere from 30 to 90 million Protestants.[60] Muslims are "conservatively estimated" to number 20 million.[61]

Article 35 of the constitution grants citizens "freedom of assembly, of association, of procession, and of demonstration." Again, Article 51 trumps these freedoms, stating that their exercise "may not infringe upon the interests of the state," without clearly specifying what that means. The limited channels for expression of discontent and the redress of grievances tends to lead to protests, which the state often violently disperses.

The state does not permit free and independent trade unions, and it suppresses attempts to organize them.[62] All unions are arms of the CCP and function as much to control workers as to represent their interests. Such is the attraction of China's market and plentiful, cheap labor supply that two staunchly antiunion U.S. companies, Wal-Mart and McDonald's, acceded to the government's pressure to unionize their stores in 2006 and 2007, respectively. In 2006, the state began to draft a Labor Contract Law to crack down on sweatshops, protect workers, and empower unions; while these steps provoked opposition from foreign investors, U.S. unions organized a campaign of support.[63] The Standing Committee of the National People's Congress passed the measure in June 2007, and it is due to take effect January 1, 2008.[64]

The days of China's strict organization into mass associations or rural collectives are over. Membership in the Communist Youth League and the CCP still conveys certain benefits, whether it is a direct career boost or the establishment of more subtle *guanxi* (connections). But more and more Chinese are participating in civic life on their own, such as in NGOs or via internet chat rooms and blogs. Chambers of Commerce, with local and foreign members, have also begun to assume an important role in Chinese life.

Recommendations

- The government should increase planning and resources devoted to enforcing constitutional provisions and existing laws guaranteeing civil liberties, and punish officers of the state who violate those rights.
- The authorities should open channels such as town-hall meetings and expand current experiments with "consultative democracy," which allow citizens to both express grievances and offer constructive opinions. The leadership should also prevent officials from interfering with this process or exacting revenge on those who participate.
- The government should work more actively and directly with religious groups in China to enrich spiritual life for believers and nonbelievers alike.

- Additional efforts should be made to protect girls and women from trafficking, and to address the gender imbalance that helps fuel the practice.

RULE OF LAW

INDEPENDENT JUDICIARY:	1.80
PRIMACY OF RULE OF LAW IN CIVIL AND CRIMINAL MATTERS:	1.17
ACCOUNTABILITY OF SECURITY FORCES AND MILITARY TO CIVILIAN AUTHORITIES:	2.50
PROTECTION OF PROPERTY RIGHTS:	2.67
EQUAL TREATMENT UNDER THE LAW:	3.00
CATEGORY AVERAGE:	**2.23**

The CCP routinely acknowledges the need for China to become a society characterized by the rule of law as opposed to the rule by law. In the former, every person and organization is equal under the law, whereas in the latter, dominant groups or individuals use the law as a malleable tool to maintain their position.

Implementing the rule of law in China is extremely difficult for several reasons. Traditionally, Chinese officials, as supposedly morally superior men, were above the law, which was seen as an instrument to enforce the rule of the state. The CCP inherited this basic approach, adding the justification that party members, as the vanguard of society, needed to use laws to protect the achievements of the revolution against class enemies. During the Cultural Revolution under Mao, the legal system collapsed along with much of the social order, adding to the current challenge.

The first laws passed in the reform era were aimed at suppressing the criminality that was still rampant following the breakdown of social order. Since 1983, the CCP has utilized "strike hard" campaigns to round up and severely punish, often with mass trials and executions, large numbers of people, particularly young people. The public, remembering the chaos of the Cultural Revolution, continues to support these harsh measures. China reputedly leads the world in executions, although exact and verifiable numbers are not available. From January 1, 2007, the Supreme People's Court regained the right to review all death penalty decisions, and the state reported that in 2006 it had meted out the fewest death sentences since 1997, without revealing any hard figures. Human rights activists put the number of executions at between 10,000 and 15,000, more than the rest of the world combined.[65] There is no plan to abolish the death penalty. After the initial period of anticrime legislation, laws to regulate the market-oriented economy were passed, along with administrative and criminal procedure codes.

Despite skepticism about the sincerity of the reform project and cynicism regarding its practical application, propaganda supporting the rule of law is ubiquitous. The print and broadcast media run detailed pieces on civil and criminal cases, as well as opinion articles, lectures, and discussions by experts and officers of the law. There are more than ninety specialized law journals. Television dramas regularly depict the legal system, police, lawyers, and judges, all with a pedagogical as well as entertainment goal. Instructional books offer help in navigating the evolving legal system,[66] and discussions in internet chat rooms address legal issues.

Nevertheless, the judiciary remains a tool of the CCP, and it rarely shows signs of independence or autonomy. The courts, including the Supreme People's Court, are answerable to the National People's Congress. At the lower levels, judges are appointed by local officials, further reducing their independence. Corruption is rife within the judicial system, but in the economic realm, particularly in cases involving foreign interests, the law is administered in a more impartial fashion.

Training of qualified judicial officials remains a work in progress. In the early reform era, police and military officers were assigned to staff the newly reconstituted legal system. They had only rudimentary training or familiarity with the law. The revival of law schools and the assistance of foreign experts, along with the support of the leadership, have helped improve the professional standards of judges, but structural constraints on the system remain significant.[67]

Suspects are not presumed innocent until proven guilty, and confessions are regularly coerced. Illegal detentions and the use of RTL are still common. Although Article 125 of the constitution guarantees public trials, this comes with a vague exception for cases involving "special circumstances," meaning many cases deemed sensitive are inaccessible even to family members of the accused. Citizens have a formal right to counsel, but many attorneys feel too intimidated to represent clients in sensitive cases. Moreover, lawyers are often treated almost as accomplices of defendants, and they are frequently prevented from meeting with their clients. In a promising development, a new cohort of activist lawyers and law professors has emerged to take on sensitive cases as part of their larger reform agenda.[68] Additionally, with backing from the Ministry of Justice, legal aid centers to provide counsel for indigent clients have sprung up rapidly, although the number of cases handled is small. Lawyers in China are required to perform pro bono work, but enforcement is problematic.[69]

Prosecutors are also agents of the party and state and thus lack independence. However, public officials and party members are regularly prosecuted for a range of crimes, most notably corruption. As in the 2006 case of Shanghai party secretary Chen Liangyu and the 2007 case of former State Food and Drug Administration director Zheng Xiaoyu, they are often detained, investigated, and punished by the party's own judicial and discipline organs before facing the ordinary courts. Zheng, whose case was linked to the international scandal of tainted Chinese food products, was subsequently sentenced to death in the formal court system. In July 2007, Chen lost his membership in both the Shanghai People's Congress and National People's Congress, though his case had yet to come to trial. In the run-up to the 17th Party Congress, the leadership wants to be seen as determined to root out and punish corruption in its ranks.

The People's Liberation Army (PLA) is the military of both the party and the state; it is overseen by the respective Central Military Commissions of the party and state, whose leaders are identical. There is a Ministry of National Defense, but it is subordinate to the state Central Military Commission and does not have direct control over the PLA. President Hu Jintao, like Jiang Zemin before him, heads both the CCP and the two Central Military Commissions. Aside from the top leadership, there is virtually no civilian control or oversight of the police, military, or internal security forces. They are rarely held accountable for abuse of power, although cases of torture have been brought to light, such as the 2003 beating death of graphic designer Sun Zhigang in a Guangzhou detention center. That case demonstrated the power of the media and especially the internet in exposing misconduct and exerting popular pressure on the state to punish violators. Nonetheless, these are exceptions, and the agents of law enforcement are not perceived as respectful of human rights.

Private property rights in the PRC have undergone a major transformation in the reform era. The state took tentative steps toward opening a space for private business, at the level of microenterprises, in 1978, and it has expanded and deepened tremendously since then. The constitution has been amended several times to reflect the standing of the private sector and to guarantee the rights of private business and property ownership. Many laws to manage the newly privatizing, market-based economy were designed to attract and reassure foreign investors, as well as to facilitate China's entry into the WTO. The Private Property Law, passed by the NPC in March 2007, was a major—although not universally applauded—step toward protecting private property more generally. The related issue of housing ownership is highly contentious. As China continues to remake its urban and rural landscape, housing, which has only recently become privatized, is regularly marked for demolition. The Chinese character for demolition, chai, is ubiquitous in the cities. Owners complain of inadequate compensation for their property, victimization by corrupt officials involved in development deals, and compulsory eviction to distant suburbs. Meanwhile, wealthy owners of luxury flats and homes in gated communities have organized homeowners' associations to defend their property rights.[70]

Recommendations
- The government should continue to reform the legal system to comply with international standards as set out in the ICCPR, which should be ratified.
- The government should consistently implement the constitutional provisions for the legal system at all levels. These include the inviolability of the freedom of persons (Article 37), and the rights to criticize and expose wrongdoing by officials (Article 41).
- The government should strengthen and monitor the system for seizure of land and compensation, ensuring that those evicted are provided with adequate time, resources, and options for resettlement.

ANTICORRUPTION AND TRANSPARENCY

ENVIRONMENT TO PROTECT AGAINST CORRUPTION:	2.80
EXISTENCE OF LAWS AND ETHICAL STANDARDS BETWEEN	
PRIVATE AND PUBLIC SECTORS:	2.50
ENFORCEMENT OF ANTICORRUPTION LAWS:	2.50
GOVERNMENTAL TRANSPARENCY:	2.14
CATEGORY AVERAGE:	**2.49**

While China today has linked itself to the global communications system, with information flowing rapidly through multiple domestic and international channels, the CCP retains much of its habitual secrecy and is disinclined to share information when it is not seen as absolutely necessary. The central government has been promulgating decrees and laws that lay the groundwork for more transparency, but actual implementation remains an enormous challenge. The authorities openly acknowledge that corruption is rampant. It is fueled by the CCP's structure and mindset; the control of significant economic assets by some party members, their families, and their client networks; and, as discussed above, the lack of an independent judiciary, a repressive media environment, and inadequate protections for petitioners and whistle-blowers.

Corruption intensified during the 1990s as economic growth accelerated and the opportunities for officials to profit from their positions multiplied.[71] Officials' personal assets are not disclosed in a reliable way, and much of their corrupt activity is conducted through family members. Many cases have involved the collection of bribes for the procurement of licenses or the manipulation of regulations, but the most flagrant examples of corruption center on land deals. While less common than the mass protests in rural areas over corrupt land deals, protests also occur in the cities, where many officials use their power to exploit the booming real-estate market.

One of the most widely publicized cases involved Politburo member and Shanghai party secretary Chen Liangyu.[72] In the fall of 2006, he was charged with involvement in corrupt land deals and misuse of the city's pension fund. Given that many bankrupt state-owned enterprises and local governments claim they cannot afford to pay promised pensions to retired and laid-off workers, the latter aspect of the Chen case proved particularly grating. He was removed from office and punished within the party before his case entered the state legal system.

Although corruption cases are being investigated at all levels—more than 6,000 officials were punished between July 2005 and the end of 2006—powerful personal networks often have significant influence over who is pursued by the authorities.[73] Chen's downfall was interpreted by many observers as a sign that President Hu Jintao had accumulated enough clout to move against the remnants of former president Jiang Zemin's Shanghai faction, which opposed him on several issues. The previously mentioned execution of Zheng Xiaoyu, meanwhile, occurred in the context of China's attempts to restore confidence in its exports and was widely seen as a demonstration of accountability for the international community rather than the result of a standard corruption investigation.

Access to higher education is in large part meritocratic, based on a national entrance examination. In recent years, however, universities have sought ways to enhance revenues in the face of reduced state support, so students from wealthy families may be able to buy special favors.[74]

The National Audit Office has been active in exposing and investigating corruption.[75] However, the sacking of the chief of the National Bureau of Statistics, Qiu Xiaohua, for suspected involvement in the Shanghai fund scandal raised doubts about the reliability of official statistics.[76]

Of the CCP's recent moves in the direction of openness,[77] some have been a response to what are literally matters of life and death. Secrecy and deception regarding the SARS outbreak in 2003 had lethal consequences and drew international outrage. The government has been more forthcoming in revealing cases of avian influenza, but figures on HIV/AIDS and an outbreak of the highly infectious blue-ear pig disease in the summer of 2007 remain problematic. The cover-up around a November 2005 toxic chemical spill into the Songhua River threatened not only the water supply of the Chinese regions it passed through, but the Russian Far East as well. This similarly attracted international condemnation. Soon after, the government issued an emergency response plan, including for natural disasters.[78]

Amid a series of revelations concerning defective, counterfeit, and unsafe Chinese products starting in the summer of 2007, the authorities issued nationalistic attacks on the safety of imported products from the United States and elsewhere, but also pledged to investigate malfeasance and provide accurate information to domestic and international consumers.

A recent decree set to take effect on May 1, 2008, recognizes the importance of transparency in its first article, and requires local governments to open their books and reveal the terms and compensation for land seizures to citizens who request the information. As might be expected, the decree also includes a catch-all clause stating that information harmful to state security and social stability cannot be disclosed.[79] If actually implemented, these regulations could have a significant effect on the behavior of local officials, to say nothing of public health and safety.

The official websites www.gov.cn, china.com.cn, and china.org.cn provide a great deal of information about the Chinese system, as well as numerous reports from the state media in a variety of languages. This means that government agencies face new requirements to disclose what they do, and are subject to popular scrutiny. Although the arrangement is hardly transparent, it is a significant breakthrough for a Leninist state, and considering the outcome associated with transparency (*glasnost*) in the Soviet Union, it is a very risky move.

One area where transparency is making some slow headway is the state budget process. While the constitution (Articles 67 and 99) grants people's congresses at all levels the power to examine and approve budgets, lack of expertise, limited time for review, and the legacy of a planned economy have made exercise of this power little more than a ritual. However, experiments with "consultative democracy" at the lowest level—township people's congresses—and the central government's collaboration with the Organization for Economic Cooperation and Development and World Bank are enhancing the capacity of delegates to perform these mandated tasks.[80]

Recommendations

- The authorities should allow the petition and court systems to play a larger role in combating corruption at local levels, with freer rein also given to the media, NGOs, and citizens to expose cases of corruption and adequate protection for petitioners, litigants, and whistle-blowers from officials who threaten them.

- More resources and autonomy should be granted to regulating agencies, both in terms of auditing state agencies and in regulating unsafe and unhealthy practices by private firms.
- The authorities should bring cases of corruption by party members into the state court system expeditiously and grant judges autonomy to adjudicate cases without political interference.
- The government should continue to disclose information about natural disasters and health risks and improve both the transparency of the information and the efficiency of its dissemination, thereby allowing Chinese and foreigners to take timely and appropriate protective measures.

NOTES

[1] "Full Text of PRC Premier Wen Jiabao's News Conference," Carter Center China Elections Project, 16 March 2007, http://www.chinaelections.org/en/readnews.asp?newsid ={52A8C4F6-A659-4137-BAED-8BF795FF1E04}&classid=1068&classname=2007 %20NPC-CPPCC.

[2] Embassy of the People's Republic of China in Brunei, "Wen: Building Prosperous, Democratic China," news release, 3 March 2007, http://bn.china-embassy.org/eng/zgxw /t300893.htm.

[3] Bruce J. Dickson, *Red Capitalists in China: The Party, Private Entrepreneurs, and Prospects for Political Change* (New York: Cambridge University Press, 2003); Margaret M. Pearson, "Entrepreneurs and Democratization in China's Foreign Sector," in *The New Entrepreneurs of Europe and Asia: Patterns of Business Development in Russia, Eastern Europe and China*, ed. Victoria E. Bonnell and Thomas B. Gold (Armonk: M.E. Sharpe, 2002), 130–155; Jonathan Unger, "China's Conservative Middle Class," *Far Eastern Economic Review* 169, no. 3 (April 2006): 27–31.

[4] Richard Levy, "Village Elections, Transparency, and Anticorruption: Henan and Guangdong Provinces," in *Grassroots Political Reform in Contemporary China*, ed. Elizabeth J. Perry and Merle Goldman (Cambridge: Harvard University Press, 2007), 20–47; Lianjiang Li, "Direct Township Elections," in *Grassroots Political Reform*, 97–116; Thomas Heberer, "Urban Elections in the People's Republic," *IIAS Newsletter* 39 (December 2005): 15; "Progress and Problems Mark Elections," *China Daily*, 10 July 2007, http:// www.chinadaily.com.cn/china/2007-07/10/content_5425062.htm; "China Punishes 192 Officials for Electoral Fraud," *China Daily*, 1 February 2007, http://www.china daily.com.cn/china/2007-02/01/content_798893.htm.

5 The German-educated president of Shanghai's Tongji University, Wan Gang, who is a member of the democratic party Zhigongdang, was appointed minister of science and technology in April 2007. Then in June, Chen Zhu, a French-educated nonpartisan hematologist, was named minister of health. The CCP has stepped up its efforts to appoint noncommunists to positions at all levels of the government. Of course, real power in Chinese organizations lies with the party committee, so the ability of these non–CCP members to determine and implement policies remains to be seen. See the cover story in *Nanfang Renwu Zhoumo* [*Southern People Weekly*] 12, 21 May 2007; Xinhua News Agency, "New Health Minister Appointed," China Internet Information Center, 29 June 2007, http://www.china.org.cn/english/GS-e/215546.htm.

6 Li Fan, "2008 Zhongguo Jiceng Minzhu Fazhan Baogao" ["2008 Report on the Development of Local Level Democracy], orig. *Jingji Guancha Bao* [*Economic Observer*], 28 December 2005, http://vip.bokee.com/110870.html; "Shanghai: Millions Turn Out to Vote in Local PC Elections," orig. *Shanghai Daily*, 13 December 2006, http://www.china elections.org/en/readnews.asp?newsid={45F2D312-5903-425A-AED74B1414843C8F} &classid=13&classname=Indirect%20Elections; Yang Tianwen and Lu Yanjuan, "A Glimpse of Local People's Deputy Elections in Changzhi, Shanxi," Carter Center China Elections Project, 29 May 2007, http://www.chinaelections.org/en/readnews.asp?newsid= {14E16C6B-9E8E-4553-A345-FE51C93CF47F}&classid=79&classname=Program%20 Special.

7 See Bruce Kam-Kwan Kwong, "Patron-client Politics in Hong Kong: A Case Study of the 2002 and 2005 Chief Executive Elections," *Journal of Contemporary China* 16, no. 52 (August 2007): 389–415. On Macao, see the section, "Politics in Post-Colonial Macau," in *Journal of Contemporary China* 14, no. 43 (May 2005), especially Herbert S. Yee, "The 2001 Legislative Assembly Elections and Political Development in Macau," 225–245, and Eilo Wing-Yat Yu, "Formal and Informal Politics in Macao Special Administrative Region Elections, 2004–2005," *Journal of Contemporary China* 16, no. 52 (August 2007): 417–441.

8 Su Yonglong, "Road to Legislating China's Property Law: Never So Tortuous, Never So Resolute," Sinopolis.com, 23 March 2007, http://www.sinofile.net/saiweng/sip_blog.nsf /d6plinks/YZHI-6ZKAZJ.

9 Tim Johnson, "In China, Civil Service Is Calling," *Seattle Times*, 13 November 2005, http://seattletimes.nwsource.com/html/businesstechnology/2002621186_bureaucrats 13.html.

10 Jason Subler, "China Cautiously Enlists NGO Help in Poverty Fight," Reuters, 8 April 2007, http://www.reuters.com/article/latestCrisis/idUSPEK14506; Jonathan Watts, "Charity: New Cultural Revolution," *Guardian*, 10 January 2006; Xiong Lei, "NGOs Finally Accepted as Valuable Partners," *China Daily*, 13 April 2007, http://www.china daily.com.cn/opinion/2007-04/13/content_849704.htm.

11 Dann Dulin, "China's Conscience," *A&U*, February 2006, 22–23, 34. In May 2007, the subject of this article, the activist Hu Jia, was detained and prevented from traveling to Europe to speak about human rights violations in China. This occurred the day after British foreign secretary Margaret Beckett called on the Chinese authorities to allow

more freedom of expression. Gao Yaojie, an octogenarian doctor who exposed the plight of poor villagers in Henan province who had become infected with HIV/AIDS by selling their blood, was initially refused permission by embarrassed local officials to go to the United States in March 2007 to receive an award for her work. International pressure and intervention from Beijing facilitated her exit, although she was subjected to house arrest upon her return. In August 2007, the government began a crackdown on AIDS organizations and international conferences. Jonathan Watts, "China Bars Activist From UK Visit in Pre-Olympic Crackdown," *Guardian*, 18 May 2007, http://www.guardian.co.uk/china/story/0,,2082996,00.html; Daniel Schearf, "China Stops AIDS Campaigner from Traveling to US to Accept Award," VOA News, 5 February 2007, http://www.voanews.com/english/archive/2007-02/2007-02-05-voa35.cfm; Human Rights Watch, "China: Harassment of HIV/AIDS Activists Intensifies," news release, 20 August 2007, http://hrw.org/english/docs/2007/08/20/china16708_txt.htm.

12 Its web address is http://www.ngorc.net.cn.

13 Jim Yardley, "Seeking a Public Voice on China's 'Angry River,'" *New York Times*, 26 December 2005; International Rivers Network, "Chinese Prefecture Cancels Dam Project on Sacred Tibetan Lake," news release, 14 November 2006, http://www.irn.org/programs/china/index.php?id=archive/061113cancel.html. The area around the Nu is part of the Three Parallel Rivers (Jinsha, Mekong, and Salween), which was named a UN World Heritage Site, but in August 2007 the United Nations warned that the site was in danger of losing this status because local officials were going ahead with several hydroelectric projects. Separately, Wu Lihong, an environmental activist, was detained by police in Jiangsu Province in April 2007 on charges of racketeering. His major campaign was against factories polluting Taihu, a famous lake in that province. In August 2007, he received a three-year jail sentence and a fine for extortion. Sun Xiaodi, another environmental activist, was harassed by local officials in Gansu after receiving an international award for his work against radioactive contamination. Yongchen Wang, "A Yellow Card for the Three Parallel Rivers," chinadialogue, 3 August 2007, http://www.chinadialogue.net/article/show/single/en/1200-A-yellow-card-for-the-Three-Parallel-Rivers; Shai Oster, "Police Hold Chinese Foe of Polluters," *Wall Street Journal* Online, http://online.wsj.com/article/SB117728245200178403.html.

14 Xiong Lei, "NGOs Finally Accepted as Valuable Partners"; Howard W. French, "For Citizens' Groups, the Struggle For Attention Is Not So Lonely in China," *New York Times*, 13 February 2007. "According to figures from the Ministry of Civil Affairs, the country had 354,000 NGOs by the end of 2006, but [Tsinghua University professor] Jia [Xijin] estimated the actual number at more than 1 million." "NGOs Have More Room to Develop," *People's Daily* Online, http://english.people.com.cn/200705/25/print20070525_377883.html. See also Chen Jie, "The NGO Community in China," *China Perspectives* 68 (November–December 2006): 29–40.

15 "Green Grow the NGOs–Oh! Says the Close-to-Government Group," *China Development Brief* (Beijing), 19 June 2006, http://www.chinadevelopmentbrief.com. On July 4, 2007, the Beijing authorities shut down *China Development Brief*, established by a Briton, Nicholas Young, in 1996. It covered a range of issues, in particular those related to the environment, AIDS, and NGOs. Young's detailed statement is available at

http://www.wilsoncenter.org/news/docs/CDB.doc. The ostensible reason was that he was conducting unauthorized surveys.

16 For overviews on the media, see Ashley Esarey, "Speak No Evil: Mass Media Control in Contemporary China," *Freedom at Issue*, February 2006; "Media and Globalization in China," NIASnytt special issue 3 (September 2005); He Qinglian, "Media Control in China," *China Rights Forum* 4 (2004): 11–28.

17 U.S. Congressional-Executive Commission on China, "Agencies Responsible for Censorship in China," http://www.cecc.gov/pages/virtualAcad/exp/expcensors.php.

18 After the Shanxi brick kiln affair (see below) was exposed, the central government issued a notice on how to spin the story and contain the damage. Separately, *New York Times* correspondent David Barboza was held, with his translator and photographer, as a "hostage" at a factory for nine hours while investigating a story on contaminated toys for export. His insight afterward was on the limits of the government in controlling local businessmen, and the collusion of businessmen and police. See "A Notice From the Central Government to Censor News Related to Shanxi Brick Kilns Event," China Digital Times, 15 June 2007, http://chinadigitaltimes.net/2007/06/a_notice_from_the_central _government_to_censor_news_rel.php; David Barboza, "My Times as a Hostage, and I'm a Business Reporter," *New York Times*, 24 June 2007. See also "Chris Buckley, "China Reporters Probing Bridge Disaster 'Beaten,'" *Guardian*, 17 August 2007, http://sport .guardian.co.uk/breakingnews/feedstory/0,,-6855986,00.html.

19 Human Rights Watch, "China: Media Freedom Under Assault Ahead of 2008 Olympics," news release, 31 May 2007. In an act reminiscent of a much earlier era, at least five newspapers ran nearly identical front pages, heavily political in content, on the weekend of August 20, 2007. Lindsay Beck, "Throwback to Mao as Chinese Newspapers Toe the Line," Reuters, 21 August 2007, http://www.reuters.com/article /worldNews/idUSPEK3781420070821?feedType=RSS&feedName=worldNews&rpc= 22&sp=true.

20 Committee to Protect Journalists (CPJ), *Attacks on the Press in 2004* (New York: CPJ, 2005), http://www.cpj.org/attacks04/asia04/china.html.

21 CPJ, *Attacks on the Press in 2005* (New York: CPJ, 2006), http://www.cpj.org/attacks05 /asia05/china_05.html.

22 Reporters Without Borders, "Information Supplied by Yahoo! Helped Journalist Shi Tao Get 10 Years in Prison," news release, 6 September 2005, http://www.rsf.org/article .php3?id_article=14884; Luke O'Brien, "Jailed Chinese Journalist Joins Suit Against Yahoo," *Wired* Blog Network, 4 June 2007, http://blog.wired.com/27bstroke6/2007 /06/jailed_chinese_.html; Rebecca MacKinnon, "Shi Tao's Case; Yahoo! Knew More Than They Claimed," RConversation, http://rconversation.blogs.com/rconversation /2007/07/shi-taos-case-y.html; Mark Magnier, "Domestic Pressure Mounts for Beijing to Clarify Laws That Let It Lock Up Troublemakers," *Los Angeles Times*, 11 June 2007.

23 Jane Martinson, "China Censorship Damaged Us, Google Founders Admit," *Guardian*, 27 January 2007, http://www.guardian.co.uk/technology/2007/jan/27/news.newmedia.

24 CPJ, *Attacks on the Press in 2005*. It should be noted that some journalists (or people posing as journalists) have extorted hush money from businesses and government agencies by threatening to print potentially damaging news. In January 2007, a reporter was

beaten to death in Shanxi province, a region notorious for illegal coal mines and terrible working conditions. While he was initially presented as a martyr, it was subsequently suggested that he was extorting payments from mine operators. There is also concern that the common practice of payments to journalists to attend media events results in bias. Edward Cody, "Blackmailing by Journalists in China Seen as 'Frequent,'" *Washington Post*, 25 January 2007; Jamil Anderlini and Mure Dickie, "China's Handouts to Journalists Skew Media Coverage," *Financial Times*, 3 August 2007.

25   For overviews, see He Qinglian, "The Hijacked Potential of China's Internet," *China Rights Forum* no. 2 (2006): 31–47; Zixue Tai, *The Internet in China: Cyberspace and Civil Society* (New York: Routledge, 2006); and Yang Guobin, "Between Control and Contention: China's New Internet Politics," *Washington Journal of Modern China* 8, no. 1 (Spring/Summer 2006): 30–47.

26   Xinhua News Agency, "China Has 144 Mln Netizens by March," *China Daily*, 18 May 2007, http://www.chinadaily.com.cn/china/2007-05/18/content_875334.htm. On a more positive note, "Senior Official Promotes 'Web Culture with Chinese Characteristics,'" News Guangdong, http://www.newsgd.com/culture/culturenews/200706050010 .htm.

27   "Chinese Bloggers to Reach 100 Million in 2007: Report," Xinhua News Agency, http://news.xinhuanet.com//english/2006-05/06/content_4513589.htm. Another potent tool for mobilization and expression of opinions is the ubiquitous cellular telephone. In May 2007, more than 1 million cell phone text messages were sent to protest the construction of a chemical plant in Xiamen, bringing it to a temporary halt while the city government reconsidered the project. In spite of warnings from officials, an estimated 10,000 citizens, including civil servants, came out to protest. The plant was being built by Chen Yu-hao, a renegade Taiwanese businessman. Mitchell Landsberg, "China City Gets the (Text) Message," *Los Angeles Times*, 1 June 2007; Edward Cody, "Text Messages Giving Voice to Chinese," *Washington Post*, 28 June 2007.

28   Howard W. French, "Chinese Discuss Plan to Tighten Restrictions on Cyberspace," *New York Times*, 4 July 2006; Reuters, "China Aims to Further Tame Web," CNN.com, 23 April 2007, http://www.cnn.com/2007/TECH/internet/04/23/china.internet.reut /index.html.

29   Richard C. Morais, "Cracks in the Wall," *Forbes*, 27 February 2006, 90–96.

30   Reporters Without Borders, "Government Gets Blog Service Providers to Sign 'Self-Discipline' Pact to End Anonymous Blogging," news release, 28 August 2007, http:// www.rsf.org/print.php3?id_article=23372.

31   Irene Wang, "Newspaper Staff Strike Over Reshuffle," *South China Morning Post*, 30 December 2005.

32   Robert Marquand, "China's Media Censorship Rattling World Image," *Christian Science Monitor*, 24 February 2006; Philip C. Pan, "The Click That Broke a Government's Grip," *Washington Post*, 19 February 2006.

33   "Southern Metropolis Daily: Where Did the Media Go Wrong Reporting the Brick Kiln Story?" China Digital Times, 6 July 2007, http://chinadigitaltimes.net/2007/07/southern _metropolis_daily_where_did_the_media_go_wrong.php; You Nuo, "We Need Inves-

tigative Journalists," *China Daily*, 18 June 2007, http://www.chinadaily.com.cn
/opinion/2007-06/18/content_896290.htm.

34 State Council of the People's Republic of China, "Regulations on Reporting Activities
in China by Foreign Journalists During the Beijing Olympic Games and the Prepara-
tory Period," Ministry of Foreign Affairs of the People's Republic of China, 1 January
2007, http://www.fmprc.gov.cn/eng/xwfw/jzfw/t326215.htm. Some local officials were
still resisting implementation, and Chinese journalists were not entitled to the same
rights. For one of the most comprehensive reports, see Human Rights Watch, *'You Will
be Harassed and Detained': Media Freedom Under Assault in China Ahead of the 2008
Beijing Olympic Games* (New York: Human Rights Watch, August 2007), http:hrw.org
/reports/2007/china0807/.

35 Rowan Callick, "The East is Read," *Weekend Australian*, 19 May 2007, accessed at http:
//chinadigitaltimes.net/2007/05/the_east_is_read_rowan_callick.php. As with Eastern
Europe under communism, China has many writers who "write for the drawer," with
little hope that their output can ever see the light of day. For a series of blogs against
"writing for the drawer," see http://tinyurl.com/2j6rks. Yan Lianke is a popular novelist
who tests the limits. Edward Cody, "Persistent Censorship in China Produces Art of
Compromise," *Washington Post*, 9 July 2007, http://www.washingtonpost.com/wp-dyn
/content/article/2007/07/08/AR2007070801063.html.

36 Office of the United Nations High Commissioner for Human Rights, "Special Rap-
porteur on Torture Highlights Challenges at End of Visit to China," news release, 2
December 2005, http://www.unhchr.ch/huricane/huricane.nsf/view01/677C1943FAA14
D67C12570CB0034966D.

37 Amnesty International, *Report 2007* (London: Amnesty International, 2007), http://the
report.amnesty.org/eng/Regions/Asia-Pacific/China; Joseph Kahn, "China Dissident Says
Confession Was Forced," *New York Times*, 10 April 2007; "Chinese Activist 'Beaten in
Jail,'" BBC News, 22 June 2007, http://news.bbc.co.uk/go/pr/fr/-/2/hi/asia-pacific
/6230148.stm.

38 "China Cracks Down on Torture and Forced Confessions," Xinhua News Agency, 17
May 2005, http://www.china.org.cn/english/China/129100.htm.

39 People also utilize petitions locally. For instance, in May 2007, citizen petitions expressing health concerns led to the suspension of the construction of a new magnetic-levitation
train between Shanghai and Hangzhou. "The People Speak, and Maglev is Put on Hold,"
Shanghai Daily, 28 May 2007.

40 Sara Davis, "China's Angry Petitioners," *Asian Wall Street Journal*, 25 August 2005; Mark
Magnier, "Seeking Justice, Dodging Capture in Beijing," *Los Angeles Times*, 28 May,
2007; Human Rights in China, "Shanghai Petitioners Detained Following Protests,"
news release, 12 April 2007.

41 Kevin J. O'Brien and Lianjiang Li, *Rightful Resistance in Rural China* (Cambridge: Cambridge University Press, 2006); Human Rights Watch, "China: Rampant Violence and
Intimidation Against Petitioners," news release, 8 December 2005, http://www.hrw.org
/english/docs/2005/12/08/china12144.htm; Carl Minzner, ed., "What Has Happened
to Petitioning in China Since the 2005 Xinfang Regulations?" Chinese Law and Politics

Blog, 18 April 2007, http://sinolaw.typepad.com/chinese_law_and_politics_/2007/04/what_has_happen.htm. The authorities declared success in resolving grievances.

42 Carl Minzner, "Are Mass Incidents Increasing or Decreasing in China?" Chinese Law and Politics Blog, 31 March 2007, http://sinolaw.typepad.com/chinese_law_and_politics_/2007/03/are_mass_incide.html.

43 Ching-Ching Ni, "Wave of Social Unrest Continues Across China," *Los Angeles Times*, 10 August 2006; Murray Scot Tanner, "Chinese Government Responses to Rising Social Unrest" (Washington, D.C.: U.S.-China Economic and Security Review Commission, testimony, 14 April 2005).

44 Edward Cody, "Chinese Police Bring Villagers to Heel After Latest Uprising," *Washington Post*, 21 December 2005.

45 Wu Jiao, "New Law to Abolish Laojiao System," *China Daily*, 1 March 2007, http://www.chinadaily.com.cn/china/2007-03/01/content_816358.htm.

46 Jerome A. Cohen, "'Rightist' Wrongs," *Wall Street Journal* Online, 26 June 2007, http://online.wsj.com/article/SB118280571701947578.html; Mark Magnier, "Parliament May Abolish the System That Gives Police A Free Hand With Petty Criminals," *Los Angeles Times*, 5 March 2007; Minnie Chan, "Kinder Face for Notorious Re-education Camps," *South China Morning Post*, 21 February 2007. Another means to harass activists and dissidents is *ruanjin* (house arrest). Brad Adams, "Hard Facts on 'Soft Arrests' In China," *Wall Street Journal*, 25 May 2007.

47 Ching-ching Ni, "China Cites Gains Made by Women," *Los Angeles Times*, 16 May 2007. The August 2007 issue of *Feminist Economics* contains a series of studies of different aspects of the situation of women in China.

48 Jonathan Watts, "Crisis Looms as 18 million Chinese Can't Find a Wife," *Observer*, 26 August 2007, http://observer.guardian.co.uk/world/story/0,,2156355,00.html. The city with the worst reported imbalance was Lianyungang in Jiangsu Province, which had a male-to-female ratio of 165 to 100.

49 See various posts at http://www.humantrafficking.org/countries/china.

50 "Canjiren Pinkun Wenti Reng Bijiao Tuchu" ["The Poverty Problem of the Disabled is Still Comparatively Obvious"], *Renmin Ribao* [*People's Daily Overseas Edition*], 29 May 2007.

51 Pankaj Mishra, "The Train to Tibet," *New Yorker*, 16 April 2007, 82–98.

52 Amnesty International, *Internal Migrants: Discrimination and Abuse; The Human Cost of an Economic 'Miracle'* (London: Amnesty International, March 2007), http://web.amnesty.org/library/pdf/ASA170082007ENGLISH/$FILE/ASA1700807.pdf.

53 Hu Shuli, "Building Human Rights, Brick by Brick," *Caijing Magazine*, 26 June 2007, http://www.caijing.com.cn/newcn/English/Editorial/2007-06-26/23309.shtml; Li Datong, "The Root of Slave Labour in China," openDemocracy, 26 June 2007, http://www.opendemocracy.net/democracy_power/china_inside/slave_labour_china.

54 Human Rights Watch, "China: A Year After New Regulations, Religious Rights Still Restricted," news release, 1 March 2006.

55 Elizabeth Rosenthal, "Pope Asks Chinese Catholics to Reconcile," *International Herald Tribune*, 2 July 2007; Adam Minter, "Keeping Faith," Atlantic Monthly (July/August 2007), http://www.theatlantic.com/doc/print/200707/chinese-bishop; Andrew Batson,

"As China's Bishops Die Off, Clash Looms With Vatican," *Wall Street Journal*, 31 January 2007, http://online.wsj.com/article/SB117018697369892678.html?mod+hpp_us _pageone. Also in July 2007, the official Chinese Catholic church selected a new bishop for Beijing. "Though the pope did not pick him, the cleric was apparently on a list of names that the Vatican had indicated it would not object to." Associated Press, "New Bishop in China, but Not Pope's Choice," *New York Times*, 19 July 2007.

56 Isabel Hilton, *The Search for the Panchen Lama* (New York: W. W. Norton, 2000).

57 "China Hosts First Buddhist Forum," BBC News, 13 April 2006, http://news.bbc.co.uk /go/pr/fr/-/2/hi/asia-pacific/4905140.stm.

58 Jane Macartney, "China Tells Living Buddhas to Obtain Permission Before They Reincarnate," *Times* (London), 4 August 2007, http://www.timesonline.co.uk/tol/news/world /article2194682.ece. The regulations are in Chinese at http://www.china.com.cn/policy /txt/2007-08/03/content_8623414_2.htm.

59 Jackie Armijo, "Islamic Education in China," *Asia Quarterly* (Winter 2006).

60 "Crossing the Communists," *Economist*, 23 April 2005, 44; Leslie Hook, "Christianity Comes to China's Cities," *Far Eastern Economic Review* 169, no. 10 (December 2006): 10–16.

61 Armijo, "Islamic Education in China."

62 Jehangir S. Pocha, "The Last 'Competitive Advantage': Letter From China," *Nation*, 4 June 2007, http://www.thenation.com/doc/20070604/pocha; "Labor Rights Activisits Imprisoned in China," *China Labour Bulletin*, E-Bulletin No. 34 (4 June 2007), http://www.clb.org.hk/public/contents/article?revision%5fid=45419&item%5fid=45418. In May 2007, a Chinese delegation walked out of a human rights dialogue meeting with the European Union in Berlin because of the presence of representatives of *China Labour Bulletin* and Human Rights in China. See *China Labour Bulletin*, E-Bulletin No. 35, 9 June 2007.

63 "Wal-Mart Unionisation Drive Ordered by Hu Jintao in March; A Total of 17 Union Branches Now Set Up," *China Labour Bulletin*, Action Update No. 3, 15 August 2006; David Barboza, "McDonald's in China Agrees to Unions," *New York Times*, 10 April 2007; Christine Buckley, "Foreign Investors Warn China Over Tough New Labour Laws," *Times* (London), 19 June 2006; David Barboza, "China Drafts Law to Empower Unions and End Labor Abuse," *New York Times*, 13 October 2006; United Steelworkers, "Steelworkers, Global Labor Strategies Counter Corporate Opposition to Worker Rights in China," news release, 26 April 2007, http://www.usw.org/usw/program /content/3965.php?lan=en; David Barboza, "Putting Aside His Past Criticisms, Teamsters' Chief Is on Mission to China," *New York Times*, 19 May 2007; Richard McGregor and Geoff Dyer, "Big U.S. Unions Court Chinese Counterparts," *Financial Times*, 23 May 2007; Nicole C. Wong, "China Plans to Empower Workers," *San Jose Mercury News*, 29 May 2007.

64 Jude Blanchette, "Key Issue for China's New Labor Law: Enforcement," *Christian Science Monitor*, 2 July 2007, http://www.csmonitor.com/2007/0702/p11s02-woap.html; "National People's Congress Approves New Labour Contract Law," *China Labour Bulletin*, 29 June 2007, http://www.china-labour.org.hk/public/contents/news?revision %5fid=46521&item%5fid=46445.

65 Xinhua News Agency, "China Metes Out Least Number of Death Sentences Last Year," *People's Daily* Online, 15 March 2007, http://english.people.com.cn/200703/15/eng 20070315_357962.html; Jim Yardley, "With New Law, China Reports a Decline in Executions," *New York Times*, 9 June 2007, http://www.nytimes.com/2007/06/09/world/asia /09china.html?ex=1339041600&en=7715c1853b37440c&ei=5088; "Death Penalty Reform Should Bring Drop in Executions," *Dialogue* no. 26 (Winter 2007): 1–2.

66 Jerome A. Cohen, "Law in Political Transitions: Lessons from East Asia and the Road Ahead for China," (Washington, D.C.: Congressional-Executive Commission on China, 26 July 2005), http://www.cecc.gov/pages/hearings/072605/Cohen.php.

67 Mei Ying Gechlik, "Judicial Reform in China: Lessons From Shanghai," *Columbia Journal of Asian Law* 19, no. 1 (Spring–Fall 2005): 97–137; Keith Henderson, "The Rule of Law and Judicial Corruption in China: Half-way Over the Great Wall," in *Global Corruption Report 2007* (Berlin: Transparency International, 2007), http://www.transparency .org/content/download/18703/255305.

68 Joseph Kahn, "A Shared Vision of Justice; Rivals on a Legal Tightrope Seek to Widen Freedoms in China," *New York Times*, 25 February 2007, http://select.nytimes.com /search/restricted/article?res=F3091FFA3A5A0C768EDDAB0894DF404482.

69 "Falu Yuanzhu" (legal aid), http://baike.baidu.com/view/15563.htm, accessed 29 August 2007; Benjamin L. Liebman, "Legal Aid and Public Interest Law in China," *Texas International Law Journal* 34, no. 211 (1999): 211–286.

70 Luigi Tomba, "Residential Space and Collective Interest Formation in Beijing's Housing Disputes," *China Quarterly* 184 (December 2005): 934–951; Benjamin Read, "Inadvertent Political Reform via Private Associations: Assessing Homeowners' Groups in New Neighborhoods," in Perry and Goldman, *Grassroots Political Reform*, 149–173.

71 Andrew Wedeman, "The Intensification of Corruption in China," *China Quarterly* 180 (December 2004): 895–921; "China's War on Corruption: Progress or Stalemate?" *CSIS Freeman Report*, March 2007, 1–2; "China Moves Up to 70th Place in Corruption Perceptions Index," China.org.cn, 9 November 2006.

72 "Shanghai Leader Stripped of Power," *China Daily*, 26 September 2006.

73 "More Than 6,600 Corrupt Officials Punished," *People's Daily*, 12 June 2007.

74 Rui Yang, "Corruption in China's Higher Education System: A Malignant Tumor," *International Higher Education* no. 39 (Spring 2005), http://www.bc.edu/bc_org/avp/soe /cihe/newsletter/News39/text011.htm.

75 Richard McGregor, "China Plans Wide Audit of Funds After Scandal," *Financial Times*, 12 December 2006.

76 "Former NBS Chief Qiu Xiaohua Sacked for Scandal," *China Daily*, 20 October 2006; David Pan, "Damn Lies and Chinese Statistics," *Asia Times* Online, 19 August 2006, http://www.atimes.com/atimes/China/HH19Ad01.html.

77 For an overview, see Yong Guo, *National Integrity System, Transparency International Country Study Report, China 2006* (Berlin: Transparency International, 2006), http://www .transparency.org/content/download/12696/125523/file/China_nis_2006.pdf. See also Human Rights in China, *State Secrets: China's Legal Labyrinth* (New York: Human Rights in China, June 2007), http://hrichina.org/public/contents/article?revision%5fid=41506 &item%5fid=41421.

78 Xinhua News Agency, "China Issues Emergency Response Plan for Natural Calamities," GOV.cn, 11 January 2006, http://english.gov.cn/2006-01/11/content_153917.htm.

79 Xinhua News Agency, "Decree to Boost Gov't Transparency," GOV.cn, 24 April 2007, http://english.gov.cn/2007-04/24/content_593208.htm; Jim Yardley, "China Sets Out To Cut Secrecy, But Laws Leave Big Loopholes," *New York Times*, 25 April 2007; Anthony Kuhn, "China Moves Toward Release of Classified Data," National Public Radio, 24 April 2007, http://www.npr.org/templates/story/story.php?storyId=9803236.

80 Joseph Fewsmith, "Exercising the Power of the Purse?" *China Leadership Monitor* 19 (Fall 2006): 1–11.

COLOMBIA

CAPITAL: Bogota
POPULATION: 46.2 million
GNI PER CAPITA: $2,740

SCORES	2005	2007
ACCOUNTABILITY AND PUBLIC VOICE:	5.02	4.56
CIVIL LIBERTIES:	4.39	3.95
RULE OF LAW:	4.21	3.78
ANTICORRUPTION AND TRANSPARENCY:	3.88	3.74

(scores are based on a scale of 0 to 7, with 0 representing weakest and 7 representing strongest performance)

Harvey F. Kline

INTRODUCTION

In 2006 and early 2007, as if Colombian democracy needed another problem apart from its endemic violence, poverty, and lack of effective law enforcement, a new quandary emerged: hard evidence of the infiltration of paramilitary groups into elections and various branches of the government. Confronting the problem—which has long been suspected by many Colombians and external observers—acquired new urgency on March 11, 2006. On that date the National Prosecutor's Office arrested Edgar Ignacio Fierro Florez, a lieutenant in the Northern Block, a demobilized paramilitary group led by Rodrigo Tovar Pupo (alias Jorge 40), which formed part of the United Self-Defense Forces of Colombia (AUC).

Fierro Florez had in his possession cash, weapons, and, most important, two computers, two flash drives, many compact discs, and a series of handwritten documents. Lists of criminal and paramilitary activities in the Caribbean coastal area were among the files found on the computer,

Harvey F. Kline is Professor of political science at the University of Alabama–Tuscaloosa. He has taught at the Universidad de los Andes in Bogota with grants from the Fulbright-Hayes Commission. He has published six books on Colombian politics.

as well as a list of 558 assassinations carried out between 2003 and 2005 in Atlantico department. The recovered files also contained the names of politicians and merchants in Caribbean coastal departments with strong ties to Jorge 40's paramilitary group.[1] In late 2006 and early 2007, what became known as the *parapolitica* (para-politics) scandal grew as evidence emerged that the paramilitary-political connections encompassed members of the National Congress, departmental assemblies, the office of the national prosecutor, large landowners, the armed forces, the national police, and even the Supreme Court.

In January 2007, the media published a document signed in July 2001 by four paramilitary leaders and thirty-two politicians calling for cooperation to work toward a new Colombia. This "Ralito Agreement" revealed complicity between paramilitary groups and future allies of the Uribe government. In February 2007, the press reported that a similar pact had been signed between six mayors and paramilitaries in Casanare department in the eastern part of the country,[2] leaving some to wonder how many other agreements there had been.

Colombia has suffered from the effects of a multisided civil war for decades. The largest insurgent group, the Revolutionary Armed Forces of Colombia (FARC), has been fighting a Marxist-based guerrilla war since the mid-1960s. Another, smaller leftist group, the Army of National Liberation (Ejercito de Liberacion Nacional, ELN), has also been active for decades. In the 1980s and 1990s, landowners increasingly began to collude with drug dealers as well as elements of the security services to provide a counter to the guerrillas in areas where state presence was weak. However, as these paramilitary groups, which eventually coalesced into the United Self-Defense Forces of Colombia (AUC), acquired strength and power, they were increasingly linked to brutal human rights violations, drug trafficking, and land seizures through coercive purchases or outright displacement. Under President Andres Pastrana (1998–2002), serious negotiations were attempted with the FARC, but these collapsed under the strain of unending violence.

The government of Alvaro Uribe Velez successfully challenged the FARC during his first term, engaging in a military offensive that pushed the rebels out of the main cities and deep into Colombia's thick jungle and high mountains. Refusing to negotiate with insurgent groups unless they entered into ceasefires, Uribe also successfully carried out the demobilization of the AUC between 2004 and 2006. Over 30,000 paramilitary troops demobilized by the end of 2006, a number larger than expected by either the government or the AUC itself. The government had less success, however, with the FARC and the ELN. In the case of the FARC, the last half of 2005 and the first half of 2006 witnessed a surge of activity, though attacks slackened considerably in the run-up to the May 2006 presidential election. The little dialogue that occurred with the government centered on the possibility of an exchange of FARC kidnapping victims for imprisoned rebels.

On December 12, 2005, the governments of Spain, France, and Switzerland submitted a proposal to the government and the FARC secretariat suggesting a meeting between the two sides in the municipality of Pradera, in the Valle del Cauca department. During the conversations the only presence would be the negotiators of the two sides, the International Red Cross, and the "political organ," made up of representatives of the three groups charged with the security of the zone. The Colombian government accepted this proposal almost immediately, but the FARC rejected it as insufficient. Although this was the first time that the Uribe government had agreed to demilitarize an area, it was not as large a zone as the FARC wanted. Messages between the two sides continued. There was cautious optimism until October 19, 2006, when the FARC set off a car bomb outside the Superior War College in Bogota. The Uribe government immediately suspended all discussions about prisoner exchange with the FARC.

In the case of the ELN, notable progress has occurred since September 12, 2005, when ELN leader Gerardo Antonio Bermudez Sanchez (alias Francisco Galan) was transferred from prison for three months to a "House of Peace" near Medellin so that he could take part in meetings with representatives of civil society. In November 2005, Galan stated in a formal communique that the ELN was ready to start a dialogue. In December 2005, Peace Commissioner Luis Carlos Restrepo met with Galan and they agreed that the ELN and the government should meet outside Colombia. This phase between Colombia and the ELN began on December 16, 2005, in Cuba, with facilitators from Spain, Norway, and Switzerland. These ELN-government talks in Cuba continued throughout 2006, began again on February 22, 2007, and were set to continue throughout the year.

ACCOUNTABILITY AND PUBLIC VOICE

FREE AND FAIR ELECTORAL LAWS AND ELECTIONS:	4.50
EFFECTIVE AND ACCOUNTABLE GOVERNMENT:	4.25
CIVIC ENGAGEMENT AND CIVIC MONITORING:	5.00
MEDIA INDEPENDENCE AND FREEDOM OF EXPRESSION:	4.50
CATEGORY AVERAGE:	**4.56**

On paper, Colombian democracy is based on regular, free, and fair elections. There is universal suffrage with multiple political parties, but violence has been common in Colombian elections for many years.

Other problems Colombia faced in 2005–2006 included the difficulty of maintaining fairness in the first presidential election in many decades in which an incumbent president was running for reelection, as well as determining what role demobilized paramilitary troops could play in politics. The first problem arose in October 2005, when the Constitutional Court declared presidential reelection constitutionally permissible on the condition that Congress pass, and the Court approve, a law to resolve the fairness issue. That November the Court deemed permissible the Law of Guarantees, which includes several stipulations designed to level the playing field: the campaign period was shortened for the incumbent, who would also be required to spend less than challengers. Moreover, several clauses were designed to ensure that media coverage and access be made as equal as possible.[3]

On the question of whether demobilized paramilitary troops could participate in the 2006 elections, President Uribe made his position clear in the last days of October 2005, when he introduced a policy, later affirmed by the Law of Guarantees, barring members of groups outside the law who had not been fully reincorporated into civilian life from participating in the campaign or providing support for candidates. As a result of this pressure, several AUC members announced their withdrawal from electoral activities later in the month. One was a member of a new party established to support Uribe's reelection.

Violence and the threat thereof affected all political parties during the congressional campaigns. It culminated with the early December 2005 assassination of Jaime Lozada, Conservative party leader and former governor and senator from Huila, allegedly committed by the FARC. Amnesty International concluded, "These killings raise serious concerns for the safety of state and elected officials in the run up to the 12 March congressional elections, and other civilians in other parts of the country in a context of similar restrictions on movement ordered by the FARC."[4]

Following the Lozada assassination, Minister of the Interior Sabas Pretelt de la Vega stated that candidates clearly needed more protection. In response, the government started a special program of security for the candidates, assigning a colonel to each candidate's campaign. In addition, the Administrative Security Department (DAS) undertook coordination of candidates' safety measures. Pretelt made it clear that the elections would not be suspended. Nonetheless, opposition party members declared that the government's measures were inadequate.

The transition of the Colombian party system continued, with many new groups offering candidates. Although an early 2006 attempt to form a single party to back President Uribe was unsuccessful, five major groups ran on the basis of supporting the chief executive and congressional candidates backing his ideas: the Social Party of National Unity (Partido Social de Unidad Nacional, commonly called the Partido de la U); the traditional Conservative party; and three new groups—Radical Change (Cambio Radical), Democratic Colombia (Colombia Democratica), and Wings Team Colombia (Alas Equipo Colombia—the recent fusion of a party with wings as its insignia and another that called itself a "team"). The opposition was made up of the traditional Liberal party and the Democratic Alternative Pole (Polo Democratico Alternativo or PDA), a new party representing the left that subsequent to the election became instrumental in advancing the para-political scandal and demanding accountability.

On paper, Colombia has tough campaign finance laws; however, over the years there have been clear cases when they were broken, most famously by drug cartels supporting Ernesto Samper's successful presidential campaign in 1994. On January 16, 2006, President Uribe ordered investigations into campaign financing in order to prevent former paramilitaries from influencing the political process. These and other investigations did not stop subsequent to the election but rather acquired an ever-faster pace toward the end of 2006 and beginning of 2007. As of February 2007, eight pro-Uribe members of Congress had been jailed on the basis of financial connections to paramilitary groups, and more than sixty former and current legislators, mayors, and other elected officials were under investigation.[5]

In the March 12, 2006 congressional elections, the Uribista coalition, led by the Partido de la U, the Conservatives, and Cambio Radical, won sixty-one senate seats (to twenty-eight for the opposition and eleven for independents), while in the lower house Uribistas captured ninety-one seats, with forty-five going to the opposition and thirty to the independents.[6]

On May 28, 2006, President Alvaro Uribe easily won a second term, the first president to do so since the nineteenth century, prevailing in the first round with 62 percent of the slightly over 11 million votes cast. Second was Carlos Gaviria of the PDA, who gained approximately 22 percent of the vote, thereby demonstrating surprising strength. Horacio Serpa, in his third try for the presidency as the Liberal candidate, finished third with only 11 percent.[7] The Organization of American States deemed the elections free and fair, reporting that the vote was conducted "in an atmosphere of freedom, transparency, and normalcy."[8] The opposition concurred that the process, including the checks on incumbent power, had functioned relatively well.

Among the new complications marking the first one hundred days of Uribe's second term was disarray within the Uribe coalition in Congress. The legislative operation of the Uribe bloc did not function with the same efficiency as its electoral apparatus. In late 2006, the coalition lost key votes due to infighting. Furthermore, the opposition parties voted as a bloc, as called for in the recent Law of Groups (Ley de Bancadas), which requires members of parties in the Congress to vote together unless the party specifies that its members may vote independently. While this could be leading to the formation of an opposition offering a coherent alternative, the practical implications of the law remain uncertain.

As in most Latin American countries, Colombia's executive branch is more powerful than the other branches of government. The Colombian Congress, however, is one of the strongest in the region and at times refuses to accept presidential initiatives. The power of the judicial branch, especially the Constitutional Court, has grown in recent years, to the point where some have suggested that the Court is usurping legislative functions. One example of the judicial branch's expanding clout occurred in February 2007, when the court, ruling that Law 54 of 1990 was discriminatory, granted gay couples inheritance rights equal to those of heterosexual unions.[9] Following the para-political revelations, the judicial branch further demonstrated its growing independence by initiating investigations of members of Congress accused of working with the paramilitary groups.

Since the beginning of his first term, President Uribe, aiming to overturn the traditional system of patronage in the civil service, has adopted a merit-based system for the selection, promotion, and naming of bureaucrats. His efforts appear to have achieved some success: according to a report by the Inter-American Development Bank, in 2006 Colombia had the fourth most efficient bureaucracy in Latin America, following only Brazil, Chile, and Costa Rica.[10]

Nongovernmental organizations (NGOs) have the freedom to operate in Colombia, although some are suspected of being allied with leftist groups and face harassment. Civil society has less influence in Colombia than in other Latin American countries, and the groups continue to play minor roles in the peace process, even though the ELN has constantly sought to include civil society. The creation of zones of martial law and the restrictions of movement for foreigners under Decree 2002 have put a damper on the activities of human rights groups, which also face direct threats. Multiple human rights groups received death threats throughout the summer and fall of 2006, and in January 2007 Yolanda Izquierda, who worked on behalf of paramilitary victims seeking restitution of their lands, was assassinated in Cordoba department.[11]

Press freedom is seriously affected by the violence in Colombia, yet government interference remains relatively limited. Until 2004, when only one journalist was killed, Colombia had one of the highest tallies of journalist deaths in the world. As a means of basic protection, journalists regularly exercise self-censorship. In its 2005 report on Colombia, Reporters Without Borders made no reference to government intervention in the media. However, it emphasized that Colombia "is still one of the region's most dangerous for journalists, with constant threats and pressure, including from guerrilla groups. Among taboo subjects are corruption, the guerrilla war and drug trafficking. More journalists fled into exile in 2005 after getting threats."[12]

The Foundation for Freedom of the Press (FLIP), a Bogota-based press watchdog, reported an increase in violations against the press in 2006, particularly surrounding the March and May elections. Two journalists were killed as a result of their reporting during 2006. In February, radio announcer Gustavo Rojas Gabaldo was shot in Cordoba by paramilitaries in retribution for criticism of links between the local government and paras. Community radio host Milton Fabian Sanchez was killed in Valle del Cauca in August 2006 following his condemnation of local drug traffickers. There were numerous reports of harassment and intimidation of journalists reporting on similar issues. The government has taken some steps to protect journalists, establishing a program to assist reporters who have received threats and a special prosecutorial unit focused on journalist assassinations.

Libel and defamation remain criminalized, though penalties seldom go beyond the obligation to rectify a statement and rarely include a fine. In 2006, the Uribe government proposed a law that would create a wider definition of libel, giving more latitude to the government. However, this proposal failed following debate in the national congress. While the national government does not use selective distribution of advertising to influence media coverage, local governments frequently do so. In early 2007, a judge issued a temporary restraining order against a Barranquilla newspaper for alleging connections between paramilitary forces and city government. The judge's decision was condemned by President Uribe and the Committee to Protect Journalists.[13] At other times, however, Uribe has been less generous with the press, such as his 2006 criticism of the newsweekly *Semana* for its reporting on the parapolitical scandal. Internet access is not hindered.

Recommendations

- The Colombian government should actively seek to prevent fraud and voter intimidation in the 2007 local elections by maintaining a law enforcement presence at all voting sites.
- Demobilized paramilitaries should not be able to run for elected office while the process of investigation and prosecution remains pending and new evidence continues to emerge regarding their criminal activities.
- The Colombian government must give adequate protection to all qualified candidates, regardless of political party.
- Members of the Uribe administration and its congressional supporters should refrain from rhetorical attacks on NGOs and human rights groups and the government should respond with immediate protection when these groups report intimidation and threats.

CIVIL LIBERTIES

PROTECTION FROM STATE TERROR, UNJUSTIFIED IMPRISONMENT, AND TORTURE:	2.86
GENDER EQUITY:	4.00
RIGHTS OF ETHNIC, RELIGIOUS, AND OTHER DISTINCT GROUPS:	3.25
FREEDOM OF CONSCIENCE AND BELIEF:	5.67
FREEDOM OF ASSOCIATION AND ASSEMBLY:	4.00
CATEGORY AVERAGE:	**3.95**

In the middle- and upper-class sectors of Colombia's major cities, civil liberties are generally respected. However, this does not hold for Colombia's poor and rural citizens, who face encroachment on their rights by state and nonstate actors. This gap in civil liberties was noted in Human Rights Watch's 2006 report, which noted that the Colombian conflict "continues to result in widespread abuses by irregular armed groups . . . as well as by the Colombian armed forces."[14] These abuses include kidnapping, torture, and murder, as well as rape, land theft, and forced conscription.

Overall statistics indicate that the level of crime has been decreasing during the Uribe era. The 2006 homicide rate was the lowest in twenty years.[15] The number of kidnapping victims declined to 621 in 2006, as compared to 3,572 in the record-setting year of 2000. The Free Country Foundation, an NGO that gives aid to victims of kidnapping, extortion, and disappearances, cited Uribe's Democratic Security Policy, initiated in 2003 and defined by the president as "the achievement of the complete control of the territory to assure the rule of law,"[16] as the reason for this decline.[17]

Torture is banned under Colombian law. However, since neither the armed forces nor the national police are effectively monitored, torture continues to occur. Recent reports indicate that prison conditions are deplorable. The number of medical doctors and provision of medicine is insufficient, while water pressure is too low for both consumption and sanitary needs. One study reported that there were forty-eight prisoners for each toilet.[18] This is a particularly unfortunate situation for citizens subjected to arbitrary arrest, which only rarely occurs in urban areas but is somewhat more common in rural conflict zones.

The Colombian constitution prohibits discrimination on the basis of gender. Colombian women have the same literacy rate as men, and their participation at all levels of the educational system equals that of males. Yet this equality does not extend to employment opportunities in either the public or private sector. Unemployment is higher among women, and those employed tend to be in inferior positions.

In January 2007, representatives of the Women's Rights section of the Inter-American Commission on Human Rights visited Colombia for the first time since June 2005. Colombian journalist Claudia Lopez suggested that the representatives would not find any improvement in the status of women since the last visit. Specifically, Lopez stated that 75 percent of the country's millions of displaced people are women and children. Overall, 28.5 percent of the households in Colombia are headed by women; however, among displaced families the figure is 40 percent, within indigenous households it is 47 percent, and among Afro-Colombians the figure reaches 49 percent. Ms. Lopez concluded that implementation of laws protecting women was lacking and that "neither the protection nor the courts have worked. The legal mandates are still ignored."[19]

Women also suffer from a high incidence of domestic and sexual violence. In late 2006, the Administrative Department of Social Well-Being of Bogota reported that 20 percent of the city's women had suffered physical violence from their husbands, while 35 percent had suffered verbal abuse. In addition, there was evidence that 11 percent had been raped.[20] The media tends to cover only sensational cases, such as that of Lizeth Ochoa in Barranquilla in July 2006, who was beaten for three hours by her husband. Ms. Ochoa declined to file civil charges, and the prosecutor's office dropped attempted murder charges.[21]

Women's groups have responded to violence and inequality in several ways. The wives and girlfriends of gang members in the central Andean city of Pereira threatened not to have sexual relations with their significant others until they disarmed and stopped their violent activities.[22] Female members of the National Congress indicated their intention to introduce a law that would require political parties to include women as 50 percent of their candidates. The proposal was not approved. However, a 2002 quota law does require that 30 percent of high posts in the executive, legislative, and judicial branches be held by women, excluding elected posts. No quota for women in elected positions was passed for 2006; in the most recent parliamentary elections, 14 out of 166 seats in the lower house and 12 out of 102 seats in the upper house were filled by women.

In May 2006, the Constitutional Court decriminalized abortion in cases of rape, when the life or health of the woman was threatened, or when there was evidence that the fetus was deformed.[23] Doctors performed the first legal abortion in Bogota in August 2006 on an eleven-year-old who had been raped by her stepfather. This procedure was quickly condemned by the Roman Catholic Church. Pedro Rubiano, archbishop of Bogota, threatened to excommunicate any woman, doctor, or judge who practiced or facilitated abortion.[24] The government, meanwhile, issued a decree regulating abortion, stating that within the limits of the Court's ruling, any woman over fourteen could have the procedure without authorization.[25]

A law adopted in 2005, Law 905, criminalizes every aspect of human trafficking, from approaching a victim to the trafficking itself. It also establishes standards of care for victims and provides a national anti-trafficking strategy.[26] Child sex tourism in resort areas on the Caribbean coast remains a problem. On December 27, 2006, Colombia ratified the Optional Protocol of the Convention on the Elimination of Discrimination against Women (CEDAW), which allows women or groups of women to submit claims of rights violations to the CEDAW committee.

The situation of Colombia's indigenous citizens, who comprise 8 percent of the national population, is dire. Indigenous reservations, which make up 30 percent of the national territory, are neglected, with insufficient medical care and children dying of malnutrition. Indigenous groups have been devastated by both indiscriminate and selective murders, massive displacement from their traditional lands, the forced recruitment of young people by insurgent groups, frequent cases of rape, the entry of the drug trade, and land seizures.

Many indigenous groups live in isolated regions, which causes further problems. The Embera people of the Pacific department of Choco, for example, suffer from malnutrition and lack of health care. In the case of the Embera of the Alto Baudo area, the nearest hospital is eight hours away by boat. As a result, between September and November 2006, seventy-five people died of malaria, of whom seventy-one were children under four years of age.[27] During a meeting of indigenous groups, the Embera also decried the assassination of fifty-two of their people and the disappearance of twenty-nine others in 2006.[28]

Guerrilla and paramilitary violence continues to have a negative effect on indigenous groups. In May 2006, the National Indigenous Organization of Colombia described how constant conflicts left indigenous groups in Choco caught between FARC guerrillas and paramilitary troops (even though the latter were officially demobilized).[29] At other times, indigenous groups have been caught in the crossfire between guerrilla and government troops. Some indigenous groups in the southern Andes have attempted to stay neutral, assisting neither the government nor the guerrillas. One of the most famous of these groups is the peace community of San Jose de Apartado in Antioquia department, which has received international recognition for its efforts to avoid the conflict. However, over 160 members of the community have been killed since 1997, and in March 2005 one of the community's leaders and seven other villagers were massacred. As of February 2007, no arrests had been made, though witnesses pointed to military involvement and dozens of soldiers were under investigation.[30]

Afro-Colombians are estimated to comprise about ten million people, nearly a quarter of the Colombian population. Though historically concentrated in villages along the coast, displacement due to the rampant violence has led to intense migration to the major cities. While there is no legal discrimination against them, they have had few representatives in high levels of politics and suffer from lower income and education levels.[31] The state has taken no recent significant action to combat discrimination against Afro-Colombians.

Over the last decade more forceful laws and regulations have been developed to enable a larger number of people with disabilities to gain equal access to education, public spaces, and the health and social security systems. These efforts, however, have not achieved their full potential as they receive insufficient funds and are not high among the government's priorities.

Freedom of religion is generally respected in Colombia. Evangelical protestant groups have grown substantially in recent decades. Roman Catholics clearly remain the dominant group, however, both in numbers and among leaders of the country. Despite the constitutional separation of church and state, in February 2007, President Uribe asked the bishop to allow him to lead prayer at a mass and asked "the Holy Virgin to help us in having a Colombia in which peace is consolidated, jobs are found, poverty is overcome, and equity is constructed."[32] The homepage of the High Commissioner for Peace includes a "Prayer to Our Lord of Peace" superimposed on a crucifix.[33] These examples demonstrate the less-than-complete separation of church and state in the country. According to a decree from the minister of education, all schools must offer classes on religion no later than April 2007.

Freedom of assembly and association are guaranteed by the Colombian constitution. Protests are generally permitted, though Colombia is not nearly as mobilized as its Andean neighbors. Labor unions have legally existed since the 1930s, although the government retains the right to suspend their activities if the law is broken. Violence against trade unionists has become a hot-button issue in the context of Colombia's attempt to forge a free-trade agreement with the United States. Since Uribe took office, over 400 trade unionists have been killed in Colombia, with only seven convictions; shockingly, this represents a decline in violence from the previous period.[34] Though much of the violence is blamed on paramilitaries, security forces have also been implicated in numerous killings. In January 2007, the National Prosecutor's Office named thirteen prosecutors to investigate the violence.[35] Also that month, a permanent new International Labor Organization office began operating in Bogota.

Recommendations
- The government should continue to curb violence through expansion of constabulary forces and organize them so that districts most affected by bloodshed receive additional forces.
- The government should provide resources to educate women regarding their rights to equal treatment in job hiring and establish a hotline that women can call to report discrimination in job hiring.
- The government should establish a unit to investigate complaints of spousal abuse and enact specific protections that will be granted to women who fear for their physical safety.
- The government should establish a greater state presence in rural areas in order to provide better protection for indigenous Colombians from illegal armed groups.

- The government should continue to emphasize that violence against trade unionists will receive special investigatory and prosecutorial focus, and direct substantial resources toward doing so.

RULE OF LAW

INDEPENDENT JUDICIARY:	5.00
PRIMACY OF RULE OF LAW IN CIVIL AND CRIMINAL MATTERS:	3.83
ACCOUNTABILITY OF SECURITY FORCES AND MILITARY TO CIVILIAN AUTHORITIES:	2.75
PROTECTION OF PROPERTY RIGHTS:	4.00
EQUAL TREATMENT UNDER THE LAW:	3.33
CATEGORY AVERAGE:	**3.78**

The inability of the Colombian state to enforce the rule of law throughout its territory is arguably the original sin from which most of Colombia's biggest problems emanate. Though conflict continues and the state still lacks significant presence in many zones, recent years have seen some efforts to broaden and deepen application of the law in the country.

The Colombian judiciary is widely regarded as more independent than most of its regional peers. This perception is based largely on the reputations of the Supreme Court and the Constitutional Court, which have each demonstrated a willingness to investigate and rule against the government in important cases. However, the fact that Colombia has four courts of maximum instance overseeing different juridical elements sometimes leads to incoherence and jurisdictional conflict that Colombians refer to as "the train wreck." For instance, when, in July 2006, the Constitutional Court overturned a decision of the Supreme Court, the head of the Supreme Court characterized the decision as "going against the juridical security of the country."[36] The primary point of dispute is use of the *tutela*, a legal mechanism used by Colombians to assert that a violation of their rights has occurred. Lower courts are considered less independent, due in large part to vulnerability to the same pressures and threats that negatively impact other aspects of Colombian society.

Inefficiency is one of Colombians' primary gripes about the justice system. Justice is bottlenecked; even as crime rates decline, the backlog of criminal cases continues to grow. In 2006 alone, 105,984 new cases entered the system, yet only 11,405 verdicts were issued.[37] Because of prison overcrowding, the Supreme Court ruled that criminals sentenced to four years or less would not have to serve any time. In May 2006, in the face of the government's refusal to implement a retroactive salary increase, 38,000 workers from the judicial branch initiated an indefinite stoppage of activities. This paralyzed all judicial proceedings taking place in the country until the strike ended in early June. Since 1995, employee salaries had been adjusted just below the inflation rate.

Under the constitution defendants are considered innocent until proven guilty and have the right and access to counsel.[38] A system is in place to provide counsel to indigent defendants and the number of public defenders has risen, but resources remain scarce. Moreover, illegally armed groups have influenced and coerced prosecutors, judges, investigators, and witnesses in Colombia, resulting in impunity and continued difficulty in consolidating the rule of law.[39]

One important, ongoing change over the last number of years is the shift away from a written, European-style justice system modeled after the Napoleonic Code to an oral, accusatory system much like the one used in U.S. courts, which went into effect in 2005 in Bogota and other cities and will extend to all regions by the end of 2008.

The most important development in recent years, however, is the beginning of legal proceedings under the Justice and Peace Law, passed in June 2005 to govern the demobilization process. The success of demobilization is critical, both in terms of removing one of the most brutal actors from the Colombian stage and by possibly establishing a mechanism for left-wing insurgents to eventually lay down their arms. For leaders of demobilized groups, it suspends traditional imprisonment, replacing it with a lighter sentence given in exchange for full confessions and the return of ill-gotten assets. Persons convicted of atrocious crimes, such as massacres, will be confined between five and eight years in government-designated locations, which could include agricultural colonies. The law encompasses only acts committed during and related to membership in an illegal group; those who lie about their crimes or return to illegal activity will be disqualified from receiving the law's benefits. Victims of paramilitary violence, human rights groups, and opposition leaders strongly objected to the law in its original form, contending it was too lenient and would perpetuate the culture of impunity already enjoyed by many paramilitaries.

In May 2006, the Constitutional Court tightened the law, removing a provision that gave prosecutors only sixty days to conduct each para investigation and decreeing that any seized assets should be used to compensate victims. In August, fourteen senior leaders were arrested pending court hearings, and a further four turned themselves in. In total, 2,695 paramilitary leaders currently charged with crimes against humanity signed up for recourse under the law.

Both accusations against paramilitaries and requests for compensation have inundated government offices. In early January 2007, Luis Gonzalez, director of the Justice and Peace section of the National Prosecutor's Office, reported that some 400 accusations against the paramilitary groups arrived in his office each day and that the total received since the law was approved was about 100,000. While Gonzalez has affirmed that the Prosecutor's Office would have enough resources if the other parts of the judicial system cooperated, many commentators have argued that far more attorneys and resources are needed to implement the law efficiently.[40]

Although more than 30,000 AUC troops had demobilized by the end of 2006, highly fraught disputes between the government and top paramilitary leaders surfaced with respect to several issues, including the conditions of confinement and the need for assurances that extradition to the United States—the paramilitaries' worst nightmare—would be avoided. By December 2006, the government had moved fifty-nine paramilitary leaders to a maximum security prison after alleging that an escape was being planned from their previous location in a run-down former recreation center. President Uribe also suggested the AUC leaders were ordering assassinations of other leaders and added, "If people who are in the peace process are killing people, those people should lose the benefits of the law, should be submitted to the ordinary laws, and if someone involved in these crimes has extradition suspended, I will immediately end the suspension."[41]

The first trial of a paramilitary leader began in December 2006, when former AUC leader Salvatore Mancuso began his deposition. He argued that the paramilitary squads existed because the government did not provide adequate protection from guerrilla groups. Coldly using a PowerPoint presentation to recount over 300 murders, he further alleged that Colombian military officers had assisted the paramilitary groups; interestingly, he only named officers who were either dead or already jailed for helping the paramilitary groups.[42] Mancuso was scheduled to continue his deposition in May 2007. Many others are slated to follow; at time of writing it remains unclear to what degree the tenets of the Justice and Peace Law will be fulfilled.

The entire existence of the AUC phenomenon underscores the complicated dynamic between civilians and security forces in Colombia. The evidence that some politicians and members of the military collaborated with paramilitaries is overwhelming, yet the ability of the state to hold such forces accountable barely existed prior to the demobilization process. Viewed from the narrow angle of civilian supremacy over the military, Colombia performs relatively well; unlike nearly all other Latin American countries, the country has been led by civilian governments since 1958. However, the persistence of conflict has meant that the military has remained a powerful actor. It has also been a troubled one, with accusations of corruption and human rights abuses common. An incident in the town of Jamundi in Valle del Cauca department in May 2006, in which ten elite antidrugs police were killed by military fire, exemplifies how far the problem can go. Though it was first characterized as a friendly fire incident, the story soon unraveled, and it became clear that the military unit was in the pay of drug traffickers; over a dozen soldiers and a colonel were eventually arrested. Soldiers have also been accused of other abuses in recent years, including keeping millions of dollars of confiscated drug money and killing civilians and dressing them as rebels in order to inflate body counts.

The military criminal justice system is also undergoing a crisis. Cases involving human rights abuses are already transferred to civilian courts. Still, due to the overwhelming number of cases in 2006 and 2007, the vice minister of defense suggested in February 2007 that the military justice system be removed from the executive branch and transformed into an independent judicial system.[43]

Property rights are guaranteed under Colombian law. Property that is being used for illegal purposes—for instance, in the drug trade—is confiscated by the government. In February 2007, the government decided to use the US$80 million in drug money found in the Cali area to build houses for poor people.[44] The Colombian government remains unable to protect the property rights of foreign investors from insurgent attacks, which has led in some cases to those investors seeking to protect themselves through alliances with paramilitaries. In March 2007, the U.S. government fined the banana giant Chiquita for paying US$1.7 million to the AUC for protection of its properties and employees since 1997.

Colombia ranks second only to Sudan in the number of internally displaced persons (IDPs), with 3.6 million. Citizens are forced from their land through threats and violent acts by paramilitary and guerrilla groups, which then use the land to consolidate their local power and further their drug operations. Some of the land is obtained by forcing the landowners to sell their property at low cost or face execution or mutilation, such as the amputation of an index finger to provide the fingerprint for false paperwork. Through collaboration with paramilitary groups and failure of the military or police to protect citizens' land rights, the Colombian government is partially responsible for the large number of IDPs. Colombia ranks poorly in contract enforcement in the World Bank's Doing Business report, and contractual disputes often lead to long and costly court cases.[45]

Recommendations

- As more information becomes available about the relationships between the armed forces and paramilitary groups, the Colombian government should intensify its efforts to punish all members of the military who have had such relationships.
- The functions of the different judicial organizations should be clarified so that resources are not lost in jurisdictional disputes.
- The government (with help from the international community) must provide sufficient investigatory resources so that paramilitary confessions can be investigated and corroborated, with those who fail to confess to all crimes, withhold the return of ill-gotten assets, or continue criminal activity disqualified from benefits under the JPL.
- As part of the overhaul of the justice system and implementation of adversarial trial proceedings, the backlog of criminal cases should be reduced through a substantial increase in funding for court proceedings.

ANTICORRUPTION AND TRANSPARENCY

ENVIRONMENT TO PROTECT AGAINST CORRUPTION:	4.00
EXISTENCE OF LAWS AND ETHICAL STANDARDS BETWEEN	
PRIVATE AND PUBLIC SECTORS:	3.75
ENFORCEMENT OF ANTICORRUPTION LAWS:	3.50
GOVERNMENTAL TRANSPARENCY:	3.71
CATEGORY AVERAGE:	**3.74**

Despite being awash in violence and drug money, corruption in Colombia is not perceived to be out of control. Nonetheless, corruption continues to infect many institutions and hinder development.

In 2006, Colombia ranked 59th in Transparency International's Corruption Perceptions Index. With 3.9 points out of 10, the country fell slightly from its 4.0 score of the previous year, ending a four-year trend of decreasing perceptions of corruption.[46] Margareth Florez, director of Transparency for Colombia, noted that corruption was far from defeated due to the weakness of political institutions, the insufficient visibility of public contracting, and "the danger of the capture of the state by large economic and delinquent groups."[47]

In December 2004, the Uribe government presented the Presidential Program of Modernization, Efficiency, Transparency, and Fight against Corruption. Its objective is to build a state policy for the fight against corruption and corresponding actions that can be used by public institutions, private enterprise, citizens, the media, and civil society organizations in the prevention, investigation, and punishment of acts of public corruption.[48] In September 2005, this plan was revised through the "State Policy Proposal for the Control of Corruption" and the National Anticorruption Program.[49] Corruption czar Rodrigo Lara Restrepo indicated the huge task of the Presidential Program when he stated that it would be applied "wherever we have evidence of corruption that involves politicians, bureaucrats, and the paramilitary groups."[50]

In February 2007, the national procurator argued that the system was beginning to work. As evidence he cited a recent report indicating that four public officials were expelled for corruption each week, with a total of 232 in 2006. The procurator argued that this was not due to greater corruption than previously, but rather because of a new disciplinary code combined with new technology to enforce it.[51] However, while the inspector general and national procurator have both been active in investigating and prosecuting graft, there is little evidence that these efforts have led to a significant decline in overall corruption. The para-political investigations in late 2006 and early 2007 revealed extensive financial connections between paramilitaries and politicians, such as those found on the computer belonging to paramilitary leader Jorge 40 (see Introduction).

Though the Colombian state traditionally has been less involved in the economy than other Latin American countries and recently has been privatizing some state enterprises, the government remains characterized by excessive bureaucratic regulations and, in many cases, low salaries that increase the probability of corruption. Furthermore, adequate protections against conflicts of interest are lacking. All government employees must make a notarized declaration of property and income. While the procurator and the comptroller are charged with investigating corruption, the quantity of allegations overwhelms their abilities. Comptrollers also exist at the departmental and local levels, but in many cases politicians have placed political friends in those posts, making these levels some of the most corrupt parts of the state apparatus. No adequate mechanisms enable victims to pursue their rights.

Legal protections are in place for whistle-blowers but they are not enforced uniformly. Prominent cases of corruption are widely reported in the national press, yet journalists investigating government corruption have been subject to harassment and violence, particularly outside the major cities.[52] Furthermore, in recent years whistle-blowers in the military have in some cases been intimidated or prevented from advancing as a result of voicing accusations against superior officers.[53]

The Colombian government provides some information to the public regarding government expenditures, and the budget is subject to legislative review.[54] The yearly budget proposal is released to the public, along with several in-year reports and an audit report. However, the Open Budget Index has stated that Colombia's year-end reports do not contain sufficient details to allow comparison between the proposed budget and actual outcomes. The constitution provides for freedom of information, and the Law Regarding Free Access to Information of Public Interest establishes unrestrained access to any documents in a public office.[55] Complicated bureaucracy and corruption, however, can at times limit the enforcement of these rights. In addition, the state makes no real efforts to provide information about government services and decisions in formats and settings that are accessible to disabled people.

Recommendations

- The Colombian government should increase transparency in its activities, focusing on rapid dissemination of information through web portals at the agency level and open-meeting laws that allow the people to know more about its operations.
- The government should increase the transparency of public contracting by ensuring that all bidding is carried out through the System of Information for Monitoring State Contracting (SICE).
- The government should improve human resource capacity within the offices of the Auditor General and the Comptroller General in order to increase the government's ability to identify and punish officials who violate anticorruption laws.
- In order to combat self-censorship regarding corruption, the government should enhance the protective and investigatory capacity of the unit in the Attorney General's office charged with protection of threatened journalists.

NOTES

[1] "Todo empezó con el hallazgo del computador de Jorge 40," *El Colombiano*, 19 October 2006, www.elcolombiano.com.

[2] "Seis alcaldes del Casanare sellaron pacto con paramilitares al estilo Ralito," *El Tiempo*, 20 February 2007, www.eltiempo.com.

[3] "Comunicado completo sobre la sentencia relativa al Proyecto de Ley Estatutaria de Garantías Electorales," *El Espectador*, 12 November 2005, www.elespectador.com/elespectador/.

[4] Amnesty International, "Colombia: AI condemns killings by FARC," http://action .amnesty.org.au/index.php/news/comments/colombia_ai_condemns_killings_by_farc/ 2 March 2006.

[5] John Otis, "Scandal forces resignation of top diplomat, Critics said her ties to others were hurting Colombia's international image," *Houston Chronicle*, 20 February 2007.

[6] "El uribismo se apoderó este domingo del Congreso de la República con una mayoría absoluta," *El Tiempo*, 13 March 2006, www.eltiempo.com.

[7] "Uribe logró triunfo de 'primera,'" *El País*, 29 May 2006, www.elpais.com.co.

[8] "U.S. congratulates Colombian president Uribe on election victory," States News Service (Washington, D.C.), 30 May 2006, accessed through Nexis, 13 April 2007.

9   "Un paso histórico: Las parejas homosexuales han empezado a existir legalmente en Colombia," *Semana*, 10 February 2007, www.semana.com.

10 *The Politics of Policies* (Washington, D.C.: Inter-American Development Bank [IDB], IPES 2006 Report), www.iadb.org/res/ipes/2006/chapter4.cfm.

11 Constanza Vieira, "Colombia: The Limits of Paramilitary Repentance," Inter-Press Service, 9 February 2007, http://ipsnews.net/news.asp?idnews=36512.

12 "Colombia—Annual Report 2006" (Paris: Reporters Without Borders [RSF]), www .rsf.org/article.php3?id_article=17418.

13 "COLOMBIA: CPJ alarmed by gag order against daily" (New York: Committee to Protect Journalists [CPJ], 30 January 2007), www.cpj.org/news/2007/americas/columbia 30jan07na.html.

14 "Colombia: Events of 2006" (New York: Human Rights Watch, 11 January 2007. http:// hrw.org/englishwr2k7/docs/2007/01/11/colomb14884.htm.

15 "Cifra de homicidios más baja en 20 años," *El País*, 3 January 2007, www.elpais.com.co.

16 "Lineamientos de la política de seguridad democrática," Presidencia de la República de Colombia, 29 June 2003, http://www.presidencia.gov.co/prensa_new/sne/2003/junio/29 /08292003.htm

17 "Siguen bajando casos de secuestro en Colombia," *El Pais*, 24 January 2007, www.elpais .com.co.

18 "Deficiente es el servicio de salud en cárceles de Colombia," *El Tiempo*, 21 September 2006, www.eltiempo.com.

19 Claudia López, "¿Año nuevo, vida nueva?" *El Tiempo*, 16 January 2007, www.eltiempo .com.

20 "11 de cada 100 bogotanas han sido violadas por sus cónyuges, dice informe del Dabs," *El Tiempo*, 27 November 2006, www.eltiempo.com.

21 "Lizeth Ochoa, golpeada por su marido, renunció a reclamar daños materiales y morales del agresor," *El Tiempo*, 29 November 2006, www.eltiempo.com.

22 "Mujeres de pandilleros en Pereira declaran 'vigilia sexual' para que dejen la Violencia," *El Tiempo*, 11 September 2006, www.eltiempo.com.

23 Juan Forero, "Colombian Court Legalizes Some Abortions," *New York Times*, 12 May 2006, www.nytimes.com.

24 Ricardo Arias Trujillo, "Sermón Permanente," *Semana*, 18–25 December 2006, www .semana.com/home.aspx.

25 "Mayores de 14 años pueden abortar sin autorización," *El Espectador*, 14 December 2006, www.elespectador.com/elespectador.

26 "Discussion Focuses on Measures to Prevent Human Trafficking as Women's Anti-discrimination Committee Reviews Colombia's Report," States News Service, 25 January 2007.

27 "75 Emberas murieron de malaria mientras esperaban ser trasladados a un lugar de atención," *El Tiempo*, 28 November 2006, www.eltiempo.com.

28 "Emberas denunciaron 52 asesinatos y 29 desapariciones durante encuentro indígena," *El Tiempo*, 25 October 2006, www.eltiempo.com.

29 "Denuncian que grupos indígenas están sitiados por combates entre las Farc y paramilitares desmovilizados," *El Tiempo*, 13 May 2006, www.eltiempo.com.

30 "Amnesty International Welcomes Advances in Investigations Into 2005 Colombia Peace Community Massacre" (New York: Amnesty International USA), 27 February 2007, http://www.amnestyusa.org/document.php?lang=e&id=ENGUSA20070227001.

31 "La comunidad afrocolombiana," *El Tiempo*, 28 May 2004, www.eltiempo.com.

32 "Uribe pide por Colombia a la virgen de los Remedios" (Bogota: Presidency of the Republic, 2 February 2007), www.presidencia.gov.co.

33 Alto Comisionado para la Paz, homepage, www.altocomisionadoparalapaz.gov.co.

34 "Colombia Fact-sheet: Murder of Trade Unionists and Impunity" (Chicago: U.S. Labor Education in the Americas Project [USLEAP], www.usleap.org/Colombia/Government %20Documents/MPS%20Document%20Analysis.pdf, accessed 13 April 2007.

35 "Los líderes sindicales de Colombia aseguran que el Estado los acorrala con muerte y amenazas, y también con leyes que terminan favoreciendo a los patronos y evitando el derecho fundamental a la asociación," *El Espectador*, 6 January 2007, www.elespectador .com/elespectador.

36 "Un nuevo choque de trenes por una tutela," *El Colombiano*, 22 July 2006, www .elcolombiano.com.

37 Corporación Excelencia en la Justicia, www.cej.org.co/scripts/index.php#.

38 *Colombia Country Report* (Washington, D.C.: Organization of American States [OAS], Inter-American Commission on Human Rights [CIDH], www.cidh.oas.org/country rep/Colombia93eng/chap.4.htm, accessed 17 April 2007.

39 "World Report: Colombia" (HRW. www.unhcr.org/home/RSDCOI/45aca29c20.html, accessed April 17, 2007.

40 "Tougher Challenges Ahead for Colombia's Uribe" (Brussels: International Crisis Group [ICG], Policy Briefing, 20 October 2006).

41 "Gobierno ordenó el traslado de los jefes de las autodefensas a la cárcel de Itagüí," *El Tiempo*, 1 December 2006, www.eltiempo.com.

42 Juan Forero, "Paramilitary Leader Submits to Justice: Seeking 'Real Truth,' Victims Gather for Testimony on Colombian Violence," *Washington Post*, 30 December 2006, http://www.washingtonpost.com.

43 "Ubicar en el poder judicial a la Justicia Penal Militar busca el Gobierno: Viceministro de Defensa," *El Tiempo*, 4 February 2007, www.eltiempo.com.

44 "Siete mil viviendas en Buenaventura y Cali serán construidas con plata de las caletas," *El Tiempo*, 13 March 2007, www.eltiempo.com.

45 "Enforcing Contracts in Colombia," in Doing Business (World Bank, 2007), www.doing business.org/ExploreTopics/EnforcingContracts/Details.aspx?economyid=46, accessed 17 April 2007.

46 "Colombia cayó al puesto 59 en el Índice de Percepción de la Corrupción (IPC) de 2006," *El Tiempo*, 1 November 2006, www.eltiempo.com.

47 "Colombia ocupa el quinto puesto de corrupción en América Latina," *El Colombiano*, 6 November 2006, www.elcolombiano.com.

48 "Propuesta de una política de estado para el control de la corrupción y Plan Nacional Anticorrupción" (Bogotá: Programa Presidencial de Lucha Contra la Corrupción, 16 September 2005), www.anticorrupcion.gov.co/control_cor/index.htm.

49 Ibid.

50 "Zar Anticorrupción propondrá que los 'paras' también confiesen casos de corrupción," *El Tiempo*, 10 January 2007, www.eltiempo.com.

51 "Destituyen a cuatro funcionarios públicos cada semana en Colombia," *El Tiempo*, 6 February 2007, www.eltiempo.com.

52 "Journalist threatened after reporting on corruption in Sincelejo municipal government" (Toronto: International Freedom of Expression Exchange [IFEX], www.ifex.org/en /content/view/full/79158, accessed 12 April 2007.

53 "Why is this man crying?" (Washington, D.C.: Center for International Policy: Colombia Program, 6 February 2005), www.cipcol.org/archives/000059.htm, accessed April 12, 2007.

54 "Colombia" in *Open Budget Index 2006* (Washington, D.C.: Center on Budget and Policy Priorities, International Budget Project, Open Budget Initiative), www.open budgetindex.org/CountrySummaryColombia.pdf, accessed 12 April 2007.

55 "Colombia" in freedominfo.org Global Survey (Washington, D.C.: freedominfo.org, 2006), www.freedominfo.org/countries/colombia.htm#7, accessed 12 April 2007.

ECUADOR

CAPITAL: Quito
POPULATION: 13.5 million
GNI PER CAPITA: $2,840

SCORES	2005	2007
ACCOUNTABILITY AND PUBLIC VOICE:	3.92	4.13
CIVIL LIBERTIES:	4.12	4.13
RULE OF LAW:	3.33	3.21
ANTICORRUPTION AND TRANSPARENCY:	3.42	3.05

(scores are based on a scale of 0 to 7, with 0 representing weakest and 7 representing strongest performance)

Andrés Mejía Acosta [1]

INTRODUCTION

For the past ten years, Ecuador has been trapped in a downward spiral of political conflict and instability that has eroded the rule of law and kept the country perched on the brink of breakdown. At the time of writing, newly elected president Rafael Correa is weathering a political storm caused by his controversial strategy of bending elected and independent government branches, including the Supreme Electoral Tribunal (TSE) and Congress, to his will regarding his plans for a constituent assembly. While President Correa's plan to overhaul the decayed political system boosted his election campaign, it also placed him in confrontation with the parties in the legislative branch that control the appointment of oversight bodies such as the comptroller general, the attorney general, and the TSE.

Andrés Mejía Acosta (a.mejia@ids.ac.uk) is a Research Fellow at the Institute of Development Studies, University of Sussex, UK. He has written extensively on Ecuadorian political institutions, including elections, political parties, and the legislature. His current work explores the impact of political institutions on fiscal outcomes in Ecuador and Latin America.

By the end of March 2007, the battle over the constituent assembly and its larger implications for political control had led to interinstitutional war in Ecuador. A political battle to determine the operating rules of the prospective constituent assembly culminated in an attempt by the congressional opposition to dismiss the head of the TSE on questionable grounds. In what appears to be a race toward institutional obliteration, the TSE responded by dismissing fifty-seven (of a total of one hundred) legislators who opposed the assembly in the form proposed by Correa. As the path toward the assembly proceeds and the fifty-seven ejected legislators undertake both violent and legal attempts to return to their seats, the rule of law in Ecuador is close to nonexistent. Despite these flagrant violations of the constitution, however, Correa remains a highly popular president in Ecuador, thus demonstrating the disdain felt by Ecuadorians toward Congress and other political elites.

Political instability has become the trademark of the Ecuadorian state. In April 2005, President Lucio Gutiérrez was ousted on the spurious charge of abandonment of office by a simple congressional resolution. A few months before the unconstitutional sacking, the third in eight years, President Gutiérrez had openly violated the rule of law by sponsoring the congressional removal of Supreme Court (CSJ) magistrates, as well as TSE and Constitutional Tribunal (TC) members. This vicious pattern of political retaliation and open conflict has dramatically affected the most salient dimensions of democratic performance. In recent years, the rule of law has been severely affected by repeated interbranch conflict; democratic accountability has been displaced by the rise and success of outsider political candidates with authoritarian tendencies; anticorruption efforts have been rendered ineffective by the political capture of oversight mechanisms; and the effective protection of civil liberties has become a political privilege rather than a right in and of itself. The problem lies not in the legal protection of civil and political freedoms but in the effective functioning of democratic practices and institutions. Ecuador's chronic political instability has eroded the capacity of the state to protect or improve individuals' quality of life.

[UPDATE: On April 15, 2007, nearly 82 percent of Ecuadorians voted in favor of convoking a constituent assembly to draft a new constitution. Elections for the 130-member assembly were officially scheduled for September 30, 2007.]

ACCOUNTABILITY AND PUBLIC VOICE

FREE AND FAIR ELECTORAL LAWS AND ELECTIONS:	4.25
EFFECTIVE AND ACCOUNTABLE GOVERNMENT:	2.75
CIVIC ENGAGEMENT AND CIVIC MONITORING:	5.00
MEDIA INDEPENDENCE AND FREEDOM OF EXPRESSION:	4.50
CATEGORY AVERAGE:	**4.13**

The 2006 presidential and legislative election represented a democratic setback in many respects. While electoral legislation was slightly improved (see below), the election was plagued by widespread accusations of fraud, vote-counting irregularities, and impunity for campaign finance violations. Organized political parties obtained less than 25 percent of legislative seats, as voters were lured by campaign promises of constitutional overhaul voiced by candidates with thin democratic credentials.

According to the constitution, all Ecuadorian adults, with the exception of the military, have the right and the obligation to vote. The TSE is appointed by the legislature for a four-year term, and its seven members mirror the political composition of congress. Presidents are elected for four years according to a majority runoff formula and cannot seek consecutive reelection.[2]

Legislators are elected for four-year terms and have no term limits. The use of a proportional representation formula for the legislature, combined with lenient electoral registration thresholds, has contributed to the proliferation of political parties, making Ecuador's one of the most fragmented party systems in Latin America.[3] This political fragmentation, which to some degree reflects the country's rich ethnic and regional diversity, has also contributed to the chronic instability and short duration of political alliances in Ecuador.

The 2006 election increased public mistrust of the TSE, and presidential candidates exchanged multiple accusations of fraud. Political controversy even reached the chief of the Organization of American States (OAS) electoral mission to Ecuador, Rafael Bielsa, when Correa accused him of bias against Correa's campaign. To avoid further controversy,

Bielsa was swiftly recalled to OAS headquarters just one day prior to the presidential runoff. Alleged irregularities in the contracting of a Brazilian exit-poll company (E-Vote) led to the invalidation of its contract and the resignation of the TSE president after technical failures left E-Vote unable to deliver a quick vote count on election day.[4]

Existing legislation establishes fixed and progressive funding allocations to all parties, offers presidential candidates free media exposure, and provides clear sanctions for candidates who do not observe spending caps or who fail to turn in campaign expenditure reports.[5] The TSE, however, has systematically failed to enforce the law—especially with respect to the imposition of sanctions for campaign finance violations—due to the highly politicized nature of its executive board. At the height of campaigning for the first round of the 2006 presidential vote, the TSE froze the bank account of presidential candidate and businessman Álvaro Noboa for exceeding the spending limit by more than 50 percent. Noboa—who had paid electoral penalties with devalued bonds for similar abuses during the 2002 election—was acquitted five days later by TSE members, some of them with close ties to his party.[6] Similar overspending was reported during the runoff elections by Citizen Participation–Ecuador (PCE), an electoral watchdog; Noboa's overspending was reported at 348 percent of the spending cap, while Correa's surpassed it by 65 percent.[7]

The Ecuadorian constitution provides for proper oversight mechanisms that in theory ensure appropriate checks and balances across government branches. In practice, however, the fragmented and shifting nature of political coalitions has turned mechanisms of oversight and control into instruments of political blackmail. In December 2004, President Gutiérrez sponsored the formation of a legislative coalition that illegally dismissed and replaced the majority of CSJ magistrates, as well as TSE and TC members. This deliberate encroachment by the executive and legislative branches on the judicial branch, which was an overt violation of democratic principles, gave the president absolute control over all three branches of the state (see Rule of Law). The sacking of Supreme Court magistrates also enabled one of the coalition parties (Roldosista Party-PRE) to annul a pending trial on corruption charges against former president and PRE founder Abdalá Bucaram, thus allowing him to return from exile in Panama. Bucaram's return triggered widespread antigovernment protests in Quito, which met with a violent response from the government. As in the 1997 crisis, when Bucaram had been declared "mentally unfit" to remain president, Ecuador's powerful congress removed a president on questionable grounds, this time dismissing Gutiérrez on the grounds of "abandonment of office," even though the president was still in the presidential palace.[8]

The politicization of government appointments has percolated to the middle and lower ranks of the government bureaucracy.[9] Legislation enacted in 2004 sought to establish merit-based and equal opportunity criteria for the selection, promotion, and remuneration of civil servants, and further legislation was adopted in 2006 to standardize these procedures across government offices. Although there is little evidence available to assess the effective impact of these norms, critical decisions regarding selection, promotion, and dismissal appear to remain for the most part a discretionary privilege of political bosses.[10]

Civic engagement and monitoring have improved thanks to the proliferation of watchdog groups that now possess greater capacity to influence the policymaking process. In recent years, a group of nongovernmental organizations (NGOs) gathered under the name of Coalición Acceso (Access Coalition) to improve auxiliary legislation to the Organic Law for Transparency and Access to Public Information.[11] In general, the creation and funding of NGOs is fully allowed by the state, although the Gutiérrez administration was accused of exerting pressure on some organizations that criticized the government.

The media in Ecuador are privately owned and outspoken. During the Gutiérrez administration, however, freedom of the press quickly deteriorated. The Inter American Press Association (IAPA) reported several violations against press freedom and journalists' rights in 2005, especially during Gutiérrez's last months in office. Several reporters were reportedly targeted in February 2005 by the Deposit Guarantee Agency (AGD)—a banking insurance bureau—and accused of outstanding debts.[12] Similarly, the government banned helicopter news coverage of protests in Quito and Guayaquil in the months leading to Gutiérrez's fall in April 2005.

Other troubling incidents related to the Gutiérrez crisis included the death of independent Chilean photographer Julio Augusto García due to asphyxia produced by tear gas, an attack on Spanish journalist Daniela Kraemer from *El País* newspaper, and the repeated intimidation and sabotage of Radio La Luna, an opposition radio outlet.

Reporters Without Borders (RSF) reported that radio director Paco Velasco and his family received death threats, seemingly associated with their active role in opposing the Gutierrez government.[13]

The situation normalized when President Gutiérrez left office, as reflected by the country's world ranking in press freedom: RSF's freedom score for the year 2005 ranked Ecuador in 87th place, with a score of 21.75; by 2006, the ranking had improved to 68th, with a score of 15.25.[14] Despite this favorable trend, in 2006 the SIP reported two gunshot attacks on *Gráficas Nacionales*, the company responsible for publishing the important Guayaquil newspapers *Expreso* and *Extra*, in a clear attempt to intimidate the press.[15] In addition, there were widespread accusations of press bias during the presidential campaign, especially from losing candidate Noboa, who shunned the press and labeled journalists for the television station Ecuavisa "accessories to the destruction of the country."[16] Correa, for his part, has also taken an aggressive stance toward the press in his first months in office, though it remains to be seen what concrete effects this will have on Ecuadorian media freedom.

Generally, the state has refrained from using libel laws to punish journalists who offend powerful actors, although libel and defamation remain criminalized. Despite isolated concerns, there is no systematic evidence that the state has imposed direct or indirect censorship of print or broadcast media. The state does not hinder access to the internet.

Recommendations

- The government should provide the necessary legal and administrative resources to apply and effectively enforce campaign finance laws. With the support of existing civil society watchdogs, it should ensure full disclosure of campaign expenditures.
- The state should strive to maintain the effective separation of powers between government branches, establish clearer legal boundaries and prerogatives for each government body, and penalize government officials whose actions encroach on other government branches.
- The prospective constituent assembly should reconfigure the appointment process and design new rules to ensure the independence of control and oversight entities such as the comptroller and prosecutor general.

- The government should confirm its commitment to press freedom by refraining from making inflammatory statements that increase polarization between the government and the press.

CIVIL LIBERTIES

PROTECTION FROM STATE TERROR, UNJUSTIFIED IMPRISONMENT, AND TORTURE:	2.43
GENDER EQUITY:	4.25
RIGHTS OF ETHNIC, RELIGIOUS, AND OTHER DISTINCT GROUPS:	3.75
FREEDOM OF CONSCIENCE AND BELIEF:	6.00
FREEDOM OF ASSOCIATION AND ASSEMBLY:	4.20
CATEGORY AVERAGE:	**4.13**

Ecuadorian legislation contains a wide array of provisions to prevent unjustified imprisonment, torture, and abuse by both state and non-state actors, and ensures citizens' right to petition when their civil and political rights are violated by state authorities. In practice, the Ecuadorian government—especially during the Gutiérrez administration—has not prevented repeated cases of politically motivated persecution of government critics as well as cases of police brutality and military misconduct. For instance, former vice-president León Roldós was severely beaten in January 2005, shortly after criticizing the government.[17] A month later, Patricio Acosta, a former cabinet minister during the Gutiérrez administration, joined other public officials in reporting the existence of a sophisticated government-sponsored espionage network that targeted government opponents.[18] In April 2005, human rights organizations denounced sixty-two cases of human rights violations against 173 citizens associated with the opposition, including death threats, beatings, and attacks on property.[19] While these accusations remain uninvestigated, reports of such incidents have declined since the end of the Gutiérrez administration.

Police brutality, disappearances, and impunity remain pervasive problems in Ecuador. Human rights watchdogs such as Amnesty International (AI) and the Ecumenical Commission of Human Rights

(CEDHU) have reported many cases of severe violations committed by the police. On August 30, 2005, the Permanent Committee for Human Rights (CDH), together with other human rights organizations, organized a rally in Guayaquil called "Acción contra el olvido" (Action against Forgetting) to protest fifty-nine cases of people who had disappeared in recent decades after being arrested as subversives by the security forces.[20] Despite these actions, the police have not yet been held accountable.

In January 2007, police arrested seventeen-year-old Paul Guañuna, accused of graffiti painting, in the presence of his two friends; the next day his body was found in a ravine with signs of torture—but the police argued that he had committed suicide.[21] Although unexplained deaths are the exception, Amnesty International sometimes reports on cases of arbitrary detention and intimidation of regular citizens, as well as human right activists and people who have raised complaints about police brutality.[22]

Ecuadorian citizens are increasingly exposed to non-state violence as a spillover effect from Colombia's military conflict. In 2005, a mission composed of national and international organizations reported several cases of *sicariato* (assassination for hire) and other crimes in the border provinces of Sucumbíos, Carchi, and Esmeraldas, which were believed to be closely linked to drug trafficking activities. According to the same report, the Colombian conflict has posed other challenges, including the devastating effects of Colombian airborne herbicide spraying of coca fields on the quality of food, water, and health on the Ecuadorian side of the border. It also highlights the fact that the local population is living under constant physical and psychological threat from members of the Ecuadorian and Colombian armed forces as well as groups of paramilitaries and guerrillas.[23]

Although the constitution establishes an ombudsman to ensure people's right to petition when constitutional rights have been violated, this office is severely constrained by its lack of legal power to enforce resolutions. Additionally, the office lacks a full national presence, and people—especially those in remote or violent areas (such as border zones)—often prefer not to complain for fear of exposing themselves to even greater danger.[24]

The problem of weak law enforcement has been aggravated by the chronic crisis in the country's jails. According to the Andean Commission of Jurists (CAJ), inmate rights are severely violated by prison overcrowding, threats to personal safety, and extended detention without sentence.[25] Prison riots and strikes are occasionally reported as inmates demand speedier and fairer trials and improved sanitary conditions. Jail workers, in turn, have demanded higher salaries and a general increase in prison budgets. An April 2006 strike led the government to declare a nationwide prison emergency.[26] Riots and violence have not decreased, and the press continues to report on deaths and injuries among inmates and prison workers.[27] Citizen watchdogs like the Latin American Development Corporation (CLD) report that as of April 2006 nearly 90 percent of inmates had been arrested for drug-related crimes, ranging from high-level trafficking to street dealing or illegal possession, while nearly 70 percent of inmates had not been sentenced.[28]

In an attempt to address this problem, the Palacio administration signed the Strasbourg Treaty in June 2005 to facilitate the repatriation of foreign prisoners within signatory nations. However, attempts to repatriate Colombian prisoners have been ineffective due to political indecisiveness and legal impediments.[29] In March 2006, Congress reformed the Code of Penal Procedures and Social Rehabilitation to stress its rehabilitating role. The National Council of Social Rehabilitation has been in charge of producing enabling regulations to implement the reform since May 2006.[30] Finally, the TC declared long-term *detención en firme* (pretrial detention) to be unconstitutional in September 2006, though controversy continues over whether the resolution should be retroactive.[31]

The government has made significant formal progress in ensuring the protection of gender and minority group rights, but the reality has not fully matched the spirit of the many legal conventions to which the country is a signatory. In 2006, President Palacio launched the Equal Opportunities Plan 2005–2009 in order to give the protection of women's rights the status of state policy and provide greater policy visibility to women's issues.[32] Women have made considerable gains in political representation in the past two years, and seven out of seventeen cabinet positions in the Correa government are held by women, including the defense and foreign affairs ministries. In terms of legislative representation, the electoral law established in 2000 required that at least 30 percent of candidates on each ballot must be women, with the quota to increase by 5 percent in each national election until it reaches 50 percent. Additionally, it established that the names of men and women competing in multimember districts should be allocated in a sequential and alternating pattern.[33] A 2006 TSE resolution, however, violated the alternation principle, allowing party leaders greater discretion regarding where to place women on the ballot.[34] As a result, twenty-six out of one hundred legislative seats were occupied by women.

The Ecuadorian constitution provides equal opportunities for men and women in the workplace, but much remains to be done to effectively prevent job and salary discrimination. According to the first time usage survey conducted in Ecuador, women work, on average, eighteen hours more per week than men. This inequality stems from the fact that there are hidden activities—like housework—that are not recognized socially or economically as work.[35] In June 2006, women's groups protested against the violations of their sexual and constitutional rights after the Constitutional Court banned the commercialization and use of the day-after pill.[36] Women and children's organizations successfully lobbied Congress in June 2005 to adopt a penal code reform that strengthened sanctions against sexual felonies and penalized activities like sexual exploitation, child pornography, and human trafficking.[37]

People with disabilities face a greater gap between legislation and practice. The state has not been able to provide for the special needs or guarantee the rights of people with disabilities. The Ecuadorian Federation for Disabled People reports that 45 percent of the 1,600,000 disabled people in the job market work in the informal sector.[38] The labor code was reformed in December 2005 to demand that employers hire a proportional share of people with disabilities, but this law has been largely ignored.[39] By contrast, religious groups have continued to enjoy full recognition and accreditation by the Ministry of Interior, which has contributed to their proliferation over the past few years.

Although the Ecuadorian Constitution of 1998 is considered one of the most progressive charters in Latin America for the multicultural and plurinational nature of its legislation, the extensive collective rights contained within have not yet been implemented, as congress has not passed enabling legislation to date. During the Gutiérrez administration, the Confederation of Indigenous Nationalities of Ecuador (CONAIE), which has been a crucial actor during the political upheaval of the last decade, suffered a severe schism around the decision to support the government. Only one branch of the movement, the Confederation of Indigenous Nationalities of the Amazon (CONFENAIE) stayed allied with the government; its head, Antonio Vargas, was appointed Minister of Welfare. CONFENAIE communities also received agricultural tools, and some leaders obtained political appointments.[40] According to some, this split was the result of a deliberate government strategy to weaken indigenous influence.[41]

While the indigenous movement maintains a strong national presence and plays a leading role in the region, its political wing, the Pachakutik party, has not avoided the electoral setbacks that affected most traditional parties; its candidates won only six out of one hundred seats in the National Congress. Pachakutik endorsed the winning presidential bid of Rafael Correa but is not part of Correa's cabinet. Nonetheless, both the indigenous movements and the highly marginalized Afro-Ecuadorian community hope to achieve substantial representation and influence in the constituent assembly.

Amnesty International has reported that oil companies have violated the civil and political rights of indigenous communities. These incidents have included death threats and intimidation against environmental and indigenous activists who opposed the Gutíerrez and Palacio governments' oil extraction policies. The state has remained inactive in the face of these violations, and in some cases it has sent the military to support oil companies.[42]

While the Ecuadorian constitution guarantees freedom of assembly, organizations including Amnesty International and CEDHU have reported several cases of human rights violations and police brutality during street protests. Victims of police brutality—and even torture—include several students arrested during street protests in Quito in April 2005 and January 2006.[43] Indigenous leader María Iza Quinatoa reportedly received death threats following her public opposition to the government's potential signing of a free-trade agreement with the United States.[44] Other protesters in the eastern provinces of Orellana and Sucumbíos encountered police brutality while demanding fairer distribution of oil resources in August 2005. During the protests, more than sixty people were reportedly injured.[45] Governments have used the declaration of state of emergency to react quickly to issues ranging from political unrest to natural disasters, but without effective oversight of executive powers, this state of expanded presidential power carries the potential for negative effects on individual civil and political liberties.

Labor unions have encountered several obstacles to forming industry and sector-wide associations. According to Human Rights Watch, Ecuadorian legislation contains loopholes that have allowed employers to bypass the freedom of association and collective bargaining rights of their employees. In September 2005, Human Rights Watch released a petition against Ecuador's being granted preferential trade benefits (ATPA) from the United States, arguing that the government has made little progress in protecting workers' right to unionize.[46] This accusation comes on top of the labor ministry's insufficient efforts to eliminate child labor, especially on banana plantations.

Recommendations

- The government should increase the financial resources and level of personnel at the ombudsman's office in order to ensure that all Ecuadorians have the ability to report human rights violations.
- The government should conduct an independent enquiry to investigate allegations of the existence of a network of espionage aimed at government officials and opposition leaders over the last five years.
- The government should continue its efforts to address the issue of prison overcrowding by doing more to facilitate the rehabilitation process and applying sentences that are proportional to the magnitude of the crime.
- The state should work to ensure the effective protection of freedom of assembly and association for all citizens, especially minority groups, by strengthening the ability of control bodies to investigate cases of abuse.

RULE OF LAW

INDEPENDENT JUDICIARY:	2.40
PRIMACY OF RULE OF LAW IN CIVIL AND CRIMINAL MATTERS:	3.00
ACCOUNTABILITY OF SECURITY FORCES AND MILITARY TO CIVILIAN AUTHORITIES:	3.00
PROTECTION OF PROPERTY RIGHTS:	4.33
EQUAL TREATMENT UNDER THE LAW:	3.33
CATEGORY AVERAGE:	**3.21**

The constitutional provisions that enable the formal separation of powers have been converted into mechanisms of blackmail and control in Ecuador. Fundamental democratic principles of checks and balances, including key tenets of the rule of law such as judicial independence and judicial review, have been systematically violated by political factions in both the government and the opposition.

Between December 2004 and April 2005, two entire and formally independent CSJs were illegally dismissed by congressional resolution, with the president's consent. The removal of judges in December 2004 was the result of a political alliance formed between President Gutiérrez and two congressional parties, the PRE and Álvaro Noboa's PRIAN. Gutiérrez was seeking legislative support to preempt possible congressional impeachment for using state resources to campaign in local elections, while congressional parties were keen on replacing CSJ magistrates associated with opposition parties.[47] Initial public support for the replacement of the CSJ magistrates, who were perceived as corrupt, disappeared when the new court invalidated the pending embezzlement trial against PRE leader and former president Abdalá Bucaram (see Accountability and Public voice). In an attempt to calm citizen outrage over Bucaram's return, and days before his own removal from office, President Gutiérrez dismissed the entire new Supreme Court in April 2005 through presidential decree. The decree was ratified by congress, but the pre-December, legitimate Supreme Court was never reinstated.

A new CSJ was appointed in November 2005 following an eight-month period of consultation and a rigorous, merit-based selection process that was monitored by the United Nations, the Organization of American States, and civil society groups. Preliminary evidence, unfortunately, suggests that the new CSJ judges and their rulings have not been exempt from political pressures.[48] The politicization of the judiciary has also undermined the rule of law in civil and criminal matters. Several months after leaving office in 2005, Gutiérrez was arrested and accused of sedition by the interim government, even though the processes necessary to enable such a charge had not been carried out.[49] The attorney general has also acted in favor of political interests. For example, interim attorney general Cecilia Armas was accused of facilitating former president Bucaram's escape from justice in December 2005.[50]

Not only did the government fail to properly investigate Armas, she actually stayed in office until 2007.

Prosecutorial independence is affected by the political maneuvering that characterizes the appointment process for the nation's top prosecutors. In principle, congress appoints the Ministro Fiscal General (Public Prosecutor) upon a nomination received from the National Judiciary Council (CNJ), an administrative body within the judiciary; congress also appoints the Procurador General (Attorney General) from a pool of three presidential nominees. Finally, Congress has the power to appoint the comptroller general, Ecuador's top auditing authority, through approval by a two-thirds majority of its members. In practice, the highly fragmented Congress has been unable to produce the necessary votes to appoint the comptroller general since January 31, 2003, and the attorney general since 2005. In the absence of officials leading these independent oversight mechanisms, it is fair to say that the actions of both the Gutiérrez and Palacio administrations remained *de facto* unchecked.

These appointments became highly controversial in 2007, as shifting legislative coalitions rallied to secure ownership of the institutions that control accountability in Ecuador. For example, the congressional appointment of the comptroller general was perceived to reflect a political concession to the Gutiérrez-led opposition in exchange for its support for the Constituent Assembly.[51] Conversely, Noboa's PRIAN party led the fight over the controversial appointment of Francisco Cucalón Rendón as attorney general; he eventually resigned in the face of protests regarding irregularities in the legislative appointment process and because he had faced corruption charges while serving as attorney general during the Bucaram administration.

The presumption of innocence until proven guilty is granted by the constitution. The 2006 declaration of unconstitutionality of extended pretrial detention by the TC marked an important step toward protecting this basic principle of justice (see Civil Liberties). The constitution establishes that all citizens are equal before the law, but it is well known that those who have money or influential connections are likely to benefit from better legal advice and speedier verdicts.

The constitution also guarantees a fair trial to all citizens and grants the accused access to independent counsel when they cannot afford it. The effective application of these rights remains severely undermined by a chronic shortage of defense attorneys. According to the CLD, the situation has not improved over the past several years. The total number of public defenders in the country is just thirty-one, they are required to defend in every single legal field without regard to specialization, and they are significantly outnumbered by the body of prosecutors in every province. In Guayas Province, for example, the ratio of prosecutors to public attorneys as of mid-2005 was fifteen to one.[52]

The armed forces remain a pivotal player in democratic politics. During periods of crisis, the armed forces have played a significant role by recognizing or withdrawing support to civilian politicians beyond their constitutional prerogatives. During the ouster of President Gutiérrez, for example, it took the armed several hours to recognize the mandate of Vice President Palacio as the new president. However, the armed forces have not systematically repressed civilians or civil movements for political purposes in recent years.

Existing legislation provides mechanisms to ensure the accountability of the police and armed forces to civilian authorities. Due to the politicization and weakness of the judiciary, however, accountability is weak, and the security forces enjoy significant autonomy when dealing with civilians. The police have received repeated warnings from international human rights organizations and have faced accusations of human rights violations and of police brutality (see Civil Liberties). An estimate by the Public Prosecutor's Office claims that the state has been obliged to pay almost US$5 million in compensation related to murders and other violations committed by the police, but the authors of such atrocities remain unidentified and unpunished.[53] According to the daily newspaper *El Comercio*, 248 police officials have been dismissed from the force by police tribunals in the past two years for violations of the police code of conduct. While this represents a noteworthy effort, the same paper reported that during 2005, the police received a total of 6,466 denunciations of rights violations.[54]

Both police and armed forces were discovered to be involved in a corruption scandal when a spectacular clandestine financial operation was uncovered in October 2005. The operation consisted of a parallel financial system that paid up to 10 percent monthly interest rates to high-profile clients, such as national politicians and high-ranking officers in the police and armed forces.[55] This shadow banking system, involving more than 160,000 deposit holders and monthly movements of between US$400 million and US$1 billion, became public upon the accidental death of its mastermind, a public notary. Although it is believed that money deposited by investors was used to finance illegal activities, such as drug and arms trafficking as well as money laundering, state authorities have not revealed official results of the investigations more than a year after the scandal was first discovered.[56] Other scandals involving law enforcement officials that have been reported by the media without receiving proper investigation from the state include accusations of police and border patrol participation in *coyoterismo* (human trafficking),[57] alleged police protection of drug trafficking suspects,[58] and theft of goods confiscated from arrested suspects.[59]

The Ecuadorian constitution recognizes and protects the right to own private property, including intellectual property rights. However, indigenous groups remain vulnerable regarding the protection of their ancestral knowledge, which has been utilized by pharmaceutical companies that seek medicinal properties in native plants and subsequently patent the useful compounds. Under current legislation, which is based on international legal instruments, this knowledge does not meet the legal criteria that would enable indigenous groups to request protected status for ancestral knowledge. The main legal limitations are the facts that intellectual property protection only covers inventions defined as "novelties" and that the owner of the rights must be an individual rather than a collective entity.[60] While this is a problem facing indigenous people around the world, the Ecuadorian state has adopted a passive attitude regarding protection of patentable knowledge by indigenous groups.

In general, contract enforceability in Ecuador is severely hindered by the weakness of rule of law. Given the conflicting nature of existing laws, court decisions are uncertain, the judiciary is prone to erratic judgments, and processes remain vulnerable to corruption. Moreover, future foreign investment is uncertain given the current political instability. A contentious dispute with the United States broke out in relation to the treatment of Occidental Petroleum, whose Ecuadorian assets were confiscated in May 2006. The United States regarded the penalties as disproportionate and pushed for international arbitration, while talks on a free-trade agreement between the two countries, already foundering, were indefinitely suspended.

Recommendations
- Significant government efforts are required to investigate, effectively sanction, and accelerate pending judiciary actions against former pres-

idents and government officials accused of wrongdoing. The government should form an autonomous commission charged with investigating and sanctioning former officials' wrongdoings.
- The government should continue to devote financial resources to expanding the capacity of the judiciary by professionally training more
judges and public attorneys nationwide.
- The repeated incidents of human rights violations by police and
armed forces should be investigated by an independent commission
with the full backing of the government.
- The government should revise and adopt the necessary legal structure
for the protection of collective and ancestral intellectual property
rights.

ANTICORRUPTION AND TRANSPARENCY

ENVIRONMENT TO PROTECT AGAINST CORRUPTION:	3.00
EXISTENCE OF LAWS AND ETHICAL STANDARDS BETWEEN	
PRIVATE AND PUBLIC SECTORS:	3.00
ENFORCEMENT OF ANTICORRUPTION LAWS:	2.50
GOVERNMENTAL TRANSPARENCY:	3.71
CATEGORY AVERAGE:	**3.05**

Despite legal reforms and greater civic activity, Ecuador continues to be
perceived as a highly corrupt country. In the 2006 Transparency International Corruption Perceptions Index, the country received a score of
just 2.3 out of 10. Worldwide, Ecuador ranks 138th out of 163 surveyed
countries, sharing the bottom of the scale in Latin America with
Venezuela.[61] According to a recent country survey, more than 50 percent of respondents described themselves as victims of corruption, with
bureaucrats and the police cited as the main agents of corruption.[62]

President Gutiérrez's efforts to adopt stricter anticorruption legislation
at the beginning of his mandate were damaged by accusations of corruption and cronyism against him and other members of his administration.
The Anticorruption System (SAE), established in 2005, sought to
strengthen existing anticorruption watchdogs and obliged high-ranking
officials to present asset declarations, but the effort remained ineffective

due to low levels of compliance and the overregulation, overlap, and even contradictory nature of the existing legal framework.[63] Like his predecessor, President Correa announced the creation of a National Anticorruption Office shortly after his inauguration. It remains unclear, however, what relationship it would have with the preceding SAE and the existing Civic Committee against Corruption (CCCC).

The state plays a predominant role in the economy. According to the Heritage Foundation's 2007 Index of Economic Freedom, the country is considered "mostly unfree," with a score of 55.3 out of 100 points, which places Ecuador 24th out of 29 Latin American countries, and 108th out of 157 countries worldwide. The report stresses low scores in areas such as business and investment freedom, where "government officials use regulatory schemes and questionable legal interpretations to solicit bribes from and otherwise take advantage of foreign investors."[64]

Independent investigative and auditing bodies have been rendered ineffective due to the increased politicization of their authority. The failure to elect a comptroller general and an attorney general for more than four and two years, respectively, illustrates this point. The internal audit and control units of the Internal Revenue Service (SRI) have limited sanctioning capacities, and some inquiries and audits of influential businesspeople, government cronies, and strategic political actors have been stalled or discouraged.[65]

The state has been unable to effectively prevent, detect, and punish cases of corruption among public officials. Obstacles include the presence of many legal loopholes and noncodified corruption activities;[66] the weak sanctioning power of anticorruption entities; and the low number of sentences and sanctions imposed in corruption cases, which reinforces the perception of impunity.[67] A government program aimed at protecting victims and witnesses of corruption has had little impact because it only covers protection in criminal cases, leaving out disciplinary or administrative ones, and it does not protect all whistle-blowers (e.g., those in the workplace); therefore, people continue to fear retaliation.[68]

Individuals responsible for upholding the country's legal standards have also commonly advanced personal economic interests at the expense of the public good. In May 2006, the director of the board of the Deposit Guarantee Agency (AGD), the government banking insurance bureau, was sent to jail for allegedly trying to collect government debts from influential bankers currently in jail or exile. Months earlier, she had denounced the fact that the state had done nothing to prosecute bankers facing corruption and embezzlement scandals.[69]

One such alleged case of impunity and exile involves Guillermo Dueñas Iturralde, CEO of the Banco de los Andes. The Superintendencia de Bancos (Banking Authority) had declared Banco de los Andes bankrupt in 1999, but a controversial judicial resolution overruled the previous declaration against the bank, allowing it to reopen in 2004. The bank, however, was forced to close again in 2006, defaulting on more than 8,000 deposit holders.[70] Dueñas fled the country to escape embezzlement charges. Although he was arrested in the United States, he was later released as the arrest warrant had been revoked by the President of the Superior Court of Justice of Quito.[71] Examples of thorough state investigation into corruption scandals and the application of legitimate and effective sanctions against private actors and public officials accused of wrongdoing are rare.

In an unprecedented move in January 2007, the CCCC made public 197 videos showing administrative personnel within the judiciary receiving money for their services. Although the videos are not admitted by the law as bona fide proof of a crime, thus shielding the accused from prosecution, those accused could face serious administrative sanctions imposed by the CNJ. In practice, there is widespread concern that the CNJ is not keen on or committed to imposing such sanctions.[72]

Privately owned media outlets are actively involved in uncovering corruption scandals, but media moguls may have significant conflicts of interest between their own assets and the corruption scandals being reported on. In a personal letter addressed to President Gutiérrez in April 2005, businessman Fidel Egas Grijalva—owner of Ecuador's largest bank and a TV station—reminded the president of a previous commitment to protecting his bank "and the financial system" from instability and warned him that his TV channel will not have a problem in uncovering repeated political mistakes of the administration. In his response, President Gutiérrez reminded the banker that his administration chartered two flights carrying a total of US$350 million in cash from the United States to boost his bank's reserves.[73] Despite the fact that a wave of corruption accusations followed this exchange, the scandal itself was never prosecuted. Journalists lack the proper training and professional incentives to investigate corruption scandals thoroughly, and new corruption cases often eclipse unsolved ones due to judicial inefficiency.[74]

In 2004, the government adopted an Organic Law for Transparency and Access to Public Information (LOTAIP), but its impact has been compromised by very low levels of compliance. According to the Access Coalition, 98 percent of the 345 institutions monitored failed to report on their websites the basic amount of information required by law.[75] Another watchdog, the Catholic University Human Rights Clinic, reported that only 14 percent of the clinic's twenty-two requests for information from government institutions and organizations received a favorable response in 2005.[76] According to CLD, this low degree of compliance is explained by the lack of awareness of both public officials and citizens of their obligations and rights, as well as the absence of proper sanctions for defiance.[77] Moreover, auxiliary legislation intended to complement the LOTAIP has sometimes contradicted and limited the full application of the law.[78]

However, there are a few success stories of LOTAIP being correctly applied to facilitate the monitoring of government activities. For instance, after a prolonged legal battle, on September 8, 2006, the Constitutional Court ruled in favor of an appeal presented by the Guayaquil newspaper *El Universo* and asked the National Congress to disclose all expense reports and other relevant administrative information.[79]

A legal framework is in place that seeks to regulate government contracting, such as the Public Contracts Law (PCL) and the Law of Consultancy (LC). In practice, these laws are often bypassed through subjective legal interpretations, and most of the bidding process remains under the control of each government contracting entity. According to an experts' report commissioned by the Inter-American Commission against Corruption, more than 36 percent of contracts placed during June 2003 and December 2005 were not regulated by the PCL or LC (accounting for roughly US$437 million).[80] Although there are provisions for reporting on the bidding, allocation, and contracting processes through an online service (Contratanet), it is mandatory only for offices and dependencies of the executive and merely optional for other public institutions; thus, its potential to become a truly effective mechanism of control and information is limited.[81] Some aspects of the energy and oil sectors, such as contracting for the provision of services and equipment, remain outside the competitive and transparent bidding process; therefore, they present significant opportunities for corruption.

The government enables the fair and legal administration and distribution of foreign assistance.

Recommendations

- The government should strengthen existing efforts to fight corruption by defining the respective roles of the National Anticorruption Office and the CCCC and augmenting their power to investigate and recommend sanctions for corruption to the judiciary.
- The government should enforce existing legislation requiring public officials to present asset declarations before and after taking office and should invoke sanctions in cases of noncompliance.
- The government should encourage and enable the active participation of civil society watchdogs to disseminate more widely the contents of the Public Access and Transparency Law, as well as ensure that contracting and other government information is disclosed in an accurate and timely manner.
- The government should extend whistle-blower legislation to guarantee job security during corruption investigations for those who report workplace corruption.
- Significant government efforts are needed to prevent private–public conflicts of interest and properly investigate and prosecute private actors, such as bankers, accused of corruption and embezzlement. These efforts could include the appointment of an independent investigating commission to handle cases of special public relevance.

NOTES

1 I want to acknowledge the invaluable research assistance and insightful comments of Juan Carlos Machado Puertas. I also thank Santiago Basabe, Julio Muñoz, Michel Rowland, and Ruben Dario Useche for sharing valuable information to include in this report.

2 No second round is needed if the leading candidate obtains more than 40 percent of the vote and leads the second candidate with more than a 10-point difference (Constitution, Article 165).

3 J. Mark Payne, Daniel Zovatto G., Fernando Carrillo Flórez, and Andrés Allamand Zavala, *Democracies in Development: Politics and Reform in Latin America* (Washington, D.C.: Inter-American Development Bank [IADB], 2002).

4 "Xavier Cazar presentó renuncia oficial al TSE," *El Universo*, 3 January 2007, http://www.eluniverso.com.

5   "Ley Orgánica Reformatoria a la Ley Orgánica de Control del Gasto Electoral y de la Propaganda Electoral," *Official Journal*, 31 March 2006, 241.

6   "Imprevista mayoría 'revive' a Álvaro Noboa," *Hoy on line*, September 21, 2006, www .hoy.com.ec.

7   Participacion Ciudadana Ecuador, "Gasto General de los Candidatos a la Presidencia de la Republica en Medios de Comunicación al 24/11/2006,"http://www.participacion ciudadana.org/reportemonitoreo/Home.aspx

8   Boletín "Viviendo la democracia," No. 18, Quito: Corporación Latinoamericana para el Desarrollo [CLD], March 2005).

9   Caridad Araujo, Andrés Mejía-Acosta, Aníbal Pérez Liñán, Sebastian M. Saiegh, and Simón Pachano. 2005. "Political Institutions, Policymaking Processes, and Policy Outcomes in Ecuador" unpublished manuscript, InterAmerican Development Bank.

10 Cucalón became attorney general during the Bucaram administration but was forced to step down three months after his appointment in 1997. "Cucalón quedó fuera del Ministerio Fiscal," *El Telégrafo*, 31 January 2007, http://www.telegrafo.com.

11 Michel Rowland, project consultant for *Proyecto Si Se Puede*. personal communication, 15 January 2007.

12 SIP, "Ecuador: Informe ante la Reunión de Medio Año, Panamá," 2005.

13 Reporters Without Borders (RSF), "Un miembro del Congreso insulta y amenaza públicamente a un periodista," 14 November 2005, www.rsf.org/article.php3?id_article =15585.

14 RSF, "Annual Worldwide Press Freedom Index -2006," (Paris: RSF, 2006), www.rsf .org/rubrique.php3?id_rubrique=639; RSF, "Annual Worldwide Press Freedom Index—2005" (Paris: RSF, 2005), http://www.rsf.org/article.php3?id_article=15331; RSF, "Annual Worldwide Press Freedom Index—2004" (Paris: RSF, 2004) http://www.rsf.org /article.php3?id_article=11715.

15 SIP, "Ecuador: Informe ante la 62ª Asamblea General, Ciudad de Mexico, Mexico," 29 September–3 October 2006, (Miami: SIP, 2006), www.sipiapa.com/pulications/informe _ecuador2006o.cfm.

16 "Ecuador: Noboa es acusado de poner en riesgo a periodistas opositores," *Agence France Presse*, 6 November 2006, accessed through Nexis.com, 14 March 2006.

17 SIP, "Ecuador: Informe ante la Reunión de Medio Año, Panamá," 2005.

18 In January 2007, the newly elected minister of energy, Alberto Acosta, denounced the existence of spying devices in his office. Shortly afterward, Rosa Maria Torres, former minister of education, supported Acosta's concerns, announcing that she was also spied upon in 2003, when she worked for the Gutiérrez administration. "Ex-Ministra pide tomar en serio denuncias de espionaje a funcionarios de Gobierno," *Ecuador Inmediato*, 22 January 2007, www.ecuadorinmediato.com.

19 Boletín "Viviendo la democracia" No. 19, Quito (CLD, April 2005).

20 Amnesty Internacional (AI), *Online documentation archive: Ecuador*, http://web.amnesty .org/library/eng-ecu/index accessed 20 August 2007; Comisión Ecuménica de Derechos Humanos de Ecuador, *Archivo de Noticias*, www.cedhu.org /html/modules.php ?name=Stories_Archive, accessed 20 August 2007.

[21]   Comisión Ecuménica de Derechos Humanos, "¡Ni un hombre mas a la cronología de la impunidad!," *Boletín de Prensa*, 7 February 2007, www.cedhu.org/html/modules.php ?name=News&file=article&sid=422.

[22]   AI, *Online documentation archive: Ecuador*.

[23]   Food First Information and Action Network (FIDH), Federación Internacional de Derechos Humanos (FIAN) , Red de Acción contra los Plaguicidas en América Latina (RAPAL), Observatorio Control Interamericano de los Derechos Humanos de los Migrantes (OCIM), Centro de Estudios y Asesoría en Salud   (CEAS) & Organizaciones e instituciones ecuatorianas miembros del Comité Interinstitucional contra las Fumigaciones (CIF): Defensoría Nacional del Pueblo, INREDH, Acción Ecológica, CEDHU, Acción Creativa, FORCCOFES, PUCE, CAS/AFSC, Plan País, SERPAJ, Comité Provincial de Derechos Humanos del Carchi, COPOCCAR, Fundación Altrópico, ECOLEX "Report of the International Mission concerning fumigations in the Ecuadorian and Colombian Border: Provincias de Carchi, Esmeraldas y Sucumbíos," No. 434/3, December 2005. http://www.fidh.org/IMG/pdf/eccl434e.pdf.

[24]   Ibid.

[25]   Comisión Andina de Juristas (CAJ), "Documento de trabajo actualizado al 5 de mayo del 2005. Sucesos en el Ecuador. Situación de la Democracia y los derechos humanos en el Ecuador" (Lima: CAJ, 2005), www.cajpe.org.pe/Banners/Texto/ecuadorsitu.pdf.

[26]   "Cárceles Reclaman presupuesto," *Hoy on line*, 24 November 2004, http://www.hoy .com.ec; "Pese a la crisis carcelaria, no se transfieren recursos," *Hoy on line*, 12 April 2006, http://www.hoy.com.ec.

[27]   "Peligrosa violencia carcelaria," *Diario Hoy*, 28 September 2005,http://www.explored .com.ec/infodat/textofinal.asp?numero=215128&texto=carcelaria; Fernando Carrion, "La violencia carcelaria" *Diario Hoy*, 26 Noviembre 2005,http://www.explored.com.ec /infodat/textofinal.asp?numero=219451&texto=carcelaria.

[28]   Boletín "Viviendo la democracia" No. 32, Quito (CLD, May 2006).

[29]   Colombia and Ecuador signed a convention on prisoners' repatriation in 1994, but the lack of compatible legislation and political volatility has hindered the application of the convention since then. For example, the repatriation process lasts longer than sentences for minor crimes (one year). Additionally, the process is not applicable to drug-related offenses, which are the prime cause of detention of Colombian nationals in Ecuador. The first repatriations took place only in 2005. Ministerio de Relaciones Exteriores de Ecuador, "Comercio/ 86 prisioneros piden su repatriación a Colombia," 24 October 2006, http://www.mmrree.gov.ec/mre/documentos/novedades/extracto/ano2006/octubre /ext024.htm; Comisión Andina de Juristas, *Cronología Andina*, Ecuador, Abril 2004, http://www.cajpe.org.pe/CRONOLOG/abrilec8.htm.

[30]   Boletín "Viviendo la democracia" No. 32 (May 2006).

[31]   "Fin de la prisión en firme," *Hoy on line*, 19 October 2006, www.hoy.com.ec.

[32]   Consejo Nacional de las Mujeres (CONAMU), "Boletín Informativo No. 11," March 2006, http://bibliotecagenero.conamu.gov.ec/boletines/institucionales/06marzo/index .html; "Plan de igualdad de oportunidades de las Mujeres Ecuatorianas" (Quito: CONAMU, 2004), http://www.conamu.gov.ec/CONAMU/files/PIO.pdf.

[33] *Ley Orgánica de Elecciones*, Article 59. It is worth noting that the 1998 constitution had already recognized a quota of 20% of women on the ballot.

[34] CONAMU, "Boletín 16," 4 August 2006,

[35] CONAMU, "Boletín 16," 4 August 2006.

[36] "Mujeres de Ecuador quieren que se venda píldora del 'día después," *Ecuador Inmediato*, 26 May 2006, www.ecuadorinmediato.com.

[37] "Interpretación al Código Penal lista para publicarse en Registro Oficial," *Ecuador Inmediato*, 4 September 2006, www.ecuadorinmediato.com.

[38] "La gente con discapacidad se alista para empleos de calidad," *El Comercio*, 15 February 2007, http://elcomercio.terra.com.ec.

[39] Ibid.

[40] "Gobierno falló en su intento de 'tomarse' la CONAIE," *Ecuador Inmediato*, 26 December 2004, www.ecuadorinmediato.com

[41] According to Bolívar González, under-secretary of welfare during the same period, "the indigenous population is divided and it has to be kept that way. Otherwise they could control all the powers." "Según Bolivar González Indígenas 'tienen' que estar divididos," *Ecuador Inmediato*, 17 January 2005, www.ecuadorinmediato.com.

[42] FIDH et al., No. 434/3, December 2005.

[43] Observatorio de Derechos Humanos, Comisión Ecuménica de Derechos Humanos de Ecuador, *Archivo de Noticias*.

[44] AI, *Acciones urgentes, AU 102/06 Temor por la seguridad / amenazas*, 21 April 2006, http://web.amnesty.org/library/Index/ESLAMR280032006?open&of=ESL-ECU.

[45] Comisión Ecuménica de Derechos Humanos de Ecuador, "Las Organizaciones de DD.HH. sobre la represión en Sucumbíos y Orellana," *Observatorio de Derechos Humanos: online news archive*, 11 December 2005, www.cedhu.org/html/modules.php?name=News&file=article&sid=391.

[46] Human Rights Watch (HRW), "Petition Regarding Ecuador's Eligibility for Atpa Designation" September 2005, http://hrw.org/backgrounder/business/ecuador0905/index.htm, 5.

[47] CAJ, "Documento de trabajo actualizado al 5 de mayo del 2005," 2005.

[48] In 2006, members of the leftist Izquierda Democrática party (ID) denounced a pact among coastal parties (PRE, PSC, and PRIAN) that allowed the return of the Gutiérrez brothers to the political arena as an electoral strategy to weaken the political opposition from the highlands. "Preocupación en la ID por nuevos vocales del TC," *Ecuador Inmediato*, 24 February 2006, www.ecuadorinmediato.com; "Para el PRE triunfo de Noboa es gestión directa de Bucaram," *Ecuador Inmediato*, 19 October 2006. www.ecuadorinmediato.com.

[49] The constitution allows for presidents and former presidents to be tried by the Supreme Court only when they have been previously impeached by congress (Article 130, 9). In this case, however, the order was issued by the president of the high court of Quito, responding to a request from the interim government. SIP, "Ecuador: Informe ante la Reunion de Medio Año, Quito, Ecuador," 2006.

50 Four days after the fall of Gutierrez's government, Armas assured Bucaram over a telephone conversation that a prison order would not be issued against him and that no one would be alerted about his leaving the country. "La Fiscal está en la polémica por una grabación," Explored, 14 December 2005, http://www.explored.com.ec; "Fiscal se niega a renunciar," El Mercurio, 27 December 2005, www.elmercurio.com.ec.

51 "Terna para contralor,"Cuenca, El Mercurio, 19 January 2007. www.elmercurio.com.ec /web/titulares.php?seccion=LPdYzLB&codigo=szX36jgTUY&nuevo_mes=01&nuevo_ ano=2007&dias=19&noticias=2007-01-19

52 Boletín "Viviendo la democracia" No. 22, Quito, (CLD, July 2005).

53 "Impunidad luego de una sancion," El Comercio, 27 February 2007, http://www.elco merci.com.

54 "248 policías separados de la Fuerza," El Comercio, 27 February 2007, http://www.elco mercio.com/solo_texto_search.asp?id_noticia=62534&anio=2007&mes=2&dia=27.

55 "Cabrera registró a 31 781 clientes," Ecuador Inmediato, 22 November 2006, www .ecuadorinmediato.com.

56 Santiago Basabe, lawyer. personal communication with author, 15 January 2007.

57 "Se destapa un nuevo escándalo para la Policía Nacional," Ecuador Inmediato, 17 November 2006, www.ecuadorinmediato.com.

58 Noticias del Congreso Nacional de la Republica del Ecuador, "Para verificar denuncias de Óscar Caranqui Comision de Fiscalización Citará a Oficiales de la Policía," 21 November 2006, http://www.congreso.gov.ec/noticias/contenido.aspx?codigo_bol=3975 &sitio=noticias.

59 "Otro escándalo envuelve a la Policía," Ecuador Inmediato, 10 November 2006, www .ecuadorinmediato.com.

60 Intellectual Property Law, Article 121 and articles that follow.

61 Transparency International (TI), "Corruption Perceptions Index (CPI) 2006," www .transparency.org/policy_research/surveys_indices/global/cpi.

62 M. Seligson and A. Córdova, "Auditoria de la Democracia, Ecuador 2006," Proyecto de Opinión Pública [LAPOP] (Nashville, TN and Quito: Vanderbilt University and Centro de Estudios y Datos [CEDATOS/Gallup Internacional], 2006, http://sitemason .vanderbilt.edu/files/jakc2k/Auditoria_de_la_Democracia_v13r_en_PDF.pdf. The study is based on sample survey of 3,000 people.

63 Michel Rowland, project consultant for Proyecto Si Se Puede. personal communication, 15 January 2007.

64 It ranks countries across different indicators related to 10 broad areas impacting upon economic freedom, such as business, trade, fiscal, monetary, investment, and financial freedom. The Heritage Foundation, "2007 Index of Economic Freedom" (Washington, D.C. and New York: The Heritage Foundation and Wall Street Journal, January 2007), www.heritage.org/index/countries.cfm.

65 Miguel Angel Játiva, public sector employee. personal communication, 22 January 2007.

66 "Informe Final Relativo a la Implementación en la República del Ecuador de las Disposiciones de la Convención Seleccionadas para ser analizadas en la Segunda Ronda, y

Sobre el Seguimiento de las Recomendaciones Formuladas a dicho País en la Primera Ronda," *Comité de Expertos del Mecanismo de Seguimiento de la Implementación de la Convención Interamericana Contra la Corrupción, Décima Reunión Del Comité De Expertos*, Sg/Mesicic/Doc.185/06 Rev. 4, 11–16 December 2006 (Washington, D.C.: OAS, 2006,), http://www.oas.org/juridico/spanish/mesicic_II_inf_ecu.pdf.

67 Michel Rowland, project consultant for *Proyecto Si Se Puede*. personal communication, 15 January 2007.

68 "Informe Final," 2006.

69 "Cantos: Se ha violentado los derechos de una persona común," *Ecuado Iinmediato*, 16 February 2006, www.ecuadorinmediato.com.

70 "Súper' ponía buenas notas a Los Andes," *Ecuador Inmediato*, 10 December 2006, www .ecuadorinmediato.com.

71 "Policía Nacional explica sobre libertad de Guillermo Dueñas," *Ecuador Inmediato*, 20 February 2007, www.ecuadorinmediato.com.

72 "Nada concreto sobre 'videojudiciales'," *Ecuador Inmediato*, 22 February 2007, www .ecuadorinmediato.com.

73 "Reactivada pelea entre Fidel Egas y Grupo Isaías," *Ecuador Inmediato*, 15 June 2005, www.ecuadorinmediato.com.

74 Michel Rowland, project consultant for *Proyecto Si Se Puede*. personal communication, 15 January 2007.

75 Boletín "Viviendo la democracia" No. 32, Quito (CLD, May 2006).

76 Ibid., No. 20.

77 Ibid., No. 32.

78 Miguel Angel Játiva, public sector employee. personal communication, 22 January 2007.

79 SIP, "Ecuador: Informe ante la 62ª Asamblea General, Ciudad de Mexico, Mexico," 2006.

80 "Informe Final," 2006, 23.

81 "Informe de Sociedad Civil sobre la Implementación de la Convención Interamericana contra la Corrupción—Cicc Segunda Ronda de Evaluación y Seguimiento de las Recomendaciones Formuladas en la Primera Ronda" (Quito: CLD, July 2006), www.oas.org/juridico/spanish/mesicic2_ecu_inf_sc_sp.pdf, 9.

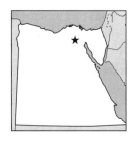

EGYPT

CAPITAL: Cairo

POPULATION: 73.4 million

GNI PER CAPITA: $1,350

SCORES	2005	2007
ACCOUNTABILITY AND PUBLIC VOICE:	2.31	1.88
CIVIL LIBERTIES:	2.18	2.06
RULE OF LAW:	3.19	2.65
ANTICORRUPTION AND TRANSPARENCY:	1.76	1.72

(scores are based on a scale of 0 to 7, with 0 representing weakest and 7 representing strongest performance)

Denis Sullivan and Kimberly Jones

INTRODUCTION

The Egyptian government, led by President Hosni Mubarak and the National Democratic Party (NDP) he controls, routinely violates its citizens' civil and political rights, including freedoms of assembly and association, as well as the right to participate in the political process as a candidate or elector. Torture and arbitrary detentions are not uncommon.

Egypt is not a military dictatorship per se, as Mubarak rules as a civilian leader. However, he and his two predecessors, Anwar Sadat and Gamal Abdel-Nasser, rose to power through and with the assistance of the military. The security apparatus—including the secret police (the *Amn al-Dawla* and *mukhabarat*) along with the legislative and judicial processes, particularly the Emergency Law and military courts—are tools used both to prevent the exercise of human rights and to curtail them. This powerful combination—executive authority (security and secret police), supported by legislative and judicial mechanisms that serve the

Denis J. Sullivan is Professor of political science and director of the Middle East Center at Northeastern University. Kimberly Jones, J.D., is doctoral candidate in political science at Northeastern University and consults on issues relating to human rights, militant groups, and the Middle East.

regime rather than the republic or the population—has ensured long reigns for all three leaders, with Mubarak in power for at least twenty-six, Sadat for eleven, and Nasser for sixteen years.

The wrath of all three leaders has been aimed squarely at the Muslim Brotherhood, the oldest (founded in 1928), most popular, and best organized opposition group. The government of Egypt refuses to recognize the Brotherhood as a party, movement, or social service organization; nonetheless, most observers consider the organization to be tolerated by the regime. The Brotherhood currently holds the largest bloc of opposition seats in Egypt's Parliament. In addition to the non-violent Brotherhood, militant religious groups, along with their alleged supporters and accomplices, also have been targets of state repression, particularly in the wake of intermittent periods of violent attack, which resumed most recently in 2002.

In 2005, the president undertook a seemingly dramatic political reform when he announced an amendment to the constitution that resulted in Egypt's first direct, multiparty presidential elections. Later that fall, Egypt held three rounds of parliamentary elections, in which the NDP, as expected, won a majority. However, the gains of the Muslim Brotherhood caused great consternation for the government. Overall, the government misused the process to cloak itself in democratic legitimacy even as the scope of opposition activity expanded and its nature shifted in 2005—resulting in a larger target group for the government's subsequent crackdown.

In December 2006, Mubarak proposed thirty-four amendments to the constitution. On March 19, 2007, the Egyptian Parliament approved the amendments, and a public referendum was scheduled for March 26. Government critics charged that the date was changed from its original April slot to impede the opposition from organizing a successful campaign against the referendum. Many human rights observers viewed some of the changes as an effort to "constitutionalize" aspects of the state's emergency legislation; Egypt has operated under a state of emergency continuously since 1981. Additionally, journalists and political pundits believe that other amendments are a direct attempt to halt popular and political advances made by the Brotherhood in the wake of the 2005 elections. The referendum passed with 75.9 percent approval in a vote characterized by extremely poor turnout.

ACCOUNTABILITY AND PUBLIC VOICE

FREE AND FAIR ELECTORAL LAWS AND ELECTIONS:	1.25
EFFECTIVE AND ACCOUNTABLE GOVERNMENT:	2.50
CIVIC ENGAGEMENT AND CIVIC MONITORING:	2.00
MEDIA INDEPENDENCE AND FREEDOM OF EXPRESSION:	1.75
CATEGORY AVERAGE:	**1.88**

The authority of the Egyptian government is not rooted in the will of the people. While Egypt holds regular elections, these are neither free nor fair in conduct or law. Suffrage is universal and equal, and electoral competition at the presidential and parliamentary levels is open to multiple, but not all parties. Approximately twenty parties are legally registered, while several others have had their registration applications consistently denied. Elections are conducted by secret ballot, but results are frequently manipulated (and often overturned) by the government.

Campaigning opportunities are not equal for those who do manage to register, and rotation of power between parties is a nonexistent concept. The Egyptian constitution (Article 5) affirms the country's multiparty political system; however, anyone seeking to mount a meaningful political challenge faces serious impediments, particularly at the presidential level.

Citizen suffrage is guaranteed by the constitution, and participation in public life is considered a national duty (Article 62). Law No. 73 of 1956, as amended by Law No. 173 of 2005 regulating the practice of political rights, stipulates that all Egyptians "shall exercise" their right to elect presidential, parliamentary, and local council candidates. In February 2005, President Mubarak initiated constitutional changes, approved by the NDP-controlled Parliament in early May, which provided for the country's first direct, multiparty presidential elections. However, the government mandated that only officially approved parties could field presidential candidates, thereby placing a nearly insurmountable hurdle for nomination in the paths of many potential candidates. Amendment opponents, both secular and Islamist, walked out of the legislative chamber before the parliamentary vote was announced.

In mid-May 2005, key opposition groups called for a boycott of the constitutional referendum. The Muslim Brotherhood, not included in the opposition statement because of the objections of a secular party, issued its own statement, also appealing for a boycott.[1] On May 25, 2005, the referendum was held and the amendment passed, although the results were disputed.[2] Voter turnout was low: estimates by nongovernmental analysts ranged from 15 percent to 20 percent, although the government estimated more than 50 percent. The validity of the referendum results, and thus the proposed changes, were questioned by various segments of society, including the Muslim Brotherhood and the umbrella opposition group Kifaya.

Following the referendum, Parliament promulgated Law No. 174 (2005), which stipulates that all parties seeking to nominate a presidential candidate must have operated for five continuous years.[3] Additionally, a party was ineligible to nominate a candidate unless it held 5 percent of the seats (the 2007 amendment process reduced this to 3 percent) in the People's Assembly and the Shura Council. An exception was made for the 2005 presidential election, when parties were permitted to nominate members of their senior leadership. To further complicate the situation, any independent (e.g., Muslim Brotherhood) applicant must be supported by 250 elected officials, including 65 from the People's Assembly, 25 from the Shura Council (Parliament's upper house), and 10 from local popular councils in at least 14 governorates. By requiring signatures from elected officials in Parliament or other "elected" bodies that are, again, all controlled by the NDP, the law plainly places enormous obstacles in the path of prospective future opposition presidential candidates. Moreover, requiring opposition parties to have at least 3 percent of the seats in Parliament in order to run their own candidate in practice excludes all but the NDP. Provisions not terribly dissimilar exist in established democracies and are considered conventional. What makes them extraordinary in Egypt is that there is little doubt on the part of objective observers that these provisions are intended to thwart democratic development.

Widespread allegations of fraud and low voter turnout marred the presidential election in September 2005. Interference with the vote included vote buying, voter coercion, and the provision of premarked, pro-Mubarak ballots that facilitated access to the polls. Independent monitors, prosecutors (including one who bore personal witness to state party corrupt behavior), and the Judges' Syndicate all blew the whistle on government electoral misconduct.[4]

Participation in the process was very low: only 23 percent of 32 million registered voters cast their ballots.[5] Still, that 23 percent was larger than in previous presidential elections in the 1980s and 1990s, when turnout was estimated to be around 15 percent. Mubarak claimed his fifth six-year term, with 88.6 percent of the vote in a field of ten contenders. Ayman Nour of the al-Ghad Party finished second with 7.6 percent of the vote; Nu'man Gomaa, of al-Wafd, was third with approximately 2.7 percent.[6]

Nour had a particularly difficult time campaigning, as he was arrested on charges of forgery, held, released, and detained again, then subsequently tried and sentenced, all in 2005. Although the charge was widely understood as trumped up to discredit his candidacy, allegations hung over him throughout the presidential campaign as well as during the parliamentary election, in which he also ran. Nour was eventually convicted and sentenced to five years' imprisonment.

After previously denying domestic monitoring groups access to the polls, the Presidential Elections Commission (PEC) announced—on election day, and under considerable international pressure and domestic demand—that civil society observers would be permitted. Following the balloting, the Independent Committee for Electoral Monitoring (ICEM), a coalition of civil society organizations, enumerated key problems, including a lack of clear voting procedures and a division of responsibility between polling agents, monitors, and supervising judges.[7]

Law No. 40, as amended by Law No. 177 (2005), provides administrative guidance and establishes the Political Parties Affairs Committee (PPAC). The PPAC controls whether or not parties come into and stay in existence through its power to approve registration of parties and halt their activities once they are established. It prohibits the formation of parties based on racial, class, or religious affiliations. The PPAC is led by the chair of the Shura Council, the upper house of the Parliament, dominated by the NDP. With the state having near absolute control of parties' ability to function, Human Rights Watch observed that the PPAC "remains the president's and ruling party's primary lever for controlling Egypt's political landscape."[8]

Law No. 173 of 2005 created a Higher Elections Commission, chaired by the minister of justice, with a mandate that includes compiling candidate rosters, monitoring compliance with electoral ethics, and declaring election results. It also provided for a variety of penal sanctions for election crimes such as fraud and intimidation, although the high level of reported and documented fraud and intimidation, and the lack of state follow-up in terms of thorough investigations, indicates that Law No. 173 is poorly implemented and enforced.

Elections for the People's Assembly are governed in part by Law No. 175 (2005), which echoes the law on presidential elections and requires campaign compliance with the "commitment to maintain national unity and abstention from using religious slogans."[9] Moreover, the 2007 addition to Article 5 of the constitution has negative repercussions for religious and ethnic groups, stating that "no political activity shall be exercised or political parties shall be established on the basis of religion or on discrimination due to gender or race."[10] These laws are notably relevant for Islamist organizations, the Muslim Brotherhood in particular, which (because it is illegal) fields candidates as independents. An amendment to Article 62 permits changes to the electoral system, moving away from the current "candidate-centered system to a mixed one that depends mostly on party lists, leaving only a small, unspecified margin for independent seats."[11] This would disadvantage the Brotherhood, which has relied on the candidate-centered setup for running members as independents.

Egypt's three-round parliamentary elections (for the People's Assembly) began in November 2005 and concluded in December. The Parliamentary Election Commission set a candidate spending limit of 70,000 Egyptian pounds (US$12,150).[12] Approximately 26 percent of the electorate turned out to vote, and the results gave 311 seats to the ruling NDP, 112 to independent candidates (including 88 seats to Muslim Brotherhood members), 6 seats to the liberal Wafd Party, 2 seats to the leftist Al-Tagammu, and 1 seat to Ayman Nour's new Al-Ghad Party. The Muslim Brotherhood's 88 seats represented a five-fold increase over their previous tally of 17 seats.

For the first time since the late 1940s, the Muslim Brotherhood (although still illegal) effectively campaigned under its own name, with candidates openly promoting their affiliation and platform. It fielded 150 candidates in a third of Egypt's 222 constituencies (each of which has two seats, for a total of 444) in order to win their eighty-eight seats. Controversy was the hallmark of the election, which was, according to domestic and international monitoring groups, characterized by widespread fraud, mistreatment of voters and candidates by thugs and gangs (apparently protected, financed, or otherwise supported by the police and security forces), and the arrest of many Brotherhood members. Mahmoud Mekki, the deputy chief justice of Egypt's Cassation Court (the highest criminal appeals court), called the elections "a farce, in which judges acted as extras."[13]

In the aftermath of the 2005 elections—which left Mubarak in power and his party still dominant, but his image damaged internally and internationally—the president postponed local council elections, scheduled for April 2006. He said they would not occur for at least two years. Although the delay was purportedly to allow for constitutional decentralization, the move was understood to have a three-fold effect: first, to allow the NDP to maintain its stranglehold on power after being threatened by opposition gains in the 2005 parliamentary elections; second, to hinder the general influence of the Brotherhood; and finally, to prevent the Brotherhood from positioning to field a viable presidential candidate in 2011.

The 2007 constitutional referendum on Mubarak's proposed amendments, likewise, created serious grievances. Numerous independent commentators suggested the government hastened the pace of the vote to prevent the opposition from mounting a meaningful campaign, resulting in a boycott by opposition groups, including the Brotherhood and Kifaya. After the election, the Judges' Syndicate alleged widespread fraud and irregularities in the vote. The Egyptian Organization for Human Rights observed premarked ballot cards and mass voting via public busing of public employees, as well as bribes and other illegal inducements.[14] Official government turnout estimates were between 23 and 27 percent; however, others asserted it was less than 10 percent.[15] Amnesty International said the amendments represented the "most serious undermining of human rights safeguards in Egypt since the state of emergency was re-imposed in 1981."[16]

Egypt's executive branch is not accountable to the legislature, and NDP dominance of both houses effectively renders hollow any theoretical separation. Historically, the judicial branch enjoyed some independence from the legislative and executive branches. The courts issued rulings that resulted in executive branch changes; they overturned elections (as in 1987 and 1990); and in the late 1990s and early 2000s, courts deemed unconstitutional a number of laws passed by Parliament (supported by the executive), including harsh laws against a free press and free association ("NGO laws"). That degree of independence waned in the 2005 elections and their aftermath. Judicial scrutiny of those processes resulted in accusations of government fraud and misconduct, primarily in the executive branch. This, in turn, led to government retaliation in April 2006, as two senior judges were called before a disciplinary tribunal and threatened with dismissal. One judge was cleared, the other reprimanded.[17] Then, as part of the 2007 constitutional amendments, limitations on judicial oversight of elections were enshrined, explicitly eliminating their supervisory role and, in its place, creating an electoral committee. A leading Egyptian paper reported judges' belief that because the government's strong-arm tactics failed to dissuade them from criticizing the vote, the state decided to constitutionally limit their role.[18]

The civil service has long been a place where personal connections, *wasta*, can be useful but not necessarily determinative. In 2006, the United Nations Development Programme (UNDP) noted the need to address corruption so that good governance values could be fostered and the civil service could become an honorable professional calling, with decent pay and merit-based opportunities for advancement.[19] This is not a new criticism of the civil service: just a few years earlier, a regional expert observed that "nepotism and favoritism in public sector recruitment and promotion continues to stifle reform."[20]

Despite the government's authoritarian oversight and one-party hegemony, Egypt has a vibrant civil society, with more than 16,000 registered nongovernmental organizations (NGOs).[21] This vibrancy is held in check, however, by stringent government control, grounded in Law 32 of 1964, a restrictive law of associations allowing for state control of private organizations. The legal regime tightened further in 2002 with Law 84, which nominally replaced Law 32 but nevertheless maintained tremendous obstacles in the path of organizations, such as continued restrictions on foreign funding and maintenance of the state's unchecked power to dissolve any NGO the government sees as a threat. Human Rights Watch characterized this law as discouraging legitimate NGO activity.[22] Nonetheless, civil society reached new levels of activism during the 2005 election season. Indeed, after the elections, Saad Eddin Ibrahim, the respected human rights activist, said "the real winner is civil society" and added that a new generation of activists had been inspired to fight for change.[23]

While the Muslim Brotherhood is the dominant opposition group among both Islamist and secularist movements, Kifaya, meaning "enough," is the best known of the secular opposition groups. The organization emerged during the 2005 electoral season, forging coalitions and mobilizing diverse supporters. However, after the election, Kifaya reportedly suffered from growing pains as internal dissent developed relating to both the power of a minority of members within the group and tensions between some Islamist and secular members.

New groups have also organized; some share Kifaya's broad reform agenda, while others have their own specific goals. For example, Aziz Sedki, a former prime minister under Nasser, formed the National Coalition (or Rally) for Democratic Change, seeking to draft a new constitution. Reporters, meanwhile, formed their own group, Journalists for Change, to "lift the grip of the state and of its security services from public journals."[24]

Egypt's media has a long and rich history, even if its current status is much diminished. It remains diverse, as state-owned, semi-official, and opposition periodicals are distributed in daily, weekly, and monthly formats.

The constitution provides for press freedom and forbids censorship except during a state of emergency (which Mubarak has maintained since coming to power in 1981) or time of war, when limited censorship is permitted. Despite the constitutional guarantee, however, restrictive media laws are in place and an assortment of press offenses are criminalized. Press legislation passed in 2006 enumerated thirty-five media offences punishable by prison sentences, including imprisonment of up to five years for "publishing false news," defamation of domestic and international heads of state, and "undermining national institutions." Notably, defamation of civil servants was decriminalized, but fines were doubled.[25] The Journalists' Syndicate strongly opposed the new law, and in protest, many opposition and independent newspapers declined to print their Sunday editions and called for a boycott of state papers.

The government rhetorically supports freedom of the press while quashing it in practice through detentions, criminal charges, and media closures. High-visibility cases include Egypt's April 2006 arrest (and subsequent release) of Al-Jazeera's bureau chief for false reporting, and a separate attack against Al-Jazeera in which the state issued criminal charges against a producer for her work related to a documentary about torture. In May 2007, the producer was convicted of "harming Egypt's national interest" and "falsely depicting events" and sentenced to six months' imprisonment and a fine.[26] Other journalists cite physical harassment, while one described difficulty gaining access to a public demonstration despite the presentation of press credentials to security forces on the scene.[27]

Many of the state's agents are perceived to be acting within the bounds of domestic law (although in violation of international norms) or carrying out official orders, and thus escape criminal or other sanction. In cases of physical abuse and mistreatment of journalists, security forces rarely face repercussions. Some journalists also admit to a degree of self-censorship, toning down articles they would otherwise (i.e., if they did not have to pass each written word through a government censor) prefer to leave more critical of the government or its allies (internal or external). Internet freedom came under government attack in early 2007 as, for the first time, an Egyptian blogger was sentenced to prison for offenses related to public order, presidential insult, and incitement against Muslims.[28]

Recommendations

- In advance of the 2010 parliamentary elections and the prospective 2011 presidential elections, the government should revisit the recent constitutional amendment ending judicial supervision of elections and prepare for meaningful judicial monitoring, or otherwise ensure adequate domestic and international supervision of those elections.
- The government should allow all parties to field candidates for parliament and president, thus eliminating the need for the PPAC, which should be abolished.
- Direct presidential elections should be democratized through the elimination of the current candidate restrictions imposed by Law 174 (2005).
- Law 84 should be abolished, and the government should engage in a meaningful dialogue with civil society leaders and international rights organizations to develop a new Law of Associations.
- The government should fully decriminalize libel and slander as a step toward ensuring freedom of the press.

CIVIL LIBERTIES

PROTECTION FROM STATE TERROR, UNJUSTIFIED IMPRISONMENT, AND TORTURE:	1.14
GENDER EQUITY:	2.25
RIGHTS OF ETHNIC, RELIGIOUS, AND OTHER DISTINCT GROUPS:	2.75
FREEDOM OF CONSCIENCE AND BELIEF:	2.33
FREEDOM OF ASSOCIATION AND ASSEMBLY:	1.80
CATEGORY AVERAGE:	**2.06**

Incidents of torture by state agents are common in Egypt due to weak legal controls and rare repercussions.[29] Human Rights Watch in 2005 and Amnesty International in 2006 reported the routine use of torture, mistreatment of political prisoners and ordinary citizens, and custodial deaths.[30] The United Nations Special Rapporteur on Torture has a pending request for a country visit to Egypt to investigate conditions and allegations.

Several notorious incidents of torture and ill-treatment have occurred in recent years. In one, four Tunisians were detained in late 2006 in connection with an alleged terrorist cell organized to fight the U.S.-led occupation in Iraq. The Tunisians claimed beatings, electroshocks, blindfolding, sleep deprivation, and the forced viewing of the torture of their cellmates.[31] In another case, Mamdouh Habib, an Egyptian national, was picked up in Pakistan and moved to Egypt, where he was allegedly tortured with techniques including suspension from hooks on a wall, sleep deprivation with dousings of cold water, and shocks with an electric cattle prod, all before being transferred to the U.S. detention facility at Guantanamo Bay, Cuba.[32]

Perhaps the most widely publicized recent case of torture involves Imad Kabir, a bus driver who had an altercation with police and was taken into custody. During his detention, officers sodomized him with a broomstick. To make the incident even more degrading, they recorded the rape with a cell phone video camera, which they broadcast in his neighborhood as a warning. Two officers involved were later arrested and scheduled for trial in 2007. However, many observers and activists believe that the only reason these officers, unlike many others, face charges is that the case brought unwanted criticism of the government after the video was publicly circulated.

The 2007 amendments to Article 179 of the constitution effectively allow the government to bring key aspects of the state's repressive emergency laws, which are maintained in the name of counterterrorism, in line with the constitution. The new language strengthens the government's hand by precluding three other constitutional articles from hindering Egypt's domestic antiterrorism campaign: Article 44 (protection of home from unwarranted search), Article 45 (privacy and security of communications), and Article 41 (freedom from arbitrary arrest or detention).

Two distinct groups already bear the brunt of arbitrary arrests and detentions: the Muslim Brotherhood and suspected religious militants.[33] State targeting of the Brotherhood is widely perceived as an effort to undermine the legitimate political opposition, while efforts directed at suspected militants are part of the domestic "war on terrorism." During the 2005 election season, news headlines in Egypt and abroad were replete with incidents of arbitrary arrests and detentions of Brotherhood members. These sweeps each resulted in the incarceration of anywhere from a couple of dozen to 1,000 members. For example, in a runoff election in late November 2005, 1,000 supporters were detained prior to and during the conduct of the poll.[34] After the elections, things did not improve: between March and October 2006, nearly 800 Brothers were detained and held. In early 2007, again, hundreds of members were arrested and detained, forty of whom face military tribunals, with no recourse to civilian appeals courts.[35] Round-ups of suspected militants also take place in the wake of attacks or any time the government finds it politically expedient.

The prison conditions that greet these detainees are extremely poor; substandard and overcrowded facilities are the norm. Amnesty International noted in 2006 that a local source estimated 16,000–20,000 people were held in appalling conditions in administrative detention without sufficient medical attention.[36] International observers were not granted access to prisons.

What Egyptians frequently refer to as "different rights" between men and women are seen by many outside Egypt as basic gender inequalities; these persist in law and in practice despite relatively strong constitutional language. Article 8 of the constitution, for instance, provides that the state "shall guarantee equality of opportunity to all citizens," and other articles likewise affirm women's rights. In contrast, personal status laws are a historic source of disempowerment. Muslim women still cannot marry Christian men, and non-Muslim women marrying Muslim men are subject to Sharia (Islamic law). In terms of positive changes, Law No. 1/2000 established a woman's right to seek and obtain a divorce from a common-law marriage, and amendments to the Nationality Law provide for parental constitutional equality regarding children's nationality.[37] However, women's ability to seek divorce has been complicated by the requirement that they forgo all financial benefit, from return of dowry to alimony, if they choose to end the marriage.

Discrimination against women as victims of domestic violence is embedded in the penal code. Article 17 permits judicial discretion in sentencing and is used to reduce punishment in cases of honor killings. The inequality of marital standing is also enshrined in Article 277, which provides that a woman's adulterous acts are understood as such no matter where they occur, whereas a man's are adulterous only when committed in the marital home. A 2005 survey compiled alarming statistics, including the fact that nearly half of all married, divorced, or separated women reported being subjected to violence after age fifteen.[38]

Female genital cutting has been illegal since 1996, and the Court of Cassation upheld the ban in 1997. Statistics, however, reveal an unfortunate reality for young women in Egypt. The U.S. Agency for International Development reported positive change between 1995 and 2000, with the proportion of young women undergoing the procedure declining from 97 percent to 81 percent.[39] However, a 2006 survey showed the practice was nearly universal among reproductive-age women.[40]

Egypt prohibits trafficking in women through Law 10 (1961). The law targets prostitution but also addresses the movement of women across borders for indecent purposes. Sources including the Protection Project nevertheless maintain that Egypt is a source, transit, and destination country for the trafficking of women and children.[41]

Islam is the official religion of the state; the constitution explicitly affirms that "Islamic jurisprudence is the principal source of legislation."[42] Article 46, however, provides for freedom of religious belief and practice. Demographically, 98 percent of the citizenry is ethnically Egyptian; ethnic minorities—2 percent or less—include Berbers, Nubians, and Bedouins, as well as Greeks, Armenians, and other Europeans. In religious terms, 90 percent of Egyptians are thought to be Muslim, mostly Sunni, with the remaining 10 percent largely Christian.[43]

The most significant religious minority in Egypt is the Coptic Christian population, consistently estimated at around 9 percent; other Christians comprise 1 percent. Discrimination against Copts does exist, although it does not reflect a systematic plot by Muslims or the state. Intermittent violence against Copts does occur, generally without public accountability or legal repercussions. Copts also face discrimination in the public and private sectors in terms of employment and political representation.

Sunni Islam dominates social, cultural, and political life in Egypt. However, within both the Sunni community and other Muslim groups in Egypt, there are different approaches to religious practice. State discrimination arises from the attempted (and failed) enforcement of a one-size-fits-all concept of the faith, institutionalized in an executive order (and subsequent policies) aimed at forging a single, government-controlled Islamic voice. To this end, the government has tried to dictate that all mosques be licensed and all sermons monitored for content. Moreover, imams are appointed and paid by the government, although many private mosques continue to operate with their own religious leaders who are not loyal to the state.

In terms of ethnic discrimination, the Bedouin suffered through suspicion and maltreatment as the state engages in its domestic antiterrorism campaign. State security crackdowns on Bedouins have followed militant attacks as they are accused of either direct involvement or complicity. In July 2005, for example, thousands were arrested after the Sharm el-Sheikh bombings that killed eighty-eight people.[44]

The Egyptian constitution recognizes the right to assembly. However, in practice, security forces frequently crack down on opposition demonstrations, arresting participants, physically abusing them on site and while in custody. For example, in May 2005, female activists were attacked and sexually molested, and some incidents were caught on camera, as was widely reported in domestic and international media.[45]

Egyptian professionals, including lawyers, doctors, teachers, and other groups, are represented by syndicates that sometimes serve as unions and licensing entities. Article 56 of the constitution provides the right to form syndicates, with participation regulated under law. Despite this guarantee, the government has taken measures to control syndicates, especially through Law 100 of 1993. In late 2006, the *Daily Star* quoted an Egyptian expert, who noted that "the syndicate system has been dominated by the authoritarian state established by the 1952 regime. . . . The syndicates have been one form of control within the system."[46]

Generally, the right to form, join, and participate in trade union activity is restricted. Workers in Egypt may form unions, but in practice the state exerts significant influence through the General Federation of Egyptian Trade Unions (GFETU), which all unions must belong to and which is closely tied to the NDP. Nonetheless, unauthorized strikes have been increasing in recent years as workers react to perceived declines in job security associated with the privatization of state-owned enterprises.

Recommendations

- The government should acknowledge past instances of torture and renounce all future use in conjunction with investigation and prosecution of those who torture and mistreat detainees.
- The government of Egypt should suspend the Emergency Law and return to the 1971 constitution.
- The government must embrace international standards on prisoners' rights and allow for better public monitoring as well as the independent and impartial review of complaints.
- The government of Egypt should ensure freedom of belief, thought, conscience, and religion by comporting with international treaties to which it is a state party.
- The government should repeal discriminatory provisions in the family and penal laws to promote a single standard of divorce for men and women.
- The government should use the full weight of the law to prevent and to punish violence against girls and women, including the existing laws against female genital mutilation.

RULE OF LAW

INDEPENDENT JUDICIARY:	3.40
PRIMACY OF RULE OF LAW IN CIVIL AND CRIMINAL MATTERS:	2.17
ACCOUNTABILITY OF SECURITY FORCES AND MILITARY TO CIVILIAN AUTHORITIES:	1.00
PROTECTION OF PROPERTY RIGHTS:	4.33
EQUAL TREATMENT UNDER THE LAW:	2.33
CATEGORY AVERAGE:	**2.65**

Egypt has an internationally well-regarded and well-trained judiciary that is considered by some to be a regional model. Judicial independence is guaranteed in Articles 165 and 166 of the constitution but not always respected in practice.

In the past, judges in the regular court system were appointed for life by the president upon recommendation by the Higher Judicial Council (HJC), led by the president of the Court of Cassation (the court of maximum instance for criminal matters) and comprised of senior judges. A 2007 amendment to the constitution, however, cancels the HJC's authority and states "Every judicial body shall assume its own affairs. A council shall be formed to join the chiefs of the judicial bodies chaired by the President of the Republic to care for its common affairs. The law shall prescribe its formation, its competencies, and its rules of action." While this could be perceived as part of an effort to grant increased independence to the judiciary, in reality, it is more likely an attempt to further consolidate executive authority over the judiciary under the guise of positive constitutional change.

Despite these legal and administrative entanglements, the judiciary is at the forefront in efforts to promote democratization in Egypt, pushing for its own independence and the accountability of other branches. Even prior to the 2007 amendment, judicial appointments and executive oversight were a long-standing point of contention. For example, in August 2001, Mubarak appointed the chief justice and five judges to the Supreme Constitutional Court from the Ministry of Justice, in defiance of the court's tradition of self-selecting the chief justice from its own ranks. Dismissal from the bench may only occur with serious cause; however, in practice, this too is problematic, as illustrated by the previously mentioned case of the two judges threatened with dismissal for electoral criticism (see Accountability and Public Voice).

Moreover, the state does not always respect judicial orders. For example, a local judge's order to allow civil society monitors into the September 2005 presidential poll was ignored.[47] Additionally, President Mubarak has failed to honor civilian court orders to release certain Muslim Brotherhood detainees who are being held for military trials.

The Ministry of Justice has historically administered and financed the court system, further entrenching executive control. However, a new Judicial Authority Law passed in 2006 and drafted by the Ministry of Justice—notably without meaningful Judges' Syndicate consultation—provides for budgetary independence. The law, however, failed to address many other long-standing substantive concerns of the syndicate.[48]

To thwart opposition, legal or otherwise, Egypt has operated two types of state military or security courts. One, now legally defunct, is termed a "state security court." Its status changed after a law passed in the summer of 2003 legally transferred its responsibilities to other criminal courts. The other special court, the State Security Court–Emergency Section, is bound only by executive oversight and offers no subsequent impartial, civil judicial relief, although the military governor may affirm the verdict or order a retrial. Additionally, one of the March 2007 amendments allows the state to refer defendants to any judicial body authorized under law. The government can thus try, without judicial review, civil rights activists, democracy activists, Islamist opponents, and secular political opponents, as well as gay men and feminists.

Egypt has grossly failed to ensure the enforcement of basic civil and political rights guaranteed under law. However, if viewed from a strict legal perspective, their record can appear misleadingly admirable. The constitution provides the legal framework for the respect of civil and political rights in civil and criminal matters. Constitutionally, people are innocent until proven guilty (Article 67); they have the right to an attorney, even when it is beyond their means (Article 67); and they are considered equal before the law (Article 60). Egypt is also a state party to the International Covenant on Civil and Political Rights. All these rights, however, are effectively suspended under the state's emergency legislation, which in April 2006 Mubarak announced would remain in effect for yet another two years.

Prosecutors, as agents of the authoritarian state, lack independence from the government, including its security forces. Prosecution of public officials and ruling party actors for corruption and other abuses of power is selective, depending on the Mubarak regime's need to eliminate and punish internal opponents by removing them publicly from their positions.

The state's security services evince a distinct lack of respect for civil and political rights. Violations of human rights include the documented use of arbitrary detention, harassment and ill-treatment of attendees at public rallies, and torture of those in custody. Accountability for human rights violations is rare but does sometimes occur in instances such as the widely publicized video of the individual sodomized while in custody (see Civil Liberties).

Egypt is not a military dictatorship per se; however, Nasser, Sadat, and Mubarak secured their power through the military. Power also derives from the secret police apparatus (*Amn al-Dawla*), the intelligence services (*mukhabarat*), and the NDP. There is no effective, democratic, civil control of the police or military; both are powers unto themselves, and the military is the dominant power of the state. Indeed, the military's budget is not subject to meaningful parliamentary oversight, and the public lacks awareness about the extent of its economic power.[49] This absence of civic accountability is critical because the military owns, runs, and profits from a significant portion of the economy, from agriculture to manufacturing to certain tourism services.

The Mubarak regime and the military and security services enjoy a relationship of mutual, if presidentially directed, dependence, with the president directing security force action within the state as necessary. There is, however, little evidence that the military or security forces take independent initiative to a degree that would threaten either the president's or the NDP's firm hold on power.

Government respect for property rights has made strides forward in recent years; however, access to and ownership of property remains unevenly divided among various socioeconomic strata. Personal property rights, especially in housing, are lacking, as many live in dwellings without official title; indeed, the Ministry of Finance estimates that more than 80 percent of residences are unregistered.[50] Beyond the basic rights issues, this puts both private citizens and the state at an economic disadvantage, as property cannot be used as collateral for further investment. The government has made progress in its willingness to promote (although as yet with minimal success) property ownership: in 2001, Law 148, the Home Mortgage Law, created an important vehicle for the purchase of private homes. Even with the option of a private mortgage, however, the initial down payment remains beyond the means of most people. Between the time of the law's implementation (2001) and 2005, only sixteen mortgages were awarded.[51] New laws regarding a flat property tax and reduction of bureaucracy in construction were on the 2007 legislative agenda.

Those who can afford legal property and a building permit face tremendous bureaucratic hurdles. In 2007, the World Bank found that property registration required seven procedures and took 193 days, at a cost of 5.9 percent of the property value. Contract enforcement was also cumbersome, requiring fifty-five procedures and more than 1,000 days, at a cost of 18.4 percent of the debt at issue.[52]

Recommendations
- Full judicial independence—from financing to appointments to dismissals—should be guaranteed in law and practice.
- The emergency court system should be fully and publicly disbanded.
- The military court system should be used only for military cases.
- The military's budget should go before the Parliament for public debate.
- The state should work to ensure people's property ownership through facilitating property registration, without penalty for noncompliance.

ANTICORRUPTION AND TRANSPARENCY

ENVIRONMENT TO PROTECT AGAINST CORRUPTION:	1.60
EXISTENCE OF LAWS AND ETHICAL STANDARDS BETWEEN PRIVATE AND PUBLIC SECTORS:	1.25
ENFORCEMENT OF ANTICORRUPTION LAWS:	1.75
GOVERNMENTAL TRANSPARENCY:	2.29
CATEGORY AVERAGE:	**1.72**

Corruption is endemic in Egypt. In the summer of 2006, Kifaya produced a scathing report, more than 200 pages in length, detailing the problems and consequences of corruption.[53] In 2006 Egypt ranked 70th out of 163 countries surveyed in Transparency International's Corruption Perceptions Index, scoring just 3.3 out of a possible 10 points.[54] Egyptian bureaucracy is entangled in red tape, providing opportunities for bribery and other corrupt behavior. The U.S. Department of Commerce found that this overregulation impedes commerce, as there is too much bureaucracy and arbitrariness and too many delays.[55] Additionally, the intervention of senior government officials is perceived as necessary to accomplish critical tasks.

Asset disclosure, a key weapon in combating bribery, is required by law at all levels of government. Judicial disclosure of assets is also specified by law; however, compliance and enforcement difficulties have been reported.[56] Moreover, public access to government officials' records is limited.[57]

Egypt's Code of Corporate Governance requires that companies have written rules on preventing conflicts of interest and procedures for internal and external audits, and stipulates criteria for the composition and disclosure of remuneration of the board of directors.[58] Egypt ratified the UN Convention against Corruption in 2005. Like most Arab countries, however, Egypt has not ratified the Organization for Economic Cooperation and Development's (OECD) Anti-Bribery Convention, and it has neither signed nor ratified the African Union's Convention on the Prevention and Combating of Corruption. Active and passive bribery are criminalized in the penal code and can result in fines and imprisonment. Protections for whistle-blowers, however, are deficient.[59] Egypt's anticorruption campaign, initiated in 2002, is government controlled, lacking substantive input from civil society groups.

Egypt's bureaucratic structure, if properly empowered, could promote transparency and fight corruption. A central auditing agency is legally authorized to monitor fiscal transparency, among other issues, and reports to parliament; however, it lacks implementing power for its recommendations.[60] The Administrative Control Authority is Egypt's anticorruption watchdog, but it lacks jurisdiction to investigate accusations of corruption against certain categories of state employees.

President Mubarak's government has garnered headlines for implementing so-called reforms, and some government officials have been investigated for corrupt behavior. For example, in February 2006, an Egyptian ferry sank in the Red Sea, taking with it the lives of 1,000 (of the 1,400) passengers. In the wake of poor government handling of the disaster and its aftermath, allegations of corruption surfaced in relation to the ferry company, Salam Maritime, and its owner, Mamdouh Ismail, a member of the Shura Council and close associate of Mubarak's chief of staff. The People's Assembly transportation committee was charged with investigating the disaster and the chair said "carelessness, indifference and corruption [were] the main culprits."[61] One year later, in February 2007, another significant corruption scandal emerged as fifty Ministry of Health officials were ordered to stay in-country until an investigation could be completed regarding their role in allowing the delivery of tainted blood to hospitals.[62]

Many analysts believe corruption charges are sometimes used selectively to create the political space necessary to ensure a smooth succession of power to Mubarak's son Gamal. These efforts serve a dual purpose: first, they are an exercise in political weeding—eliminating significant opposition to the dynastic succession—and second, they are a limited attempt at appeasing domestic and international audiences concerned about state accountability. Gamal currently serves as the assistant secretary-general of the NDP and heads the key policy-making committee within the party.

Regarding transparency and public scrutiny, there is a distinct lack of public access to information. In terms of budget transparency, in 2006, the International Monetary Fund (IMF) said further progress was needed but lauded the government's efforts to carry out reforms in terms of increased transparency and efficiency.[63] The former Article 115 stated that the People's Assembly could not effect any modification in the draft budget. However, as part of the package of constitutional amendments of March 2007, greater parliamentary scrutiny of the budget is envisaged, including the ability to amend expenditures. There are government procurement laws and some protections for bidders; concerns, however, exist about procedural transparency.[64] Even higher education is not immune from corrupt practices. Hundreds, and frequently thousands, of students are packed into auditoriums in a lecture format. To get the attention of the professor, and to get good grades, all too often students must approach the lecturer for "private lessons"; these may legitimately take place, but more often result in the exchange of money for a good grade, without the professor actually meeting the student outside of class.

The international donor community, led by the United States and European Union, struggles to ensure that its aid to Egypt is administered legally and distributed fairly. The United States congressional oversight and Government Accountability Office (GAO) audits have highlighted Egypt's inability to absorb the billions of dollars it receives annually, especially in economic assistance (military aid is absorbed much more readily). The United States' aid to Egypt (over US$60 billion from 1979 to 2007) has been deemed a political handout, an encourage- ment and reward for Egypt's maintenance of peace with Israel, and an incentive to maintain a strategic partnership with the United States and support its policies in the Middle East. There are few, if any, American governmental reports (GAO, congressional, or otherwise) that suggest Egypt's administration and distribution of aid is a source of corruption. Still, media reports frequently question the size as well as the sources of Mubarak's enormous personal wealth—that is, whether it is a direct result of the scores of billions of dollars in aid Egypt has received during his rule.[65]

Recommendations

- The government should accept NGOs and the press as partners in the campaign against corruption by engaging in an open and ongoing dialogue at the national and local levels.
- The government should champion public administration reform, streamlining processes such as business and property registration, which currently suffer from bureaucratic delays and offer opportuni- ties for corrupt practices.
- The government should redouble its campaign against corruption and look to independent judicial reformists to head up the effort through public education, criminal investigations, and prosecutions.
- The government should enable its corruption watchdog agencies to operate independently from the executive.

NOTES

[1] Essam El-Din, "NDP Reacts Coolly to Boycott Call," *Al-Ahram Weekly Online*, 19–25 May 2005, http://weekly.ahram.org.eg/2005/743/fr2.htm.

2 See Egyptian State Information Service (SIS), "Political Reform in Egypt," SIS, http://constitution.sis.gov.eg/en/4.htm.

3 Constitution of the Arab Republic of Egypt, Article 76.

4 "Not Yet a Democracy; Egypt's Election," *Economist*, 10 December 2005.

5 "Landslide Win for Egyptian Leader," BBC News, 9 September 2005, http://news.bbc.co.uk/2/hi/middle_east/4231338.stm.

6 Mona El-Nahhas, "Ghad's Bigger Battles," *Al-Ahram Weekly*, 15–21 September 2005, http://weekly.ahram.org.eg/2005/760/eg7.htm.

7 Independent Committee for Election Monitoring, *Preliminary Report on Election Day Voting and Counting Process* (Cairo: Ibn Khaldun Center for Development Studies, 8 September 2005), http://www.eicds.org/english/activities/news/preliminaryreport05.htm.

8 Human Rights Watch (HRW), *Monopolizing Power—Egypt's Political Parties Law* (New York: HRW, January 2007), http://hrw.org/backgrounder/mena/egypt0107/2.htm#_ftn5.

9 Law No. 175 of 2005 on the People's Assembly, http://www.sis.gov.eg/En/Politics/Parliamentary/laws/041306000000000003.htm.

10 Constitution of the Arab Republic of Egypt, Article 5, as amended.

11 Amr Hamzawy, "Where Machiavelli Errs," *Al-Ahram Weekly*, 5–11 April 2007, http://weekly.ahram.org.eg/2007/839/op55.htm.

12 "Guide to Egypt's Election," BBC News, 8 November 2005, http://news.bbc.co.uk/2/hi/middle_east/4417150.stm.

13 "Egypt: Parliamentary Runoffs Marred by Reports of Violations," IRIN, 17 November 2005, http://www.irinnews.org/report.asp?ReportID=50191&SelectRegion=Middle_East&SelectCountry=EGYPT.

14 Egyptian Organization for Human Rights (EOHR), "Results of the Monitoring of the Public Referendum over the Constitutional Amendments," news release, 26 March 2007, http://www.eohr.org/press/2007/pr0326-2.shtml.

15 Mona Salem, "Few Egyptians Vote in Controversial Referendum," Agence France-Presse, 26 March 2007.

16 Amnesty International (AI), "Egypt: Proposed Constitutional Amendments Greatest Erosion of Human Rights in 26 Years," news release, 18 March 2007, http://www.amnestyusa.org/document.php?lang=e&id=ENGMDE120082007.

17 AI, "Egypt: Violent Attacks and Arrests of Peaceful Protesters Must Stop," news release, 23 May 2006, http://www.amnestyusa.org/document.php?lang=e&id=ENGMDE120102006.

18 Mona El-Nahhas, "Judges Call for Monitors," *Al-Ahram Weekly*, 25 January 2007.

19 United Nations Development Programme (UNDP), "Egypt Human Development Report 2005 Launched Under the Title 'Choosing Our Future: Towards a New Social Contract,'" news release, 12 February 2006, http://www.undp.org.eg/news/press/NHDR2005.htm.

20 Samir Radwan, "Towards a Coherent Employment Strategy," *Al-Ahram Weekly*, 14–20 October 2004, http://weekly.ahram.org.eg/2004/712/ec2.htm.

21 Kareem Elbayar, "NGO Laws in Selected Arab States," *International Journal of Not-for-Profit Law* (September 2005), http://www.icnl.org/knowledge/ijnl/vol7iss4/special_1.htm.

22 HRW, *World Report 2007* (New York: HRW, January 2007), http://hrw.org/wr2k7/pdfs/egypt.pdf.

23 "Egypt: Focus on Presidential Elections," IRIN, 12 September 2005, http://www.irinnews.org/Report.aspx?ReportId=25468.

24 Mona Salem, "Reformist Groups Mushroom in Egypt," *Middle East Online*, 6 June 2005, http://www.middle-east-online.com/english/?id=13687.

25 Reporters Sans Frontieres (RSF), *Annual Report 2007* (Paris: RSF, 2007), http://www.rsf.org/country-43.php3?id_mot=152&Valider=OK.

26 Committee to Protect Journalists (CPJ), "Cairo Court Sentences Al-Jazeera Producer to Six Months in Jail," news release, 2 May 2007, http://www.cpj.org/news/2007/mideast/egypt02may07na.html.

27 RSF, *Annual Report 2007*.

28 HRW, "Egypt: Blogger's Imprisonment Sets Chilling Precedent," news release, 22 February 2007, http://hrw.org/english/docs/2007/02/22/egypt15379.htm.

29 Egyptian Organization for Human Rights, *Torture in Egypt: An Unchecked Phenomenon* (Cairo: Egyptian Organization for Human Rights, 2004), http://www.eohr.org/report/2004/re4.htm.

30 HRW, *World Report 2007*; AI, Report 2006 (New York: AI, 2006), http://web.amnesty.org/report2006/egy-summary-eng#6.

31 AI, "Urgent Action: Egypt—Forcible Return/Torture/Fear of Further Torture," news release, 5 January 2007, http://www.amnestyusa.org/actioncenter/actions/action7869.pdf.

32 See Dana Priest and Dan Eggen, "Terror Suspect Alleges Torture," *Washington Post*, 6 January 2005, http://www.washingtonpost.com/wp-dyn/articles/A51726-2005Jan5.html.

33 This is not meant to imply that militants in Egypt constitute a cohesive group like the Brotherhood.

34 William Wallis, "Opposition Hit by Crackdown in Egypt's Election," *Financial Times* (London), 29 November 2005.

35 Heba Saleh, "Egypt Cracks Down on Illegal Muslim Group," *Financial Times*, 7 February 2007, http://www.ft.com/cms/s/3077672a-b6e7-11db-8bc2-0000779e2340.html.

36 AI, "EU-Egypt Association Council Meeting" (briefing paper, AI European Union Office, Brussels, 13 June 2006), http://www.amnesty-eu.org/static/documents/2006/EU_Egypt_Association_Council_briefing_paper_2006.pdf.

37 SIS, "Boosting Women's Status in Egypt," SIS, 2005, http://www.sis.gov.eg/En/Women/empowerment/100500000000000001.htm.

38 Fatma El-Zanaty and Ann Way, *Egypt Demographic and Health Survey 2005* (Cairo: Ministry of Health and Population, National Population Council, El-Zanaty and Associates, and ORC Macro, 2006), http://www.measuredhs.com/pubs/pdf/FR176/17Chapter17.pdf.

39 U.S. Agency for International Development (USAID), "Empowering Women by Changing Attitudes," USAID, http://www.usaid.gov/stories/egypt/fp_egypt_female.html.

40 El-Zanaty and Way, *Egypt Demographic and Health Survey 2005*.

41 Protection Project, *Egypt* (Washington, DC: Protection Project, 2005), http://www.protectionproject.org/egypt.doc.

42 Constitution of the Arab Republic of Egypt, Article 2.

43 U.S. Central Intelligence Agency (CIA), *World Factbook 2007* (Washington, D.C.: CIA, 2007), http://www.cia.gov/cia/publications/factbook/geos/eg.html.

44 Harry De Quetteville, "Suspicion Over Egypt Bombings Falls on Bedouin," *Daily Telegraph* (London), 31 July 2005, http://www.telegraph.co.uk/news/main.jhtml?xml=/news/2005/07/31/wegypt31.xml&sSheet=/?news/2005/07/31/ixnewstop.html.

45 Michael Slackman, "Assault on Women at Protest Stirs Anger, Not Fear, in Egypt," *New York Times*, 10 June 2005.

46 Liam Stack, "Experts Fear Fraud in Upcoming Election," *Daily Star* (Egypt), 3 November 2006, http://www.dailystaregypt.com/article.aspx?ArticleID=3768. Stack quoting Nabil Adel Fattah, the deputy director of Al-Ahram Center for Political and Strategic Studies.

47 Charles Levinson, "Who'll Watch Egypt's Historic Vote?" *Christian Science Monitor*, 6 September 2006, http://www.csmonitor.com/2005/0906/p04s01-wome.html.

48 Amira Howeidy, "The Battle Is Not Over," *Al-Ahram* (Cairo), 29 June–5 July 2006, http://weekly.ahram.org.eg/2006/801/fr2.htm.

49 The CIA's World Factbook estimated it at US$2.44 billion for 2002.

50 Ahmed A. Namatalla, "Ministry of Finance to Present New Property Tax Law to Parliament in January," *Daily Star*, 2 January 2007, http://www.dailystaregypt.com/article.aspx?ArticleID=4741.

51 Overseas Private Investment Corporation (OPIC), *Egypt: Overview of the Housing Sector* (Washington, D.C.: OPIC, July 2005), http://www.opic.gov/pdf/Issues_Egypt HousingOverview_July05.pdf.

52 World Bank, "Doing Business—Explore Economies—Egypt," World Bank International Finance Corporation, 2007, http://www.doingbusiness.org/ExploreEconomies/Default.aspx?economyid=61. Data listed for 2006.

53 See Kifaya, *Corruption in Egypt: The Black Cloud is Not Disappearing* (Cairo: Kifaya, July 2006), http://www.ikhwanweb.net/images/Kefayafasad.doc.

54 Transparency International (TI), *Corruption Perceptions Index 2006* (Berlin: TI, 2006), http://www.transparency.org/policy_research/surveys_indices/cpi/2006.

55 U.S. Department of Commerce, *Doing Business in Egypt: A Country Commercial Guide for U.S. Companies* (Washington, D.C.: U.S. Department of Commerce, Commercial Service, 2007), http://www.buyusa.gov/egypt/en/ccg01.html.

56 Outline Report of the State of the Judiciary in Egypt (Beirut and Washington, D.C.: Arab Center for the Development of the Rule of Law and Integrity and the International Foundation for Election Systems, January 2004), http://www.arabruleoflaw.org/Files/128085836818735000_BriefOutline--StateoftheJudiciaryReportforEgypt.pdf.

57 Global Integrity, "2006 Country Reports: Egypt," Global Integrity, http://www.global integrity.org/reports/2006/EGYPT/scorecard.cfm?subcategoryID=51&countryID=9.

58 Cairo and Alexandria Stock Exchanges (CASE), "Egypt Code of Corporate Governance," CASE, August 2005, http://www.egyptse.com/index.asp?CurPage=rules_regulations.html.

59 Global Integrity, "2006 Country Reports: Egypt," http://www.globalintegrity.org/reports/2006/EGYPT/scorecard.cfm?subcategoryID=56&countryID=9.

60 UNDP Programme on Governance in the Arab Region (POGAR), "Financial Transparency—Egypt," POGAR, http://www.pogar.org/countries/finances.asp?cid=5.

61 Gamal Essam El-Din, "Corruption of All Sorts," *Al-Ahram*, 16–22 February 2006, http://weekly.ahram.org.eg/2006/782/eg4.htm.

62 "Egypt Bans 50 Health Officials from Travel over Corruption Probe," BBC Monitoring International Reports, 25 February 2007.

63 International Monetary Fund (IMF), *Arab Republic of Egypt: 2006 Article IV Consultation—Staff Report* (Washington, D.C.: IMF, July 2006), http://www.imf.org/external/pubs/ft/scr/2006/cr06253.pdf.

64 Office of the U.S. Trade Representative, *2006 National Trade Estimate Report on Foreign Trade Barriers* (Washington, D.C.: U.S. Trade Representative, March 2006), http://www.ustr.gov/Document_Library/Reports_Publications/2006/2006_NTE_Report/Section_Index.html.

65 The speculation has been rife for more than a decade. See, for example, Mamoun Fandy, "Egypt Sliding into Crisis," *Christian Science Monitor*, 30 July 1993, 18.

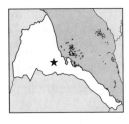

ERITREA

CAPITAL: Asmara
POPULATION: 4.9 million
GNI PER CAPITA: $200

SCORES	2005	2007
ACCOUNTABILITY AND PUBLIC VOICE:	0.67	0.44
CIVIL LIBERTIES:	1.54	0.95
RULE OF LAW:	1.03	0.71
ANTICORRUPTION AND TRANSPARENCY:	1.71	0.86

(scores are based on a scale of 0 to 7, with 0 representing weakest and 7 representing strongest performance)

Dan Connell

INTRODUCTION

Eritrea showed considerable promise upon winning its de facto independence in May 1991 after a thirty-year war against successive U.S.- and Soviet-backed Ethiopian governments that had laid claim to the former Italian colony. Eritrea formalized its status as Africa's newest nation in a near unanimous vote for sovereignty (99.8 percent) in a UN-monitored referendum in which 98.5 percent of the 1,125,000 registered voters participated.[1] Over the next three years, the transitional government established new state institutions—executive, legislative, and judicial branches presiding over a three-tiered administration (national, regional, local); a streamlined civil service; professional armed forces; and new police and security forces, while also managing a highly participatory constitution-making process.

However, the leadership of the independence movement was deeply divided in its commitment to democratic governance. Regime hardliners, who got the upper hand during a series of regional conflicts capped in 1998–2000 by a bloody border war with Ethiopia, plunged

---

Dan Connell, the author of six books and numerous articles on Eritrea, teaches journalism and African politics at Simmons College in Boston.

the new country into a cycle of military mobilization and political repression that stymied the country's development prospects and reversed progress toward democracy. This situation worsened in 2006 with an increase in politically motivated arrests, torture and deaths of political prisoners, persecution of religious minorities, and tightened restrictions on nongovernmental organizations (NGOs) and aid agencies.

The victorious Eritrean People's Liberation Front (EPLF)—renamed the People's Front for Democracy and Justice (PFDJ) in 1994—today rules with an iron fist under the leadership of former military commander, now president, Isaias Afwerki. The constitution, ratified in 1997, has yet to be implemented; national elections, repeatedly postponed, have yet to be held. Meanwhile, other political parties and independent NGOs are prohibited, and what few private media emerged in the immediate post-independence years have been shut down. Thousands of people have been detained for political offenses ranging from public dissent to noncompliance with open-ended national service requirements. Among the more prominent political prisoners are eleven former independence movement leaders and government ministers—dubbed the Group of 15—jailed in September 2001 after publicly criticizing the president's undemocratic practices. Detainees also include journalists, mid-level officials, merchants, businessmen, young people resisting conscription, and church leaders and parishioners associated with banned religious organizations.

Eritrea is a nation in a perpetual state of emergency, under siege by its own leaders, with a population denied the most basic freedoms of speech, assembly, press, and religious practice. The continuing confrontation with Ethiopia not only dominates the political discourse to the point where all dissent is branded as treason, it also provides cover for militarizing the new state from top to bottom and for exporting instability to neighboring states—among them Sudan and Somalia—in an effort to weaken Ethiopia. The unresolved border conflict serves as justification for President Isaias to maintain a near-total monopoly on all forms of domestic political and economic power. The absence of any independent media and the complete suppression of civil society preclude the development of a legal opposition within the country—or of any organized public discussion of what such an opposition might look like, were it to be permitted. The ruling party itself is largely a shell through which the president exercises one-man rule that he shows no sign of relinquishing voluntarily. Under these conditions, national elections, when eventually conducted, will only serve to confirm the current dictatorship.

ACCOUNTABILITY AND PUBLIC VOICE

FREE AND FAIR ELECTORAL LAWS AND ELECTIONS:	0.00
EFFECTIVE AND ACCOUNTABLE GOVERNMENT:	1.25
CIVIC ENGAGEMENT AND CIVIC MONITORING:	0.00
MEDIA INDEPENDENCE AND FREEDOM OF EXPRESSION:	0.50
CATEGORY AVERAGE:	**0.44**

The EPLF's political culture has long been predicated on secrecy and the exercise of absolute power, often by violent means. Throughout the 1970s and 1980s, the EPLF was led by the clandestine Eritrean People's Revolutionary Party (EPRP), a group chaired by Isaias and strongly influenced by Maoist political currents. Founded in secret in 1971, the EPRP defined the EPLF from its earliest days. It ran a cadre school that trained organizers who convened thrice-weekly political education sessions for all EPLF members. It secretly met to draft the EPLF's program prior to its congresses and to select slates for leadership before elections. Its central committee doubled as the EPLF's political bureau, positioning the party to run the Front on a day-to-day basis. Disobedient party members were punished mercilessly and then suddenly rehabilitated; this replicated the practice in China, where Isaias received military and political training at the height of the Cultural Revolution in 1968–1969. Dissidents were imprisoned for long periods or, in some cases, summarily executed.

Although the EPRP was frozen in 1989 and officially disbanded in February 1994, this secretive pattern of rule remained during the construction of the state in the 1990s, and it continues today. The EPLF established a provisional National Assembly in 1992 by adding seventy-five delegates chosen in party-run regional elections to its own seventy-five-member Central Council. This body confirmed Commander Isaias as the acting president in an uncontested ballot that was closed to the media and the public, as are all National Assembly meetings. President Isaias then personally selected cabinet ministers, regional governors, upper-echelon judges, an auditor-general, the governor of the national bank, new ambassadors, top military commanders, and many mid-level officials and civil authorities. Today, he presides over all meetings of both the party's Central Council and the National Assembly and has the exclusive power to call either body into session.

Although the new government initially appeared to establish a separation of powers—an executive office with a cabinet of ministers, an interim parliament, and a nominally independent judiciary—it was largely an illusion. The cabinet did not provide a forum for debate or decision making. Instead, it served as a clearinghouse for determining how to implement the policies of the president's inner circle. Even the military remained under the president's personal control, as Isaias leapfrogged his own defense ministry to exercise direct command through five zonal commanders, most of whom he brought with him from the clandestine EPRP.

Eritrea's constitution, ratified by a 527-member constituent assembly on May 23, 1997, guarantees citizens "broad and active participation in all political, economic, social and cultural life of the country," but it also says that these rights can be limited "in the interests of national security, public safety or the economic well-being of the country, health or morals, for the prevention of public disorder or crime or for the protection of rights and freedoms of others."[2] Government officials have said the constitution will go into effect once national elections are conducted, but such elections, first scheduled for 1998 and delayed by the outbreak of war, rescheduled for 2001 and then delayed again by the political crisis that engulfed the ruling party, have yet to be set.

Over the past decade and a half, Eritrea has conducted regional and local elections with balloting open to men and women of all religious and ethnic backgrounds, but no forms of new political organization, such as independent parties or caucuses within the PFDJ, have been permitted. All voting for local public office has been conducted in town meeting–style sessions presided over by PFDJ cadres. Campaigns are not permitted, as there are no legal organizations to put them together, apart from those run by the government. Individuals are not allowed to set up organized political operations during PFDJ-run elections. Public discussion prior to elections is centered on the character of the candidates and their loyalty to the ruling party. There is no debate over policy options or initiatives in public forums and no outlet for new proposals or critiques of existing policies. New programmatic initiatives or policies can appear only if prepared by party functionaries and vetted by the president's office before being made public. During Eritrea's first post-independence decade, the only exchanges over political issues among the country's new leaders took place behind closed doors at party-run seminars or leadership meetings. However, since 2001, when such exchanges spilled into public view, all dissenters were imprisoned and even these backroom debates have been squelched.

As there are no legal parties in Eritrea apart from the PFDJ, and as there have been no national elections of any kind, no rotation of power has been or is likely to be possible. A special parliamentary commission in 2001 drafted a party law that legalized multiple parties and laid the groundwork for national elections, but the president refused to implement it and placed the commission chair, former minister of local government Mahmud Sherifo, in prison.

All opposition groups—of which there are many—are based outside Eritrea and are unable to operate openly within the country. Though these opposition groups have little visible influence within Eritrea, their polemics are avidly followed by many urban dwellers via the internet, and several, especially those deriving from splits in the ruling PFDJ, maintain clandestine lines of communication with members of the state bureaucracy and the military. Nonparty critics of the regime organized in a network of civil society organizations post frequent bulletins about human rights abuses, often within hours of their occurrence, thereby demonstrating extensive links with contacts on the ground. There are signs that such groups are beginning to influence members of the diaspora to diminish their financial contributions to the government—contributions that have until now been the regime's primary source of foreign exchange.

Over four decades of chronic turmoil in the country's original independence movement, the Eritrean Liberation Front (ELF) produced numerous splinters, ranging from the ruling EPLF/PFDJ, which broke off in 1970, to the Sudan-based Eritrean Islamic Jihad, which formed in the 1980s. In 2005, a coalition of more than a dozen externally based factions grouped themselves together as the Eritrean Democratic Alliance (EDA) to oppose the PFDJ-controlled government. Most maintain military bases or offices in neighboring Ethiopia or Sudan and seek to oust the Isaias regime by extralegal means. Member organizations, winnowed to eleven by February 2007, when the coalition split into two blocs, included the ELF (the largest of the former ELF factions, led by Adbella Idris); the ELF-Revolutionary Council; the Eritrean National Salvation Front (ENSF); the Eritrean Democratic Party (EDP, led by EPLF founder and G-15 member Mesfun Hagos); two Islamic factions; and several smaller groups organized around regional interests. The ELF-RC, the EDP, and the ENSF form a secular nationalist bloc, while the others, led by the ELF, tend to represent regional, religious, and ethnic constituencies.[3] Nearly all the groups claim to support democracy and human rights; their organizational practices, however, do not reflect these ideals. In addition, the governments of the states in which these factional groups operate have maintained strict control over their operations, sharply limiting their ability to implement democratic reforms among refugee populations within their borders. Tensions among opposition groups tend to reflect rivalries among their leaders and legacies of conflict in the field, as well as differences over such issues as land policy, language, the role of religion in politics, and whether to reorganize the state through some form of ethnic or regional federalism.

The civil service in Eritrea, initially based on a mix of merit and political loyalty, has become increasingly dysfunctional as experienced personnel have fled the country, to be replaced by unskilled national service conscripts, many of whom are subject to political manipulation and engage in petty corruption. There are no published guidelines, no legal recourse in the event of dismissal, and no transparent competitive process for securing civil service positions or gaining advancement. Ministerial portfolios are frequently shuffled to keep rivals from developing power bases of their own. High-ranking officers and government officials who question the president's judgment over minor issues often find themselves subjected to the Maoist Chinese practice of *midiskal* (freezing) in which they are removed from their posts and kept on salary but not permitted to work, then abruptly brought back into the fold when they are perceived to be "rehabilitated."

Eritrea has not permitted the formation of politically oriented civil society groups, think tanks, policy organizations, or other independent NGOs. The only indigenous NGO recognized by the government that is not directly under PFDJ control is the Citizens for Peace in

Eritrea, which focuses solely on peacebuilding with Ethiopia. International NGOs have seen their work strictly limited to the provision of relief under government supervision. In fact, international groups are not permitted to establish local chapters in Eritrea, and global human rights organizations have been blocked from carrying out local investigations.[4]

The only media in Eritrea today are those controlled by the state or the ruling party: EriTV, which began broadcasting in Asmara in 1993; Dimtsi Hafash (Voice of the Masses radio), which broadcasts in six languages with a transmission power of 1,000 kilowatts; three newspapers, all of which carry roughly the same information and opinion, one published in Tigrinya (*Hadas Eritrea*), one in Arabic (*Eritrea al-Hadisa*), and one in English (*Eritrea Profile*); a government-run press service, the Eritrean News Service (EriNA); several small publications and radio programs run by party-controlled social organizations (women, workers, youth); and a party-controlled website, Shaebia.org. The Ministry of Information, headed by Ali Abdu Ahmed, uses the media to propagandize without permitting opposing views to be published or broadcast.

A 1996 Press Law guaranteed the freedom of the press but prohibited, among other things, the dissemination of material that "promotes the spirit of division and dissension among the people" or that contains "inaccurate information or news intentionally disseminated to influence economic conditions, create commotion and confusion and disturb the general peace."[5] These vague proscriptions afforded the state broad discretion to harass the country's new private newspapers after they began publishing critiques of the president and the conflict with Ethiopia in 2000 and early 2001, and to shut down the private press altogether in September 2001. The law also banned foreign funding of indigenous press, the contravention of which was the government's unofficial rationale for the press closures.

The Committee to Protect Journalists termed Eritrea "one of the world's worst jailers of journalists" in 2006, while Reporters Without Borders rated Eritrea 166 out of 168 countries in its 2006 Worldwide Press Freedom Index, ahead only of Turkmenistan and North Korea.[6] Amnesty International reported that fourteen journalists remained in prison at secret locations without charge at the end of 2006 and that at least one of them—Fessehaye Yohannes, the former editor of Eritrea's largest-circulation daily, *Setit*—had probably died in prison.[7] An unconfirmed report first posted on an Ethiopian website and termed credible by Amnesty International and Reporters Without Borders, among other watchdog organizations, claimed that three journalists held under harsh conditions at the E'era-E'ero Prison in the coastal desert lowlands, along with other prominent political prisoners, had also died.[8] Eritrea allowed only two resident foreign reporters in 2006—from Reuters and Agence France-Presse—and severely restricted their movements, along with those of all foreigners in the country.

The information and independent analysis of domestic and international issues that reaches Eritreans does so largely through radio and web-based media originating abroad. The two most consistent opposition broadcasters from outside the country are the EDA, whose short-wave programming originates in Ethiopia, and the Tesfa Delina Foundation, which airs programs via satellite that are produced by civil society groups based abroad. One opposition radio station—al-Sharq, broadcasting nine hours a day from Sudan starting in 2005—was shut down after Sudan and Eritrea signed an accord to cooperate with one another on November 3, 2006.[9] Most opposition groups also maintain active websites, as do several unaffiliated NGOs and human rights groups in Eritrea's very active diaspora, most of them highly critical of the Isaias regime. Eritrea has seen an explosion of internet connectedness, particularly among young people in the main towns and cities. However, the four private internet service providers are monitored internally by the state, email is routinely monitored, and foreign broadcasts are periodically jammed, while all cultural exchanges are managed by the state.

Recommendations

- Eritrea's already-ratified constitution should be implemented without further delay.
- The government should approve the party law legalizing multiple parties and laying the groundwork for national elections.
- The government should grant amnesty to members of opposition political movements based outside the country and allow these organizations to re-enter after renouncing violence. The government should allow them to join the political process as legal entities competing with the ruling PFDJ on a level playing field.

- An independent commission should be established to organize Eritrea's first national elections, with adequate safeguards for competing parties and open campaigns and with extensive international monitoring throughout the process.
- The 1996 Press Law should be rescinded and constitutional protections for free media respected by permitting the reestablishment of independent newspapers and the creation of independent broadcast media.

CIVIL LIBERTIES

PROTECTION FROM STATE TERROR, UNJUSTIFIED IMPRISONMENT, AND TORTURE:	0.29
GENDER EQUITY:	3.50
RIGHTS OF ETHNIC, RELIGIOUS, AND OTHER DISTINCT GROUPS:	0.75
FREEDOM OF CONSCIENCE AND BELIEF:	0.00
FREEDOM OF ASSOCIATION AND ASSEMBLY:	0.20
CATEGORY AVERAGE:	**0.95**

The as-yet-unimplemented constitution bans torture (Article 16), but former detainees claim to have been routinely subjected to it. Amnesty International reported in February 2006 that Eritrea held "several thousand prisoners of conscience" for their religious or political beliefs, with many in secret locations, where they were tortured or treated poorly.[10] Human Rights Watch reported "frequent" use of torture throughout 2006 at severely overcrowded detention facilities, including cargo containers located in areas of "unbearable hot and cold" in conditions of "extreme starvation, lack of sanitation, and hard labor."[11] No public officials have ever been prosecuted for torturing or abusing prisoners.

Conditions for many current political detainees are impossible to ascertain, as the prisoners are denied all access to visitors. The location of many political prisoners is secret; these include private houses in the major cities, as well as specially constructed facilities in rural areas, such as Zara in the barren western mountain area near Sudan, Adi Abeito in the highlands north of Asmara, and Dongolo and E'era-e'ero in the scorched coastal lowlands. Arrests for political infractions are frequent, arbitrary, and rarely accompanied by formal charges, although Eritrea's constitution theoretically guarantees the right of habeas corpus (Article 17), and the Eritrean penal code limits detention without charge to thirty days. Estimates of the number of political prisoners detained since 1991 run to the thousands, but it is impossible to get an accurate count as no charges have been filed against any of them and no formal trials have been held. There are widespread reports of members of opposition groups such as the ELF held under detention since the early 1990s. At least one of the G-15 is reported to have died of natural causes, but there are no confirmed reports of executions of dissidents. No one detained for his or her political beliefs has been brought to trial.

Numerous governments, multilateral organizations, and human rights organizations, including the U.S. Department of State, have called for the release of Eritrea's political prisoners, particularly those arrested in September 2001. However, the Asmara government insists that it holds no prisoners for political reasons, claiming those who are incarcerated are criminals or security risks. In March 2004, the African Commission on Human Rights issued an advisory ruling that the continued detention of the eleven former high-ranking government officials taken in September 2001 was illegal. On the fifth anniversary of their arrests, the Council of the European Union renewed its call for either "a free and fair trial" or their unconditional release.[12]

Hundreds of Eritreans who were forcibly deported from Malta in 2002 and Libya in 2004 remained in detention at the end of 2006, most in secret prisons on the island of Dahlak Khebir.[13] Amnesty International reported in February 2007 that an additional 430 Eritrean nationals facing deportation in Libya, many of them young people fleeing conscription into the Eritrean armed forces, will return home to arrest and torture.[14] All Eritrean men between the ages of eighteen and forty-five and all women between eighteen and twenty-seven are required by law to perform eighteen months of national service in the armed forces or government-run public works projects. Since the outbreak of war with Ethiopia in 1998, however, conscripts have been kept in service on a continuous basis, many serving in low- or no-paying jobs in state- and party-controlled enterprises. There have been frequent, often brutal, house-to-house roundups to identify, induct, or detain evaders. Reinduction for those who have already served has been used as political punishment for members of the press and others who have expressed public criticism of government policies. Parents of those refusing to serve or those who have left the country without permission have been arrested and held as hostages in lieu of the return of the offending youth or payment of fines equivalent to US$3,500.[15] A steady flow of refugees into neighboring Sudan and Ethiopia is an outcome of this policy.

Women played a central role in Eritrea's independence war, constituting more than 30 percent of the 95,000-strong liberation army and playing a wide range of nontraditional roles. Their postindependence participation in public life presents a mixed record, as conservative social values have reasserted themselves and destructive traditional practices such as female circumcision, child marriage, and virginity testing have become increasingly common. The constitution prohibits discrimination based on race, ethnic origin, color, and gender and mandates the National Assembly to legislate measures designed to eliminate such inequality (Article 14). Although this has yet to be put into effect, the state has already acted to diminish oppressive cultural practices and has effectively blocked trafficking in women and children. The government has declared International Women's Day an official holiday and ratified the Convention on the Elimination of All Forms of Discrimination against Women (CEDAW). Women held three ministerial portfolios in 2007—Justice, Tourism, and Labor and Social Affairs. However, programs aimed at improving women's economic and social conditions are not initiated or monitored in an organized manner; like other social groups, women are prohibited from forming their own advocacy groups apart from the party-sanctioned National Union of Eritrean Women.

The government has increased educational opportunities for girls and opened schools in remote areas of the country for children of minority groups, offering primary education in all nine of the country's indigenous languages. Elementary school enrollment rose 270 percent from 1991 to 2001.[16] Secondary and postsecondary education is state subsidized and free to students, who are accepted largely on merit, though the poorly performing economy limits the number of children subsistence farm families can afford to send to school. Social pressures weed out many of the female students as sons are given priority within the family.

The situation of the disabled is similar to that of women; the government runs programs for them and places disabled people—mainly disabled war veterans—in jobs, but there is no articulated policy to which disabled people can hold the government accountable or institutional body to which they can appeal when there is a perception of abuse or discrimination. Those with disabilities not arising from "national service" are forced for the most part to rely on family support systems or the handful of charities that exist in Asmara, mainly for the blind and deaf.

Eritrean society as a whole is ethnically and religiously diverse. Tigrinya speakers, mostly Christian sedentary farmers and urban dwellers concentrated on the highland plateau, make up nearly half the population. Tigre-speaking Muslims, many of them agro-pastoralists living in the western lowlands and the coastal plains, are the second-largest group, making up close to a third of the population. The remaining fraction comprises six mostly Muslim minorities, plus the Kunama, who hold traditional religious beliefs. There is no official language, although Tigrinya, Arabic, and English prevail in business and commerce.

This ethnic potpourri is almost evenly divided between Sunni Muslims and Christians (most of whom are Orthodox, along with Catholic and Protestant minorities tracing to the precolonial period), with a small minority (2 percent) who practice traditional beliefs. Among these groups, there is little institutional discrimination based on faith, although Orthodox Christians of the Tigrinya-speaking ethnic group dominate the economy and hold most high-level political posts. However, the government actively suppresses evangelical Protestant denominations that have made recent inroads. Although the as-yet-unimplemented constitution guarantees all citizens "the freedom to practice any religion and to manifest that practice" (Article 15), the government has banned what it terms new churches—referring to minority evangelical Christian denominations and mission groups, which have experienced rapid growth over the past decade. The government has also intervened directly in the affairs of even those churches with legal recognition.

In May 2002, the government proscribed all religious denominations except for Islam, the Eritrean Orthodox Church, the Roman Catholic Church, and the Evangelical Church of Eritrea (Lutheran). Members of the prohibited denominations—less than 2 percent of the population, but with growing influence among Eritrea's youth—were forbidden from worshipping anywhere in Eritrea, even in private homes. By the end of 2005, Amnesty International reported that at least 26 members of the proscribed clergy and more than 1,750 parishioners had been detained, along with a smaller number of Muslims, many of them taken prisoner during clandestine wedding ceremonies and private prayer meetings. Among the detainees are Jehovah's Witnesses—whose members have been denied basic civil rights since declining, on religious grounds, to participate in the 1993 referendum establishing Eritrea's independence—and members of at least thirty-six evangelical and Pentecostal churches, along with followers of the Baha'i faith. Detainees were held incommunicado alongside political prisoners and frequently ill-treated or tortured in an effort to force them to renounce their beliefs and sign documents pledging not to attend future religious meetings.

Popular gospel singer Helen Berhane, who had recently released an album of Christian music, was jailed on May 13, 2004, and held in a shipping container at the Mai Serwa military camp until her release in October 2006. On May 28, 2005, police arrested the bride and groom and 200 guests, including the pastor of the Meseret Krisos Church and gospel singer Essey Stefanos, at a wedding in Asmara. On September 30, 2005, dozens of evangelical church members were arrested in sweeps across Asmara, including many from the Rema Church, and on October 3, police arrested the twenty staff members of the Kale Hiwot Church, which runs an orphanage, nursery and primary schools, and an emergency feeding center. Dozens of Muslims belonging to new Islamic religious groups were also detained in September 2005.[17] Another seventy-five evangelical Christians, half of them women, were jailed on February 1, 2006, for reading the Bible while at the military training camp at Sawa. Many evangelicals who were later released showed evidence of severe physical maltreatment. Two members of an evangelical church south of Asmara were reportedly tortured to death on October 17, 2006, while a third died after "persistent torture" in an Assab prison four months later.[18] Authorities also stripped Eritrean Orthodox Patriarch Abuna Antonios of his ecclesiastical authority and placed him under house arrest on August 25, 2005, after he protested government interference in Eritrea's largest legal religious institution.[19]

The U.S. State Department has imposed sanctions on Eritrea under the 1998 Religious Freedom Act for failing to address the persistent violations of religious freedom. Nevertheless, the crackdown continued unabated into 2007, as authorities arrested sixty-eight evangelical Christians in three raids in January, according to the California-based mission organization Open Doors, which ranked Eritrea thirteenth worst out of fifty countries on its 2007 World Watch List of countries that persecute Christians.[20]

Meanwhile, the Eritrean government has come under attack from Islamist terrorists based in neighboring Sudan, chiefly the Eritrean Islamic Jihad Movement (EIJM). EIJM was originally founded in Sudan in 1980 and was affiliated with Osama bin-Laden's terrorist network in the 1990s. After the group underwent a split earlier this decade, the largest faction took the name Eritrean Islamic Party for Justice and Development and affiliated itself with the secular nationalist EDA opposition coalition, one of two Islamic groups to do so. The EIJM is blamed for a rash of landmine incidents, ambushes, and bombings over the past decade, including the May 25, 2004, bombing in the western town of Barentu that injured ninety people. This confrontation has led to increasingly stringent, and often repressive, government controls over the mostly Muslim inhabitants of the western and coastal lowlands.

With no outlet for political protest in Eritrea, the Islamist resistance has become the default channel for the rising popular dissatisfaction among Eritrean Muslims. Issues that feed the movement's growth include a litany of perceived cultural slights: the government's refusal to accept Arabic as an official language; government interference in the selection of leadership in Islamic religious institutions, including the appointment of the Grand Mufti in Asmara; the virtual colonization of the lowlands by Tigrinya-speaking Christian entrepreneurs, who own most of the shops, businesses, hotels, and other urban enterprises and control most local commerce and trade; the denigration of pastoralism as a way of life, reflected in government policies and services favoring settled farmers; resentment over a postindependence trend toward unequal representation for Muslims in state and party leadership; fears that the official (but haphazardly implemented) land reform will impinge on traditional grazing rights, a concern that has been reinforced by the recent resettlement of war-displaced civilians and refugees returning from Sudan in the fertile western plains; and, most important, outrage over the conscription of women into an army where they reportedly suffer extensive abuse. These trends have politicized religious identity and strengthened the Islamist appeal among many Eritrean Muslims, especially those in rural areas.

The only nonreligious membership-based organizations permitted to operate in Eritrea today are those under the party's direct control—

the National Confederation of Eritrean Workers, with an estimated 20,000 members in five federations; the National Union of Eritrean Women, with 200,000 members; and the National Union of Youth and Students, with 170,000 members.[21] The trade unions are not permitted to organize any segment of the workforce without state and party permission, nor are strikes permitted under any circumstances. Independent trade union organization is not allowed by individuals or groups outside these party-controlled structures. Three trade union leaders were arrested in 2005—two on March 30, one on April 9—on unspecified charges after rumors of impending labor protests.[22] Women's and youth organizations are largely service providers and do not engage in policy advocacy or protest. Donations to these organizations are closely monitored by the state, which bans unrecognized organizations from accepting foreign funds. The PFDJ pre-selects the leadership slates and sets the priorities for these organizations, which are then confirmed at periodic organizational congresses.[23]

No group larger than seven is permitted to meet without government permission, and no organized public protest is tolerated. On July 30, 2001, the president of the University of Asmara Student Union, Semere Kesete, was arrested after criticizing the forced labor imposed on students during the summer months. When University of Asmara students protested his arrest the next day outside the High Court in Asmara, they were rounded up and sent to a summer work camp, where at least two died from extreme climate conditions. In the aftermath, the university's student union was disbanded by the authorities and replaced by a chapter of the PFDJ-controlled National Union of Eritrean Youth and Students.[24]

All other instances of public remonstration since independence—by liberation front fighters upset over the lack of pay in May 1993, by disabled veterans protesting their banishment from major urban centers in 1994, and by young National Service conscripts in 2004—have been forcibly put down, with their leaders detained for lengthy periods without trial.

Recommendations

- The government should either release or bring to public trial all political prisoners, including, but not limited to, the former liberation front leaders and government officials identified with the Group of 15.

- Allegations of state torture should be investigated promptly and fully, and the government should ensure appropriate prosecution and punishment of perpetrators.
- A law on religion should be adopted that provides legal protections for all religious groups, as mandated by Eritrea's as-yet-unimplemented constitution, and prompt legal action should be taken against those who attack members of minority faiths.
- The national service program should be depoliticized and restructured; it should not be used as a vehicle for coerced, underpaid labor for state and party operations.
- Full and unfettered freedom of public assembly should be permitted, as guaranteed by Eritrea's as-yet-unimplemented constitution.

RULE OF LAW

INDEPENDENT JUDICIARY:	1.20
PRIMACY OF RULE OF LAW IN CIVIL AND CRIMINAL MATTERS:	0.00
ACCOUNTABILITY OF SECURITY FORCES AND MILITARY TO	
CIVILIAN AUTHORITIES:	0.00
PROTECTION OF PROPERTY RIGHTS:	1.33
EQUAL TREATMENT UNDER THE LAW:	1.00
CATEGORY AVERAGE:	**0.71**

The Eritrean judiciary functions as an arm of executive authority, with judges appointed or dismissed at the discretion of the president's office. In some cases, panels of military and police officers have sentenced offenders in secret proceedings that flout basic international fair trial standards. Detainees are not informed of the accusations against them, have no right to defend themselves or to have legal counsel, and have no recourse to independent judges to challenge abuses of their rights. Most political detainees never come to trial and are held indefinitely on a presumption of guilt that is not subject to challenge. Families inquiring after jailed relatives are told, "You have no right to ask."[25]

The president created a system of secret military tribunals called special courts in 1996 to hear cases of corruption and other unspecified abuses by government and party officials. These courts are directly accountable to his office and are presided over by military officers with no formal training in the law. Hundreds have been sentenced by them, and they are closed to the public. The trials are conducted without legal representation for the accused or any right of appeal. Prisoners are sent to secret security prisons and military camps scattered around the country, which are not open to public scrutiny or even family visits. In July 2001, the chief judge of the High Court, Teame Beyene, was removed from his post after complaining of executive interference in judicial proceedings and calling for the dismantling of the special courts. Although the multitiered judicial system has suffered greatly from severe shortages of trained personnel, no new licenses have been issued for lawyers to engage in private practice in seven years, and most judges in the civilian court system lack legal training.

The military remains under the president's personal control, as he exercises direct command over the five theater-operation generals—the most powerful figures in the country after the president and, as such, the de facto governors of the country's five *zobas* (provinces)—while frequently ignoring General Sebhat Ephrem, his minister of defense. The country's feared national security service is independent of the armed forces and is headed by a longtime Isaias loyalist, Brigadier General Abraha Kassa, but, like the armed forces, its personnel remain under the president's personal control.

All land is the property of the state under a land reform proclaimed in 1995. This decree guaranteed usage rights to all citizens for agricultural and residential land, but it remains incompletely implemented. Prior to this, most land in Eritrea was communally controlled under tenure arrangements that varied widely between and within ethnic groups. After the sharp decline in Eritrea's economy following the outbreak of war in 1998, the government began offering long-term leases for cash payments and threatened to strip the land rights of citizens living abroad if they became involved in dissident political activities or failed to fulfill their tax obligations. With exports extremely low and new investment not forthcoming, the economy survives largely on remittances from the diaspora, whose members are required to pay a 2 percent asset tax in order to maintain rights to purchase land, secure inheritances, and take advantage of other privileges within Eritrea.

Recommendations

- Executive interference in the judiciary should be halted, and judges should be permitted to function independently.
- The special courts should be abolished immediately and their functions taken over by civilian bodies.
- Those accused of any crime—political or otherwise defined— should be informed of the accusations against them, have access to legal counsel, and be able to appeal.
- Access to residential and agricultural land should not be subject to political conditions. All land transactions should be open and transparent, with conditions for lease or extended use made clear and adhered to by both parties.

ANTICORRUPTION AND TRANSPARENCY

ENVIRONMENT TO PROTECT AGAINST CORRUPTION:	1.00
EXISTENCE OF LAWS AND ETHICAL STANDARDS BETWEEN PRIVATE AND PUBLIC SECTORS:	1.50
ENFORCEMENT OF ANTICORRUPTION LAWS:	0.50
GOVERNMENTAL TRANSPARENCY:	0.43
CATEGORY AVERAGE:	**0.86**

Throughout the postindependence years the economy has been dominated by the state and the PFDJ, which share ownership of the country's major financial and commercial institutions, agricultural and industrial enterprises, utilities, services, communications facilities, and transport companies. The PFDJ itself holds dozens of businesses in banking, trade, construction, shipping, metalworking, auto repair, road surfacing, and well-drilling, among other industries, and it holds controlling stakes in a number of joint ventures with foreign investors for other large-scale undertakings, such as mining.[26] These enterprises, set up in the 1980s and 1990s, had been operated by the Liberation Front, and the PFDJ has since expanded them with state favor. While the state has divested itself of some large and medium-size enterprises, it continues to play a commanding role in the economy. Privatization has gone slowly, in part out of would-be investors' fear of party interference in economic ventures and in part due to the precarious security situation since 1998.

Personal corruption among individuals has historically been low in Eritrea and severely punished when uncovered, but the state and the ruling party, often acting in concert, have made extensive use of economic levers for political ends. It is common, for example, for the PFDJ to pressure enterprises to include it as a partner in new ventures and then exact payment or a percentage of profits in exchange for government cooperation. Meanwhile, strict controls on travel by Eritrean citizens, such as the raising of the minimum age for men to apply for travel abroad without the support of a high-level government official to fifty in March 2005, have generated a lucrative business in such documents as highly prized exit visas. In the process, the practice of graft and corruption among state bureaucrats has grown, particularly at middle and lower levels, where pay rates have stagnated as inflation rates have soared. The militarization of much of the country, with zonal commanders outranking civilian administrators, has also fostered widespread corruption in the allocation of housing, management of local businesses, and control of trade. Transparency International placed Eritrea in a five-way tie for 93rd out of 163 nations in its 2006 Corruption Perceptions Index, scoring the country 2.9 on a scale of 1 to 10.[27]

Brigadier General Estifanos Seyoum, a high-ranking member of the PFDJ and a veteran of the independence war, was relieved of his post in the Ministry of Finance in August 2001 after questioning the equity of tax collection from PFDJ-owned enterprises. A signatory of the May 2001 "Open Letter to the PFDJ," he was detained with the other members of the G-15 in September 2001 and has not been heard from since.[28] No questions about tax collection or government expenditures have been raised in public forums since then. Nor is there any independent auditing body with authority to take up such issues. Under the constitution, the president appoints an auditor general, but this position has not been functional. There is no public record of the party's economic operations, no published line item national budget for the state, no detailed accounting for tax collection or remittances—no fiscal transparency of any kind for either state or party finances. In fact, the line items for the national budget remain a well-guarded secret—not only from the general public but also from most members of the cabinet and the ruling party.[29]

Meanwhile, according to the International Monetary Fund (IMF), since the outbreak of war with Ethiopia, "GDP declined, inflation rose, the external current account worsened, international reserves were nearly depleted, and banking assets were severely compromised." This has led the government to reverse course on privatization and increase its role in the economy, a practice the IMF warned could "endanger fiscal sustainability by lowering growth prospects" while increasing Eritrea's reliance on foreign assistance, even as new policies made it more and more difficult for aid agencies to operate in Eritrea.[30] Faced with chronic shortages of both skilled labor and foreign exchange, the government has squeezed the anemic small-business sector and cracked down heavily on black marketeering. Hope for economic recovery depends on substantial expansion of gold and mineral exploration, expected to produce results by 2008, and the establishment of tax-exempt free zones near the Red Sea ports of Assab and Massawa.

On March 28, 2005, the government announced penalties of two years in prison and fines of more than US$130,000 for those caught using foreign currency without permission.[31] That June, the government began requiring businesses to answer extensive questionnaires as to whether employees and their extended families, including those residing outside Eritrea, had fulfilled their national service obligations and paid their taxes.[32] In July 2005, the government announced tough new rules for the thirty-seven international aid agencies working within the nation, including a requirement that they maintain in-country accounts with at least US$2 million on deposit, and an imposition of taxes on imported aid, leading many to close their operations. On March 20, 2006, the government shut down three of the remaining thirteen agencies after issuing a statement criticizing their work in the country. These were the American charity Mercy Corps International, the Irish agency Concern Worldwide and the Britain-based consortium ACORD, agencies that had been involved in Eritrea since the independence war.[33] Two months later, the government tightened the already extensive restrictions on in-country travel by requiring permits for all foreigners to leave the capital.[34]

With an executive-dominated government running a one-party state that prohibits independent media, quashes nonparty NGOs, and detains without trial or recourse to appeal those who dissent individually, in Eritrea there are no whistle-blowers for misconduct of any kind. Under these conditions of rigid, one-man rule, there are no avenues for substantive change open to the citizenry at present. This is unlikely to change until President Isaias steps down or is removed from power under pressure from an aroused populace and a restless military.

Recommendations

- The financial affairs of the state and the People's Front for Democracy and Justice should be fully disentangled and made transparent with the help of international financial advisors.
- A comprehensive line item national budget for revenue, operational expenses, and capital expenditures should be prepared, published annually, and made easily accessible to the public.
- Tax policies and procedures should be open, transparent, and subject to independent review.
- The practice of requiring exit visas to leave the country should end. Collection of bribes and favors for issuing government permits and documents should be thoroughly investigated, and laws should be passed to prevent it in the future.
- The government should implement safeguards to protect whistleblowers on institutional and personal corruption from retributive action by those whom they expose.

NOTES

1. *Eritrea: A Country Handbook* (Asmara: Ministry of Information, 2002), 23–24.
2. Eritrea Constitution, Articles 7, 26, http://unpan1.un.org/intradoc/groups/public/documents/CAFRAD/UNPAN00464.pdf.
3. For a "family tree" tracing the origins and interrelationships of these and other Eritrean political movements, see "Eritrean Political Organizations: 1961–2007" (Elk Grove, Calif.: Awate Foundation, 4 March 2007), http://www.awate.com/portal/content/view/4485/9; for a breakdown of EDA membership, see "EDA will hold its congress" (Elk Grove, Calif.: Awate Foundation, 15 February 2007), www.awate.com/portal/content/view/4469/3.
4. Amnesty International delegates were refused visas in July 2002 and have not been permitted to enter Eritrea since then. Neither Human Rights Watch nor the Committee to Protect Journalists has had representatives in Eritrea since 2003.
5. Passed by the National Assembly in its 22–24 January 1996 session as Proclamation 90/98 and published by the Ministry of Information.
6. "North Korea, Turkmenistan, Eritrea the worst violators of press freedom" (Paris: Reporters Without Borders [RSF], 23 October 2006), http://www.rsf.org/rubrique.php3?id_rubrique=639.

7   "Eritrea: Five years on, members of parliament and journalists remain in secret deten-
    tion without trial, with fears that some may have died in custody" (London: Amnesty
    International [AI], 18 September 2006), http://web.amnesty.org/library/Index/ENGAFR
    640092006; see also "Eritrea: Prominent journalist reported dead in secret prison" (AI,
    15 February 2007), web.amnesty.org/library/Index/ENGAFR640022007.

8   "The Secret PFDJ Prison at E'era-E'ero" (Cerritos, Calif : Asmarino.com, 31 August
    2006), http://zete9.asmarino.com/index.php?itemid=585.

9   "Eight state media journalists still held in police-run 'Agip' centre in Asmara" (RSF, 1
    December 2006), http://www.rsf.org/article.php3?id_article=19955.

10 "Report 2006: Eritrea" (AI, New York, May 2006), http://web.amnesty.org/report
    2006/eri-summary-eng.

11 "World Report: 2007" (New York: Human Rights Watch, 2007), http://www.hrw
    .org/wr2k7/wr2007master.pdf.

12 "Declaration by the Presidency on behalf of the European Union on political prisoners
    in Eritrea" (Brussels: Council of the European Union, 18 September 2006), http://
    www.consilium.europa.eu/ueDocs/cms_Data/docs/pressData/en/cfsp/90996.pdf.

13 "Testimony of Eritreans deported from Malta, jailed in Dahlak," (Elk Grove, Calif.:
    Awate Foundation, 22 July 2005), http://awate.com/artmen/publish/article_4190.shtml.

14 "Libya: Forcible return/Torture and ill-treatment" (AI, 8 February 2007), http://web
    .amnesty.org/library/Index/ENGMDE190042007?open&of=ENG-2D3.

15 "Eritrea: Over 500 parents of conscripts arrested" (AI, 21 December 2006), http://web
    .amnesty.org/library/Index/ENGAFR640152006.

16 Eritrea: A Country Handbook, 99.

17 "Eritrea: Religious Persecution" (AI, 7 December 2005, http://web.amnesty.org/library
    /index/engafr640132005.

18 "Eritrea: Christian dies in military jail," Compass Direct News, 22 February 2007, http:
    //www.compassdirect.org/en/display.php?page=news&lang=en&length=long&idelement
    =4779; see also "Eritrea: Torture/Prisoners of conscience" (AI, 3 November 2006),
    http://web.amnesty.org/library/Index/ENGAFR640132006?open&of=ENG-380.

19 "Eritrean Patriarch Uncanonically Deposed," Glastonbury Review (British Orthodox
    Church), February 2006, http://www.britishorthodox.org/113a.php.

20 "Recent clampdown in Eritrea reveals new government tactic," Mission Network News,
    Grand Rapids, Mich., 13 February 2007, http://www.mnnonline.org/article/9588.

21 Eritrea: A Country Handbook, 50–52.

22 "Eritrea: Fear of torture/arbitrary detention" (AI, 6 May 2005), http://web.amnesty
    .org/library/Index/ENGAFR640022005?open&of=ENG-ERI.

23 Numerous interviews by the author with leaders and members of NUEW, NCEW,
    NUEYS, Asmara, 2001, 2002, and subsequent interviews with high-ranking youth and
    women's union leaders in the U.S. in 2005–2006, including the former head of NUEYS,
    Mohedin Shengeb, after he fled Eritrea in 2005.

24 Interviews by the author with Asmara University students and members of NUEYS,
    Asmara, October 2001, February 2002; Boston, November 2003; New York, May 2005.

25 "Eritrea: Five years on, members of parliament and journalists remain in secret detention without trial, with fears that some may have died in custody" (AI, 18 September
   2006), http://web.amnesty.org/library/Index/ENGAFR640092006.

26 Interview by the author with PFDJ economic affairs head Hagos Gebrehewit, Asmara,
   14 February 2002.

27 "2006 Corruption Perceptions Index" (Berlin: Transparency International, 6 November
   2006), http://www.transparency.org/news_room/in_focus/2006/cpi_2006__1/cpi_table.

28 "Another Critical Official Sacked," IRIN, 7 August 2001, http://allafrica.com/stories
   /200108070236.html.

29 Interviews by the author with Eritrean government officials, Asmara, August–September
   2001, February–March 2002.

30 "Fiscal Sustainability—The Case of Eritrea" (Washington, D.C.: International Monetary Fund [IMF], January 2004), http://www.imf.org/external/pubs/ft/wp/2004/wp0407
   .pdf. See also "IMF Board Concludes Article IV Consultation with Eritrea" (February
   2005), http://www.imf.org/external/np/sec/pn/2005/pn0518.htm.

31 Ed Harris, "Eritrea cracks down on black market currency trade," Reuters, 14 April
   2005, http://www.sudantribune.com/article.php3?id_article=9066.

32 "Eritrea: Family's party loyalty pre-requisite to acquiring business licenses" (Elk Grove,
   Calif.: Awate Foundation, 28 June 2005), http://www.awate.com/artman/publish
   /article_4151.shtml.

33 "Eritrea: Authorities expel three foreign NGOs" (New York: UN Office for Coordination of Humanitarian Affairs, 23 March 2006), http://www.irinnews.org/report.aspx
   ?reportid=58532.

34 "New travel rules in Eritrea," Agence France-Presse, 31 May 2006, http://dehai.org
   /archives/dehai_news_archive/may-jun06/0582.html.

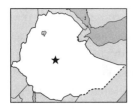

ETHIOPIA

CAPITAL: Addis Ababa

POPULATION: 77.1 million

GNI PER CAPITA: $180

SCORES	2005	2007
ACCOUNTABILITY AND PUBLIC VOICE:	1.88	1.85
CIVIL LIBERTIES:	2.83	2.85
RULE OF LAW:	2.06	2.35
ANTICORRUPTION AND TRANSPARENCY:	2.76	2.36

(scores are based on a scale of 0 to 7, with 0 representing weakest and 7 representing strongest performance)

Edmond J. Keller

INTRODUCTION

In May 2005, Ethiopia held its third-ever multiparty parliamentary elections. The first had been held in 1995, four years after the Ethiopian Peoples' Revolutionary Democratic Front (EPRDF) succeeded in toppling the Marxist-Leninist regime that had ruled the country since 1974. Over the past decade and a half, the EPRDF regime has made substantial progress in transforming Ethiopian society, but further steps are required. While in some respects the political system is much more open than at any other time in Ethiopia's history, it is far from resembling a liberal democracy.

Edmond J. Keller is director of the Globalization Research Center Africa and Professor of Political Science at the University of California at Los Angeles (UCLA). He is the former director of the James S. Coleman African Studies Center at UCLA, president of the African Studies Association, and a current member of the Council on Foreign Relations, the Overseas Development Council, and the Pacific Council on International Policy. Professor Keller has been a visiting researcher at the Institute for Development Studies at the University of Nairobi (Kenya) and a policy analyst with the United Nations Economic Committee for Africa. He is the author of more than one hundred articles on African politics, two monographs, and four co-edited volumes. The most recent is a co-edited volume with Donald Rothchild entitled *Africa-US Relations: Strategic Encounters* (2006).

When it came to power in 1991, the EPRDF organized a conference that led to the implementation of a transitional charter and government. This was achieved by means of pact-making among the leaders of thirty-one different political movements, most of them based on ethnicity and region. A Council of Representatives in the Transitional Government was created in which the EPRDF had the largest single bloc (thirty-two seats out of a total of eighty-seven), followed by the Oromo Liberation Front (OLF) with twelve seats. The aim of the body was to secure the support of the leadership of the most significant ethnic groups in Ethiopia so that this multiethnic state could hold together.

Initially, the most significant ethnic groups were given both a stake in the new regime and more regional autonomy than at any time in modern history. However, over the next year the ruling coalition narrowed further until it finally included only the EPRDF and ethnically based regional parties beholden to it, so-called People's Democratic Organizations (PDOs). This was fueled in part by the EPRDF's sense of insecurity; the core of the party is the Tigray People's Liberation Front (TPLF), and the Tigray people make up less than 10 percent of the country's population. Despite a public pronouncement that it was committed to redressing past inequities and injustices toward various ethnic communities, the EPRDF chose to deal with non-Tigray groups only through the PDOs. In retrospect, the EPRDF's decision not to compromise with other leaders, who at the time were perceived as threats, was a grave error.

Very early in its rule, the EPRDF initiated policies designed to demonstrate that it was dedicated to social justice and respect for the country's ethnic diversity. Examples of this could be seen in the creation of a federal system based on what are at least nominally ethnically based states as well as a constitutional provision allowing for "self-determination up to and including separation."[1] Coupled with this was the creation of mechanisms to devolve administrative and political authority from the center to the regional states and subregional governments, including a revenue-sharing formula based on a system of block grants. Notably, the World Bank saw the merits of such a strategy and has over the years been one of the strongest supporters of Ethiopia's decentralization and social-equity policies.

However, politics continues to serve as a significant drag on rapid and steady socioeconomic and political development. For instance, the regime benefited from widespread support during its 1998 to 2000 war with Eritrea, but after a ceasefire was declared, support turned to criticism. Many in Ethiopian society wanted nothing less than the total defeat of the Eritreans. Hard-liners in the TPLF threatened Prime Minister Meles Zenawi and his supporters from within, while other groups, some today represented in the formal opposition parties Coalition for Unity and Democracy (CUD) and United Ethiopian Democratic Forces (UEDF), criticized the regime from without.

Over the past decade and a half, three nominally democratic national elections have been held in Ethiopia. However, until May 2005, the opposition did not present a formidable challenge to the EPRDF. In the latest elections, opposition parties were able to secure 173 out of a total of 546 seats in the unicameral Parliament, the House of Peoples' Representatives,[2] up considerably from the meager twelve they held in the previous Parliament. This electoral success seems to have emboldened certain members of the opposition, who to this day continue to cry fraud in reference to the May 2005 balloting, arguing that they should have gained even more seats. The EPRDF has consequently cracked down on internal opposition and seems to be again on a war footing over the situation on the Eritrean border. The EPRDF regime also feels threatened by the designs of Somali Islamists on Ethiopia's southeastern border. Late in 2006, Ethiopia launched a massive invasion in support of the fragile transitional government of Somalia, routing the Union of Islamic Courts forces that had come to control most of southern Somalia.[3]

Armed opposition to the regime generally manifests itself in low-intensity warfare in regions like the Somali state and parts of Oromia. However, the government has recently become increasingly concerned with the activities of a group calling itself the Ethiopian People's Patriotic Front that operates primarily in the Gondar area of the Amhara state and parts of the Gambella region. The movement is in the early stages of development, and it is unclear whether it will present a formidable military challenge.[4]

Despite the country's continuing political instability, there are prospects in 2007 for important political reforms. For example, in response to the demands of the opposition following the 2005 elections, the Parliament is presently considering an amendment of the proclamation regarding the composition and work of the National Elections Board that would make it more broadly representative. Other proclamations, such as those regulating nongovernmental organizations (NGOs) and land-related issues, will also be presented to parliament for discussion. Additionally, the parliament is expected to enact a new press law, though critics expect more restrictions rather than an expansion of press freedom.

ACCOUNTABILITY AND PUBLIC VOICE

FREE AND FAIR ELECTORAL LAWS AND ELECTIONS:	1.25
EFFECTIVE AND ACCOUNTABLE GOVERNMENT:	3.25
CIVIC ENGAGEMENT AND CIVIC MONITORING:	1.67
MEDIA INDEPENDENCE AND FREEDOM OF EXPRESSION:	1.25
CATEGORY AVERAGE:	**1.85**

By the time of the run-up to the 2005 national elections, the EPRDF had begun to successfully tackle some very difficult problems of economic development, such as poverty alleviation and food security. It was receiving considerable support and praise for its performance from international actors such as the United States, the European Union, and the World Bank. At the same time, Ethiopia was being pressured by international donors to further open its political system.

The National Election Board of Ethiopia is responsible for organizing elections and for ensuring that the whole process is free and fair. However, entering the 2005 elections, opposition parties felt that the membership of the board had been stacked in favor of the ruling party. They pressed for a more representative board, but in the end were able to win only limited concessions from the regime.

The EPRDF had initially agreed to allow international and national observer groups to monitor the May 2005 elections. However, some would-be international observers, including three U.S.-based organizations—the National Democratic Institute, the International Republican Institute, and the International Foundation for Electoral Systems—that in the early spring of 2005 had been conducting civic education exercises in the country, were ordered in April to leave within forty-eight hours. They were accused of being in the country illegally and engaging in activities that had not been approved by the government. The organizations denied those charges but left amid protests from the U.S. government.

The run-up to the elections was fraught with tensions, despite the fact that the political system was much more open than at any other time in the country's history. For example, opposition parties and candidates had relatively open access to the state media, and the candidates took part in live, televised debates. Both the opposition and the EPRDF held peaceful mass rallies. All of this led to a huge voter turnout, which the Carter Center estimated as high as 90 percent of the country's twenty-six million registered voters.[5]

Even as it was opening up the political system, credible reports indicated that the EPRDF regime was engaging in activities to intimidate, silence, or eliminate some elements in the opposition, particularly in the countryside.[6] Amnesty International reported that the government had subjected opposition party members to beatings, detention on trumped-up charges, harassment, and disappearances.[7] Opposition supporters in Eastern Gojjam and other locations were allegedly shot dead by government forces. Additionally, there were claims that prospective opposition voters were illegally dropped from the voting rolls, while EPRDF supporters were given multiple voter registration cards in different locations. In some cases, voter registration cards were even given to children. This pattern continued up to the actual elections in May 2005. While putting on a democratic face for the international community, the EPRDF operated behind the scenes in an unaccountable manner, structuring the elections in its own favor.

Although the government had pledged to make local election monitoring possible, it imposed tough new rules in the spring of 2005 that effectively barred thousands of local observers from monitoring the elections. It was announced that electoral officials would accredit only monitors who were registered as poll observers when their organization was first established. This requirement affected the majority of such groups, as the idea of local monitors had only recently begun to be contemplated and planned for by the country's civil society organizations.

Rather than accepting this as a defeat, several civil society organizations took the matter to the Supreme Court. Just days before the elections, the court declared the new rules to be illegal. This was an apparent victory for the groups, but the last-minute ruling gave them little time to prepare, and they also faced logistical problems in getting their monitors out into the field.

Despite its best efforts, the EPRDF was forced to come to grips with the dramatic success of the opposition parties at the polls. For its part, the opposition, rather than celebrating its gains, immediately cried fraud. International observers from the European Union and the Carter Center corroborated this charge in at least some places, but the opposition became increasingly strident in its claims, demanding that the results be overturned in some constituencies and the vote rerun in others. The CUD, the largest opposition group, rejected the results, with some members refusing to take their seats in Parliament. In early July, postelection tensions exploded when the government tried to impose a ban on public assemblies. Protesters took to the streets and were greeted with a violent government response. In initial clashes in Addis Ababa, Ethiopia's capital, police and the military killed at least thirty-six civilians and wounded more than 100, while thousands of other protesters were arrested throughout the country. The violence abated somewhat when the government and main opposition parties tried to negotiate a way forward by agreeing on which local elections would be subject to independent review.

These negotiations broke down in November 2005, and protests resumed. This time, at least forty-six people were killed, 200 were wounded, and more than 10,000 were arrested in Addis Ababa and other towns. The government then ordered the arrests of several dozen opposition leaders, journalists, and civil society activists. Those arrested were accused of infractions including outrage toward the constitution, incitement to riot, treason, and conspiracy to commit genocide against the Tigray people. The treason and genocide charges allowed the government to detain those charged indefinitely without trial. At the time of writing, 111 individuals were being detained, with thirty-five more to be tried in absentia. All of those being held maintain their innocence, and, except for three civil society activists, they have refused to put up a formal defense. The treason trial began in May 2006 and at time of writing remained in its early stages. However, in March 2007, the Supreme Court ordered that twenty-five detained journalists be freed. In addition, the prosecution dropped the most serious charges, those relating to genocide.

[UPDATE: During the spring and summer of 2007, a number of journalists and prominent opposition leaders being held in connections with the 2005 protests, including some who had been convicted of various crimes, were released by the government. On April 9, twenty-five opposition members and journalists were acquitted and freed by the High Court. On July 20, an additional thirty-eight opposition leaders who had been convicted were pardoned, while on August 16, thirty-two more opposition members who had been held without charge were released.]

Although the constitution clearly articulates the separation of powers among the various branches and levels of government, the executive branch operates according to its own whims. The Parliament is so heavily dominated by the EPRDF and its PDO partners that it often serves as no more than a rubber stamp for the executive branch. For example, on the eve of Ethiopia's 2005 parliamentary elections, the government coerced Parliament into quickly enacting four articles of the draft press law. On the same day, two new government radio and television stations were approved.[8] While the judiciary does sometimes issue rulings that do not favor the government's position, the executive has maintained significant power over the judiciary, primarily through hiring and firing practices.

Within the executive branch, the EPRDF regime recognizes the need to professionalize public administration at all levels. However, civil service reform and training have been slow. Although Ethiopia's civil service is fairly independent compared with those of other countries at a similar level of development, it continues to be an area of weakness and inefficiency in the federal system. In a sign of limited progress, the Civil Service College graduated 575 students in August 2006,[9] but it will take time to train and appropriately place the much-needed administrators.

The government in 2006 allowed open debates over policies, giving citizens at least symbolic access to the decision-making process. The government also uses television and radio to reach out to the population, and claims to make a particular effort to consult with civil society organizations and the private sector. However, overall, civil society and the press have faced a more difficult environment since the 2005 elections and their aftermath. During this time, the EPRDF regime has repeatedly suppressed freedom of expression despite strong pressures from the donor community, including the curtailment of much-needed development assistance.

Until the preelection period, Ethiopia was developing what many observers felt was a substantial and vibrant civil society, with active groups in all parts of the country. By 2006, there were at least 1,200 nongovernmental organizations (NGOs) in the country, up from about twenty-four in 1994.[10] Particularly in the run-up to the elections, civil society organizations took advantage of Ethiopia's new political openings, engaging in civic education activities and organizing candidate debates on television and radio. Most notable were the roles played by a coalition of thirty-five civil society organizations known as the Election Observation Coalition, and by another group, the Organization for Social Justice in Ethiopia. These two organizations took the lead in bringing the successful Supreme Court challenge to the sudden electoral law changes aimed at barring civil society organizations from providing local election observers.[11] Since the elections, however, civil society has fallen on hard times. The new elections law being considered by Parliament in early 2007 would severely restrict opportunities for civil society groups to register as poll monitors.

Most Ethiopian organizations are concerned with economic and social development issues rather than political matters. However, highly active civil society organizations focused on political issues do exist, mainly in Addis Ababa. The most prominent local human rights organization is the Ethiopian Human Rights Council (EHRCO). Even before the events of 2005, EHRCO was routinely accused of being antigovernment. As a consequence, its staff members were often subject to government harassment and intimidation. In 2005, the organization's founder, Mesfin Wolde Mariam, was jailed along with others accused of engaging in acts that threatened the stability of the country. Although EHRCO has not been completely shut down, it was less active after late 2005.[12] It is important to note that since the crises of 2005, civil society groups have not vigorously attempted to influence government policies for fear that their members will be harassed or even jailed.

Despite the existence of laws guaranteeing freedom of expression, it is clear that the media's rights are not upheld in practice. By 2006, Ethiopia had dropped twenty-nine places in Reporters Without Borders' Worldwide Press Freedom Index following the recent shift away from political liberalization. It now ranks 160 out of 168 countries in the index.[13]

Whereas between 1992 and 2000 there was a movement toward greater political openness and press freedom, in the past five years this trend has been steadily reversed.[14] According to the Committee to Protect Journalists, in 2007 Ethiopia was one of three African countries that, despite some political progress, have turned increasingly repressive toward the press.[15] Still, the independent press has taken advantage of the freedoms of expression that were supposedly guaranteed by the Press Law of 2003, even while complaining about its shortcomings.[16] Ethiopia has eighty-two weekly and thirty-two monthly newspapers, although critics argue that journalists face harassment and imprisonment on a regular basis. In fact, of those currently on trial, fourteen are editors and reporters charged with serious crimes ranging from outrage against the constitution to treason. Even though these journalists are not formally members of the opposition, they are accused of having published articles sympathetic to the opposition as well as interviews with their leaders.

Following the 2005 elections and subsequent civil unrest, the government raided newsrooms, blocked newspapers from publishing, and expelled two foreign reporters. Ethiopia is currently the third-leading jailer of journalists in the world, after China and Cuba. Today, fewer than ten private newspapers are being published in Addis Ababa, compared with more than twenty before the violence in November 2005.[17] The OpenNet Initiative, a group dedicated to open access to websites, charged that the Ethiopian government has gone so far as to censor antigovernment websites and blogs, although the government denies the allegation.[18]

Ethiopia's Broadcast Law, which allows private broadcasters, has been in place since 1999, but until April 2006 no privately owned radio stations had actually received licenses to operate. The two stations that were licensed to launch that month were said to have been selected based on their programming and financial status. Many Ethiopians appear to view this as a positive step by the government, but some journalists are skeptical, feeling that the EPRDF regime cannot be trusted to uphold the law. The new stations reach only the Addis Ababa area, leaving out the rest of the country.[19] In late 2005, two foreign radio stations that had a national reach, Voice of America and Deutsche Welle, were ordered to stop operating in Ethiopia because they had broadcast critical reports.[20]

Recommendations

- The EPRDF regime should make a serious effort to reach accommodation with opposition parties and further liberalize the political system. The government should present a detailed plan for future elections in order to build confidence among opposition parties and the public at large.
- The government should review the past work of the National Board of Elections and broaden its membership to include elements from civil society and opposition parties.
- The Parliament should follow through on passing a new and improved press law in 2007 that grants the media more access to government and legal proceedings and bars censorship of newspapers and internet sites. Lawmakers should systematically engage members of the press during the decision-making process.
- The government should continue to grant licenses to private media and allow closed newspapers to resume operations.

CIVIL LIBERTIES

PROTECTION FROM STATE TERROR, UNJUSTIFIED IMPRISONMENT, AND TORTURE:	2.00
GENDER EQUITY:	3.25
RIGHTS OF ETHNIC, RELIGIOUS, AND OTHER DISTINCT GROUPS:	3.00
FREEDOM OF CONSCIENCE AND BELIEF:	4.00
FREEDOM OF ASSOCIATION AND ASSEMBLY:	2.00
CATEGORY AVERAGE:	**2.85**

Increased threats to and violations of civil liberties were a consequence of the political tensions that sprang from the flawed 2005 elections. Prior to the elections, the EPRDF appeared ready to allow civil rights to expand and receive legal protection. As early as 1997, the government proposed a National Human Rights Commission, but it was not established until 2004 and did not begin functioning for another year. In its first years, the new commission did not show any signs of vigorously upholding human and civil rights laws, nor did it actively cooperate with local or international human rights organizations.[21] In early 2005, the Ministry of Justice registered the Human Rights League, an Oromo human rights organization, some of whose founding members had spent four years in prison before being acquitted of violent conspiracy.[22] However, the Human Rights League has remained inactive to date.[23]

Starting with the arrests of opposition leaders in November 2005, the government reverted to its traditional practice of denying basic civil liberties. For example, beginning in September 2006, anyone caught with copies of a political manifesto written by CUD's Berhanu Nega, which had been smuggled out of prison and published in Uganda, was detained. Individuals who possessed a so-called civil disobedience calendar, containing pictures of the opposition leaders on trial and calling for nonviolent civil disobedience, were also subject to detention. According to the official report of the government's commission of inquiry into the violence following the elections, 199 people were killed and 30,000 people were arrested during the June and November 2005 crackdowns.

Government repression and violations of civil liberties occurred throughout the country. In Oromia, for example, the government cracked down on the OLF, accusing it of sedition and arresting a number of its leaders. Once arrested, these leaders regularly had their human rights violated. Teshale Aberra, a president of the Oromo Supreme Court who fled to Britain in November 2006 to escape threats and harassment, maintains that illegal detention and torture are commonplace, as do many international human rights groups. The Oromo assert that the central government tends to exaggerate when expressing its concerns about the OLF's armed struggle for secession.

In the troubled Somali regional state there have been growing claims of arbitrary detentions and killings linked to the long-running irredentist sentiment in the region. In Gambella, hundreds of Anuak people have been killed by government forces and local militia since 2003, and others have been detained without trial. Although there was an official inquiry into the 2003 killings, the military received no blame. Since then, arbitrary arrests, rapes, beatings, and extrajudicial killings have continued. For those who are detained, conditions are difficult: Ethiopian prisons are extremely overcrowded and the provision of food and medical care do not adequately meet prisoners' needs.

Article 35 of the 1994 constitution explicitly guarantees gender equity, stating, "Women shall, in the enjoyment of rights and protections provided for by this Constitution, have equal right with men." However, given historical discrimination against women, the full implementation of this pledge will require consistent enforcement by all levels of government over a significant period of time.[24]

In May 2005, the revised criminal code made female genital mutilation a criminal offense punishable by up to ten years' imprisonment. It also increased the punishment for the traditional practice of abduction for the purpose of marriage from three to as many as ten years in prison, and made the offense subject to punishment as rape, thereby ending the impunity previously enjoyed by suspects who married their victims.[25] Other evidence of the government's intent to better protect women's rights can be seen in its efforts to cooperate with the Ethiopian Women Lawyers Association (EWLA). EWLA has been providing training on women's rights issues to the police force, and it has urged the police to combat violence against women.[26]

Despite these efforts, women continue to be abused and discriminated against in the private sphere. Culture and religion continue to dominate social attitudes about the rights of women, especially in rural areas. There are organizations to assist women and raise awareness of gender-based violence, but they lack public support.[27]

As in other parts of Africa, women bear the brunt of the HIV/AIDS epidemic because of their general lack of control over sexual relations, as well as a lack of knowledge of the disease and how it is transmitted. Fifty-five percent of individuals living with the disease in Ethiopia are women.[28] Girls also continue to lag behind boys when it comes to education. They are less likely to attend school, with only about 16 percent achieving secondary education.[29]

The U.S. State Department classifies Ethiopia as a Tier 2 country in its annual Trafficking in Persons reports, meaning the government does not meet minimum standards but is attempting to do so. Although anti-trafficking laws exist, enforcement efforts remain insufficient. Ethiopia is not a signatory to the UN Protocol to Prevent, Suppress and Punish Human Trafficking. Women are subject to trafficking for sexual and employment purposes, from rural to urban areas as well as to foreign countries.[30]

Much of the previously described internal conflict arises from the delicate ethno-linguistic balance in Ethiopia. From the founding of the modern Ethiopian state in 1855, the Amhara ethnic group, with the strong support of the Ethiopian Orthodox Church, was politically dominant. It was on this basis that the imperial state of Ethiopia was created. Present-day Ethiopia has a population of over seventy million, and is evenly divided among Christians and Muslims. However, the largest ethnic group is the Oromo people, who comprise 40 to 45 percent of the population. They are followed by the Amhara, who make up about 25 percent of the population, and the politically powerful Tigray people, who represent about 9 percent. The remainder of the population consists of sixty-seven other ethnic groups. Since the imperial state was built on conquest, groups such as the Oromo and Somalis have resented Amhara (and now Tigray) domination and have increasingly pressed for either first-class Ethiopian citizenship or complete separation. Ethiopia's strongly federal system is an attempted response to this issue.

Eritrea, which was formerly an Ethiopian state, gained independence in 1993, but the two states fought a bloody border war between 1998 and 2000; even after subsequent international negotiations, exact territorial delimitations remain unresolved. Despite a constitutional provision allowing foreigners to acquire Ethiopian citizenship, people of Eritrean origin who were not expelled from the country after the outbreak of the 1998 border fighting have often felt like second-class citizens or stateless individuals. It is now possible for Eritreans to receive a document acknowledging their nationality and allowing them to continue to live and work in Ethiopia, and they have rights beyond those of other foreign nationals, but in practice Eritreans are routinely treated as aliens.[31]

Article 27 of the constitution declares that all citizens have the right to freedom of religion, conscience, and thought. In general, this right is upheld, except when groups opposed to the EPRDF regime on political grounds express their opposition in religious terms. Such has been the case with radical Islamists operating in the Somali regional state. In recent years, supporters of groups opposed to the EPRDF regime have been systematically harassed, subjected to extrajudicial punishment, or even killed. Evangelical Christian groups and smaller sects have also complained of facing bureaucratic hurdles, especially when attempting to gain access to land to be used for religious purposes.

Freedom of assembly is enshrined in the constitution but problematic in practice, especially since the 2005 postelection crackdown. While that episode provides the clearest evidence of limitations on the ability to protest, it is far from being the only such example in recent years. The federal police, in particular, are blamed for many violent repressions of public demonstrations. Student demonstrators in Oromia have been subjected to harsh treatment on several occasions; in early 2007, beatings by federal police resulted in at least one death and numerous wounded students.[32]

Ethiopia permits the formation of unions, but the government regularly interferes in their operations, harassing and intimidating labor activists. The Ethiopian Teachers' Association (ETA) has a particularly contentious relationship with the government due to its perceived political activism. In recent years, ETA members have been detained on numerous occasions, including several who were held in connection with the postelection protests.

Recommendations

- The Human Rights Commission should be given more independence and authority to investigate government entities so that it can become an effective monitor of human rights.
- Both local and international human rights groups should be allowed to do their work without intimidation or harassment, and all levels of government should protect them from such threats regardless of the political affiliations of the aggressors.
- The government should prioritize affirmative action for women and work with women's rights groups to educate and assist rural women with respect to domestic violence and AIDS.
- The government should broaden and deepen civic education programs so that the civil and human rights provisions of the 1994 constitution are more widely known among the public, in the civil service, and in the military.

RULE OF LAW

INDEPENDENT JUDICIARY:	2.00
PRIMACY OF RULE OF LAW IN CIVIL AND CRIMINAL MATTERS:	2.17
ACCOUNTABILITY OF SECURITY FORCES AND MILITARY TO	
CIVILIAN AUTHORITIES:	2.25
PROTECTION OF PROPERTY RIGHTS:	1.67
EQUAL TREATMENT UNDER THE LAW:	3.67
CATEGORY AVERAGE:	**2.35**

The 1994 constitution makes an unmistakable commitment to the rule of law. Article 37, "Right of Access to Justice," states that "everyone has the right to bring a justiciable matter to, and to obtain a decision or judgment by, a court of law or any other competent body with judicial power."[33] However, this commitment is not always observed in practice, partly due to Ethiopia's low human resource capacity and the challenges of operating a truly federal system.

Generally, a rule of law culture has not yet developed evenly throughout the country; moreover, the legal system is subject to strong political pressure.[34] While at the federal level judges tend to be well trained and professional, at lower levels quality and independence decline. This is particularly true at the local level, where judges are often uneducated, poorly paid or not paid at all, and not fully conversant in the laws they are expected to uphold. Police are also poorly educated, inadequately trained, and lacking in legal knowledge. Consequently, bribery and abuse of power are common. Human Rights Watch found that local officials use "social courts" run by untrained EPRDF appointees. The courts act only after very long delays and show little independence or concern for defendants' procedural rights.[35]

Even in cases where judges are capable, there may be outside interference with court deliberations, depending on the prominence of the individual on trial. High-profile defendants who are seen as threats to the regime are likely to face interventions by federal or local officials. Amnesty International has reported that in recent years a number of judges have been relieved of their duties when they were seen to have delivered judgments unfavorable to the government.[36] Judge Teshale Aberra, the president of the Oromo Supreme Court who fled to the United Kingdom in November 2006, maintains that the government is appointing a large number of friendly judges to the courts. Although Article 20 of the constitution gives criminal defendants the right to counsel, defendants often decline to exercise this right in the face of intimidation, or meet with obstruction when they try.

Nonetheless, the government touts the recent implementation of its Justice System Reform Program, which aims to improve training and judicial administration, as evidence of its commitment to judicial independence.[37] In January 2007, the Federal Supreme Court handed down judgments against former members of the deposed Marxist-Leninist regime who were accused of crimes against humanity and genocide dating back to the infamous Red Terror of the late 1970s. The government said that even though it took years to reach verdicts, the pursuit of the cases was necessary and demonstrated the diligence of the Office of the Special Prosecutor in ensuring that justice was achieved. The seventy-two defendants on trial had been incarcerated for twelve years; thirty-four were present in court, and another twenty-five—including Mengistu Haile Mariam, former head of the ousted regime—were tried in absentia. Mengistu and eleven of his top associates were sentenced to life in prison.

Further evidence of the improving performance of the Ethiopian court system can be found in Oromia.[38] State courts there recently passed judgment on 311,023 cases out of 396,768 filed in 2005, or 78 percent of the year's cases. This has significantly reduced backlogs and delays in the state court system. The Oromia Supreme Court has also been providing short- and long-term training to judges and support staff, and the Oromia state cabinet recently approved a judicial training center. Furthermore, the Federal Supreme Court has for the first time introduced a judges' performance evaluation regulation to provide judicial accountability and monitor judges' independence.

The military has generally remained loyal to civilian authority. However, in August 2006, a dissident Oromo general defected to Eritrea with 100 of his troops and pledged his support for the armed wing of the OLF. This moved the government to begin a systematic purge of soldiers it viewed as potentially disloyal.[39] Additionally, in a series of surveys taken in 2005, the public expressed concerns about the "public integrity of the armed forces."[40] This concern stems not only from events surrounding the flawed elections of 2005 but also from the way various groups, such as the Anuak, Somalis, and Oromo, have been treated by military forces called in to put down popular unrest.[41] Accountability for abuses perpetrated by the security forces is rare. An example is the commission of inquiry on the 2005 postelection violence: although in the end the commission officially exonerated the security forces of using "excessive force," it soon emerged that an earlier commission vote had found that excessive force was indeed applied.

Article 40 of the constitution upholds the rights of all citizens to own private property, except for land, which is exclusively owned by the state in common with Ethiopia's various peoples. The government may also appropriate private property in the interest of the public good. Judges are often too inexperienced, and the system is often too understaffed, to properly enforce existing commercial and bankruptcy laws.[42]

Recommendations

- The government should continue the implementation of the judicial reform program and expand it to include all local courts.
- Efforts to improve the training of police and judicial officials should be stepped up, and the training and retraining of civil service employees in legal matters should be given higher priority.
- The authorities should grant NGOs or international observers access to "prisoners of conscience," so as to demonstrate their commitment to transparency in the application of the rule of law. Officials should also uphold the constitutional rights of the accused to a fair and speedy trial.
- The government should ensure the full implementation of the judicial performance evaluation regulation that was recently issued by the Supreme Court.

ANTICORRUPTION AND TRANSPARENCY

ENVIRONMENT TO PROTECT AGAINST CORRUPTION:	2.40
EXISTENCE OF LAWS AND ETHICAL STANDARDS BETWEEN PRIVATE AND PUBLIC SECTORS:	3.00
ENFORCEMENT OF ANTICORRUPTION LAWS:	1.75
GOVERNMENTAL TRANSPARENCY:	2.29
CATEGORY AVERAGE:	**2.36**

By the standards of some countries in Africa, public corruption in Ethiopia is not overwhelming. However, it has been on the rise in recent years. There is evidence of institutional corruption, with the public citing graft by certain government officials, as well as petty corruption, in which individuals report having to pay bribes to receive services.

Transparency International's 2005 Global Corruption Barometer found that Ethiopian respondents perceived corruption to be widespread.[43] The most corrupt public institutions were said to be taxation agencies (scoring 3.8 points out of 5, with 5 representing the most corrupt). Business and private sector groups, also with a score of 3.8, are viewed as part of the problem. The Ethiopian public was similarly concerned about corruption involving political parties (3.6), the police (3.7), and the judiciary (3.7). Respondents felt that the least corrupt institutions were civil society organizations and religious bodies, which scored 2.5 and 2.4, respectively. Ethiopia has a high incidence of bribery. In the same Transparency International report, 30 percent of respondents said they had paid a bribe in the past year, while about half said they were asked for a bribe. Offering bribes to avoid problems with authorities is common, with nearly half of respondents saying they did so.[44]

Ethiopia's corruption is in part influenced by the difficulties of operating a federal system with a public bureaucracy that is low in human capacity. Officials are underpaid and often unaccountable. Common forms of corruption include bribes to receive certain permits and contracts or to get a public official to act more favorably in the issuing of a license. There is additional evidence that the public is concerned about the number of companies that, because of their political connections, enjoy above-average access to information, contracts, and finance.[45] Lawmakers regularly consult with business allies while formulating the state budget, though the state has made progress in disseminating budget information to the public.

The government is ostensibly pursuing economic liberalization, but the World Bank found that ongoing state control of the economy has held back the private sector. Some industries have been privatized, but the state still owns the major utilities and dominates the financial sector. Moreover, high-level party officials have undue privileges as business entrepreneurs.[46]

In 2001, the EPRDF unveiled the Federal Ethics and Anti-Corruption Commission (FEACC). It is widely held in Ethiopia that the commission was created principally to pursue powerful figures who had fallen out of favor with the regime. However, the FEACC has recently been active in fighting high-level corruption. For example, twelve senior officials of the Development Bank of Ethiopia were arrested in May 2006 and charged with violations of bank policy and illegal overseas transfers. In a separate reform move, the Federal Inland Revenue Authority (FIRA) in 2006 installed a new tax administration system to help improve the efficiency of revenue collection.[47] The FEACC also established a mechanism for whistle-blowers to confidentially report cases of corruption and pledged to protect them from retribution; although the testimony of whistle-blowers has indeed been utilized in corruption cases, the politicization of corruption cases may limit their effectiveness. In addition, the lack of media freedom clearly inhibits the press' ability to freely conduct investigative journalism or widely air accusations of corruption in an unbiased fashion.

A January 2007 Economist Intelligence Unit (EIU) report stated that Prime Minister Meles Zenawi in November 2006 had sacked the long-serving federal auditor general, Lema Argaw, for allegedly interfering in politics. According to the EIU, in July 2006 Argaw had reported that some federal money allocated to regional governments had not been properly accounted for. The government declared that in doing this, he had overstepped his authority, since regional funds were not part of his purview. The EIU report suggests that the prime minister did not have the authority to fire Argaw, citing a constitutional provision that gives such power to Parliament.[48]

Ethiopia has an ombudsman, but it is not clear that he is free from political pressure. Human Rights Watch claims that he was appointed without adequate debate or discussion.[49] The government's Plan for Accelerated and Sustained Development to End Poverty (PASDEP) includes measures to improve reporting by federal institutions, make this information available to the public, and improve accountability and transparency at the local government level.[50] Generally, although access to state information has increased, Ethiopia still lacks systematic legislation governing such access. There is no freedom of information law; the draft press law includes a section regarding access to state information, but leaves ambiguous the constraints that the state may place on citizen requests.

Recommendations

- The government should continue reform of the taxation agencies and the current system of tax collection by expanding the workforce and using newly available technologies to improve efficiency.
- Officials must create a more systematic method of granting licenses, permits, and contracts to avoid bribery. This could be done by centralizing such functions or providing improved oversight of lower-level bureaucrats.
- The authorities should focus more attention on fighting corruption at the local level, as increasing local accountability will improve the flow of accurate information to higher officials regarding patterns of corruption.
- Government at all levels should uphold freedom of information in law and in practice, which could greatly improve both accountability and effectiveness.

NOTES

[1] In some ways, the EPRDF regime's public commitment could be considered nothing more than a fiction, as not all states are ethnically homogeneous. Three of the nine regional states (Gambella, Beneshngul/Gamuz, and the Southern Nations, Nationalities, and Peoples' Region) comprise several different ethnic groups.

[2] Ethiopia also has the House of the Federation, a deliberative and consultative body of 108 members who represent the various regional states. It is not a legislative body.

[3] Jeffrey Gettleman, "Ethiopian Warplanes Attack Somalia," *New York Times*, 24 December 2006. It is widely believed that the United States was complicit in this invasion and even provided tactical and logistical support.

[4] See the group's website, http://www.eppf.net/eppfNews.htm.

5 See Carter Center, "Ethiopia Elections: Dispatch from Addis Ababa," news release, 16 May 2005, http://www.cartercenter.org/news/documents/doc2098.html; Terrence Lyons, "Ethiopia in 2005: The Beginning of a Transition?" *Africa Notes* no. 25 (January 2006), http://www.csis.org/media/csis/pubs/anotes_0601.pdf.

6 "Ethiopian Election 2005," BBC Monitoring Service, 13 October 2005, http://and enet.com/Ethiopian_Election_2005_News.pdf.

7 See Amnesty International (AI), *Ethiopia: The 15 May 2005 Elections and Human Rights—Recommendations to the Government, Election Observers and Political Parties* (London: AI, 29 April 2005), http://web.amnesty.org/library/index/engafr250022005.

8 Amare Aregawi, "How Free is Our Speech?" *Developments Magazine* no. 30 (25 July 2005), http://www.developments.org.uk/articles/how-free-is-our-speech.

9 "Ethiopia: Civil Service College Graduates 575 Students," *Ethiopian Herald*, 22 August 2006.

10 The 1,200 number is from Bizuwork Ketete and Kassaye Amare, "Assessment of the Operating Environment for CSO/NGOs in Ethiopia" (Addis Ababa: Christian Relief & Development Association," December 2006, http://www.crdaethiopia.org/Documents /Assesment%20of%20NGOs%20Operating%20Environment%20in%20Ethiopia.pdf. For the 1994 information see Rahmato Desselegn, "Civil Society Organizations in Ethiopia," in *Ethiopia: The Challenge of Democracy from Below*, ed. Bahru Zewde and Siegfried Pausewang (Uppsala: Nordiska Afrikainstitutet, 2002).

11 Lahra Smith, *Implications of the 2005 Elections for Ethiopian Citizenship and State Legitimacy* (unpublished paper, African Studies Association annual meeting, San Francisco, CA, November 2006), 17.

12 Human Rights Watch (HRW), "Ethiopia," in *World Report 2007* (New York: HRW, 2007), 5.

13 Reporters Without Borders (RSF), *Worldwide Press Freedom Index 2006* (Paris: RSF, 23 October 2006), http://www.rsf.org/rubrique.php3?id_rubrique=639.

14 "Ethiopia: Several Bills Before Parliament," *Reporter*, 16 October 2006.

15 The other two countries are Gambia and the Democratic Republic of Congo. See Associated Press, "Ethiopia Tops List of Countries Where Press Freedom is Deteriorating," *International Herald Tribune*, 2 May 2007, http://www.iht.com/articles/ap/2007/05/02 /africa/AF-GEN-Ethiopia-Press-Freedom.php.

16 Julia Crawford, "'Poison,' Politics and the Press," *Dangerous Assignments* (Spring/Summer 2006), http://www.cpj.org/Briefings/2006/DA_spring_06/ethiopia/ ethiopia_DA_spring _06.html.

17 Ibid.

18 See Associated Press, "Ethiopia Tops List of Countries Where Press Freedom is Deteriorating."

19 "US Jampro to Install FM Towers in Ethiopia," *Sudan Tribune*, 19 April 2006, http://www.sudantribune.com/article.php3?id_article=15136; United Nations Office for the Coordination of Humanitarian Affairs (OCHA), news release, 4 April 2006, http://www.irinnews.org.

20 Meera Selva, "Ethiopia Purges All Opposition With Treason and Genocide Charges," *Independent*, 23 December 2005.

21 AI, *Report 2006* (London: AI, 19 January 2007), http://web.amnesty.org/report2006 /eth-summary-eng.

22 Ibid.

23 HRW, "Ethiopia."

24 Constitution of the Federal Democratic Republic of Ethiopia (1994).

25 AI, *Report 2006.*

26 "EWLA Provides Training to Police Members on Women's Rights," *Ethiopian Herald*, 1 September 2006.

27 OCHA, "Ethiopia: Domestic Violence Rampant, Says UNFPA," news release, 12 October 2005, http://www.irinnews.org/Report.aspx?ReportId=56682.

28 "Ethiopia: Inequality, Gender-Based Violence Raise HIV/AIDS Risk for Women," Plus-News, 8 January 2007, http://www.plusnews.org/report.aspx?reportid=64382.

29 OCHA, "Ethiopia: Domestic Violence Rampant, says UNFPA."

30 U.S. Department of State, *Trafficking in Persons Report 2007* (Washington, D.C.: U.S. Department of State, 2007), http://www.state.gov/g/tip/rls/tiprpt/2007.

31 Embassy of Ethiopia, *Directive Issued to Determine the Residence Status of Eritrean Nationals Residing in Ethiopia* (Washington, D.C.: Embassy of Ethiopia, 2001), http://www .ethiopianembassy.org/RstatusEr.shtml.

32 Georgette Gagnon, "Letter to Ethiopian Ministers on Human Rights Violations Against Students" (New York: HRW, 20 February 2007), http://hrw.org/english/docs/2007 /02/20/ethiop15368.htm.

33 Constitution of the Federal Democratic Republic of Ethiopia (1994).

34 Heritage Foundation, *2007 Index of Economic Freedom* (Washington, D.C.: Heritage Foundation, 16 January 2007), http://www.heritage.org/index/country.cfm?id=Ethiopia.

35 HRW, "Ethiopia."

36 AI, "Ethiopia: Treason Trial of Prisoners of Conscience Opens in Addis Ababa," news release, 2 May 2006, http://web.amnesty.org/library/Index/ENGAFR250152006.

37 "Ethiopia: Ruling on Derg Officials Shows Independence of Judiciary: Ministry," *Ethiopian Herald*, 15 January 2007.

38 "Ethiopia: Oromia Courts Pass Judgment on Over 311,000 Cases," *Reporter*, 6 October 2006.

39 "Army Security Moves to Identify Dissenters," *Ethiopian Life, Politics, Culture and Arts*, http://seminawork.blogspot.com/2006/08/army-security-moves-to-identify.html.

40 Transparency International (TI), *Global Corruption Barometer 2005* (Berlin: TI, 9 December 2005), http://www.transparency.org/content/download/2160/12762/file /Global_Corruption_Barometer_2005_(full_report).pdf.

41 Cedric Barnes, *Ethiopia: A Socio-political Assessment* (Writenet: Commissioned by United Nations High Commissioner for Refugees, Status Determination and Protection Information Section, May 2006), 23–28, http://www.unhcr.org/home/RSDCOI/44f29d704 .pdf.

42 Heritage Foundation, *2007 Index of Economic Freedom.*

43 TI, *Global Corruption Barometer 2005.*

44 Ibid.

45 Barnes, *Ethiopia: A Socio-political Assessment.*

46 Economist Intelligence Unit (EIU), *Ethiopia Country Report* (London: EIU, 2007), http://portal.eiu.com/report_dl.asp?issue_id=1021731487&mode=pdf.

47 Ibid.

48 Ibid., 16–17.

49 HRW, "Ethiopia," in World Report 2005 (New York: HRW, January 2005), http://hrw.org/english/docs/2005/01/13/ethiop9833.htm.

50 "Ethiopia: Building on Progress" (Addis Ababa: Ministry of Finance and Economic Development), September 2006, http://www.mofaed.org/macro/PASDEP%20Final%20English.pdf.

HONDURAS

CAPITAL: Tegucigalpa
POPULATION: 7.1 million
GNI PER CAPITA: $1,200

SCORES	2005	2007
ACCOUNTABILITY AND PUBLIC VOICE:	3.81	3.97
CIVIL LIBERTIES:	3.88	3.74
RULE OF LAW:	3.35	3.56
ANTICORRUPTION AND TRANSPARENCY:	2.96	3.14

(scores are based on a scale of 0 to 7, with 0 representing weakest and 7 representing strongest performance)

Orlando J. Perez

INTRODUCTION

For most of its history, Honduras has been among the poorest nations in Latin America. It has a per capita income of US$1,200, about two-thirds of its seven million people live in poverty, and income is very unequally distributed. The UN Development Programme's Human Development Index in 2006 ranked Honduras 117 out of 177 countries.[1] The country also suffers from high unemployment and underemployment. It has been subject to political and military domination by its neighbors, its economy is dependent on foreign banana companies, and its population is relatively uneducated. Nevertheless, since 1982, when the military returned to the barracks, Honduras has made great strides toward democratic governance. The process, however, is by no means complete.[2]

Orlando J. Perez is a Professor of Political Science at Central Michigan University in Mount Pleasant, Michigan. He teaches courses in comparative politics, Latin American politics, and U.S.–Latin American relations. His work has appeared in the *Journal of Interamerican Studies and World Affairs, Hemisphere, South Eastern Latin Americanist, Political Science Quarterly,* and *Journal of Political and Military Sociology.* He received his M.A. and Ph.D. in political science from the University of Pittsburgh.

In the 1990s, Honduras benefited from regional peace and cooperation as it worked to make its economy viable and independent of U.S. aid. In 1992, the government concluded an agreement with El Salvador that largely settled the border controversy between the two countries; the last disputed section of the border was demarcated in 2006. Late in 1998, Honduras was devastated by Hurricane Mitch, one of the worst natural disasters of the century in the Western Hemisphere. The storm left 5,600 people dead and thousands missing, devastated the road network and other public infrastructure, crippled key sectors of the economy, and destroyed several thousand schools and nearly 83,000 homes. Mitch was estimated to have caused more than US$3 billion in damage in Honduras alone.

According to data from the World Bank, the percentage of the population living below the poverty line went from 74.8 percent in 1991 to 63.3 percent in 2002, while the portion of the population living in extreme poverty went from 54.2 percent in 1991 to 45.2 percent in 2002. The reduction in poverty was greater in urban areas, where both extreme and total poverty declined, than in rural areas, where total poverty fell but extreme poverty actually increased between 1991 and 2002.[3]

Honduras has experienced a rise in violence due to its growing role as both a transit point and a final destination for small arms from Guatemala, El Salvador, and Nicaragua.[4] Crime has also flourished as a result of the activities of semi-organized youth gangs known as *maras*, which have spread throughout the country. The maras are structured on gangs of Salvadoran youth in the United States, which spread to Guatemala and Honduras through El Salvador, and continue to maintain links to the United States.

While progress toward democracy has been achieved, significant problems remain. They relate primarily, though not exclusively, to the lack of accountability within the judicial system and supporting agencies such as the police. Particularly troubling issues include arbitrary, extrajudicial executions; poor prison conditions and frequent detainee abuse; a culture of impunity for violations of human rights; a lack of judicial independence; discrimination against indigenous people and homosexuals; and minimal labor law enforcement.

ACCOUNTABILITY AND PUBLIC VOICE

FREE AND FAIR ELECTORAL LAWS AND ELECTIONS:	4.75
EFFECTIVE AND ACCOUNTABLE GOVERNMENT:	2.75
CIVIC ENGAGEMENT AND CIVIC MONITORING:	4.00
MEDIA INDEPENDENCE AND FREEDOM OF EXPRESSION:	4.38
CATEGORY AVERAGE:	**3.97**

Citizens have the constitutional right to change their government peacefully in periodic, free, and fair elections in which the president, vice president, and members of the National Congress are chosen by universal suffrage. The executive branch in Honduras, headed by a president who is elected by a simple majority, has traditionally dominated the legislative and judicial branches of government. After two successive Liberal governments, the National Party came to power in 2002; the Liberals returned in 2005, with Jose Manuel Zelaya Rosales as president.

One of the biggest challenges facing the future of Honduran politics is the fact that the two traditional, dominant parties, the Liberal Party of Honduras (PLH) and the National Party of Honduras (PNH), emphasize voting based on personalities and regionalism rather than platform and ideology, which are similar in the two parties. Thus, voters have been presented with little real choice.

The 2005 election was the seventh democratic ballot held since 1982, and despite extensive confusion in the vote count, which resulted in Nationalist candidate Porfirio Lobo Sosa refusing to concede for ten days, it was generally considered free and fair. Observers from the Organization of American States (OAS) noted some irregularities but no systematic fraud. In May 2004, a new Electoral Law was passed in an attempt to make elections more democratic.[5] For the first time in Honduran history, internal party primaries were held as a way to nominate candidates; moreover, 30 percent of all candidates were supposed to be women, although none of the parties followed this provision to the letter.[6] The new law abolished the old National Electoral Tribunal, which was dominated by the traditional parties, and replaced it with a Supreme

Electoral Tribunal appointed by the National Congress.[7] Additionally, the new law changed the manner of voting in congressional elections, allowing citizens in each of the country's eighteen departments to cast ballots for several individual candidates, potentially from different parties, rather than choosing a single party list.

Honduras has five registered political parties: the PNH, the PLH, the Social Democrats (Partido Innovacion Nacional y Social Democrata, PINU-SD), the Christian Democrats (Partido Democrata-Cristiano, DC), and Democratic Unification (Partido Unificacion Democratica, UD). The PNH and PLH have alternately ruled the country for decades. In this deeply entrenched party system, traditional community and family allegiances generally dominate voting decisions. This is reflected in the poor level of platform development and weak discourse in election campaigns, with little substantive discussion about critical issues such as poverty and vulnerability to natural disasters. Political finance rules were modified in 2004 to include more transparency and increased public funding, but Transparency International reported that the changes have yet to be put into practice.[8] Members of the Honduran congress, especially those from the PNH and PLH, are generally seen as more beholden to their respective party leaders than to the electorate, and their actions tend to serve the interests of the country's highly concentrated political and economic elite.[9]

In a recent article, Ismael Moreno described the Liberal Party as a federation of parties that are clearly in competition and confrontation with each other, as evidenced by the seven different candidates who contested the party primaries in February 2005.[10] Upon winning the election, Zelaya divided power among these many factions rather than trying to assert control over them. This has had negative effects on the capacity of the government to develop and implement a cohesive agenda. Governance was further undermined when the incoming administration adhered to the partisan tradition of replacing the bulk of the civil service, agency, and institution heads at every level, including basic posts. The purge left the government seriously depleted of experienced and capable officials and has effectively prevented continuity in the majority of public policies. As a report from the Center for Global Development stated, "Both [Inter-American Development Bank] and World Bank have experienced significant stoppages to their programs

. . . in past political transitions in Honduras. One World Bank official explained that disruptions in Honduras are among the worst in the region . . . everyone from ministers to entry-level technocrats turns over every four years."[11]

Underscoring the shortcomings of this system, a major shakeup of the cabinet occurred in January 2007. Several ministers were dismissed after an assessment conducted by the Ministry of the Presidency—at the direction of the president—found a number of deficiencies and instances of administrative waste.[12] Meanwhile, as there is little cohesion in Zelaya's cabinet or within the Liberal Party in Congress, the legislative process has become an arena for contesting interests, and various cross-party pacts have been made to get required legislation passed.

The status of civil society in Honduras remains tenuous. While non-governmental organizations (NGOs) and other groups are allowed to operate, these groups complain of onerous registration requirements and government interference in their work. Moreover, with the exception of some business groups, the government has generally exhibited little inclination to take the views of civil society into account when formulating policy. The significant presence of international donors, however, has led to an increase in pressure on the government to increase cooperation with civil society.[13]

Freedom of speech and of the press are constitutionally protected; however, the government generally does not respect these rights in practice. On a positive note, on May 9, 2005, the Supreme Court declared that the defamation law, which had criminalized criticism of public officials and created a "special realm of protection" around them, was unconstitutional. The court held that provisions of the law violated both national and international norms concerning freedom of expression.[14] Nonetheless, restrictive press laws are still often used to subpoena journalists for reporting on official corruption, drug trafficking, and human rights abuses.

President Zelaya often criticizes the media when he perceives news reports as being unfriendly to his government. He has accused journalists of exaggerating the government's mistakes and minimizing its accomplishments. During 2006, journalists faced a number of legal prosecutions from political figures. On September 4, Ernesto Rojas, a reporter for Radio San Pedro, was sued by city council member

Guillermo Villatoro Hall, while Francisco Romero, a reporter on the program "Hablemos de Noche de Honduras," was sued by Yansen Juarez, the national coordinator of programs and projects in the Ministry of Public Education. Both suits were considered to be on charges of harassment.

The number of threats and physical attacks against journalists has generally diminished, but some incidents did occur in recent years, particularly following the publication of articles on organized crime or corruption. In July 2005, unidentified individuals in San Marcos de Ocotepeque tried to kill radio journalist Jose Aleman by firing several shots at him as he was returning home from the station. Aleman revealed that he had received death threats after reporting on problems with the water supply for the community. Politically motivated attacks against the press were common as well. On November 5, 2005, Liberal Party supporters forced the temporary closure of Virtud Stereo radio and made death threats against its manager, Jaime Diaz, as a result of party rivalry during the election. In April 2006, Liberal Party representative Romualdo Bueso Melghem tried to strangle community journalist Martha Vasquez during a public meeting. Vasquez is a contributor for the website Indymedia.com. Separately in April, Wendy Guerra, host of the Santa Rosa de Copan city–based Channel 49 news program "Denuncias 49," was fired following political pressure felt by the station's manager, who is a member of the Liberal Party. In May, Guerra was rehired after a public outcry.

Honduras has around nine daily papers, including the popular *El Heraldo* and *El Tiempo*. There are six private television stations and five nationally broadcasting radio stations—one state owned and four independent. Although both print and broadcast outlets are predominantly privately owned, media ownership is concentrated in the hands of a few powerful business conglomerates with intersecting political and economic ties; this has led to self-censorship. Corruption among journalists also has an unfavorable impact on reporting. In addition, the government influences media coverage through bribes, the granting or denial of access to government officials, and selective placement of official advertisements. The government did not restrict access to the internet; however, less than 5 percent of the population used the internet in 2006.

Recommendations

- The 30 percent quota for female candidates mandated by the new Electoral and Political Organization Law should be enforced.
- The Electoral Law should be amended to enhance the level of representation in Congress through the election of deputies by districts.
- Regulations on political party and campaign financing in the new Electoral Law should be enforced and additional safeguards implemented to ensure fair and competitive electoral processes.
- Media ownership concentration should be monitored, and independent media outlets and journalists should be protected against intimidation and harassment. Police and judicial independence must be guaranteed in the investigation and resolution of cases involving harassment of independent, rural, and indigenous media outlets.
- Reforms of the Civil Service Law are needed to significantly reduce partisan influences on government employees, particularly in low- and mid-level positions. The government should amend the Civil Service Law and its regulations to ensure equity and objectivity in the selection of applicants for civil service posts.

CIVIL LIBERTIES

PROTECTION FROM STATE TERROR, UNJUSTIFIED IMPRISONMENT, AND TORTURE:	2.71
GENDER EQUITY:	3.25
RIGHTS OF ETHNIC, RELIGIOUS, AND OTHER DISTINCT GROUPS:	2.75
FREEDOM OF CONSCIENCE AND BELIEF:	6.00
FREEDOM OF ASSOCIATION AND ASSEMBLY:	4.00
CATEGORY AVERAGE:	**3.74**

Honduras is plagued by violations of civil liberties, including unlawful killings by police and former members of the security forces, detainee abuse by security forces, the disappearance of dissidents, lengthy pretrial detention, and lack of due process of law. Government corruption, impunity for lawbreakers, and gang violence exacerbate these problems.

In November 2004, Honduran President Ricardo Maduro took the first step toward accepting state responsibility for the security forces' violations of human rights beginning in the 1980s. Complying with previous decisions by the Inter-American Court of Human Rights and the Inter-American Commission on Human Rights, he apologized for the 1992 extrajudicial killing of Juan Humberto Sanchez and the 1995 disappearance of Dixie Miguel Urbina. He also reported the establishment of an Inter-Institutional Commission on Human Rights for the country, and promised to ensure well-funded investigations and progress reports for victims' family members. Human rights groups and the media, while hailing the developments, voiced skepticism about whether the government would follow through on its pledges.[15] Two years later, little concrete action had been taken, and allegations of new abuses continue to be reported.

In the country's prisons, inmates endure overcrowding and unsanitary conditions. A total of some 13,000 prisoners are housed in facilities with an intended capacity of 6,000, and all but one of the facilities were originally built for other purposes, including military barracks, schools, and offices. Poor urban and rural residents are disproportionately represented in the prison population, with only a small minority from the middle and upper classes. Rape and other prison violence are common, and guards are subject to bribery by inmates, enabling escapes and the smuggling of contraband including weapons and drugs. Because mara members are often sequestered from other inmates and offered no rehabilitation, they are more likely to continue their criminal activity.[16] The presence of such gangs contributes to large-scale riots, uprisings, and arson. A May 2004 blaze at the San Pedro Sula prison killed 107 gang members, and the resulting investigation remains unresolved to date.

Gang violence is one of the most serious problems facing the country, and Honduras has one of the highest crime rates in Central America. There were 36,000 gang members in Honduras at the end of 2003, according to police statistics. A new Anti-Mara Law went into effect in August 2003, amending Article 332 of the criminal code. It aimed to combat the rise in youth violence by rounding up gang members for "illicit association," and allowed police to detain youths merely for appearing to belong to gangs—due to tattoos or other insignia—and gathering in their neighborhoods.[17] Thus, one effect of the Anti-Mara Law has been a fresh surge in the prison population. Moreover, the law restricts freedom of assembly and association, contradicting provisions of the constitution and international treaties. Since its promulgation, it is estimated that more than 1,000 mareros have been arrested and imprisoned, though the majority of them have never faced trial.[18]

On December 23, 2004, twenty-eight people were massacred on a public bus in San Pedro Sula. While President Maduro claimed that the massacre was a gang retaliation for his crackdowns, others suggested that the killings were part of a turf battle between the Mara Salvatrucha and M-18 gangs.[19] Two Mara Salvatrucha members were convicted of the crime in February 2007, but two others were acquitted due to lack of evidence, and other possible suspects remained at large. Juan Bautista Jimenez, a gang leader who was believed to have ordered the attack, was found hanged to death in prison in early 2005.[20]

The Zelaya government, after an initial move away from hard-line tactics and toward dialogue and rehabilitation programs, has recently taken action to crack down on the gangs, arresting hundreds in September 2006. Zelaya also proposed doubling the size of the existing police force and forming an elite special forces unit. The latter plan drew criticism for potentially militarizing the civilian police.[21]

The Violence Observatory at the National Autonomous University of Honduras issued a report on the number of violent deaths—including homicides, traffic accidents, and suicides—in Honduras in 2006. The report found that the number of homicides had increased by 24.9 percent from 2005 to 2006, and that of the 4,736 violent deaths in 2006, an overwhelming 3,018 were homicides. This made the homicide rate 46.2 for every 100,000 Hondurans.[22] President Zelaya announced on August 30, 2006, a new plan to stem the tide of violence. Operacion Trueno (Operation Thunder) was designed to develop close cooperation between police, military, and private security forces. In the first days of action in September, the program made the headlines for operations in which security forces detained more than one hundred "delinquents" in a single night. Operacion Trueno will add 30,000 to 60,000 "often untrained and mainly unregulated private security [personnel] . . . to bolster 10,000 experienced and usually better-trained Honduran armed service personnel as well as 8,000 police officers who are now thinly spread across the country," according to the Council on Hemispheric

Affairs.[23] Similar, repeated efforts to apply a strong-arm solution to the problems of crime and youth gangs have previously failed to stem the tide of criminal activity, and in most cases have made things worse.

At the beginning of 2007, the UN Committee on the Rights of the Child examined Honduras' compliance with the convention, and expressed concern over the high number of disappearances and extrajudicial killings of minors, and the lack of response from both the state and the public. The committee urged the government to curb mara-related violence through education, gang prevention, and rehabilitation programs, as well as a renewed focus on the abundance of firearms in the country.[24]

Violence against women is rampant in Honduras. Special domestic violence courts were reportedly overwhelmed by the tens of thousands of complaints received in recent years. Amnesty International reports that, according to the special prosecutor for women's affairs, nearly a third of the women who submitted domestic abuse complaints were eventually killed by their abusers.[25] The special prosecutor in January 2007 announced the formation of investigative units in the capital and six other cities that would be devoted to solving murder cases with female victims. In 2006, 171 women were killed.[26]

The Women's Movement for Peace has argued that judicial bias consistently favors male perpetrators in domestic-violence cases. The group reported in late 2006 that alleged victims had won only 204 of the 6,628 suits filed that year, noting that wealthy and powerful men were especially likely to prevail in court. Gladys Lanza, the organization's coordinator, listed a number of public officials who had faced allegations of domestic abuse.[27] The constitution and laws prohibit gender-based discrimination in employment, but the regulations are often ignored. Patriarchal attitudes pervade employment practices, and the state does not do enough to curtail abuses or enforce the law. The majority of women hold low-skilled jobs, primarily as domestic workers or in maquiladoras.

Discrimination and violence against gays and lesbians is rampant. In a March 2007 case reported by Amnesty International, gay rights activist Donny Reyes was severely abused in police custody in Tegucigalpa. He was allegedly beaten by the officers who detained him, then assaulted and raped by other detainees in a jail cell over the course of several hours, with the alleged encouragement of police.[28]

At least 7 percent of the population of Honduras is considered part of an indigenous group, amounting to more than 500,000 people. Article 346 of the Honduran constitution states that "it is the duty of the government to protect the rights and interests of existing indigenous communities in the country, especially with respect to the land and forests where they are settled."[29] However, the state has not fully enforced those rights. Indigenous groups have been subject to intimidation, violence, and harassment, and some activists are imprisoned, tortured, and killed. In addition, the government has failed repeatedly to protect indigenous land rights. In March 2007, the Civic Council of Popular and Indigenous Organizations (COPINH) reported a recent incident in which local officials and heavily armed police allegedly used force and arson to disperse an indigenous Lenca community on behalf of a landowner. The officers, overseen by a public prosecutor and local police commissioner, reportedly burned forty homes and a coffee nursery at the settlement, located about eighty kilometers northwest of the capital. The blazes spread to adjacent forests and scorched some 800 acres, COPINH said.[30]

Environmental groups have also become targets of harassment and intimidation, particularly by landowners and logging interests. After President Zelaya announced a ban on logging in parts of Olancho province in May 2006, environmentalists reported receiving multiple death threats, presumably because they had campaigned for the new restrictions. The Environmental Movement of Olancho (MAO) soon asked the Inter-American Commission on Human Rights to compel Honduran authorities to protect its personnel. However, two MAO leaders were shot to death in the main plaza of the town of Guarizama in December 2006, and the organization claimed that the national police had summarily executed them. One of the victims, Heraldo Zuniga, told witnesses at the scene that employees of the Sansone logging firm had hired a police sergeant to kill him. Two days after the men's deaths, the human rights commission ordered officials to provide security for MAO activists.[31]

The Honduran constitution protects freedom of religion.[32] Roughly 80 percent of the population is believed to be Roman Catholic, although Protestant denominations have apparently been expanding in recent years. There is little serious friction between religious groups.

The Honduran constitution guarantees both freedom of association and freedom of assembly. Trade union rights have been an area of conflict; workers attempting to organize often face intimidation, blacklisting, and other forms of retribution. Banana plantations and the *maquila* export processing zones are particularly conflictive areas with respect to labor rights.

Hondurans are generally able to utilize their right to protest and numerous demonstrations occurred in the last two years, many involving environmental and indigenous activists. Some activists have denounced the "illicit association" element of the anti-mara laws, which is ambiguous enough to be used against non-mara groups, including the oft-persecuted gay community.

Recommendations

- The Anti-Mara Law should be revised so as to enhance due process protections, particularly habeas corpus rights, and reduce pretrial and arbitrary detentions.
- A concerted effort must be made to remedy the deplorable conditions in the nation's prison system. Particularly important is alleviation of overcrowding and elimination of harassment and abuse of prisoners. Efforts should be made to promote policies aimed at rehabilitation and prevention rather than focusing exclusively on incarceration.
- Significant resources should be dedicated to preventing domestic violence. The Law Against Domestic Violence should be revised so that judges oversee the law's implementation and perpetrators face serious criminal penalties instead of community service, which the law currently prescribes.
- The government should immediately implement the Law for Integrated Youth Development and the National Youth Policy Proposal (Ley Marco para el Desarrollo Integral de la Juventud y Propuesta de Politica Nacional de Juventud), an initiative aimed at dealing with youth and gang violence that was approved in September 2005 but has yet to be fully funded or implemented.
- The government must protect indigenous communities' efforts to organize and mobilize in support of their constitutional rights in the face of assault by private landowners and businesspeople. It is particularly important to stop police and judicial authorities from intimidating and harassing indigenous activists.

- The government must provide greater protection for threatened environmental and social activists and ensure prompt and effective prosecution of those accused of killing or intimidating them.

RULE OF LAW

INDEPENDENT JUDICIARY:	3.20
PRIMACY OF RULE OF LAW IN CIVIL AND CRIMINAL MATTERS:	3.33
ACCOUNTABILITY OF SECURITY FORCES AND MILITARY TO CIVILIAN AUTHORITIES:	3.25
PROTECTION OF PROPERTY RIGHTS:	4.00
EQUAL TREATMENT UNDER THE LAW:	4.00
CATEGORY AVERAGE:	**3.56**

The judicial branch of government in Honduras is subject to intervention and influence by both the elected branches and wealthy private interests. Incoming presidential administrations commonly ensure the replacement of judicial officeholders with their own appointees, and pervasive corruption enables the manipulation of court decisions by outside actors. The rule of law is further undermined by the government's general failure to protect the public from violent crime and police abuses, and the lack of physical security in turn encourages vigilantism and other forms of lawbreaking. According to one report, less than a fifth of the population trusts the justice system, with rural residents and the lower classes expressing the least confidence.[33]

The judiciary is administered by the fifteen-member Supreme Court of Justice, which is also the country's highest court of appeal. The court submits the budget for the judicial branch to the National Congress for approval, governs the organization of judicial districts, and oversees the public defender service. Supreme Court judges are elected for seven-year terms by the Congress, leaving them dependent on political support and patronage. Since the court, and specifically its president, is responsible for appointing and dismissing subordinate judges, this political influence extends into the lower courts and affects job security. Appointments and promotions are often made in violation of legal and ethical guidelines and without regard to merit. Judges at all levels commonly ignore the official code of ethics, which also applies to attorneys and their clients.[34]

The constitution contains ample and detailed provisions to ensure the protection of fundamental criminal procedure rights. Warrants are required for arrests unless the suspect is caught in the act (Article 84). Detention without charges is limited to twenty-four hours without a judge's order, or up to six days with court approval (Article 71). Suspects are guaranteed legal aid, protection against coerced self-incrimination, and the presumption of innocence (Articles 83, 88, and 89).[35] However, many of these provisions are not fully enforced or are enforced in the breach, particularly with respect to gang members.

The criminal procedure code that took effect in February 2002 replaced the inquisitorial system with one based on the adversarial model, leading to greater transparency and a reduction in procedural delays. The proportion of prisoners held without sentence fell from 76 percent to 62 percent between 2002 and March 2006.[36] Despite such improvements, many problems remain, such as deplorable prison conditions, inordinately long pretrial detention, and the woefully inadequate public defenders' office. These issues continue to delay and too often deny justice for many Honduran citizens.

The National Human Rights Commission in Honduras received 9,390 complaints of human rights violations in 2006, including illegal detention, abuse of authority, and due process violations. Although justice officials and education personnel were listed among the accused perpetrators, security agencies were the subjects of the most complaints.[37]

The transition from military to civilian rule and the subsequent establishment of civilian control over the military has proceeded steadily, if not always smoothly, for a quarter of a century. Fearful of the impact of the Sandinista revolution in Nicaragua and apprehensive about the U.S.-supported military build-up in El Salvador, both the military and the traditional political class went to great lengths to accommodate the United States during the 1980s.[38] The military has stayed in the barracks since 1982; during this time, and particularly since the turn of the century, civilian control has increased considerably. Control of the military budget, however, has ensured that the military continues to hold influence in the Honduran economy.[39]

Honduran security forces have still largely not been held account-able for human rights abuses inflicted during the 1980s. After a visit to the country at the end of January 2007, the UN Working Group on En-forced Disappearances noted that the lack of serious investigation had resulted in de facto amnesty for past rights abusers. Notably, unlike in some Latin American countries, there is no specific crime for forced dis-appearance in Honduras, making the investigation and prosecution process more difficult. According to Honduran special prosecutor San-dra Ponce, however, the government was working on a bill to criminal-ize forced disappearance.[40]

Protection of property rights is weak in Honduras. The shortcom-ings of the judiciary, along with an outdated commercial code, make enforcing contracts a difficult and time-consuming process. The gov-ernment has begun to make improvements in intellectual property pro-tection and the civil procedures code, largely as a result of its obligations under the Central American Free Trade Agreement (DR-CAFTA) with the United States.[41] Starting with the 1962 agrarian reform law, Hon-duras has a history of land redistribution from large estates to small-scale farmers. These reforms, however, have been largely negated in recent decades, especially after the passage in 1992 of the Law for Agrarian Modernization. Despite the predominantly rural landscape of Honduras, peasants have limited or no access to land ownership, a situation which continues to cause conflict and occasional land invasions.[42]

Recommendations
- The Judicial Career Law should be amended to protect against dis-crimination and the distortion of objective criteria in the selection of judicial officials.[43]
- The Justice Ministry should be provided with its own investigative police force to strengthen the investigative capacities of the public prosecution and to help ensure guarantees for defendants.
- The state should fully enforce the new criminal procedure code, which will ensure the release of all detainees held under the old code who have been acquitted in the first instance.
- Public defenders should be provided with improved training and material resources, such as offices, computers, and vehicles, in order to function more effectively.

ANTICORRUPTION AND TRANSPARENCY

ENVIRONMENT TO PROTECT AGAINST CORRUPTION:	3.20
EXISTENCE OF LAWS AND ETHICAL STANDARDS BETWEEN	
PRIVATE AND PUBLIC SECTORS:	3.25
ENFORCEMENT OF ANTICORRUPTION LAWS:	3.25
GOVERNMENTAL TRANSPARENCY:	2.86
CATEGORY AVERAGE:	**3.14**

Corruption in Honduras is deeply rooted and present at all levels of society. Approximately US$526.3 million is lost to corruption annually, challenging the nation's ability to achieve sustained progress in the political, social, and economic spheres.[44] The country's entrenched culture of impunity has many interrelated causes, ranging from a restricted media, low levels of citizen participation, and lack of transparency to institutional shortcomings such as weak judicial independence and unaccountable legislators. In a country as poor as Honduras, the undermining of the rule of law and the transfer of funds from development projects to the pockets of corrupt individuals carries particularly pernicious effects.[45]

According to the 2007 Index of Economic Freedom produced by the Heritage Foundation and the *Wall Street Journal,* Honduras's economy is 60.3 percent free, making it the world's 76th freest economy among 157 nations.[46] The report praises the level of fiscal and financial freedom in the country as well as its tax levels and a slowly improving banking sector. Negatives include weak property rights and low levels of business freedom, including difficulties related to commercial licensing and business closure costs.[47]

The 2006 Transparency International Corruption Perceptions Index gives Honduras the fifth worst score in the Western Hemisphere, 2.5 out of 10, a level indicative of uncontrolled corruption. This leaves Honduras with a ranking of 121 out of 163 countries in the survey. Honduras's score in 2005 had been slightly better, at 2.6 out of 10.[48]

On November 23, 2006, the Honduran Congress passed the Transparency and Access to Public Information Law, becoming the sixth Latin American country to adopt such a law.[49] The law established the National Institute for Access to Public Information (IAIP) as the clearinghouse for processing citizens' information requests.[50] While the principle behind the law was lauded by many civil society groups, they pointed to numerous loopholes that will allow the government to shield large numbers of documents from public scrutiny, especially in the name of national security. Government ministers will also be able to restrict any document that is believed to threaten economic stability or governance. Other major drawbacks include restrictions on information about humanitarian aid, ambiguous provisions regarding the purging of files, the weakness of the IAIP, and the inapplicability of the law to large numbers of high-ranking officials.[51]

On February 10, 2007, an estimated 30,000 Hondurans marched in Tegucigalpa to protest corruption and demand transparency. The high attendance lost some of its power, however, following allegations that at least 2,000 people had been paid by the Liberal Party to participate in the march and provide assurances that cheers would outweigh heckles when President Zelaya spoke.[52]

Corruption among the police remains alarmingly high. Police involvement in drug trafficking, extrajudicial killings, and intimidation of human rights groups remains a major problem. More than fifty police officers have been removed or prosecuted for involvement in corrupt activities ranging from taking bribes to murder. Police corruption seems to be worse in rural areas, where officers are routinely used by landowners, large corporations, or prominent politicians to intimidate political opponents or social activists.

A report by the Federation of Organizations for Development in Honduras (FOPRIDEH) revealed that the four government institutions with the highest number of corruption-related media stories in 2006 were the Executive Directorate of Income (the revenue collection agency), municipal governments, the immigration agency, and the justice ministry. One of the major scandals during 2005 and 2006 was the so-called *gasolinazo*, in which 500 tankers of gasoline were brought into the country illegally, costing the government about 67 million lempiras (US$3.5 million) in taxes. Reports indicate that officials of the National Agrarian Institute linked with the then-ruling National Party benefited from the operation.[53] Another area of concern was the selling of Honduran visas by immigration officials to ineligible foreign citizens so they could obtain entry into the United States. In 2006, the U.S. government suspended the issuing of entry visas in Honduras until Honduran officials provided assurances that firm steps would be taken to curb corruption in the immigration agency.[54] Despite some limited efforts to that end, immigration and customs services remain among the most corrupt agencies in the Honduran government.

While Honduras has laws to protect civil servants and to promote transparency in government procurement processes, many of them are lightly enforced, lack teeth, or are contradictory. In general, Honduras lacks adequate mechanisms for auditing public accounts. The Superior Court of Accounts is not fully equipped to handle all of the responsibilities the law requires. Additionally, conflict-of-interest regulations are poorly enforced, and private-sector influence on government continues to distort public policy decisions. The Honduran budget process was judged by the Open Budget Initiative to be only "minimally" open, with little information provided to citizens by the executive, and no public hearings.[55] Restraints on the media and the lack of specific and effective legislation to protect whistle-blowers also make the reporting of corruption less likely.[56]

Recommendations

- The Law of Transparency and Access to Public Information should be revised to close loopholes and contradictions that permit the classification of large numbers of documents that should be available for public scrutiny. These reforms should be accompanied by stronger mechanisms for public participation and scrutiny of government decisions.
- Significant efforts should be made to stem the tide of corruption in the national police force. The government of Honduras should fully implement Article 8 of the Organic Law of the National Police, which calls for an Internal Affairs Unit under the direct supervision of the minister of security and with independent powers to investigate illegal and corrupt actions by police officers. The unit should also be able to coordinate its investigative activities with the Justice Ministry in order to ensure that crimes by police officers are swiftly prosecuted.
- Training programs for public servants should be increased in order to raise the standards of conduct, and to improve mechanisms for preventing conflicts of interest.[57]
- The government should adopt and implement specific measures for protecting civil servants who report acts of corruption, ensuring that they are not subjected to threats or reprisals.[58]

• The government should provide the Superior Court of Accounts with the resources it needs to fully carry out its functions.

NOTES

1 Honduras's HDI ranking remained largely unchanged between 1998 and 2004.

2 For a comprehensive analysis of Honduran political history in the twentieth century, see Alison Acker, Honduras: *The Making of a Banana Republic* (Boston: South End Press, 1988); Thomas P. Anderson, *Politics in Central America: Guatemala, El Salvador, Honduras, and Nicaragua*, 2nd ed. (New York: Praeger, 1988); John A. Booth, Christine J. Wade, and Thomas W. Walker, *Understanding Central America: Global Forces, Rebellion, and Challenge* (Boulder, CO: Westview Press, 2006); Dario A. Euraque, *Reinterpreting the Banana Republic: Region and State in Honduras, 1870–1972* (Chapel Hill: University of North Carolina Press, 1996); Donald E. Schulz and Deborah Sundloff Schulz, *The United States, Honduras, and the Crisis in Central America* (Boulder, CO: Westview Press, 1994); Mark B. Rosenberg and Philip L. Shepherd, eds., *Honduras Confronts its Future: Contending Perspectives on Critical Issues* (Boulder, CO: L. Rienner Publishers, 1986); James A. Morris, *Honduras: Caudillo Politics and Military Rulers* (Boulder, CO: Westview Press, 1984); Kirk S. Bowman, *Militarization, Democracy, and Development: The Perils of Praetorianism in Latin America* (University Park: Pennsylvania State University Press, 2002).

3 World Bank, "Memorandum of the President of the International Development Association and the International Finance Corporation to the Executive Directors on a Country Assistance Strategy for the Republic of Honduras," 29 May 2003, http://wbln0018 .worldbank.org/lac/lacinfoclient.nsf/8d6661f6799ea8a48525673900537f95/bcf2ecb585 a5fbcb85256d4e00776112/$FILE/main.pdf.

4 William Godnick, with Robert Muggah and Camilla Waszink, *Stray Bullets: The Impact of Small Arms Misuse in Central America* (Geneva: Small Arms Survey, 2002).

5 Ley Electoral y de las Organizaciones Politicas, Tribunal Supremo Electoral de Honduras, http://www.tse.hn.

6 Marcela del Mar Suazo, *Mujer y Ciudadania Politica en Honduras: Valoracion Preliminar del Impacto de la Ley de Igualdad de Oportunidades y la Ley Electoral* (New York: United Nations Development Programme [UNDP], 7 April 2005), http://www.undp.un.hn /proddal/pdf/Marcela_Suazo_070405.pdf.

7 The qualifications include being a natural-born Honduran citizen, a minimum of twenty-five years old, and in full exercise of one's constitutional and civil rights (Constitution of the Republic of Honduras, Chapter 5, Article 52).

8 Transparency International, "Elections Activity Chart," 2006, http://www.trans parency.org/content/download/6642/39834/file/TI-ElectionsActivityChart.doc.

9 U.S. Agency for International Development (USAID), *Regional Strategy for Central America and Mexico, FY 2003–2008; Volume 2: Annex B: Honduras Country Plan* (Washington, D.C.: USAID, 30 September 2003), 27, http://pdf.dec.org/pdf_docs/PDABZ 673.pdf.

10 Ismael Moreno, "Nadie espera nada del nuevo gobierno," *Revista Envio* no. 291 (June 2006).

11 Sarah Lucas, "Honduras Field Report," MCA Monitor, Center for Global Development, April 2007, http://www.cgdev.org/doc/MCA/Honduras_fieldrpt.pdf.

12 "Honduras: Cabinet Shake-up Causes Disquiet," *Latin America Regional Report: Central America & Caribbean,* January 2007.

13 Honduras Center for the Promotion of Community Development (CEHPRODEC), *From Consultation to Participation: CIVICUS Civil Society Index Report for Honduras* (Tegucigalpa: CIVICUS, November 2006), http://www.civicus.org/new/media/CSI _Honduras_Country_Report.pdf.

14 International Media Lawyers Assocation (IMLA), "Defamation, Insult, False News," IMLA Thematic Newsletter, January 2007, http://www.internationalmedialawyers.org /cgi-bin/blog/blosxom.cgi/newsletter_first_thematic.html.

15 May I Speak Freely? (MISF), "Honduras' Slow Road to National Reparation," news release, 25 October 2006, http://www.mayispeakfreely.org/index.php?gSec=doc&doc _id=160.

16 Ismael Moreno, "Honduras' Prison Massacres Reflect a Social and Political Crisis," *Revista Envio* no. 294 (January 2006), http://www.envio.org.ni/articulo/3201; Lisa J. Adams, "Honduran President Calls for Crime Reform," Associated Press, 2 February 2006.

17 Harold Sibaja, Enrique Roig, Anu Rajaraman, Hilda Caldera, and Ernesto Bardales, *Central America and Mexico Gang Assessment, Annex 3: Honduras Profile* (Washington, D.C.: USAID, April 2006), http://www.usaid.gov/locations/latin_america_caribbean /democracy/honduras_profile.pdf.

18 Amnesty International (AI), "Honduras: 102 Deaths In Prison: An Independent Inquiry Is Required Along With a Review of Government Security Policies," news release, 19 May 2004, http://web.amnesty.org/library/Index/ENGAMR370042004?open&of =ENG-HND.

19 Mark P. Sullivan, "Honduras: Political and Economic Situation and U.S. Relations" (Washington, D.C.: Congressional Research Service, 3 May 2005), http://fpc.state.gov /documents/organization/47138.pdf.

20 MISF, "Two Gang Members Convicted for 2004 Bus Massacre," Honduras News in Review, 26 February 2007, http://www.mayispeakfreely.org/index.php?gSec=doc&doc _id=255.

21 Sullivan, "Honduras: Political and Economic Situation"; Sibaja, Honduras Profile.

22 MISF, "State University Reports Over 3,000 Violent Deaths in Honduras in 2006," Honduras News in Review, 26 March 2007, http://www.mayispeakfreely.org/index .php?gSec=doc&doc_id=259.

23 Council on Hemispheric Affairs, "Honduras' Operacion Trueno: An Audacious Proposal That Must Be Reformed and Renovated," news release, 16 October 2006, http://www .coha.org/2006/10/16/honduras%e2%80%99-operacion-trueno-an-audacious-proposal- that-must-be-reformed-and-renovated.

24 MISF, "UN Committee Concerned Over Summary Executions of Minors," Honduras News in Review, 13 February 2007, http://www.mayispeakfreely.org/index.php?gSec =doc&doc_id=251.

25 AI, *Report 2006* (London: AI, 2006), http://web.amnesty.org/report2006/hnd-summary-eng.

26 MISF, "Funding Approved for "Femicide" Investigation Units," Honduras News in Review, 30 January 2007, http://www.mayispeakfreely.org/index.php?gSec=doc&doc_id=249.

27 MISF, "Women's Group Says Domestic Violence Not Taken Seriously in Honduran Courts," Honduras News in Review, 4 December 2006, http://www.mayispeakfreely.org/index.php?gSec=doc&doc_id=219.

28 AI, "LGBT Activist in Honduras Beaten by Police and Raped at Police Station by Detainees, Says Amnesty International," news release, 20 March 2007, http://www.amnestyusa.org/document.php?lang=e&id=ENGUSA20070330001.

29 AI, "Justice Fails Indigenous People," AI Library, 1 September 1999, http://web.amnesty.org/library/Index/ENGAMR370101999?open&of=ENG-2AM.

30 MISF, "Police Burn Indigenous Settlement in Effort to Force Residents Off Land," Honduras News in Review, 12 March 2007, http://www.mayispeakfreely.org/index.php?gSec=doc&doc_id=257.

31 MISF, "Police Kill Two Environmental Leaders; Human Rights Commission Orders Protective Measures," Honduras News in Review, 9 January 2007, http://www.mayispeakfreely.org/index.php?gSec=doc&doc_id=233.

32 Constitution of the Republic of Honduras, Article 77, http://pdba.georgetown.edu/Constitutions/Honduras/hond82.html.

33 USAID, *Regional Strategy for Central America and Mexico; Working Group on Arbitrary Detention, Report of the Working Group on Arbitrary Detention, Addendum: Mission to Honduras* (New York: UN Human Rights Council, December 2006), http://daccessdds.un.org/doc/UNDOC/GEN/G06/152/64/PDF/G0615264.pdf?OpenElement.

34 Working Group, *Report of the Working Group; Edmundo Orellana, State of the Judiciary Report: Honduras 2003* (Washington, D.C.: IFES, April 2004), http://www.ifes.org/publication/5b50fbf181a756d24a794251fc569f23/SOJ_Honduras_english.pdf.

35 Working Group, *Report of the Working Group*; Constitution of the Republic of Honduras.

36 Working Group, *Report of the Working Group*.

37 MISF, "Human Rights Commission Received More Than 9,000 Complaints in 2006," Honduras News in Brief, 26 March 2007, http://www.mayispeakfreely.org/index.php?gSec=doc&doc_id=259.

38 Richard J. Millett and Orlando Perez, "New Threats and Old Dilemmas: Central America's Militaries in the 21st Century," *Journal of Political and Military Sociology* 33, no. 1 (Summer 2005): 59–79, http://calbears.findarticles.com/p/articles/mi_qa3719/is_200507/ai_n14904111/pg_1.

39 UNDP Evaluation Office, *Country Evaluation: Assessment of Development Results: Honduras* (New York: UNDP, 2006), 26, http://www.undp.org/eo/documents/ADR/ADR_Reports/ADR_Honduras.pdf.

40 MISF, "UN Working Group Investigates Disappearances from 1980s," Honduras News in Review, 13 February 2007, http://www.mayispeakfreely.org/index.php?gSec=doc&doc_id=251.

41 *Doing Business In Honduras: A Country Commercial Guide for U.S. Companies* (Washington, D.C., and Tegucigalpa: U.S. Foreign Commercial Service and Department of State, 2007), http://www.buyusa.gov/honduras/en/ccg2007.html.

42 Suzanne York, "Honduras and Resistance to Globalization," International Forum on Globalization, http://www.ifg.org/analysis/globalization/Honduras2.htm.

43 Mechanism for the Follow-Up on the Implementation of the Inter-American Convention Against Corruption, *Republic of Honduras: Final Report* (Washington, D.C.: Organization of American States [OAS], 15 December 2006), 16, http://www.oas.org /juridico/english/mesicic_II_rep_hnd.pdf.

44 MISF, "30,000 March Against Corruption in Honduras," Honduras News in Review, 26 February 2007, http://www.mayispeakfreely.org/index.php?gSec=doc&doc_id=255.

45 USAID, *Regional Strategy for Central America and Mexico*, 29.

46 Tim Kane, Kim R. Holmes, and Mary Anastasia O'Grady, *2007 Index of Economic Freedom* (Washington, D.C., and New York: Heritage Foundation and *Wall Street Journal*, 2007), 221, 223, http://www.heritage.org/research/features/index/downloads/Index 2007.pdf.

47 Ibid.

48 Transparency International, *Corruption Perceptions Index 2006* (Berlin: Transparency International, 6 November 2006), http://www.transparency.org/policy_research /surveys_indices/cpi/2006.

49 International Freedom of Expression Exchange (IFEX), "Congress Approves Access to Information Law," news release, 30 November 2006, http://www.ifex.org/en/content /view/full/79666/.

50 Ibid.

51 Thelma Mejia, "A Murky Transparency Law," Inter Press Services, 22 February 2007, http://www.globalpolicy.org/nations/launder/regions/2007/0222transparency.htm.

52 MISF, "30,000 March Against Corruption in Honduras."

53 "Conexion 'gasolinazo'-INA," *El Heraldo*, 20 April 2006, http://www.elheraldo.hn/nota .php?nid=49081&sec=12&fecha=2006-04-20; Federacion de Organizaciones para el Desarrollo de Honduras (FOPRIDEH), "Informe Sobre el Estado de los Casos de Corrupcion en Honduras 2006," August 2006, http://www.cna.hn/uploads/files/II _INFORME_CORRUPCION_FORPIDEH.pdf.

54 "Prometen 'destapar la olla' en el RNP," *El Heraldo*, 19 June 2006, http://www.el heraldo.hn/nota.php?nid=52070&sec=12&fecha=2006-06-19.

55 International Budget Project, "Honduras," in *Open Budget Initiative 2006* (Washington, D.C.: Center on Budget and Policy Priorities, 2006), http://www.openbudgetindex .org/CountrySummaryHonduras.pdf.

56 Mechanism for the Follow-Up, *Republic of Honduras: Final Report*, 16.

57 Mechanism for the Follow-Up, *Republic of Honduras: Final Report* (Washington, D.C.: OAS, March 12, 2005), 38, http://www.oas.org/juridico/english/mec_rep_hnd.pdf.

58 Ibid.

IRAN

CAPITAL: Tehran

POPULATION: 71.2 million

GNI PER CAPITA: $3,000

SCORES	2005	2007
ACCOUNTABILITY AND PUBLIC VOICE:	1.75	1.63
CIVIL LIBERTIES:	1.89	1.74
RULE OF LAW:	2.70	2.17
ANTICORRUPTION AND TRANSPARENCY:	1.73	1.85

(scores are based on a scale of 0 to 7, with 0 representing weakest and 7 representing strongest performance)

Stephen C. Fairbanks

INTRODUCTION

Ayatollah Ruhollah Khomeini's 1979 Islamic revolution depended on mass participation nationwide, but the clerics who took up the reins of power have since refused to submit to democratic accountability. The authority of the ruling Shiite ayatollahs, who claim to represent God's will, is bolstered by the Islamic Republic's constitutional system. The supreme leader, who is not directly elected by the Iranian populace, sits at the pinnacle of the system. He is supported by the unelected Council of Guardians, which blocks legislative attempts at reform and vets candidates for elected office.

Iran's political system has been dominated since 1979 by conservative clerics and politicians. They have worked over the years to preserve the uprising's Islamic and revolutionary values—and to keep themselves in power. The result is an authoritarian regime that demands public compliance with traditional Islamic laws, affecting people's social interactions

Stephen C. Fairbanks is a specialist on Iranian affairs who previously served as the political analyst on Iran for the U.S. Department of State and as director of the Radio Free Europe/Radio Liberty Persian Service. He earned a Ph.D. in Iranian studies at the University of Michigan.

and private lives. It strongly resists many forms of modernity and the notion of an open society.

Substantial sectors of Iranian society are at a disadvantage under the Shiite and exclusively male-dominated regime. The officially imposed Islamic laws bar many women from playing significant economic or political roles. The political engagement of religious minorities, including Sunni Muslims, is very limited, and ethnic minorities such as Kurds, Arabs, and Baluchis—who make up nearly half the population—are granted little room for participation.

Advocates for political reform and an open civil society made significant progress in the late 1990s, but at present their efforts to boost civil liberties and democratic participation are stalled. The reform movement launched by then president Mohammad Khatami in 1997 was eclipsed after conservatives won a majority in the Majles (parliament) in 2004 and Mahmud Ahmadinejad won the presidency in 2005. A backlash against reform measures was perhaps inevitable, since conservatives saw gradual liberalization as a threat to regime longevity, just as it had been in the Soviet Union and Eastern Europe. In addition, the reformists themselves admit that they lost voter support by concentrating too soon on political development rather than basic economic needs.

The reform movement is not dead, even if reformist politicians are currently out of power. Dissenters continue to voice criticism of government policies, though journalists, intellectuals, students, and proponents of human rights have become more wary, imposing a measure of self-restraint in order to avoid a crackdown by the authorities.

Developments in neighboring Iraq and Afghanistan have increased the Iranian regime's sense of insecurity and helped harden its exclusionary and repressive tendencies. Apprehensive that Washington seeks regime change in Tehran, the ruling clerics have tightened restrictions on freedom of expression and remain distrustful of broader political participation.

Nonetheless, politics in Iran remain dynamic. Voter turnout is impressively high, as most Iranians value what little democratic process is available to them, despite the entrenchment of the ruling clerics and the economic and political incompetence of successive elected administrations. Even within the narrow spectrum of regime-approved candidates, election outcomes can be unpredictable. An abundance of political parties, though often ephemeral and ineffective by Western standards, provide an important forum for political debate.

The constant ebb and flow of Iranian politics has caused some significant setbacks for Ahmadinejad and his hard-line allies. Increasingly blatant criticism in the press after his first year in office was followed by the crushing defeats of his political supporters in nationwide elections in December 2006.

ACCOUNTABILITY AND PUBLIC VOICE

FREE AND FAIR ELECTORAL LAWS AND ELECTIONS:	1.75
EFFECTIVE AND ACCOUNTABLE GOVERNMENT:	1.75
CIVIC ENGAGEMENT AND CIVIC MONITORING:	2.00
MEDIA INDEPENDENCE AND FREEDOM OF EXPRESSION:	1.00
CATEGORY AVERAGE:	**1.63**

Iran's present state system is designed to perpetuate the domination of the Shiite clerical hierarchy. Candidates for elective office must express fealty to the principle of *velayat-e faqih*, or rule by a religious jurist, which stipulates that only highly qualified experts on Islamic law are suitable to head the state. This empowers Ayatollah Ali Khamenei in his lifetime position as supreme leader, even if his jurisprudential credentials fall far short of those of his predecessor, Ayatollah Ruhollah Khomeini.

Regular nationwide elections offer some relief from the authoritarian, unelected entities that effectively control the state. For the theocratic regime, elections add a measure of popular legitimacy to the authority it claims to derive from God. The populace, meanwhile, gains some sense of democratic participation by choosing from among officially vetted candidates for the presidency, parliament, local councils, and the Assembly of Experts, a body of loyal senior clerics who choose the supreme leader.

Suffrage is universal in Iran, unlimited by gender or ethnicity. The minimum voting age rose to eighteen in January 2007 after remaining at only fifteen for many years; the change was seen as a measure to counteract the comparatively high popularity of reformists among younger voters.

A comprehensive election bill, under consideration by the Interior Ministry and the Majles since August 2006, promises to codify numerous electoral regulations, but its passage remains uncertain.[1] Among the issues being debated is a proposal to tighten the screening process for Majles candidates by requiring them to have a university degree and a minimum of five years' executive experience. Opponents charge that this narrows democratic representation, particularly in smaller provincial cities where fewer citizens hold university degrees.[2]

Campaign financing is not transparent, and in the absence of campaign finance laws there appear to be few restraints on privileged interests wielding influence over the electoral process. Certain politically active clerical organizations, the oldest and most important of which are the Militant Clergy Association (*Jame'eh-ye Rowhaniyat-e Mobarez*) and the Qom Seminary Lecturers Association (*Jame'eh-ye Modarresin-e Howze-ye Elmiye-ye Qom*), endorse their favored candidates in every election. They have access to the enormous resources that accrue from religious tithes and endowments to mosques, but precisely how they provide money to candidates, or how much, is difficult to determine. Information on campaign contributions by other interests, in the business community, the military, or government organizations, is also unavailable. Occasionally, though, the media carry veiled references to the Tehran municipality's use of public resources to back candidates it prefers.

Balloting is secret, and the process is monitored by electoral authorities from the Interior Ministry and the paramilitary Basij organization. Several reformist groups claimed numerous cases of ballot-box fraud in the presidential elections of 2005 and in the December 2006 local council elections; in the latter polling, even the Justice Ministry acknowledged some 290 cases of election offenses in Tehran alone.[3] A spokesman for the main reformist coalition complained that the election supervisory board for Tehran ignored demands for a recount, and the interior minister was unresponsive to concerns raised by former presidents Khatami and Hashemi Rafsanjani as well as Mehdi Karrubi, a former Speaker of the Majles and 2005 presidential candidate.

There is, however, genuine competition between the two broad political factions, the conservatives and the reformists, with both comprising a mix of clerical and lay leaders loyal to the regime. Conservatives, who refer to themselves as *osulgarayan* (fundamentalists), currently control the political process and advocate a return to what they perceive to be Islamic and revolutionary values. Reformists seek democratic reforms, greater freedom of expression, an easing of repressive Islamic social strictures, and less confrontational foreign relations.

Conservatives and reformists enjoy a limited rotation of power, resulting from what are sometimes fiercely contested elections. However, interference by unelected institutions centered on the supreme leader has facilitated domination by the conservatives since 2004, making it difficult to present significant policy options in the manner possible under more competitive political systems.

Although all candidates are allowed to put up posters in public places, campaign opportunities are not always equal for everyone. Reformist candidates, unlike conservatives, complain that they are not granted permission to hold political rallies or to speak at university gatherings.

The dominant, conservative side of Iran's political spectrum remains distrustful of parties that would broaden access to the political system. The Freedom Movement of Iran, a liberal Muslim party that supports the Islamic Republic but is less supportive of the need for clerical rule, is banned from elections. No strictly secular party is granted permission to operate.

There are more than 200 political parties in Iran, as well as influential political groups, such as the conservative Militant Clergy Association, that play a similar role. Most political parties have very limited membership and are usually built around a few noteworthy politicians. The parties are generally idle during the stretches between national elections. Nearly all are centered in Tehran, though in recent years some have established provincial offices. Parties try to form coalitions at election time, but rivalries are often too intense for anything but the most ephemeral partnerships.

Iran's parties have been ineffective in promoting democracy. One of their few functions is to decide on which candidates to endorse, but after numerous and often contentious meetings of their central committees, some parties fail to achieve even that. The parties can rarely agree on platforms, so voters frequently find it difficult to understand what candidates stand for.

President Ahmadinejad was elected without the support of any formal party organization and shows little interest in parties. His minister of culture was roundly criticized for declaring in January 2007 that in Iran the Basij paramilitary organization and the "culture of martyrdom" have taken the place of parties both organizationally and ideologically.[4]

The twelve-member Council of Guardians limits and determines Iranians' political choices. Supreme Leader Khamenei directly appoints half of the council, and the judiciary chief—himself appointed by Khamenei—chooses the other half with the approval of the Majles. The council rules on whether legislation conforms with Islamic law and the constitution; it rejected most laws passed by the reformist Majles of 2000–2004.

The antidemocratic power of the Council of Guardians is most apparent in its vetting of candidates for the presidency, the Majles, and the Assembly of Experts. In the 2004 Majles elections, the council rejected 44 percent of prospective candidates, nearly all of them reformists, for vaguely stated reasons related to insufficient support for the Islamic system of government. In 2005, it rejected all reformist candidates for the presidency, but the ensuing public outcry prompted Supreme Leader Khamenei to order the council to approve one reformist, Mostafa Mo'in. His ultimate defeat was assured when his party's newspaper was shut down some weeks prior to the election.

For the Assembly of Experts elections of December 15, 2006, the Council of Guardians barred the candidacy of all women, laymen, and junior clerics, and nearly all reformist and hard-line clerics. It used unprecedented written and oral exams on Islamic jurisprudence to keep all but traditional, conservative clerics out of the assembly, making the elections more like a system of appointments.

Other inequities were apparent in the nationwide elections for more than 100,000 positions on city and town councils, held concurrently with the Assembly of Experts contest. Candidates for these seats were more closely vetted than ever before by the Electoral Supervisory Board—which is appointed by the Council of Guardians—as well as the Interior and Intelligence ministries. Numerous reformist candidates were barred, sometimes on the basis of allegations that were impossible to prove, such as narcotics use or immoral sexual behavior, or more often for not being committed sufficiently to Islam or to the principle of *velayat-e faqih*. Reformist politician Mohsen Armin observed that Ahmadinejad had abandoned his 2005 campaign promise to breach the wall blocking access to power and was now building an even taller barrier to deny such access to others.[5]

The separation of the executive, legislative, and judicial branches of the government is stipulated in the constitution, but the supreme leader, ranking above all three, has no true constitutional accountability. It is highly unlikely that the Assembly of Experts would ever use its constitutional authority to dismiss him if he proved incompetent, since its members are vetted by the Council of Guardians, whose members are in turn chosen directly or indirectly by the supreme leader.

The accountability of the supreme leader has been debated, but so far he has never been called before any state body for questioning. In December 2006 Ayatollah Mohammad Taqi Mesbah-Yazdi, a hard-line member of the Assembly of Experts, told his followers that while accountability is a requirement of democracy and is therefore suitable for a president, it is not to be expected from the supreme leader, who is above the constitution because he is appointed by God.[6]

The executive branch is generally responsive to Parliament, and ministers are regularly interpellated and sometimes impeached. However, the judicial branch, whose head is appointed by the supreme leader, is not accountable to the other branches, and the courts have summoned deputies for offenses that include speeches made in the Majles, despite a doctrine of parliamentary immunity. Further questions concerning the separation of powers arose when President Ahmadinejad appointed the judiciary spokesman to serve simultaneously as minister of justice.

Iran's bloated and inefficient civil service is plagued by redundant offices and nonmeritocratic preferences for war veterans, members of the Basij paramilitary forces, and relatives of the many clerics with government connections. Cronyism has increased during the Ahmadinejad administration, despite his campaign promise to eliminate it. By the end of his first year in power he was being openly accused of having given numerous government positions to friends from his years in the Islamic Revolutionary Guard Corps (IRGC) and his university, as well as to numerous relatives.

Limited civic engagement regarding government policy and legislation takes place through political parties and the newspapers and websites that often serve as their mouthpieces. These groups comment on pending legislation and the policies of both the executive branch and the Council of Guardians, but they are strictly enjoined from criticizing any policies explicitly set or endorsed by the supreme leader.

Nongovernmental organizations (NGOs) are not prohibited from registering in Iran, but their situation has worsened in the past three years. The optimistic expectations that were engendered by the rapid rise of NGOs during the administration of President Khatami have been tempered by the current government's mistrust of and sometimes hostility toward them. Emadoddin Baqi, head of the Society to Defend Prisoners' Rights and one of Iran's bolder NGO leaders, recently compared the situation of NGOs under Khatami and Ahmadinejad: "When Khatami was president, we could contact the Majles and correspond with the government, even with the minister of intelligence . . . and eventually even the judiciary was replying to us in a completely open fashion. Once Ahmadinejad took over, however, every link began to break and now we have lost access to the government."[7]

According to Mashallah Shamsolvaezin, the head of Tehran's journalists guild, no more than 10 percent of the approximately 8,300 officially registered NGOs are able to stand on their own feet financially. These organizations are "nongovernmental," yet much of their funding comes from government grants, which have been dwindling since Ahmadinejad took office. Shamsolvaezin adds that Washington's threats of regime change and its announced democracy-support program have caused some Iranian NGO leaders to limit their activities out of fear of being accused either of espionage or of being financed by the United States.[8] For the regime, this is a convenient pretext for undermining the activities of civil society institutions and inhibiting donor support.

Restrictions on freedom of expression have worsened under Ahmadinejad. Newspapers have been shut for increasingly arbitrary reasons, and reporters' physical security has been compromised by threats and imprisonment. Seeing this, and having already witnessed more than one hundred publications shut down during the Khatami era, journalists eventually had to become very cautious after Ahmadinejad entered office. Reformist newspapers are fewer in number than their conservative counterparts because most have been closed down by the conservative judicial authorities. Those that remain are able to promote reformist viewpoints, but they reach a much more limited audience than radio and television.

All radio and television broadcasting, the main source of news and information for nearly all Iranians, is strictly under the control of the supreme leader's office and provides only official points of view. No private broadcasting is allowed. This gives conservative candidates a strong advantage during electoral campaigns. There is media vibrancy, though, among internet-based news agencies and news websites.

The Ahmadinejad administration is far less tolerant of media criticism than the Khatami government had been. It characterizes criticism of its failures as insults, slander, and lies; the president's press adviser declared that "spreading lies against the government is like injecting deadly poison into the country's atmosphere of freedom."[9] Notably, the strength of the government's reaction shows that the press does carry views and reports unfavorable to the president and his administration.

Coverage guidelines appear to be elastic, conforming to the non-transparent decisions of such bodies as the Supreme National Security Council and the supreme leader's office. The government's primary instrument of control has been the Press Supervisory Board of the Ministry of Culture and Islamic Guidance. The board licenses newspapers and warns them if they have violated the law. According to the head of the Supreme Administrative Court, Dorri-Najafabad, the board can recommend a publication to the judiciary's Press Court if it deems it to be in violation, and can ban it temporarily until the court date arrives.[10] Reformists have complained that the board imposes the views of the hardliners who support Ahmadinejad, but in mid-2006, when traditional conservatives turned away from Ahmadinejad, the Press Supervisory Board began to be less restrictive.[11] Language advocating relations with the United States, for example, was formerly forbidden, but it now appears in at least the reformist press, as does criticism of Ahmadinejad's handling of the nuclear issue. Such changes in guidelines may be a means for the regime to introduce eventual policy shifts or to gauge public reactions.

The reformist daily *Sharq* became the best-known victim of efforts to control newspapers that are critical of the government. After publishing many critical articles, culminating with a cartoon that subtly insulted the president, the Press Supervisory Board closed it in September 2006 for not complying with orders to change its management. It eventually resumed publication in the spring of 2007.

Other minor papers, several of them provincial and most of them reformist, have also been shut down, but their closures provoked little public outrage, probably because of their limited circulation. Publication of a staunchly conservative paper that supported Ahmadinejad, *Siyasat-e Ruz*, was suspended in early February 2007; conflicting reasons were given as to why. The temporary closure nevertheless raised an outcry from reformists, who saw the case as relevant to their own civil liberties concerns.

Together with some vocal critics in the Majles, the print media and reformist news websites commenced spirited attacks against the administration in the summer of 2006, ostensibly after giving Ahmadinejad a fair chance by allowing him a full year to get his government in order. With the defeat of Ahmadinejad's allies in the December 15, 2006, local council and Assembly of Experts elections, and amid impending UN economic sanctions and threats from Washington, the media went on the attack, targeting the administration's economic failures and confrontational diplomacy. *Sharq* was a key reformist voice, but other reformist papers such as *Aftab-e Yazd, E'temad, E'temad-e Melli, Farhang-e Ashti, Kargozaran,* and *Mardomsalari* also contribute to a certain level of vitality in the press.

The Press Court, a branch of the conservative-controlled judiciary, uses vague libel laws, or even vaguer charges of "insulting Islamic sanctities" or "undermining the state," to suspend or permanently shut down reformist papers. Anything negative about the supreme leader, of course, is prohibited, as are criticisms of Islamic precepts, disapproval of the concept of the Islamic Republic, and rejection of the principle of *velayat-e faqih*.

Journalists, particularly younger and less well-known ones, have little protection from arbitrary arrest and detention. They can be held and imprisoned for violations far beyond ordinary press laws and can fall into the grasp of courts of other jurisdictions. The case of Arash Sigarchi, the former editor of *Gilan-e Emruz*, from the Caspian Sea city of Rasht, illustrates how national security concerns are often invoked to silence journalists. In February 2005, Sigarchi was sentenced to fourteen years in prison by the Gilan Province Revolutionary Court for collaborating with an unnamed "hostile government," inciting the general public, insulting the late Imam Khomeini, and engaging in propaganda activities against the regime. However, an appeals court reduced his sentence to three years, and he was eventually allowed to go outside the prison to receive treatment for cancer.[12]

The internet has been a vexing problem for the Iranian state, which is unable to effectively control it as a source of information and dissident opinion. It is a vehicle for oppositionists outside the country and, more importantly, for dissidents within Iran, particularly political activists and politicians on the margins of the ruling system. Despite several well-publicized cases in which bloggers were jailed, the state has been unable to stop bloggers from using the internet to express frustration with the regime's social and political strictures. The state appears caught between attempting to suppress the internet and allowing access as a safety valve for Iranians expressing their discontent.

Web-based Iranian news services and news websites have proliferated in the past three years, helping significantly to diversify news sources for Iranians. Many are politically oriented, ranging from religiously and politically conservative to reformist. Several have run afoul of government censors, including Baztab, which became officially filtered in February 2007. Affiliated with the conservative secretary of the Expediency Council, Mohsen Reza'i, it apparently offered reports that were too critical of administration officials. In September 2006, the Ministry of Culture and Islamic Guidance sent newspapers a list of news agencies they were permitted to use for their publications. Many well-known agencies, including Baztab, were absent from the list.

In the area of cultural expression, there has been some regression from the blossoming in literature and the arts that characterized the Khatami era. Music in Iran has come under the scrutiny of Saffar-Harandi, the current minister of culture and Islamic guidance, who has taken measures to expunge foreign influences. Convinced that the West is subjecting Iran to a "cultural onslaught" aimed at turning its youthful population against Islamic rule, he even told a visitor from the UNESCO-affiliated International Music Council that the government's "cooperation" with the Iranian music industry has prevented Iranian music from "falling into vulgarism."[13]

Recommendations

- The Shiite clerics' domination of the political realm should be greatly reduced, and membership in the Assembly of Experts should be open to laypeople, including women.
- The Council of Guardians' role in vetting candidates for presidential and parliamentary elections should be eliminated.
- The government should support the activities of political parties and NGOs by reinstating, on a fair and nonpartisan basis, the grants to parties that the Khatami government had provided and which the Ahmadinejad administration has cut off. It should also end its baseless denunciations of NGOs as foreign agents.
- The government should enforce its own standards against cronyism, particularly in granting positions to former members of the IRGC.
- The state should permit unfettered freedom of expression by ending prosecutions of journalists, website operators, and other individuals for peacefully expressing their opinions; ending direct regime control

of the broadcast media; and ceasing the review and prior censorship of books and films.

• Press laws pertaining to newspapers and websites must be applied fairly and without regard to political orientation, so that conservative media outlets are held to the same standards of journalistic responsibility as reformist ones.

CIVIL LIBERTIES

PROTECTION FROM STATE TERROR, UNJUSTIFIED IMPRISONMENT, AND TORTURE:	1.14
GENDER EQUITY:	1.75
RIGHTS OF ETHNIC, RELIGIOUS, AND OTHER DISTINCT GROUPS:	2.00
FREEDOM OF CONSCIENCE AND BELIEF:	2.00
FREEDOM OF ASSOCIATION AND ASSEMBLY:	1.80
CATEGORY AVERAGE:	**1.74**

The Iranian government continues to violate the civil liberties of its citizens. In July 2005, Iran's judiciary officially acknowledged widespread violations of prisoners' rights, claiming at the same time that reforms had been enacted to address the problems. However, solitary confinement, imprisonment without charge, and torture continue to be reported.

Abuses of prisoners are so prevalent in Tehran's notorious Evin prison that four Iranian human rights groups have courageously called on the United Nations to investigate. Political prisoners held in Section 209, which is controlled by the Intelligence Ministry to the exclusion of Iran's prison organization and even Evin's prison officials, are reportedly beaten and deprived of sleep and medical care. In 2006, prominent human rights lawyer Abdolfateh Soltani was detained in a small cell for more than seven months, two of them in solitary confinement.[14] There are persistent complaints that violent felons are housed with political prisoners and often beat them up. The death penalty is applied more frequently in Iran than in any country except China. In recent years, international human rights organizations have repeatedly decried Iran's use of the death penalty against minors and for nonviolent crimes such as adultery.

There are few checks on arbitrary arrests; citizens are imprisoned for long periods without charge and without notification to their families. The spring 2007 detentions of four Iranian Americans with dual citizenship, still unresolved as of the writing of this report, is a prominent case in point.

On a more positive note, Iran's law enforcement forces, intelligence services, and the IRGC do take very seriously the protection of citizens against violent crime, working to prevent and punish acts of violence by both common and organized criminals.

Iran is less efficient, however, in combating other criminal activity, such as drug trafficking, gasoline smuggling to neighboring countries, and white-collar crime. In October 2006, Iran's prosecutor general, noting poor relations between prosecution offices and institutions relating to the judiciary, called for a better organized and more professional approach to confronting organized crime.[15]

Citizens often have no means of redress when they suspect that state authorities have violated their rights. When political prisoners Akbar Mohammadi and Feyz Mahdavi were reported to have died—on July 30, 2006, and September 6, 2006, respectively—because of mistreatment by authorities at Evin Prison, the head of the Supreme Administrative Court, Ayatollah Dorri-Najafabadi, simply dismissed the allegations by saying that we all die sooner or later. He said that the authorities had expressed condolences to the families but that he did not believe anyone would intentionally cause someone's death in prison.[16]

Attacks on peaceful activists and political dissidents occur with regularity and with little or no intervention by the state. On university campuses, student demonstrators are often attacked by student members of the paramilitary Basij organization or by outside vigilantes.

Gender equity remains a distant goal in Iran, where traditional Islamic laws deprive women of equal rights in marriage, divorce, child custody, inheritance, and other areas. A woman's testimony in court has half the value of a man's, for example, and women need the written permission of their father or husband to travel. Segregation of men and women in public, institutionalized since the 1979 Islamic revolution, appears to be on the increase. As of early 2007, plans were under discussion for a new women-only park in Tehran as well as single-sex hospitals.

It is increasingly common for women to work outside the home, though it was long taboo in Iran and was considered an insult to the man in the family. According to a Majles report in December 2005, 12 percent of the female population is employed. Even though more than half of the country's university student population is female, most women graduates have difficulty finding employment. The Majles report indicated that 75 percent of working women have jobs that have nothing to do with their education.[17] President Ahmadinejad outraged many women in October 2006 when he said that women should, at most, only work part time and devote more time to their main job of raising children.

State engagement on issues relating to women falls far short of international standards. Women can be elected to the Parliament and local councils, but they cannot run for the presidency or the Assembly of Experts; women's rights activists perennially seek to gain equality in all four arenas. Following the 2004 election, women held 12 seats in the 290-seat Majles.

A plan to institute gender quotas that would limit admission of female students to universities was being debated in the Majles in January and February 2007. In January, the government shut down a website set up by women's rights activists inside Iran to collect signatures in a bid to reform discriminatory laws.

Ethnic tensions have increased in the past three years, reflecting a perception among Iran's Azeris, Kurds, Baluchis, and Arabs that Persians regard them as culturally and linguistically inferior. The discontent has not reached the level of widespread popular support for separatist movements, however.

Tehran has mixed tougher security measures with efforts to alleviate ethnic dissatisfaction. It also regularly alleges that the American and British forces in neighboring Iraq are fanning unrest within Iran's Arab, Kurdish, and Azeri provinces.

Azeri unrest and street protests erupted in Tabriz and several other western Iranian cities following the May 19, 2006, publication of a cartoon in the state-owned and Tehran-based *Iran* daily newspaper that depicted an Azeri as a cockroach. The state's sensitivity to Azeri concerns was evident in the ensuing closure of the paper and the replacement of its management when it eventually reopened. Khamenei, Ahmadinejad, and others sought to make amends with numerous conciliatory speeches.

In an apparent effort to sooth local tensions, President Ahmadinejad made a visit, extensively covered on state television, to West Azerbaijan province from August 31 to September 2, 2006. Ahmadinejad has also visited Iranian Kurdestan, Baluchestan, and the ethnic Arab province of Khuzestan, promising in each case that Tehran would pay much greater attention to local concerns. His ability to deliver on such promises, which are similar to those he made to every one of Iran's thirty provinces, has been severely constrained by a lack of central government resources.

The state has responded harshly to terrorist acts in Ahvaz, Khuzestan, attributed to Arab separatists, whom it says are sent by the British from Iraq. Ten ethnic Arabs were given death sentences in November 2006 for armed activity against the state. Three were executed that December and three more on February 14, 2007, reportedly in front of their families. Three UN human rights rapporteurs and several human rights groups, including Amnesty International and Human Rights Watch, said that the trials did not meet international standards. The UN experts said the trials "made a mockery of due process requirements" and that the convictions were based on confessions extracted under torture.[18]

In Baluchestan, the Sunni militant group Jundallah was responsible for several recent attacks against government targets, including a February 14, 2007, attack on an IRGC bus near Zahedan that killed at least eleven people. Widespread arrests followed the incident, adding to the list of smoldering local grievances.

The problems with Iranian Baluchis are religious as well as ethnic. The Baluchis are Sunnis, and the 10 percent of the Iranian population that is Sunni is treated as inferior in the Islamic Republic, where Shiite Islam is the state religion. As of 2006, there was still no Sunni mosque in Tehran. In the past year, as Iranian leaders spoke repeatedly against Sunni-Shiite violence in neighboring Iraq, they also spoke of Sunni-Shiite harmony within Iran, although it is likely they were more motivated by international tensions than a sincere desire to remedy inequities at home.

The state maintains careful control over the appointment of Shiite religious leaders, vetting them according to their loyalty to the Islamic Republic and its principles. Clerics must retain the approval of the state, which can dismiss any it deems insufficiently loyal. The regime expects religious leaders of Sunni and non-Muslim minorities to be loyal as well, though it is unclear whether the state plays any role in their appointment or dismissal.

The constitution recognizes Zoroastrians, Jews, and Christians as religious minorities, and they are allowed to worship, although all of their activities are subject to vetting by the government. These groups have a set number of parliamentary seats reserved for them but are barred from senior government positions.

Adherents of the Baha'i faith, who at more than a quarter of a million comprise Iran's largest non-Muslim religious minority, enjoy no such rights. Deemed heretics by Iran's Shiite clerics for holding that prophecy did not end with Muhammad, they are sometimes alleged to be a security threat and are accused of being agents of foreign powers, despite their lack of political involvement. In November 2006, for example, Majles Cultural Committee member Sattar Hedayatkhah told a conservative daily that Baha'ism is not a religion but an "imperial sect" that will threaten Iran's youth if officials do not take it seriously.[19] Rumors of a resurgence of the banned, anti-Baha'i Hojjatiyeh Society have appeared in the Iranian press. The accusation of apostasy, punishable by death according to a hard-line interpretation of Islamic law, hangs over the Baha'i community.

The situation of the Baha'is has worsened over the past two years. According to UN Special Rapporteur on Freedom of Religion Asma Jahangir, the chairman of the command headquarters of the armed forces in Iran sent a secret letter on October 29, 2005, to the Intelligence Ministry, the IRGC, and the police, demanding that they identify and monitor Baha'is, on the orders of Ayatollah Khamenei.[20] The Baha'i International Community reports growing threats that include a pattern of arrests—fifty-four in Shiraz in May 2006—and an August 2006 order by the Interior Ministry requesting that provincial officials report the circumstances and activities of local Baha'is, including their "financial status," "social interactions," and "association with foreign assemblies."[21] The conservative daily *Keyhan*, which is reputedly close to the supreme leader, ran a series of anti-Baha'i articles attempting to show that Baha'is are collaborators with and spies for Israel and America.[22]

Although Article 27 of Iran's constitution includes the principle of freedom of assembly, its application is limited in practice. Permission must be sought to hold demonstrations and public protests, and it is not granted in a consistent manner, in part because of differing interpretations of the constitution's vague stipulation that such meetings must not abuse Islamic "fundamentals." According to the government, a women's rights rally in Tehran on June 12, 2006, took place without the necessary permit. After two hours it was broken up by police, including club-wielding policewomen, resulting in numerous arrests and allegations of police brutality.

Although the Islamic Republic of Iran is a member of the International Labor Organization (ILO) and has agreed to ILO Convention 87, which calls for freedom of association and the right to organize, Iran has no free and independent trade unions. The unions that exist are closely monitored by the state. Under Ahmadinejad, the state has increasingly become involved in the elections of union leaders. In August 2006, for example, the Ministry of Labor banned the election of the board of directors of the Trade Union of Journalists without explanation, even though the union had held such elections six times previously.[23]

The regime denies workers the right to strike. Mansur Osanlu, head of the Tehran bus workers' syndicate—a union affiliated with the International Transport Workers' Federation but not recognized by the government—spent most of 2006 in prison for organizing a bus drivers strike in December 2005. Hundreds of drivers and union organizers were also arrested.[24] The government is even cracking down on demonstrations by government-organized unions. In February and March 2007, the Teachers' Union held a series of rallies in Tehran to demand higher salaries, resulting in the arrests of the union's secretary general and numerous teachers.[25]

Recommendations

- Iran should uphold its constitutional prohibition against torture and ill treatment and vigorously enforce the 2004 law banning torture, arbitrary arrests, and forced confessions.
- Judicial authorities should end long-term "temporary" detention without trial and prolonged solitary confinement, and inform families about the location and status of their detained relatives.
- Discriminatory laws against women should be revoked, and women should be given the freedom to demand their rights and seek equity in employment. Existing labor laws that prohibit gender-based wage discrimination and provide job training for women should be enforced.
- The government should end constitutional discrimination against the Baha'i faith and grant its adherents the same rights as other Iranians.

RULE OF LAW

INDEPENDENT JUDICIARY:	2.20
PRIMACY OF RULE OF LAW IN CIVIL AND CRIMINAL MATTERS:	1.83
ACCOUNTABILITY OF SECURITY FORCES AND MILITARY TO	
CIVILIAN AUTHORITIES:	1.50
PROTECTION OF PROPERTY RIGHTS:	3.67
EQUAL TREATMENT UNDER THE LAW:	1.67
CATEGORY AVERAGE:	**2.17**

While the judiciary is closely allied with the supreme leader, who chooses its head and sets its general guidelines, it is independent from the executive and legislative branches. It often clashed with the reformist administration of President Khatami and, more recently, has sometimes come into conflict with the hard-line administration of President Ahmadinejad. Noting that court judgments must not be affected by politics, Ayatollah Hasan Mar'ashi, a member of the Assembly of Experts and the judiciary's former deputy for judicial affairs, has claimed that the judiciary moves on a more moderate and logical course than the administration in power, whether that administration is conservative or reform-minded.[26] For instance, in some cases in 2007 in which the Ministry of Culture and Islamic Guidance sought to ban newspapers that it found too critical of the administration, the judiciary indefinitely postponed taking action.

At the same time, lawyers' independence is endangered. Several have been jailed for defending political activists and individuals charged with espionage. A bill before the Majles at the time of writing would threaten the independence of the bar association by bringing it under the jurisdiction of the Justice Ministry.[27] This bill, if enacted, would violate the constitutional principle that lawyers confront judges on behalf of the people.

The Islamic Republic pays lip service to the rule of law but applies it unevenly. The law is particularly ill-defined when it comes to "political offenses," which consist mostly of vague charges such as "undermining the system." In 2006 and 2007, academics and NGOs with extensive foreign contacts have been subjected to an increasing number of political-offense accusations. Several have been charged with seeking to effect a "velvet revolution" by promoting democratization. Giving un-authorized interviews to foreign radio outlets or meeting with pro-democracy organizations abroad is particularly risky, and accepting money from such organizations is treated as a subversive political act. A bill that aimed to define political crimes was drafted by the Interior Min-istry and sent to the Majles in 2000, but it was never passed. In Febru-ary 2006, the Expediency Council, which adjudicates disputes among the judicial, executive, and legislative branches, called on all three to cooperate in drawing up a new bill, but as of August 2006 there was still no agreement. The judiciary spokesman declared at the time that there was already a "competent court" to deal with political offenses, even though the term still lacked a clear definition.[28]

Numerous due process rights that are explicitly guaranteed in the constitution are routinely and blatantly ignored, including freedom from arbitrary arrest (Article 32), the right of access to competent courts (Arti-cle 34), the right to select an attorney or be provided with legal counsel (Article 35), and the presumption of innocence (Article 37). A prime example of Iran's failures to apply the rule of law to protect its citizens from unconstitutional abuses is the case of Ali Akbar Musavi-Khoini, a former reformist lawmaker and head of the Alumni Association of the Office for the Consolidation of Unity student group. He was arrested at a women's rights demonstration on June 12, 2006, and jailed for two months under a temporary detention order, which was subsequently re-newed for another two months. Musavi-Khoini's defense attorney com-plained that he had been given no opportunity to meet his client, be informed of the charges, or arrange for independent physicians to exam-ine the detainee after reports that he had been beaten.[29] After a 131-day detention, Musavi-Khoini was released on bail.

Lawyers who defend those accused of acting against national secu-rity are at risk of facing similar charges themselves. That was the fate of seven lawyers in 2006 who tried to defend the alleged terrorist bombers in Ahvaz. The Public and Revolutionary Prosecutor's Office in Ahvaz charged them with acting against national security after several websites published a letter in which they criticized revolutionary courts for mis-handling the case and refusing to let them meet their clients. Five of the seven were acquitted in February 2006, but as of this writing the cases of two of the lawyers, Javad Tariri and Faisal Sa'idi, remain open.[30]

Pervasive politicization of the judicial system undermines the rule of law. While government officials are sometimes criticized for abuses of power or for violations of human rights, they are rarely, if ever, prosecuted or held accountable while still in office. The wealthy and powerful in general are rarely prosecuted.

The military and the IRGC are barred by law from interfering in politics, and even law enforcement officers must resign before registering as candidates for political office. However, numerous former IRGC officers serve in the legislative and executive branches, and in the past year reformist political leaders have warned that encroachment into politics by the military is a very real danger. Following the December 15, 2006, local council and Assembly of Experts elections, fifteen reformist Majles representatives complained to Defense Minister Mostafa Najjar that commanders of the Basij Resistance Force, the millions-strong paramilitary branch of the IRGC, had illegally supported some conservative candidates.[31]

Both the IRGC and the Basij, in their official role of combating counterrevolutionaries at home, have engendered concerns of human rights violations. The IRGC is sometimes brought in to control crowds and quell antigovernment disturbances. They have the power of arrest and control a wing at Tehran's notorious Evin prison. On university campuses, members of the "student Basij," under the direction of IRGC officers, are commonly brought in to break up rallies by reformist students.

Property rights are generally upheld in Iran, in accordance with a long Islamic legal tradition of respecting private property. Ethnic and religious minorities such as Arabs and Baha'is, however, have been subject to eviction with inadequate assistance or compensation. In addition, contract enforcement is hampered by the inefficient and politicized judicial system.

Recommendations

- The government must no longer hold political prisoners and other prisoners of conscience, especially when it is unable to define what constitutes a political offense.
- The state should provide for fair trials by informing detainees of the charges against them, giving all detainees access to counsel, and mandating that all trials, including those in "national security" cases, be conducted in public.

- The government should prevent security forces from cracking down on peaceful rallies by citizens demanding their rights and place more controls on the operations of the Basij militias.
- The property rights of ethnic and religious minorities should be respected, with adequate compensation paid for expropriated land.

ANTICORRUPTION AND TRANSPARENCY

ENVIRONMENT TO PROTECT AGAINST CORRUPTION:	1.40
LAWS AND ETHICAL STANDARDS BETWEEN PRIVATE AND	
PUBLIC SECTORS:	2.50
ENFORCEMENT OF ANTICORRUPTION LAWS:	1.50
GOVERNMENTAL TRANSPARENCY:	2.00
CATEGORY AVERAGE:	**1.85**

Economic and financial corruption is endemic in Iran. Privileged elites and their families control both legitimate and underground monopolies. Excessive state involvement in the economy—resulting from state control of the oil industry, nationalization of major privately held industries from the prerevolutionary era, and state economic planning left over from the Iran-Iraq war—fosters close cooperation between political and economic interests. Furthermore, income-tax collection is enforced unevenly at best, a result not only of the prevailing bribery and favoritism but also of the oil-based economy, which makes the state much less dependent on taxation from individuals and businesses and helps soften demands for accountability.

The privatization of state-owned industries has resulted in uncontrolled corruption. According to Mohammad Nahavandiyan, president of the Tehran Chamber of Commerce and the economic deputy of the Supreme National Security Council, the lack of transparency in the privatization process engenders favoritism and prevents fair competition for concessions.[32]

Excessive bureaucratic regulations and a poorly paid bureaucracy make bribery and petty corruption a normal part of daily life. In 2006, the Majles Research Center released a poll finding that more than

40 percent of managers acknowledged having to pay bribes to facilitate their work.[33] Provisions against conflicts of interest between the private and public sectors exist on paper but are rarely enforced.

Regime leaders often call for a crackdown on corruption and promise to remedy the lack of transparency that fosters it, but so far they have offered no concrete solutions. On April 30, 2001, Supreme Leader Khamenei issued a major decree to the heads of the legislative, executive, and judicial branches, rallying them to an organized struggle against economic corruption aimed at rooting out abusers of state resources, greedy individuals, and monopoly seekers. He urged the State Inspectorate Office, the State Audit Office, and the Intelligence Ministry to cooperate closely, but negligence, confusing laws, prolonged legal procedures, redundant investigative institutions, and a lack of transparency and accountability have all stymied the fight against corruption.

Judiciary Chief Ayatollah Mahmud Shahrudi has often spoken out against corruption in Iran's governmental and banking institutions. However, he appeared to ignore the *bonyads*, endowed foundations that account for a sizable but undetermined portion of the country's economic activity. Several *bonyads* constitute large industrial conglomerates that are beyond public scrutiny and are controlled by regime insiders—senior clerics, former officials and politicians, and former IRGC leaders. Shahrudi has called for the implementation of more transparent laws related to financial and administrative performance to stop the corruption and capital flight that undermine Iran's economy. The flawed legal environment offers no protection for whistle-blowers or anticorruption investigators.

The judiciary chief has also grandly demanded that secret information within government organizations be made "available to all, transparently and simultaneously," and has called for reducing the multiplicity of supervisory organizations that he says undermine anticorruption efforts.[34] He has explained that the dual nature of Iran's economic system—a mix of state-owned and private enterprises—breeds corruption, as do the many complicated banking, customs, and tax laws. So far, however, he has not elaborated on what could be done to remedy these legal and structural shortcomings.

Meanwhile, Shahrudi has told the Majles that judiciary, security, and law enforcement officials must tread carefully with economic corruption cases because of their "highly sensitive" nature.[35] That cautious approach only helps ensure that allegations of corruption are not given a wide and unbiased airing in the news media. There have been considerable complaints in the Majles and the media that the public cannot learn even the names of those being investigated.

A Tehran daily, noting that the judiciary does not even reveal how many anticorruption cases are in progress, concluded that it "only prosecutes small fries [sic] while the big fish boldly pile on their illegal wealth."[36] Moreover, Majles Research Center head Ahmad Tavakoli complained in 2005 that the judiciary's excessive consideration for corrupt individuals undermined the fight against corruption.[37]

Redundant judicial and supervisory institutions foster serious inefficiencies and rampant embezzlement in state agencies. For example, the State Audit Court, which is supervised by the Majles, is little more than a ceremonial body because judges appointed by the regular judiciary often overturn its verdicts. The parallel institutions of the State Audit Organization and the State Inspectorate Organization also hamper the audit court and its investigative work. Sometimes several inspection agencies simultaneously investigate a single case.[38]

A Majles deputy who was overseeing the State Audit Court in December 2005 revealed numerous examples of embezzlement in state agencies. He cited the state-owned Iranian Telecommunications Company, which sold a company to the private sector for a fraction of its real value, and the minister of cooperatives, who gave 4,500 gold coins to his relatives as gifts. The courts convicted individuals in several cases, but the lawmaker charged that the judiciary avoided implementing the sentences.[39]

Iran's oil industry remains the most lucrative sector for embezzlement and corruption, despite Ahmadinejad's campaign promises to combat what he called the "oil mafia." The Audit Court reported in June 2006 that US$6 billion in oil revenues had not been deposited in the national treasury during the previous fiscal year.[40] The bonds between Ahmadinejad's administration and the IRGC may explain how the Corps won three huge construction contracts, worth US$7 billion, in 2006. The headquarters of Khatam ol-Anbiya, the IRGC's engineering corps, won a US$3 billion contract to develop the South Pars oil field, a deal to expand the Tehran Metro, and a contract to build a 900-kilometer gas pipeline in the Persian Gulf, all without competitive bidding and other legal formalities.[41]

The state provides some mechanisms, of questionable effectiveness, for people to register complaints about corruption, particularly regarding public officials. Public complaints increased over 500 percent in 2006 when the state inspectorate set up a telephone hotline for the purpose,[42] and President Ahmadinejad, who made anticorruption promises a key part of his 2005 presidential campaign, has received thousands of written complaints about corruption during his regular visits to provincial towns. So far, however, the complaints do not seem to have made much difference.

The state has a relatively transparent budget process, in which the government draws up a budget and submits it to the Majles for extensive debate, and it is then submitted for approval by the Council of Guardians. However, there is enough lack of clarity in the budget details, as well as insufficiently accurate accounting of expenditures, to foster suspicions of profiteering by regime insiders.

Recommendations

- The state should reveal the names of officials and private figures being investigated for corruption and allow the news media to report on these cases.
- The state should remove redundant investigative agencies so that cases can be pursued efficiently.
- The judiciary and investigative agencies should be required to report openly to the Majles on the progress of their anticorruption efforts.
- Privatization of state-held industries and properties must be conducted transparently and in full compliance with clearly defined laws.

NOTES

1. The Islamic Republic News Agency (IRNA) on January 16, 2007, reported that by March 19, 2007, the Interior Ministry was to submit the bill to the Majles, where legislators would debate it for "months."
2. "Denying Citizenship Rights," *E'temad-e Melli*, 25 December 2006.
3. "Head of Justice Department in Tehran Province Announces Statistics on Election Violation Cases," Iranian Students News Agency [ISNA], 23 December 2006.
4. "Party Politics, a Necessity for the Country's Better Government," *Aftab-e Yazd*, 21 January 2007. The issue was covered extensively in several other reformist papers.
5. "Armin: Interior Ministry Officials Should Answer for the Conduct of Executive Boards," *Aftab-e Yazd*, 16 November 2006.

6 "Mesbah-Yazdi: Only Some Parts of the Powers of the Vali-ye Faqih Have Been Included in Constitution," *E'temad*, 27 December 2006.
7 "Baqi: The Prisoners' Society's Contact with the Government Is Lost," *E'temad*, 21 January 2007.
8 International Crisis Group (ICG), *Iran: Ahmadi-Nejad's Tumultuous Presidency* (Brussels: ICG, 6 February 2007).
9 "Javanfekr: Following the Establishment of President's Weblog, the Younger Generation Will Become Better Acquainted with Ahmadinejad's Ideas," *Aftab-e Yazd*, 21 August 2006.
10 "Prosecutor-General: Press Supervisory Board Can Ban Publications Temporarily," *Hemayat*, 19 September 2006.
11 Ali Reza Ahmadi, "The Competition Between the Governmental and Non-Governmental Sector," *Mardom Salari*, 4 October 2006.
12 "Arash Sigarchi Given a Month's Prison Leave," *Aftab-e Yazd*, 2 October 2006.
13 "Saffar-Harandi: Music in Iran Will Never Promote Vulgarism," IRNA in English, 9 January 2007.
14 Golnaz Esfandiari, "Iran: Rights Groups Want Investigation of Evin Prison," Radio Free Europe/Radio Liberty (RFE/RL), 24 October 2006.
15 "Prosecutor General Criticizes Organized Crime Investigation," *Hemayat*, 2 October 2006.
16 "Prosecutor-General: Press Supervisory Board Can Ban Publications Temporarily," *Hemayat*, 19 September 2006.
17 "Head of the Majles Committee on Women and the Family: 75 Percent of Women Have Jobs That Have Nothing to Do with Their Education," *Hemayat*, 3 December 2005.
18 Golnaz Esfandiari, "Iran: UN Experts Urge Tehran Not to Execute Ethnic Arabs," RFE/RL, 15 January 2007.
19 "Hedayatkhah, Member of Majles Cultural Committee: 'Officials Should Take Danger of Baha'ism Seriously,'" *Siyasat-e Ruz*, 12 November 2006.
20 Golnaz Esfandiari, "Iran: UN, U.S. Concerned Over Situation of Baha'is," RFE/RL, 30 March 2006.
21 Bahai'i International Community, "Iran Steps Up Secret Monitoring of Baha'is," news release, 2 November 2006, http://www.bahai.org/persecution/iran.
22 "Keyhan Publishes 'A Silhouette of Baha'ism' That Exposes Secrets of Baha'ism," *Keyhan*, 27 January 2007.
23 Sanaz Allahbadashti, "Efforts to Curb Civil Institutions," *E'temad-e Melli*, 5 August 2006.
24 "Iranian Union Leader 'Abducted,'" BBC News, 11 July 2007
25 Shirzad Abdollahi, "Teacher Arrested at School," *E'temad-e Melli*, 17 April 2007.
26 "Ayatollah Mar'ashi: As Long as Poverty Exists, Corruption Will Exist as Well," *Aftab-e Yazd*, 28 January 2006.
27 Iraj Jamshidi, "Threatening the Independence of the Bar Association," *E'temad*, 23 December 2006.
28 "Karimi Rad: Concept of Political Offence is Defined," *Mardom-Salari*, 27 August 2006.

29 "Musavi-Khoeini's Lawyer Asks for Independent Medical Check for Client," *Aftab-e Yazd*, 2 October 2006.

30 "Court Acquits Five of Ahvaz Bombing Lawyers," Iranian Labor News Agency (ILNA), 6 February 2007.

31 "Fifteen MPs of Majles Minority Faction Asked the Defense Minister for an Explanation About the Activities of Some Military Commanders," Fars News Agency, 2 January 2007.

32 "Fear and Hope," Kargozaran, 10 July 2006.

33 "The Majles Research Center Announced: 40% of Iranian Managers Have to Pay Bribes," *Mardom Salari*, 2 July 2006.

34 "Judiciary Chief Calls for Identification of Elements that Cause Unprecedented Flight of Capital," *Mardom Salari*, 19 September 2005.

35 "Majles Closed-Door Session Discusses Corruption in Economic and Administrative Sectors of Society," IRNA, 2 November 2005.

36 S. Sadeqi, "Accountability Needed," *Iran Daily*, 19 November 2005.

37 "Tavakkoli: Judiciary Power Must Adopt the Alawite Model in Fighting Corruption Instead of Showing Mercy and Consideration," *Iran*, 26 November 2005.

38 "Construction and Reform Administrations Broke the Record for Corruption," *Ya Lesarat ol-Hoseyn*, 21 December 2005.

39 Ibid.

40 "Member of Majles Article 90 Committee States Account Receiving $6 Billion of Oil Revenue Is Unknown," *Siyasat-e Ruz*, 14 June 2006.

41 "Three Contracts—$7 Billion Dollars: Khatam ol-Anbiya Headquarters Largest Contractor in the Country," *E'temad-e Melli*, 1 July 2006.

42 "Head of the State Inspectorate: Lack of Transparency in Fight Against Corruption Itself Breeds Corruption," *Aftab-e Yazd*, 18 June 2006.

LAOS

CAPITAL: Vientiane
POPULATION: 5.9 million
GNI PER CAPITA: $500

SCORES	2005	2007
ACCOUNTABILITY AND PUBLIC VOICE:	1.19	1.16
CIVIL LIBERTIES:	2.16	2.39
RULE OF LAW:	1.63	1.99
ANTICORRUPTION AND TRANSPARENCY:	1.51	1.64

(scores are based on a scale of 0 to 7, with 0 representing weakest and 7 representing strongest performance)

Martin Stuart-Fox

INTRODUCTION

In December 1975, after a thirty-year struggle, the Lao People's Revolutionary Party (LPRP) seized power from the former Royal Lao regime, abolished the monarchy, and established the Lao People's Democratic Republic (LPDR). The institutions of government of the new regime were modeled on those of the former Soviet Union. Today the LPDR is one of only five remaining Marxist-Leninist states, two of which (China and Vietnam) are its powerful neighbors. It is also one of only five Theravada Buddhist countries, three of which (Burma/Myanmar, Cambodia, and Thailand) comprise its other three neighbors. The paradox of contemporary Laos—a country whose communist leaders at the same time portray themselves as good Buddhists—reflects its position on this fault line.

During its first ten years in power, the LPRP pursued orthodox socialist policies: it nationalized industry and cooperativized agriculture. However, plummeting production and peasant opposition forced a

---

Martin Stuart-Fox is Emeritus Professor at the University of Queensland, Australia. He has written six books and more than fifty articles and book chapters on Lao politics and history.

reconsideration. In 1986, the ruling party introduced what it called the new economic mechanism. Over the next decade, land rights were returned to their peasant owners, state-owned industries were privatized (except for a few designated as strategic), the economy was opened to foreign capital, and development aid was welcomed from any country prepared to give it. Over this period, Laos reduced its close dependency on Vietnam, and in 1997 both countries joined ASEAN, the Association of Southeast Asian Nations.

Like other countries in the region, Laos was affected by the Asian economic crisis of 1997–1998. Capital inflow collapsed, inflation mushroomed, and some, but not all, of the economic gains of the previous decade were lost. Since 2000, investment has again picked up—mainly in tourism, hydropower, and mining—and the economic outlook is relatively rosy, with projected GDP growth for 2007 estimated at 7.1 percent.[1]

Over all this time the LPRP has never relaxed its grip on power. Taking China and Vietnam as its models, the party has presided over the change from a centrally planned to a free-market economy while refusing to contemplate even the most minimal democratic reforms. The LPRP is the sole political party. It controls the National Assembly, the government, and all mass organizations. The bureaucracy is a highly politicized arm of the party, as is the media. As a result, what passes for civil society is severely stunted. Corruption has become endemic, and rule of law is honored more in the breach than the observance.

The degree of control exercised by the LPRP is not readily evident to visitors to Laos, however. While the tiny Christian community is suspect for its overseas links, Buddhism is encouraged. Lines of orange-clad monks make their daily begging rounds, while members of the Politburo make their obeisance to senior monks at important Buddhist festivals. Most Lao pursue their daily lives as they have always done; the power of the party is felt mainly by those who would challenge it. No criticism, or even political debate, is permitted outside the confines of the highly secretive party, which recruits its membership from the ambitious and the educated. Without the support of the party, promotion in government and the bureaucracy or success in business is impossible. As everyone knows in Laos, a powerful political patron is the key to advancement for any individual and his or her family—and for such party connections, citizens in Communist Laos give thanks to the Buddha.

ACCOUNTABILITY AND PUBLIC VOICE

FREE AND FAIR ELECTORAL LAWS AND ELECTIONS:	0.50
EFFECTIVE AND ACCOUNTABLE GOVERNMENT:	1.75
CIVIC ENGAGEMENT AND CIVIC MONITORING:	1.00
MEDIA INDEPENDENCE AND FREEDOM OF EXPRESSION:	1.38
CATEGORY AVERAGE:	**1.16**

For the first fifteen years of the Lao PDR, the LPRP ruled without a constitution. During this period, revolutionary justice prevailed: the party was the law. The 1991 constitution was extensively amended in 2003, the better to reflect the political and economic reality of contemporary Laos. The amended constitution was passed by the National Assembly and promulgated by presidential decree, but only after first being endorsed by the Politburo. In fact, the president of the Politburo was the same state president who decreed the promulgation of the constitution. Such is the overlap between the ruling party and the organs of state in Laos.

Article 3 of the 2003 constitution states that the rights of the multiethnic Lao people are exercised and ensured by the political system (as set out in the constitution) "with the Lao People's Revolutionary Party as its leading nucleus."[2] Article 5 stipulates that the parliament (the National Assembly) and "all other state organizations" function by a process of "democratic centralism." What this means is that they are organized in the same way as the ruling party, as hierarchical organizations in which information (about social issues and concerns, for example) flows up the hierarchy, while decisions flow down. This effectively concentrates all power in the hands of a tiny ruling elite at the apex of the party and the state. The degree of concentration of power is all the more apparent when one considers that all but one of the twenty-eight ministers comprising the Cabinet, all but two of 115 National Assembly deputies, and almost all senior bureaucrats are party members, subject to the party discipline implicit in the concept of democratic centralism.

Articles 3 and 5 of the 2003 constitution essentially define the political system of the Lao PDR, for they define the role of the LPRP and the mode of functioning that enables it to monopolize political power.

While they remain in place, it is difficult to see how any significant reform in the direction of democratic processes can even be introduced. Because the ruling party is all-powerful in Laos, it is necessary to understand how it works before turning to the National Assembly or the government. The LPRP has a typically Leninist cellular structure. Party branches exist at all administrative levels from the village through the district and province to the Central Committee of the party, which is elected by party congresses held every five years. Cells also exist in all government ministries, in the four officially sanctioned mass organizations (the Lao Front for National Construction, the Lao Women's Union, the Lao People's Revolutionary Youth Union, and the Federation of Lao Trade Unions), and in the military. Theoretically, each lower level delegates a representative to the next level up. In practice, delegates are appointed through the patronage of senior party officials, who thus gain networks of supporters within the party.

Patron–client relationships include, first and foremost, members of the client's extended family. They may also be based on home region (still very important in Laos), school class, party connections, and common business interests. At the higher levels, patron–client networks may be cemented by intermarriage between families. Patronage is provided in a variety of ways (see below), for which gratitude is shown in monetary form. Political advantage is gained by placing members of one's network in key positions (in the party, the government, or the bureaucracy). Thus, much of the substance of politics is about whose clients get what; for agreement, trade-offs are essential. How all this works is highly secret, though rumors abound in the lead-up to important political events. Patronage politics constitutes the core of Lao political culture.

The most significant events in the Lao political calendar are the five-yearly LPRP congresses, the last of which, the eighth, took place in March 2006. It was expected, and hoped, that several aging generals who had dominated the Politburo for the last decade would retire. But the only retirement was of General Khamtay Siphandone as party (and state) president. He made way for Lieutenant-General Choummaly Sayasone to take his place (in both offices), but all the other old generals remained. As one had died in office, two places became vacant in the eleven-member Politburo. They went to the long-serving former foreign minister and to the first woman, and the first Hmong, to be elected to the Politburo. The only hopeful sign was that nineteen out of the fifty-five members of the Party Central Committee were new faces. They are not likely to endorse any democratic reform, but being younger and better educated they may be persuaded to back some further economic or legal reforms.

Within weeks of the congress, elections were held for the National Assembly; these occurred ten months early in order to bring them into line with the congress and allow a new assembly to endorse a new government. All NA candidates require endorsement by the party-controlled Lao Front for National Construction, whose structure parallels that of the party. A handful of independent candidates were permitted to stand, two of whom were elected. The other 113 are members of the LPRP, including a few senior party officials slated to become key figures in the new government.

The elections were relatively fair, in the sense that individual candidates could try to convince people to vote for them, and voters were not coerced into voting for one candidate or another out of the slate of candidates presented in each province. From the party's point of view it did not much matter who got in, as all party members would toe the party line; however, preferred candidates headed each provincial list, which was enough to ensure their election. In the event, over 60 percent of those elected comprised new faces, though there was little prospect that the new assembly would be any less politically accommodating than previous ones. Its first acts were to put in place the state office holders (president and vice president) and endorse the government already decided upon by the Party Central Committee.

Most ministers in the new government are not members of the National Assembly and are not answerable to it. In reality, no matter what the constitution says, the government is answerable only to the LPRP Politburo, of which the new prime minister, Bouasone Bouphavanh, and his four deputy prime ministers are all members. Another thirteen ministers are members of the Party Central Committee. Again, however, the dozen new ministers tended to be younger and better educated than those they replaced and therefore, perhaps, more open to arguments that improved governance is necessary to prevent Laos from falling further behind its ASEAN partners.

What is unlikely to change is the prevailing political culture, which encourages political intervention in staffing and promotion issues in the civil service, in cases of law, in business dealings, even in school enrollments and health care. Nor will there be any encouragement of civic or nongovernmental organizations (NGOs) free of political control. No criticism of the party is permitted, and no public discussion of party policy takes place either. All is decided by the ruling elite.

As a result, civil society hardly exists. Foreign NGOs are allowed to function only in accordance with government controls,[3] and there is no such thing as a Lao NGO. Organizations such as the Lao Bar Association, established by government decree in 1996,[4] or the Lao National Chamber of Commerce and Industry, established by a statute passed by the National Assembly in December 2001, are semi-governmental and not independent.[5] The only popular associations permitted in Laos are organizing committees for religious functions, peasant producer and water-user associations, school associations, and sporting clubs. None are remotely political. Even attempts to set up cultural and historical associations have failed to receive permission from the Ministry of Information and Culture (MIC), presumably because they were potentially political.

The MIC controls all media in Laos. There is no freedom of the press and no legal protection for Lao journalists who fail to reflect the party line. In fact, most Lao journalists are party members attached to the MIC. There was an understandable note of weariness, therefore, in the 2006 report on Laos by Reporters Without Borders, which began: "Nothing changes in Laos."[6] Foreign correspondents are treated as spies and prevented as much as possible from making contact with any person or group who might be critical of the government or the party. Two Hmong who assisted foreign journalists in contacting Hmong dissidents still holding out against the Lao People's Army are serving long prison sentences for "obstructing justice" and "possession of arms."[7]

In an open letter to President Choummaly Sayasone soon after his appointment to office, Reporters Without Borders called for "radical reforms" that would both establish an independent press in Laos and protect journalists. It wants these provisions included in the media law that the government has been in the process of drafting since 2001 but which has yet to come before the National Assembly. The letter also called for a presidential pardon for the two Hmong and for a Lao author arrested in 1999 for prodemocracy activities and imprisoned in a secret location.[8] There is no likelihood that any of these requests will be met. What is more likely is that "slandering the State, distorting party and state policies, inciting disorder, or propagating information or opinions that weaken the State" will continue to draw a penalty of imprisonment for journalists under the Lao penal code.[9]

Use of the internet is slowly increasing in urban areas, stimulated by the demands of foreign backpackers. Estimates for 2006 were that 25,000 Lao were using the internet, with connections entirely confined to urban areas.[10] In 2002, the National Internet Control Committee installed filters to block unwanted information. Anyone attempting to bypass the filters can be fined, while anyone circulating news reports critical of the party or the government can be prosecuted under the penal code. Satellite TV dishes are more readily available than internet connections, on payment of a license fee, but most Lao confine their viewing to Thai soap operas.

In addition to monitoring the internet, the government keeps an eye on cultural expression to ensure that no political criticism creeps in. The Lao Writers' Association, with a membership of just over one hundred, is closely tied to the MIC. Visual and performing arts sound two themes, traditional and revolutionary, and eschew social criticism. Effectively, therefore, though the government does promote traditional Lao and ethnic minority culture, there is no artistic freedom.

In conclusion, the Lao PDR remains entirely under the control of the LPRP, which permits no form of political opposition. Civil society is virtually nonexistent, and the media is tightly controlled by the ruling party.

Recommendations

- The Lao authorities should further amend the 2003 constitution to eliminate both the special role allotted to the Lao People's Revolutionary Party and all reference to democratic centralism, to allow the organization of other political parties and their participation in National Assembly elections.
- The National Assembly and its Standing Committee should undertake the full range of activities set out in the 2003 constitution, in particular the new articles permitting questioning of government ministers (Article 63) and the drafting of laws by the new National Assembly Standing Committee for presentation to and debate by the National Assembly (Article 59).

- The Lao authorities should eliminate political interference in the civil service and introduce a competitive, merit-based system of appointments and promotions.
- The Lao authorities should permit the establishment of independent professional and cultural organizations and associations and encourage the development of a vibrant civil society.
- The government should enact a media law that permits the establishment of independent media outlets, enshrines press freedom, and protects working journalists from politically motivated prosecution.

CIVIL LIBERTIES

PROTECTION FROM STATE TERROR, UNJUSTIFIED IMPRISONMENT, AND TORTURE:	1.14
GENDER EQUITY:	3.25
RIGHTS OF ETHNIC, RELIGIOUS, AND OTHER DISTINCT GROUPS:	2.75
FREEDOM OF CONSCIENCE AND BELIEF:	3.00
FREEDOM OF ASSOCIATION AND ASSEMBLY:	1.80
CATEGORY AVERAGE:	**2.39**

Civil liberties for Lao citizens are set out under Chapter 4 of the 2003 amended constitution, which covers obligations as well as fundamental rights. Four of the eighteen articles are new—the rights to vote, to work, to lodge complaints and petitions, and to be free of arrest or search without a court order. Of these, the last is the most significant, for it provides some guarantee against arbitrary arrest and reinforces the slow evolution toward rule of law.

The constitution guarantees Lao citizens equality before the law, notably in terms of gender, ethnicity, and personal beliefs. A separate article endorses gender equality, while another guarantees freedom of religious belief. These constitutional guarantees are reassuring, but a large gap exists in Laos between the letter of the law and the reality of the human rights enjoyed by Lao citizens.

Take, for example, "the right and freedom of speech, press and assembly" that Article 44 guarantees Lao citizens, along with the right "to set up associations and to stage demonstrations which are not contrary to the laws." As one of the constitutional obligations of all citizens is to respect the laws of the land (Article 47), and as the penal code has very broad definitions of what constitutes "betrayal of the nation," rebellion, and improper gathering and use of intelligence (Articles, 51, 52 and 53),[11] the state effectively has the legal means to curtail any or all of these rights at any time. And it does so by the simple expedient of requiring permits for any media outlet, association, or public demonstration of any kind. As such permits are never issued, attempts to claim these constitutional rights are effectively denied.

Given this catch-22 situation, it is hardly surprising that Lao citizens are most reluctant to test the extent of the rights they supposedly enjoy. The last time any form of public demonstration took place was in October 1999, when a small group of about thirty students tried to unfurl a banner calling for greater political freedom. The demonstration was immediately broken up by police, who arrested five ringleaders. The five were apparently sentenced in June 2001, though the trial and its outcome were never reported in the Lao press. Since then one student has died from mistreatment.[12] The Lao authorities have refused officially to confirm any of this. Indeed, they claim not to know the whereabouts of two of the students (who may be known under alternative names.) The other two are in Vientiane's notorious Samkhe prison, where a number of political prisoners are held along with the worst criminal offenders.

Access to prisons in Laos is denied to human rights organizations, such as Amnesty International, but conditions are considered to be very poor. Amnesty has long accused the Lao government of using torture and other degrading treatment on prisoners, charges which the Lao authorities reject. Some idea of conditions can be gained from the experiences of Kay Danes, an Australian held with her husband for eleven months in 2001 on charges of embezzlement in relation to a failed business venture. They were incarcerated not in Samkhe, but in the Phonhong detention center for foreigners, which comes under the jurisdiction of the Ministry of Foreign Affairs. Other prisons are run by the Ministry of Security. If conditions are as bad in Phonhong as the torture and deprivation Kay Danes reported, one can only imagine what they are like in Samkhe prison.[13]

Political prisoners in particular may be held incommunicado for long periods, often without charges being brought. Prisoners who have completed their sentences may be released only if they have paid any costs incurred in prison. Families of prisoners with the right personal and political connections (and money) may provide additional food and medicines to inmates and even have their cases brought to the appeals court. Payment is always required by prison authorities for any service performed, even to act on an order for release.

The usual Lao government response to concerns expressed about the lack of safeguards against mistreatment of citizens by the state, including unjustified imprisonment, is simply to deny that any such abuses take place. Therefore, the Lao authorities argue, there is no reason to define procedures to redress such nonexistent abuses. As a result, the only defense anyone has, in the face of a defective legal system, is through whatever influence can be brought to bear by means of personal and political networks and judicial bribery.

Several political prisoners known to be in Lao jails are Hmong. The Hmong insurgency dates back to the earliest years of the regime and had its roots as much in fear of reprisals as in political opposition. It has been largely kept alive through support from Hmong refugees outside Laos. After a quiescent period, a series of attacks on buses in 2003 was blamed on Hmong "bandits" and led to a crackdown by government security forces. The following year, the first Western journalists managed secretly to make contact with Hmong insurgents and brought their plight to public attention. Since then small groups of mainly women and children have surrendered to Lao authorities, while others have fled to join more than 6,000 Hmong refugees still in Thailand who have been resisting both repatriation to Laos (under the auspices of the UNHCR) and resettlement in the United States.[14]

The Hmong are only one of forty-nine ethnic groups listed in the 2005 census, though with a population of 451,946 they are the second largest minority, after the Khamu (with 613,893), out of a total populations of 5.622 million. During the Vietnam War, the Hmong were divided: some were recruited into the CIA's secret army; others fought for the Pathet Lao revolutionaries. While most Hmong associated with the secret army were either airlifted out with their leader, General Vang Pao, or fled as refugees, those who fought for the Pathet Lao were rewarded. Hmong have risen through the Lao People's Revolutionary Party to become provincial governors and members of the Central Committee, and in 2006 a Hmong woman (Pany Yathothu) was elected to the powerful Politburo. Two other Hmong are government ministers, one the minister of justice and the other an adviser to the prime minister.

Many Hmong have been resettled, along with other upland ethnic minorities, from hilltop villages, where they practiced slash-and-burn agriculture and grew opium poppies, to land where they can supposedly practice permanent agriculture and have better road access. There has been considerable criticism of this internal resettlement program, whose stated purpose is to preserve forest resources and improve government services, but whose actual effect is to threaten minority cultures.[15] Resettlement is supposed to be voluntary, but coercion has been used at times. Promised government services have not materialized, and poverty has increased.

Other minority representatives are, like the Hmong, recruited into the party and the army, and some have reached positions of power. Additional political influence has been exerted by minorities through membership in the Lao Front for National Construction (LFNC). Over the past few years, however, the LFNC has been losing political clout. It is now little more than an arm of the party whose principal task is to quell any political criticism or social unrest. So far the government has done little to improve living conditions and opportunities for ethnic minorities. Indeed, disparities between urban and rural standards of living and incomes continue to grow.

Many ethnic minorities are animists of one kind or another, but some have converted to Buddhism or Christianity. Indeed, while a large proportion of Catholics are ethnic Lao,[16] the majority of Protestants (most members of the Lao Evangelical Church) are from ethnic minorities (including Hmong and Khamu). But Christians are regarded with some suspicion because of their international links, and evangelization, though theoretically permitted by the 2002 decree on religious practice, is prohibited on the grounds that it might create social division.[17] Some Christians have been arrested and reportedly forced to renounce their faith.[18]

Other religions have not been so targeted. There are small congregations of Baha'i and Muslims in Laos, but almost two-thirds of the population (including virtually all ethnic Lao) are Buddhists. The remainder are classed as animists, whose religious practices are accepted as part of their culture.[19]

The Lao United Buddhists Association functions under the watchful eye of the party, but monks no longer have to study Marxism-Leninism. Buddhism is even encouraged as being central to Lao culture and history by a ruling party seeking to bolster its ideological appeal through the embrace of Lao nationalism. There is reason to believe that the party took a hand in deciding who became head of the Lao monastic order, but as Buddhism in Laos becomes increasingly free of direct party control (provided it remains apolitical), it may refrain from direct intervention in the future.

Another minority is the officially estimated 1 percent of the total population who have some form of disability.[20] Of these, a declining proportion suffered war injuries (8 percent). In fact, over 55 percent were aged between six and eighteen years and so were born after the war ended. Their disabilities were overwhelmingly congenital (36 percent) or due to illness (41 percent). Only 1 percent were disabled by encounters with unexploded ordnance, but these amounted to 65 percent of all amputees, plus 13 percent of all cases of paralysis. The total number of unexploded ordnance (UXO) victims was 5,094.[21]

Very little is being done to assist these people. There is some physical and mental rehabilitation for UXO victims, especially children, but little in the way of special training or employment. A national strategy for people with disabilities is supposedly in place, coordinated by the Ministry of Labor and Social Welfare, but most assistance is provided by international NGOs, UN agencies, and some aid programs of friendly states.

The Lao government has been more active in protecting women and in demonstrating its commitment to gender equality. The 2004 Law on the Development and Protection of Women enshrines the leading role of the Lao Women's Union (LWU) in promoting both goals.[22] It defines development as ensuring "good health, knowledge, capabilities and revolutionary ethic." In November 2005, the Gender Resource Information and Development Center, a project of the LWU, published the first *Lao PDR Gender Profile*.[23] This comprehensive report brings together all the literature on women in Laos and sets out an enabling legal environment for gender equality, the role of women in the economy, women's health and education, women's special vulnerabilities, and women's involvement in decision making. It will provide the basis for all future policies with respect to gender.

While a good first step, there is a long way to go. The *Profile* recommends a series of practical measures to be adopted, including programs to enhance gender awareness among senior (male) officials and to promote socioeconomic development, especially among ethnic minority women. It also aims to increase the social status and political participation of women. According to the 2005 census, 31 percent of government employees are women, but they are disproportionately represented at the lower levels. Twenty-nine women were elected to the 2006 National Assembly (23 percent); two are government ministers (out of twenty-eight); and one is a member of the Politburo (out of eleven). At the provincial and district levels, however, female participation in decision making is far less evident.

The *Profile* took special note of the growing problem of trafficking of women and proposed a number of legal and educational measures to combat it. Though the *Profile* provided no figures, it is believed that up to 20,000 Lao are trafficked annually to neighboring countries. About a third are men who are exploited as bonded labor. Some women and girls are sold as wives, but most end up in prostitution. The Lao government is aware of the problem but has been slow to act. In 2005, the government amended the penal code to include child trafficking and imposed penalties of twenty years' imprisonment.[24] A few cases have been prosecuted, but outside Vientiane some local officials are believed to be protecting the perpetrators. Most of the impetus for the government to improve matters, and to provide care for victims of trafficking, has been due to pressure from international donors.

Workers' rights are supposedly protected and promoted by the Federation of Lao Trade Unions. However, this is an organization under close party control, whose purpose is rather to keep wages at levels that will attract foreign investment. Groups of workers are not free to form their own trade unions.

Recommendations

- The government should refine the penal code to limit the comprehensiveness of what constitutes anti-state activity.
- The government should permit citizens to exercise their freedoms as set out in the constitution and refrain from using penal provisions to punish them when they do so.

- The government should provide access to its prisons for international inspection and should investigate all prisoner complaints of abusive treatment.
- The government should establish mechanisms to ensure that its resettlement programs for ethnic minorities do not contravene their essential human rights.
- The government should allow access by human rights organizations and international NGOs to all former Hmong insurgents who surrender to the Lao authorities.

RULE OF LAW

INDEPENDENT JUDICIARY:	1.80
PRIMACY OF RULE OF LAW IN CIVIL AND CRIMINAL MATTERS:	1.17
ACCOUNTABILITY OF SECURITY FORCES AND MILITARY TO CIVILIAN AUTHORITIES:	1.00
PROTECTION OF PROPERTY RIGHTS:	3.00
EQUAL TREATMENT UNDER THE LAW:	3.00
CATEGORY AVERAGE:	**1.99**

Upon coming to power, the LPRP replaced all the laws of the former Royal Lao regime with its own socialist law administered by people's courts. Not until January 1983 was a Supreme People's Court (SPC) established that could act as a court of appeal to review decisions taken by these people's courts. Civil and criminal codes were not promulgated until 1989 and 1990, respectively. Only when the constitution of the LPDR was finally enacted in August 1991 was the Lao legal system provided with a proper constitutional underpinning.

Under the amended 2003 constitution, the National Assembly appoints the president of the Supreme People's Court and the supreme public prosecutor, on the recommendation of the state president. They in turn appoint and preside over a supposedly independent judiciary. Judges are appointed by the National Assembly Standing Committee, on the recommendation of the president of the SPC. They do receive some legal training, and there are foreign-assisted programs to improve their command of the law and legal procedures.

The Public Prosecutor's Office (PPO) is supposed to monitor implementation of all laws by the government, the civil service, and mass organizations and to take them to court for any transgressions. This is an impossible task, both because the PPO is understaffed and because it too is an arm of the party (which is not going to prosecute itself). Not surprisingly, no government department or instrumentality has been charged with any breach of any law. The legal provisions of the constitution make no mention of either the ruling party, which is supposedly policed by its own Control Commission, or the security apparatus or the military (which has its own courts).

No channels exist for making new laws known to the people, apart from a column in the party newspaper. Among urban professionals, knowledge of the growing body of laws and decrees is often sketchy, although increasingly, educated and informed Lao citizens do refer to the law to defend themselves or others against arbitrary decisions or actions by party or government officials. However, as the rural population is largely illiterate and ignorant of the law, they tend not to use it. Instead they resort to the methods they understand: the influence of relatives, friends, and patrons, and the payment of bribes. So in rural areas the party still determines the law.

The interpretation of many laws requires testing, but in Laos there is no constitutional court in which to do this. Whether or not a law is constitutional or an interpretation valid is decided by the Standing Committee of the National Assembly (NA), comprising the president and vice president, plus the presidents of the six NA commissions. In any case, application of the law seldom depends on the letter of the law and its proper interpretation. Three other factors influence judgments: payment of bribes; conformity with party policy; and extralegal pressure in the form of intervention by politically powerful friends or relatives. This is the most efficacious means of winning a legal case, especially a civil dispute. So, as the Lao say, it all depends on who has "the strongest string."

From the point of view of legal authorities, political intervention in sensitive cases may be a double-edged sword, for they may find themselves evaluating a case not on the basis of law but on which of two conflicting sets of phone calls and other private interventions represents the more powerful political interests, with failure carrying severe professional risk.

For those arrested, there is no presumption of innocence even in criminal cases, much less in political ones. Prisoners may be held for months while prosecutors assemble the case against them. There is no legal aid program, though the UNDP is assisting in establishing one. Finally, it should be noted that judgments in all cases with political or security ramifications are routinely submitted to senior party leaders before being handed down. Despite frequent statements by the party and government that they are committed to establishing the rule of law, until the court system is fully independent of the party, this will remain a chimera.

In the meantime, the rule of law in Laos is highly compromised. The security forces are under close party control and are beyond the reach of public scrutiny. They are not held accountable for any abuse of power they commit, and there is no means by which they could be. It is routinely assumed that anyone charged with an offence by the security forces must, prima facie, be guilty—otherwise they would not have been arrested in the first place. Judges, whatever the level of their training, are not free and independent in cases "endangering the security of the state"; they are expected to hand down guilty verdicts.

Lao citizens do have property rights in relation to their dwellings and personal possessions. But land is another matter. Over the past decade a land titling project has been under way for urban areas, beginning with Vientiane. This has led to a large number of disputes, which are resolved by a court of arbitration. Once again payments and influence are crucial to obtaining a desired outcome, so land ends up in the hands of the wealthy and well connected.

In rural areas, most farmland reverted after cooperativization to its original owners in the form of "use rights," which can be transferred (through sale or exchange) or passed on to designated family members. The ownership of all land resides in the "national community" and is managed by the state.[25] All land not in agricultural use belongs to the state, including forest land traditionally used for slash-and-burn farming by ethnic minorities. Since 1996, a proportion of this land has been distributed to villages under the Land and Forest Allocation Program in the form of both individual and communal use rights.[26] While the program provides some security of tenure, it also effectively limits access to land previously used for slash-and-burn farming or to gather forest products—a vital part of the economy of poor villagers.[27] Areas of "protected forest" remaining in the hands of the state can be leased for a fee, either to villagers (if they can pay) or to loggers or large companies for plantation agriculture—to the benefit not of local villagers but of party officials.

This is not so say that incremental improvements are not being made in implementing the rule of law. A body of law is slowly being developed and applied in the courts. For it to be more broadly accepted, however, a rigorous separation of powers will be necessary between the judiciary and the party. Moreover, general acceptance and application of the rule of law will require a much better-educated population than exists at present. Conservatively, it will require another generation before the rule of law is widely accepted and applied in Laos—and even then law is unlikely to be free of patronage politics.

Recommendations

- The LPRP should penalize party members who are determined to have interfered in any way in legal processes.
- The government should devote more resources to educating the population, rural and urban, about new laws as they are promulgated and about relevant legal procedures.
- The government should introduce measures to protect citizens from abuse by the security forces, including defining the powers of the police by law and establishing a complaints tribunal or an independent ombudsman's office.

ANTICORRUPTION AND TRANSPARENCY

ENVIRONMENT TO PROTECT AGAINST CORRUPTION:	1.80
EXISTENCE OF LAWS AND ETHICAL STANDARDS BETWEEN	
PRIVATE AND PUBLIC SECTORS:	1.75
ENFORCEMENT OF ANTICORRUPTION LAWS:	1.00
GOVERNMENTAL TRANSPARENCY:	2.00
CATEGORY AVERAGE:	**1.64**

What counts as corruption depends to a large extent on how it is defined and what is considered acceptable or unacceptable in a given culture. In traditional Lao society, it was considered natural for resources (wealth) and power to be concentrated in the hands of the ruling elite (the nobility), by virtue of their karma, which determined their birth and social status. Power derived from networks of obligation and loyalty given in return for protection and assistance in times of need; in other words, from the judicious distribution of resources. But for that to happen, ruling elites had to gain control over resources to distribute.

Under the French, the traditional structure of Lao society hardly changed, except that the punitive tax regime encouraged evasion and contempt for the law. Once Laos obtained independence, the flood of American aid provided the opportunity for those in positions of power to enrich themselves. So scandalous did corruption become that it provoked U.S. congressional investigation. Criticism of the corruption of wealthy families gained the Pathet Lao considerable public support and became a factor in their campaign to seize power in 1975.

Under the Lao People's Democratic Republic, corruption was initially limited to the exercise of power rather than the accumulation of wealth, but within a decade, with the introduction of a free-market economy, financial corruption began to increase. Some mid-level bureaucrats were charged with corruption and imprisoned in 1983–1984,[28] but this was partly political, and no high officials have been charged since, not even after the National Audit Office reported mismanagement and irregularities in the construction of irrigation and other infrastructure projects (in its 2003 report to the NA).[29] This compares with much more recent trials and convictions of high-ranking officials for corruption in both China and Vietnam. All that has happened by way of punishment of spectacularly corrupt high Lao party officials is that they have been quietly reprimanded, transferred, and/or demoted in the party ranking, which has not precluded their later return to powerful positions in government and the party.[30]

By the time Laos entered the twenty-first century, corruption had become deeply rooted in the political culture of the country.[31] Apart from the usual bribes and evasion of duties and taxes, the most damaging forms have been the plunder of the banking system by those with political connections, who obtain loans, often by way of state-owned enterprises, that are never repaid; and debasement of the legal system through rulings decided by bribery and political pressure. Illegal timber smuggling (especially by the military), cronyism in the awarding of contracts, and land grabbing are also widespread, lucrative forms of corruption. In tertiary education, the powerful make sure that their children obtain good marks and overseas scholarships, which means that more talented, but less well-connected students miss out.

Despite being nominally Marxist-Leninist, direct state involvement in the economy in Laos is limited to some two dozen "strategic" state-owned enterprises (SOEs), including natural monopolies such as electricity generation and distribution and water, plus enterprises such as Air Lao and the state printer. Indirect involvement is pervasive, however, in the form of bureaucratic registration and regulation of all business ventures, which allows officials to demand payment for almost everything they do. Delays and corruption associated with foreign investment have been reduced, however, by streamlining procedures under the Planning and Investment Committee, presided over by a senior minister.

The passage of new laws has done little to help, as the problem of lax enforcement remains. In fact, in some cases the effect of new laws has actually been to increase corruption because more officials have to be paid not to apply them. For example, environmental protection laws have done little to protect the environment: they just require that rangers appointed to look after "protected areas" be paid off in addition to the usual provincial party officials.

As no protection is provided by the state (in the form of an ombudsman's office or legislation protecting whistle-blowers) for those who report corruption, no one does. It is assumed that whatever is happening has been cleared with someone in authority (in the party), and so people prefer to mind their own business. And speaking of business, senior public officials from the president on down have business interests on the side, which everyone needs to supplement their meager government incomes, and to which no conflict-of-interest rules apply. As no public official in Laos is required to reveal his or her personal assets, however, word-of-mouth and rumor are the only means of knowing who owns what.

In such an environment, permeated by the power of a single ruling party, no auditing system can be independent of political pressure. Instead, auditors simply become complicit in the corruption they are supposed to contain. Their proceedings are wrapped in the secrecy that envelops everything the party does. The National Audit Office (established in 2001) is not politically independent: it reports to the Office of the Prime Minister, and any action taken on its findings requires a political decision. So great has been the financial mismanagement of some state-owned enterprises that oversight has been tightened by the Ministry of Finance. Also, the government is progressively publishing more information, in the form of policies, reports, and statistics (for example, the results of the 2005 national census), but nothing appears on the deliberations of the party. And there is no free media able even to speculate on what might be going on.

This lack of transparency extends from the party to the government to the bureaucracy. No one knows how decisions are made. Even relatively senior civil servants are reluctant to take decisions in their areas of competency, preferring to refer them up the hierarchy. When decisions are made, reasons tend not to be given. They are acted upon in the spirit of "democratic centralism"; that is, unquestioningly. This especially applies to the award of government contracts and other decisions with financial implications, such as tax rulings or exemptions.

International financial institutions have long criticized the lack of transparency in Laos. Under such pressure a procurement monitoring office was established in 2003 within the Ministry of Finance, which is supposed to improve procurement processes, and since 2002 documentation on the budget has been regularly published in the official government gazette. The budget itself is debated by the NA, but its provisions are seldom questioned, and it is always passed as presented, along with the financial statements of government ministries. Extrabudgetary expenditures escape any scrutiny, and military expenditures are completely opaque and not subjected to public audit.

Only in the areas of foreign investment (see above) and foreign aid have attempts been made to provide more transparent procedures—for the obvious reason that senior Lao authorities want the projects and programs to go ahead. Investment provides employment and aid improves living conditions and services; allowing government officials not only to take credit, but also to recommend employees. So the system perpetuates itself, without checks and balances, but with indirect foreign support, which Western governments continue to provide, despite "leakages," in preference to permitting Laos to slip entirely into China's widening orbit.

Recommendations

- The government should ensure that the provisions of all anticorruption legislation are fully implemented and that corrupt officials are prosecuted in the courts.
- Public finances should be made more transparent and debated more freely by the National Assembly.
- More information should be made available by the government, and the media should be permitted freely to discuss government policy and decisions.
- The press should be allowed to report freely on corrupt practices, and anonymity and protection should be provided for whistle-blowers.

NOTES

1 According to the IMF. See http://www.imf.org/external/country/LAO/index.htm.
2 Constitution of the Lao People's Democratic Republic, http://www.laoembassy.com/news/constitution/constitution.htm.
3 For a list of foreign NGOs in Laos, see http://www.directoryofngos.org/. The decree permitting NGOs to operate in Laos can be found at http://www.mofa.gov.la/decrees/DecreeOnNGO.htm. See also *A Study of NGOs. Lao People's Democratic Republic* (Manila: Asian Development Bank [ADB], 1999), http://www.adb.org/NGOs/docs/NGOLaoPDR.pdf.
4 There are currently fifty-six members (as of 22 January 2006). See http://www.laobar.org/about_lba.html. This site, which includes a number of useful legal documents, was unavailable on 3 May 2007, but is to be reestablished.
5 For a list of member associations and business groups of the Lao National Chamber of Commerce and Industry, see http://www.lncci.laotel.com/Page%20Associations%20and%20Groups.htm.
6 At http://www.rsf.org/country-50.php3?id_mot=577.
7 Ibid.
8 A copy of this letter can be found at http://www.rsf.org/print.php3?id_article=18109.
9 Quoted in ibid.
10 According to http://www.internetworldstats.com/stats3.htm.
11 Accessible at http://www.apwld.org/pdf/lao_penalcode1989.pdf.
12 *Annual Report—2006* (London: Amnesty International [AI], 2006), http://web.amnesty.org/web/web.nsf/print/8CFC832FF2D820CB802571650031837C, states that this death was the result of torture.
13 Kay Danes, *Nightmare in Laos* (Bangkok: Maverick House, 2006); see also http://www.phaseloop.com/foreignprisoners/prison-phonthong.html.
14 See *Annual Report—2006* (AI); see also http://www.huntingtonnews.net/national/061221-kinchen-hmong.html, accessed 24 January 2007.

15 See, for example, Olivier Evrard and Yves Goudineau, "Planned Resettlement, Unexpected Migrations and Cultural Trauma in Laos," *Development and Change* 35, 5 (2004): 937–62.

16 There are 42,000 Catholics in Laos and a roughly similar number of Protestants. In Pakse recently, the first local priest in fifty years was ordained. See http://www.zenit.org/english /visualizza.phtml?sid=101595, accessed 25 January 2007.

17 This is another catch-22 situation. Under Article 9 of the constitution, all acts "creating divisions between religions and classes or people" are banned. On these grounds requests for permission to proselytize, required under the 2002 decree that permits such proselytizing, are routinely rejected.

18 See *Annual Report—2006* (AI).

19 The *Report on Religious Freedom—2005* (Washington, D.C.: U.S. Department of State, 2005), http://www.state.gov/g/drl/rls/irf/2005/51517.htm, accessed 25 January 2007, includes a useful section on the religious demography of the Lao PDR.

20 This estimate is based on 1995 data, giving a figure of around 56,000. *Country Profile on Disability: Lao People's Democratic Republic* (Tokyo: Japan International Cooperation Agency, March 2002), http://www.jica.go.jp/english/global/dis/pdf/lao_eng.pdf, accessed 25 January 2007.

21 UXO continue to cause injuries, especially among children. The United States government has refused to accept responsibility for UXO remaining in Laos and has provided very little assistance to get rid of it.

22 The law was passed by the Lao National Assembly in November 2004. The March 2006 UNDP draft translation can be found at http://www.na.gov.la/eng/laws/wmn_law.pdf.

23 Accessible at http://siteresources.worldbank.org/INTLAOPRD/Resources/Lao-Gender-Report-2005.pdf.

24 See *Trafficking in Persons Report* (Washington, D.C.: U.S. Department of State, 2006), http://www.state.gov/g/tip/rls/tiprpt/2006/65989.htm.

25 See Amended Land Law (2003) at http://www.na.gov.la/eng/laws/econ/land_law.pdf.

26 See the 1997 Land Law, http://sunsite.nus.edu.sg/apcel/dbase/laos/primary/laalnd.html.

27 See, for example, Yayoi Fujita and Khamla Phanvilay, "Land and Forest Allocation and Its Implication on Forest Management and Household Livelihoods," and Daovorn Thongphanh, "Does Decentralisation Meet the Needs of Local People? Implementing Land and Forestland Allocation in Two Local Communities, Lao PDR" (Oaxaca, Mexico: International Association for the Study of Common Property, Tenth Biennial Conference, papers, 9–13 August 2004), http://dlc.dlib.indiana.edu/, accessed 30 January 2007.

28 Martin Stuart-Fox, *A History of Laos* (Cambridge: Cambridge University Press, 1997), 188.

29 Rarely does the Lao press report on corruption. This report in *Le Rénovateur*, 9 October 2003, was in the context of an article on the National Assembly. On 27 November 2003, *Le Rénovateur* returned to the subject of corruption in a report on a two-day anticorruption seminar by its editor, Khamphout Xayasomroth, titled "La corruption, cheval de bataille du Gouvernement." More recently, in an opinion piece for the *Vientiane Times*

titled "New hope for media freedom," Ekaphone Phouthonesy pointed to the role the press could play in combating corruption.

30 For example, Sisavath Keobounphanh was dropped from the Politburo at the Fifth Party Congress in March 1991 and demoted to fifteenth position on the LPRP Central Committee. No reason was given, but popular rumor focused on corruption. Yet at the Sixth Party Congress in March 1996, Sisavath regained his place in the Politburo and was appointed vice president of the LPDR. In the government reshuffle of 1998, which saw Khamtay Siphandone become state president, Sisavath took his place as prime minister.

31 See Martin Stuart-Fox, "The Political Culture of Corruption in the Lao PDR," *Asian Studies Review* 30, 1 (March 2006): 59–76; see also Patrick Keuleers, *Corruption in the Lao PDR: Underlying causes and key issues for consideration* (Bangkok: United Nations Development Programme [UNDP], March 2004).

LIBYA

CAPITAL: Tripoli
POPULATION: 6.2 million
GNI PER CAPITA: $7,380

SCORES	2005	2007
ACCOUNTABILITY AND PUBLIC VOICE:	0.56	0.68
CIVIL LIBERTIES:	1.17	1.55
RULE OF LAW:	1.12	1.85
ANTICORRUPTION AND TRANSPARENCY:	0.19	0.66

(scores are based on a scale of 0 to 7, with 0 representing weakest
and 7 representing strongest performance)

Alison Al-Baddawy

INTRODUCTION

In recent years, Libya has succeeded in ending its isolation and transforming itself from a pariah state into a full member of the international community. Colonel Muammar Qadhafi's announcement in December 2003 that he would abandon his weapons of mass destruction programs was a major step forward in this respect. It opened the way for the resumption of bilateral relations with the United States and the lifting of international sanctions. In May 2006, Libya was finally removed from the U.S. state sponsors of terrorism list, marking its full rehabilitation.

This new international climate raised hopes that the Libyan regime would take the opportunity to engage in domestic reforms that would

Alison Al-Baddawy is a Research Fellow at Kings College London, where she specializes in North Africa with a particular focus on Libya. She has conducted numerous research projects on Libya and published widely on the topic. Her other main research area is on Muslim communities in Europe and on political Islam and radicalization. She has carried out a range of research projects in this field and is about to publish a book on radical Islam in Europe by I. B. Tauris.

bring the country more in line with international standards. This was partly prompted by a new reformist discourse adopted by some parts of the regime, which called for economic transformation and flagged issues such as human rights and respect for the rule of law. However, while there have been some tentative steps in the field of economic reform, political change has remained largely off the agenda. Colonel Qadhafi has shown no willingness to alter the fundamentals of the Libyan political system, the Jamahiriyah (State of the Masses). Political parties are banned, and there are no genuinely independent civil society organizations. While there has been an easing in recent years whereby the regime is allowing some degree of criticism of certain aspects of the government and is encouraging former dissidents to return to the country, anyone daring openly to challenge the regime or the Libyan state is in danger of arrest, torture, and imprisonment. As a result there is no real opposition movement in the country.

The Jamahiriyah, introduced by Qadhafi a few years after the revolution of 1969, is a highly personalized and idiosyncratic political system. It is based on a mixture of Arab nationalism, socialism, and Islam, and through it Qadhafi has been able to impose his own ideology on the population and ensure complete uniformity and control. Indeed, the formal mechanisms of government notwithstanding, Qadhafi and his hand-picked clique of advisers are the real power brokers in the country. Qadhafi has been able to maintain power for so long through his ability to manipulate these informal power networks, a complex hierarchy of security structures and the country's tribal alliances. He has also come increasingly to rely on his own family and members of his own tribe, the Qadhadfa, to shore up his regime.

Although there have been some attempts to open Libya's tightly controlled economy, private sector activity remains limited, and bureaucracy is still highly problematic. Corruption is also a major problem, not only through the payment of bribes but also because much of Libyan life still hinges on personal and tribal connections. In addition, the country is still blighted by persistent socioeconomic dilemmas, such as unemployment and housing shortages. Although there are signs that the regime, or at least certain parts of it, are making serious efforts to deal with some of these issues, the enormous scope of the challenge makes meaningful reform extremely difficult to implement.

ACCOUNTABILITY AND PUBLIC VOICE

FREE AND FAIR ELECTORAL LAWS AND ELECTIONS:	0.25
EFFECTIVE AND ACCOUNTABLE GOVERNMENT:	1.00
CIVIC ENGAGEMENT AND CIVIC MONITORING:	0.33
MEDIA INDEPENDENCE AND FREEDOM OF EXPRESSION:	1.13
CATEGORY AVERAGE:	**0.68**

Political parties are banned in the Jamahiriyah, and membership in any illegal party is punishable by death under Law 71 of 1972. In theory, the Jamahiriyah is a system of direct, or people's, democracy whereby every citizen over the age of eighteen can participate in government at the local level through Basic People's Congresses. The decisions reached at these congresses are then fed up to a higher body, the General People's Congress (parliament), and are implemented by the General People's Committee (cabinet). Marking his ongoing commitment to the Jamahiriyah, in January 2006 Qadhafi announced that the number of Basic People's Congresses was to be increased to 30,000. These congresses have limited influence, however, as key decisions are still made by the informal power structures that make up the Libyan regime, with Qadhafi at the helm. In fact, although Colonel Qadhafi has no official leadership role, preferring to refer to himself as "Brother Leader" or "Guide of the Revolution," all power rests with him.

In theory, the General People's Congress chooses the secretaries (ministers) who are appointed to the General People's Committee. In reality, people who fill these posts are chosen by Qadhafi, with the decisions rubber-stamped by the congress. Moreover, the same few individuals have remained in positions of power for the past three decades, with Qadhafi simply rotating their posts. The majority of the secretaries in the General People's Committee as of January 2007 have been in government positions for many years. Even the power of the General People's Committee is limited, however, and its members are often considered to be little more than technocrats. This reflects the fact that personality and links to the leader are always more important than official positions. In addition, the General People's Committee is often hostage to the whims of the General People's Congress. The former general secretary of the General People's Committee, Shukri Ghanem, repeatedly complained that he was not even able to appoint his own cabinet, as decisions had to be approved by the congress, and that the General People's Congress also blocked his reform plans.

Elections are held every four years to choose the members of the Basic People's Congresses who represent their local area in the General People's Congress. Citizens are able to put themselves forward as candidates but must be approved by a special committee in order to stand. In the July 2004 elections, the regime introduced a new system that it claimed would increase transparency: it did away with traditional voting booths and forced voters to declare their choice in front of a committee. No effective mechanisms prevent those with economic privilege from exerting undue influence on the voting process, and no attempts are made to stop candidates from offering money and other goods in return for votes. It was reported that in the July 2004 elections, candidates had set up tents to provide people with food, as well as offering cigarettes and money to try to attract voters.

Parallel to the formal political system Qadhafi has also created a network of paralegal bodies that wield significant power and carry with them the authority of the revolution. The most important is the Revolutionary Committees Movement, formed in the 1970s; its members have been responsible for some of the worst abuses committed by the regime. Although these excesses have been curtailed in recent years, the Revolutionary Committees remain a powerful interest group who are given special privileges and who continue to dominate many sectors and institutions, including the General People's Congress and the Basic People's Congresses. There are also a number of loyal Revolutionary Committees members in the General People's Committee who have tried to block those of a more reformist bent. In fact, Qadhafi's son Saif al-Islam is reported to be locked in a battle to try to limit the Committees' power.

Qadhafi also draws upon the Popular Social Leaderships as a key instrument of power. These consist of important tribal leaders who represent their own communities and localities within the organization, enabling Qadhafi to manipulate the country's tribal alliances better and keep the more rebellious tribal groupings in line.

Qadhafi's children are also highly influential in both the political and economic spheres. Currently, the most important of them is Qadhafi's son Saif al-Islam. Despite the fact that he claims to represent civil society, he takes an active role in the political and economic running of the country. He has been responsible for negotiating international agreements, such as the La Belle disco bombing compensation in 2004, and is involved in the ongoing negotiations to resolve the case of the Bulgarian and Palestinian medics convicted of deliberately infecting over 400 children in a Benghazi hospital with the HIV virus. In September 2006, he participated in a meeting of the National Oil Corporation (NOC) held to discuss the next bidding round for foreign companies seeking oil exploration rights. All five of Qadhafi's other children also exercise significant influence in other spheres.

The regime follows a socialist-style system in which the state is the main employer, guaranteeing many people jobs in the public sector. Wages, however, are not generally sufficient to live on, and many people take second jobs in order to make ends meet. The whole public sector is characterized by chaos and inefficiency. In September 2005, Shukri Ghanem complained of the scores of "ghost employees" who take a state salary each month yet who never turn up to work or who do not even exist.[1]

Selection and promotion for many public sector jobs, especially high-ranking ones, is made on the basis of personal contacts and the degree of loyalty the applicant displays toward the regime. In November 2005, in an attempt to encourage younger, better-qualified people to enter the government, Shukri Ghanem announced the formation of a "Getting New Blood into the Leadership Committee." However, no further information has surfaced about whether this committee is active or what it has achieved.

The regime continues to take an arbitrary approach toward dismissal from the public sector. There were numerous reports in 2005 of public companies being closed or restructured for privatization and of employees being pushed out with no form of compensation. News also emerged in December 2006 that 5,000 teachers in the Benghazi area had been suspended from their jobs for not being sufficiently qualified. It was reported that they were warned not to speak to the press while their files were being assessed by the People's Committee for the Labor Force. This initiative was later withdrawn, however, and the teachers were allowed to remain in their posts. In January 2007, General Secretary Baghdadi Mahmoudi announced that in its efforts to pare the public sector, the state was going to lay off 400,000 workers, and that each released public employee would be given a full salary for three years or granted up to 50,000 dinars in loans to start a business.

Genuinely independent civic groups do not exist in Libya, as any organization has to be sanctioned by the state and must conform to the ideals of the Libyan revolution. Thus the many groups that present themselves as nongovernmental organizations (NGOs) are neither independent nor in a position to genuinely comment on or influence government policy or legislation. In recent years, Saif al-Islam has presented himself as the leader of civil society through his charity, the Qadhafi Development Foundation. This organization has enhanced Saif al-Islam's ability to play a major political and economic role in the country. Qadhafi's daughter Aisha runs a charitable foundation, Watassimu, that also claims to be independent. It would also be impossible for anyone not linked to the state to secure funding to set up a civic group, and any money given from abroad must be channeled through the authorities before it can be delivered.

The media is another sector that is dominated by the state and by the Revolutionary Committees in particular. State newspapers serve as propaganda tools for the regime. The television service is also state-run, as are the radio and news agencies. In recent years, Saif al-Islam has been keen to promote alternative media sources; in 2006, his One Nine Media company announced that it was entering into a partnership with international printing houses to distribute foreign newspapers inside Libya and that it would be setting up a new satellite television channel called Al-Mishri in 2007. The regime has also tolerated the presence of the semi-opposition online magazine *Libya al-Youm*, which allows space for those who support the reformist agenda of Saif al-Islam. This publication publishes criticism of the institutions of government and raises issues such as corruption and the failings of public companies and utilities. Criticism of Qadhafi, his family, or the regime, however, is firmly off-limits.

Libel laws exist in Libya, but information is limited in the public domain about whether libel cases are prosecuted. The state provides no mechanism to protect journalists who face intimidation or threats. In May 2005, the mutilated corpse of journalist Daif al-Ghazal was found in Benghazi after he had begun speaking out about corruption and had threatened to publish documents that would implicate officials. Prior to his death, al-Ghazal allegedly made several statements alluding to his fears that he would be killed, but he received no protection from the state.[2] The regime has repeatedly promised to open a full investigation into the killing, although as of March 31, 2007, there appeared to have been limited progress on this issue.

The internet is widely available in Libya, although the sector is heavily monitored. The state has blocked the sites of Libyan opposition groups abroad, but many Libyans appear able to circumvent these restrictions. This can have serious consequences. In January 2005, the security services arrested Abdel Razak al-Mansuri after he had posted a series of articles critical of the regime on the internet. Al-Mansuri was sentenced to eighteen months in prison on charges of possessing a pistol. He was eventually released in March 2006. Since his release, he has continued posting critical articles on his website and does not appear to be being persecuted for doing so.

The state strictly controls publishing houses and printing presses. The main publisher in Libya, Al-Ferjani, is private, but it is in fact heavily linked to the state. Foreign newspapers are not generally available. Indeed, the regime only publishes around 3,000 copies of its own newspapers each day, and consequently, it is difficult to obtain copies. Satellite television channels are readily accessible. Cultural expression is restricted, and writers and artists are at risk of imprisonment if they produce what are deemed anti-revolutionary works of art. The Libyan Writer's Union is heavily dominated by the Revolutionary Committees Movement.

Recommendations

- The regime should lift the ban on political parties.
- The government needs to open space for genuinely independent civil society actors to operate.
- Open competition and promotion based on merit should be encouraged within the public sector.
- The state should ensure that compensation measures for those public sector employees who are to be laid off are adequate and are implemented properly.
- The regime should encourage a genuinely independent press that fosters debate. It should also try to inject some dynamism into its local media.

CIVIL LIBERTIES

PROTECTION FROM STATE TERROR, UNJUSTIFIED IMPRISONMENT, AND TORTURE:	1.29
GENDER EQUITY:	3.00
RIGHTS OF ETHNIC, RELIGIOUS, AND OTHER DISTINCT GROUPS:	1.00
FREEDOM OF CONSCIENCE AND BELIEF:	1.67
FREEDOM OF ASSOCIATION AND ASSEMBLY:	0.80
CATEGORY AVERAGE:	**1.55**

Libyan legislation prohibits the use of torture, but according to international human rights organizations, torture is still employed by the security services. In line with its new reformist discourse the regime has openly condemned the use of torture. In December 2006, during an interview with the Al-Jazeera channel, Saif al-Islam declared that he would come forward to speak publicly about human rights violations that had been committed in the name of the revolution. Nevertheless, he also made it clear that certain individuals rather than the state were going to be made to take responsibility for such acts. He indicated that those accused of practicing torture will be asked publicly to name the official who instructed them and that these officials will in turn be tried and punished. While this is a positive step, it looks as though the regime intends to make scapegoats out of certain officials as a means of turning a page on the past and is unwilling to admit its own role in having sanctioned such practices.

Prison conditions are generally poor, with serious overcrowding and inadequate sanitary, recreational, and medical facilities. In October 2006, a riot erupted in the Abu Slim prison in Tripoli, sparked by a number of prisoners who are members of militant Islamist groups. As the violence spread, the security forces entered the prison and began shooting, killing one inmate and injuring a number of others.

There is no effective protection against arbitrary arrest. The security services operate with relative impunity, and there is no recourse against the state in such instances. Nevertheless, in a number of cases in 2006 and 2007, individuals were able to secure compensation through the courts for having been wrongly arrested. While things have improved in recent years, anyone criticizing the regime or suspected of opposition activity is at risk of arrest and detention. Political prisoner Fathi el-Jahmi, who criticized the regime after his release from prison in March 2004 and was subsequently rearrested, remains in prison. In November 2006, unconfirmed reports appeared of preemptive arrests in the Bani Walid area, allegedly carried out to deter Libyans from going to join the jihad in Iraq.

The regime has taken steps, however, to release some of its political prisoners. This includes the group of more than 150 Muslim Brotherhood prisoners who were arrested in 1998 and convicted of belonging to an outlawed organization. They were eventually released in March 2006 under the clemency of Qadhafi, and Saif al-Islam has been working to reinstate them in their jobs in spite of resistance from hard-line revolutionaries. They are clearly not permitted to engage in any sort of political activity outside the framework of the Jamahiriyah. The regime is also engaged in negotiations with more militant Islamist prisoners to secure their release under similar terms and conditions, and in January 2007, a group of sixty Islamists was freed. Negotiations between the imprisoned leadership of the Libyan Islamic Fighting Group—the most influential Libyan militant group, which was largely crushed at the end of the 1990s—and the regime are continuing, with the regime trying to convince the movement to renounce violence. In addition, the regime has tried to lure back dissidents residing abroad, leading a number of high-profile opponents to return to the country in 2006. Therefore, the situation is easing for those opponents willing to cut a deal with the regime. Moreover, Libyans are trying to use Saif al-Islam as a vehicle through which to channel protest. In January 2007, a group of Libyans from Benghazi wrote to Saif al-Islam's charity to complain about the security services in their area, which had arrested a group of residents after they objected to a number of security officials appropriating public land so that investors could build on it. The extent to which Saif al-Islam will tolerate such complaints is yet to be seen.

Long-term pretrial detention is very common in Libya. The law limits the amount of time a suspect may be detained, but this cutoff is not enforced. In July 2004, prisoners in pretrial detention were estimated to make up 56.8 percent of the total prison population.[3] Moreover, prolonged incommunicado detention is also practiced.

Although generally no nonstate actors are powerful enough to commit acts of abuse, some of the offspring of high-ranking figures within the regime are not held accountable for their actions, and there have been reports of their intimidation of others with violence. The security services have been unwilling to step in on these occasions for fear of retribution.

The state has promoted the concept of the equal civil and political rights of men and women. In fact, Qadhafi has actively championed women's rights as part of his progressive revolutionary ideology. Aside from some parts of family law, such as inheritance, in which general principles of the Maliki school of Sunni Islam are practiced, Libyan legislation provides for the equal treatment of men and women. However, much of Libyan society remains highly conservative, and discrimination persists. For example, although Libyan labor legislation holds that employers must pay equal wages to men and women if the nature and conditions of their work are the same, in reality women are often paid less than their male counterparts.

Human trafficking is a problem, especially regarding women from sub-Saharan Africa being trafficked into Europe through Libya. Articles 415 and 420 of the penal code criminalize prostitution and prostitution-related activities, including sexual trafficking.[4] The state has arrested some of those involved, but there is little information about exactly what steps the regime has taken. Libya has, however, begun working with European governments and with the European Union to tackle the problem of illegal immigration more generally.

The Libyan regime does not acknowledge any ethnic minorities, despite the presence of the Berbers and Tuareg. Until recently it was illegal for a child to be given a Berber name. In January 2007, however, following an announcement by Saif al-Islam the previous August to the same effect, the General People's Committee issued a decree ruling that Libyans could give their children names that "express the origins of Libyans," suggesting that Berber names are now acceptable. This would indicate some easing of pressure on the Berber minority in terms of cultural and linguistic rights, although any sign of political activity around the Berber issue is still out of bounds.

There is limited awareness about the rights of people with disabilities in Libya, as in much of the Arab world. No special legislation has been introduced to protect people with disabilities against discrimination, and they often face social stigma. Under Law 30 of 1981, disabled people are entitled to various benefits, including admission to specialized institutions if they need full-time care, receiving care services at home, exemption from income tax if working, and other entitlements. *Landmine Monitor* reported in 2006, however, that poor awareness of disabilities, low incomes, and the lack of home care and social safety networks hamper the integration of people with disabilities.[5]

As for the issue of religious discrimination, Libya is a Muslim country that follows the Maliki school of Sunni Islam. The government is broadly tolerant of other faiths, largely because they do not represent a threat, and a number of Christian churches and communities operate in the country. Being an atheist is extremely difficult in Libya, as in the rest of the Arab world, and anyone professing a lack of belief in God would be subject to severe social stigma. The state's main concern, however, remains that of politicized Islam. Despite the fact that it has released a number of Islamist prisoners of late, anyone suspected of being involved in or sympathizing with outlawed religious groups risks heavy persecution. Although Islamic dress appears to be increasingly tolerated, wearing the *niqab* (complete covering of the body and face) or sporting a long beard is still likely to attract suspicion. The regime ensures that mosques remain open for only fifteen minutes before and after prayer time in order to prevent potential unauthorized political activity. It also has total control over the appointment of imams and other spiritual leaders. Mosques are generally controlled by the state, which also supervises the *khoutbas* (Friday sermons). It also maintains strict control over what is taught in terms of religious education.

Freedom of association is enshrined in the Great Green Charter of Human Rights of the Jamahiriyah Era.[6] There are numerous trade unions in Libya, although they are strictly controlled by the regime through the Labor Secretariat. Workers may join the General Trade Union Federation of Workers (GTUFW), which is administered by the People's Committees, but all independent trade union activity is banned.[7] Foreign workers are not permitted to join the GTUFW. The notion of collective bargaining exists in law but is undermined by the fact that the government remains the most important single employer and the unions form part of management.[8] Assemblies, strikes, sit-ins, and demonstrations are all banned under Law 45 of 1972, and anyone engaging in such practice is liable to severe mistreatment. It was reported that when airline workers approached their GTUFW-affiliated union over their concerns about having to fly aircraft that did not meet technical safety standards, they were told they should not protest and should continue working.[9]

It is strictly prohibited for any kind of group to organize, mobilize, or advocate for peaceful purposes. Demonstrations and public protests are banned in Libya unless they have been orchestrated by the state in advance. When spontaneous protests do occasionally break out, the regime does not refrain from using excessive force. In February 2006, the Revolutionary Committees orchestrated a demonstration in Benghazi to protest against the Danish cartoons depicting the prophet. The demonstration, however, got out of hand as protesters attacked the Italian consulate, began burning cars, and also turned against the regime. The security forces opened fire on the protesters, killing eleven and arresting many others. After the events, however, the regime immediately suspended the minister for public security and began investigations into the affair. Although this was done partly in response to the fact that the events were broadcast on the international media, it did mark a more mature approach toward such a public outburst.

Recommendations

- The government should commit resources to improve prison conditions and limit practices such as lengthy pretrial detention.
- The state should follow up on Saif al-Islam's promises to bring those who have perpetrated torture to justice and provide compensation to those who have been the victims of torture.
- The government should implement the existing legislation that protects against discrimination against women and carry out an information campaign at the grassroots level to make women more aware of their rights in this respect.
- The state needs to allow genuinely independent trade unions to form and to establish links with international trade union bodies.

RULE OF LAW

INDEPENDENT JUDICIARY:	1.00
PRIMACY OF RULE OF LAW IN CIVIL AND CRIMINAL MATTERS:	2.00
ACCOUNTABILITY OF SECURITY FORCES AND MILITARY TO CIVILIAN AUTHORITIES:	0.25
PROTECTION OF PROPERTY RIGHTS:	3.00
EQUAL TREATMENT UNDER THE LAW:	3.00
CATEGORY AVERAGE:	**1.85**

The Libyan justice system cannot be considered free from political influence; it is deeply intertwined with the interests of other institutions of the revolution. Although Article 31 of the 1991 Promotion of Freedoms law states, "Judges are independent in their decisions and there is no authority above them apart from the law,"[10] judges and magistrates are not protected from interference by the regime, especially in cases of a political nature. Moreover, while under the law all parties are treated equally before courts and tribunals, in reality Libyan society still operates on personal and tribal connections, and bribery is an effective mechanism within the justice system.

January 2006 brought a positive step, however, when Libya abolished its People's Courts. These chambers, set up in the 1980s as a parallel court system to try political cases, were heavily criticized by international human rights groups for failing to comply with minimum standards for fair trial. Following their abolition, a number of cases that had originally been conducted in the People's Courts were reheard in the criminal courts. This includes the case of the Muslim Brotherhood prisoners who were retried in a regular court in 2006. Their verdicts were ultimately upheld, although they were released in March 2006 under the clemency of Qadhafi.

The Supreme Council for Judicial Authority is the administrative authority of the judiciary, handling matters of discipline.[11] It acts as a technical consultant committee, tasked with studying legislation and improving the laws in accordance with the principles of the Jamahiriya.[12] It is also responsible for appointing, transferring, and dismissing judges, although in many cases, having the right connections within the regime is the key to appointment. It is also very rare for a judge ever to be dismissed in Libya. In order to practice law in Libya, citizens must complete a law degree and then train for two years with a legal firm. Libya has an estimated 2,500 lawyers working in private legal practice.[13] These are represented by the Libyan Bar Association. The regime has worked to restrict the activities of this association, preventing it from choosing its own representatives and imposing its own personnel on the organization. In October 2006, the security services took over the association's Benghazi office and prevented its members from holding a meeting in its Tripoli office.

According to Article 31 of the Constitutional Declaration of December 1969, defendants are presumed innocent until proven guilty. In political cases, however, the results are generally predetermined. Libyan lawyers have complained that in many cases they receive the file for the case only in the first trial session.[14] On some occasions they have also been prevented from being able to defend their clients, and the defendants have been assigned alternative state lawyers. Little information exists in the public domain about criminal cases; however, it seems that ordinary citizens have access to fair and public trials, although not necessarily timely ones.

Those being tried on political charges did not have the right under the People's Court system to independent counsel and had attorneys imposed upon them from the state Popular Lawyers Office. It is not clear whether, given the abolition of these courts, defendants are now able to choose their own counsel. In criminal cases, the state provides legal representation for those who cannot afford to pay their own legal fees. However, this process is likely to be subject to corruption. Public officials are prosecuted for wrongdoing if the regime decides to make an example of them, but the process appears to be arbitrary. In 2005, those accused of torturing confessions out of the foreign medics convicted of infecting children from Benghazi with the HIV virus were brought to trial but all ten defendants were acquitted.

There is no effective civilian control of the armed forces, and there is no defense ministry or defense minister within the General People's Committee. Qadhafi has the rank of colonel; all matters relating to defense are in his hands and in the hands of high-ranking military personnel within the upper echelons of the regime such as Brig. Abu Baker

Younis Jaber, who is Secretary of the General Committee for Defense. Qadhafi has created a multilayered and complex network of security services and agencies that are all ultimately answerable to him. It is impossible to distinguish who is responsible for which parts of these various organizations at any one time. However, Qadhafi has drawn many of his security personnel from certain tribes, such as the Warfalla tribe. Qadhafi's sons have also been able to wield influence within the armed forces. In 2006, Saadi Qadhafi was appointed to head the Special Forces, and Moatassim Qadhafi has his own brigade, which is reputed to be particularly powerful. Moatassim was also recently appointed to head the new National Security Commission, which was set up in October 2006 to act as an overarching body bringing together the existing internal and external security sectors.

The police force is subordinated to the Ministry for Public Security but in reality is answerable to Qadhafi. In a speech to new graduates of the Public Security Services in April 2004, Qadhafi announced that the police were to become a military force to defend the country from terrorists. He also announced that, as with the armed forces, he would take personal responsibility for promoting police officers.

The police, military, and internal security agencies, including the Revolutionary Committees Movement, do not appear to be held accountable for abuses of power for personal gain, and they are as subject to corruption as any other institution. The personnel of these agencies have scant regard for human rights and still practice torture and intimidation regularly.

When Libya relaxed its property laws in 2004, it became legal for any Libyan national to buy property for investment and to rent it out. At the same time, the government introduced a special scheme under which citizens could apply to banks for loans to build their own houses. However, the scheme was soon beset with problems due both to the bureaucracy involved in the application and approval process and because it became subject to corruption.

The state enforces property rights and contracts provided they are within the framework of the Jamahiriyah system. As the Libyan regime asserts that it has no ethnic minorities, no special provisions are made for Berber or Tuareg property customs. The state does not protect people from confiscation of property or possessions. In fact, confiscating property is one method that has traditionally been used by the regime to intimidate those it deems to have been disloyal, and the Revolutionary Committees have been known in the past to bulldoze the houses of regime opponents. Yet the regime appears in some cases to be receptive to the demands of former regime opponents who, on returning to the country from exile in 2006, began lobbying to have their property and possessions returned to them.

All persons are entitled to equal protection under the law and are equal before the courts and tribunals. In practice, however, those who curry special favor with the regime or who are linked in some way to the country's informal power brokers clearly fare much better within the system.

Recommendations

- The government should ensure that every citizen has the right to independent counsel and can choose their own defense lawyer.
- The state should open the judiciary to external scrutiny and set up training courses for lawyers, with external assistance.
- The state should take steps to free the housing loan scheme from excessive corruption and bureaucracy.
- The government should work to limit corrupt practices in the judiciary.

ANTICORRUPTION AND TRANSPARENCY

ENVIRONMENT TO PROTECT AGAINST CORRUPTION:	0.80
EXISTENCE OF LAWS AND ETHICAL STANDARDS BETWEEN	
PRIVATE AND PUBLIC SECTORS:	0.75
ENFORCEMENT OF ANTICORRUPTION LAWS:	0.50
GOVERNMENTAL TRANSPARENCY:	0.57
CATEGORY AVERAGE:	**0.66**

Libya is steeped in bureaucracy and regulatory controls. These offer ample opportunity for bribery and corruption, and both are rife. As part of its new openness the regime has made tentative steps toward liberalizing Libya's economy and has allowed a greater degree of private sector activity, although this remains on a small scale. Moreover, most of the more lucrative opportunities have been snatched up by members of Qadhafi's own family or by the families of high-ranking officials within the inner circle. There is little separation between private interests and public office. Many of those on the boards of important Libyan companies that profess to be private also hold important government posts. There is also no protection against conflicts of interest in the private sector.

Libya legislates against corruption, and sentences for such offenses are severe. The Supreme Audit Institution reportedly promotes financial transparency, and the Board of the General Peoples Control is tasked with curbing corruption. In addition, the regime has established endless monitoring, auditing, and supervisory committees that are supposed to guard against corruption, but in fact these bodies themselves tend simply to increase opportunities for corrupt practices. In September 2006, Qadhafi announced that all public officials would be given until the end of December to declare their assets and sources of income. Special Transparency Committees were set up to oversee the process, and it was announced that any official failing to complete and return the form declaring their wealth by the December deadline would be liable to prosecution under criminal law. This appears to have been the first serious large-scale attempt in many years by the regime to curb corruption by state officials; it was reported that a number of public officials fled the country for extended periods to avoid detection. In December, however, the deadline was extended until March 2007, and it is rumored that it will be extended again to the end of 2007. Moreover, while the scheme appears to be a bold move by the regime, whether it will make any serious inroads into the core problems with transparency and conflicts of interest is doubtful. Given that large patronage networks underpin the Jamahiriyah, it seems unlikely the regime would clamp down entirely on such practices.

Despite this legislation and a robust anticorruption discourse, corruption remains a significant problem. Libya was ranked 105 out of 163 in Transparency International's 2006 Corruption Perceptions Index.[15] The punishment of officials accused of corruption continues to be arbitrary. In November 2006, for example, an appeals court in Benghazi ruled that the Secretary of the People's Committee for the Zwaitina area and two of his colleagues should be imprisoned, fined, and prevented from holding public office as they had allegedly been involved in a corruption scam forging expense claims and siphoning money from the public purse. However, others have not been brought to trial for such practices.

No effective mechanisms exist to assist victims of corruption. Although the regime is allowing its citizens a little more breathing space insofar as it is now easier to complain openly about such issues, bringing anyone to justice for corrupt practices remains extremely difficult unless one has the necessary connections within the regime. Corruption is receiving greater attention in the Libyan media, especially in the *Libya al-Yom* online publication. However, there are no specific mechanisms to protect whistle-blowers or investigators who report corruption, as the murder of journalist Daif al-Ghazal demonstrated.

The higher education system is not immune from bribery either. Like most of Libya's institutions, the Revolutionary Committee Movement has a significant influence within this sector. Individual academics who have tried to resist such corruption have found themselves subject to harassment and in some cases threats of physical violence.

The Libyan tax system is also subject to corruption and inefficiency; the amount of tax people pay appears to be relatively arbitrary. No effective internal audit mechanisms ensure the accountability of tax collection. In 2005 the International Monetary Fund recommended that the Libyan authorities simplify their tax system, develop tax payment arrangements for corporations, restructure the tax and customs departments, and upgrade controls as well as human resources and buildings and equipment.[16]

The main auditing body is the Board of Inspection and Popular Control, which was established in the late 1980s with the aim of exercising financial, administrative, and technical control over all authorities. However, this is an organ of the state and as such is neither free from political pressure nor independent. The Revolutionary Committees still act as a monitoring and supervisory body, although their task is to "safeguard the revolution," and as such they do not perform as a genuinely independent investigative or authoritative body that is autonomous from the state.

Access to government information is limited, and legal, regulatory, and judicial processes are not transparent. The regime makes little of its information public, partly because of excessive bureaucracy. However, some improvements have occurred in providing basic statistical information in recent years, with the National Organization of Information and Documentation of the Planning Secretariat having set up a website that publishes data.[17] Under the leadership of former general secretary Shukri Ghanem, the General People's Committee set up its own website in July 2005, which enabled individuals to contact the premier directly by email.[18] Other Libyan institutions have also set up their own websites. Libyan legislation is becoming increasingly accessible as laws are posted on government websites and in some state media outlets.

Citizens do not have the legal right to obtain information about government operations or to petition for it. Anyone without the necessary connections would not be able to question or demand information about any part of the Libyan system, as this could have severe consequences. No special attempts are made to offer information accessible to disabled people.

Despite the fact that the budget is passed by the General People's Congress, in reality its content is decided by Qadhafi and his advisers; it is then filtered down to the population as and when the regime sees fit. For example, in a January 2006 speech to a special budgetary session of the General People's Congress, Qadhafi declared that the defense budget should be cut because, as he explained, the country did not need planes, tanks, or missiles because the Libyan population were ready to defend themselves with Kalashnikovs and explosive belts. At the same time, Qadhafi declared that from that time onward each year's budget must be allocated to a specific sector in order to bring each sector up to scratch, beginning with the housing sector. The budget is not subject to any review or meaningful scrutiny. Detailed expenditure accounting is not available, although some details are provided through the National Information and Documentation Office.

Government contracts are not generally awarded in an open, transparent way that ensures effective competition. However, the National Oil Corporation (NOC) won praise from investors and international media in 2005 when it conducted its EPSA IV bidding round, in which foreign energy companies bid for oil exploration rights in a genuinely open and transparent manner.

All foreign assistance is prohibited unless it goes through government channels. No information is made available about its administration and distribution.

Recommendations

- The government needs to ensure that the anticorruption drive introduced in September 2006 is followed up on and, where possible, extended to higher-ranking state officials.
- The government should run an information campaign to warn against corrupt practices and encourage and protect those who have been the victims of corruption to come forward with their grievances.
- The administration should build on the positive developments already undertaken in terms of providing information through the internet and make more documents and information available in this format.
- The government should take steps to reform the tax sector in line with the International Monetary Fund (IMF) recommendations.

NOTES

1 "Lika'at: al-Doctor Shukri Ghanem [Interviews: Dr. Shukri Ghanem]," *Libya Today*, 20 September 2005 (in Arabic).

2 "Daif Al-Ghazal, Biography of a Libyan Journalist who stood up to corruption" (London: Arab Press Freedom Watch, 10 June 2006), http://www.apfw.org/indexenglish .asp?fname=news%5Cenglish%5C2006%5C06%5C13085.htm.

3 "Libya Prison Brief," International Centre for Prison Studies, Kings College London, http://www.kcl.ac.uk/depsta/rel/icps/worldbrief/africa_records.php?code=28.

4 "Libya Country Report," (Washington, D.C.: Protection Project, 2002), http://www .unhchr.ch/tbs/doc.nsf/(Symbol)/CCPR.C.102.Add.1.En?Opendocument

5 "*Landmine Monitor* Report 2006: Libya" (Ottawa: International Campaign to Ban Landmines, 2006), http://www.icbl.org/lm/2006/libya.html.

6 Great Green Charter of Human Rights of the Jamahiriyan Era (12 June 1988), http://www.geocities.com/Athens/8744/grgreen.htm.

7 "Libya: Annual Survey of Violations of Trade Union Rights" (Brussels: International Confederation of Free Trade Unions, 2006), http://www.icftu.org/displaydocument .asp?Index=991223877&Language=EN.

8 Ibid.

9 Ibid.

10 "Libya: Time to Make Human Rights a Reality" (London: Amnesty International [AI], MDE 19/002/2004, April 2004).

11 "Libya Judiciary" (Beirut: UNDP Programme on Governance in the Arab Region [POGAR], http://www.pogar.org/countries/judiciary.asp?cid=10.

12 "Libyans For Justice," www.libyans4justice.com (in Arabic).

13 "Libya: Emerging from isolation" (Law Society of England and Wales, 12 May 2005) http://www.lawsociety.org.uk/newsandevents/newsletters/international/archive/view= article.law?NEWSLETTERID=238508.

14 "Libya: Time to Make Human Rights a Reality" (AI).

15 "Corruption Perceptions Index 2006" (Berlin: Transparency International [TI]), http://www.transparency.org/policy_research/surveys_indices/cpi/2006.

16 "The Socialist People's Libyan Arab Jamahiriya: 2005 Article IV Consultation—Staff Report; and Public Information Notice on the Executive Board Discussion" (Washington, D.C.: International Monetary Fund, IMF Country Report No. 06/136, April 2006).

17 www.nidaly.org.

18 www.gpc.gov.ly (in Arabic).

MAURITANIA

CAPITAL: Nouakchott
POPULATION: 3.1 million
GNI PER CAPITA: $740

SCORES	2005	2007
ACCOUNTABILITY AND PUBLIC VOICE:	2.00	3.56
CIVIL LIBERTIES:	2.39	2.94
RULE OF LAW:	2.12	2.51
ANTICORRUPTION AND TRANSPARENCY:	1.97	2.67

(scores are based on a scale of 0 to 7, with 0 representing weakest
and 7 representing strongest performance)

Cédric Jourde

INTRODUCTION

Ever since the bloodless coup d'etat that ousted Colonel Maaouya Ould
Sid Ahmed Taya and brought to power the Military Council for Justice
and Democracy (CMJD) in August 2005, Mauritania has epitomized
the metaphor of a "country at the crossroads." The government is
presently seeking to carry out an effective transition toward democracy
and away from the previous regime, in which de jure democratic reforms
could barely hide the de facto authoritarian functioning of the state. The
postcoup transition period has generated significant changes in the formal rules of the political game; elections, the independence of the judiciary, and freedom of the press have been greatly improved. However, it
is still unclear whether the new democratic infrastructure will be

Cédric Jourde is an Assistant Professor at the School of Political Studies, University of
Ottawa. His research focuses on the politics of ethnicity, the processes of democratization and authoritarian restoration, and political Islam in Mauritania. He has published
articles in journals such as *International Studies Quarterly, Comparative Politics,* and the
Journal of Contemporary African Studies. He has also written chapters in volumes edited
by William F. S. Miles, Zekeria Ould Ahmed Salem, Charles-Philippe David, and David
Grondin.

415

reflected in practice and help Mauritania move away from its authoritarian past.

Since achieving independence in 1960, Mauritania has been governed by authoritarian regimes (either civilian or military), including that of Colonel Taya. Although he first came to power in a 1984 military coup, the system Taya oversaw after 1991 included the formal elements of democracy, such as a constitution that provided for political pluralism and recognized universal human rights; an uninterrupted cycle of multiparty elections at the municipal, legislative, and presidential levels; and a flourishing independent press. However, an authoritarian reality stood behind the democratic façade, and ruling elites skillfully manipulated liberalizing reforms. For instance, although elections were organized on a regular basis, the regime never put itself at risk. Taya won all three presidential elections he contested in a process that was generally seen as unfair. In the National Assembly, the presidential party and its smaller allies controlled 100 percent of the seats in 1992, 99 percent in 1996, and 87 percent in 2001. Meanwhile, the government cracked down on alleged Islamist leaders, harassed and jailed opposition leaders, and disbanded opposition parties. In fact, those who successfully ousted Taya were military officers who he thought were his most loyal collaborators.

Three interrelated issues are critical for the fate of the latest democratic transition. The first is the issue of whether the military will accept subordination to civilian control. With the victory of Sidi Ould Cheikh Abdellahi in a March 2007 presidential election, the last stage of the transition was completed, but considering that military officers have been in power without interruption since 1978, the effective retreat of the military from political and economic affairs remains uncertain. The second issue is whether the neopatrimonial and clientelistic management of public offices and resources is going to be gradually replaced by more transparent and equitable processes. Though a certain degree of neopatrimonialism may coexist with a more democratic form of government, the problem in Mauritania is so extensive that significant reforms will be needed. The third issue concerns whether the new government will finally come to terms with the 1989–1991 state-sponsored massacres and expulsions of non-Arabic-speaking communities (the Haalpulaar, Wolof, and Sooninke) and the marginalization of Haratin (also called black Moors, the former slaves of lighter-skinned, Arabic-speaking Moors known as Bidhan). If these minority groups are not fully included in the political and social spheres, Mauritania's democratization will remain glaringly incomplete. The reforms under way in the country are quite promising on paper, but their actual implementation will be a major test for the new government.

ACCOUNTABILITY AND PUBLIC VOICE

FREE AND FAIR ELECTORAL LAWS AND ELECTIONS:	3.50
EFFECTIVE AND ACCOUNTABLE GOVERNMENT:	2.75
CIVIC ENGAGEMENT AND CIVIC MONITORING:	4.00
MEDIA INDEPENDENCE AND FREEDOM OF EXPRESSION:	4.00
CATEGORY AVERAGE:	**3.56**

The leader of the transitional CMJD that ousted Taya in August 2005 was Colonel Ely Ould Mohamed Vall, who had served as chief of national police since 1984. He admitted that the democratic institutions adopted under the former regime had been subverted into a de facto single-party system, dominated by Taya's Democratic and Social Republican Party (PRDS).[1]

During the postcoup transition period, a constitutional referendum (June 24, 2006) and four different elections were held, including a two-round municipal election, a two-round legislative election (both municipal and legislative elections were held on November 19 and December 3, 2006), a two-round senatorial election (January 21 and February 4, 2007), and a two-round presidential election (March 11 and 25, 2007). Changes in electoral rules and practices made the transitional elections more fair and transparent than those held under Taya, all of which were dominated by the PRDS and smaller pro-Taya parties. A first important change was the creation of an Independent National Electoral Commission (INEC) in November 2005.[2] Previously, only the Interior Ministry was allowed to organize and monitor elections, which created problems in terms of partiality. Under the new system, the Interior Ministry organizes the elections, but INEC monitors and supervises the process and appoints electoral officials.[3] However, the establishment of

INEC was not without flaws. The CMJD unilaterally appointed the INEC chairman, a retired colonel, without consulting opposition parties.[4] In addition, INEC was inadequately funded and staffed, which limited the extent of its territorial coverage and monitoring capacity.[5]

A second important move was the taking of a census (RAVEL).[6] It was carried out in the spring of 2006 to establish a new, more reliable electoral list and make the electoral process more transparent. After an initial census was conducted in February 2006, prior to the June referendum,[7] a second round was held to include the many voters who were left off the list in the first round as well as young citizens who had just reached voting age.[8] The fact that RAVEL was conducted under the sole jurisdiction of the Interior Ministry, with no INEC monitoring, was highly problematic.[9] Moreover, leaders of the opposition and independent newspapers claimed that in the Senegal River Valley, many individuals from non-Arabic-speaking minorities were not included in the census on the grounds that they did not have appropriate identification cards.[10] Considering that members of minority communities often had their ID cards taken away or were expelled to neighboring Senegal and Mali during the 1989–1991 period of state-sponsored violence against them, the issue of ID cards should have been seriously dealt with by the transitional authorities. These allegations, if proven, reveal a significant weakness in the reliability of the electoral census and therefore in the protection of minorities' political rights.

Another improvement to the electoral framework was a decree that compels military personnel to vote only in those districts where they are registered.[11] Under the Taya regime, military personnel could vote in any electoral district, and trucks loaded with soldiers were sent to districts where the opposition presented a serious challenge so as to guarantee a victory for the PRDS.

In a change that was perhaps more problematic, the CMJD authorized electoral bids by independent candidates; in past elections, only those associated with a political party could seek office.[12] The presence of independent candidates opened the door for a personalization of the vote and facilitated deceptive electoral financing. Newspapers reported that the head of state met with tribal leaders and rural notables and allegedly told them that they should encourage their populations to vote for the independents.[13] Opposition parties denounced the decision, but to no avail.

In 2006–2007, independent candidates won a majority in the National Assembly, the local councils, and the Senate, having benefited from the financial and political support of people connected to the Taya regime or the junta in power (often the same individuals). Most independent candidates were former members of the PRDS who resigned from the party after the coup, or members of powerful families who were connected to Taya's government. For instance, the leader of the independent deputies, Lemrabott Cheikh Ahmed Ould Sidi Mahmoud, was the interior minister in Taya's last government, and also served as his foreign minister and minister of rural development; he terminated his membership in the PRDS after the coup.

In June 2006, less than a year after the coup, some 97 percent of voters approved a set of constitutional amendments in a national referendum. International observers were generally satisfied with the voting process.[14] INEC reported some problems, however, including the exclusion of local nongovernmental organizations (NGOs) from the electoral monitoring team, the partiality of the personnel of the administration in several districts, the omission of duly registered voters from the electoral list, and the exclusion of some INEC representatives from polling stations by local state officials.[15]

The municipal and legislative elections, held simultaneously in late 2006, nevertheless confirmed the improving conditions of the electoral process. International observers, including a European Union (EU) team, viewed the two rounds positively, even noting some improvements between the first and second round, including more neutrality on the part of the administration. The elections were also more open in that the transitional government allowed military officers who had been jailed under the Taya regime for their participation in a failed June 2003 coup to have their own party. Similarly, the government allowed Islamist activists who were frequently arrested and oppressed under Taya to run in the elections. However, they could do so only on an individual basis, as the transitional government maintained Taya's policy of denying Islamists the right to form a party. EU observers raised some concerns about the partiality of staff members at various polling stations. They also criticized the absence of a mechanism to restrict and control electoral spending. The team noted the weak coverage of national monitoring teams and the limited access of political parties to the state-owned television and radio network. Finally, pointing out that more than 15 percent of the ballots were declared invalid in the first round and 6 percent were rejected in the second round, EU observers said more flexible rules were needed in order to forestall a perception that political factors had motivated the ballots' rejection.[16]

In all four elections, independent candidates and their allies from the PRDS asserted their dominance over the Taya-era opposition parties. In the National Assembly, the coalition of the independent representatives, who are tied to the CMJD and the former regime (thirty-eight seats), and the political parties associated with the Taya regime (sixteen seats) won a total of fifty-four out of ninety-five seats, while the coalition of Taya-era opposition parties won forty-one seats. At the municipal level, the results were similar, as the coalition of independent candidates and former pro-Taya parties won a majority of city and town councils.

Elections to the Senate in early 2007 were the least democratic of all the voting that occurred during the transition. Though any adult citizen can be a Senate candidate, the pool of voters is restricted to mayors and municipal council members. The limited electorate provided an incentive for widespread vote buying and intimidation. INEC reported that "material and moral pressures are being exerted upon local councilors to influence their voting."[17] Part of this pressure came directly from the CMJD. In fact, the new Senate includes the wives of two officers on the military council, as well as three brothers of CMJD members.[18] The independent candidates and those from Taya's party control two-thirds of the Senate (thirty-seven out of fifty-six seats), while the opposition won only sixteen seats (the three seats reserved for "Mauritanians living abroad" were still not allocated at the time of writing).

Finally, the two-round presidential election of March 2007 ended the transition period. In the first round, independent candidate Sidi Ould Cheikh Abdellahi finished first with 24.8 percent of the vote, while Ahmed Ould Daddah, leader of the largest opposition party, got 20.7 percent. Behind them were Zeine Ould Zeidane (15.3 percent), Messoud Ould Boulkheir (9.8 percent), and three other candidates with weaker support. The first two candidates moved to the second round, which Abdellahi won with 52.9 percent of the vote.

In an unusual move for an African election, in the second round the two presidential contenders participated in a debate aired on public television and radio. Furthermore, the election was observed by both local and international monitoring groups. The EU mission reported that the voting took place in a "calm and transparent" context, with the administration remaining generally neutral and all candidates receiving fair and equitable access to public media. However, the EU team reported some problems, including the absence of limits and a monitoring mechanism for campaign financing.[19] Once the Interior Ministry confirmed Abdellahi's victory, his second-round opponent publicly acknowledged the outcome, providing further legitimacy to the vote.

Though the constitutional amendments adopted in the 2006 referendum slightly restricted the power of the president by imposing a two-term limit and prohibiting him from leading a political party, the 1991 constitution sanctions "the preeminence of the Head of State."[20] The legislative and judicial branches are in a condition of political subordination. The president appoints and dismisses the cabinet, and can dissolve the National Assembly, which cannot remove him from office except in cases of high treason. He appoints three of the six judges of the Constitutional Council (including its president), which is tasked, among other things, with validating electoral results. Under the previous regime, the executive's power was strengthened through informal political channels that linked the presidency to local rural leaders, powerful businesspeople, and public servants. The politicization of public institutions was a method of rewarding loyalty to the regime and punishing opposition. Whether this will change under the new elected leadership is difficult to predict. The central government often overawes local elected officials, and representatives of the Interior Ministry and the Defense Ministry currently enjoy unchecked powers in rural areas.

Heavy restrictions were placed on civil society organizations under the previous regime. Organizations with a social or political agenda, such as those aimed at defending Haratin or critiquing the government's human rights record, were denied official recognition. However, in the weeks prior to the 2005 coup, the Taya regime began to change its approach, deciding to hold official talks with the groups and eventually granting them official recognition.[21] The same policy was pursued after the coup, when the CMJD confirmed the organizations' status. It is too early to say whether the new government will maintain the same liberal stance if it confronts civic organizations that strongly criticize its policies. There are no major financial obstacles to the formation of civic organizations, and donors do not face major governmental impediments. Though these groups have had no serious effects on government actions in the past, this may change if the political liberalization process moves forward.

The transitional government sent a positive signal with respect to freedom of the press when, in December of 2005, it created a commission to advise the government on reforms of the media sector. The commission submitted its report in March 2006, and the resulting Ordinance on the Freedom of the Press was adopted in June.[22] The ordinance removed legal mechanisms used under the Taya regime to censor the press, including the infamous Article 11 of the Law on the Press, which forced newspapers to submit a copy of each issue to the interior ministry for approval prior to publication.[23] However, new restrictions have appeared in the form of ambiguously worded regulations that open the door to censorship. Financial and penal sanctions can be imposed if journalists "offend the President of the Republic" (Article 35), if they "attack the honor" of governmental institutions or officeholders (Articles 37–39), or if they threaten "the state's interior or external security" (Article 33). In other ambiguous language, foreign media can be unilaterally censored by the interior ministry if they "undermine Islam or the reputation of the state, if they go against the public interest, or if they threaten public order and security."[24]

The new Law of the Press was combined with the creation of a High Authority for the Press and Broadcast Media (HAPA) in October 2006.[25] HAPA's main task consists of monitoring public communications and enforcing political parties' and candidates' equal access to the media during electoral periods, which it did successfully during the presidential election. HAPA will also monitor the liberalization of television and radio stations, which are presently state monopolies. Under the previous regime, the state-owned media were highly propagandistic, but this changed during the transition period. Whether the new government will pursue the reform of its broadcast outlets remains to be seen. The print media, the internet, and foreign satellite television stations operate with relative freedom, but radio broadcasting, with its low cost and accessibility to illiterate people, constitutes the most popular medium.

There were no cases of internet censorship. Access to the internet is on the rise in the capital, and a few attempts have been made to connect large rural towns to the medium. During the transition period, no journalists were arrested or arbitrarily detained. One journalist was physically attacked, allegedly by a former high-ranking official of the Taya regime.[26]

The cultural expression of non-Arabic-speaking communities is increasingly tolerated. For instance, the government authorized the celebration of the twentieth anniversary of a Haalpulaar cultural association in June 2006. The association, like many others, had been the target of state repression in the 1980s and 1990s.[27] Nevertheless, Arabic continues to dominate the state-owned television and radio stations.

Recommendations

- To avoid the radicalization of Islamists, the new government should allow the creation of any political party, including an Islamist party.
- A well-financed and independent institution within the civil service should be created to address the problems of nonmeritocratic and patronage-based appointments.
- In addition to the abolition of Article 11 of the Law on the Press, the provisions concerning criticism of the president and representatives of the state should be removed to prevent government censorship.
- Electoral rules should provide mechanisms for the monitoring of campaign spending, including clear funding limits and disclosure requirements for funding sources.
- Elected local councils should be granted more power vis-à-vis the central government. State representatives should be accountable to local officials on at least some issues, such as land distribution.

CIVIL LIBERTIES

PROTECTION FROM STATE TERROR, UNJUSTIFIED IMPRISONMENT, AND TORTURE:	2.86
GENDER EQUITY:	2.75
RIGHTS OF ETHNIC, RELIGIOUS, AND OTHER DISTINCT GROUPS:	2.25
FREEDOM OF CONSCIENCE AND BELIEF:	2.67
FREEDOM OF ASSOCIATION AND ASSEMBLY:	4.20
CATEGORY AVERAGE:	**2.94**

Article 13 of the Mauritanian constitution protects citizens from torture and inhumane treatment in prisons. A mediator of the republic (similar to an ombudsman) was established in 1993, both to investigate the abuse of citizens by state representatives and to make recommendations for settling such disputes.

With respect to protection from state terrorism, torture, and unjustified imprisonment, recent history can be clearly divided into two distinct sections: before and after the 2005 coup. During the period leading up to the coup, oppressive practices continued on a regular basis. Political opponents were routinely arrested, whether they were leaders of opposition parties, Islamists, or military personnel allegedly involved in coup plots. For instance, in November 2004 three top leaders of the opposition were arrested, and an opposition member of the National Assembly was detained in May 2005.[28] Moreover, following the coup attempt of June 2003 and the alleged coup attempts of August and September 2004, about 200 soldiers and civilians were arrested. Allegations of torture were made by the prisoners, their lawyers, and their family members. It is very difficult to independently confirm or refute such allegations, given the obstacles to prisoner visits by journalists and representatives of human rights organizations.[29] More than eighty of the detainees were issued guilty verdicts in February 2005, and four received life prison sentences, but all were released after the 2005 coup.[30]

Islamists were frequently arrested under the Taya regime, and no proof of wrongdoing was presented to the public.[31] More than thirty Islamists were released a few weeks after the 2005 coup, and around one hundred others were granted an amnesty.[32] About twenty-four prisoners remained in jail, however, while arrests of other alleged Islamist terrorists continued in June and September 2006 and January 2007, still without the public disclosure of any proof of wrongdoing, without trial, and for a duration that exceeded the legal limit of thirty days.[33]

The transitional government announced that it would address the problem of prison conditions, acknowledging that conditions under the previous government had violated basic human rights. In November 2005, the new justice minister promised major improvements through his proposed reform of the justice system. The plan included a pledge to increase the budget for detainees' medical services and food by 75 percent.[34] The government also built a new prison to deal with overcrowding at Nouakchott's central prison, as well as a new detention facility for women.[35] In a sign of the seriousness of the problem, detainees at the central prison rebelled against their guards on July 18,

2006, calling for improvements in their conditions. An important challenge remains in ensuring that detainees no longer fear being "suicided," or killed in a staged suicide, when they enter a police station.[36] The police claimed in one case that "the suspect committed suicide by hitting his head on his cell's wall."[37]

The CMJD adopted a reform of penal code procedures in December 2006.[38] Prisoners now have the ability to contact their families during the first hours of preventive detention (*garde a vue*) and the right to contact a lawyer. Also, the duration of garde a vue in cases of threats against the security of the state was curtailed from thirty days to five days. An extension can be authorized by the justice ministry, but not beyond fifteen days. Another important reform is the creation of a Court d'Accusation, which deals with such issues as provisional release demands and accusations against judicial police officers. The critical step will be to ensure that these new legal reforms are implemented in practice.[39]

The treatment of women in Mauritania varies according to ethnicity, status group (or "caste"), urban-rural setting, and class. In this Muslim country, the Islamic legal tradition applies to personal and family matters and entails certain forms of gender discrimination. These inequalities are maintained in the personal status code adopted in 2001.[40] Although the code includes certain improvements in gender relations, such as the obligation to obtain a woman's consent for marriage, these provisions are rarely respected in practice. The code remains ambiguous also, for instance, with respect to underage marriage. Article 6 states that a "legal guardian [who must be a man, as stated in Article 10] can authorize the marriage of a girl under 18 if there is an interest in it [*sic*]." This vague phrase is repeated in Article 9, which states that the marriage must be "in the interest of the woman."[41]

In the formal political arena, a significant effort was made during the municipal and legislative elections to increase the number of female officeholders. For instance, 20 percent of the seats in municipal councils are reserved for women, and at least 20 percent of the candidates on party lists must be women. At the national level, quotas are also imposed for party lists, the size of which depends on the number of seats for each electoral district.[42] Legislative electoral results did not reach expectations, as women comprise only 18 percent of the legislature, but that was an improvement compared with previous elections. The EU monitoring team reported that the participation of women, both in the organization of the elections and within political parties, "remains weak."[43] Furthermore, there are no women among the country's regional governors and local prefects. The conditions for Haratin women remain difficult. Though the government denies the existence of slavery, many are still forced into servitude, a practice that could be dealt with more effectively if serious criminal penalties were enacted and applied (see below on the issue of Haratin).

Under pressure from international organizations such as the UN Development Programme and local NGOs, the government has attempted to address important gender issues, especially violence against women. Training sessions were organized to raise police officers' understanding and sensitivity toward domestic violence in November 2004.[44] Also, a pilot project was created in Nouakchott to care for girls and women who have been victims of domestic violence.[45] In opposing female genital mutilation (FGM), which affects about 70 percent of Mauritanian women, the government obtained the support of religious leaders, who issued a *fatwa* against the practice in 2006.[46] The transitional government has also adopted a Law for the Penal Protection of Children, some provisions of which deal with FGM.[47] Article 12 of the law remains ambiguous, however. It states that penal sanctions will apply when "an offense [*une atteinte*] is committed against girls' genitals . . . if this act has resulted in a prejudice for her." The last phrase opens the door to contradictory interpretations.[48] More generally, despite these efforts, the transitional government's minister of women's affairs stated that violence against women is still on the rise in Mauritania.[49] The main problem remains the gap between official policy and its effective implementation.

One defining aspect of Mauritania's political system continues to be the political, economic, and social status of minority ethnic groups (with "minority" referring more to their political weight than to their number): the non-Arabic-speaking groups (the Haalpulaar, Sooninke, and Wolof) and the Haratin. The transitional government refused to address the 1989–1991 state-sponsored killings and expulsions of Haalpulaar, Sooninke, and Wolof residents. It took no measure to compensate the victims and their families, to allow the collective return of Mauritanian refugees living in Senegal and Mali (as well as the restitution of their stolen property and the reintegration of former civil servants), or even to acknowledge the role played by the government during the violence.

At the time of this writing, the 1993 Law of Amnesty, which protects military personnel involved in the massacres of 1989–1991, was still in effect. It is not clear whether the National Commission for Human Rights, a consultative body created in early 2007, is able to look into the matter; Article 5 of its bylaws states that it cannot deal with events that occurred prior to its creation.[50]

With respect to Haratin, the transition did not bring about significant changes. As in the precoup period, the official policy was to admit the existence only of the "consequences" of ancient slavery practices, not ongoing slavery itself. The transitional government's justice minister nonetheless organized a conference in March 2006 to discuss the issue and even invited NGOs that were prohibited by the Taya regime. A central problem remains, however: though slavery and the trafficking of individuals are legally forbidden, the practice of slavery is not prosecuted as a criminal offense. As an official from the justice ministry admitted, the current law (the 1983 Penal Code) "does not identify the practice of slavery as a crime against Humanity."[51] Neither the 2003 Law on the Traffic of Persons nor the 2003 Labor Code mentions the words "slavery" or "slave."[52] In rural areas, regardless of what legal texts state, when disputes erupt between freeborn clans and their former slaves, local officials often take the side of former masters at the expense of the Haratin.[53]

The rights of people with disabilities do not seem to have been affected substantially by the recent political changes. In December 2005, during the International Day of Disabled People, the transitional government promised to work on the integration of disabled people into Mauritania's social and economic life. A draft law was adopted in 2006 that aims to promote disabled people's access to basic social services, including health care, education, and infrastructural accommodations.[54]

The government does not prevent the few non-Muslims—limited to Western expatriates and West and Central African immigrants—from practicing their faiths. The state's interference with religious practices applies only to Islam. Under the Taya regime, the state appointed loyal clerics to official Islamic positions, such as the High Council for Muslim Affairs. Apparently hoping to capitalize on U.S.-led antiterrorism efforts worldwide,[55] the Taya government frequently arrested outspoken Muslim figures and raided mosques in Nouakchott.[56] At the time of this writing, the Law on Mosques, adopted in 2003 to transform mosques into government-monitored religious facilities, was still in place. The transitional government did not take the same repressive approach toward prominent Islamists.

Officially, the state recognizes the right of citizens to assemble, to form independent trade unions, and to demonstrate peacefully. It does not compel people to join specific organizations. In reality, some nuances must be noted. With respect to freedom of association, the Taya regime would prohibit an organization if the issue around which it mobilized was considered politically sensitive, such as antislavery or political Islam. The current government maintains the policy of not allowing moderate Islamists to form a political party. The transitional government did not prohibit or shut down other civic or political organizations. Both before and after the coup, however, the government has generally been quick to break up demonstrations. For instance, in November and December 2006, the police took action against longshoremen at the Nouakchott port and cracked down violently on students who were protesting the difficult conditions at Nouakchott University.[57]

Mauritanian unions are relatively small, covering mostly workers in the small industrial sector and civil servants. Under the Taya regime, they were under the tight control of the government and subject to repression when they became too critical. Since the transition, however, unions have become much less submissive and have not been targeted by the authorities.

Recommendations

- The new elected authorities should both officially acknowledge the state's role in the 1989–1991 massacres and expulsions of Haalpulaar, Sooninke, and Wolof citizens and call for an investigation to identify those responsible. The 1993 Law of Amnesty that protects individuals who have committed human rights violations should be abolished.
- The government should put in place an official mechanism to allow and facilitate investigations of detention conditions and allegations of torture and illegal arrest by state forces.
- The authorities must unambiguously declare slavery a criminal offense. In order to end controversies about the existence of slavery in the country, the judicial system must proceed in a transparent and prompt way when citizens report cases of slavery, trafficking of persons, and forced labor.

- The government must implement a nationwide network of shelters for victims of domestic violence (replicating the pilot project instituted in a Nouakchott neighborhood) and ensure the effective implementation of laws criminalizing violence against women.

RULE OF LAW

INDEPENDENT JUDICIARY:	3.20
PRIMACY OF RULE OF LAW IN CIVIL AND CRIMINAL MATTERS:	2.33
ACCOUNTABILITY OF SECURITY FORCES AND MILITARY TO CIVILIAN AUTHORITIES:	2.00
PROTECTION OF PROPERTY RIGHTS:	2.00
EQUAL TREATMENT UNDER THE LAW:	3.00
CATEGORY AVERAGE:	**2.51**

The Mauritanian judicial system combines French and Islamic (Malikite rite) legal traditions. Article 89 of the constitution guarantees the independence of the judiciary in theory, and an organic law also protects judges from undue influence. However, even after the postcoup reforms of the judiciary, the system entails the formal domination of the executive over the judiciary.

The president heads the Conseil Supreme de la Magistrature (Superior Council of Magistrates), whose tasks include the nomination of judges. The constitution allows the president to appoint three of the six members of the Constitutional Council, including its chairman, whose voice predominates in case of a split vote. The president also appoints all five members of the High Islamic Council, which advises him on matters of Islamic law.

Formal subordination of the judiciary was reinforced by informal practices during the Taya regime. Specific examples were acknowledged in a report published by the transitional government's commission on justice.[58] The commission's "Final Report on Justice" identified problems such as the "political instrumentalization of the judiciary" and a "crisis of confidence" in which "no verdict, even when correct, avoids suspicion of partiality."[59] Very few judicial decisions ever went against the

Taya government. Coming from an official panel, the uncompromising tone of the report is unprecedented in Mauritania. The state-owned newspaper, which in the past never criticized the government, asserted that the justice system under the previous regime "greatly suffered from its lack of independence" and was "plagued by clientelism and mal-administration."[60] Even though the constitution considers citizens innocent until proven guilty, the fate of those charged with crimes under Taya depended mostly on their personal connections with powerful people, or lack thereof. Civilian public officials and members of the ruling PRDS were never prosecuted.

To deal with these problems, the transitional government adopted important reforms of the justice system. It created a special interministerial commission in the fall of 2005 whose task was to propose major changes. Three main goals were cited: greater judicial independence, improved quality and quantity of human resources and capacities, and improved material infrastructure. On the last two points, the justice minister identified specific problems, explaining that about twenty courts across the country could not function normally because they simply had no judges; he also said that 60 percent of the buildings owned by the justice ministry were currently rented to private individuals.[61]

Reforms implemented since the publication of that report include changes to the Code du Statut de la Magistrature (magistrature status code), passed in June 2006. The new code aims to address the lack of human resources by allowing the magistrature to seek new members among law school professors, private sector legal experts, and clerks of the court, all of whom were previously excluded by recruitment rules. The new code also provides for greater judicial independence by suspending the president's ability to head the Superior Council of Magistrates when disciplinary actions are taken against magistrates who have committed professional faults.[62] Also, in December 2006 the government adopted a bill that reformed penal code procedures and included a stricter, more transparent framework for preventive detention (see above).

In December 2005, the government adopted a draft bill designed to improve poor people's access to legal services.[63] The government also created a National Council for Legal Assistance, and set up offices in each of the country's regions to facilitate and coordinate the delivery of legal aid.[64]

Now that the formal rules of the justice system are improving, the main task is to ensure that they are effectively implemented, as suggested by the chair of the Mauritanian bar, who publicly demanded at the outset of the transition that more independence be granted to the justice system.[65]

The political power of the military began to rise when Mauritania fought a war in Western Sahara in 1975. Between 1978 and 2005, every change in leadership occurred through a military coup d'etat. Although the 1991 constitution provides for a civilian form of government, in reality the military has always been the key pillar of the state. To a large extent, the armed forces' loyalty is secured through the distribution of significant political and economic advantages to top officers, and it can be lost when such distribution fails.[66] Security matters, which are very broadly defined, are the exclusive domain of the military, as are the armed forces' internal affairs. The elected government's biggest challenge is to obtain both legal and practical civilian control over the military.

Article 15 of the constitution ensures the right to own property. The Law on Land Tenure, adopted in 1983, guarantees private ownership of land. However, it also states that the government can evict citizens, with compensation, to help meet larger "economic and social development needs." Communities that, in accordance with their customs, oppose the individual ownership and sale of land must create cooperatives and officially register as associations. In rural areas, de facto expropriation of land by powerful agents with connections to high-ranking civil servants is common. Such activity was in part responsible for the tensions between state officials and communities of the Senegal River region—the homeland of the Haalpulaar, Sooninke, and Wolof ethnic minorities—that eventually resulted in the state-sponsored killings and evictions of thousands of black African citizens between 1989 and 1991. Conflicts between Haratin and Bidhan masters also broke out in rural areas when the former claimed land ownership on the basis that they were the ones actually working the land. In urban centers, shantytowns have mushroomed, most often without any official property titles, and they have frequently been the targets of violent and sudden evictions by state officials.

A Code of Investments was promulgated in 2002 to facilitate and protect foreign direct investment. Also, to make the local legal environment more secure for business transactions, the transitional government specifically created in 2006 two "tribunals of commerce," in Nouakchott and Nouadhibou.

Recommendations

- The constitutional independence of the judiciary must be upheld in practice to provide for a universal and effective respect for the rule of law. Specific policies should include confirmation mechanisms that would allow the Senate or National Assembly to assess the president's judicial nominees and prevent excessive executive domination of the judiciary.
- The military must be effectively monitored and bound by transparent forms of civilian control, in keeping with the spirit of the 1991 constitution. The exclusive jurisdictions and policy domains of the military and security agencies, whether formal or informal, should be subjected to autonomous civilian oversight.
- The government must implement transparent procedures to prevent the arbitrary seizure of land in rural areas, including safeguards against unlawful decisions by local representatives of the state, such as governors, prefects, and gendarmes. Similarly, fair and open mechanisms for land titling in large urban areas must be established.
- The coverage of tribunals of commerce, which are currently located only in the two large cities of Nouakchott and Nouadhibou, must be extended to the entire country to prevent the development of a two-tiered system that leaves the rest of the country with no reliable legal foundations for business transactions.

ANTICORRUPTION AND TRANSPARENCY

ENVIRONMENT TO PROTECT AGAINST CORRUPTION:	2.80
EXISTENCE OF LAWS AND ETHICAL STANDARDS BETWEEN	
PRIVATE AND PUBLIC SECTORS:	3.00
ENFORCEMENT OF ANTICORRUPTION LAWS:	2.75
GOVERNMENTAL TRANSPARENCY:	2.14
CATEGORY AVERAGE:	**2.67**

In the period prior to the coup, state economic policy began to be more clearly defined through the adoption of an investment code, the simplification of the tax system, and the elimination of many bureaucratic regulations from the economy. However, political clientelism, or the weak separation of public office from the personal and political interests of state officials, remained widespread and nurtured corruption. Management of public resources, whether those generated within the country or those derived from international development aid, was strongly influenced by political and private imperatives.

Under the Taya regime, public access to government information was both limited and unreliable. Even public institutions, such as the different commissions of the National Assembly, the Senate, and the Cour des comptes (comptroller and auditor general), faced great difficulties in gaining access to government information and monitoring the policy-making process.[67]

Major private economic actors, both individuals and firms, enjoyed great economic freedom, so much so that they formed an oligopoly with close family, clan, and personal ties to the presidency.[68] Postcoup events suggest that this oligopoly has not changed, although its internal hierarchy has shifted, with those closer to the new junta's leaders gaining special access to state contracts and licenses, such as cellular telephone licenses and deals involving Mauritania's airlines. They control most sectors of the market economy, including transport, banking, telecommunications, food importation, and construction.

The Taya regime never cracked down on corruption at the highest levels of the state. The country's auditing body, the Cour des comptes, failed to fulfill its role; its lack of independence stemmed from its subordination to the president, who appointed its chairman.[69] In September 2005, the transitional government indicated its willingness to fight corruption by creating the Inspection Generale de l'Etat (State Inspectorate General, or IGE), led by an inspector general nominated by the prime minister. Its task is to "promote good governance, healthy management of public affairs, fight against corruption and against economic and financial crimes."[70] In the words of the inspector general, IGE can "control who it wants, when it wants."[71] A number of unwarranted spending decisions were disclosed by the IGE, suggesting that it is indeed able to tackle the problems of corruption and mismanagement effectively.[72] Still, it is not clear how this new institution differs from the existing Cour des comptes and the General Inspectorate of Finance, leaving open the possibility of a significant functional overlap.[73] It remains to be seen whether the new government will provide the IGE with the resources and political support it needs to carry out its mission. The CMJD sent a mixed signal concerning corruption when its leader declared that people who had committed economic crimes under the previous regime would not be prosecuted.[74]

The accountability of tax collection is hampered by weak human and material capacity. An International Monetary Fund (IMF) report pointed out, in diplomatic language, the possibility of "inadequate supervision by the revenue-collecting agencies," noting that they "are not obliged to provide annual reports to the legislature on their activities."[75] Some reforms have been adopted since the coup, including the implementation of a single identifying number for each taxpayer and the reform of different strategic sectors, such as fisheries and hydrocarbons.

A few months before the coup, important measures were promulgated to deal with transparency and corruption, such as Mauritania's participation in the IMF's General Data Dissemination System (2004), the standardization and computerization of the budgetary and spending process (2004),[76] the creation of internal auditing institutions in each ministry,[77] and the creation of an Anti-Corruption Police service.[78] Following pressure from the IMF, the Taya government acknowledged in May 2005 that the bulk of the data (1992–2005) it had provided to the fund was inaccurate. As stated by the IMF, "The revisions of most economic and financial data since 1992 confirmed that over many years fiscal and monetary policies had been substantially looser than previously reported to the Fund."[79] These false data, including major unacknowledged, extrabudgetary military spending,[80] led the IMF to suspend Mauritania from further negotiations and to demand the reimbursement of monies allocated through Poverty Reduction and Growth Facility (PRGF) accords. Factors behind this fraud included "the lack of program ownership and low accountability of government institutions, combined with their deficient domestic oversight."[81] In mid-2006, the new government provided revised data to the IMF, which then decided to resume its relations with Mauritania. However, this scandal raises doubts about the reliability of data in other sectors that are of less concern to the IMF, including social indicators.

The transitional government announced that Mauritania had joined the Extractive Industries Transparency Initiative (EITI) to ensure the transparent management of revenues generated by the oil sector. A special account was set up in April 2006 specifically to receive oil money, to be overseen by the newly created National Committee for the Monitoring of Hydrocarbon Revenues.[82] While the decision presents a positive development, its actual implementation and duration will be a major test of transparency. The IMF argues that more efforts are needed "to strengthen the finance ministry's oversight over oil revenue collection, and to proceed with the appointment of an auditor of international reputation,"[83] while the World Bank states that the government-owned Societe mauritanienne des hydrocarbures (Mauritanian hydrocarbon company) should "enhance its openness to public scrutiny to avoid conflicts of interest and prevent it from becoming a 'state within the state.'"[84]

Under the previous regime, legislators had neither the necessary training nor adequate access to information to provide sufficient oversight of the budget-making process. So far, no reform on that subject has been adopted. It remains to be seen whether the newly elected National Assembly will be better equipped.

In theory, a safe legal environment for citizens who denounce cases of corruption is provided by the mediator of the republic, the penal code, and the constitutional right of expression. Under the Taya regime, the reliability of this framework was undermined by the institutional and empirical weakness of the mediator (see Civil Liberties), the judicial system's lack of independence, and government censorship of newspapers when they attempted to report detailed allegations of corruption.

With respect to higher education, living and working conditions at universities remain inadequate, and faculty often come under pressure to favor well-connected students. Some changes have been implemented during the transition to improve the situation. For instance, in 2006 the distribution of much-valued fellowships to study abroad was more transparent than before. But some sources also reported that several individuals who held key positions in the previous regime and were known for their corrupt practices were still sitting on the fellowship distribution committee after the coup. Family ties seem to be an asset that increases the likelihood of obtaining such grants.[85]

Recommendations
- The new institution in charge of the management of oil revenues should be made as transparent as possible. Related control mechanisms should be created within the energy ministry and the Societe mauritanienne des hydrocarbures.

- In light of the positive work undertaken by the Inspection Generale de l'Etat, internal and external auditing bodies should be granted full independence from the presidency, protected against informal influences, and provided with the resources to carry out their mission.
- An effective mechanism must be set in place to investigate and condemn cases of private appropriation of public resources. This could be done by making the mediator of the republic fully independent of the presidency, by allowing all citizens (not just elected representatives) to lodge a complaint with the mediator, and by providing the mediator with more human and material resources.
- In order to combat petty corruption in education, the faculties and staff of educational institutions should be provided with better salaries and working conditions. An independent body should be created to investigate illegal pressures on faculty by parents and administrative superiors.

NOTES

[1] "Premiere conference de presse du President du Conseil Militaire pour la Justice et la democratie," *Horizons* no. 4079 (10 October 2005).

[2] "Transition democratique: la CENI officiellement instituee," *Horizons* no. 4099 (9 November 2005).

[3] "Conseil des ministres: elargissement des attributions de la CENI," *Nouakchott Info Quotidien* no. 1142 (4 January 2007).

[4] The term "opposition parties" refers to parties that were in the opposition during the Taya regime.

[5] "Adoption du bulletin unique: la bataille des couleurs," *Le Calame* no. 537 (10 May 2006).

[6] RAVEL stands for Recensement a Vocation Electorale.

[7] "Processus electoral: demain, le recensement," *Horizons* no. 4165 (15 February 2006).

[8] "Rapport d'evaluation du vote referendaire par la CENI: Qui veut voyager loin menage sa monture!" *Nouakchott Info Quotidien* no. 1044 (9 August 2006); "RAVEL II: Une autre opportunite pour se faire recenser," *Horizons* no. 4305 (4 September 2006).

[9] "La CENI a le tournis: les ravages du RAVEL," *Le Calame* no. 528 (8 March 2006).

[10] Ibid.

[11] "Vote militaire: une nouvelle reglementation," *Le Renovateur* no. 109 (14 November 2006).

[12] "Politique: de la candidature independante," *L'Authentique Quotidien* no. 235 (30 December 2005).

[13] "Processus Democratique: Ely jette un pave dans la mare," *L'Authentique Quotidien* no. 361 (18 September 2006).

14 "Les observateurs internationaux satisfaits," *Horizons* no. 4255 (24-26 June 2006).

15 "Rapport d'evaluation du vote referendaire par la CENI…," *Nouakchott Info Quotidien* no. 1044 (9 August 2006); "Exclusion des observateurs nationaux du referendum: la polemique," *Le Calame* no. 544 (28 June 2006).

16 "Observateurs de l'union: Bien, mais peut encore mieux faire," *Nouakchott Info Quotidien* no. 1116 (22 November 2006); "Point de presse de la mission d'observation de l'Union Europeenne: des ameliorations a apporter au processus electoral," *L'Authentique Quotidien* no. 403 (7 December 2006).

17 As reported in "Mauritania," *Country Report* (London: Economist Intelligence Unit [EIU], January 2007), 14.

18 "La victoire des colonels: senatoriales 2007," *L'Authentique Quotidien* no. 424 (22 January 2007).

19 "Mission d'observation electorale (MOE): Le scrutin du 11 mars s'est deroule dans la transparence," *Nouakchott Info Quotidien* no. 1192 (15 March 2007). The EU observation mission's preliminary report can be found on the mission chair's website: http://maib.info/1/spip.php?article514.

20 Djibril Ly, "L'Etat de droit dans la constitution mauritanienne du 20 juillet 1991," *Revue mauritanienne de Droit et d'economie* 9 (1993): 50.

21 "La reconnaissance des ONG s'inscrit dans la droite ligne de l'ouverture politique," *Nouakchott Info Quotidien* no. 780 (19 May 2005).

22 The new ordinance on freedom of the press can be found here: http://www.ami.mr/fr/texteslegislatifs.html.

23 "Conseil des Ministres: Adoption de la nouvelle loi sur la presse," *Nouakchott Info Quotidien* no. 1002 (8 June 2006).

24 Ordinance of the Freedom of the Press, Article 21.

25 A copy of the ordinance can be found in "Ordonnance 2006-034 portant institution de la Haute autorite de la presse et de l'audiovisuel (HAPA)," *Horizons* no. 4340 (20 October 2006); see also "Liberalisation de la presse: la Haute Autorite sur les rails," *Le Calame* no. 555 (27 September 2006).

26 Reporters Without Borders, "Editor attacked after receiving death threats," news release, 17 February 2006, http://www.ifex.org/en/content/view/full/72347/.

27 Personal observations during that event, Nouakchott, June 2006.

28 "Apres l'interpellation et la liberation d'un depute RFD: les deputes de l'opposition se solidarisent avec leur collegue," *Nouakchott Info Quotidien* no. 770 (2 May 2005).

29 "Qui torture qui? Dossier 8 juin et Co.," *Le Calame* no. 460 (3 November 2004): 1, 3.

30 "Proces des putschistes: plaidoyers, etat de siege et querelles de procedures," *L'Authentique Quotidien* no. 179 (23 November 2004); "Mauritania," *Country Report* (EIU, April 2005).

31 "Un delit politique: detention des chefs islamistes," *Le Calame* no. 466 (15 December 2004); "Victimes de la loi sur la presse," *Le Calame* no. 462 (17 November 2004): 3; "Greves des avocats," *L'Authentique Quotidien* no. 197 (17 May 2005); "Islamistes en prison: la defense denonce des sevices contre deux detenus," *Le Calame* no. 493 (23 June 2005).

32 "Declaration du ministre de la Justice a la presse: 115 individus, dont 32 etaient en prison, ont beneficie de l'amnistie," *Horizons* no. 4054 (5 September 2005).

33 "Deux presumes salafistes ecroues: on deterre la loi sur le terrorisme," *Le Calame* no. 554 (20 September 2006); "Nouvelle serie d'arrestations dans les milieux 'salafistes': la 'guerre contre le terrorisme' continue," *Le Calame* no. 572 (17 January 2007); "Serie d'arrestations de presumes islamistes," *L'Authentique Quotidien* no. 418 (11 January 2007).

34. "Reforme de la justice: affirmation de l'independance du magistrat," *Horizons* no. 4286 (8 August 2006).

35 Ibid.

36 "Les droits fondamentaux, dans les prisons et les commissariats: Projet d'ordonnance portant revision du Code de Procedure Penale," *Nouakchott Info Quotidien* no. 1147 (11 January 2007).

37 "Journee mondiale contre la torture: menace sur l'integrite du corps humain en Mauritanie," *L'Authentique Quotidien* no. 203 (27 June 2005); "Tortures et meurtres attribues a la police: le FONADH denonce," *Le Calame* no. 494 (30 June 2005).

38 Agence mauritanienne d'information, "Le porte parole du gouvernement commente les travaux du Conseil des ministres," news release, 27 December 2006.

39 "Les droits fondamentaux, dans les prisons et les commissariats: Projet d'ordonnance portant revision du Code de Procedure Penale," *Nouakchott Info Quotidien* no. 1147 (11 January 2007); "Reforme de la justice: affirmation de l'independance du magistrat," *Horizons* no. 4286 (8 August 2006); "Reforme de la justice et du droit: Le plus grand travail de la transition," *Le Calame* no. 585 (4 April 2007); "Nouvelles dispositions du Code de Procedure Penale: Detention preventive et controle judiciaire," *Le Calame* no. 586 (18 April 2007).

40 The entire Personal Status Code is available on the justice ministry's website: http://www .justice.gov.mr/NR/rdonlyres/81255DB5-4489-448C-9574-DB9711B39718/0/Code statutpersonnelFr.pdf.

41 "Nouveau Code de Statut Personnel: la loi qui libere," *Nouakchott Info Quotidien* no. 813 (18 July 2005).

42 "Presence des femmes aux cercles de prise de decision: Pour plus de place au soleil," *Le Calame* no. 529 (15 March 2006).

43 Quoted in "Observateurs de l'Union: Bien, mais peut encore mieux faire," *Nouakchott Info Quotidien* no. 1116 (22 November 2006).

44 "Session de formation des policiers sur la prise en charge psycho sanitaire des filles et femmes victimes de violence sexuelle: evaluer l'ampleur du phenomene pour apporter une meilleure assistance aux victimes," *Horizons* no. 3850 (13 November 2004).

45 "Inauguration d'un centre pilote de prise en charge psycho-sanitaire et sociale des filles et femmes victimes des violences physiques," *Horizons* no. 3896 (18 January 2005).

46 See a report by the German international aid agency, GTZ, "Mutilations genitals feminines en Mauritanie," available at: http://www.gtz.de/de/dokumente/fr-fgm-pays -mauritanie.pdf. See also "Tolerance zero aux mutilations genitales féminines: les Ulemas mauritaniens decretent une fatwa," *Le Calame* no. 524 (8 February 2006); "Mutilations genitales feminines: pour agir contre cette pratique," *Le Calame* no. 474 (9 February 2005).

47 The law can be found on the justice ministry's website: http://www.justice.gov.mr/NR /rdonlyres/5EBA5298-9830-4234-8022-960D614F303C/0/ordonnancen2005015.doc.

See also "Formation sur le code de la protection penale de l'enfant," *Horizons* no. 4234 (26–27 May 2006).

48 "Tolerance zero aux mutilations genitales feminines," *Le Calame* no. 524 (8 February 2006).

49 "Violence a l'egard des femmes: necessite de nouvelles juridictions," *Horizons* no. 4112 (28 November 2005).

50 "La Commission Nationale des Droits de l'Homme chez le colonel Ely," *Le Calame* no. 586 (18 April 2007).

51 "Droits de l'Homme: Consensus pour une lutte sans merci contre l'esclavage," *Nouakchott Info Quotidien* no. 955 (27 March 2006); "Journee de reflexion sur l'esclavage: comment tuer le monstre?" *Le Calame* no. 531 (29 March 2006).

52 See the interview with the leader of SOS-Esclave in "Entretien avec Boubacar Ould Messaoud, President de SOS Esclave," *La Tribune* no. 295 (16 March 2006).

53 For an example of that pattern, see "Trarza: un fait divers qui risque d'etre amplifie par les rancoeurs ethno-tribales," *Nouakchott Info Quotidien* no. 1126 (11 December 2006).

54 Agence mauritanienne d'information, "Commentaire du ministre de la communication," news release, 11 October 2006; "L'accessibilite numerique, theme de la journee internationale: handicaps," *Horizons* no. 4376 (15–17 December 2006); "Journee internationale des personnes handicapees: la Mauritanie oeuvrera a une meilleure integration des personnes handicapees," *Horizons* no. 4116 (5 December 2005).

55 Cedric Jourde, "The International Relations of Small Neoauthoritarian States: Islamism, Warlordism, and the Framing of Stability," *International Studies Quarterly* (June 2007).

56 "Affaires des islamistes: perquisitions et arrestations dans plusieurs mosquees," *Eveil Hebdo* no. 580 (17 May 2005); "Decouverte de plans visant a conduire une 'revolution' islamiste," Agence France-Presse (AFP), 18 May 2005.

57 "Universite de Nouakchott: Interpellations au sein de l'UNEM," *Tahalil Hebdo*, 14 December 2006; "Journee sanglante a l'universite de Nouakchott," *Al Akhbar Info* (27 December, 2006), available at: http://fr.alakhbar.info; "Poursuite des affrontements entre la police et les etudiants a Nouakchott," *Al Akhbar Info* (28 December 2006).

58 "Faciliter l'acces au droit et a la justice aux categories les plus defavorisees," *Horizons* no. 4084 (17 October 2005); see also "Reforme de la justice: au chevet de la grande malade," *Le Calame* no. 511 (31 October, 2005).

59 The entire document is available on the government's webpage: http://www.mauritania .mr (in Arabic) or http://www.mauritania.mr/french.default (in French). See page 12 of that document.

60 "Reforme de la justice: affirmation de l'independance du magistrat," *Horizons* no. 4286 (8 August 2006).

61 Ibid.; see also interview with justice minister in "Mahfoudh Ould Bettah, Ministre de la Justice: Les reformes entamees vont etre poursuivies," *Le Calame* no. 535 (26 April 2006).

62 "Adoption du nouveau statut de la magistrature: la reforme de tous les dangers," *L'Authentique Quotidien* no. 321 (13 June 2006).

63 "Faciliter l'acces au droit et a la justice aux categories les plus defavorisees: le ministre de la justice a Horizons," *Horizons* no. 4084 (17 October 2005); Agence mauritanienne

d'information, "Commentaire du Ministre de la Communication," news release, 21 December 2005.

64 "Point de presse: creation d'un conseil national pour l'assistance judiciaire," *Nouakchott Info Quotidien* no. 897 (22 December 2005); "Decret sur l'aide juridique et judiciaire," *Le Calame* no. 580 (7 March 2007).

65 Agence mauritanienne d'information, "Le batonnier de l'Ordre des Avocats reclame plus d'independance et de modernisation de la justice," news release, 16 January 2007.

66 Zekeria Ould Ahmed Salem, "La democratisation en Mauritanie: une 'illusio' postcoloniale?" *Politique Africaine* 75 (October 1999): 140–41.

67 *Report on the Observance of Standards and Codes—Fiscal Transparency Module* (Washington, D.C.: International Monetary Fund [IMF], Country Report No. 02/268, December 2002); *Groupe Technique Thematique, "Gestion Ressources Publiques," Rapport Provisoire* (Islamic Republic of Mauritania, February 2004), 7; *Country Financial Accountability Assessment* (Washington, D.C.: World Bank and the Islamic Republic of Mauritania, Report No. 27065, Vol. 1, November 2003), 46–47; *Programme d'appui a la mise en oeuvre du Programme national de bonne gouvernance, 2003–2005* (New York; United Nations Development Programme, March 2003), 63.

68 *Project Performance Assessment Report* (World Bank, Report No. 29615, 1 July 2004), 25.

69 *Report on the Observance of Standards and Codes . . .* (IMF, Country Report 02/268), 13–14.

70 "Inspection generale d'Etat: un gadget de plus?" *La Tribune* no. 273 (26 September 2005).

71 "Entretien avec M. Mohamed Ould Horma Ould Abdi, Inspecteur General d'Etat: toutes les institutions seront controlees en 2006," *Horizons* no. 4215 (27 April 2006).

72 Ibid., see concrete examples of cases of corruption and mismanagement.

73 Ibid.

74 "Premiere conference de presse du President du Conseil Militaire pour la Justice et la democratie," *Horizons* no. 4079 (10 October 2005); see also "Faut-il punir ou excuser les auteurs des detournements des deniers publics?" *L'Authentique Quotidien* no. 214 18–24 October 2005.

75 *Report on the Observance of Standards and Codes . . .* (IMF, Country Report 02/268), 7–8, 14.

76 "Chaine des depenses publiques: un pas vers la modernisation, deux pas vers la transparence," *Nouakchott Info Quotidien* no. 694 (12 December 2004).

77 "Parachever la reorganisation de l'administration et des finances publiques pour une gestion plus saine: le ministre de la communication et des relations avec le parlement, porte-parole officiel du gouvernement," *Horizons* no. 3927 (5 March 2005).

78 "Creation de nouvelles structures pour combattre le detournement des biens publiques et la corruption," *Horizons* no. 4010 (3 July 2005); see also "Balayer devant sa porte: Commissariat special de lutte contre les crimes economiques," *L'Authentique Quotidien* no. 204 (5 July 2005).

79 *Islamic Republic of Mauritania: 2006 Article IV Consultation—Staff Report; Staff Statement; Public Information Notice and Press Release on the Executive Board Discussion; and Statement by the Executive Director for the Islamic Republic of Mauritania* (IMF, Country Report No. 06-272, July 2006), 3.

80 Ibid., 4.

81 Ibid., 7.

82 The official text for this commission can be found at: http://www.tresor.mr/static/arrete-cnsrh.doc.

83 Ibid., 20.

84 *Second Poverty Reduction Strategy Paper/Mauritania* (World Bank, Report No. 38116-MR, 29 November 2006), 6.

85 See two articles on that subject: "Enseignement superieur: Bourses de la transparence," and "Les 10 grandes injustices de la Commission Nationale de Bourses CNB," *La Tribune* no. 295 (16 March 2006): 3

MOZAMBIQUE

CAPITAL: Maputo
POPULATION: 20.4 million
GNI PER CAPITA: $340

SCORES	2005	2007
ACCOUNTABILITY AND PUBLIC VOICE:	4.13	4.27
CIVIL LIBERTIES:	4.49	4.39
RULE OF LAW:	3.39	3.92
ANTICORRUPTION AND TRANSPARENCY:	2.78	3.23

(scores are based on a scale of 0 to 7, with 0 representing weakest and 7 representing strongest performance)

Robert B. Lloyd

INTRODUCTION

The December 2004 presidential and legislative elections marked a major transition in Mozambique's political evolution. After eighteen years as the nation's president, Joaquim Chissano stepped down in February 2005. Under his leadership, Mozambique ended a brutal sixteen-year civil war, abandoned its Marxist rhetoric and political system, introduced a democratic constitution, allowed competitive elections, and instituted economic reforms that resulted in a decade of impressive economic growth. Chissano left office, however, amid complaints of government corruption, a rising crime rate, and with Mozambique increasingly experiencing the devastating impacts of the HIV/AIDS pandemic.

Robert B. Lloyd is an Associate Professor of International Relations and Chair of the International Studies and Languages Division at Pepperdine University in Malibu, California. Dr. Lloyd received his Ph.D. from The Johns Hopkins School of Advanced International Studies. He worked in Mozambique in the 1990s with SIL, a nongovernmental educational organization, and has since maintained close ties with the country. He has published numerous articles on conflict resolution and democratization in Southern Africa.

His successor, Armando Guebuza, is a wealthy businessman with a hardliner past. Trained as a guerrilla fighter for Mozambique's independence from Portugal, Guebuza stirred controversy through his actions as a government leader after the country's independence in 1975. He became referred to as "20-24" in response to his ultimatum to Portuguese settlers to leave the country with 20 kilograms of baggage in twenty-four hours. In the 1980s, his "Operation Production" forcibly removed Mozambicans from cities into the countryside in a futile attempt to increase food production and reduce urban unemployment. Later, he led the government's negotiations with the Mozambique National Resistance (RENAMO) rebels, which eventually resulted in the Peace Accord in 1992. As Mozambique made a transition in the 1990s from Marxism to capitalism, Guebuza developed financial interests in a wide variety of business concerns, earning him the nickname "Mr. Gue-Business."

Guebuza's election cemented the control of the Front for the Liberation of Mozambique (known by its Portuguese acronym as FRELIMO) over the country. The opposition RENAMO, which transformed itself from a rebel group to a political party following the end of the civil war, saw its political influence slump. RENAMO's share of representation in the 250-seat legislature (Assembly of the Republic) fell from 117 to 90. FRELIMO increased its share from 133 to 160, which is just below the two-thirds threshold required to change the constitution. The continued electoral losses of RENAMO suggest that Mozambique increasingly displays a "predominant party" system, with FRELIMO being seen at the "natural" party of government.

Mozambique is a country in transition. Its great achievement has been the political and economic liberalization of a nation whose foundation was marked by colonial subjugation, Marxist repression, and civil confrontation. For Mozambique's political and economic transformation to continue, it must be supported by a strengthening of the judiciary, the professionalizing of the police force, and a reduction in the opportunities for corruption. The president has asked for, and received, a mandate to address these particular issues. Early indications are that he is beginning to address these issues that have undermined the country's political and economic reforms.

ACCOUNTABILITY AND PUBLIC VOICE

FREE AND FAIR ELECTORAL LAWS AND ELECTIONS:	3.75
EFFECTIVE AND ACCOUNTABLE GOVERNMENT:	3.75
CIVIC ENGAGEMENT AND CIVIC MONITORING:	5.33
MEDIA INDEPENDENCE AND FREEDOM OF EXPRESSION:	4.25
CATEGORY AVERAGE:	**4.27**

Mozambique has a democratic multiparty political system based on universal suffrage, an independent judiciary, and freedoms of assembly, religion, and speech.[1] The 1990 constitution guided the historic 1994 national and provincial elections that marked the first multiparty democratic vote in Mozambique's history. The country has had two election cycles since then, most recently in 2004. FRELIMO has won every election, but the RENAMO opposition party has provided stiff electoral competition.

FRELIMO candidate Armando Guebuza, running on an anticorruption and anticrime platform, emerged the victor in the December 2004 general elections, garnering 63.7 percent of the national vote, compared with 31.7 percent for RENAMO leader Afonso Dhlakama. Representing a range of political interests, twenty parties competed on a party-list, proportional electoral system. The elections were peaceful, but election observers noted serious electoral deficiencies, including ballot-box stuffing, the politicization of the National Election Commission (CNE), and a lack of transparency.[2] Mozambique's Constitutional Council accepted the election results but was highly critical of the way in which the CNE conducted the contest.[3]

Despite equal campaigning opportunities and government campaign funding for all parties, FRELIMO nevertheless enjoys a decided electoral advantage as it has been in power for three decades, is better able to tap into state resources for political campaigning, and has built a national presence. Laws requiring political parties to publish the sources and uses of funds are not enforced, making it difficult to determine the influence of economically privileged interests on the political process.

Tensions from the civil war still exist; the two main parties frequently accuse one other of physically harassing supporters in their respective political strongholds. The constitution requires that political parties be national in scope, uphold national interests, and not advocate violence.[4] Political parties often reflect regional and ethnic interests: the main opposition base is located in the central part of the country, while FRELIMO's base is in the south and the north.

The constitution separates the executive, legislative, and judicial branches. Revisions to the constitution in 2004 strengthened an already strong executive, permitting the Council of Ministers to introduce "decree laws" that automatically become law if parliament does not challenge them during the session following their publication.[5] The executive branch also tends to dominate the judicial branch, in part due to its ability to select judges. Mozambique is a unitary state and the government is highly centralized, but a limited devolution of power is beginning to occur. The Mozambican national parliament in late 2006 approved a bill creating locally elected provincial assemblies, which are tasked to approval of the provincial government's budget and plan and verification of its fulfillment. Provincial assemblies cannot pass laws, but do have the ability to provide closer public scrutiny of local governments. In some provinces this could provoke conflict, with RENAMO-dominated provincial assemblies clashing with governors and district governments appointed by the central—and FRELIMO-controlled—government.

The civil service is generally selected on the basis of open competition and merit.[6] However, relatively low pay, inadequate resources, and a lack of trained personnel undermine its efficiency and professionalism.

The government of Mozambique is engaged in initiatives that reflect the interests of women and ethnic and religious groups. The constitution recognizes that men and women are "equal before the law in all spheres of political, economic, social, and cultural affairs." The government mandates that at least 30 percent of the National Assembly and cabinet must be women,[7] and women hold key positions in the Guebuza government. While Portuguese is the official language, the use of local languages in education and as a means of communication is encouraged. The constitution establishes a secular state but "recognizes and values" religious groups. It also grants people with disabilities the same rights and responsibilities as other citizens, though poverty makes it less able to accommodate special needs.

Foreign nongovernmental organizations (NGOs), largely European and American, operate freely throughout the country and influence the political process through grants and technical assistance. The Program Aid Partnership, for example, is a group of donor countries that collectively provides a significant portion of the state budget and plays a notable role with government agencies. However, such groups are generally oriented toward technical issues and are reluctant to involve themselves in electoral issues. NGO consultation was formalized in January 2005, when a newly established Council of State included representatives of civil society to advise the president. Some NGOs have complained about registration delays, but there are no reports of registration denial or state pressure on their financial patrons.

The constitution guarantees "freedom of the press, and the independence of the media." There is no direct censorship of the media, and President Guebuza has publicly affirmed the government's commitment to media freedom.[8] Journalists report a generally open environment for press freedom, except when reporting on corruption by government officials. Reporters Without Borders (RSF) ranks Mozambique 45th out of 168 countries in its 2006 press freedom index, up from 49th place in 2005 and 64th in 2004.

In general, the state protects individuals from imprisonment for the free expression of their views, although there are no shield laws to protect journalists. Nevertheless, reports occasionally surface of party and government officials threatening and detaining journalists, claiming libel.[9] The constitution provides a fundamental right to defend one's honor, good name, and reputation. Conviction for libel can result in prison sentences, but courts have not applied these provisions in recent years. In February 2005, for example, the city council of the provincial capital of Pemba briefly threatened to sue the local weekly newspaper, *Horizonte.* The paper had printed a series of articles critical of the city and its garbage collection and made allegations of corruption against the mayor.[10]

Despite the general improvements there are still isolated incidents of harassment, unlawful detention, and violence against members of the press.[11] In 2000, Carlos Cardoso, a Mozambican investigative journalist, was gunned down in public. At the time of his death he had been investigating allegations of bank fraud at the Commercial Bank of Mozambique. Despite many outstanding questions related to the murder, six individuals were eventually arrested, tried, convicted, and given lengthy prison sentences. RSF cited these heavy sentences as a major reason for the rankings jump between 2004 and 2005. The murder and trial received widespread and extensive media attention. During the trial, three of the accused stated that the President's son, Nyimpine Chissano, had ordered the murder. This charge was strongly denied by Nyimpine Chissano. In May 2006, the government opened an investigation into the younger Chissano's alleged "moral authority" behind the murder of Cardoso.[12]

Additionally, police authorities in Maputo, the capital, acknowledged that local police manhandled and threatened with guns journalists covering the return to the country of Anibal dos Santos Junior, one of the men convicted of Cardoso's murder.[13] In a separate incident, police in Maputo beat and detained two journalists with the *Zambeze* newspaper who had observed municipal police beating street vendors and seizing their products. The municipal police commander later apologized and stated the officers would be punished, although it is not known if this occurred.[14]

While the government owns and operates print, radio, and television media, there is no evidence of censorship. Most Mozambicans receive news from the state-owned Radio Mocambique, which has been commended by the Committee to Protect Journalists for its nonpartisan coverage.[15] State-owned Televisao de Mocambique operates the only national network. *Noticias*, the major newspaper in the capital, is state-managed. Mozambique also has a number of privately owned newspapers and television and radio stations (including a religious one) that operate freely.[16] The government does not restrict access to the internet,[17] the number of internet service providers is growing, and the environment is competitive.[18] Nonetheless, RENAMO argues that some media coverage is biased in favor of the ruling party, citing the government-funded Mozambique News Agency.[19] The constitution guarantees free artistic expression and intellectual property rights. There have been no reports of government restriction on cultural expression, but pirating of internationally copyrighted software, music, and film is not uncommon.

Recommendations

- The National Assembly should pass shield legislation to protect journalists from libel lawsuits arising from reporting on public officials.
- The government should increase compensation for civil servants, including the police, to reduce the attraction of corruption.
- The government should reform the National Elections Commission (CNE) to make it smaller in membership, nonpartisan and depoliticized, and more professional and transparent both in its internal operations and supervision of elections.
- The state should ensure that international election observers have access to all aspects of elections, especially the tabulation process.

CIVIL LIBERTIES

PROTECTION FROM STATE TERROR, UNJUSTIFIED IMPRISONMENT, AND TORTURE:	2.86
GENDER EQUITY:	3.75
RIGHTS OF ETHNIC, RELIGIOUS, AND OTHER DISTINCT GROUPS:	4.00
FREEDOM OF CONSCIENCE AND BELIEF:	6.33
FREEDOM OF ASSOCIATION AND ASSEMBLY:	5.00
CATEGORY AVERAGE:	**4.39**

Mozambique is slowly moving in a direction of greater protection for civil rights and liberties, but this progress is hindered by police misconduct, judicial understaffing, improper pretrial detention, and poor prison conditions.

The constitution prohibits torture and cruel or inhumane treatment, and the death penalty is illegal. In 2005, Amnesty International (AI) found fewer reports of police torture of detainees than in previous years. In Manica province, the government charged fourteen police officers with a number of offenses, including assault, extrajudicial execution of suspects, extortion, and theft. These officers have not yet gone to trial.[20] AI also reported several instances of attacks against peaceful activists in 2005. In one incident, police beat and then opened fire on vendors at the Limpopo market in the city of Xai-Xai who were peacefully marching to the municipal offices to air their grievances about market conditions. In another, striking students at Eduardo Mondlane University in Maputo were beaten by police. No investigations were conducted into whether force was used legally.[21] There are no effective protections against arbitrary arrest, particularly in the more rural areas.

Multiple reports continue to highlight inhumane conditions in prisons. In 2006, the Open Society Initiative for Southern Africa released an extensive report that included a review of prison conditions in Mozambique. The organization noted understaffing, procedural delays in bringing criminal cases to trial, severe overcrowding, poor physical infrastructure, and a lack of sanitary conditions and access to basic health care. In addition, youthful offenders are not well separated from older and more hardened criminals.[22] For example, in early 2005 the *Noticias* newspaper reported that the main prison in the central Mozambican city of Beira contained 630 prisoners, although it is designed to hold just 150, and that most of the inmates were ill. Only 97 of the prisoners had been tried and convicted.[23] Also early in 2005, prisoners injured in a fight at a high-security Maputo prison were left without medical care for some time, and one of the prisoners later died. In response, the attorney general stated that prisoners had a right to medical care.[24] In 2005, the justice minister cited three prisons where ongoing facility refurbishment is designed to separate hardened criminals from youth.[25]

Part of the problem is the slow pace of justice. The constitution limits pretrial detention and provides prisoners the right to judicial review of their detention, but understaffing and a lack of the funds necessary to post bond has led to many accused people being held in prison. Furthermore, there are allegations of detainees being held past their prison term. The constitution does permit citizens to seek redress for damage caused by illegal state acts and recourse for any act that violates constitutional guarantees.

Since the beginning of multiparty democracy in 1994, there has been no systematic and widespread abuse of citizens by nonstate actors. Periodically, the leader of the RENAMO opposition has threatened to form another army, and this "Presidential Guard" could pose a threat to citizens if RENAMO chose not to participate in the government.[26] Crime is a serious problem, and combating it is a difficult issue confronting the government. In some cases, criminals have been released from detention back into the community, which has led to public lynchings. Between August and November 2006, for example, more than twenty alleged criminals were beaten or burned to death in the capital.[27] This widespread vigilantism is due in part to a lack of access to the formal judicial system and a relatively low level of incarceration compared to other African countries. These developments underscore the state's lack of legal and judicial capacity. The police are widely seen by Mozambicans as corrupt. Training is inadequate, and deaths due to HIV/AIDS both deprive the government of trained police forces and necessitate the training of additional police officers each year.

The constitution guarantees equal civil and political rights for men and women: "Men and women shall be equal before the law in all spheres of political, economic, social, and cultural affairs." These provisions are not always upheld, although government officials publicly stress their importance.[28] In recent years, the government has undertaken major revisions of legislation that discriminated against women. In December 2005, the parliament voted unanimously to ratify the Protocol to the African Charter on Human and People's Rights and the Rights of Women in Africa. Justice Minister Esperanca Machavela publicly stated that civil servants should adopt a culture of human rights, and supported the creation of a National Humans Rights Commission to help protect civil rights.[29]

The question of abortion remains in dispute. Mozambique criminalizes abortion, but the Protocol permits it in cases of rape, incest, and danger to the well-being of the mother. The government is also working on legislation to criminalize domestic violence against women.[30] Traditional African customs, however, do not always conform to the view of the roles of men and women expressed in state law or international norms. Thus, it is not clear, particularly in the rural areas, how much of an impact government laws will have on such traditional practices as the husband's family not permitting property inheritance by a widow, polygamy, and sexual inheritance of the wife by her late husband's brother.[31]

Mozambique is also a signatory to the International Labor Organization Convention on the Abolition of Forced Labor and the UN Protocol to Prevent, Suppress, and Punish Trafficking in Persons, Especially Women and Children. This convention provides a definition of human trafficking and criminalizes this activity. Despite these legal safeguards,

Mozambique is considered a source country for human trafficking, both internally and internationally. In 2006, police in the northern province of Nampula arrested a Bangladeshi citizen who admitted to trafficking sixty-six Bangladeshis previously detained in the port city of Nacala.[32] There are also allegations of organ trafficking, most notably in a Human Rights League report released in October 2006. However, the government had earlier investigated these claims and found no evidence to support them.[33] HIV/AIDS is a growing problem—with the government estimating 15.6 percent of the population between fifteen and forty-nine infected—which leaves orphaned children at particular risk of neglect, abandonment, and even exploitation. In March 2007, the government introduced legislation that makes the trafficking of children a criminal offense.[34]

Ethnolinguistic diversity has been one source of tension in a country of 19 million people and thirty-nine spoken languages. Addressing this issue, the constitution guarantees freedom of association and equal rights before the law, regardless of ethnic origin or religion, and outlaws discrimination based on these criteria. While Portuguese is the official language, the government actively promotes the development of Mozambique's languages.[35] In some cases legislation has favored citizens' constitutionally based civil rights over traditional ethnic or religious practices. Finally, the constitution guarantees the right to assistance in the case of disability, but the number of people with disabilities—many as a result of the civil war—combined with the poverty in the country has made it difficult for the government to address this issue.

The religious landscape in Mozambique is complex. The majority of the population adheres to some form of Christian belief. Muslims comprise nearly 20 percent of the population and are concentrated in the north, largely along the coast. However, many Mozambicans, including those who also call themselves Muslims and Christians, follow traditional African religious beliefs and practices to varying degrees.[36] The constitution guarantees freedom of religion and does not place restrictions on religious observance and education. These rights are respected by the government, which permits Christian and Muslim schools, has sought good relations with religious groups, and regularly grants foreign missionaries residence visas. The government refrains from interference in the appointment of leaders of religious organizations and does not sponsor religious groups. However, some limited restrictions on religious expression do exist. For example, religious groups are required to register with the government and may not organize as political parties.

The constitution reflects the government's pro-labor heritage in guaranteeing work, just payment, safe working conditions, and the rights to form unions, strike, and take paid holidays. Citizens are not compelled by the state to belong to any association, either directly or indirectly. Civic, business, and political groups are permitted to organize, mobilize, advocate, and publicly demonstrate for peaceful purposes. However, police do occasionally disrupt public demonstrations. For instance, in 2005 in the city of Nampula, police violently broke up a demonstration by high school students. They used batons to disperse the students, who were banging tin cans, and took a number of the students to local jails. The students claim to have informed the education authorities of their intention to demonstrate, and local education authorities condemned the attack.[37]

Recommendations

- The prison system should be reformed, including mandatory posting of laws governing detention and prison conditions, construction of additional prisons to alleviate overcrowding, and separation of violent from nonviolent offenders and juveniles from adults.
- The state should ratify and begin active implementation of the provisions of the United Nations Convention Against Transnational Organized Crime and its related protocols. These include the Protocol to Prevent, Suppress and Punish Trafficking in Persons, Especially Women and Children, and the Protocol against the Smuggling of Migrants by Land, Sea and Air. Specific implementation measures for Mozambique include applying security and border controls to detect and prevent trafficking and securing technical assistance programs for law enforcement and judicial training.
- The government should develop a comprehensive public/private orphanage system to respond to the projected increase in the number of AIDS orphans. This will also help protect children from sexual exploitation and trafficking.
- The requirement that citizens and foreigners be required to carry identification papers when in public should be abolished.
- The government should move forward with the establishment of the proposed National Human Rights Commission.

RULE OF LAW

INDEPENDENT JUDICIARY:	3.60
PRIMACY OF RULE OF LAW IN CIVIL AND CRIMINAL MATTERS:	3.50
ACCOUNTABILITY OF SECURITY FORCES AND MILITARY TO CIVILIAN AUTHORITIES:	4.50
PROTECTION OF PROPERTY RIGHTS:	3.33
EQUAL TREATMENT UNDER THE LAW:	4.67
CATEGORY AVERAGE:	**3.92**

The constitution states that the judiciary is charged with guaranteeing and strengthening the rule of law and promoting the rights and freedoms of citizens. Additionally, the judiciary is designed to be independent of any religious bodies, and judges are to be obedient to the constitution and the law, impartial, and disinterested.

The selection of judges, however, does in fact reflect political considerations. If one party controls both the assembly and the presidency, that party can exercise substantial political influence over the Supreme Court, the highest judicial body. Currently, the president, who is FRELIMO, selects trained, professional judges to the court through a judicial advisory body. These nominees must be ratified by the assembly. The Supreme Court president and vice-president have five-year, renewable terms. The assembly also votes in elective, lay judges—drawn from civil society organizations—to the court. As FRELIMO has a majority of the votes in the parliament, judges may be more sympathetic to FRELIMO policies—a point the RENAMO opposition has made from time to time. A 2006 report on judicial independence by the Open Society Initiative for Southern Africa found that decades of FRELIMO rule had entrenched a culture of political influence in the lower tiers of the judiciary. The justice minister, however, has denied these allegations.[38]

Mozambique's Constitutional Council, which became fully operational only in 2003, assesses whether legislation is consistent with the constitution, resolves conflicts between branches of government, and oversees elections. This body is chosen by the president and assembly. As yet, courts have not ruled against the executive on any major legislative or executive decision. The Constitutional Court did issue a withering report on the conduct of the 2004 elections but did not annul the overall outcome of the presidential and legislative elections. The Supreme Court is the final court of appeals for criminal and civil cases. The 2004 constitutional amendments established a new layer of appeals courts between the provincial and Supreme Court in order to reduce the number of cases heard by the Supreme Court, but these new courts have not been implemented.

Judges and court personnel do not always have adequate training. The president of the Supreme Court noted in 2005 that the country had 184 judges, but of those only 91 had a university degree. While court clerks should have a bachelor's degree, only 3 percent possessed such a degree and just over half did not have a high school diploma. Up to 2004, an average of five Mozambicans with law degrees chose to become judges each year, but a recent major salary boost increased significantly the number choosing a career as a judge. Nevertheless, the President of the Supreme Court stated in March 2005 that the judicial system needed at least an additional 500 judges to meet the demands placed on it. This shortage of trained personnel was cited as one reason for the severe backlog (over 100,000) of pending cases.[39] In addition, necessary reference materials such as legal documentation are lacking at many offices. The 2004 constitution recognized community courts, and in many areas these courts are the only mechanism for adjudicating disputes. Nevertheless, technical, administrative, and financial impediments to implementation of these constitutional provisions mean many of these local courts are essentially autonomous.[40]

Everyone charged with a crime is presumed innocent until proven guilty, and each defendant, including those who lack financial resources, has a right to independent counsel. However, while suspects may be held up to six months without being formally charged, the backlog of cases in the judicial courts means that a case may then not be heard for several years. In 2006, four pretrial detainees died in a mudslide while working at a gold mine in Manica province. The government opened an inquiry into why detainees were used as prison labor when such a practice is usually reserved for convicted prisoners.[41] Police have also released those accused of crimes before trial, sometimes due to overcrowding in the jails and in some cases due to alleged cooperation with the criminals. The public believes this catch-and-release policy helps fuel crime and is another factor in the rise in public lynching (see Civil Liberties).[42]

There are allegations, but no clear and systematic evidence, of prosecutors being influenced by political officials. Important public officials have not been prosecuted for abuse of power or other wrongdoing. In May 2006, however, the government opened an inquiry into the involvement of the former president's son in the death of a prominent journalist (see Accountability and Public Voice).

The military, internal security forces, and the police fall under the jurisdiction of the president. While these groups refrain from involvement in the political process, the government's control over the police is less certain. The government admits that organized crime rings have infiltrated the police.[43] At times they have been held accountable for corruption and human rights abuses. In October 2005, for example, a court sentenced eight policemen to three- to ten-year prison terms for the murder of eight prisoners between 2001 and 2005 in the provincial capital of Chimoio. The prisoners were shot execution style outside the city. The court believed the prisoners were murdered to cover up information regarding corruption among the police.[44] In 2004, AI reported that a police officer convicted of beating a sixty-year-old woman and her daughter received a three-month sentence of imprisonment in Xai-Xai. In another case, a police officer in Beira received a seven-year sentence and a fine for shooting dead an eighteen-year-old man.[45]

The constitution guarantees equality before courts and tribunals. Discrimination on grounds of gender, ethnic origin, and nationality are prohibited, and reported instances of such discrimination are lacking. The government has been cautious on the question of sexual orientation, neither supporting the legalization of homosexuality nor actively discriminating against homosexuals.[46] There is no evidence of widespread bias against ethnic, religious, or gender groups seeking equal treatment from the court. Nevertheless, a 2005 government-sponsored survey of public perceptions of government corruption indicated that a strong majority of respondents believed that "only the poor and weak are unable to evade the laws." The survey also indicated public ambivalence about the honesty and independence of the courts.[47]

Property title is historically a hot-button issue due to the country's colonial and Marxist legacies. Article 86 of the constitution guarantees the right to ownership of property, and the state may expropriate property only in accordance with the law, for the public interest, and with just compensation. Individual property rights over land, however, are severely restricted. Traditional law views the land as communal and allocated by the chief. Reflecting its Marxist heritage, Articles 46–48 of the 1990 constitution enshrine state ownership of land and its use. Mozambique employs a system of land tenure/usage rights in lieu of actual ownership. In urban areas, increasing population pressures have led to illegal land sales by individuals who were allotted land but never built on the parcel. Local governments have not always enforced the law, which states that a building must be constructed on a parcel within six months of its allocation.[48] In late 2006, the government introduced urban land-use reform regulations intended to reduce property transaction costs and time.[49] In rural areas, land cannot be used as collateral for loans, which hinders development of the agricultural sector.

The state promotes the private sector, encourages foreign investment, and guarantees the right of inheritance. In the past few years, foreign investment has increased substantially, indicating a generally favorable business climate. However, the lack of judicial capacity is one issue that the government has acknowledged as a constraint.

Recommendations

- The government should implement provisions of the 2004 constitution that created new regional appeals courts between the supreme and provincial courts in order to improve citizen access.
- The state should clarify, strengthen, and fund the community courts and train community court judges as one way to address the lack of access to the judicial system which is helping to fuel growing vigilantism.
- The government should increase salaries and judicial-training programs to meet the pressing need for qualified judges.
- The availability of legislation, jurisprudence, and other necessary reference materials, particularly at the district level should be augmented.
- The state should examine procedures for the possible future privatization of land title, long-term leases of land, and stronger property rights for urban areas.

ANTICORRUPTION AND TRANSPARENCY

ENVIRONMENT TO PROTECT AGAINST CORRUPTION:	2.80
EXISTENCE OF LAWS AND ETHICAL STANDARDS BETWEEN	
PRIVATE AND PUBLIC SECTORS:	3.00
ENFORCEMENT OF ANTICORRUPTION LAWS:	3.25
GOVERNMENTAL TRANSPARENCY:	3.86
CATEGORY AVERAGE:	**3.23**

The issues of corruption and transparency take a prominent place in Mozambique's political landscape. Indeed, President Guebuza has publicly stated that the administration faces serious problems in this regard.[50] Transparency International's 2006 Corruption Perceptions Index (CPI) ranked Mozambique 99 out of 163 countries surveyed. The CPI score (10 being the least corrupt) was 2.8, the same as for the previous two years.[51]

In order to combat the problem, the government has upgraded its Anticorruption Unit to a Central Office for Combating Corruption, infusing the unit with staffing and financial resources. AI noted that the unit had been effective in investigating and prosecuting several high-profile cases.[52]

However, effective legislative and administrative safeguards to prevent, detect, and punish corruption of public officials remain weak. High-ranking state officials must submit yearly asset declarations, but these are archived in the offices of the Constitutional Council and are not publicly released.[53] Mozambican law requires political parties to disclose their accounts regularly, but none has ever done so. This has given rise to charges that funds include illicit sources of income, though there is no evidence to support these charges. In April 2006, the parliament ratified the United Nations Convention against Corruption, which explicitly bans the use of such illicit funds for political parties.[54] This convention also includes provisions to protect whistleblowers, though it is unclear how this legislation may affect the behavior of individuals who draw attention to actual cases of corruption.[55]

The investment climate is generally favorable, but corruption and bureaucratic inefficiency remain key impediments to foreign investment.

Still, foreign direct investment has increased substantially, especially for so-called mega-projects such as the Mozal aluminum smelter near Maputo. The government has been seeking to reform its bureaucracy to reduce the time and simplify the paperwork associated with the business registration process. It has also been pursuing a policy of privatization for several years. Nonetheless, Mozambique still has a number of state-owned firms. In 2006, the state gained 85 percent ownership of the massive Cahora Bassa dam, which the government purchased from Portugal. This private-public affinity increases the opportunities for—and accusations of—rent-seeking behavior by officials.[56]

The government conducts internal audits of state administrative units but lacks the capacity to conduct them effectively. Another challenge is the proper auditing of the new provincial legislatures. One area where the government has continued to make reforms that increase transparency is in the administration of customs.[57] Mozambique has an Administrative Tribunal, an independent auditing body administratively and financially independent from the executive. This body examines and certifies the government budget and its management, and departments must respond to questions posed by the tribunal. However, the long-term effectiveness of this auditing body is still to be determined.

In 2006, the government introduced revenue administration reforms to ensure greater accountability of tax collection. The reforms included the introduction of a new general tax law, the creation of the Central Revenue Authority to improve the efficiency of tax administration, establishment of new tax tribunals staffed with professional judges, and an increase in tax audits.[58] Furthermore, the government has already begun to implement a software accounting system (e-SISTAFE) to better track funds.

The 2004 constitutional revisions also allowed for the creation of an ombudsman. Currently, the attorney general is tasked with investigating allegations of wrongdoing. Accusations of corruption are investigated, but it is not clear how free this process is from political influence. There is also intrusive legislative oversight of corruption investigations, with parliamentarians inquiring as to the status of investigations.

The state provides mechanisms by which victims of corruption may pursue their rights. However, in the case of police corruption, proving a case may be difficult. Moreover, lack of capacity in the judiciary may make it difficult to pursue a claim in a timely and effectual manner.

In 2006, eighteen key foreign aid donors, collectively called Program Aid Partners, who provide financial support for the government budget, stated that the government had made "no progress in implementation" of the anticorruption initiative. Some key international donors believe that one reason the government has not always ensured the judiciary's complete independence is to avoid close scrutiny of government corruption. This view is based on perceived delays in the pace of justice reform, notably regarding the 1997 plundering of the newly privatized Banco Austral. The newly appointed director of the bank, Antonio Siba-Siba Macuacua, was murdered in 2001, soon after he began investigating the bank's finances. No investigation was subsequently made of either the bank fraud or Siba-Siba's murder. Donor pressure for an audit eventually led to confirmation of misconduct by senior FRELIMO individuals, but as yet none has been prosecuted.[59] A second serious allegation is that profits from the country's reported status as a heroin transit point may indirectly fund FRELIMO.[60] To combat such activity, the parliament is considering adopting in 2007 a new anti-money laundering law, which would enable the creation of a new financial investigation unit.

The existence or pervasiveness of corruption in the primary, secondary, and tertiary educational sectors is unclear. Given the relatively low level of salaries paid to teachers and the overcrowding of classrooms, it would be surprising not to discover the types of corrupt practices reported in some other African countries.

In July 2006, Mozambique began the consultative process that forms part of the African Union's African Peer Review Mechanism. This self-evaluation process on good governance specifically includes public consultation.[61] Public sector information is published regularly, while the annual Government General Accounts Report is published after its approval by the assembly. The government has advanced toward ensuring greater transparency in the budget-making process. The annual budget must be approved by the legislature, and the budget and related budgetary legislation are available on the internet. The Ministry of Planning and Finance makes available additional reports that relate to budgetary matters. Finally, the Bulletin of the Republic also publishes government information.

Citizens have a legal right to government information. In practice, however, this right has been undermined by a lack of bureaucratic capacity, the cost of disseminating information to the broader public, and, according to media accusations, government stonewalling.[62] The media proposed in 2005 a draft freedom of information bill that fosters greater transparency and tackles corruption through publication of government documents.[63] By the end of 2006, the proposal had not yet gained a sufficient number of deputy sponsors to introduce the legislation into parliament's agenda.[64] The degree to which information about government services and decisions is made available to persons with disabilities is unclear. Government efforts are directed largely toward the broad dissemination of information via print, radio, and television.

In recent years most of the influx of foreign direct investment has been in extractive industries mega-projects. Given the importance of this sector to the country—and the great potential for corruption—the government committed itself in 2006 to following the Extractive Industries Transparency Initiative (EITI), a move strongly endorsed by the International Monetary Fund (IMF). However, this commitment has not yet been formalized in any specific legislation.[65] Since 2006, the government has been in the process of implementing a new software auditing system for more transparent and effective budget execution for the procurement of goods and services. Off-budget expenditures are now being included in an overall budget accounting system, which should provide a more detailed and accurate picture of all development projects.

The state attempts to ensure transparency, open bidding, and effective competition in the awarding of contracts. Procurement and bidding rules exist for the purchases of goods and services, with purchases above a certain threshold requiring bids. Some businesses have stated that these rules are not always observed. The IMF has urged procurement reform as a method to improve governance.

Mozambique is a low-income country that is heavily dependent on foreign assistance. This has allowed foreign donor agencies to exert considerable influence on government administration and distribution of foreign assistance; there were no reports of large-scale foreign aid fraud in recent years.

Recommendations

- The state needs to provide more effective oversight of the procurement process.

- The government needs to adhere fully to the IMF EITI principles.
- All public officials and political parties should be required to disclose publicly their assets and sources of funds.
- The parliament should debate and pass the media-proposed freedom of information law.

NOTES

1 *1990 Constitution of Mozambique.*

2 "Carter Center and Electoral Observatory Cite Irregularities" (Amsterdam: Association of European Parliamentarians for Africa [AWEPA], 21 December 2004); "Harsh Criticism from EU, Which Also Says Irregularities Could Reduce RENAMO Parliamentary Seats" (AWEPA, 20 December 2004), http://www.awepa.org/index2.php?option=com _content&task=view.

3 "Results analysis confirms fraud and misconduct in 2004 presidential election," AWEPA, *Mozambique Political Process Bulletin* 33 (1 November 2006).

4 *1990 Constitution of Mozambique*, Articles 31–43.

5 "Judiciary Not Always Independent, Report," UN Integrated Information Networks, 5 October 2006, http://www.allafrica.com/stories/printable/200511110176.html.

6 "RENAMO Claims Political 'Exclusion,' FRELIMO Denies," Mozambique News Agency, 30 November 2006, http://www.allafrica.com/stories/printable/200612020 10525.html; "Government Denies Practicing 'Social Exclusion'," Mozambique News Agency, 2 November 2005, http://www.allafrica.com/stories/printable/200511020382.html.

7 *Conceição Osório, Subvertendo o poder político? Análise de género das eleições legislativas em Moçambique, 2004* (Maputo: Women and Law in Southern Africa [WLSA] Moçambique, 2005); review in AWEPA, *Mozambique Political Process Bulletin* 33 (1 November 2006):16.

8 "Guebueza Reaffirms Press Freedom," Mozambique News Agency, 16 July 2006, http://www.allafrica.com/stories/printable/200607170311.html.

9 Ibid.

10 "City Council Threatens to Sue Independent Weekly," Mozambique News Agency, 18 February 2005, http://www.allafrica.com/stories/printable/200502210083.html.

11 "Africa 2006" (New York: Committee to Protect Journalists, 20 January–8 December 2006), http://www.cpj.org/regions_06/africa_06/africa_06.html#moz.

12 "Son of Former Head of State Charged in Cardoso Murder Case," allAfrica,com, Reporters Without Borders, 12 May 2006, http://www.allafrica.com/stories/printable /200605150954.html.

13 "Half-Hearted Police Apology to Journalists," Mozambique News Agency, 31 January 2005, http://www.allafrica.com/stories/printable/200501311158.html.

14 "Journalists Assaulted, Equipment Confiscated," Mozambique News Agency, 29 June 2005, http://www.allafrica.com/stories/printable/200506300826.html.

15 "Mozambique," *Afrobarometer*, May 2006, http://www.afrobarometer.org/mozambique .htm.

16 "Country profile: Mozambique," BBC News, 17 January 2007, http://news.bbc.co.uk/2 /hi/africa/country_profiles/1063120.stm.

17 "Internet Filtering Map" (Toronto: OpenNet Initiative, 2006), http://www.opennet .net/map/index2.html.

18 "Internet Access on the Increase," Mozambique News Agency, 20 October 2006, http:// www.allafrica.com/stories/printable/200610200625.html.

19 "Abolish AIM!, Shrieks RENAMO Deputy," Mozambique News Agency, 9 November 2005, http://www.allafrica.com/stories/printable/200511090609.html.

20 Ibid.

21 Mozambique, Covering January–December 2005 (London: Amnesty International [AI], 23 May 2006), http://web.amnesty.org/report2006/moz-summary-eng.

22 Mozambique: Justice Sector and the Rule of Law, 2006 (Johannesburg: Open Society Initiative for Southern Africa, 2006), http://www.afrimap.org/english/images/report /Mozambique%20Justice%20report%20(Eng).pdf.

23 "Hundreds of Prisoners Await Trial for Over Two Years," Mozambique News Agency, 1 February 2005, http://www.allafrica.com/stories/printable/200502010250.html.

24 "Prisoners Have Right to Medical Care—Madeira," Mozambique News Agency, 13 January 2005, http://www.allafrica.com/stories/printable/200501140246.html.

25 "Law Faculties Must Strengthen Legality—Minister," Mozambique News Agency, 8 November 2005, http://www.allafrica.com/stories/printable/200511080527.html.

26 "No Intention of Reintroducing One-Party State—FRELIMO," Mozambique News Agency, 29 June 2005, http://www.allafrica.com/stories/printable/20061108136.html.

27 Bayano Valy, "Citizens Become Judge, Jury, and Executioner," Mozambique News Agency, 7 November 2006, http://www.allafrica.com/stories/printable/2006110801 36.html.

28 "Gender Equality Is Human Rights Issue—Garrido," Mozambique News Agency, 11 November 2005, http://www.allafrica.com/stories/printable/200511110176.html.

29 "Human Rights League Launches Report," Mozambique News Agency, 5 May 2005, http://www.allafrica.com/stories/printable/200505050258.html.

30 "Female Genital Mutilation in North," Mozambique News Agency, 8 December 2006, http://www.allafrica.com/stories/printable/200612080439.html.

31 "Assembly Ratifies Protocol on Rights of African Women," Mozambique News Agency, 8 December 2005, http://www.allafrica.com/stories/printable/200512080369.html.

32 "Leader of People Trafficking Racket Arrested," Mozambique News Agency, 12 April 2006, http://www.allafrica.com/stories/printable/2006104120538.html.

33 "Human Rights League Violates Rights," Mozambique News Agency, 26 October 2006, http://www.allafrica.com/stories/printable/200610260464.html.

34 "Mozambique: New Legislation on Children," Mozambique News Agency, 29 March 2007, http://www.allafrica.com/stories/200703290750.html.

35 "Languages of Mozambique," in Raymond G. Gordon Jr., Ethnologue: Languages of the World, 15th ed. (Dallas, TX: SIL, Inc., 2005), http://www.ethnologue.com/show _country.asp?name=Mozambique (accessed February 2007).

36 "The World Factbook, 2007" (Springfield, VA: U.S. Central Intelligence Agency, 2007), https://www.cia.gov/cia/publications/factbook/index.html.

[37] "Police Attack Nampula Students," Mozambique News Agency, 11 February 2005, http://www.allafrica.com/stories/printable/200502110548.html.

[38] "Judiciary Is Losing its Fear, Claims Minister," Mozambique News Agency, 5 January 2006, http://www.allafrica.com/stories/printable/200601050373.html.

[39] "Huge Backlog of Cases in Mozambican Courts," Mozambique News Agency, 1 March 2005, http://www.allafrica.com/stories/printable/200503010575.html.

[40] "Interview with a community court judge, Nampula province," 11 August 2005, p. 128, *Mozambique: Justice Sector and the Rule of Law, 2006* (Johannesburg: Open Society Initiative for Southern Africa, 2006), http://www.afrimap.org/english/images/report/Mozambique%20Justice%20report%20(Eng).pdf.

[41] "Prisoners Die in Mozambique Mine," BBC News, 30 October 2006, http://news.bbc.co.uk/go/pr/fr/-/2/hi/africa/6100324.stm.

[42] "Public Image 'Very Poor'—Deputy Minister," Mozambique News Agency, 15 March 2006, http://www.allafrica.com/stories/printable/200603150551.html.

[43] "FRELIMO Members Criticize State of Justice System," Mozambique News Agency, 11 December 2006, http://www.allafrica.com/stories/printable/200612120044.html.

[44] "Policemen Jailed for Executing Prisoners," Mozambique News Agency, 5 October 2006, http://www.allafrica.com/stories/printable/200610050636.html.

[45] *Mozambique, Covering January–December 2004* (AI, 25 May 2005), http://web.amnesty.org/report2005/moz-summary-eng.

[46] Salane Muchanga, "Mozambique Discovers its Gay Minority," Afrol News/Savana, 2 February 2007, http://www.afrol.com/articles/22322.

[47] "Survey Finds Police the Most Dishonest Institution," Mozambique News Agency, 9 June 2005, http://www.allafrica.com/stories/printable/200506090443.html.

[48] "Matola Officials Sacked for Illegal Land Sales," Mozambique News Agency, 13 February 2006, http://www.allafrica.com/stories/printable/200602130700.html.

[49] "Republic of Mozambique: Letter of Intent, Memorandum of Economic and Financial Policies, and Technical Memorandum of Understanding" (Maputo: Government of Mozambique, 24 October 2006), http://www.imf.org/External/NP/LOI/2006/moz/102406.pdf.

[50] "Guebuza Denounces Corrupt Civil Servants," Mozambique News Agency, 26 April 2005, http://www.allafrica.com/stories/printable/20050426059.html.

[51] "Corruption Perceptions Index" (Berlin: Transparency International, 2004, 2005, 2006), http://www.transparency.org.

[52] *Mozambique, Covering January–December 2005* (London: Amnesty International [AI], 23 May 2006), http://web.amnesty.org/report2006/moz-summary-eng.

[53] "Call for Alliance Against Corruption," Mozambique Information Agency, 8 December 2005, http://www.allafrica.com/stories/printable/200512080370.html.

[54] "Assembly Ratified Anti-Corruption Conventions," Mozambique News Agency, 26 April 2006, http://www.allafrica.com/stories/printable/200604260688.html.

[55] "No Progress in Anti-Corruption Campaign," Mozambique News Agency, 14 September 2006, http://www.allafrica.com/stories/printable/200609140800.html.

[56] "New Hydro Plant for Mozambique," *Energy in Africa*, 13 December 2006, http://www.energyinafrica.net/brief/power/521210.htm.

57 Evan Davies, "Mozambique Learns to Build from Within," BBC News, 7 May 2005, http://news.bbc.co.uk/go/pr/fr/-/1/hi/business/4654455.stm.

58 "Republic of Mozambique: Letter of Intent . . ." (Government of Mozambique), http://www.imf.org/External/NP/LOI/2006/moz/102406.pdf.

59 "Donors and government at loggerheads over governance, corruption," AWEPA, *Mozambique Political Process Bulletin* 33 (1 November 2006): 11–13.

60 "Q&A: Mozambique Votes," BBC News, 29 November 2004, http://newsvote.bbc.co.uk /mpapps/pagetools/print/news.bbc.co.uk/2/hi/africa/4051707.stm; "Corruption, Law, and Justice" (AWEPA, 17 February 2005), http://www.awepa.org/index.php?option =com_content&task=view&id=462.

61 "Mozambique Sets Up Peer Review Forum," allAfrica.com, Mozambique Information Agency, 13 July 2006, http://www.allafrica.com/stories/printable/200607130661.html.

62 "Journalists Welcome Access to Information Bill," allAfrica.com, International Freedom of Expression Clearing House, 11 August 2005, http://www.allafrica.com/stories/print-able/2005081100009.html.

63 "Note on the Draft Law of Mozambique on Access to Official Sources of Information" (London: Article 19—Global Campaign for Free Expression, June 2005), http://www .article19.org/pdfs/analysis/mozambique-july-2005.pdf.

64 "Mozambique: Journalists Welcome Draft Information Bill," allAfrica.com, UN Integrated Regional Information Networks, 2 August 2005, http://www.allafrica.com /stories/printable/200508020942.html.

65 "Republic of Mozambique: Letter of Intent . . ." (Government of Mozambique), http://www.imf.org/External/NP/LOI/2006/moz/102406.pdf.

PARAGUAY

CAPITAL: Asunción
POPULATION: 6.1 million
GNI PER CAPITA: $1,400

SCORES	2005	2007
ACCOUNTABILITY AND PUBLIC VOICE:	4.10	4.29
CIVIL LIBERTIES:	4.06	4.03
RULE OF LAW:	3.92	3.32
ANTICORRUPTION AND TRANSPARENCY:	3.28	3.33

(scores are based on a scale of 0 to 7, with 0 representing weakest and 7 representing strongest performance)

Peter Lambert

INTRODUCTION

In 2007, the Colorado Party celebrates sixty years in power, having successfully negotiated periods of political instability, civil war, dictatorship, and democratic transition. Since the end of the dictatorship of General Alfredo Stroessner in 1989, the Colorado Party has won all four presidential elections, despite administrations repeatedly characterized by economic mismanagement and inefficiency, rampant corruption, and almost constant interfactional power struggles within the party. Indeed, to a great extent, established political and bureaucratic elites in the Colorado Party have successfully defended their privileges in the new democratic environment and controlled many aspects of the (unconsolidated) transition.

Overall, progress has been slow in the strengthening of political institutions, participation, and representation, as well as the implementation of rule of law. The opposition remains divided and ineffectual, unable to unite and seriously challenge Colorado hegemony, while significant

Peter Lambert is a Senior Lecturer in Latin American Studies at the University of Bath, UK. He has written extensively on different aspects of Paraguayan politics.

sections of the population remain broadly skeptical about democracy as a political system. The possibility of elections bringing authoritarian or populist politicians to power remains high, as witnessed by the continued support for ex-general Lino Oviedo, imprisoned since 2004 on charges relating to his failed 1996 coup attempt.

Central to the growing sense of disillusionment with the performance of democracy has been the lack of socioeconomic progress. Despite improvements over the past three years, Paraguay ranks behind only Bolivia in South America in terms of human development and suffers from low coverage of basic healthcare, education, and sanitation. Paraguay is one of the most unequal countries in the continent in terms of land and income distribution, with a GINI Index rating of 57.8.[1] It is also one of the poorest, with a per capita income of just US$1,280— significantly below the poverty line. According to government figures, 38.2 percent of the population lives in poverty and 15.5 percent lives in extreme poverty.[2] This is exacerbated by combined unemployment and underemployment affecting 37.9 percent of Paraguayans; furthermore, an estimated 60 percent to 70 percent of workers do not even receive the minimum wage of approximately US$180 per month.[3] Despite a reduction in poverty levels since 2003, years of underinvestment in social spending make it unlikely Paraguay will meet the 2015 target for achieving its Millennium Development Goals.

Faced with these challenges, President Nicanor Duarte Frutos promised economic recovery, anticorruption measures, and increased social spending when he came to power in 2003. Following years of stagnation and recession, in the past three and a half years the government has avoided the widely predicted economic collapse and overseen macroeconomic recovery. It has attacked corruption and inefficiency in public management and increased targeted social spending, correctly identifying these as the key governance issues. Nevertheless, progress has been limited by opposition in Congress as well as by powerful vested interests, mainly from within the Colorado Party. Crucially, in May 2005, the Minister of Finance, Dionisio Borda, widely seen as the key figure behind progressive, democratic reforms in the first two years of the administration, resigned. His departure reflected the strength of conservative pressures within the ruling party and was seen as a significant blow to the administration's reform efforts.

ACCOUNTABILITY AND PUBLIC VOICE

FREE AND FAIR ELECTORAL LAWS AND ELECTIONS:	3.75
EFFECTIVE AND ACCOUNTABLE GOVERNMENT:	3.25
CIVIC ENGAGEMENT AND CIVIC MONITORING:	5.67
MEDIA INDEPENDENCE AND FREEDOM OF EXPRESSION:	4.50
CATEGORY AVERAGE:	**4.29**

Although in principle democratic institutions and procedures provide ample possibility for the effective rotation of power among different political parties, in practice the Colorado Party has won all four presidential elections since 1989.[4] Despite electoral irregularities in some polling stations and accusations of misuse of state assets in electoral campaigns, however, there have been no reports of systematic nationwide irregularities, and elections have been broadly free and fair, especially following the partial introduction of electronic voting since 2003. Due to its powerful electoral machinery and deep clientelistic networks in rural areas, the Colorado Party has maintained tight control of government and the state and has used limited power-sharing effectively in recent years (1995, 1999–2003, and 2005) to pass key legislation. This lack of effective opposition reflects the weakness of a party system that is characterized by clientelism, working practices designed to capture votes rather than articulate or channel social interests, and a lack of ideological differentiation between parties. There is a widespread perception of political corruption within Congress, with the buying and selling of votes seen as commonplace.[5]

The political system in general is subject to low levels of confidence and legitimacy in Paraguay, as evidenced not only by low levels of electoral participation, but also by an apparent decline in citizen support for democracy. According to the 2005 Latinobarómetro Report, Paraguayans, when compared with other Latin Americans, offer the least opposition to the acceptability of military rule (just 31 percent compared with the Latin American average of 62 percent), the least support for democracy (just 32 percent compared with a Latin American average of 53 percent), and a level of satisfaction with the performance of democracy of just 17 percent.[6] Further disillusionment is perhaps reflected in signs of increasing support for ex-president Stroessner (before his death in August 2006) in the form of demonstrations to celebrate his birthday, opinion polls rating him as the most popular president since 1950, and the rise of a powerful neo-stronista faction within the ruling Colorado Party.[7]

In November 2005, President Duarte announced his intention to run for the Colorado Party presidency, in apparent violation of the constitution, the electoral code, and the party statute, all of which prohibit the president from holding any other professional post. Following an ambiguous ruling by the Superior Tribunal of Electoral Justice (TSJE) in January 2006 that he could stand but not hold the party presidency, in February 2006 Duarte won the internal Colorado Party elections with 63.4 percent of the vote. The Supreme Court then upheld his right to hold both posts, prompting political uproar and large-scale public demonstrations against both Duarte and what was seen as a politicized Supreme Court. Under increasing pressure, Duarte was inaugurated as party president and then immediately ceded the post to party vice president José Alberto Alderete.

Meanwhile, the president continued to push for constitutional reform to strengthen executive powers and allow for presidential reelection. His case was bolstered, at least in his own eyes, by the victory of the Colorado Party in the municipal elections in November 2006, which Duarte saw as a public endorsement both of his administration and of his plans for constitutional reform. With the opposition failing to put forward joint candidates in many municipalities, the Colorado Party won around 50 percent of the vote and 150 out of 231 municipalities, including the capital, Asunción, where Evanhy de Gallegos became the first female mayor. Immediately following the results, the Colorado Party announced it would formally push for an amendment of Article 229 of the constitution to allow for Duarte's reelection. However, the president faces an uphill struggle. Even if he were to secure a majority in Congress and the Senate—the latter of which is unlikely—he would then need to win a popular referendum—a difficult challenge given that according to polls in December 2006, his plans for constitutional reform have the support of just 31 percent of the population.[8] While the need for constitutional reform—in order to prevent the opposition in Congress from repeatedly blocking crucial initiatives (such as banking reform, civil service reform, and tax reform) for sectarian reasons—is widely recognized, there is a fear that it could be used inappropriately to alter the balance of power between executive, legislature, and judiciary in favor of the former, reducing the ability of the other two to act as an effective check on excessive executive power.

Despite continued pressure from such groups as Transparency Paraguay, no reform of legislation on party campaign financing has taken place. With state funding for party campaigns limited and based on previous election results, the bulk of party finances are private. However, as parties are not required to reveal their funding sources and few effective checks and balances are in place, there is a lack of transparency and clarity regarding the origins and uses of funds. This, added to the widespread practice of awarding congressional seats (through allocation of high positions on party electoral lists) in exchange for personal contributions to electoral campaigns, has allowed privileged interest groups direct access to political power and influence. Moreover, due to a lack of transparent accountancy, misuse of public funds and state resources for electoral campaigns is common among all parties, especially the ruling Colorado Party, which maintains an extensive (and expensive) clientelistic network as its electoral base.

Although the 1996 electoral code requires a 20 percent minimum of female candidates on electoral lists, the Colorado Party (2005) and the opposition PLRA (2006) have both increased their minimum to 33 percent.[9] However, no party has adopted a system of alternate gender listing in order to counter the common practice of placing male candidates higher up on the party electoral lists. Although there are no legal impediments to their participation, women are significantly underrepresented in public political life, especially at senior levels. There are just eight female deputies (out of eighty), six senators (out of forty-five), one departmental governor (out of seventeen), and one female member of the Supreme Court of Justice (out of nine). Of the three female cabinet members in 2003, only one remains (in Education and Culture), although Mónica Pérez was named new head of the Central Bank of Paraguay in 2005. There are no indigenous people in high office.

The state sector remains highly politicized and is closely tied to the ruling Colorado Party, representing a vital source of its electoral support. Appointments and promotions are frequently made on the basis of political allegiance, and in elections since 1989, political harassment of personnel opposed to ruling party candidates has been reported. The sector is also characterized by high levels of institutionalized corruption, extreme informality, lack of institutionalization, and low levels of efficiency and effectiveness, as well as a notable lack of transparency.[10] Crucial civil service reform—in the form of Law 1626, passed in December 2000 to introduce new transparent, merit-based systems for civil service selection and promotion—remains suspended in the Supreme Court, demonstrating the endurance of a clientelistic political culture. Efforts by President Duarte to reform the state sector have met with some success (see Anticorruption and Transparency) but have often been blocked by vested political interests, generally within the Colorado Party.

Despite entering the transition weak and fragmented, Paraguay's civil society has seen significant growth since 1989. This is especially true of nongovernmental organizations (NGOs), which are free to operate without undue government interference and have played an active role in promoting policy reform on a broad range of issues, including human rights, government transparency and accountability, citizens' (including women's and indigenous peoples') rights, compulsory military service, and protection of the environment.[11] Groups representing more powerful—especially landowning—sectors, such as the Asociación Rural del Paraguay, enjoy significant political influence and leverage.

Freedom of the press and media is guaranteed by the constitution and generally upheld by the state. The government does not attempt to influence media content through illegal methods (such as bribery), nor does it fund specific media outlets for propaganda purposes. However, press freedom is threatened by two constraints. First, the constitutional requirements that reporting be "accurate, responsible and even-handed" (Article 28) and that expression not "exceed the bounds of acceptable criticism" (Article 151) mean that the (politically motivated) threat or use of defamation and libel laws is often applied to intimidate and silence journalists and media outlets. In a notorious, but by no means isolated case in 2006, the Supreme Court upheld the criminal defamation conviction and a fine of US$200,000 against Aldo Zucolillo, director of ABC Color, a paper renowned for its role in the struggle for democracy, brought by a senator from the Colorado Party. Zucolillo currently faces eighteen lawsuits over articles his paper has published on corruption and abuse of power.

Second, journalists who undertake political investigations, especially into corruption and drug trafficking, continue to risk intimidation, threats, and violence and receive minimal police protection. In February 2006, journalist Enrique Galeano disappeared following his investigations into drug and arms smuggling in Concepción, northern Paraguay. Despite accusations that prominent local authorities, including the police and Colorado Party representatives, were implicated, as well as national pressure for a public inquiry, nobody was prosecuted and the case was closed.

Recommendations

- Reform of party financing is required to include greater monitoring of public and private funding of political parties, tighter controls on misuse of state funds, and greater transparency in terms of party expenditures and accounts.
- Political parties should adopt rules requiring gender alternation on party lists in order to fulfill their commitment to increasing women's presence in the government.
- The state should ensure that defamation cases do not hamper the full enjoyment of freedom of speech or lead to censorship. Moreover, the state should reconsider Article 28 of the constitution with a view to prevent preemptive or punitive political libel suits against journalists.
- A thorough state reform program, in the form of or based on Law 1626, needs to be implemented in order to introduce merit-based systems of appointment and promotion throughout the state sector.

CIVIL LIBERTIES

PROTECTION FROM STATE TERROR, UNJUSTIFIED IMPRISONMENT, AND TORTURE:	2.57
GENDER EQUITY:	4.00
RIGHTS OF ETHNIC, RELIGIOUS, AND OTHER DISTINCT GROUPS:	3.00
FREEDOM OF CONSCIENCE AND BELIEF:	6.00
FREEDOM OF ASSOCIATION AND ASSEMBLY:	4.60
CATEGORY AVERAGE:	**4.03**

Although torture is specifically prohibited under the constitution and penal code, numerous examples of police abuse committed in order to punish, intimidate, or gain confessions have been compiled by the Attorney General's Office. Furthermore, following a visit in November 2006, UN human rights expert and Special Rapporteur Manfred Nowak reported that torture is still widely used in police custody and called for the practice to be fully criminalized, measures put in place to prevent it, and all perpetrators to be prosecuted.[12] The establishment of a Special Human Rights Unit within the Office of the State Prosecutor in 2005 was widely seen as an important step forward. However, there have still been no convictions for torture since the criminal code entered into force in 1999, reflecting high levels of impunity and ineffective systems for investigation, protection, and redress. The continuation of torture, despite pressure from international organizations ranging from Amnesty International to the United Nations High Commissioner for Human Rights, is due to a number of factors, including the failure of the state to widen the definition of torture in the criminal code to comply with Article 1 of the UN Convention against Torture so that the practice be fully criminalized.

Following widespread criticism of prison conditions, three independent, interinstitutional commissions have been set up since 2004 in compliance with the Optional Protocol to the Convention against Torture. Comprising representatives from human rights NGOs, diplomatic personnel, unions, and the Senate Human Rights Commission, these commissions carry out unannounced inspections of Paraguay's prisons. Their reports severely criticized appalling conditions, which include: severe overcrowding (for example, the country's largest prison, Tacumbú, holds 3,166 inmates although its capacity is just 1,500[13]); inadequate basic health, medical, and sanitation facilities; rampant corruption; mistreatment of prisoners, including torture; neglect of prisoners suffering from mental health problems; failure to separate juveniles from adults, men from women, the condemned from those awaiting trial, and serious from minor offenders; and lack of adequate staffing, with an average of just one guard for every eighty inmates.[14] The government has authorized new prison facilities, but overall the prison system remains desperately underfunded. A further key contributory factor is that prisoners do not in practice have the right to a swift trial. Pretrial detention accounts for 75 percent of inmates, and it is common practice to release prisoners before trial on the basis that they have already completed the minimum sentence for their alleged crime.[15]

There are no political prisoners in Paraguay, and the constitution prohibits arbitrary arrest and guarantees habeas corpus. Although in theory the accused is presumed innocent until proven guilty, detentions without corresponding judicial orders or other requirements established under law are common, with those arrested often held in detention for excessive periods. Although the accused have the right to a defense lawyer at public expense, the state lacks the resources to provide counsel for many poor defendants, who often go to trial with no legal representation. Past abuses of human rights, however, are being dealt with more effectively. The combined efforts of the Human Rights Ombudsman (Defensor del Pueblo), established in 2001, and the nonpartisan Truth and Justice Commission, set up in 2004 to investigate abuses committed under the Stroessner dictatorship, have so far resulted in 1,069 victims of torture being awarded compensation totaling approximately US$14 million, with many outstanding cases still to be compensated.[16]

Following widespread criticism of the armed forces for enforced conscription of minors and mistreatment of conscripts, the Duarte administration established a human rights office within the military with the aim of reviewing procedures, holding unannounced inspections, and investigating and reporting on conditions and abuses. The office also has a remit to help NGOs investigate illegal recruitment and abuse. However, both practices continue, and no prosecutions have yet been brought.[17]

The government has also been criticized for tolerating excessive use of force by the police and army when they are dealing with demonstrations, especially by landless peasants. Other forms of peasant protest, such as roadblocks and land occupations, have been subjected to particularly excessive responses either directly by state security forces, or—more commonly—by private security forces organized by landowners. The state has consistently failed to intervene to protect against such abuse and shown little interest in pursuing those guilty of perpetrating such violence.

In October 2005, Paraguay presented its 2nd Periodic Report on Human Rights to the UN Human Rights Committee.[18] Despite some areas of limited praise, the committee criticized the insufficient mechanisms for judicial protection, compensation, and remedy against discrimination for disadvantaged groups, including children, women, indigenous people, and people with disabilities.

Overall, significant progress has been made in creating a more favorable legal framework for gender equality since 1989, in great part due to an active women's movement that has pushed for progressive legal reform. Paraguay has ratified all international conventions protecting women's rights and introduced an array of posts and programs, including the highly effective Secretariat for Women's Affairs, which promotes gender equality in public policy.

However, despite institutional and legal advances, four factors illustrate the many structural obstacles facing women. First, sexual and domestic violence remain widespread, with insufficient mechanisms for protection of victims or prosecution. According to the Secretariat for Women's Affairs, reports of violence against women increased from 426 in 2000 to 2,036 in 2005.[19] Although domestic violence is a criminal offense, it must be habitual before being seen as such, and is then only punishable by a fine. Second, discrimination in the workplace means women suffer lower pay, poorer training opportunities, and fewer chances for promotion. This is especially the case in the unregulated informal sector, which accounts for over 40 percent of the workforce, and within that, domestic service, a sector in which approximately 25 percent of the female workforce is employed.[20] There has been no revision of the norms that govern the conditions and rights in this area. Third, Paraguay suffers from high rates of maternal mortality, especially in rural areas, related to a lack of adequate healthcare and, according to women's groups, the continued penalization of abortion (dating from 1910), which leads to unsafe, illegal abortions at potential risk of life and health. Fourth, anecdotal evidence suggests that hundreds of women are trafficked abroad annually for sexual exploitation, especially through the Tri-Border Area, the notoriously lawless zone between Paraguay, Brazil and Argentina. Despite the establishment in 2005 of a new office to deal with trafficking in this region, support for victims remains virtually nonexistent, while law enforcement agencies remain underfunded and convictions of traffickers rare.

Equal opportunity for people with disabilities is guaranteed under the constitution, which also stipulates that the state must provide disabled people with healthcare, education, and professional training. However, in practice, the absence of appropriate legislation means disabled people are not provided for and face significant discrimination in terms of public attitudes and access to the labor market, public transport, and public and private buildings.[21] Nor are government services and decisions made available in formats accessible to disabled people. The appalling conditions (lack of adequate sanitary facilities, lack of trained staff, and lack of adequate nutrition), suffered by the 460 residents of the Neuropsychiatric Hospital in Asunción, which became headlines in 2006, underline the depth of discrimination.

Indigenous people (approximately 1.7 percent of the population) have the lowest indicators in terms of social development of any sector in Paraguayan society and suffer from extreme poverty, marginalization, and exclusion. Favorable legal and constitutional protection is routinely circumvented or ignored and masks continued neglect by the state and a lack of judicial and police protection. This was highlighted by two recent rulings of the Inter-American Commission on Human Rights (IACHR). In 2005, the court found in favor of the Yaskye Axa community, while in March 2006, it found in favor of the Sawhoyamaxa community—in both cases for displacement of communities from ancestral lands. In the case of the latter, the court ordered the return of lands with compensation and also emphasized that it is the responsibility of the state to ensure full equality in land, education, health, and judicial protection. In August 2006, the government paid US$12,000 of the US$18,000 the court had ordered in compensation.[22]

Indigenous people are largely excluded from political and economic participation due to a lack of adequate access to land, financial resources, and basic social services such as education and health care; additionally, they have no high-level political representation. In terms of work, they suffer routine violations of basic labor rights and protection, reflected in extremely low or nonexistent pay and unacceptable working conditions, especially in the Chaco region. Discrimination and inequality are deeply embedded and reflected in economic, social, and cultural marginalization. For example, illiteracy rates are approximately 64 percent for indigenous people, compared with 6 percent for the population as a whole; child malnutrition is 13.7 percent nationally but 41 percent among indigenous children; 58 percent of the population nationally have access to safe drinking water but only 2.5 percent of indigenous people; and primary school completion is 70 percent nationally but less than 20 percent among indigenous children.[23]

Freedom of religion is respected both in the constitution and in practice, with no undue state interference or restrictions. The Catholic

Church freely criticizes the government, especially over issues of poverty, corruption, and inequality.

Although freedom of assembly is generally recognized, there are several restrictions. For example, in Asunción demonstrations are restricted to certain times and places, while nationally there are limits on the time, place, and nature of protest (for example, road closure is prohibited), and demonstrations require prior police authorization. Such restrictions have been criticized as "neither reasonable nor necessary in a democratic society, have no legitimate objective, and are not motivated by pressing social need."[24] Those who violate them in peaceful acts of civil disobedience, however, are subject to criminal prosecution.

Freedom of association is generally respected, including the right to form and join trade unions, in both the public and private sectors (with the exception of the armed forces and the police), and citizens are not compelled to belong to any association. Despite constitutional protection, union activity remains inadequately guaranteed by the state, and violations of international labor standards, such as harassment and firing of union organizers, the establishment of competing company unions, and violations of collective agreements and contracts are common. Fear of reprisal and economic insecurity contribute to the weakness of the union movement, which includes only 6.4 percent of the workforce.[25]

Recommendations

- A reform of the prison system needs to be introduced and should include an increased budget to permit improvements in infrastructure, facilities, and conditions to comply with constitutional and legal requirements.
- The efficiency of the judicial system needs to be improved in order to reduce the excessive proportion of prisoners held in extended preventive, pretrial detention. For minor offences, prosecutors and judges should set firm court dates within the prescribed legal period or free accused criminals at nominal bail.
- The police need appropriate training in the observance of human rights and public order. Cases of torture, impunity, and excessive use of force should be dealt with expeditiously and transparently.
- The criminal code needs to be amended to classify torture in full accordance with Article 1 of the UN Convention against Torture and

permit full implementation of its procedures regarding investigation, prosecution, punishment, and compensation.

- The state needs to be proactive in the protection of constitutional and international human rights of indigenous people, with particular emphasis on stronger legal protection of ancestral lands, greater access to basic social welfare services, and protection from labor and other exploitation.
- Legislation needs to be passed to modify Law 1066/97, which regulates the right of public assembly, in order to guarantee full rights to peaceful demonstration.

RULE OF LAW

INDEPENDENT JUDICIARY:	3.00
PRIMACY OF RULE OF LAW IN CIVIL AND CRIMINAL MATTERS:	3.67
ACCOUNTABILITY OF SECURITY FORCES AND MILITARY TO CIVILIAN AUTHORITIES:	3.25
PROTECTION OF PROPERTY RIGHTS:	3.67
EQUAL TREATMENT UNDER THE LAW:	3.00
CATEGORY AVERAGE:	**3.32**

There is still no objective public system for selection and designation of judges, district attorneys, and prosecutors to ensure that selection and promotion are based on merit. Instead, the judiciary continues to be subject to a high level of party political interference, which undermines the integrity of the system of checks and balances and the independence of the sector. Members of the Supreme Court of Justice, the High Court of Electoral Justice, and the Council of the Judiciary—as well as others lower down in the judiciary—are all designated on the basis of agreements between political parties, in accordance with the number of congressional seats held. Hence appointments are made on grounds of political service, allegiance, and loyalty rather than merit and expertise, experience, or qualifications, raising serious doubts about the impartiality and independence of the judicial system from political pressures.[26] Although rulings may occasionally go against the government (with which the government will comply) the Supreme Court is ultimately a political body, with loyalties weighted towards the Colorado Party.

Despite internationally funded reform projects, the judiciary is widely seen as inefficient, corrupt, insufficiently funded, and unable either to combat corruption and impunity or to protect citizens' (especially poor citizens') rights. Local judges and prosecutors often have not received adequate training and are subject to undue pressures from local economic and political elites who seek to block or delay investigations or influence individual judges. The overloaded and underfunded system is simply unable to deal with the enormous backlog of cases; indeed, long-running cases are routinely dropped after four years (except for those involving human rights abuses committed by state actors during the dictatorship). The law grants access to independent counsel but in practice the government lacks resources to provide it to the vast majority of defendants. Although some progress has been made over the past few years, there are still only 148 public defenders in the country, with the result that most Paraguayans are forced to rely on private finance, thus limiting adequate defense to those who have the necessary assets.

The reform of the Supreme Court by President Duarte in 2003 epitomized the problems facing the judicial system. Given the court's reputation for institutional corruption, the president's actions received widespread support. Resulting negotiations between political parties over replacement members, however, revealed the level of politicization of the process. Some of the court's subsequent decisions, such as upholding President Duarte's right to run for the presidency of the Colorado Party in early 2006, also were seen as reflecting the high level of politicization of the Court—and of the judiciary as a whole. Two further cases in 2006 reflect the ambiguity of progress. First, advances were illustrated when Heriberto Galeano, commander of the Presidential Guard and personal friend of President Duarte, was retired from his post and later arrested for illicit enrichment. In contrast to this success, efforts to prosecute the president of Congress, Víctor Bogado, for the same crime were blocked by the Colorado Party in Congress on the grounds of congressional immunity.[27] Both cases were brought by Arnaldo Guizzio, the widely respected anticorruption state prosecutor. As a result, the Supreme Court came under intense (but eventually unsuccessful) pressure from Colorado Party interests to refuse the renewal of Guizzio's appointment in December 2006, provoking a public outcry over political intervention in judicial affairs.

The police are inadequately funded and staffed and poorly trained in all aspects of their work, from public order to investigative procedure. Such is the inefficiency of the police that it is common for those who can afford the cost to employ private investigators to pursue criminal investigations. The police are also widely perceived as institutionally corrupt. There is evidence of continued police involvement in crime and links to local and national mafias, and police enjoy a high level of impunity in terms of corruption, excessive use of violence, and abuse of human rights. Reform of the national police has mainly focused on equipment improvements, although the new administration has promised to implement measures to professionalize the organization.

Following their central role in the dictatorship, there has been a noticeable depoliticization of the military in the past decade. Despite three bouts of political instability involving sectors of the armed forces in 1996, 1999, and 2001, the military no longer plays an overt role in politics. Troops have routinely been used in quelling disturbances of public order, especially in recent land disputes and occupations, but overall the military appears to be firmly under civilian control. However, this does not mean that it is accountable to the public: impunity is still widely seen as characteristic of the armed forces, and there have been no prosecutions of members of the armed forces for human rights abuses during the dictatorship. Nor is the military free from political interference. In November 2006, President Duarte agreed to opposition demands to retire the head of the armed forces, General José Key Kanawaza, and twelve other military commanders, as part of a political deal, despite the fact that the professional conduct of those retired was not in question.

The state's monopoly on the use of force is not constant throughout the country, especially in areas in the eastern border region next to Brazil. This is complicated by the growing Brazilian population in the region, as well as the presence of trafficking in contraband, arms, and drugs. However, despite U.S. fears of the Tri-Border Area being used as a base for international terrorism, investigations by representatives from Paraguay, Brazil, Argentina, and the United States led to a joint declaration in December 2006 that "no terrorism activities" had been detected.[28]

Property rights are a contentious issue in a country that is renowned for its inequality of land ownership: 30 percent of peasants are landless, while just 10 percent of the population owns 66 percent of the land.[29] Conflict erupted in 2004–2005, with nationwide marches, road closures, demonstrations, and land occupations by organized peasants as they attempted to force the government to address the lack of land reform. The occupations led to violent conflicts between peasants and both public and (increasingly) private security forces, and peasants were subject to threats, violence, and unlawful arrest by police and local judges. In 2006 there were eight politically motivated killings of peasant activists, none of which have yet led to convictions.[30] In one incident in Caaguazú in June 2006, two peasants were shot dead and five injured when paramilitary forces, acting with the apparent complicity of the police, opened fire on land occupiers.[31] Despite the conflict, and government promises, there has been little advance in terms of land reform, and the underlying problems of vast inequalities in land ownership and distribution as well as high levels of landlessness remain unaddressed and unresolved.

Perhaps most worrying has been the emergence of Citizen Security Committees, armed groups often created by powerful local (often land-owning) interests, which are tolerated and even encouraged by the authorities. Complaints against these groups related to threats, torture, harassment, illegal arrest, and extrajudicial killings led Senator José Nicolás Morínigo, president of the Senate Human Rights Commission of the, to present a bill in mid-2006 to prohibit civil organizations that aim to maintain public order. As of March 2007, the bill remains before Parliament.

In eastern Paraguay, indigenous communities have frequently complained of nonrecognition of land titles as well as illegal, often violent, expropriation of traditional lands by private individuals, groups, and companies—usually for intensive agricultural production (such as soya). As the IACHR found in 2006, the state is failing to provide adequate protection of indigenous territory or to protect communities from uncontrolled and increasing deforestation and ecological degradation. In practice, there are insufficient police or legal safeguards to protect indigenous land from illegal occupations, and almost half of all communities have no definite, legal assurance of land ownership. INDI, the state assistance body, is currently in a state of near collapse due to the failure of the congress to allocate full funds for the sixth consecutive year.[32]

Recommendations

- Professionalization of the judiciary should include special provisions for the implementation of an objective, transparent, merit-based system for selection, designation, and promotion of judges, district attorneys, and prosecutors. An appropriate system of penalties for misconduct and the prohibition of political influence on the judiciary at all levels is needed.
- Greater resources are needed to improve the role and accessibility of public defenders and to provide training to improve police investigative capacity.
- To combat impunity, a clear judicial complaints system needs to be established, to include guarantees of anonymity and protection for the plaintiff, transparency of investigation, and a set framework of investigative and disciplinary procedures.
- The state should pass legislation to prohibit Citizen Security Committees, as well as all other nonstate armed groups, and act to dissolve and disarm all such groups immediately.
- The government must comply with its commitment to introduce a thorough and long-overdue land reform program to defuse rising tensions and conflict in the countryside.

ANTICORRUPTION AND TRANSPARENCY

ENVIRONMENT TO PROTECT AGAINST CORRUPTION:	2.80
EXISTENCE OF LAWS AND ETHICAL STANDARDS BETWEEN	
PRIVATE AND PUBLIC SECTORS:	3.75
ENFORCEMENT OF ANTICORRUPTION LAWS:	3.50
GOVERNMENTAL TRANSPARENCY:	3.29
CATEGORY AVERAGE:	**3.33**

When the dictatorship collapsed in 1989, Paraguay was already notorious for endemic, systemic corruption. However, it is widely believed that corruption has actually increased during the transition, pervading all levels of society and reaching the highest levels of government. Currently, two of the country's four democratic ex-presidents (Raúl Cubas

Grau and Luis Ángel González Macchi) are serving prison sentences for illicit enrichment, while one (Juan Carlos Wasmosy) is still under investigation and facing criminal proceedings; the fourth (Andrés Rodríguez) only escaped prosecution through his death in 1997.

Despite international pressure, principally from the United States, to enforce measures to combat narcotics, money laundering, trafficking in people, and contraband and infringements of intellectual property rights, Paraguay remains a major regional centre and conduit for narcotics and arms smuggling, contraband, money laundering, and counterfeit and pirated goods from East Asia. This reflects a range of problems from weak implementation of laws and international agreements to pervasive and institutionalized corruption in law enforcement agencies. Despite international pressure, there is still no centralized, freely operating unit focusing on corruption, such as an anticorruption ombudsman.

The public sector is characterized by a lack of real controls and oversight as well as the overlapping of authority and functions, and remains institutionally and structurally corrupt. Efforts since 2000 to reduce excessive, loss-making state involvement in the economy through privatization have failed due to the lack of procedural transparency and the scale of corruption and inefficiency involved in the few completed transfers to the private sector. Indeed, under intense civil pressure, Duarte announced in June 2005 that the government would not pursue privatization of Paraguay's oil and cement companies, specifically due to public concern over corruption. The lack of transparency with respect to those officials responsible for state assets, and even administration and distribution of foreign aid and loans, is exacerbated by poor internal auditing systems that are often subject to corruption. There is no effective legislation providing for public financial disclosure by government personnel or appropriate ethical standards to separate public and personal interests. Moreover, boundaries to prevent conflicts of interests in the private sector are lacking. Corruption severely affects the general population in its dealings with the state sector; according to Transparency Paraguay, the total cost to civilians of routine administrative bribery in dealings with state representatives (police, ministries, civil service) in 2005 was approximately US$30 million.[33]

Despite media investigations of corruption, the effectiveness of prosecutions is severely hindered by the inefficiency and corruption within the judiciary and the police, as well as the fear that many citizens have in coming forward as witnesses or plaintiffs. In addition to the case of the journalist Enrique Galeano (see Accountability and Public Voice), the 2005 kidnapping and subsequent murder of Cecilia Cubas, daughter of the former president, revealed high levels of corruption in both the police and the public prosecutions office, leading President Duarte to sack the minister of the interior, Nelson Mora, and thirty senior police officers.

Supported by the international community, the Duarte administration has, however, made anticorruption policy a central pillar of its efforts to introduce good governance. Anticorruption measures focused initially on creating an island of integrity in the Ministry of Finance, which under Dionisio Borda (2003–2005) made significant advances in reducing corruption and increasing public transparency and accountability, especially in terms of internal auditing and prevention of tax evasion, previously running at an estimated 70 percent.[34] Likewise, customs underwent thorough internal reform, with the introduction of a merit-based appointment and promotion system designed to end its previous politicization, corruption, and lack of efficiency. Again, this led to significant improvements in income generation.

Crucially, an Office of Public Procurement was established within the Ministry of Finance, alongside external auditing of all public enterprises, to ensure that all 301 state institutions adhere to new strict regulations on planning and transparency (including all tendering, bidding, and adjudication).[35] This led to an estimated 30 percent savings on the annual government procurement bill.[36] Overall, primarily as a result of anticorruption measures, tax revenues increased by 74 percent between 2003 and 2006,[37] while overall government income increased by 122 percent in the same period.[38] Reflecting the progress made in the past three years, Paraguay's ranking in the TI CPI has risen from 129th out of 133 countries, with a score of just 1.6 in 2003, to 111th out of 160 countries, with a score of 2.6 in 2006.[39]

Access to information in practice remains extremely difficult, despite pressures for the introduction of a freedom of information law from a joint body of NGOs established in 2004. Proper legislative review of the budgetary process, which receives wide media coverage, and the publication of detailed statistical information on websites by a number of government ministries do reflect some progress in increasing internal transparency and access to information, in line with continued government promises.

For the first time, Paraguay has a government in power that has committed itself to implementing a serious program to combat corruption by focusing on state reform, modernization, improved tax accountability, and greater transparency. Furthermore, the creation of a Citizens' Anticorruption Observatory in 2006, comprising ten NGOs, as well as the growing profile of Transparency Paraguay, reflect greater organization within civil society. However, this struggle necessarily challenges the interests of established elites, especially within the Colorado Party, who have become wealthier through illicit enrichment during the transition.[40] It is widely believed that the resignation of Finance Minister Dionisio Borda in 2005 was due to pressures from within the ruling party to oust a minister who threatened not only the financial interests of elites but also the Colorado Party's clientelistic base within the state sector. Given the scale and deeply embedded, pervasive nature of corruption, further reform will be a task that is not only difficult and dangerous, involving taking on powerful mafias that allegedly exercise a considerable degree of influence over the legislature and the judiciary, but also one that could threaten a crucial bastion of Colorado Party electoral and political dominance.

Recommendations

- Appropriate funds and political and judicial support should be devoted to investigating and punishing alleged corruption, especially among politicians, members of the public sector, and the security forces.
- All government agencies should seek to emulate and promote as good practice the significant progress already made in the Ministry of Finance in terms of internal auditing, transparency, publication of budgets via the web, and anticorruption strategies.
- As a basic tool to strengthen democracy, a bill should be introduced to strengthen, regulate, and protect in practice and under law the right to information, while establishing hierarchies of accessible and responsible personnel to ease bureaucratic complexities.
- The government should consider the creation of an independent anti-corruption ombudsman to play a public role in investigating and denouncing abuses and promoting reforms, as well as the creation of an independent Office of the Inspector General in all key ministries.

NOTES

1   *United Nations Human Development Report 2006* (New York: United Nations Development Programme [UNDP], 2006), http://hdr.undp.org/hdr2006/statistics/indicators/147.html.

2   *Principales Resultados de la Encuesta Permanente de Hogares: Empleo y Pobreza* : Dirección General de Estadística, Encuestas y Censos [DGEEC], Asunción, 2006), 13, http://www.dgeec.gov.py/publicaciones/biblioteca/presentacion_empleo2005/boletin_empleo_y_pobreza_2005.pdf.

3   Ibid, 3.

4   The only national election the Colorado Party has lost was the extraordinary vice presidential election in 2000, when PLRA candidate Julio César Franco, supported by the dissident Colorado faction PUNACE, narrowly defeated the Colorado Party candidate.

5   *Paraguay Country Profile* (London: Economist Intelligence Unit [EIU], 2006), 8.

6   *Latinobarómetro Report* (Santiago Chile: Corporación Latinobarómetro, 2006), 51, 56, 58 respectively, http://www.latinobarometro.org/uploads/media/2005_02.pdf.

7   *Latin American Weekly Report* (LAWR), 8 November 2005, 8.

8   LAWR, 12 December 2006, 9.

9   The Partido Liberal Radical Auténtico (Authentic Radical Liberal Party) has been the main opposition party since the transition began in 1989.

10 R. A. Nickson, "Reformando el Estado en Paraguay" in *Estado, Economía y Sociedad: Una Mirada Internacional a la Democracia Paraguaya* (Asunción: Centro de Analisis y Difusion de Economia Paraguaya [CADEP], 2005), 41–72.

11 For an in-depth analysis of civic action, see C. Soto, L. Bareiro, Q. Riquelme, and R. Villalba, "Sociedad Civil y Construcción Democrática en Paraguay" in M. Albuquerque, *La Construcción Democrática desde abajo en el Cono Sur* (Sao Paolo: Instituto Polis, 2004), 135–193.

12 "Special Rapporteur on Torture Ends Mission to Paraguay" (New York: Office of the United Nations High Commissioner for Human Rights [OHCHR], press release, 29 November 2006), www.unhchr.ch/huricane/huricane.nsf/view01/509BA4239456B976C12572350077E647?opendocument.

13 "Situación Penitenciaria," in *Informe Derechos Humanos en Paraguay 2006* (Asunción, Paraguay: Coordinadora de Derechos Humanos del Paraguay [CODEHUPY]; Litocolor; Instituto de Estudios Comparados de Ciencias Penales y Sociales [INECIP], 2006), 52.

14 Ibid., 53.

15 Based on figures from the General Prison Supervisor's Office of the Supreme Court (INECIP, October 2006), 59.

16 *Pagos a Víctimas de la Dictadura* (Asuncion: Office of the Presidency of the Republic, 5 December 2006), http://www.presidencia.gov.py/visitas_pdf/Victimas%20de%20la%20Dictadura.pdf.

17 *Report 2005: Paraguay* (London: Amnesty International [AI], http://web.amnesty.org/report2005/pry-summary-eng.

18. *Concluding Observations of the Human Rights Committee: Paraguay* (New York and Geneva: United Nations Human Rights Committee, 24 April 2006), www.unhchr.ch /tbs/doc.nsf/(symbol)/CCPR.C.PRY.CO.2.En?opendocument.

19. M. González Vera and V. Villalba, "Un estado que desatiende los derechos de las mujeres" in CODEHUPY (2006), 106.

20. Ibid., 114.

21. C. Pacheco and M. Horvath, "La Situación de las Personas con Discapacidad en las Políticas Sociales Nacionales," in *Informe Derechos Humanos en Paraguay 2004* (Asunción, Paraguay: CODEHUPY; Litocolor, 2004), 147–151.

22. O. Ayala and M. J. Cabello, "Entre la realidad y los avances de la justicia internacional," in CODEHUPY (2006), 364.

23. Figures from *Draft Country Programme Document: Paraguay* (New York: UNICEF, 2006), 3, http://www.unicef.org/about/execboard/files/06-pl50_Paraguay_Rev1(1).pdf.

24. *Informe Alternativo de CODEHUPY al Segundo Informe Periódico del Estado de Paraguayo* (CODEHUPY, 2005), 14, www.omct.org/pdf/procedures/2005/85th_hr _commission /ngo_reports/hrc85_paraguay_informe_alt.pdf.

25. R. Villalba, "El Movimiento Sindical: aun mucho por resolver," in CODEHUPY (2004), 202.

26. L.E. Escobar Faella, "Estalla la crisis del sistema del Justicia" in CODEHUPY (2004), 61–70.

27. Bogado was accused of significant financial irregularities while he was president of CONATEL, the state telecommunications company, between 2002 and 2003.

28. LAWR, 12 December 2006, 16.

29. LAWR, 26 July 2005, 7.

30. Q. Riquelme, "Otro año de reclamos sin soluciones de fondo" in CODEHUPY, (2006), 217.

31. Report 2006: Paraguay (AI), http://web.amnesty.org/report2006/pry-summary-eng.

32. *Informe Alternativo*, CODEHUPY (2005), 16.

33. *Encuesta Nacional sobre Corrupción* (Asunción: QR Producciones Gráficas; Transparencia Paraguay, 2005), 30.

34. *Latin America Monitor: Southern Cone* 19, 9 (September 2002): 7.

35. A law was passed in 2004 creating the Dirección General de Contrataciones Públicas, an office answerable to the Ministry of Finance, to promote and monitor transparency in procurement. All deals are now published on the website, as well as the conditions and results for all bidding processes. See www.contratacionesparaguay.gov.py.

36. Nickson, "Reformando el Estado en paraguay" (2005), 62.

37. *Informe de Recaudaciones Tributarias*, Octubre 2006 (Asuncion: Gabinete Técnico del Ministerio de Hacienda, 2006), 6, http://www.presidencia.gov.py/visitas_pdf/IngTrib 102006.pdf.

38. *Resultados de Reformas y Mejoras en la Gestión* (Gabinete Técnico del Ministerio de Hacienda, 2006), 18, http://www.presidencia.gov.py/programas/resultdic06.pdf.

39. *Corruption Perceptions Index* (Berlin: Transparency International), http://www.trans parency.org/policy_research/surveys_indices/global/cpi.

40. A. Miranda, *Dossier-Paraguay: Los Dueños de Grandes Fortunas* (Asunción: Mirando y Asociados, 2000).

PERU

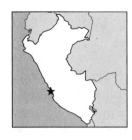

CAPITAL: Lima
POPULATION: 27.9 million
GNI PER CAPITA: $2,920

SCORES	2005	2007
ACCOUNTABILITY AND PUBLIC VOICE:	4.65	4.30
CIVIL LIBERTIES:	4.64	4.43
RULE OF LAW:	3.84	4.07
ANTICORRUPTION AND TRANSPARENCY:	3.21	3.49

(scores are based on a scale of 0 to 7, with 0 representing weakest and 7 representing strongest performance)

Jake Dizard

INTRODUCTION

On July 28, 2006, Peruvian president Alejandro Toledo concluded his five years at the helm of Peru's frail democracy. As the successor to authoritarian ruler Alberto Fujimori, Toledo was expected to lead Peru toward enactment of the deep reforms necessary to raise living standards and consolidate democracy. Unfortunately, by the end of his term Toledo had narrowly avoided impeachment and had long since lost the ability to set the political agenda. Despite nearly five full years of economic growth averaging over 5 percent, poverty rates had fallen only slightly, and job growth was weak. Toledo had been given a difficult task. Structural, historical, and political factors make governing Peru difficult and unpredictable. Social tension is ever-present, institutions are underdeveloped, and political culture is anomic. While Toledo's commitment to democracy was largely unquestioned, his leadership abilities were widely criticized. Despite economic gains, some notable reforms, and

Jake Dizard is a Research Analyst at Freedom House and is the Assistant Editor of *Countries at the Crossroads*. He also serves as the Andean region analyst for the Freedom House publications *Freedom in the World* and *Freedom of the Press*.

the maintenance of democracy, the foundations of Peruvian stability remained unsteady.

Toledo's successor, former president Alan Garcia, was not at first glance the obvious candidate to prosper in a campaign atmosphere dominated by disillusionment with government. After all, during his first term, from 1985 to 1990, the economy collapsed, a medium-intensity civil war reached its peak, and corruption and human rights abuses were rampant. However, during his subsequent years out of office, Garcia remained a masterful politician, projecting an image of authority that voters found appealing in comparison to the indecisive Toledo. Having finished second to Toledo in the 2001 race, Garcia found in the 2006 campaign an ideal foil in the person of Ollanta Humala, a fiery anti-system candidate who emerged as the voice of discontented Peruvians. Although Humala secured a first-round victory, the fear of instability—or even authoritarianism—he inspired allowed Garcia to assume the unlikely role of safe choice, which was enough for him to win the presidency with 52 percent of the vote.

The ineffectiveness of the Peruvian state at performing the fundamental tasks of governance, from carrying out justice to tackling entrenched poverty, is a primary cause of the discontent that Peruvians unfailingly express when polled regarding attitudes toward democracy. Problems of day-to-day life, including crime, joblessness, and corruption are ever-present reminders of the state's failures. However, less tangible concerns are often voiced as well. The broadest is the theme of exclusion, which in the Peruvian context essentially describes the lack of integration between historically excluded sectors (both socioeconomic and ethnic) and the relatively modern, largely urban portion of the Peruvian state, society, and economy. Humala's outsider candidacy—and near victory—in the 2006 election was a symptom of the dissatisfaction with not just the candidates but the overall political model offered by the contemporary ruling class.

Nevertheless, in 2007 Peru finds itself in a position of real opportunity. Although economic growth has not created many new jobs and is largely based on high commodities prices, six years of expansion capped by 8 percent GDP growth in 2006 have filled state coffers, thus providing for the novel possibility of strategic planning. Decentralization, a potentially powerful tool for closing the distance between citizen and state, has received a new focus and has been greeted enthusiastically by citizens. At the time of writing, President Garcia's approval ratings remain above 50 percent, even though in a March 2007 poll nearly 80 percent of Peruvians responded that the president had demonstrated little or no compliance with his campaign promises.[1] On the surface, the Garcia government has as good an opportunity as any administration in recent decades to tangibly improve the lives of Peruvian citizens.

There are sound reasons, however, to be wary of the new government. Despite substantial overall improvements since the end of the civil war and the fall of Fujimori, institutions remain feeble. President Garcia's inauguration speech was notable for the absence of any mention of human rights or anticorruption issues, leading to doubts about the government's will to confront entrenched impunity. The detailed recommendations of the Comision de la Verdad y Reconciliacion (Truth and Reconciliation Commission—CVR) remain largely unimplemented. Furthermore, members of Garcia's American Popular Revolutionary Alliance (APRA) party have demonstrated little patience with civil society and only a grudging inclination to cooperate on the resolution of past human rights abuses. Even Prime Minister Jorge del Castillo, regarded as a moderate, referred to victims' lawyers as "useful idiots of Shining Path-ism." President Garcia's personalist tendencies are well established, and his overall vision for the next five years remains unclear; the lack of a coherent opposition means that checking his populist instincts or forcing issues onto the agenda that APRA would rather not confront could be difficult.

ACCOUNTABILITY AND PUBLIC VOICE

FREE AND FAIR ELECTORAL LAWS AND ELECTIONS:	5.50
EFFECTIVE AND ACCOUNTABLE GOVERNMENT:	3.50
CIVIC ENGAGEMENT AND CIVIC MONITORING:	3.33
MEDIA INDEPENDENCE AND FREEDOM OF EXPRESSION:	4.88
CATEGORY AVERAGE:	**4.30**

Both the first and second rounds of the 2006 Peruvian elections for congress and the presidency generally fulfilled international standards regarding free and fair elections. Suffrage is universal and obligatory, and turnout in each of the two rounds was close to 90 percent. The Organization of American States characterized the April election, which comprised both legislative and first-round presidential balloting, as "strongly positive" as well as "orderly and dignified,"[2] while June's second-round presidential vote was deemed "calm, orderly, and transparent."[3] The main problem noted by observers was the persistent problem of Peruvians lacking identity documents, which may have diminished the electorate by up to 1 million voters.[4]

Elections are conducted by a tripartite system of electoral entities. The National Registry (RENIEC) is responsible for voter registration, the National Office of Electoral Processes (ONPE) administers the electoral process, and the National Electoral Board (JNE) resolves election-related legal questions and challenges. Although many analysts support the separate organs as more specialized and effective, others—especially within the JNE—argue that the system leads to duplication of efforts and cost inefficiencies and that the ONPE (and possibly the RENIEC) should be merged into a body headed by the JNE. During the 2006 elections, tensions between the JNE and ONPE emerged over ballot design as well as party and candidate registration. As of early 2007, the congress was considering a plan, submitted with the support of President Garcia, that would merge the two.

Congressional elections are held concurrently with the first round of the presidential election. Congressional voting is carried out through open-list proportional representation, with the number of representatives for each department determined by population. No party won a majority in the 2006 elections; the single largest legislative grouping corresponded to the on-again, off-again alliance of the Peruvian Union (UPP) Party and Humala's Peruvian Nationalist Party (PNP), which gained forty-five seats. APRA was second with thirty-six; other important shares went to National Unity (UN) with seventeen seats and the pro-Fujimori Alliance for the Future with thirteen seats. The election represented the first in which parties were required to reach an electoral hurdle of 4 percent of the national vote. If no candidate wins a first-round majority in the presidential contest, a second round is held between the top two finishers; in 2006 this meant Humala and Garcia.

Serious violence was associated with the local and regional elections conducted on November 18, 2006. Nearly two dozen districts were rocked by protests in which election offices were ransacked and ballot boxes burned. Much of the violence was blamed on voters angry about the effects of "votos golondrinos," or ballots cast by voters who had transferred their place of registration in the midst of the campaign. The ONPE later acknowledged that there had been insufficient time to properly analyze the addresses listed on voter rolls.[5]

Campaigning opportunities are unhindered for Peruvian political parties. Limitations on campaigning in Peru are more likely to be self-imposed, as few parties have the geographic reach, organizational structure, and ideological coherence to appeal broadly throughout the country. However, the rise and fall of parties generally occurs organically, and a rotation of parties in power is the rule. Peruvian ruling parties have been largely personalist vehicles for many decades; with the partial exception of APRA, once a given party leader is no longer president, that party's strength dwindles. Toledo's Peru Possible party is a good example: in 2001 it captured forty-seven seats; in 2006, just two. Fujimori's series of "instant" parties and the failure of APRA to compete seriously for the presidency without Alan Garcia on the ticket further illustrate the problem. Generally, the weakness of Peruvian parties is regarded as a major reason for Peru's political instability and difficulties in building momentum toward institutional consolidation.

Campaign finance laws have been strengthened, with all candidates and parties now required to list all donations. The electoral office lacks sufficient resources, however, to investigate all filings adequately, and the use of *testaferros* (third parties) is considered common. In the 2006 campaign, Humala was accused of receiving funds from the Venezuelan government, although the accusation has not been confirmed. Money from sources linked to drug trafficking led to the exclusion of several candidates in the local and regional elections. With resources generally scarce, parties often recruit candidates on the basis of their ability to self-finance and contribute to the party; those who can contribute most are placed higher on the party list.[6]

Although Peru is a strongly presidential system, the executive does not exercise absolute control over the legislative and judicial branches. While presidents have historically been granted broad decree powers by the congress, during Toledo's term the percentage of legislation passed by decree declined significantly.[7] The weakness of political parties, however, often limits their effectiveness as a check on the executive. Furthermore, congressional oversight of the executive corresponds to a large extent with political point-scoring potential rather than a consistent vision of the limits and standards of the executive's role. The judiciary is constitutionally autonomous (though troubled; see Rule of Law), and the Constitutional Tribunal, in particular, has shown a willingness to rule against other branches of government as well as the military.

State hiring practices remain inefficient and politicized. Provisions for formal, meritocratic selection processes exist but are time-consuming. Therefore, an increasing number of public employees are hired on a temporary basis; Peruvian labor law provides little precedent or guidance as to the rights of these workers.[8] Legally mandated projects to improve job descriptions and establish incentives programs have not been implemented. There are also discrepancies between the perceived high caliber of personnel in "technical" agencies such as the Finance Ministry and the lower quality of those in "social" agencies.

Peruvian civil society is highly active. Nongovernmental organizations (NGOs) saw their ability to work freely greatly expanded in the wake of Fujimori's downfall. Cooperation between government and civil society reached a high point under the Valentin Paniagua-led post-Fujimori transitional government and in the first year of Toledo's term. In some respects, consensus within civil society has continued to expand; for instance, business groups, previously focused on narrower market and economic themes, have started to emphasize social issues as well.[9]

There are several realms of conflict, however, between the state and civil society. Cooperation between the state and NGOs has diminished significantly under the APRA government, which is perceived as wary of NGO motivations. Given the lack of a coherent opposition in congress, NGOs are seen by the government almost as opposition political parties. This puts them in a difficult position: the more vigorously they oppose government actions, the more the government view that they are political entities is validated. President Garcia has also expressed his disapproval of the tactics used by groups protesting operations in the extractive industries, suggesting they hinder economic development and encourage violent conflict.

More controversially, in December 2006 final amendments were passed to a new law that imposed new registration rules on all NGOs operating in the country. The law, which technically updated the charter of the Peruvian Agency for International Cooperation (APCI), requires that all NGOs register with APCI and divulge details of the provenance and intended use of all donated funds. For money channeled through APCI, the agency—which as an arm of the foreign affairs ministry is an executive branch institution—will have the ability to "prioritize" spending in line with national development goals, as well as impose sanctions on organizations that are deemed noncompliant with the new regulations.

The government argued for the need for transparency in NGO operations, while also noting that most of the new rules were already on the books but were unenforceable. NGOs, however, see the law as unconstitutional in its terms and chilling in its message. Many NGOs believe the law will result in less criticism from groups that fear being arbitrarily targeted by the government. They also note that in the international competition for donor aid, Peruvian groups will be less likely to receive assistance if the donors perceive the government role as overly intrusive. With respect to the law's legality, NGOs and their congressional allies argue that the measure violates freedom of association and the right to free contract. Moreover, the coalition behind the law's passage rang alarm bells. The law was presented by Congressman Rolando Souza, Fujimori's former lawyer, and supported by APRA, the Fujimori bloc, and National Unity. Some observers suggest that Garcia continues to worry about investigations into human rights practices during his first administration and is also attempting to maintain cordial relations—or even an outright alliance—with legislators aligned with Fujimori, who are adamantly opposed to the activities of many Peruvian human rights and anticorruption NGOs.

In the final passage, the law's structure was changed to exempt aid not channeled through the state from the prioritizing clause. However, this did not satisfy NGOs, who collected the 10,000 signatures necessary to challenge the measure before the Constitutional Tribunal, a process unresolved at the time of writing.

Freedom of the press is constitutionally protected in Peru, and the media is vibrant and active, especially at the national level. Bribe-induced media support was one of the pillars of the Fujimori regime. Although the press recovered strongly under Toledo, the media has not fully regained Peruvians' trust, and controversies related to Fujimori's media control continue to resurface occasionally. In 2005, for instance, the Wolfenson brothers, who had been convicted of accepting bribes from Vladimiro Montesinos, Fujimori's shadowy right-hand man, were set free after a law was passed allowing house arrest to count toward prison sentences.[10]

Libel and defamation remain classified as criminal offenses in Peru, and journalists continue to be prosecuted, receiving large fines and jail sentences, although the jail terms are generally suspended. While abuses occur, not all accusations of defamation can be regarded as attempts to intimidate the press: journalistic ethics in Peru remain a work in progress. Many journalists, especially low-paid provincial ones but also those based in Lima, are willing to accept bribes in return for favorable coverage.[11] Additionally, unsubstantiated stories regarding corruption and other official malfeasance, as well as stories linking individuals to criminals or other unsavory characters, remain a problem.

Especially at the local and regional levels, journalism is a dangerous profession in which reporting on local scandals can lead to intimidation, harassment, and serious attacks. The number of alerts issued by IPYS, a local press watchdog, increased dramatically from 2005, when sixty alerts, including thirty-one attacks and death threats, were registered, to 2006, when the ninety-six total alerts included fifty-six attacks and threats. In March 2007, journalist Miguel Perez was murdered in the northern department of Cajamarca after reporting on local corruption. Indeed, allegations of corruption against local officials and coverage of drug trafficking are the themes most commonly linked to attacks on the press. In the days after Perez's death, thousands marched to demand justice in the case, and at the time of writing an ongoing investigation had already led to several arrests. Impunity for threats and aggression, however, remains the norm.

The Peruvian government refrains from direct and indirect censorship of the media, and most outlets are privately owned. Both print and broadcast media remain reliant, however, on advertising dollars from limited sources such as government (at the local level) and a few large companies (especially retailers) at the national level. Media concentration has also increased at the national level; for example, the El Comercio group now owns four of Lima's most prominent newspapers. Internet access is unhindered and is widespread in the cities, although it remains rare in rural and jungle areas. Freedom of cultural expression is generally unrestricted.

Recommendations

- Congressional elections should be changed from open-list to closed-list in order to strengthen the decision-making power of parties and diminish the competition for candidates with high name recognition but little ideological coherence.
- In order to standardize selection mechanisms and limit patronage opportunities, the Law of Public Employment should be passed and implemented without delay.
- The changes in registration requirements for NGOs should be rescinded immediately and measures taken to improve dialogue between civil society and the government.
- The government should increase the resources devoted to protecting threatened journalists and investigating attacks against the press.

CIVIL LIBERTIES

PROTECTION FROM STATE TERROR, UNJUSTIFIED IMPRISONMENT, AND TORTURE:	3.71
GENDER EQUITY:	3.75
RIGHTS OF ETHNIC, RELIGIOUS, AND OTHER DISTINCT GROUPS:	3.50
FREEDOM OF CONSCIENCE AND BELIEF:	6.00
FREEDOM OF ASSOCIATION AND ASSEMBLY:	5.20
CATEGORY AVERAGE:	**4.43**

The Toledo government used the momentum of the transition to make important advances in the sphere of human rights. Most crucial was the work of the CVR. In August 2003, the final report was released, shocking Peruvians with its finding that 69,000 citizens perished between 1980 and 2000. More than half of the deaths were attributed to the terrorist group Shining Path, but state security forces were deemed responsible for large-scale human rights violations as well. Since then, the detailed recommendations contained in the report have been considered the touchstone for human rights efforts in Peru. In addition, a comprehensive National Human Rights Plan for 2006–2011, formulated with significant input from civil society, was approved in December 2005. Implementation during 2006 was weak, however; just one of the envisioned series of regional meetings was held, and the Garcia government announced its intention to revisit the plan by widening civil society consultations, a move that was seen as a delaying tactic.[12]

Overall, despite a few advances, the Garcia administration so far has shown hostility toward the process of coming to terms with past human rights violations. The behavior of the APRA and Fujimori blocs in the congress has provided substantial support to analysts who claim that an "alliance for impunity" exists between the two groups. An early sign was Garcia's unsuccessful attempt to enact his popular (and populist) campaign vow to apply the death penalty to child rapists and terrorists, an action that would clearly violate the Inter-American Convention on Human Rights.

In December 2006, the Inter-American Court of Human Rights ruled that the state owed reparations and a public apology to victims of the massacre of forty-two inmates at the Castro Castro prison in 1992. Fujimori sympathizers and ex-military members presented the ruling as a victory for terrorists and restated the call for renunciation of the San Jose pact. Only after the boiling controversy drew significant international outcry did Prime Minister Jorge del Castillo and, eventually, Garcia explicitly state that Peru would not pull out of the system. These incidents, however, as well as the overall aggressive posture by accused human rights abusers during the administration's early months, have led the human rights community to worry that the frustrating impunity for abuses—some of which now date back two decades or more—will strengthen under Garcia.

Another worrying sign is the increase in threats and intimidation against Peruvian human rights defenders (including the war's victims as well as members of the human rights community), a phenomenon that in 2006 drew the attention of the Inter-American Commission on Human Rights. According to the National Human Rights Coordinator (CNDDHH), incidents of threats and intimidation increased from sixteen in 2005 to thirty-six in 2006.[13] In September 2006, the congress began to consider a measure to strengthen the preexisting Effective Collaboration Law and extend its protection to vulnerable human rights defenders, but the project remains pending.[14]

Torture by state security forces remains an occasional problem in Peru. Members of the CNDDHH reported at least sixteen cases of torture in 2006, declaring that this most likely reflected only a small portion of the true number.[15] Most observers agree, however, that torture is no longer practiced in a systematic way. Prosecutions for reported cases continue to occur only sporadically and affect only low-level officers.

The Peruvian prison system has not improved in recent years. Prisons are overcrowded by 75 percent,[16] facilities are falling apart, corruption and disease are rampant, and violence is frequent. The idea of rehabilitation is nearly nonexistent; instead, politicians speak of toughening rules, especially by reopening Challapalca prison, an unheated facility at roughly 15,000 feet altitude that was closed in 2005 on the recommendations of the Truth and Reconciliation Commission and the IACHR.

As with torture, arbitrary arrest is a problem that has decreased by orders of magnitude since the end of the internal conflict. After a December 2006 attack by Shining Path remnants in Machente, Ayacucho, killed five police officers and three civilians, eight peasants were arrested and charged with both the crime and being members of a subversive group. Although doubts were quickly raised about their culpability—the men had alibis and police accounts were inconsistent—national politicians trumpeted the arrests as reflecting a successful police investigation. Only several weeks later, after the intervention of the human rights ombudsman known as the People's Defender (DP), were the accused liberated. This case served to show that in high-profile cases, procedural abuses remain possible.

Long-term pretrial detention is an ongoing issue in Peru. According to the prison institute's statistics, nearly 70 percent of jailed Peruvians are held under pretrial detention. Indeed, a significant number of Peruvian arrestees never serve time under formal sentence, as the maximum pretrial detention period of twenty-four months (thirty-six for serious crimes) is reached with no formal verdict, and prisoners are released.[17]

Remnants of the Shining Path, now associated with cocaine producers, continue to attack security forces sporadically in coca-growing zones, resulting in repeated extensions of the states of emergency in these areas. In December 2005, thirteen police officers and civilians were killed in two attacks,[18] while the Machente attack was the most severe in 2006. Ominously, Mexican cartels are now operating in Peru. In

August 2006, a judge presiding over the trial of accused members of the Tijuana cartel was assassinated at a cafe in Lima. Notably, in October 2006, Shining Path leaders Abimael Guzman and Elena Iparraguirre received life sentences in retrials held to atone for the undemocratic trial procedures used during the Fujimori era.

Crime has steadily increased in Peru, although it is still far below the level found in many Latin American countries. Indeed, according to analysts, the perception of lack of safety is growing much faster than crime itself. A general sense of discontent, along with institutional fragility, the legacy of political violence, and the rising visibility of street gangs all contribute to this perception. Despite sensationalistic media coverage of murders, burglary and muggings are far more common. The response of the police in recent years has been deficient. Various plans have been enacted; most recently a policy of "districtization," intended to put more police on the streets and in stations easily accessible to citizens, was put into effect. However, a strategic vision is lacking, and crude, ineffective tools of repression continue to be emphasized over sustained, community-based efforts.[19]

Peruvians whose rights have been violated have an important tool of redress in the institution of the ombudsman. Constitutionally autonomous, with a highly regarded staff, the ombudsman accepts complaints about alleged rights violations ranging from torture to no-show teachers. Although findings are not binding, ombudsman reports carry an important moral weight. The CNDDHH notes that the ombudsman's intervention was decisive in getting the accused campesinos liberated after the incident in Machente.[20]

One of the most important advances in recent years related to applying the CVR recommendations occurred in July 2006, when the government issued implementing regulations for victims' reparations. In order to postpone resolving the politically fraught issue of which individuals are to receive compensation, initial reparations will be communal in nature, focusing on infrastructure, monuments, and other civic benefits.[21]

Peruvian men and women are guaranteed equality under the constitution. In practice, however, Peruvian women suffer from many of the ills associated with *machista* culture and underdevelopment. Domestic abuse is rampant, affecting an estimated 50 percent of Peruvian women.[22] Women living in rural areas face particularly difficult obstacles. Health infrastructure is extremely deficient, and a lack of cultural sensitivity and indigenous language ability among health workers results in a reluctance on the part of rural indigenous people to visit clinics. For pregnant women, this results in a vicious circle: babies are born outside of clinics and therefore do not receive birth certificates, which leads to further marginalization from social services as they grow up. The Garcia government has established consultative councils with civil society groups, but it remains unclear whether the goodwill gesture will translate into action.

Peru, like many countries in the region, has been designated a source country for trafficking in women. Laws against trafficking comply with international norms, and some prosecutions have occurred. Sexual abuse of domestic employees is also a serious problem, although in January 2007 the government increased penalties for rape of domestic workers.

On March 9, 2007, President Garcia signed the Law of Opportunities, which is intended to combat discrimination in employment, including the 30 percent pay differential between men and women.[23] Implementation will be a challenge, however, as the Ministry of Women's and Social Development (MIMDES) remains underfunded. Another bright spot is national political representation; the congress elected in 2006 included thirty-five women, or 30 percent of the total, which fulfilled the intended electoral quota.

Deeply ingrained discrimination remains a massive stumbling block in Peru's attempts to achieve a more developed and equitable society. Racial identity is not as strong in Peru as in neighboring Bolivia and Ecuador, due in part to the centrality of class-based ideologies in Peruvian history.[24] This has slowed efforts to confront the pervasive phenomenon of discrimination against Quechua and Aymara speakers, Afro-Peruvians, Amazonian indigenous groups, and citizens with Andean features. In recent years, consciousness about the need to confront racism has been growing. Efforts, however, are still largely led by civil society rather than the state. When the government is involved, it is often at the municipal rather than the national level.

The state has enacted some measures, however. Laws against discrimination, which is already a criminal offense in Peru, were tightened in August 2006. Fines have been issued to establishments that discriminate with regard to clientele. In February 2007, the ombudsman, for the first time, suggested criminal prosecution against four teachers who had refused to teach a young girl with a disability.[25]

Peru is a signatory to ILO Convention 169, which requires consultation with indigenous groups when legislation affecting them is passed. Indigenous groups argue that the state has not complied with its duties. In particular, conflict related to natural resource exploitation has surged along with investment and exploration. As of March 2007, the congress was considering a measure to halt resource exploitation in zones populated by isolated tribes.[26]

The Peruvian government has been diligent about ratifying international charters, forming commissions, and enacting laws regarding the rights of people with disabilities. In 2006, Peru formulated its second Plan of Equal Opportunities for Disabled Persons, which will guide efforts from 2007 to 2012. The new plan is meant to create mechanisms to ensure that government agencies comply with Peruvian laws guaranteeing access to public buildings. Currently, compliance is greatest among federal agencies, while municipalities lag far behind, with a mere 1 percent achieving accessibility.[27] Access to education has increased, and mild affirmative action exists: Peruvians with disabilities are granted a 3 percent quota in public agencies and a 15 percent benefit on civil service tests. However, CONADIS, the agency in charge of disabled rights, is underfunded and lacks data regarding the number of disabled Peruvians. Furthermore, the fusion of CONADIS, which had been independent, into MIMDES in December 2006 disappointed disabled rights activists.

Most Peruvians are Catholics, although the popularity of evangelical faiths has grown in recent years. Freedom of religion is strong in Peru, despite the special relationship that the state has with the Catholic Church, the result of a concordat signed with the Vatican in 1980. The Catholic Church and its clergy receive special tax benefits and subsidies from the state. Since 2004, other faiths have been eligible to register for similar benefits, but the process is designed to accommodate the structural and doctrinal qualities of the Catholic Church. Religious discrimination is not considered a problem, interference in religious observance is rare, and the state does not interfere with internal organizational processes or the naming of leaders of any faith.

The once-strong Peruvian labor movement has weakened considerably in recent decades; the unionization rate declined from 18 percent in 1980 to just 3 percent in 2007.[28] Increasing this rate would be challenging, as Peruvian law requires a minimum of twenty workers to form a union, a number that excludes 98 percent of Peruvian businesses. Although it is formally difficult to obtain permission to strike, work stoppages occur with great regularity. The teachers' union, which is the most active and radical group, has been demonized by the government and the media as Marxist-dominated and uncaring about the education of Peruvian children. In both the public and private sectors, businesses have increasingly circumvented rigid labor laws by hiring temporary workers.

The Peruvian state generally recognizes freedom of association and assembly, rights that Peruvian citizens are not shy about exercising. Mobilizations and protests are a daily occurrence throughout the country. These range from peaceful demonstrations by a wide range of civic and political groups, which generally occur without incident, to more radical protests that sometimes transcend a single issue and become protests against the nature of the Peruvian state. Violence on the part of both protesters and the authorities is common, with dozens of injuries to protesters and police and several protester deaths reported in both 2005 and 2006. The protests that most often result in violence are generally those conducted by coca growers, although demonstrations against extractive industries companies have increased in militancy in recent years.

Recommendations

- The government should overhaul prison management, placing all prisons under the authority of the National Penitentiary Institute, and greatly increase the resources devoted to rehabilitation programs inside all jails and prisons. The government should also refrain from reopening Challapalca prison.
- The Justice Ministry should heed the recommendation made by the People's Defender in October 2006 and create a unit specializing in the provision of defense for victims of human rights violations.
- The state should systematically implement the recommendations of the CVR in the areas of reparations and prosecution of human rights abuses. The proposed expansion of the Effective Collaboration Law should be approved.
- The state should greatly increase its efforts to provide essential services in areas such as health and justice in Quechua and other non-Spanish languages.

RULE OF LAW

INDEPENDENT JUDICIARY:	4.00
PRIMACY OF RULE OF LAW IN CIVIL AND CRIMINAL MATTERS:	4.00
ACCOUNTABILITY OF SECURITY FORCES AND MILITARY TO CIVILIAN AUTHORITIES:	4.00
PROTECTION OF PROPERTY RIGHTS:	4.33
EQUAL TREATMENT UNDER THE LAW:	4.00
CATEGORY AVERAGE:	**4.07**

The institutions responsible for administering and upholding the rule of law in Peru suffer from extremely low credibility in the eyes of the public. Opinion polls consistently show the judiciary and the police as the two most distrusted national institutions. The sheer magnitude of problems makes legal reform one of Peru's most vexing issues. For most of the past few years, the perception was that improvement was slow to nonexistent. In early 2007, however, signs appeared of an increased determination within the judicial branch to curb some of the worst abuses and root out bastions of corruption. However, the profound systemic and cultural changes that are necessary for the judiciary to regain citizens' confidence will take significant time, resources, vigilance, and political will.

Serious structural, economic, and cultural problems hinder the independent and impartial administration of justice. The system is generally underfunded; administrative workers, in particular, are viewed as susceptible to corruption. Jurisprudence, especially in lower-level courts, is unpredictable and excessively formal. The caseload far outstrips judicial capacity.

In recognition of this, overhauls are periodically proposed. The most comprehensive and ambitious of these reforms was the Special Commission on General Justice Reform, known as CERIAJUS. The project, which brought together civil society, judges, and policy makers, was presented in August 2004. As with so many other best-laid plans, however, political will to implement the project was not sustained over the next two years. Nonetheless, CERIAJUS provided the architecture for a thorough transformation of Peruvian justice. In January 2007, incoming

Supreme Court president Francisco Tavara (who is also administrative head of the Judicial Power—PJ) announced a forty-nine-point plan to initiate judicial reform that was based substantially on CERIAJUS. The early stages of the new plan emphasize reducing corruption and increasing transparency. The judiciary's investigative unit, the Office of Judicial Control (OCMA), has increased its activity in 2007, suspending dozens of judges suspected of improprieties. The judicial financial secrecy privilege has also been lifted for judges under investigation. Furthermore, in March 2007 the Supreme Court began the process of publishing all decisions on its website.

One of the harmful legacies of the Fujimori era was the damage he inflicted on the independence of the judiciary. Hundreds of judges were sacked and replaced with provisional appointees lacking job security and, therefore, independence. Partially as a result of a history of government interference in the judiciary, the PJ zealously guards its autonomy. While history, as well as doubts about the APRA government's commitment to a depoliticized judiciary, dictates that watchfulness is warranted, autonomy has sometimes served as an excuse to prevent reform efforts and protect powerful vested interests.

The one judicial organ that has a demonstrated history of independence from other branches is the Constitutional Tribunal (TC), which is independent of the PJ. This court has issued a series of decisions in recent years that have been applauded for checking questionable executive and legislative branch decisions. Frictions exist, however, between the TC, the Supreme Court, and the JNE, which all see themselves as courts of maximum instance. Additionally, four of the seven TC members' terms expire in June 2007; as new judges are selected by a two-thirds vote of the congress, whether the next court will demonstrate similar independence is unpredictable. Early signs in 2007 pointed to a less than fully transparent selection process.

Compliance with judicial decisions usually occurs but can be inconsistent and slow at times. In late 2006, however, the congress blatantly disregarded a TC ruling stating clearly that members of the military charged with human rights violations were to be tried in civilian courts.[29] The abuse of tools such as the *amparo*, a legal stay that prevents decisions from entering into effect, has harmed the judiciary's ability to have its decisions enforced. The amparo is widely viewed as inviting corruption; on multiple occasions, judges have issued a decision, only to see another judge, often not even in the relevant jurisdiction, issue an amparo that prevents the original decision from taking effect. One of Tavara's early moves was to rein in this abuse by requiring that all judges notify a superior when issuing an amparo.

The National Council of Magistrates (CNM) is constitutionally charged with the appointment, promotion, and dismissal of judges, while training is the domain of the Judicial Academy (AMAG). By the end of Fujimori's term, over 70 percent of all Peruvian judges were provisional. In recent years, the proportion of provisional judges has fallen and currently is less than 15 percent.[30] In 2006, the CNM implemented new, improved regulations for judicial hiring. The Supreme Court, however, contains a large number of provisional judges, a fact that received renewed attention in August 2006 with the arrest of a provisional Supreme Court justice caught accepting a US$300 bribe from a policeman.

All Peruvians charged with a crime are considered innocent until proven guilty. The difficulty, especially for poor or rural citizens, lies in navigating the justice system. Poor Peruvians often find that there is little place to turn when adjudication or punishment is required. Occasional lynchings and the frequent outbreaks of social conflict are only the most dramatic examples of the lack of judicial intermediation in many parts of Peru. In recent years the state has attempted to increase the numbers of community-selected justices of the peace, as well as hire additional translators and exempt the poor from legal fees, but resources for such projects remain scarce.

Most observers consider the gradual introduction of a new code of criminal procedure to be the most important reform in many years. The new system, which replaces the traditional inquisitorial system with an adversarial, oral testimony–based trial procedure, will be implemented gradually throughout the country. According to the CNDDHH, the early signs are positive; in the first province where it was implemented, pre-trial resolution has been achieved in 40 percent of cases under the new system, ten times the rate in 2005.[31] Citizens have the right to independent counsel, but the resources provided for legal assistance are meager. Prosecutors function out of the Public Ministry, which is a branch of the PJ. Like judges, their independence is affected by a significant rate of provisionality. In November 2006, human rights groups were angered when the attorney general's office dismissed Cristina Olazabal, a human rights prosecutor in Ayacucho who was considered to be one of the most effective investigators of war-related human rights violations.[32]

Despite the high-level corruption cases aired publicly following Fujimori's fall, prosecution of public officials and ruling-party actors for abuse of power remains weak. Corruption prosecutions do occur but are somewhat arbitrary and very slow. Impunity for human rights violations in the 1980–2000 period is a critical unresolved issue in Peru. In its final report the CVR identified 47 emblematic cases; another 260 have been added through subsequent investigation. Resources have been limited, however, and the vast majority of cases remain stuck in the investigation phase. Indeed, for all the thousands of dead, only one middle-ranking and no high-ranking military officials have been convicted and sentenced.

Civilian control over the military has been consolidated in Peru; security forces do not unduly interfere in the political process. Garcia's choice for minister of defense, Allan Wagner, is seen as having a modernizing vision, centered on the idea of fortifying the defense minister's office in relation to the generals and increasing management capacity through specialized vice-ministries.

Another important project is to achieve a clearer delineation of the military's role in internal security. Currently, the military can, under certain circumstances, be deployed to support the police even without the declaration of a state of emergency. This works to the advantage of politicians, who can send in the armed forces without assuming the political cost of declaring a state of emergency. The military, however, is increasingly conscious of its public image and wants clearer rules in order to avoid being placed in tense situations at little cost to politicians.[33] One other important achievement in recent years was the October 2005 adoption of new code of military ethics, which fulfilled one of the CVR's recommendations.[34]

There are several caveats to the military's basically positive agenda. One is the continuing issue of military corruption, which surfaced several times in 2006, most notably when a massive scheme involving ordering and selling surplus gasoline was uncovered. The other major caveat is the military's intransigence in the face of investigations and judicial processes against soldiers accused of human rights violations in the 1980s and 1990s. In March 2006, Human Rights Watch wrote President Toledo a letter deploring the lack of cooperation by the military in providing investigators with useful information, above all regarding the names behind the aliases commonly used by soldiers during the conflict.[35] Additionally, in November 2006 the military announced that it would henceforth pay the legal costs of servicemen facing investigation for abuses during the conflict, a provision that human rights groups found frustrating in the face of the state's miserliness with assistance for victims of the conflict. Finally, Garcia's naming of Luis Giampietri as his vice president was viewed as a signal that the military's unease about exposure to prosecution would not be ignored. Giampietri is accused of ordering a violent response to unrest at El Fronton prison in 1986; he was considered a fierce defender of the military's role in the fight against Shining Path and has been at the forefront of verbal attacks on Peru's human rights community.

All of the aforementioned complications regarding past justice come in the context of the possible return to Peru of former president Fujimori, who arrived in Chile in November 2005 and announced his intention to return to Peruvian politics. At the request of Peru, Chile arrested the fugitive leader and held him while Peru prepared the case for extradition on ten counts of corruption and two counts of human rights violations related to the death squad known as the Colina Group. Although he was barred from participating in the 2006 presidential elections, the strong possibility of Fujimori's return has contributed to the polarization regarding resolution of past human rights issues. While most advocates of human rights and democracy relish the possibility of seeing Fujimori in a Peruvian jail cell, Garcia and APRA have been notably ambivalent regarding the efforts to achieve his extradition.

Property rights are semi-predictable in Peru. The country was an early innovator in land titling, and efforts continue to regularize new urban settlements as well as agricultural lands. Contract enforcement in Peru remains problematic due to the erratic functioning of the legal system. The Commercial Court system, however, which began operation in 2005, has significantly increased the speed and predictability of contract dispute resolution. Most citizens are protected from unjust deprivation of property. Laws safeguarding indigenous territories are considered fairly strong, but these lands can be bought and sold, and loopholes in the regulations have contributed to the environmental conflicts noted above.

Recommendations

- The judiciary should work with congress and the president to implement the reforms proposed by CERIAJUS while maintaining a regular dialogue with civil society groups regarding the pace and sequencing of reforms.
- The government should provide the necessary resources to implement the new penal code on the originally proposed schedule, with the entire country covered by 2011.
- The military should provide, without delay, all requested information regarding aliases used by military officers during the 1980–2000 armed conflict and cooperate with ongoing human rights trials in the civilian courts.
- The state should dramatically increase the resources allocated to the preliminary investigation phase of cases of human rights violations.

ANTICORRUPTION AND TRANSPARENCY

ENVIRONMENT TO PROTECT AGAINST CORRUPTION:	3.40
EXISTENCE OF LAWS AND ETHICAL STANDARDS BETWEEN PRIVATE AND PUBLIC SECTORS:	3.25
ENFORCEMENT OF ANTICORRUPTION LAWS:	3.75
GOVERNMENTAL TRANSPARENCY:	3.57
CATEGORY AVERAGE:	**3.49**

The massive scale of the corruption that occurred during Fujimori's decade in power remains unprecedented and unsurpassed in Peruvian history. However, despite efforts to prosecute high-level civil and military officials from the 1990s and improve government transparency, as well as a heightened level of citizen and media vigilance, there is little question that corruption remains a serious problem in Peru.

The Peruvian web of regulations and bureaucratic errands vastly increases the opportunities for petty corruption. Nevertheless, there has been some simplification; for instance, the state has attempted to cut the number of steps needed to open a business. The World Bank's annual Doing Business report boosted Peru from seventy-eighth place in 2005 to sixty-fifth in 2006, with improvements in the ease of starting a business and getting credit accounting for much of the change.[36] In comparison with regional neighbors and other developing countries, the Peruvian state is not excessively involved in the economy. Foreign investment is generally welcomed, and although the pace of privatization has slackened considerably since Fujimori's selling spree, both the Toledo and Garcia governments have eagerly promoted privatization and concessions when they are politically feasible.

The state has some mechanisms to separate public office from the personal interests of officeholders. All functionaries are required to fill out asset declarations, which are submitted to the Comptroller General's office for scrutiny. These forms, however, are often incomplete, and only summaries are available to the general public. One notable step occurred in March 2007, when a candidate for the Supreme Court was ruled ineligible because he had filed for bankruptcy recently.

The effort to formulate and enforce an effective process to detect, investigate, and prosecute public officials for corruption is a major issue in Peru, given the nature of the Fujimori/Montesinos regime. The process is highly politicized and, to a substantial degree, media driven, although the comptroller's office also investigates possible acts of corruption. Efforts to investigate and prosecute ministers, members of the congress, and members of the judiciary are harmed by attempts by these officials to hide behind immunity rules for public functionaries. In February 2007, for instance, a number of members of congress attempted to block a regulation that would deny immunity for investigations initiated prior to entry into public office.

Victims of corruption generally assume that they have few mechanisms to pursue their rights. According to anticorruption NGO Proetica's yearly poll, in 2006, 94 percent of Peruvians said they do not report bribery solicitations, and 78 percent characterized the results of corruption denunciations as "little" or "not at all" effective.[37] With weak confidence in institutions, Peruvians are apathetic, perceiving that there is little to be gained by reporting corruption.[38]

SUNAT, the national tax agency, is generally viewed as having increased in efficiency and transparency. Tax collection has improved and has achieved a broader base in recent years. The primary independent auditor in Peru is the Comptroller General of the Republic (CGR), who is appointed by the president for a seven-year term and must be approved by the congress. The comptroller's office is legally, although not constitutionally, autonomous and is responsible for scrutinizing everything from state purchases to asset-declaration forms. The CGR lacks sanctioning power, however, relying instead on the agencies concerned to take action when improprieties are found.

The effectiveness of the investigation and prosecution system at combating corruption is questionable. Impunity, however, is not universal, including for high-level officials. The current anticorruption legal subsystem was set up during the transitional Paniagua government. Efforts to trace money illicitly acquired during the Fujimori administration continue, although the pace of convictions and reclamation of money has slowed. Many analysts have criticized the Garcia government for a lack of zeal regarding corruption since entering office. One of the few investigations that have received official attention is the inquiry into corruption and wasteful spending by Toledo and his wife, Eliane Karp, and many see this as largely political theater.

The Peruvian news media is perhaps the primary driver of discussion about corruption-related issues. National newspapers and television programs, as well as some regional and local media, constantly unearth new instances of corruption. Some of the most significant recent scandals, including the early 2007 attempted purchase of overpriced police patrol cars that resulted in the resignation of Interior Minister Pilar Mazzetti, came to light after being reported in the media. The return of APRA to power has reinvigorated the watchdog instinct within the press. The absence of whistle-blower laws in Peru inhibits the willingness of public employees to speak out about corruption within the government. A measure originally proposed in 2003 nearly passed the congress in 2006 but has fallen off the agenda.[39] More generally, anticorruption activists can be subject to intimidation, especially at the local level.

The Peruvian government, although still often opaque, has measurably improved its transparency in recent years. The Law on Transparency and Public Information has been valid since 2002 and imposes significant transparency obligations on the state. Citizens may petition the state for information, and compliance is slowly improving as knowledge of the law spreads. The process is highly bureaucratic, however; according to an investigation by Article 19, functionaries continue to delay the handing over of documents due to fear of being punished by their superiors.[40]

The Peruvian executive's budget-making process is rated as a model for developing countries in terms of transparency and timeliness. The 2006 Open Budget Index ranked Peru seventh out of fifty-nine countries evaluated, ahead of such industrialized nations as Sweden, South Korea, and Norway.[41]

The publication of expenditures is handled at the agency level. Compliance with the law, which requires that websites be fully updated quarterly, varies by agency. The Peruvian Press Council (CPP), which monitors compliance with the law, reported in January 2007 that twenty-seven out of the forty-one state institutions it evaluated had not adequately updated relevant financial information; in particular, the presidential web portal lacked detailed spending information.[42]

The awarding of government contracts and concessions is an area of vulnerability in Peru. Laws governing research on market prices are unclear, although the CGR has proposed introducing a more transparent price-filtering tool known as the "witness price." The Mazzetti affair was just one of numerous scandals to emerge in relation to government purchases. The government has taken some actions to improve state contracts. Transparency has increased, and technology is being gradually implemented to facilitate reverse-auction and other mechanisms intended to maximize efficiency.

Recommendations

- The constitution should be amended to guarantee permanently the autonomy of the Comptroller General of the Republic by making it an independent organ.
- As suggested by CERIAJUS and Supreme Court President Tavara, the statute of limitations should be lifted for crimes involving public corruption.
- The proposed whistle-blower law should be passed and steps taken to assure that repercussions against whistle-blowers are investigated and punished.
- The state should formulate and enact an effective system of research for all state purchases in order to guarantee market prices and quality control.

NOTES

1 Maria Elena Castillo, "El 58% aprueba a Garcia, pero mayoria senala que no cumple con sus promesas," *La Republica*, 9 February 2007, www.larepublica.com.pe/content /view/142364/483/.

2 "Electoral Observation Mission of the OAS Presents Preliminary Report on Second Round of the Presidential Election in Peru" (Washington: Organization of American States [OAS], OAS Press Advisory, 6 June 2006), www.oas.org/OASpage/press_releases /press_release.asp?sCodigo=EOM-PE-04.

3 "Electoral Observation Mission . . . Preliminary Report . . ." (OAS, 6 June 2006), www .oas.org/OASpage/press_releases/press_release.asp?sCodigo=MOE-PE-5E.

4 Lack of identity papers caused many other problems related to rights as well. See Civil Liberties. The 1 million number is disputed. See "Peru Election 2006" (Vancouver: University of British Columbia, Department of Political Science, 9 June 2006), http://weblogs .elearning.ubc.ca/peru/archives/027810.php for a useful dialogue regarding its validity.

5 Interview with Dra. Magdalena Chu, Chief of ONPE, 26 March 2007.

6 Interview at Institute of Legal Defense, Lima, 2 April 2007.

7 Cynthia Sanborn and Eduardo Moron, "The Pitfalls of Policymaking in Peru: Actors, Institutions, and Rules of the Game" (Washington, D.C.: Inter-American Development Bank [IADB], Research Network Working Paper, April 2006), 46. Garcia, however, received decree power on tax and security issues in the first year of his term.

8 Koldo Echebarría, ed., "Informe sobre la situación del servicio civil en América Latina" (IADB, May 2006), 423.

9 This newfound interest in social issues is mainly the result of fear that if social exclusion is not ameliorated, the 2011 election could result in the victory of Humala or some similarly populist candidate.

10 Ramiro Escobar, "Crime: Public Starting to Lose Faith in Peru's Corruption Battle," IPS Inter-Press Service (Lima), 15 July 2005, Lexis-Nexis.

11 Interview with Adriana Leon of the Institute for Press and Society, Lima, 26 March 2007.

12 Interview at Asociacion Pro-Derechos Humanos (APRODEH), Lima, 28 March 2007.

13 Bajo el signo de un gobierno con pasado: Informe Anual 2006 (Lima: Coordinadora Nacional de Derechos Humanos [CNDDHH], April 2007, 44, www.dhperu.org/index .php?link=24&pag=4.

14 Ibid.

15 Ibid., 104.

16 Interview at Defensoria del Pueblo, Lima, 30 March 2007.

17 Interview at Institute of Legal Defense, 2 April 2007.

18 "Sendero Kill Eight in Ambush," *Latinnews Daily*, 21 December 2005, Lexis-Nexis.

19 Interview at Institute of Legal Defense, Lima, 30 March 2007.

20 *Informe Anual 2006* (CNDDHH).

21 "Terapia Colectiva," Caretas 1969 (29 March 2007): 38.

22 This figure includes both physical and psychological abuse. Interview with Cecilia Olea of Flora Tristan Women's Center, 27 March 2007.

23 Antonio Zapata, "Educacion y trabajo de la mujer en el Peru," *La Republica*, 7 March 2007.

24 The leftist-nationalist military government initiated by Juan Velasco in 1968 discouraged the use of the word "indigena," instead preferring the more class-relevant "campesino." See Wilfredo Ardito, "Racismo en el Peru Republicano," *Revista Aportes Andinos* (Quito: Universidad Andina Simon Bolivar, April 2004), www.uasb.edu.ec /padh/revista9/articulos/wilfrido%20ardito.htm#pasado.

25 Ardito, "Primer Juicio Penal por Discriminación," *Reflexiones Peruanas* 135, 28 February 2007, http://reflexionesperuanas.blogspot.com/2007/02/rp-135-primer-proceso-penal-por.html.

26 Ardito, "Y usted . . . no sera tambien indigena?" *Reflexiones Peruanas* 137, 10 May 2007, http://reflexionesperuanas.blogspot.com/2007/05/reflexiones-peruanas-137-y-usted-no-ser.html.

27 Interview with Ricardo Zevallos of Risolidaria, Lima, 28 March 2007.

28 Interview at Centro de Asesoria Laboral de Peru (CEDAL), Lima, 27 March 2007.

29 *Informe Anual 2006* (CNDDHH), 41.

30 Interview with Dr. Francisco Tavara, President of Peruvian Supreme Court, Lima, 29 March 2007.

31 *Informe Anual 2006* (CNDDHH), 47.

32 "APRODEH Lamenta y Cuestiona Destitucion de Fiscal Cristina Olazábal" (Lima: APRODEH, press release, 3 November 2006), www.aprodeh.org.pe/notapress/notas /03nov06.htm.

33 Interview at Institute of Legal Defense, Lima, 2 April 2007.

34 *Informe Anual 2006*, 36.

35 Jose Miguel Vivanco, "Letter to President Toledo on the Military's Failure to Cooperate with Investigations" (New York: Human Rights Watch [HRW], 16 March 2006), http://hrw.org/english/docs/2006/03/13/peru13045.htm.

36 "Peru" in Doing Business (Washington, D.C.: The World Bank, 2006), www.doing-business.org/ExploreEconomies/Default.aspx?economyid=152.

37 *Cuarta encuesta nacional sobre corrupcion* (Lima: Proteica, October 2006), www.proetica .org.pe/Descargas/PPT/presentacion.ppt.

38 Interview at Proetica, Lima, 30 March 2007.

39 Interview at Contraloria General de La Republica, Lima, 29 March 2007.

40 Javier Casas, "A Legal Framework for Access to Information in Peru," in *Time for Change: Promoting and Protecting Access to Information and Reproductive and Sexual Health Rights in Peru* (London: Article 19, 2006), 48.

41 Open Budget Index 2006 (Washington, D.C.: Center on Budget and Policy Priorities, 2006), 37, www.openbudgetindex.org/SummaryReport.pdf.

42 Alejandra Nieto, "CPP: Gobierno no cumple con la Ley de Transparencia," *La Republica*, 25 January 2007, www.larepublica.com.pe/content/view/140168/483.

PHILIPPINES

CAPITAL: Manila

POPULATION: 88.7 million

GNI PER CAPITA: $1,420

SCORES	2005	2007
ACCOUNTABILITY AND PUBLIC VOICE:	4.46	4.16
CIVIL LIBERTIES:	3.92	3.85
RULE OF LAW:	3.30	3.29
ANTICORRUPTION AND TRANSPARENCY:	3.50	3.38

(scores are based on a scale of 0 to 7, with 0 representing weakest and 7 representing strongest performance)

Paul D. Hutchcroft

INTRODUCTION

At first glance, the Philippines might be perceived as a thriving democracy. Since its transition from authoritarian rule in 1986, general elections have been held in 1992, 1998, and 2004. Midterm elections—for positions ranging from the local level to the national Senate and House of Representatives—have been held on schedule in intervening years. The May 2004 elections involved a wide array of political parties and brought forth impressive levels of voter turnout. Civic involvement was extensive, as hundreds of thousands of volunteers went to polling stations to try to safeguard the electoral process. Midterm elections in May 2007 continued these patterns and resulted in substantial gains for the opposition in the Senate.

On the whole, Philippine democracy has combined popular exuberance with the major flaws of elite dominance and institutional weakness.

Paul D. Hutchcroft is a Professor of Political Science at the University of Wisconsin–Madison. He has written extensively on Philippine politics and political economy, and is the author of *Booty Capitalism: The Politics of Banking in the Philippines* (Cornell, 1998). His current book project, *The Power of Patronage: Capital and Countryside in the Twentieth-Century Philippines*, analyzes territorial politics in the Philippines from the early U.S. colonial period through the Local Government Code of the 1990s.

The political structures implanted and nurtured under U.S. colonial rule in the early twentieth century were characterized by the exclusion of the masses, patronage-infested political parties, a spoils system that undermined bureaucratic coherence, and (under the 1935 constitution) opportunities for overbearing executive authority. While suffrage expanded after independence in 1946, the country's "cacique democracy" fell far short of the democratic ideal. In essence, there was rotation of power within the elite without effective participation by those at the bottom of highly inequitable socioeconomic structures.[1] Authoritarian enclaves could be found in many locales throughout the archipelago.

In 1972, President Ferdinand Marcos concentrated power in his own hands by declaring martial law. He proclaimed that he would replace the "old oligarchy" with his "New Society" and lay down stronger foundations for democratic renewal, but it soon became clear that his ultimate goal was the creation of a new oligarchy centered on his own family. By the time he was removed from office via the "People Power" uprising of 1986, the economy was a shambles. Incoming president Corazon Aquino (1986–1992) focused on restoring the structures of pre–martial law elite democracy, and the old clans stepped forward to reclaim their places in Congress. Aquino's successor, former general Fidel Ramos (1992–1998), achieved substantial success in promoting important economic reforms through skillful manipulation of old-style patronage politics. Elements of a vibrant civil society, meanwhile, sought to keep up the pressure for much-needed social reforms.

When former movie star Joseph Estrada was elected to the presidency by a landslide in 1998, he promised material improvements for the masses but instead devoted his presidency to taking care of himself, his (multiple) families, and his cronies. Anger over allegations of corruption, abuse of power, and involvement with gambling syndicates led to impeachment proceedings. In January 2001, when the trial became stalled in the Senate, huge crowds took to the streets in protest. After the military withdrew support from his administration, Estrada left the palace and Vice President Gloria Macapagal Arroyo assumed the presidency with the imprimatur of the Supreme Court. She served out the remainder of Estrada's term and was then elected to her own six-year term in 2004.

Analysis of recent trends suggests that Asia's oldest democracy has become increasingly dysfunctional in several important ways. First, deepening concerns about the competence and integrity of the Commission on Elections (COMELEC) have further undermined public confidence in its capacity to adjudicate election results with accuracy and fairness. While the Philippines has often exhibited deficiencies in electoral administration, these problems were manifested most dramatically in the May 2004 elections. More than a year later, in the wake of allegations that the president herself had played a role in fixing the vote count, the Arroyo government nearly collapsed. Second, the Philippines has dozens of political parties but no party system per se. Because most parties are loosely organized vehicles with little programmatic coherence, voters lack substantive choice when they cast their ballots. Politicians frequently move from one party or party alliance to another, and few parties have any serious institutional apparatus (it is notable that presidents give little attention to the development of their own ruling parties). Third, the influence of money and coercion skews electoral outcomes in favor of those who can successfully buy votes and/or coerce voters. Fourth, there is strong evidence of military involvement in the killings of hundreds of leftists, activists, and church personnel. In the wake of a recent fact-finding mission, a UN Special Rapporteur expressed concern about the impact of these killings on the democratic process: "It intimidates vast numbers of civil society actors, it sends a message of vulnerability to all but the most well connected, and it severely undermines the political discourse which is central to a resolution of the problems confronting this country."[2] Fifth, press freedom is undermined by killings of journalists and a poor record of prosecuting those responsible. A more recent trend involves increasing numbers of libel suits against journalists by people close to the current administration. In light of these developments, many freedom indicators for the Philippines have declined since 2005.

ACCOUNTABILITY AND PUBLIC VOICE

FREE AND FAIR ELECTORAL LAWS AND ELECTIONS:	3.25
EFFECTIVE AND ACCOUNTABLE GOVERNMENT:	3.25
CIVIC ENGAGEMENT AND CIVIC MONITORING:	6.00
MEDIA INDEPENDENCE AND FREEDOM OF EXPRESSION:	4.13
CATEGORY AVERAGE:	**4.16**

The Republic of the Philippines has a presidential system and a bicameral legislature. Under the current constitution, adopted in 1987, the president and vice president are elected by popular vote for single six-year terms. The twenty-four members of the upper house, the Senate, are elected from a single, nationwide district.

In the 2004 elections, President Arroyo received 40 percent of the popular vote, and in the final vote count she exceeded the tally of her closest contender by more than 1 million votes. Arroyo proved to be an indefatigable campaigner, highly adept at deploying the many advantages of incumbency and cutting deals with local politicians and religious groups that could deliver the votes of their constituencies. In the wake of the elections, Arroyo's ruling party alliance controlled the Senate and the House. However, given the weakness of party loyalties and party discipline, ongoing control and influence over legislators must regularly be renewed through the dispersal of patronage and public resources.

In line with historical patterns of high voter turnout, nearly 75 percent of registered voters cast their ballots in the May 2004 elections.[3] For the first time, rights of suffrage were given to the millions of overseas Filipino workers who had previously been excluded from the electoral process. Unfortunately, a mere 233,000 chose to exercise their right to vote.[4]

The 2004 elections revealed many flaws in the system of electoral administration. As many as 2 million voters appeared at polling places to find that their names were not on official COMELEC lists.[5] In the absence of clear patterns of favoritism, this disenfranchisement seems to have been the result of administrative incompetence. Most damaging to COMELEC credibility was the release, in mid-2005, of audiotapes thought to contain conversations between the president and a notorious COMELEC official. In these conversations, a distinctive female voice was apparently seeking assistance in ensuring a million-vote margin in the presidential race.[6] The scandal that the tapes provoked not only threatened the survival of the Arroyo administration but also severely undermined the legitimacy of the electoral process.

The Philippine ballot is probably one of the most archaic in the world, as attempts at modernization have bogged down amid allegations of corruption. Voters are required to fill in, by hand, the names of all candidates for whom they are voting. The vote tally is then conducted manually; with 35 million ballots, each containing votes for twenty-five to thirty positions, election officials face the gargantuan task of counting about a billion preferences in all. This laborious process has proven to be highly susceptible to fraud: as official election tallies begin their long migration from local precincts to Manila, politicians can use a variety of tactics to supplement retail vote purchases with wholesale manipulation of the vote count. Allegations of fraud were prevalent throughout the tallying period in May and June 2004, but the results were given some validity by a leading vote-monitoring group. The 2005 vote-fixing allegations against the president tainted both the 2004 elections and those who had previously chosen to give them a stamp of approval.[7]

In addition, both COMELEC and the national police failed in their obligation to ensure the security of candidates and voters during the election period. According to police statistics, there were 148 killings in election-related violence in 2004, more than double the total from the last general elections in 1998. Moreover, the insurgent New People's Army (NPA) was reportedly extorting permit-to-campaign fees in the areas that it controlled, and is alleged to have killed rivals on the left. While most election-related violence occurred in provincial towns or rural areas and may not have affected the results elsewhere, voters in areas where violence or the threat of violence existed were not free to make informed political choices and were thus effectively disenfranchised.[8]

[UPDATE: While the May 2007 elections took place after the period examined in this report, the results deserve brief summary. Voter turnout declined to an estimated 66 percent of registered voters, lower than in the 2004 general elections. One election-monitoring group, Bantay Eleksyon, speculates that this may be due to "stricter monitoring by citizen groups [preventing] the padding of votes in many places."[9] The vote count was conducted at a customarily slow pace, with major contention over the twelfth place finisher in the senatorial races (the winner was not declared until July). The Philippine national police reported 121 election-related killings, less than the 148 deaths in the 2004 general elections but marginally more than the 111 people killed in the last midterm elections in 2001. A broad alliance of disparate opposition forces won the majority of seats in the Senate, but the ruling party alliance enjoys overwhelming control of the House. Given the weakness of party alliances, this balance may shift. In the Senate, the palace will likely be able to woo some of the opposition senators to its side. In the House, although the president and Speaker Jose de Venecia have enjoyed a long-standing alliance, apparent tensions in their relationship merit close observation.[10]]

Aside from problems of administration, the Philippine electoral system in its very design encourages politics based on personalities and patronage rather than platforms and parties. Candidates from well-known families, along with newscasters and movie stars, are favored by the antiquated, non-preprinted ballot. There is no option to vote according to a party ticket. Even the posts of president and vice president are elected separately, often leading to a situation in which the two top national officials claim allegiance to rival political parties or factions. Bloc voting for the Senate encourages rivalries within parties; since all candidates are competing within one nationwide district, each senatorial candidate is required to forge his or her own alliances with local political clans who can deliver votes from across the archipelago. One might expect the election of one-fifth of the House through proportional representation (PR) to strengthen parties somewhat, but this outcome is undermined by the highly unconventional nature of Philippine PR. While a conventional PR system requires a *minimum* level of electoral success in order to gain seats, Philippine PR imposes a *maximum* limit of three seats per party regardless of the number of votes received.[11]

A final concern relates to inequities in the financing of political parties and candidates. Although all parties and candidates have equal campaigning rights, the prohibitive cost of campaigns privileges wealthy candidates. The 1985 omnibus election code bars campaign contributions from specific individuals and entities, including financial institutions, public utility operators, government contractors, government civilian and military personnel, and foreigners and foreign corporations. There are no limits, however, on the size of contributions from individuals or entities not covered by the prohibition. Moreover, the code specifies limits on expenditures for election purposes, but enforcement of such limits is doubtful. As a result, those with money exert a disproportionate influence on election results. This includes not only traditional political-economic elites but also those who have close ties to gambling syndicates, drug lords, and other members of the under-world.[12] If election administrators cannot with any degree of accuracy maintain voter lists or count vote results, it is unrealistic to suppose that they would be able to enforce the provisions of a campaign finance law—no matter how well intentioned the writing of such legislation might be.

Democratic accountability is reinforced by the countervailing power of the three branches of government (executive, legislative, and judicial) and two houses of the legislature (the House and the Senate). Recent impeachment attempts against Arroyo (in 2005 and 2006) have failed, as the administration has been able to count on the support of House Speaker Jose de Venecia and the legislators whose loyalty he rewards. However, late in 2006, efforts by the presidential palace and the speaker to push through major constitutional changes were blocked by the Supreme Court. A palace-backed "people's initiative" had gathered sig-natures from throughout the country in support of a plebiscite on shift-ing the country from a bicameral presidential system to a unicameral parliamentary system. The high court ruled that the campaign did not fulfill constitutional requirements.[13] In subsequent weeks, senators offered further opposition to reforms designed to abolish their chamber. These episodes indicate the capacity of separate branches of government to oppose abuses of power and to force a more deliberative approach on such important issues as constitutional reform.

At the same time, corruption and inefficiency nurtured by a well-entrenched spoils system frequently undermine the bureaucracy's capac-ity to implement laws that have been passed by the legislature and signed by the president. Corruption can be found at all levels of government, and graft accusations are a staple of opposition challenges to incumbents. Every administration promises measures to clean up government, and in some cases they can claim certain degrees of success in targeted areas. Structural obstacles, however, generally frustrate sustained improvement. The electoral process privileges the dispensing of patronage over the de-livery of good governance, thus limiting the ability of voters to demand policy-based accountability from elected officials.[14] The high expense of elections encourages corrupt behavior on the part of politicians, and there is little incentive for a national administration to enforce corrup-tion laws at the local level except against opposition figures. Poorly paid bureaucrats have their own individual incentives for corrupt behavior, and are often able to engage in corrupt acts with impunity.

Institutional problems notwithstanding, the democratic impulse within Philippine society is deep and enduring. Civil society organizations are strong and have in the past nurtured free-election movements intent not only on combating vote fraud but also on countering the tendency of patronage politics to corrupt democracy and undermine good governance. In 1986, these organizations came together in an ad hoc coalition that was able to topple the corrupt and authoritarian regime of Ferdinand Marcos. The pattern was repeated against Joseph Estrada in 2001.

As part of the post-Marcos antiauthoritarian impulse, Philippine non-governmental organizations (NGOs) have been actively and formally incorporated into decision-making processes. A prime example is the 1991 Local Government Code, which mandates the representation of NGOs on local councils. While this incorporation has often been resisted by local politicians, the provisions of the law do provide new opportunities for organized societal groups to influence the decisions of development councils, school boards, and bidding committees. The state does not subject NGOs and other civic organizations to onerous registration requirements, nor does it harass donors and funders of these organizations.

A final historical strength of Philippine democracy is its boisterous media scene, which plays a major role in publicizing allegations of corruption. Since the fall of the Marcos regime in 1986, the media have been free from direct state censorship. Philippine media enjoy a very substantial degree of freedom, whether one is examining traditional print and broadcast media, works of cultural expression, or access to the internet. The bulk of the media is under private ownership, and the government does not impose overly burdensome registration requirements.[15] Despite these broad freedoms, recent increases in the harassment of journalists are integrally related to broader concerns about the declining condition of Philippine democracy.

The widespread killing of journalists led Reporters Without Borders to declare that "after Iraq, the Philippines is the most dangerous country for journalists." According to the Committee to Protect Journalists, thirty-two reporters have been killed for their reporting in the fifteen years between 1991 and 2006. Fewer than 10 percent of the cases have led to convictions. A recent government commission on media and activist killings points the finger at "local politicians, warlords, or big business interests" driven by a range of mainly local motives.

A newer mode of media harassment comes from those close to the national leadership. In 2006, the president's husband, "First Gentleman" Jose Miguel Arroyo, filed libel suits against forty-three journalists. The lawsuits seek a total of US$1.4 million in damages for stories accusing him of involvement in vote rigging and corrupt actions; if convicted, the journalists could also face imprisonment for six months to six years. In response, 600 journalists and thirty supporting organizations have issued a petition urging the decriminalization of libel. A government attempt to charge other journalists with sedition in the wake of a February 2006 coup attempt was blocked by the Supreme Court.[16] It is not clear to what extent these legal charges will intimidate or embolden the media, particularly given that libel and sedition laws have not in the past been an effective means of curbing media criticism of government officials. Combined with the killings, however, the legal charges must be viewed as a disturbing attack on one of the major bulwarks of Philippine democracy.

Recommendations

- COMELEC needs thoroughgoing reform, from the national to the local level, so that it can develop the capacity to maintain accurate lists of voters and execute an accurate and expeditious vote count. Allegations of election fraud, particularly postelection, wholesale manipulation of the vote count involving politicians and COMELEC officials, need to be investigated by independent prosecutors who are willing and able to press charges for wrongdoing.
- The government should ensure the modernization of the ballot and the automation of the vote-tallying process prior to the next general elections in 2010.
- The national police and COMELEC should work together to reduce election-related violence. The effort must include prompt investigation, prosecution, and punishment of violent acts.
- The government should ensure that murders of journalists result in the prosecution and punishment of perpetrators. The national leadership must exhibit the political will to reverse the current culture of impunity.

CIVIL LIBERTIES

PROTECTION FROM STATE TERROR, UNJUSTIFIED IMPRISONMENT, AND TORTURE:	2.00
GENDER EQUITY:	4.00
RIGHTS OF ETHNIC, RELIGIOUS, AND OTHER DISTINCT GROUPS:	3.50
FREEDOM OF CONSCIENCE AND BELIEF:	5.33
FREEDOM OF ASSOCIATION AND ASSEMBLY:	4.40
CATEGORY AVERAGE:	**3.85**

While the 1987 constitution enshrines a range of civil liberties, the government has an inconsistent record of putting these guarantees into practice. Those who have the means to hire lawyers fare much better than those who do not, and those who attract the gaze of the national media can generally defend their constitutional rights more effectively than those in distant provinces. Although in some cases the government has taken additional legal steps to ensure that citizens enjoy their rights, in other cases fundamental constitutional rights have been circumvented—particularly in the fight against those labeled insurgents or terrorists. Along with central policy directives, many problems arise from the national government's seeming lack of control over its own security forces.

An alarming development in recent years has been the killing of hundreds of leftists, activists, and church personnel. The murders are most common in areas where the government battles the Communist Party of the Philippines, whose NPA is engaged in a nearly three-decade-long armed struggle against the government. Although the number of people killed since the Arroyo administration took power in 2001 is in dispute (136 according to the national police and 836 according to one local human rights group), Amnesty International (AI) reported a substantial increase in 2005 and 2006. In June 2006, the government declared "all-out war" against Communist rebels. The killings have been given increasing national and international attention since 2006, through an August 2006 report by AI, a February 2007 report by a special government commission, March 2007 hearings in the U.S. Senate, a June 2007 Human Rights Watch report, and a report by a UN Special Rapporteur scheduled for release in mid-2007. President Arroyo's own commission concluded that "some elements in the military were behind the killing of activists" and that ranking armed forces personnel have failed in their duty to investigate, punish, and prevent the killings.[17] In general, prosecution of the killings is hampered both by a long-standing culture of impunity for human rights abuses and continuing fears among potential witnesses of the danger of reprisals for cooperating with the police. According to Human Rights Watch, not a single perpetrator has been successfully prosecuted.[18]

In areas where the insurgency is strong, the government is likewise unable to prevent killings of civilians by the left. As the military is quick to emphasize, the NPA has a history of killing civilian opponents and in the 1980s undertook gruesome purges of its own members.[19] In some cases, it is alleged, the NPA plays the role of hired gun in disputes among rival elite politicians. Security forces are also deficient in securing the citizenry against such crimes as homicide, assault, theft, and rape; even worse are charges that some elements of the security forces have ties to criminal syndicates.[20]

In February 2006, rebellious military officers botched an attempt to combine a popular uprising with a coup d'etat. In response, the Arroyo government declared a state of emergency "in a hurriedly drafted proclamation that sounded eerily like the one Marcos signed when he declared martial law in 1972." Many feared the loss of democratic rights, but the Arroyo government encountered considerable opposition to its measures and the Supreme Court later ruled that the official acts promulgated under emergency rule were illegal. Although the main perpetrators were within the military, the primary targets of government repression were on the left, including Congress members. A recent report by the American Bar Association (ABA) voices concern over the "misuse" of rebellion and sedition charges and the impact that this has on the country's civil liberties.[21]

A new antiterrorism bill, enacted in March 2007 and effective in July, gives the government formal authority to detain suspects for three days without charges. In addition, it provides new authority to conduct surveillance, initiate wiretaps, and seize assets. Critics, including the Catholic bishops conference and UN human rights experts, fear that a broad definition of "terrorism" invites abuse of civil liberties.[22]

The constitution guarantees protection against torture and deprivation of liberty without due process. Indeed, as stipulated in the constitution, a Commission on Human Rights was created in 1987 with the power to investigate, on its own or after receiving complaints, violations of these guarantees as well as other civil and political rights. Yet arbitrary arrests, long-term detention without trial, and even torture persist, primarily in cases of suspected insurgents and their sympathizers. In a 2003 report, AI noted a "serious discrepancy" between laws on the books prohibiting torture and its use by law enforcement officials. Within a larger context of "intimidation and fear of reprisals," the burden of proof is on the victims—thus making it extremely rare for acts of torture to be prosecuted.[23] Government and nongovernmental human rights groups are seeking to reverse patterns of impunity through the passage of a law that criminalizes acts of torture.[24]

In April 2006, President Arroyo commuted the death sentences of 1,230 prisoners in what is probably "the world's largest ever mass commutation." Two months later, the death penalty was abolished by law.[25] The next humanitarian challenge will be to improve conditions for Philippine prisoners, who are commonly housed in deplorable, unsanitary facilities designed for much smaller populations. System-wide, facilities that measure 56,000 square meters house more than 60,000 prisoners. Basic necessities, including toilets and sleeping space, are in short supply. The superintendent of prisons laments the lack of funds for building new facilities and predicts a 13 percent annual increase in the prison population over the next eight years.[26] Children are sometimes detained in adult facilities and, like women, face risks of physical and sexual abuse.[27]

Citizens whose rights are violated by the state can legally petition for redress through the judicial system. But the judicial system, while in the process of reform, is still biased against those of little means (see Rule of Law). The poor majority often lack the education and financial resources necessary to navigate the courts.

The government can point to some progress in achieving the goal of gender equity, as societal groups encourage it to fulfill a clearly stated mandate in the 1987 constitution (Article II, Section 14). Often in response to lobbying by women's groups, the government has enacted many laws promoting women's rights. At the pinnacle of power, women often play a very visible role. Two out of the four post-Marcos presidents have been women, although in both cases their political careers followed those of prominent politician relatives—for Corazon Aquino, her husband, and for Gloria Macapagal Arroyo, her father. While President Arroyo's cabinet was overwhelmingly male as of mid-2007, a substantial proportion of cabinet members were women in earlier years of the administration.[28] The Senate and the House are 17 percent and 16 percent women, respectively.[29] More than half of government employees are female, but they hold only about 35 percent of top-level positions in the bureaucracy.[30] One-third of the judges of the Supreme Court and the Court of Appeals are women, as are 23 percent of judges in trial courts at all levels.[31] One half of students in law school are female, and women play a very prominent role in the professions more generally.[32]

Further down the socioeconomic ladder, Filipino women face much more substantial obstacles, and achievements on the ground often fall short of promises in the law. Female factory workers often labor in harsh conditions without benefit of union protections. Women who seek work abroad in the entertainment industry sometimes find themselves victimized by criminal syndicates. Sex workers throughout the country are exploited by brothel owners, pimps, customers, and police officers.[33] Legal measures have been adopted to address major concerns of women, including a 2003 act addressing trafficking of women and children and a 2004 law criminalizing domestic violence against women and children.[34] Their success has yet to be ascertained. In the view of one UN agency, however, "progressive laws are not always enforced, and despite the existence of equality under the law, women still suffer discrimination in many areas."[35]

The 1987 constitution calls for the state to give priority to the needs of "the underprivileged, sick, disabled, women, and children" (Article XIII, Section 11). Because most disabled people live in poverty,[36] efforts to improve their condition are often part of larger programs of poverty alleviation. The National Anti-Poverty Commission, established in 1998, seeks to encourage cooperation among national government agencies, local government leagues, and representatives from fourteen "basic sectors" of society, including people with disabilities. While some progress has been made in integrating the disabled into mainstream society, in large part due to the efforts of NGOs, they continue to face problems of access to basic social services, housing, education, and employment.[37]

The government has a relatively strong record with respect to freedom of conscience and belief. The vast majority of Filipinos are Roman Catholic (85 percent); Protestants make up 9 percent, and Muslims 5 percent. While Catholics predominate in government, the state does not interfere in the appointment of religious leaders or the internal activities of other peaceful faith-related organizations, nor does it place restrictions on religious observance, religious ceremony, or religious education. Non-Catholic Christians, as well as Catholics out of favor with elements of the church leadership, are able to succeed in the political arena. President Ramos (1992–1998) was a Protestant, and President Estrada (1998–2001) received a strong electoral mandate despite the opposition of key members of the Catholic hierarchy. Muslim politicians, however, have had little success at winning national office. Since 1987, only two Muslims have won seats in the Senate, partly due to the nationwide electoral district. Representation of Muslims in presidential cabinets, moreover, is minimal at best.

While Filipino Muslims are free to practice their religion, the post–World War II flood of Christian settlers to traditionally Muslim areas in Mindanao led to increasing tensions over land ownership and control of political and economic resources. Muslim elites' historical accommodation with Manila came under fire from those seeking to challenge structures of discrimination against Muslims and protect communities against Christian paramilitary groups. The current armed conflict between the government and Muslim groups can be traced to the 1972 declaration of martial law, which closed off opportunities for peaceful conflict resolution. In an effort to address Muslim concerns, the architects of the 1987 constitution provided for the creation of an autonomous region in Muslim Mindanao (ARMM). But the establishment of ARMM did not end the insurgency, as many in the region objected both to its boundaries and to Manila's efforts to interfere in the determination of its leadership.

Since a historic 1996 accord between Manila and the Moro National Liberation Front (MNLF), the major secessionist movement in Mindanao has been the Moro Islamic Liberation Front (MILF). The MILF split from the MNLF in 1978 and is estimated to have 12,000 fighters.[38] Although founded with a commitment to form an independent Islamic state, the MILF has in fact demonstrated significant capacity for negotiation and compromise. Negotiations with Manila have been and continue to be complicated by government vacillation between conciliation and aggression, alleged links between the MILF and transnational extremist organizations such as Jemaah Islamiah (JI), and the MILF's lack of operational control over many of its ground units.[39] Meanwhile, militarization of the area due to the conflict has created many opportunities for violations of the rights of civilians, both Muslim and Christian. The International Crisis Group declares the Philippines to be "the region's weakest state—effectively a failed state in parts of the south where JI fugitives and others find sanctuary."[40]

In stark contrast to the MILF, the Abu Sayyaf Group (ASG) is estimated to have a mere 200 fighters. It has previously expressed ideological goals, had tenuous links with al-Qaeda, and is widely thought to have associations with JI. ASG has also been blamed for urban bombings. However, it has largely degenerated into a bandit organization devoted to piracy and kidnapping foreign tourists for ransom. Given Manila's weakness in controlling the country's periphery, it is only with the assistance of U.S. forces that these "entrepreneurs in violence" have been contained.[41]

Along with the Muslim minority, indigenous (largely upland) communities have long felt discriminated against by the government and the dominant lowland Christian majority. Those classified by law as indigenous constitute 15 percent to 20 percent of the population.[42] Roughly 60 percent of these indigenous peoples have their ancestral homes in Mindanao, while another 33 percent live in Luzon.[43] A UN report notes "significant human rights violations" against indigenous communities as the result of "economic activities such as logging, mining, multi-purpose dams, commercial plantations, and other development projects. . . . Sometimes . . . entire areas are reported to have been devastated without regard to the wishes and rights of indigenous communities."[44]

The constitution enshrines the right to form associations for purposes not contrary to the law as well as the right to mobilize and advocate for peaceful purposes. The state does not compel citizens directly or indirectly to belong to particular associations. The wide array of organizations in the country indicates the substantial freedom of association that Filipinos enjoy. In 2003, over 20 percent of the total number of paid employees in the country belonged to trade unions.[45] While citizens are free to join groups and mobilize for peaceful protests, the government often fails to exercise restraint when dispersing demonstrators.

Historically, rallies of peasant farmers and urban poor have frequently evolved into violent clashes.

Recommendations

- National leaders should consistently and unambiguously condemn the recent political killings and vigorously pursue the prosecution of all who are responsible.
- Rebellion and sedition charges, as well as new antiterrorism provisions, should not be used to harass the political opposition or narrow the scope of legitimate political discourse.
- Allegations of torture and violations of due process should be investigated promptly and fully, and the government should ensure appropriate prosecution and punishment. The first step toward this goal is the passage of a law criminalizing acts of torture.
- Prison conditions, notably the lack of basic sanitation and sleeping space, need urgent attention as prison populations rapidly increase. Laws designed to protect children in custody should be strictly enforced. Female offenders should have separate facilities supervised by female staff.
- The government should ensure the more consistent enforcement of laws against the trafficking of women and children, as well as those criminalizing domestic violence.
- Training for law enforcement personnel should include techniques on negotiating with demonstrators in order to reduce the use of force. Law enforcement personnel found to have used force indiscriminately should be appropriately punished.

RULE OF LAW

INDEPENDENT JUDICIARY:	3.80
PRIMACY OF RULE OF LAW IN CIVIL AND CRIMINAL MATTERS:	3.00
ACCOUNTABILITY OF SECURITY FORCES AND MILITARY TO CIVILIAN AUTHORITIES:	2.00
PROTECTION OF PROPERTY RIGHTS:	4.33
EQUAL TREATMENT UNDER THE LAW:	3.33
CATEGORY AVERAGE:	**3.29**

The Philippine constitution provides formal safeguards for judicial independence, and in recent rulings the Supreme Court has exhibited a considerable degree of independence from the executive and legislative branches. Major problems, however, plague the Philippine judicial system as a whole. Especially troubling in the overall assessment of rule-of-law indicators are recent trends in civil-military relations.

While there are many judges who fearlessly uphold the rule of law even in the face of substantial personal risk, the Philippine judicial system suffers from chronic inefficiency and widespread perceptions of corruption. As summarized in an acronym coined by a recent chief justice of the Supreme Court, there are "urgent ACID problems that corrode justice, namely, limited access to justice by the poor, corruption, incompetence, and delay in the delivery of quality justice."[46] Many express a lack of confidence in the impartiality and competence of the judiciary. The late Jaime Cardinal Sin, archbishop of Manila, once denounced the "judicial Judases" found throughout the judicial system and observed that the study and practice of law in the Philippines are "as different as heaven and hell."[47] Current reforms are designed to enhance the judiciary's independence, competence, probity, timeliness, and impartiality, but a persistent problem is the severe lack of resources provided to the judiciary.

The court system extends from local-level courts up through regional trial courts, the Court of Appeals, the Sandiganbayan (Anti-Graft Court), and the Supreme Court. The selection of judges for these and other more specialized courts begins with the Judicial and Bar Council (JBC), which has four ex-officio members (the chief justice, the secretary of justice, a member of the House of Representatives, and a member of the Senate) as well as four members appointed by the president with the consent of the joint House-Senate Commission on Appointments. The JBC considers the suitability of applicants based, at least formally, on a range of important minimum qualifications. It forwards a list of three candidates for each vacancy to the president, who then makes the appointment without legislative confirmation. A recent study team of the ABA reports that "the perception as to fairness in the Presidential appointment power was uniformly negative." At every step of the selection process, it is noted, personal connections outweigh professional expertise. "It was reported that politicians may call an applicant and ask what the judge would do for them if they supported the nomination." Judges enjoy a good deal of independence once in office, but "'gratitude' to the appointing authority may remain an issue" along with the influence of personal and familial connections.[48] This feeds long-standing concerns about the vulnerability of Philippine judges to political influence.

The 1987 constitution guarantees fiscal autonomy to the judicial branch: appropriations must be automatically released by the executive and cannot be reduced below the amount appropriated the previous year. In relative terms, however, the judiciary's share declined from 1.17 percent of the national budget in 1998 to 0.88 percent of the national budget in 2004.[49] The lower courts sometimes have difficulty paying their telephone and electric bills and often lack basic equipment (computers, photocopying machines, and the like). It is not uncommon for local courts to be beholden to local governments for the provision of their basic needs; in such a situation, local politicians can choose to deprive judges of their phone service. Courthouses are often in poor physical condition and uniformly lack basic security staff.[50]

The judicial system is bogged down by a huge backlog of cases, numbering over 800,000 at the end of 2005. One factor is the 30 percent vacancy rate in prosecutorial positions. As the ABA study team explained, slow justice contributes to the overcrowded prison conditions discussed above; as a result, "many accused languish in jails in violation of their constitutional rights." Further factors behind these judicial delays are the reluctance of judges to use contempt and subpoena powers to speed up the judicial process and the alleged corruption of process servers, sheriffs, and police.[51]

As part of the Action Program for Judicial Reform (APJR), initiated by former chief justice Hilario G. Davide in 2001, there was a 100 percent increase in judicial salaries between 2002 and 2006. This development has reportedly helped increase the number of applicants for vacant judgeships.[52] Nonetheless, according to a study recently cited by a Supreme Court justice, the salaries of upper-level judges are roughly one-sixth the salaries of their counterparts in the private sector. As he concluded, "a judiciary that has to be concerned on how to earn its own income for its very subsistence is not fully independent as it is not free from fear or free from want."[53] A recent survey revealed that judges are also concerned about their own physical safety. Between 1999 and 2006, ten judges were killed.[54]

The public continues to perceive substantial corruption in the judiciary. According to the ABA report, "many litigants apparently come to their attorneys expecting to have to pay for a favorable result, and some attorneys have apparently lost clients when they refuse" to make such a payment. Some credit the APJR and other reforms with helping to reduce the scope of corruption,[55] but reformers will continue to face the problem in the years to come.

To the extent that money buys justice, those without resources suffer most from the system's lack of impartiality. In a country with huge disparities of wealth and power, issues of access loom particularly large. Only 40 percent of respondents in a 2003 survey agreed with the statement: "Whether rich or poor, people who have cases in court generally receive equal treatment."[56] Those with wealth or political connections are able not only to hire the best lawyers but also to purchase a favorable result from prosecutors or judges. Lack of English skills disadvantages many poor Filipinos as they confront the legal system. Public defenders are given minimal salaries, and vacancy rates for such positions are even higher than those for prosecutorial jobs. This further aggravates the inability of the poor to gain access to justice, and undercuts the constitutionally guaranteed presumption of innocence. People with resources, meanwhile, know how to work the system to their advantage. It is rare for high-ranking government officials to be prosecuted, and convictions are even rarer. In 2004, the ombudsman admitted that it had been at least fifteen years since a "big fish" had been successfully prosecuted.[57]

It is important to emphasize, however, that the Supreme Court has demonstrated its capacity to resist political pressures from both the executive and the legislative branches of government. Most recently, as noted above (see Accountability and Public Voice), the Supreme Court in November 2006 blocked the joint attempt of the palace and the Speaker of the House to push through a "people's initiative" to amend the constitution. This was all the more notable given that a majority of the high court's members had been appointed by the president herself. This and other judgments in closely watched cases have been accepted as the law of the land and served to demonstrate the independence of the judiciary.

The Philippines has a long history of civilian control over the military, even during the martial-law regime headed by Ferdinand Marcos (who was, unlike many other authoritarian leaders in the region, a politician rather than a general).[58] The challenge of the post–martial law years has been military adventurism rather than military dominance. In the late 1980s, a total of nine coups were attempted against the government.[59] They were all failures, but they revealed the military's high degree of factional division, weak chain of command, and very low degree of institutionalization. Retired military officers have gone on to play important roles in the government, including the leading defender of constitutional government (future president Ramos, elected in 1992) and the most prominent leader of the post–Marcos coups (future senator Gregorio Honasan, elected in 1995). Their shift to electoral politics is often read as an indication of military power within civilian institutions, but in many ways it reflects instead the historical dominance of civilian institutions over those of the military.

Even so, the power of the military cannot be discounted. It is most apparent when there is division within or among civilian institutions, at which point the military has been able to tip the balance. The prime example is the decision of Joseph Estrada to leave the presidential palace in 2001 once he lost the support of senior military and police officers. Military factions are also capable of undermining confidence in the government even when their putschist actions fail; they demonstrate dissatisfaction with civilian leaders, who commonly increase favors to the military in response. A July 2003 mutiny in the financial district of Metro Manila was easily put down, for example, but not without unnerving the palace and encouraging special attention to the needs of top commanders.[60] Most recently, military adventurism brought an apparent coup attempt in February 2006, intended to coincide with the twentieth anniversary of the downfall of Ferdinand Marcos. The coup plans were leaked, and the plotters failed to garner the support they had hoped for. In the aftermath, the government took the opportunity to crack down on a range of opponents while assiduously cultivating top military officials. Political institutions have been weakened in the pursuit of regime preservation, and civil liberties have often been set aside. In such an environment, the military may again be the deciding factor between contending civilian factions.

As in the judicial system, a major constraint on property rights in the Philippines stems from unequal access to legal protections. The country has a long history of land grabbing, in which privileged elites dispossess the poor of their lands through both coercion and superior knowledge of the law. The postwar years have not witnessed the sustained success with land reform found elsewhere in East Asia. For those who can afford to initiate civil cases to protect property rights, there are frequent delays in contract enforcement and resolution of bankruptcy disputes. These delays bring insecurity to property owners, inhibiting investment. A recent index of property rights protections lists the Philippines in the third quartile of seventy countries surveyed worldwide.[61]

Indigenous communities' legal hold over ancestral domains has long been threatened by government allocation of resource rights to logging and mining interests. Building on previous legal efforts to improve security of tenure,[62] the 1987 constitution commits the state to protect the rights of "indigenous cultural communities" to ancestral lands, "subject to the provisions of this Constitution and national development policies and programs" (Article XII, Section 5).[63] The 1997 Indigenous Peoples Rights Act (IPRA) provided new legal avenues for securing community-based property rights and created a National Commission on Indigenous Peoples to promote indigenous people's rights and well-being. Mining interests challenged IPRA in the courts, but its constitutionality was confirmed by the Supreme Court in late 2000. On paper, these constitutional and statutory provisions provide an exemplary foundation for upholding indigenous rights. In practice, several factors inhibit their effectiveness: the government's lack of commitment and institutional capacity, indigenous communities' distrust of government agencies, legal inconsistencies, insufficient grassroots access to legal expertise, and continuing threats from the mining and lumber industries and their supporters within the government.[64]

Recommendations

- It is important to sustain the momentum of judicial reforms initiated in recent years. Particular attention should be given to reforms seeking to reduce the politicization of the judicial appointment process. In addition, salaries of judges should be further increased to attract sufficient numbers of qualified candidates.
- More resources should be devoted to ensure that poor defendants are provided with appropriate counsel and that citizens in rural areas have easier access to courts.
- The principle of civilian control over the military should be continually reaffirmed. Discontent among junior officers should be addressed

not by appeasing the top ranks but by addressing allegations of corruption within military structures. At the same time, acts of rebellion by the military should be vigorously investigated and prosecuted.

- Recognition of indigenous land rights should be accompanied by broader government measures taken to support, not undermine, the livelihood of indigenous peoples.

ANTICORRUPTION AND TRANSPARENCY

ENVIRONMENT TO PROTECT AGAINST CORRUPTION:	3.00
EXISTENCE OF LAWS AND ETHICAL STANDARDS BETWEEN PRIVATE AND PUBLIC SECTORS:	3.00
ENFORCEMENT OF ANTICORRUPTION LAWS:	3.50
GOVERNMENTAL TRANSPARENCY:	4.00
CATEGORY AVERAGE:	**3.38**

Corruption is extensive throughout the Philippine state apparatus, from the lowest to the highest levels. Bribes and extortion seem to be a regular element of the complex connections among bureaucrats, politicians, businessmen, the press, and the public. In the 2006 Transparency International Corruption Perceptions Index, the Philippines tied with Russia for 121st out of 163 countries (within the region, it placed ahead of Indonesia, Cambodia, and Myanmar and behind Singapore, Malaysia, Thailand, Laos, and Vietnam).[65]

Philippine public institutions display a weak separation between the official and private spheres, and special access to the state apparatus has been the major avenue for private wealth accumulation. Indeed, the term "crony capitalism" was created to describe the plunderous activities of the Marcos regime. Limited attempts at economic reform under the administration of Corazon Aquino were launched amid ready acknowledgement that "the base for crony capitalism" survived Marcos's downfall in 1986. Among the most forceful official attacks on these practices came at the 1992 inauguration of President Fidel Ramos, who declared that the Philippine economic system "rewards people who do not produce at the expense of those who do . . . [and] enables [those] with political influence to extract wealth without effort from the economy."

Economic reforms, particularly those of the Ramos administration, sought to shrink the state's role in the economy and thereby reduce corruption. This involved extensive privatization, trade liberalization, and substantial deregulation of such basic industries as telecommunications and shipping. Large family conglomerates remain important, but external openness has limited monopoly power and provided a fair and even test to new entrants in areas including manufactured exports, information technology, and e-business.[66] Even in the wake of changes brought about by years of deregulation and liberalization, however, the country remains hampered by what the World Bank sees as "the inability of public institutions to resist capture by special interests" and a "limited ability to provide public goods and services."[67]

While well-crafted anticorruption laws are on the books and there is no lack of graft allegations, the enforcement of prohibitions on corruption is often woefully deficient. The media reports freely—often rambunctiously—on corruption charges, and journalists themselves are sometimes accused of collecting bribes for publishing both attacks and defenses of public officials (a system known as AC–DC, or "Attack Collect–Defend Collect"). Election campaigns regularly revolve around allegations of corruption, and political alliances are a central factor in determining who is currently under investigation. The administration of nursing board exams was rocked by a cheating scandal in 2006,[68] but in general the country's system of higher education seems to be relatively insulated from pervasive corruption.

Major contracts are voided because of perceptions of corruption, including a 2003 COMELEC attempt to modernize the electoral system that was subsequently nullified by the Supreme Court.[69] Perhaps the most dramatic story relates to the Manila international airport, described by one international newspaper as "a $500 million monument to the unpredictability of doing business in a country known for corruption and political turbulence." Scheduled to open in late 2002, the badly needed facility sits unused to this day. On the basis of allegations of corruption, the Supreme Court in 2004 confirmed an executive decision declaring previous government contracts with private partners for the construction of the airport to be null and void. Negotiations continue amid allegations against contending parties, with little expectation that the government will seek to punish anyone responsible for corrupt acts. At this point, the overarching goal is simply to open the airport for business.[70]

There are many well-established mechanisms to fight corruption. The oldest is the Commission on Audit (COA), a constitutionally mandated agency that can trace its history to 1900. The COA's authority is limited to exposing corrupt acts; it does not have the authority to prosecute or punish corrupt officials. The main agency charged with investigating as well as prosecuting corruption cases is the office of the ombudsman (OMB), a special body mandated by the 1987 constitution and established in 1988. Charges are brought before the Sandiganbayan, a court specifically tasked with adjudicating cases of graft. The Sandiganbayan was established in 1973 and its mandate was continued in the 1987 constitution.

Constitutional provisions seek to guarantee the OMB's political independence. The ombudsman serves a seven-year fixed term of office with no possibility of reappointment and is removable only by impeachment. The OMB's record, however, indicates that institutional independence does not guarantee efficacy in the fight against corruption. Under the leadership of the first ombudsman (1988–1995), the OMB was notoriously inefficient. By the end of 1994, the office had a backlog of 14,652 cases.[71] The second ombudsman's record (1995–2002) was no better. Indeed, confidence in his integrity dropped so low that impeachment proceedings were initiated against him for bribery and betrayal of the public trust. The third ombudsman was well regarded by advocates of clean government but resigned before the end of his term. He was replaced in 2005 by the head legal counsel to President Arroyo. Critics express ongoing concerns that the OMB has yet to go after "big fish," focusing instead on petty charges. They remain particularly distraught over the OMB's September 2006 dismissal of charges against the head of COMELEC for the automation contract that had been voided by the Supreme Court in 2004. Many hoped that such charges could have led to an overhaul of the poll body.[72]

However, with what is often the strong and creative support of international organizations and domestic civil society groups, there have been gains on other fronts in recent years. Responding to estimates that 20 percent of the funding for government contracts goes to kickbacks and commissions, a Government Procurement Reform Act was signed into law in 2003.[73] Its passage was aided by the earlier creation of a monitoring and advocacy organization, Procurement Watch Inc., which mounted a media campaign and received international support as well as the backing of NGOs that banded together in the Transparency and Accountability Network.[74] The goal is to rationalize the legal framework for procurement, and in the process "increase transparency, competitiveness, efficiency, accountability, and public monitoring of both the procurement process and the implementation of awarded contracts."[75] But even the law's most ardent supporters estimate that "it may very well take a decade to get it fully implemented and working across all levels of government."[76]

Another recent initiative has been the use of "lifestyle checks" to determine whether government officials have "accumulated properties and/or who has incurred expenditures and/or who has ostentatiously displayed wealth manifestly out of proportion to his or her legitimate income." The effort unites anticorruption agencies with accredited NGOs and has been funded by the European Union.[77] In 2006, the presidential palace noted in an annual report that such checks on officials of director rank or higher had resulted in thirteen dismissals.[78] Critics, however, fear that this anticorruption strategy could be used instead to conduct witch hunts against personal rivals or to exact vengeance against superiors. It may also privilege sanctions against lower-level officials whose behavior is easier to monitor; higher officials, meanwhile, can simply engage in capital flight and money laundering.[79] The government's Medium Term Philippine Development Plan for 2004 to 2010 urges the passage of a Whistle-blower's Protection Act to encourage public officials to expose corruption in their units.[80]

It is difficult to measure the success of these various efforts, but one recent survey showed that "the proportions of managers saying that 'most' or 'almost all' of the companies in their line of business give bribes to win public sector contracts" declined somewhat in most areas of the country between the 2003–2005 period and 2006. Still, for all the efforts that have been undertaken to combat corruption in the Philippines, there is little progress to show. As a recent World Bank report acknowledges, "the country has not had much success in combating corruption. Despite relatively intense media attention and the proliferation of so-called anticorruption agencies, corrupt exchanges have continued to pervade government activities."[81]

Ultimately, curbing corruption depends not on piecemeal measures but on a concerted, long-term drive to build stronger institutions—

particularly the bureaucracy and political parties. Bureaucratic reforms should aim to promote and enforce a clearer division between public and private, beginning with a targeted effort to build specific "islands of strength" and moving outward to other agencies. Effective bureaucratic reform, however, depends in turn on challenging the spoils system and the dysfunctional set of political incentives that it engenders. As long as politics is dominated by pork and patronage rather than programs and policies, politicians will continue to undermine even the best-laid plans for bureaucratic integrity. A promising first step would be well-conceived electoral reforms, through which the country could begin the long and challenging process of building stronger and more programmatic political parties.

The Philippine budget process involves legislative review and scrutiny but is nonetheless characterized by a high degree of executive prerogative. As in the pre–martial law years, presidential discretion in the release of appropriated funds encourages members of Congress to affiliate with the ruling party after presidential elections, thus undermining the goal of party cohesion discussed above.[82] The constitution allows the legislature to decrease but not increase the budget items proposed by the president. Legislators are also able to adopt special-purpose appropriations,[83] so-called lump-sum operations that now constitute 60 percent of the total budget. Some government revenues, such as the substantial earnings from gambling and sweepstakes programs, are not subject to legislative oversight. One recent evaluation of budget transparency and accountability gave the Philippines a 51 percent ranking (out of a possible 100 percent), noting many areas in which information is available to the public but also suggesting that there is much room for improvement. Congressional budget hearings are open to the public, but many decisions take place out of public view. This is particularly true at the final stage of budget legislation, when bicameral committees meet and are influenced by what is said to be substantial executive intervention.[84]

While the Philippines does not yet have a freedom of information law, the 1987 constitution very clearly recognizes "the right of the people to information on matters of public concern" (Article III, Section 7). This, along with statutory provisions and court rulings, gives the country "the most liberal information regime in Southeast Asia." Even so, investigative journalists have suggested many ways in which government data could be more consistently and readily available to the public.[85]

Recommendations

- Piecemeal attempts to fight corruption can produce valuable incremental gains, but the struggle for good governance ultimately requires a fundamental restructuring of the political system. A comprehensive reform agenda should be crafted around the challenging but essential long-term goals of strengthening bureaucratic coherence and encouraging the emergence of more institutionalized political parties.
- The prosecution and punishment of corrupt acts involving top officials is critical in the fight against corruption. To that end, the government should institute measures that ensure the integrity and independence of the office of the ombudsman.
- A law providing legal protections for whistle-blowers should be adopted.
- The current budget process, which privileges presidential discretion and undermines the cohesion of political parties, should be reformed to establish a more equal distribution of authority between the executive and legislative branches.

NOTES

1 Benedict Anderson, "Cacique Democracy in the Philippines: Origins and Dreams," in *The Spectre of Comparisons: Nationalism, Southeast Asia and the World* (London: Verso, 1998). For further broad historical analysis of Philippine democracy, see Paul D. Hutchcroft and Joel Rocamora, "Strong Demands and Weak Institutions: The Origins and Evolution of the Democratic Deficit in the Philippines," *Journal of East Asian Studies* 3, no. 2 (May–August 2003): 259–292.

2 United Nations Office at Geneva, "UN Expert Says Extrajudicial Killings in Philippines Have a Corrosive Effect on Civil Society and Political Discourse," news release, 22 February 2007, http://www.unog.ch/80256EDD006B9C2E/(httpNewsByYear_en)/CDD628AE9A86E2C0C125728A003E9F31?OpenDocument.

3 National Citizens' Movement for Free Elections (Namfrel), "The Terminal Report to NAMFREL Operation Quick Count 2004," 30 June 2004, 2.

4 Data from COMELEC's *Statistical and Narrative Report—2004 National Elections*, available at http://www.comelec.gov.ph/oav/oav_2004report_part04.html. In 2006, the country's 8 million overseas workers sent home remittances totaling US$12.8 billion, or roughly 10 percent of the country's economy. See "Filipino Remittances Hit $12.8bn," BBC News, 15 February 2007, http://news.bbc.co.uk/2/hi/business/6364143.stm.

5 Namfrel, "The Terminal Report," 2.

6 Transcripts of "the alleged taped conversations between Pres. Gloria Macapagal-Arroyo and Comelec Commissioner Virgilio Garcillano" can be found on the Philippine Center for Investigative Journalism (PCIJ) website at http://pcij.org/blog/wp-docs /hellogarci-transcript-final.pdf, with perhaps the most commonly quoted conversation on page 16.

7 See Roberto Verzola, "The True Results of the 2004 Philippine Presidential Election Based on the NAMFREL Tally," *Kasarinlan* 19, no. 2 (2004): 92–118.

8 Alecks Pabico, "Were the 2007 Elections Less Violent?" PCIJ, 5 July 2007, http://i-site.ph/blog/?p=217#more-217; Amnesty International (AI), *Philippines: Political Killings, Human Rights and the Peace Process* (London: AI, 15 August 2006), 3, 27, http://web .amnesty.org/library/Index/ENGASA350062006?open&of=ENG-PHL.

9 See the full 3 July 2007, Bantay Eleksyon final report at http://www.iper.org.ph/CER /bantayeleksyon2007/reports/final-report-07-election.html.

10 For comprehensive analysis of the election and its aftermath, see the "Special Post-Election Issue" of *Newsbreak*, July–September 2007.

11 Based on a new formula being promulgated by Supreme Court Chief Justice Artemio V. Panganiban, the number of seats allocated by PR would shrink further. For his explanation of the changes, see Artemio V. Panganiban, "Criticisms of the Panganiban Formula," Inquirer.net, 22 July 2007, http://www.inquirer.net/specialfeatures/eleksyon 2007/view.php?article=20070722-78042.

12 Alfred W. McCoy, "Covert Netherworlds: Clandestine Services and Criminal Syndicates in Shaping the Philippine State," in *Government of the Shadows*, ed. Tim Lindsey and Eric Wilson (London: Pluto Press, forthcoming 2007).

13 Sheila S. Coronel, "The Philippines in 2006: Democracy and Its Discontents," *Asian Survey* 47, no. 1 (2007): 175–182, at 178.

14 See, for example, two outstanding works on corruption edited by Coronel, then of the PCIJ: *Pork and Other Perks: Corruption and Governance in the Philippines* (Quezon City: PCIJ, 1998) and *Betrayal of the Public Trust: Investigative Reports on Corruption* (Quezon City: PCIJ, 2000). A third volume, for which Coronel served as lead author, provides an excellent account of the distinctive character of the pork barrel, the centrality of pork to the political system, and the way in which Philippine-style patronage politics undermines bureaucratic cohesion and the overall quality of governance. Coronel et al., *The Rule-makers: How the Wealthy and Well-Born Dominate Congress* (Quezon City: PCIJ, 2004).

15 In 1999, the Estrada administration filed a lawsuit against one newspaper and organized a boycott of advertisers against another, but "this attack on the media galvanized middle-class sentiment against Estrada." Randolf S. David, "Erap: A Diary of Disenchantment," in *Between Fires: Fifteen Perspectives on the Estrada Crisis*, ed. Amando Doronila (Metro Manila: Anvil Publishing and the *Philippine Daily Inquirer*, 2001), 148–179, at 157–158 (quote at 158).

16 Reporters Without Borders (RSF), *Annual Report 2006* (Paris: RSF, 2006), http://www .rsf.org/article.php3?id_article=17359&Valider=OK; Committee to Protect Journalists, *Attacks on the Press in 2006* (New York: Committee to Protect Journalists, 2007), http: //www.cpj.org/attacks06/asia06/phil06.html; Report of the Independent Commission to Address Media and Activist Killings (chaired by retired Supreme Court justice Jose

A. R. Melo), 22 January 2007, 48–49; RSF, *Annual Report 2007* (Paris: RSF, 2007), http://www.rsf.org/article.php3?id_article=20795&Valider=OK.

17 Melo Commission Report, 1, 58; Marie Hilao-Enriquez, "Statement to the Hearing of the Subcommittee for East Asian and Pacific Affairs, Senate Foreign Relations Committee of the 110th U.S. Congress" (Washington, D.C., 14 March 2007), http://foreign .senate.gov/testimony/2007/EnriquezTestimony070314.pdf; AI, *Philippines: Political Killings, Human Rights and the Peace Process*, 2, http://web.amnesty.org/library/Index / ENGASA350062006?open&of=ENG-PHL; Human Rights Watch (HRW), *Scared Silent: Impunity for Extrajudicial Killings in the Philippines* (New York: HRW, June 2007), http://hrw.org/reports/2007/philippines0607/philippines0607web.pdf. The forthcoming UN report will be issued by Philip Alston, the Special Rapporteur on extrajudicial, summary or arbitrary executions.

18 T. Kumar, "Extrajudicial Killings in the Philippines: Strategies to End the Violence" (testimony, U.S. Senate Committee on Foreign Relations, Subcommittee on East Asian and Pacific Affairs, Washington, D.C., 14 March 2007), 8; AI, *Philippines: Political Killings, Human Rights and the Peace Process*, 1–2; HRW, Scared Silent, 3. On the long-standing culture of impunity, see McCoy, *Closer Than Brothers: Manhood at the Philippine Military Academy* (New Haven: Yale University Press, 1999), 299–338.

19 Melo Commission Report, 14–15; HRW, *World Report 2007* (New York: HRW, 2007), http://hrw.org/englishwr2k7/docs/2007/01/11/philip14840.htm; Robert Francis Garcia, *To Suffer Thy Comrades: How the Revolution Decimated Its Own* (Quezon City: Anvil, 2001).

20 McCoy, "Covert Netherworlds."

21 Coronel, "The Philippines in 2006," 176; AI, *Report 2007* (London: AI, 2007), http://thereport.amnesty.org/eng/Regions/Asia-Pacific/Philippines; American Bar Association (ABA) Asia Law Initiative, *Judicial Reform Index for the Philippines* (Washington, D.C.: ABA, March 2006), 23, http://www.abanet.org/rol/publications/philippines_jri _2006.pdf.

22 See the compilation of news summaries on the *Jurist* website, http://jurist.law.pitt.edu /jurist_search.php?q=anti-terrorism%20law%20in%20philippines.

23 AI, *Philippines—Torture Persists: Appearance and Reality Within the Criminal Justice System* (London: AI, 24 January 2003), http://web.amnesty.org/library/Index/ENGASA 350012003?open&of=ENG-PHL.

24 "CHR to Step Up Lobby for Anti-torture Law," *Sun-Star Davao*, 15 July 2006, http:// www.sunstar.com.ph/static/dav/2006/07/15/news/chr.to.step.up.lobby.for.anti.torture .law.html. See also Asian Human Rights Commission, "Law Needed to Stop Torture and Systemic Negligence in the Philippines," news release, 31 March 2006, http:// www.ahrchk.net/statements/mainfile.php/2006statements/469.

25 AI, "Philippines Abolishes the Death Penalty," news release, 1 September 2006, http:// web.amnesty.org/library/Index/ENGACT530032006?open&of=ENG-PHL.

26 Agence France-Presse, "Philippine Prison System a Living Hell Reminiscent of 19th Century," *Khaleej Times*, 3 February 2007, http://www.khaleejtimes.com/DisplayArticle New.asp?xfile=data/todaysfeatures/2007/February/todaysfeatures_February6.xml&sec tion=todaysfeatures&col=.

27 AI, *Report 2005* (London: AI, 2005), http://web.amnesty.org/report2005/phl-summary-eng.

28 See Republic of the Philippines, Office of the President, "The Cabinet and Other Officials," http://www.op.gov.ph/cabinet.asp; National Commission on the Role of Filipino Women (NCRFW), *Report to the United Nations Committee on the Elimination of Discrimination against Women* (New York: United Nations, 2 August 2004), 74, http://www.unifem-eseasia.org/projects/Cedaw/docs/countryreports/philippines/CR-5-6_Philippines.pdf.

29 Congress of the Philippines, House of Representatives, "Congressional Profile," http://www.congress.gov.ph/members/profiles.

30 NCRFW, *Report*, 75.

31 On the Supreme Court, see http://www.supremecourt.gov.ph/justices/index.php; on the Court of Appeals, see http://ca.supremecourt.gov.ph/images/references_corner/div-20070326.pdf. Data on the trial courts is calculated from NCRFW, *Report*, 74.

32 ABA Asia Law Initiative, *Judicial Reform Index for the Philippines*, 18; NCRFW, *Report*, 94–95.

33 NCRFW, *Report*, 99, 59–60.

34 Ibid., 61, 65.

35 UNIFEM, "Philippines: Country Snapshot," UNIFEM East and Southeast Asia Regional Office, 2007, http://www.unifem-eseasia.org/projects/Cedaw/countryprogramme_philippines.html.

36 Japan International Cooperation Agency, *Country Profile on Disability: The Republic of the Philippines* (Tokyo: Japan International Cooperation Agency, March 2002), 8, http://www.jica.go.jp/english/global/dis/pdf/phi_eng.pdf.

37 Foundation for International Learning, *Identifying Disability Issues Related to Poverty Reduction: Philippines Country Study* (Manila: Asian Development Bank, 2002).

38 International Crisis Group (ICG), *Philippines Terrorism: The Role of Militant Islamic Converts* (Brussels: ICG, 19 December 2005), 20, http://www.crisisgroup.org/home/index.cfm?id=3844.

39 Joseph Chinyong Liow, *Muslim Resistance in Southern Thailand and Southern Philippines: Religion, Ideology, and Politics* (Washington, D.C.: East-West Center, 2006), 21–22.

40 ICG, *Philippines Terrorism*, 20.

41 "U.S. Helps Fight Against Abu Sayyaf," BBC News, 2 April 2007, http://news.bbc.co.uk/2/hi/asia-pacific/6499589.stm; ICG, *Philippines Terrorism*, 1; HRW, *World Report 2007*; Eric Gutierrez, "From Ilaga to Abu Sayyaf: New Entrepreneurs in Violence and their Impact on Local Politics in Mindanao," *Philippine Political Science Journal* 24 (2003): 145–178; Herbert Docena, *Unconventional Warfare: Are U.S. Special Forces Engaged in an 'Offensive War' in the Philippines?* (Quezon City: Focus on the Global South, 2007), http://www.focusweb.org/index.php?option=com_remository&Itemid=105&func=fileinfo&id=23.

42 The Philippine Indigenous Peoples Rights Act (IPRA) defines indigenous peoples as "homogeneous societies identified by self-ascription and ascription by others, who have continuously lived as organized community on communally bounded and defined territory, and who have, under claims of ownership since time immemorial, occupied, pos-

sessed and utilized such territories, sharing common bonds of language, customs, traditions and other distinctive cultural traits, or who have, through resistance to political, social and cultural inroads of colonization, non-indigenous religions and cultures, become historically differentiated from the majority of Filipinos."

[43] Special Rapporteur on the Situation of Human Rights and Fundamental Freedoms of Indigenous People, *Mission to the Philippines* (New York: United Nations Economic and Social Council, Commission on Human Rights, 5 March 2003), 7, http://www.unhchr .ch/Huridocda/Huridoca.nsf/0/568f8e64e2800006c1256cf7005d2593/$FILE/G031152 1.pdf.

[44] Special Rapporteur, *Mission to the Philippines*, 13.

[45] Philippine Department of Labor and Employment, "Extent of Unionism," *Labstat Updates* 8, no. 13 (October 2004).

[46] Artemio V. Panganiban, "Message from the Chief Justice," in *Annual Report 2005* (Manila: Supreme Court of the Philippines, 2006), 5, http://www.supremecourt.gov.ph /announce/sc_annual_report_2005.pdf.

[47] Paul D. Hutchcroft, *The Philippines at the Crossroads: Sustaining Economic and Political Reforms*, (New York: Asia Society, 1996).

[48] ABA Asia Law Initiative, *Judicial Reform Index for the Philippines*, 15.

[49] Ibid., 6, 26. The Supreme Court, which administers all lower courts, proposes that the judicial branch receive 2 percent of the national budget. Arcie M. Sercado, "SC Justice Tinga Speaks on Declining Judicial Pay, Calls for Judicial Budget Increase," news release, Supreme Court Public Information Office, 4 April 2007, http://www.supremecourt .gov.ph/news/courtnews%20flash/2007/04/04040703.php.

[50] ABA Asia Law Initiative, *Judicial Reform Index for the Philippines*, 26, 28–29, 45.

[51] Ibid., 2, 22, 24–25.

[52] Ibid., 1, 27. According to a late 2006 poll, the percentage of judges who consider their compensation "inadequate" has dropped from 81 percent a decade ago to 61 percent today. Mahar Mangahas, Linda Luz Guerrero, and Marlon Manuel, "New Diagnostic Study Sets Guideposts for Systematic Development of the Judiciary," news release, Social Weather Stations (SWS), 10 December 2006, http://www.sws.org.ph.

[53] Sercado, "SC Justice Tinga."

[54] Mangahas, "New Diagnostic Study"; ABA Asia Law Initiative, *Judicial Reform Index for the Philippines*, 3.

[55] ABA Asia Law Initiative, *Judicial Reform Index for the Philippines*, 3.

[56] SWS, *2003–2004 Surveys*, 43.

[57] Simeon V. Marcelo, "Ombudsman's Briefing Paper on its Anti-Corruption Program" (presentation at the Combating Corruption Conference, Makati, Philippines, 22 September 2004).

[58] Eva-Lotta E. Hedman, "The Philippines: Not So Military, Not So Civil," in *Coercion and Governance: The Declining Political Role of the Military in Asia*, ed. Muthiah Alagappa (Stanford: Stanford University Press, 2001), 165–186.

[59] McCoy, *Closer than Brothers*, 4.

[60] An official investigation into the 2003 mutiny brought forth a very well-considered agenda for reform, responding in part to junior officers' grievances over corruption within

the military. See "Findings of the Feliciano Commission," *Manila Times* Internet Edition, 23 October 2003, http://www.manilatimes.net/others/special/2003/oct/26/2003 1026spe1.html.

61 Alexandra C. Horst, *International Property Rights Index (IPRI) 2007 Report* (Washington, D.C.: IPRI, 2007), http://internationalpropertyrightsindex.org/UserFiles/File/PRA _Interior_LowRes.pdf.

62 Daniele Perrot-Maitre and Lynn Ellsworth, "The Philippines Indigenous Peoples' Rights Act of 1997," in *Deeper Roots: Strengthening Community Tenure Security and Community Livelihoods* (New York: Ford Foundation, 2003), http://www.fordfound.org/elibrary /documents/515/030.cfm.

63 For a list of relevant provisions, see International Work Group for Indigenous Affairs (IWGIA), "Constitutional Rights Relevant for Indigenous Peoples in the Philippines," 2006, http://www.iwgia.org/sw16705.asp.

64 Perrot-Maitre and Ellsworth, "The Philippines Indigenous Peoples' Rights Act"; Special Rapporteur, *Mission to the Philippines*, 9–12; IWGIA, "Constitutional Rights"; Rorie R. Fajardo, "Alien Nation: Still Strangers in Their Own Land," *i Report* Online Edition, 25 July 2007, http://www.pcij.org/i-report/2007/indigenous-peoples.html.

65 Transparency International (TI), *Corruption Perceptions Index 2006* (Berlin: TI, 2006), http://www.transparency.org/policy_research/surveys_indices/cpi/2006.

66 Emmanuel S. De Dios and Paul D. Hutchcroft, "Political Economy," in *The Philippine Economy: Development, Policies, and Challenges*, ed. Arsenio Balisacan and Hal Hill (New York: Oxford University Press, 2003, and Quezon City: Ateneo de Manila University Press, 2002).

67 Philippines Country Management Unit, *Country Assistance Strategy for the Philippines, 2006–2008* (Washington, D.C.: World Bank, 2005), 13.

68 See Carlos H. Conde, "Scandal over Nurses' Exams Stirs Unease in Philippines," *New York Times*, 21 August 2006, http://www.nytimes.com/2006/08/21/world/asia/21nurses .html?ex=1186200000&en=62863c83cbb6e7e2&ei=5070.

69 *Information Technology Foundation of the Philippines et al. v. Commission on Elections et al.* (Philippine Sup. Ct. No. 159139, 13 January 2004).

70 Carlos H. Conde, "Free Flow: Airport Snag Hurts Outlook in Manila," *International Herald Tribune*, 27 October 2005, http://www.iht.com/articles/2005/10/26/business /transcol27.php; Roel Landigin, "A Commercial Compromise: A Less-Than-Perfect Solution May be the Only Way to Open NAIA-3," *Newsbreak*, 11 February 2006, http://www.newsbreak.com.ph/index.php?option=com_content&task=view&id=2409&I temid=88889053.

71 Cecile C. A. Balgos, "Ombudsman," in *Pork and Other Perks*, ed. Coronel.

72 Kristin L. Alave, "Watchdog to Gov't: Where's Big Fish?" *Philippine Daily Inquirer*, 2 August 2007; "The Street Ombudsman," *Newsbreak*, 21 November 2006; Transparency and Accountability Network, "Press Statement," 16 October 2006, http://www.tan .org.ph/files/home.asp.

73 Procurement Watch Inc., "Procurement Reform in the Philippines: Changing the Rules of the Game" (PowerPoint presentation, n.d., involving Ed Campos, Tina Pimentel, and Jacinto Gavino), http://www.worldbank.org/wbi/governance/pdf/11iacc_cam_pim_gav .pdf.

74 J. Edgardo Campos and Jose Luis Syquia, *Managing the Politics of Reform: Overhauling the Legal Infrastructure of Public Procurement in the Philippines* (Washington, D.C.: World Bank, 2006).

75 TI, *Global Corruption Report 2004* (London: Pluto Press, 2004), 237.

76 Campos and Syquia, *Managing the Politics of Reform*, 32.

77 "COA Joins 14 Government Agencies, NGOs in Lifestyle Check Coalition," *COA News* 4, no. 2 (April–June 2003), http://www.coa.gov.ph/COA_News/2003/v4n2/news6_v4n2.asp; see also TI, *Global Corruption Report 2004*, 238.

78 Presidential Management Staff, "2006 State of the Nation Address: Technical Report," July 2006, 74, http://www.gov.ph/sona/2006sonatechnicalreport.pdf.

79 TI, Global Corruption Report 2004, 238–39. The latter problem is to be addressed by the Anti-Money Laundering Act, passed in 2003 under pressure from the intergovernmental Financial Action Task Force.

80 Asian Institute of Management (AIM), *Whistleblowing in the Philippines: Awareness, Attitudes and Structures* (Makati: AIM–Hills Governance Center, 2006), http://www.aim-hills.ph/projectpage/prs/research3.htm.

81 SWS, *The 2006 SWS Survey of Enterprises on Corruption* (Quezon: SWS, 6 July 2006); Campos and Syquia, Managing the Politics of Reform, 3–4.

82 Gabriella R. Montinola, "Parties and Accountability in the Philippines," *Journal of Democracy* 10, no.1 (January 1999): 126–140, at 136, 139. As she notes, "this system provided overwhelming disincentives to party loyalty . . . , meaningful electoral choice, and democratic accountability."

83 Global Integrity, "Philippines: Integrity Scorecard," in *2006 Country Reports* (Washington, D.C.: Global Integrity, 2007), http://www.globalintegrity.org/reports/2006/philippines/scorecard.cfm?subcategoryID=45&countryID=28.

84 The International Budget Project Open Budget Initiative, "The Philippines: Open Budget Index 2006" (Washington, D.C.: Center on Budget and Policy Priorities, 2006), http://www.openbudgetindex.org/CountrySummaryPhilippines.pdf; Rorie Fajardo, "Lack of Transparency in Gov't's 'Special-Purpose Funds' Rapped," GMA News Services, 8 November 2006, http://www.openbudgetindex.org/GMA%20News%20Services.pdf.

85 Yvonne T. Chua, "The Philippines: A Liberal Information Regime Even without an Information Law," freedominfo.org, 17 January 2003, http://www.freedominfo.org/features/20030117.htm.

RUSSIA

CAPITAL: Moscow
POPULATION: 141.7 million
GNI PER CAPITA: $5,780

SCORES	2005	2007
ACCOUNTABILITY AND PUBLIC VOICE:	2.88	2.38
CIVIL LIBERTIES:	3.72	3.31
RULE OF LAW:	3.41	3.14
ANTICORRUPTION AND TRANSPARENCY:	2.79	2.70

(scores are based on a scale of 0 to 7, with 0 representing weakest and 7 representing strongest performance)

Kathryn Stoner-Weiss[1]

INTRODUCTION

Russia's movement toward democracy and the rule of law has been halting at best since the heady days of the collapse of communism in December 1991. Although Russia has maintained many of the formal institutions of democratic governance through the 1990s and into the twenty-first century, the quality of its democracy has fluctuated greatly. Indeed, by 2005, having endured significant rollbacks of electoral rights, Russia could no longer be considered a democracy at all according to most metrics. The country has come to resemble the autocratic regimes of Central Asia more than the consolidated democracies of Eastern Europe that have recently joined the European Union.

Kathryn Stoner-Weiss is senior research scholar and associate director for research at the Center on Democracy, Development, and the Rule of Law, Freeman Spogli Institute for International Studies, Stanford University. Before coming to Stanford in 2004, she taught at the Woodrow Wilson School of Public and International Affairs and the Politics Department at Princeton University for nine years. Stoner-Weiss is the author of *Resisting the State: Reform and Retrenchment in Post-Soviet Russia* (Cambridge, 2006), *Local Heroes: The Political Economy of Russian Regional Governance* (Princeton, 1997). She is also the co-editor (with Michael McFaul) of *After the Collapse: the Comparative Lessons of Post-Communist Transitions* (Cambridge, 2005).

549

Although the constitution forged in 1993 by Russia's first post-Soviet president, Boris N. Yeltsin, has survived as the blueprint of Russian politics, the political system under Yeltsin's handpicked successor, President Vladimir V. Putin, has become ever-more dominated by the executive branch, at the expense of the legislature and judiciary. The nascent political party system of the 1990s has been replaced by a set of political organizations loyal primarily to the president and largely dependent on him for their existence. Over the past few years, with the demise of parties on both the right and the left, a functioning political opposition has ceased to exist in Russia. Democracy has been curtailed further by the state's gradual takeover of independent media. Finally, in the past two years in particular, civil society and nongovernmental organizations (NGOs) have been stifled through legislation that imposes onerous re-registration requirements. A few of these organizations have been unceremoniously raided and closed by the authorities, while human rights and democracy groups have been accused of pushing an agenda that benefits foreign states. More generally, civil society finds itself increasingly unable to serve as an effective check on abusive state practices at a time when the hollowing out of political opposition has increased the importance of external monitoring.

Notwithstanding these rather dramatic leaps off the democratic path that the country had appeared to be following in the early 1990s, Russia remains undeniably freer than it was during the Soviet period. Russian citizens are not tightly controlled by the state in every aspect of their lives as they were under communism. At the same time, they are not free to express their opinions about political leaders, to assemble freely, or to read whatever they like in the Russian press. Despite formal constitutional guarantees, in Russia today there are informal but firm guidelines regarding what sorts of protest speech and organizations are permitted or prohibited by the state.

Russia is certainly not reverting to communism, a specific political and economic system based largely on fear and bureaucratic fiat. Nonetheless, there has been a steady erosion of the content, if not the formal institutions, of Russian democracy. President Putin has accomplished this in part by increasing the importance of the security apparatus in governing the country. Particularly notable has been a shift in emphasis from the impartial rule of law to a preferential rule *by* law, aimed at rewarding government supporters and punishing those perceived to be threats or enemies of the regime.

Russia is even less democratic in 2007 than in 2005. Power is increasingly concentrated in the presidency, and the human and legal rights of Russian citizens are less secure than they have been at any point since 1991. Political pluralism and press freedom have been similarly afflicted. The still-unsolved October 2006 murder of Anna Politkovskaya, a reporter known for her pioneering coverage of the Chechen conflict, underscored the fragility of independent journalism in contemporary Russia.

Perhaps because his administration tightly monitors the media, President Putin remains hugely popular, though many of his policies are not. His attempt to reduce subsidies to pensioners in January 2005 sparked a series of demonstrations, the war in Chechnya continues to be of concern to the Russian public, and various civil society groups have protested their circumscribed rights. Still, none of this has made up for the lack of a meaningful political opposition.

In 2008, Putin's second term as Russia's president will expire. The constitution requires that he leave office, and he has stated on several occasions that he intends to do so. However, it is clear that Russian voters will not be given a completely free hand to choose the next president from an open field of candidates. The selection of Putin's possible successors is being tightly choreographed by the Kremlin, and the lingering uncertainty as to whether elections will even be permitted indicates that the future of Russian democracy is in serious jeopardy.

ACCOUNTABILITY AND PUBLIC VOICE

FREE AND FAIR ELECTORAL LAWS AND ELECTIONS:	2.00
EFFECTIVE AND ACCOUNTABLE GOVERNMENT:	3.00
CIVIC ENGAGEMENT AND CIVIC MONITORING:	2.00
MEDIA INDEPENDENCE AND FREEDOM OF EXPRESSION:	2.50
CATEGORY AVERAGE:	**2.38**

Just prior to the collapse of the Soviet Union, Russia initiated compet-itive and semicompetitive elections. Under the Soviet system, partici-pation in elections was mandatory, leading to traditionally high voter turnouts. However, there was no choice between candidates, all of whom were members of the Communist Party.

Since 1993, elections at the national level have occurred regularly and in accordance with electoral laws. Registration requirements for can-didates have fluctuated, and officials at the regional and national levels have used the rules to prohibit candidates who are unpalatable to the Kremlin and local business leaders. Nonetheless, the basic rules of elec-tions are known and published, and campaigns are often, but not al-ways, competitive. Incumbents who control the media and access to campaign financing from private business groups have a clear advantage. The increased control of the media by the Kremlin has reduced the competitiveness of elections at the national level.

Since Putin's ascent to power—as prime minister in August 1999, acting president in January 2000, and president in March 2000—elec-tions at the regional and national levels have become more managed by the presidential administration. The Kremlin's dominance over the elec-toral process at the national level began in 1999 with the parliamentary victory of Unity, now known as United Russia. Putin does not claim a formal membership in any political party, but on United Russia's offi-cial website, Putin is featured as the "moral leader" of the party.[2] United Russia dominated parliamentary elections in 2003, winning 37 percent of the popular vote.

In the March 2004 presidential election, Putin won a second term with slightly more than 70 percent of the vote. His closest competitor, the Communist-backed Nikolai Kharitonov, garnered 13.7 percent. While there was some suspicion that voter rolls had been cut to inflate turnout (the required minimum turnout was 50 percent), and irregu-larities were reported in several regions, there was little doubt that Putin had been the voters' first choice. The election results were confirmed by the Central Electoral Commission.[3]

The federal Law on Political Parties originally came into effect on July 14, 2001. However, it has been revised and tightened in the past two years, making it more difficult for political organizations to regis-ter as parties. The law required each political party to demonstrate by January 2006 that it had at least 50,000 citizens as members and branches with at least 500 members each in more than forty-five of Russia's regions.[4] As of February 2007, seventeen parties have confirmed participation in the December 2007 elections for the State Duma, the lower house of parliament; however, this number may rise by the time a review of registration is completed later in the year.[5]

Although multiple parties are permitted to run, the field has narrowed ahead of the 2007 elections. This is partly a natural process of attrition and consolidation of what had been a very broad spectrum of parties in the 1990s. However, it is also due to administrative and legal obstacles that prevent a truly competitive electoral system. For instance, over the past two years, candidates in local elections have been denied registration on questionable grounds, including accusations that they falsified signatures or improperly filed the necessary paperwork. In March 2007, the opposition party Yabloko was barred from St. Petersburg's municipal elections after the local electoral commission ruled that over 10 percent of its signatures were invalid.

Moreover, in advance of the Duma elections, the minimum threshold for parties to gain representation has been increased from 5 percent of the vote to 7 percent. This step is likely to eliminate small, liberal opposition parties, including Yabloko and the Union of Rightist Forces (SPS), which drew close to 5 percent in the last Duma elections in 2003. Furthermore, in 2007 the Duma will be elected exclusively according to party lists in a proportional-representation system, ending the previous mixed system and its bloc of single-mandate seats. While this is not necessarily a less democratic method of electing representatives to parliament, in the current context the new system will only further entrench the status quo or enhance the standing of United Russia.

In December 2006, President Putin signed a law amending electoral rights. It enlarged the list of citizens ineligible to participate in elections to include those sentenced to prison terms for serious crimes and for crimes of an "extremist" nature; those imprisoned for public display of Nazi symbols; and those convicted of "extremist acts" against a state, regional, or local body of power. Given that these acts are not clearly defined, there is understandable concern that a broad interpretation could seriously imperil electoral rights in the future.

The new electoral law included restrictions on political parties' use of television airtime to campaign against opponents. It also eliminated the minimum turnout requirement for elections at the national, local, and regional levels, allowing even elections with scant voter participation to be accepted as valid.

The upper house of the Russian parliament, the Federation Council, serves as a rubber stamp for the Kremlin and a compliant Duma. Its members are selected by regional executives and legislatures, and many are patronage appointments who may have never visited the regions they ostensibly represent. The Federation Council is one more way for informal networks to help allies gain power. Although elected officials in theory control the Russian state, current and former members of the security services have assumed a growing role in government under Putin, who had himself been an officer in both the Soviet-era KGB and the Federal Security Service (FSB), its main domestic successor.

In January 2006, Putin signed a controversial law designed to bring foreign and domestic NGOs under tighter state control. He defended the law as a necessary step to prevent foreign interference in Russian politics. Critics said the law was designed to limit the previously vibrant civil society that had arisen after the Soviet collapse.

The law required all groups to reregister with the justice ministry by mid-October 2006 and file an annual "work plan" beginning in 2007. Many groups failed to meet the first deadline due to the relatively onerous registration process. As a result, they were forced to close until they were able to supply the necessary documentation. Some ceased to function completely in Russia. Notable among the roughly ninety international organizations forced to close their doors at least temporarily were Human Rights Watch, Amnesty International, the National Democratic Institute, the International Republican Institute, and Internews.

Most of these groups eventually reregistered, but virtually all reported the process to be cumbersome, and most expect further bureaucratic interference associated with new obligations to report regularly on daily activities and funding. The concern is that the law will give the Russian government unprecedented authority to regulate NGO operations and decide which projects are acceptable. The true test of the law's effect on NGOs will come in the spring and summer of 2007, when reports on the groups' activities are due.

The media remain tightly controlled by the presidential administration, and over the last seven years Russia has been one of the three most dangerous places in the world to be a journalist (behind Iraq and Colombia). Since Putin assumed office in 2000, 13 journalists have been killed in contract-style murders. There have been no convictions in any of the cases.[6] The murder of forty-eight-year-old Anna Politkovskaya in her apartment building on October 7, 2006, refocused national and international attention on the problem.

Politkovskaya was a special correspondent for the Russian newspaper *Novaya Gazeta*. For seven years she had fought to bring the story of the Chechen conflict to light despite the dangers involved and the irritation it caused among Russian military and political officials. Politkovskaya had been threatened and detained for writing stories about human rights abuses against Chechen civilians by the Russian military and Chechen forces.

Days after her murder, Putin described Politkovskaya as an "insignificant" figure and dismissed the notion that there was any official involvement in her killing. (At the time of writing, there is no clear evidence that the state was involved.) However, the poisoning approximately one month later of former Russian spy Aleksandr Litvinenko in London fueled theories that the Kremlin had begun to systematically murder critics at home and abroad. Litvinenko had been a critic of the Putin administration and had allegedly begun to investigate Politkovskaya's murder when he was evidently poisoned with polonium 210, a radioactive substance used as, among other things, an initiator for nuclear weapons. Through painstaking investigation in London and Moscow, British authorities uncovered a trail of the substance leading from the restaurant where Litvinenko ate his last meal. Before dying in a London hospital in November 2006, Litvinenko himself accused Russian authorities of orchestrating his poisoning. Putin has denied this charge. The investigation into how polonium 210 was smuggled across Europe to London and then slipped into Litvinenko's meal is still under way at the time of writing. Although it remains unclear whether the Russian state is culpable, Litvinenko's unusual death has apparently buttressed a popular impression that the Kremlin is capable of, and amenable to, eliminating its critics one way or another (see the discussion of Mikhail Khodorkovsky in Rule of Law).

Other media developments in recent years have also been troubling. In 2006, in advance of the G-8 summit in St. Petersburg, the Duma passed a bill, later signed by Putin, that broadened the definition of extremism to include criticism of public officials in the media. Several reporters have been charged under this new law, according to the Committee to Protect Journalists, including Dmitry Tashlykov of the regional paper *Vladimirsky Krai*, who allegedly defamed the governor of the Vladimirov region in an internet chat room.[7]

The Russian government and Kremlin-allied businessmen have steadily consolidated their control of Russian print and television outlets over the past several years. This trend continued with business magnate Alisher Usmanov's purchase of the newspaper *Kommersant* in the fall of 2006. He assured *Kommersant* journalists that he would not interfere with the paper's sometimes critical editorial line, but the acquisition is generally seen as part of an effort to silence possible critics in the run-up to the 2007 Duma elections and 2008 presidential election. Indeed, the International Research and Exchanges Board (IREX) Media Sustainability Index for 2005 noted a steady decrease in freedom of the press since 2001. There is also a lack of fairness in the issuing of broadcast licenses, a process overseen by the culture ministry, such that competitive licensing bids depend on loyalty to particular officials or groups. There is little transparency in broadcasting regulation, although politics clearly plays a role, as evidenced by the recent decision to effectively prohibit local rebroadcasting of Radio Free Europe/Radio Liberty in Russia.[8]

Recommendations

- The vote threshold for parties to gain representation in the State Duma should be lowered back to 5 percent to allow for the entry of smaller parties and a broader political discourse.
- The government should repeal the January 2006 NGO law so that NGOs receiving foreign funding can operate without fear of arbitrary closure. More generally, NGOs should be permitted to operate freely and without close monitoring by the justice ministry.
- The government should devote greater resources and more consistent effort to fully investigating violence against journalists and bringing the perpetrators to justice.
- The culture ministry should award broadcasting licenses through a truly competitive and transparent process.

CIVIL LIBERTIES

PROTECTION FROM STATE TERROR, UNJUSTIFIED IMPRISONMENT, AND TORTURE:	2.57
GENDER EQUITY:	4.00
RIGHTS OF ETHNIC, RELIGIOUS, AND OTHER DISTINCT GROUPS:	3.00
FREEDOM OF CONSCIENCE AND BELIEF:	4.00
FREEDOM OF ASSOCIATION AND ASSEMBLY:	3.00
CATEGORY AVERAGE:	**3.31**

Russia's human rights record, particularly with respect to the ongoing conflict in Chechnya, is grim. Although the law prohibits torture or inhumane treatment of prisoners, ill-treatment of detainees by police is not uncommon. When it occurs, abuse generally comes in the first few hours after arrest and includes beating with fists or batons, electric shocks, and denial of access to medical help. Reports of brutal beatings, rape of male and female prisoners in Chechen detention centers, and detention without trial are widespread, especially in cases of suspected collaboration with Chechen rebels.[9]

Russian NGOs recorded 114 cases of torture by police in eleven regions of Russia between 2001 and 2005, not including the North Caucasus and the detention facilities near Chechnya.[10] There is little systematic evidence, but disciplinary action against police for such behavior appears to be rare. In November 2006, Amnesty International reported that poorly trained and low-paid police officers routinely use forced confessions—obtained without an attorney present—to "solve" crimes.[11] Confessions obtained in this way become the basis for criminal charges and convictions.

Russia's imprisonment rate is among the highest in the world, with 670 prisoners per 100,000 residents.[12] Prison conditions are notoriously poor, and common health risks include HIV, tuberculosis, and other deadly diseases. Sanitary conditions are negatively affected by erratic water supplies and lack of hot water;[13] many pretrial detention centers do not have flush toilets, and detainees are forced to use buckets instead.[14] Overcrowding is common, and drug addiction among inmates has soared since 2000.

Police, on occasion, fail to keep accurate detention records, allowing suspects to remain in detention beyond the legal limit of forty-eight hours without seeing a judge. Moreover, the threat of torture deters detainees from reporting the excessive time in jail.[15]

Crime is a persistent problem in post-Soviet Russia. According to the country's statistics agency (Roskomstat), crime has increased steadily since 1990, jumping rather dramatically from 2004 onward. Murder rates have remained relatively steady at over 30,000 per year since the mid-1990s, while robbery and drug smuggling have been particular areas of growth. The number of incidents classified as "terrorism" has increased since 2000, with spikes occurring in 2002 and 2003.[16] Individual security in Russia today, therefore, is in serious question. This is particularly true of women and children, for whom sex trafficking into Asia and Central and Eastern Europe is a severe problem.[17] In 2004, it was alleged that 92 percent of all Russian women who leave to work abroad end up forced to work in the sex industry.[18]

The Russian military is notorious for hazing recruits and mistreating servicemen. One well-known case took place in December 2005 at the Chelyabinsk Tank Academy, where nineteen-year-old private Andrei Sychyov and several other conscripts were forced by more senior soldiers to squat for several hours while being brutally beaten. After four days without treatment, Sychyov developed an infection that resulted in the amputation of his legs and genitals. Had military doctors not covertly reported Sychyov's condition to the civic organization the Union of the Committees of Soldiers' Mothers, the incident might well have gone unnoticed by senior army officials and the media. The Union of the Committees of Soldiers' Mothers estimates that 80 percent of hazing incidents go unreported in the Russian military.[19] Moreover, several cases of soldiers being forced into male prostitution by senior officers surfaced in March 2007.[20]

Gender equity is a continued challenge in contemporary Russian society, and not enough is done to ameliorate the effects of gender imbalances in the political sphere in particular. Women are generally absent at high levels of executive authority; the only woman ever to be a governor is Putin ally Valentina Matvienko of St. Petersburg. Representation by women in the State Duma had decreased from 13.5 percent in 1993 to 9.8 percent by 2003. Female candidates in Russia have generally performed better under single-mandate voting than proportional representation, in part because political parties tend to place women's names lower on their lists. The elimination of single-mandate constituencies for the 2007 Duma elections is likely to depress female representation even further.

The Russian constitution declares not only equality of gender before the law but also equality of religion and freedom of conscience, religious worship, and practice (Article 28). Notwithstanding these guarantees, the Orthodox Church of Russia has sought to assert and maintain its dominance in the face of challenges from foreign missionary organizations. A controversial law passed in 1997 asserted that only Russian Orthodoxy, Judaism, Islam, and Buddhism had full legal standing. Other religious groups were required to demonstrate that they had been registered to operate in the Soviet Union and then Russia for at least fifteen years. Without legal status, religious organizations are unable to open bank accounts or own property, among other activities.

A number of religious groups have experienced bias and harassment in recent years. These include Roman Catholics, Jehovah's Witnesses, members of the Church of Scientology, and Seventh-Day Adventists.[21] Anti-Semitism remains a serious problem, although President Putin has publicly pronounced that discrimination against Jews is intolerable, and prosecution for hate crimes has apparently increased. Attacks against Jews are currently outnumbered by attacks against migrants from the Caucasus and Central Asia—Chechnya and Georgia especially. Still, in 2005 and 2006 a number of violent attacks against Jews, Jewish monuments, and synagogues occurred in Moscow, St. Petersburg, and other major cities in Russia.[22]

Conditions for ethnic minorities have worsened in the past several years. In part this is a result of the ongoing conflict in Chechnya and terrorist attacks by Chechen and other Muslim rebels elsewhere in Russia. Poor relations between Russia and Georgia have also meant increased stops on the streets for anyone who does not have classically Slavic looks. Perhaps most startling, though, is the introduction of a new state regulation forbidding certain categories of shops and markets from hiring foreigners after April 1, 2007. The law is intended to crack down on the approximately 10 million illegal migrants who come from Central Asia, the Caucasus, and China to work in Russia. It also smacks of a racist form of Russian nationalism.

Freedom of assembly has become increasingly circumscribed in recent years. Licenses and permits for rallies are growing more difficult to obtain in major cities. Nonetheless, a few political rallies and meetings have taken place with the specific aim of challenging the political leadership. Perhaps the most notable were January 2005 protests by Russian pensioners against the new law that stripped disabled citizens, pensioners, and war veterans of benefits such as free public transportation and medications, replacing them with cash sums instead. In St. Petersburg, more than 10,000 people protested, with some even calling for Putin to resign.[23] Other demonstrations took place across Russia, in the Siberian regions, and as far east as Sakhalin Island. In some regions, the protests were actually effective, prompting local politicians to repeal, or at least delay, some of the benefit reforms.

On March 3, 2007, an umbrella group of organizations and civic activists known as the Other Russia staged a political rally on the streets of St. Petersburg, with several thousand demonstrators protesting the infringement of civil and political rights in Russia.[24] Although they were formally denied permission to demonstrate and were initially blocked from the city center, the crowd broke through police barriers and marched down Nevsky Prospekt, the city's main artery. A similar rally in December 2006 in Moscow was less successful, as about 4,000 riot police blocked 2,000 protesters from marching into the center of the city.

The transition from the Communist system to a market economy in the 1990s brought about a sharp decline in living standards for Russian workers. Discredited Soviet-era trade unions were not well equipped or inclined to provide relief or support in the face of the dramatic decreases in the value of wages that followed the end of price controls in 1992 and the wave of privatizations later in the decade. More recently, however, there have been reports of an increase in unionization, particularly in the automobile and oil industries, with new unions forming spontaneously to demand better pay for workers.[25]

Recommendations
- The government should create a special, independent task force to investigate reports of abuse in the military. Senior officials who fail to report abuse need to be held accountable.

- The guarantees of freedom of assembly in the constitution should be evenly applied and upheld. The state should ease the process of obtaining permits and licenses for public demonstrations.
- Russian police and detention facilities should be more closely monitored by the public prosecutor's office, and accusations of prisoner abuse should be fully investigated and prosecuted where appropriate.
- The government should invest greater resources in police training, particularly focusing on the rights of suspects and detainees.

RULE OF LAW

INDEPENDENT JUDICIARY:	3.20
PRIMACY OF RULE OF LAW IN CIVIL AND CRIMINAL MATTERS:	3.00
ACCOUNTABILITY OF SECURITY FORCES AND MILITARY TO CIVILIAN AUTHORITIES:	2.50
PROTECTION OF PROPERTY RIGHTS:	3.33
EQUAL TREATMENT UNDER THE LAW:	3.67
CATEGORY AVERAGE:	**3.14**

There is a noticeable gap in Russia between the existence of laws on paper and their implementation in practice, creating uncertainty about the rule of law. Laws are often applied inconsistently to suit exigent circumstances or political purposes.

By the letter of the constitution the judiciary is independent of the legislative and executive branches of government, but in practice members of government, wealthy individuals, and powerful businesses interfere in judicial decisions. Judges often report feeling pressured by federal authorities.[26]

Trial by jury was introduced experimentally in 1994 in several regions in Russia. In November 2001, the Duma passed a criminal procedure code extending the right to a jury trial in cases involving crimes that carry a minimum sentence of ten years, effective in January 2003. Although the number of jury trials has increased in recent years, juries currently adjudicate only 8 percent of all criminal cases. The conviction rate in jury trials (81 percent) is notably lower than in non-jury trials

(99 percent),[27] perhaps due to a higher standard of evidence required by juries. Some analysts also cite the legacy of Soviet oppression, which might lead jurors to side with defendants.[28]

The Russian Supreme Court has expressed concern over the gap between jury and non-jury acquittal rates, questioning whether members of the public are capable of serving on juries and arriving at reasonable decisions. Annual statistics provided by the court indicate that acquittals are appealed more often than convictions, and that the Supreme Court overturns a much higher percentage of acquittals than convictions.[29] As double jeopardy is not prohibited, in a few cases prosecutors have obtained a guilty verdict after two or even three jury acquittals.[30] In 2005, 14.5 percent of appealed guilty verdicts were overturned by the Cassation Chamber of the Russian Supreme Court, while 49 percent of acquittals were overturned and sent back to the appropriate court for retrial.[31] This high rate of reversed jury acquittals is likely to undermine the availability or usefulness of jury trials in the future.

The quality and impartiality of judges in Russia is uneven. Some help prosecutors present evidence or remind them of evidence they may be omitting at trial.[32] At times, judges overlook procedural violations or allow evidence that is technically not permissible.[33] Moreover, sentencing for cases of similar nature is inconsistent. In 2004, in an effort to combat judicial corruption, the Russian government raised judicial salaries markedly, but this has not eradicated bribery. Corruption is greater at the trial court level, where only one judge presides, than at the appellate level, which involves panels of several judges.

The prosecutor general is appointed by the president of Russia. Prosecutors at all levels are generally closely monitored by officials in the executive branch, who do not hesitate to interfere in prosecutions for political or business purposes. Executive accountability for decisions on judicial and prosecutorial dismissals and appointments is low. For example, Putin dismissed Russia's long-serving chief prosecutor in 2006 with essentially no explanation. There was widespread speculation that it was part of a Kremlin shake-up in advance of the 2008 presidential election, but since the executive is essentially free from public, legislative, or media scrutiny, analysts were left in the dark as to why this change occurred.

Security forces have maintained their privileged position in the Russian system under Putin, in part due to his background as a KGB officer in the Soviet period. He has appointed many of his former colleagues to positions of influence in the Russian government. It is estimated that of the 1,000 leading political figures in Russia, 78 percent have worked with the KGB or FSB.[34] As a result, law enforcement has become more centralized under the control of authorities in Moscow.[35]

The right to private property is protected under Article 35 of the constitution, but the enforcement of contracts and property rights remains uneven. This is one of the key obstacles to increased foreign investment in Russia outside the oil and gas industry, where most foreign investment is concentrated.

The International Property Rights Index, a composite measure comparing relative property rights among seventy countries, assigns Russia a score of 3.2 out of the best possible 10. In particular, Russia scores poorly on judicial independence, physical property rights protection, and intellectual property rights protection. Russia's cumulative scores on the index put it near the bottom of world rankings, at 63 out of 70.[36]

Although the index is a snapshot of Russian property rights relative to a limited group of countries, it is illustrative of a lack of confidence on the part of investors and businesspeople in the safety of property rights in Russia. The government's criminal prosecution of politically active billionaire Mikhail Khodorkovsky and its parallel campaign against his now-defunct oil firm, OAO Yukos, have undoubtedly contributed to the perception of Russia as an unstable business environment. In the wake of the Yukos case, major foreign companies have come under pressure to give up controlling stakes in oil and gas projects to state-owned firms, threatening a key source of outside investment.

Recommendations

- Immediate steps should be undertaken to guarantee judicial independence, including stricter penalties for attempting to influence judges' decisions.
- Greater resources need to be invested in the training of judges, especially regarding proper court procedures.
- The state should introduce the principle of double jeopardy in criminal proceedings to protect against spurious and repetitive prosecutions.
- Additional mechanisms need to be developed to ensure equitable and just enforcement of property rights, particularly with respect to arbitrary property seizures.

ANTICORRUPTION AND TRANSPARENCY

ENVIRONMENT TO PROTECT AGAINST CORRUPTION:	2.40
EXISTENCE OF LAWS AND ETHICAL STANDARDS BETWEEN	
PRIVATE AND PUBLIC SECTORS:	3.00
ENFORCEMENT OF ANTICORRUPTION LAWS:	2.25
GOVERNMENTAL TRANSPARENCY:	3.14
CATEGORY AVERAGE:	**2.70**

Since assuming the presidency in 2000, Putin has repeatedly declared his intention to bring corruption to heel. However, progress in this regard has been minimal. In fact, Russia's corruption score on Transparency International's Corruption Perceptions Index worsened from 2.7 in 2004 to 2.5 in 2006.[37]

Business regulations in Russia remain complicated and amorphous. Typical bureaucratic hurdles in opening a business include a cumbersome licensing process, arbitrary inspections, and unpredictable tax collection. Registration requirements and excessive documentation rules in general are also frequently noted as problems by new firms in Russia. Bureaucratic inefficiency and corruption are consistently cited by foreign and domestic investors as one of the "principal obstacles to investment in Russia today."[38]

There is also little uniformity in doing business across the country's many regions. Officials at the regional and city level exercise wide discretion in assessing licensing and registration fees and determining when to conduct inspections. Aside from bribing government officials and politicians, businesspeople report having to pay protection money to organized criminal groups. Given that there is no national procurement system, it is also typical to pay bribes to obtain government contracts, according to another World Bank study.[39] As a result, Russia has attracted little foreign direct investment (FDI) relative to its economic potential. For example, the Organization for Economic Co-operation and Development (OECD) reports that FDI in Russia in 2005 was 3 percent of gross domestic product, compared with 4.9 percent in Poland.[40]

The OECD confirms that the Russian state is expanding its role in the economy, particularly in "strategic" sectors like oil and gas.[41] This began in earnest in 2004 with the seizure of Mikhail Khodorkovsky's oil company Yukos and the Kremlin-orchestrated transfer of its assets to a state-owned firm. Khodorkovsky and his colleague Platon Lebedev were arrested in 2003 on charges of tax evasion. After an eleven-month trial in 2004 and 2005, both men were found guilty and sentenced to nine years in prison. Meanwhile, virtually all of Yukos's key assets were sold in dubious state-sponsored auctions to pay off huge tax assessments. Khodorkovsky is widely believed to have been targeted because of his resistance to Kremlin control and possible presidential ambitions.

The OECD notes that in Russia, "the expansion of state ownership in important sectors will probably contribute to more rent-seeking, less efficiency and slower growth."[42] State auditing and inspection bodies are used selectively and for political purposes. Recent examples include the investigation of former prime minister Mikhail Kasyanov, an opposition figure and possible contender for the presidency in 2008. Kasyanov was placed under federal investigation in 2005 for alleged fraud related to a property purchase he made in 2004 while still in office. As in the Khodorkovsky case, the target of the probe may well have broken the law, but he appears to have been singled out for political reasons while those in better standing with the Kremlin go unpunished.

Tax collection in Russia has greatly improved since the introduction of a flat personal income-tax rate early in Putin's first presidential term, but tax laws are still complicated, and there is a pervasive culture of tax evasion. Corporations are pursued for tax arrears inconsistently and sometimes for political purposes.

Russia has no meaningful conflict-of-interest laws; many senior officials in the president's administration serve on the boards of the country's major oil and gas firms. The high price of oil on world markets in recent years has created ever-greater incentives for the state to involve itself in this crucial sector of the economy. Finally, as Russia's laws on disclosure of the assets and incomes of state officials are underdeveloped, there is little to stop elected and appointed officials from exploiting their positions for personal gain. Freedom of information is guaranteed in Article 29 of the Russian constitution. However, this right to know is limited as the state lacks mechanisms through which citizens can obtain such information.

Bribery continues to be a concern in higher education. Admission to postsecondary institutions can often be obtained with a bribe to the right official. Cases of typically low-paid professors being convicted of taking bribes in exchange for higher grades have come to light in Moscow and other big cities. In an effort to curb corruption in education, in February 2007 the Duma moved to introduce a standardized testing system for Russian students in their final years of high school. In initial testing in selected regions of Russia, however, unusually high scores were reported, and officials suspected cheating. Ironically, the head of the Federal Test Center, the organization tasked with grading exams and test papers, was suspended following allegations of corruption and fraud involving misuse of test-center funds. The prosecutor general has opened a criminal investigation.[43]

In general, reporting instances of official corruption is a risky endeavor. A 2006 report on whistle-blowing noted that since 1998, the European Court of Human Rights in Strasbourg, France, had received 28,000 complaints from Russia. Most apparently concerned abuse of power and corruption by police and judicial officials. The number of complaints from Russia is reportedly higher than from any other member state of the Council of Europe, suggesting in part that victims are unable to obtain justice within the Russian system. Of the total, the court has ruled on 106 and found the Russian state guilty in 90, or about 85 percent of the cases. Reports of intimidation aimed at complainants abound.[44] At the time of writing, Russian whistle-blowers are not formally protected by law, so their fates depend on individual circumstances, including the mercy of employers against whom they may be complaining and the interest and activity of international and domestic NGOs intervening on their behalf.[45]] In the wake of Putin's attacks against the free operation of NGOs in Russia, however, these groups represent an increasingly weak source of protection for those choosing to make formal complaints against an arm of the state.

Recommendations

- Senior government officials should be required to report their personal and professional ties to private and state companies. Enforceable conflict-of-interest laws should be introduced to ensure greater transparency in both business and political life.
- Business regulations and licensing needs to be simplified and streamlined in order to reduce opportunities for bribery.

- Anticorruption NGOs must be granted greater access to government procedures and information. Freedom of information regulations should be enforced.
- The parliament should provide, and the courts should uphold, formal legal protections for those reporting corruption, environmental damage, or human rights abuses.

NOTES

1   The author is grateful to Micah Cratty and Karina Qian for research assistance.
2   See Edinii Rossii Ofitsialnii Sait Partii at http://www.edinros.ru.
3   Robert Coalson, "Tsik Moves to Cut Off Discussion of the Presidential Election," Radio Free Europe/Radio Liberty (RFE/RL), 8 April 2004.
4   Federal Law No. 175-FZ, "On the Election of Deputies of the State Duma of the Federal Assembly of the Russian Federation" (11 December 2002).
5   "Amendments to Elections Legislation" (Vienna: Organization for Security and Cooperation in Europe [OSCE], Office for Democratic Institutions and Human Rights, December 2006), http://www.osce.org/odihr.
6   For the ranking of Russia as third most dangerous for journalists after Iraq and Colombia, as well as the number of journalists murdered since 2000, see Committee to Protect Journalists, "Attacks on the Press in 2006, Europe and Central Asia: Russia," http://www.cpj.org/attacks06/europe06/rus06.html.
7   Committee to Protect Journalists, "Russian Journalist on Trial for Defaming Local Governor in Internet Chat Room," news release, 23 February 2007, http://www.cpj.org /news/2007/europe/russia23feb07na.html.
8   *Russian Media Sustainability Index* (Washington, D.C.: International Research and Exchanges Board [IREX], 2005).
9   See Human Rights Watch at http://www.hrw.org for documentation of this phenomenon from 1999 to 2006.
10 *Russian NGO Shadow Report on the Observance of the Convention Against Torture and Other Cruel, Inhuman or Degrading Treatment or Punishment by the Russian Federation for the Period from 2001 to 2005* (Moscow: UN, Office of the High Commissioner for Human Rights, May 2006), http://www.ohchr.org/english/bodies/cat/docs /ngos/joint-russian-report-new.pdf. See also Claire Bigg, "Russia: Law Enforcement Organs Accused of Widespread Torture," RFE/RL, 29 March 2007, http://www .rferl.org/featuresarticle /2007/03/ae51d94d-72f4-46e5-a5c6-6c8de6afd851.html.
11 Amnesty International (AI), "Russian Federation: Beating Out 'Confessions' in Police Detention," news release, 22 November 2006, http://news.amnesty.org/index/engeur 460602006; AI, *Russian Federation: Torture and Forced 'Confessions' in Detention* (London: AI, 22 November 2006), http://web.amnesty.org/library/index/ENGEUR460562 006.

[12] Alexey Bobrik, Kirill Danishevski, Ksenia Eroshina, and Martin McKee, "Prison Health in Russia: The Larger Picture," *Journal of Public Health Policy* 26, 1 (2005): 33.

[13] Ibid., 36.

[14] Ibid., 41–42.

[15] AI, *Russian Federation: Torture and Forced 'Confessions' in Detention.*

[16] All of the statistics in this paragraph come from "10.1 Chislo Zaregistrirovannikh Prestuplenii po Vidam (1990–2005)" available through the Federal'naya Sluzhba Gosudarstvennoi Statistiki at http://www.gks.ru/free_doc/2006/b06_13/10-01.htm.

[17] "Human Trafficking and Modern-day Slavery: Russian Federation 2006" at http://gvnet.com/humantrafficking/Russia.htm

[18] Anastasia Lebedev, "Russia's Willing Sex Workers Find Enslavement Abroad," *Moscow News*, 22 April 2004, article viewed at http://www.waytorussia.net/news/2004-04/women-foreigners.html.

[19] Claire Bigg, "Brutal Hazing Incident Rocks Army," RFE/RL, 27 January 2006, http://www.rferl.org/features/features_Article.aspx?m=01&y=2006&id=B84F149F-7911-4F94-B7CD-A43808F2FDB3.

[20] Patrick Moore, "Rights Group Says Conscripts Forced into Prostitution," RFE/RL, 13 February 2007, http://www.rferl.org/newsline/2007/02/1-RUS/rus-130207.asp.

[21] Oleg Liakhovich, "Religious Freedom in Russia: A Long and Winding Road," *Moscow News*, 25 March 2005, http://www.mosnews.com/feature/2005/03/25/religiousfreedom.shtml.

[22] *Chronicle of Antisemitism in Ukraine and Russia: 2005–2006* (Washington, D.C.: Union of Councils for Jews in the Former Soviet Union [UCSJ], 2 February 2007), http://www.fsumonitor.com/stories/020207Report.shtml.

[23] Valentinas Mite, "Russia: Pensioners' Protests Mount Growing Challenge to Putin," RFE/RL, 17 January 2005, http://www.rferl.org/features/features_Article.aspx?m=01&y=2005&id=CFDD7D73-5BFF-48D9-AAE6-81CD8096A951.

[24] Masha Lipman, "Breaking the Cordon," *Moscow Times*, 12 March 2007, 10.

[25] Boris Kagarlitsky, "Rebirth of Unions in Russia," *Moscow Times*, 22 September 2006.

[26] International Bar Association Human Rights Institute, *Striving for Judicial Independence: A Report into Proposed Changes to the Judiciary in Russia* (London: International Bar Association, June 2005), http://www.ibanet.org/images/downloads/2005_06_June_Report_Russia_Striving%20for%20Judicial%20Independence_Final_English.pdf.

[27] Peter Finn, "Fear Rules in Russia's Courtrooms: Judges Who Acquit Forced Off Bench," *Washington Post*, 27 February 2005, http://www.washingtonpost.com/ac2/wp-dyn/A56441-2005Feb26?language=printer.

[28] Andrei Kolsenikov, "Is Russia Ready for Jury Trials?" RIA/Novosti, 3 August 2006, http://en.rian.ru/analysis/20060803/52236722.html.

[29] Kristi O'Malley, "Not Guilty Until the Supreme Court Finds You Guilty: A Reflection on Jury Trials in Russia," *Demokratizatsiya* 14 (Winter 2006).

[30] Finn "Fear Rules in Russia's Courtrooms."

[31] O'Malley, "Not Guilty . . . ," 4.

32 Noel C. Paul, "Rundown Jury: Twelve Not-So-Angry Russians," *Legal Affairs* (July/ August 2004), http://www.legalaffairs.org/issues/July-August-2004/scene_paul_julaug 04.msp.

33 O'Malley, "Not Guilty…," 3.

34 See, for example, "Federal Security Service (FSB) History" at http://www.global security.org/intell/world/russia/fsb.htm.

35 Brian D. Taylor, *Power Surge? Russia's Power Ministries from Yeltsin to Putin and Beyond* (CSIS PONARS, Policy Memo No. 414, December 2006), http://www.csis.org/media /csis/pubs/pm_0414.pdf.

36 International Property Rights Index (IPRI), *Russia* (Washington, D.C.: IPRI, 2007), http://internationalpropertyrightsindex.org/index.php?content=cdata&country=Russia.

37 Transparency International (TI), *Corruption Perceptions Index* (Berlin: TI, 2005, 2006), http://www.transparency.org/policy_research/surveys_indices/cpi.

38 Organization for Economic Cooperation and Development (OECD), *Economic Survey of the Russian Federation, 2006* (Paris: OECD, November 2006), 7, http://www .oecd.org/dataoecd/58/49/37656835.pdf.

39 World Bank, "Progress on Anti-Corruption Mixed in Russian Federation: Corruption Eased in Transition Countries, 2002–2005," news release, 26 July 2006, http://web .worldbank.org/WBSITE/EXTERNAL/COUNTRIES/ECAEXT/RUSSIANFEDER-ATIONEXTN/0,,contentMDK:21007237~menuPK:305605~pagePK:141137~piPK:1 41127~theSitePK:305600,00.html.

40 OECD, "Russia Should Do More to Attract FDI Following Convertible Rouble Move, Says OECD," news release, 7 May 2006, http://www.oecd.org/document/50/0,3343,en _2649_201185_37049074_1_1_1_1,00.html.

41 OECD, *Economic Survey of the Russian Federation*, 2006.

42 Ibid., 6.

43 Associated Press, "Russia Sets out to Fight Corruption in Education with a New Standardized Test," *International Herald Tribune*, 2 February 2007, http://www.iht.com /articles/ap/2007/02/03/europe/EU-GEN-Russia-Education-Reform.php?page=1.

44 These statistics and reports come from Anna Nemtsova, "Russia: A Phone Call to Putin, How do Kremlin Authorities Deal with Whistle-Blowers? Silence Them," *Newsweek International*, 13 March 2006, http://www.msnbc.msn.com/id/11677921/site news week/.

45 Rashid Alimov, "Russian Nuke Whistleblower Files for Asylum in Finland," Bellona Foundation, 11 March 2005, http://www.bellona.org/english_import_area/interna tional/russia/envirorights/info_access/40553.

RWANDA

CAPITAL: Kigali
POPULATION: 9.3 million
GNI PER CAPITA: $250

SCORES	2005	2007
ACCOUNTABILITY AND PUBLIC VOICE:	1.48	1.43
CIVIL LIBERTIES:	2.21	1.86
RULE OF LAW:	1.22	1.24
ANTICORRUPTION AND TRANSPARENCY:	1.97	2.48

(scores are based on a scale of 0 to 7, with 0 representing weakest and 7 representing strongest performance)

Jennie E. Burnet

INTRODUCTION

Thirteen years after the 1994 genocide, in which more than 800,000 Tutsi and moderate Hutu were slaughtered in less than three months, the Rwandan government has made enormous progress in bringing stability and economic development to the country. The genocide ended when the Rwandan Patriotic Front (RPF), a rebel movement that had been fighting a civil war with the government since 1990, seized most Rwandan territory and drove the genocidal regime into exile. Since 1994, the RPF has ruled, first under a consensual dictatorship in which it shared power with a limited number of political parties, and since 2003 under a nominal democracy following national elections.

President Paul Kagame and the RPF-dominated legislature were elected by a landslide; the elections, however, were marred by bias and intimidation, which precluded any genuine challenge to the RPF. While many international observers and diplomats based in Kigali viewed the 2003 elections as part of a continuing evolution toward democracy in the country, the elections allowed the RPF to consolidate its monopoly

Jennie E. Burnet is Assistant Professor in the Department of Anthropology at the University of Louisville.

on power in the Parliament, the presidency, and the ministries. The regime allows very little space for independent voices and, according to some analysts, has become even more repressive since the end of the transition period in 2003.[1] The legislative and judicial branches of government have done little to counterbalance the executive or mitigate the influence of the military in policy making. In practice, power remains concentrated in the hands of a small inner circle of military and civilian elites known as the *akazu*. Critical voices in civil society and the media have been almost completely silenced.

The government states that genocide prevention is one of its main priorities. While Rwanda's Hutu, Tutsi, and Batwa ethnicities—all of whom share a common language and culture—have achieved a substantial measure of peaceful coexistence, ethnic divisions remain a concern. In enforcing the 2001 Law on Discrimination and Sectarianism, which established stiff penalties for those guilty of "divisionism," the government has continued to silence critics of its policies or practices. Politically motivated accusations of divisionism can carry criminal penalties and have continued to be used to attack civil society organizations, the press, and individuals. Accusations of divisionism or "genocidal ideology" are among the most effective tools for silencing critics.

Achieving justice for the 1994 genocide remains an intractable problem. In a positive step, the government began implementing Gacaca courts, loosely based on a traditional conflict resolution mechanism (also called Gacaca) nationwide in 2005 following a pilot phase, reforms, and numerous delays. In 2002, the government had decided to implement the courts to try the bulk of genocide cases. Yet it now appears as if the Gacaca courts may fill the prisons rather than empty them. In March 2005, following the preliminary phase of trials, approximately 761,000 suspects stood accused of genocide.[2] The majority of these suspects remain in their communities as the Gacaca courts continue trials; however, unknown numbers have been arrested or rearrested and returned to prison.

Transitional justice has been and continues to be largely one-sided as Gacaca will not be used to prosecute revenge killings or war crimes by the RPF in Rwanda between 1990 and 1995 or in the Democratic Republic of Congo between 1996 and 2000. These crimes are not nearly on the same scale as crimes of genocide, yet failure to address them adequately has led to the perception that the government is carrying out victors' justice.

ACCOUNTABILITY AND PUBLIC VOICE

FREE AND FAIR ELECTORAL LAWS AND ELECTIONS:	1.25
EFFECTIVE AND ACCOUNTABLE GOVERNMENT:	1.75
CIVIC ENGAGEMENT AND CIVIC MONITORING:	1.33
MEDIA INDEPENDENCE AND FREEDOM OF EXPRESSION:	1.38
CATEGORY AVERAGE:	**1.43**

Rwanda holds regular elections for parliament and the presidency, district councils and administrators, and local-level administrative positions. Yet elections are not conducted by secret ballot at all levels. In February 2006, Rwandans voted in local elections to fill administrative positions following the redrawing of district and provincial boundaries in January.[3] In contests at the lowest administrative levels, citizens voted by lining up behind their chosen candidates and thus were not guaranteed ballot secrecy.[4] Contests for officials at the next higher level used secret ballots, but Human Rights Watch reported numerous irregularities, including stuffing of ballot boxes and intimidation of candidates.[5] In a number of contests, voters did not have a choice, as only one candidate stood for election.[6]

There is no meaningful competition between political parties and thus no real opportunity for rotation of power; since 2003, the RPF has dominated all levels of government. While Rwandan law guarantees the free operation of political parties, attempts to launch new parties have been stifled through targeted persecution of their leaders. Virtually all political parties included in the current government joined an RPF coalition in 2003. The New Partnership for African Development (NEPAD) peer review, conducted in 2005 and published in September 2006, was very favorable toward Rwanda and praised its achievements in economic development and security, yet the report characterized political participation in the country as "rehearsed."[7]

Rwanda boasts one of the most effective bureaucracies and civil services in all of Africa. On a day-to-day basis, the government operates effectively in terms of administration and implementation of policies. In general, government officials are educated, well trained, and hold the requisite skills to perform their duties.

The 2003 constitution established the executive, legislative, and judicial branches as independent entities designed to provide checks and balances. In practice, however, the legislative and judicial branches have little independence from the RPF political party and little ability to oversee the actions of the executive. While the Parliament has the greatest proportion of women of any legislative body in the world, it is dominated by RPF representatives. Since the destruction of opposition political parties prior to the national elections in 2003, the Parliament has operated largely as a rubber stamp to policy initiatives emerging from the ministries and the president's office. In addition, the judiciary has yet to establish itself as an independent arbiter (see Rule of Law).

Civil society organizations speak publicly and influence policy decisions when their views are in line with those of the government and the RPF. Between 2004 and 2007, government dominance of civil society organizations increased. The 2001 Law on Non-Profit Associations gave government authorities the power to control projects, budgets, and hiring of personnel and required all organizations to obtain a renewable certificate of registration from the Ministry of Local Government, Good Governance, Community Development and Social Affairs (MINALOC). This certificate is granted on the basis of the organization's mission statement and annual report. The registration process allows government authorities to monitor the activities of nongovernmental organizations (NGOs) and control their publications.[8] Between 2004 and 2007, numerous organizations encountered difficulties in registering or renewing their registration.

At the end of June 2004, a report by a parliamentary commission on genocidal ideology recommended the dissolution of several international and local NGOs that "preached genocidal ideology and ethnic hatred." The organizations mentioned on the list included the only local human rights organization willing to criticize the government publicly and document human rights abuses committed by government authorities. Almost all the local civil society organizations named in the report closed their doors between July 2004 and January 2005. In 2006, all international NGOs and local civil society organizations with ties to France, or which promoted the French language or culture, were either ejected from the country or forced to close following the diplomatic row over the indictment of several RPF leaders by a court in France overseen by the anti-terrorism judge Jean-Louis Bruguière. The effect of these events was to quell any autonomous civil society in Rwanda, as the surviving civil society organizations are very careful to avoid criticizing the government, the RPF, the president, or their policies.

Since February 2004, when the government began easing restrictions on broadcast media, the radio airwaves have become more diverse, with several local and international radio stations broadcasting on the FM bands. By the end of 2005, at least nine commercial, community, and religious radio stations were operating in the country along with new provincial stations belonging to state-owned Radio Rwanda.[9] In a crackdown related to the diplomatic conflict over the Bruguière indictments, the government stopped the FM transmission of Radio France International on November 27, 2006.[10]

Despite the relaxation of tensions with broadcast media, overall media independence and freedom of expression have declined. Basic legal guarantees of freedom of expression and the media were contained in the media law adopted in 2002. The law states that the press is free and that censorship is forbidden, yet in practice the media are still tightly controlled by the government. Articles of the same law impose criminal sanctions on the media for a wide range of offenses such as divisionism and genocide ideology, punishable by one to five years in prison. Accusations of these crimes are used to intimidate and silence journalists.

Several periods marked by courageous journalism criticizing the government, the RPF, and the president have been followed by crackdowns on the media. Since 2005, one of the few independent newspapers, the biweekly *Umuco*, and its personnel have been repeatedly harassed and threatened for their criticism of the government, and the publication has been censored. In September 2005, Rwandan authorities seized issues of *Umuco* at the Ugandan border as the paper was being brought from the printer and detained its editor for seven hours.[11] In January 2006, and again in August, *Umuco*'s editor was forced into hiding after articles critical of the ruling RPF party led to threats and a police summons.[12] In a positive turn, an *Umuco* journalist was released from prison on July 28, 2006, after spending nearly eleven months in jail on a murder charge related to the 1994 genocide, a charge of which he had been acquitted several years earlier.[13] The journalist had been arrested in 2005, just after he published an article in which he accused Gacaca officials in Gitarama province of mismanagement and witness tampering.[14] Another independent newspaper, *Umuseso*, has been the target of similar harassment, intimidation, and censorship since it was founded in the early

2000s. Several of its journalists were forced to flee the country,[15] and in August 2006, Rwanda's highest court upheld a ruling imposing a one-year suspended prison sentence and ordering *Umuseso* editor Charles Kabonero to pay the equivalent of US$2,000 in damages for defaming the deputy speaker of parliament in a 2004 article.[16]

Reporters Without Borders reported in August 2006 that Bosco Gasasira, the editor of the weekly *Umuvugizi*, had been receiving threatening phone calls and had been under surveillance by military intelligence for criticizing economy and finance minister James Musoni.[17] In February 2007, Gasasira was attacked and injured by three men wielding crowbars. One of the attackers was arrested but has not yet been charged, although police said they had completed their investigation.[18] The director of *Umurabyo* was jailed in January 2007 for publishing an anonymous letter that criticized the administration of President Kagame.[19]

Media activities have also been curtailed through public smear campaigns against specific journalists as well as the media in general. In January 2006, President Kagame and Joseph Bideri, director of the Rwandan Information Office (ORINFOR) publicly criticized the news media and singled out two journalists for exaggerating criticism of the Rwandan government by international human rights organizations and being biased against the government.[20] As the largest advertiser in Rwanda, the government influences the media by only advertising in publications that support the RPF line.

The state does not hinder access to the Internet; however, the only Internet provider is the state-owned telecommunications company, RwandaTel. As a result, many internet users assume that their online communications can be and are monitored by the government.

Recommendations

- The electoral laws should be amended to ensure greater transparency in the electoral process (including registration of voters and candidates), the independence of the electoral commission, and freer campaigning. The government should hold elections for public office at all levels of the government by secret ballot. In order for such amendments to pave the way for free and fair elections in practice, however, the government must also open up space for independent political thought.

- The government should not interfere with attempts to establish and operate new political parties.
- The legislature, through amendments to the 2001 Law on Discrimination, should give a clear and restricted definition to the crimes of promoting "divisionism" or "genocide ideology" so that they are less apt to be used to punish critics of the regime.
- The government should stop interfering with civil society and the media, and should encourage these groups to exercise their roles as independent monitors of government policy.
- The government should thoroughly investigate all attacks against journalists and bring those responsible to justice.

CIVIL LIBERTIES

PROTECTION FROM STATE TERROR, UNJUSTIFIED IMPRISONMENT, AND TORTURE:	1.14
GENDER EQUITY:	2.75
RIGHTS OF ETHNIC, RELIGIOUS, AND OTHER DISTINCT GROUPS:	2.00
FREEDOM OF CONSCIENCE AND BELIEF:	2.00
FREEDOM OF ASSOCIATION AND ASSEMBLY:	1.40
CATEGORY AVERAGE:	**1.86**

The majority of the Rwandan population has enjoyed relative security between 2004 and 2007. Nonetheless, repercussions of the 1994 genocide continue to be felt. The vast majority of survivors and families of those who were killed have yet to receive any reparations. Large numbers of survivors, especially women—many of whom were raped during the genocide and suffer from AIDS—live in extreme poverty. Many Rwandans continue to suffer the effects of trauma. The government has established a Fund for Assistance to Genocide Survivors that provides some support to defray the costs of education and health care. However, a law on reparations has never been finalized.

With the launching of Gacaca courts nationwide in 2005, many segments of society began to feel less secure. In some regions, genocide survivors have been threatened by people who did not want to be accused of genocide crimes, and Gacaca judges have been threatened or harassed.

In December 2006, potential witnesses and Gacaca judges in Eastern province were killed.[21] Many other Rwandans, particularly Hutu, have worried that the Gacaca jurisdictions might be used to settle other scores (see Rule of Law below).

Since initial presidential reprieves in 2003, the government has released tens of thousands of prisoners, many who had been detained for many years awaiting trial. Additional releases have followed as part of the government's efforts to implement justice via the Gacaca courts. This was a positive step toward reducing the prison population, improving prison conditions, and ending the imprisonment of thousands of people who had not yet stood trial. Authorities provisionally released nearly 20,000 detainees in July 2005 and another 36,000 in August 2006.[22] Another wave of releases began in February 2007. Many of the released prisoners had confessed to participating in the 1994 genocide but had already served the maximum sentence for their category of crimes.[23] Many others were old and in poor health or had been children at the time of the genocide. Released prisoners attended a six-week reeducation camp before returning to their home communities. After returning home, many of the released prisoners were rearrested because the local Gacaca jurisdiction rejected their confessions as incomplete or untrue.[24]

The government and security forces continue to arrest, detain, or "disappear" critics of the government, the RPF, or the president. In March 2005, Alberta Basimongera, former dean of the Law School at the National University, was arrested because of a text he had edited in 1995 that was highly critical of the RPF.[25] Jean-Népomuscène Nayinzira, a presidential candidate in the 2003 elections and a former minister, was detained by police in May 2005 and continually harassed after he firmly critiqued the regime's governance policies in an interview on the Voice of America.[26] Physical coercion and torture are often used during interrogations or detentions of suspects. Police officers, prison guards, and soldiers who engage in torture are not held accountable.

Progress toward ending prolonged pretrial detention has been made with the release of prisoners charged with genocide. Yet in May 2006, Human Rights Watch reported that hundreds of children were being illegally held in an unofficial detention center in the capital city of Kigali in "deplorable conditions."[27] According to authorities, the facility was intended as a "transit center" for "undesirable persons," such as street children, beggars, street vendors, and sex workers, who had been arrested in the city and were being sent back to their communes of origin.[28] Shortly after the Human Rights Watch report was published, the center was closed, and detainees were forced to leave in the middle of the night.[29] Some detainees were returned to their districts of residence while others were left outside the city limits. In general, prison conditions in Rwanda remain poor, with a lack of food, sanitation, and adequate medical care. Other than limited assistance provided by the International Committee of the Red Cross and religious charities, prisoners must rely on family members to bring them food, drinking water, clothing, and other basic needs.

Since late 2006, the number of extrajudicial executions and arbitrary killings by police has been on the rise. According to Amnesty International, at least three prisoners at the Mulindi military detention center were killed and more than twenty were seriously wounded when military police fired upon unarmed prisoners while responding to a protest by prisoners in the center.[30] In Eastern province several detainees were shot while "trying to escape," according to authorities, but forensic evidence indicated that the detainees had been executed.[31]

With the massive backlog in the criminal justice system as a result of the 1994 genocide and efforts to prosecute its perpetrators, the police and judicial system have very limited resources to protect citizens from abuse by non-state actors. Crime is a growing problem in the country, with petty theft being the most common offense. In 2006 and 2007, reports of home invasions by well-armed bandits increased.[32] In most cases, victims do not seek assistance from the police or state for fear that the thieves will return and kill them.

In 2001, the Parliament passed a law that made divisionism and genocidal ideology crimes, yet the legislation did not clearly define these terms. Since then, the government has used accusations of divisionism to weed out dissent from government or RPF policy. Between 2004 and 2007, the government's campaign against divisionism and genocidal ideology spread beyond the parliament and opposition political parties to include attacks on civil society organizations, schools, and the media. According to Human Rights Watch, authorities compiled a list of hundreds of persons suspected of such ideas in 2005 and 2006.[33] A priest was sentenced to twelve years' imprisonment in September 2006 for "minimizing the genocide" by suggesting that prosecutors had been wrong to call persons who participated in genocide "dogs."[34] In February 2007, Prime Minister Bernard Makuza said that more than 600 cases against people menacing genocide survivors, people accused of divisionism, or "genocide revisionists" had been prosecuted under a program set up by the Supreme Court.[35]

More positively, the Rwandan government continues to be a leader on the African continent in promoting women's rights and ensuring gender equality in law and policy. The 2003 constitution set quotas guaranteeing women at least 30 percent of all positions in decision-making bodies. Women are well represented throughout the government, often holding more than the number of places set aside by quotas. At the end of 2006, 42.3 percent of representatives and senators in the National Parliament were women.[36] However, with the reduction of public space in which civil society organizations operate, women's organizations that had been very effective in lobbying the government on women's issues in the past have avoided tackling issues that are not in line with the government's policy directives.

Despite the advances in promoting women's rights in the law and government, it has proven more difficult to overcome gender-based discrimination in practice. Many women face unwanted sexual advances from superiors in the workplace or from government administrators. In these cases, women do not know where or how to seek assistance.

Important gaps remain in legal protections, especially to prevent violence against women. Although the penal code defines rape as a crime, prosecutions are rarely pursued. The government has made a priority of trying individuals accused of sexually abusing or raping children but has lacked sufficient resources to address the problem adequately. Police and investigators have little or no training in effective investigation of sexual assault or rape, and there is no standard protocol for conducting such inquiries. Few genocide prosecutions have included charges of sexual violence, despite recognition of sexual violence as a tool of the genocide. The open, public forum of Gacaca trials and severe social repercussions for victims of sexual assault make it almost impossible for victims of rape in the genocide to confront their abusers in court. Trafficking of women and children is a crime, but due to lack of resources it is rarely investigated and never prosecuted.

Since 1994, the government has implemented a policy known as "national unity," whereby citizens should consider themselves first and foremost as Rwandan rather than as Hutu, Tutsi, or Batwa. Notations of ethnic identity were removed from the national identity cards early in the transition period, and it became illegal to discriminate on the basis of ethnic affiliation. While some observers question whether the government's true intent is to eliminate discrimination, the Rwandan government maintains that this is indeed its intention and that this is the best way to prevent another genocide. Discussions about ethnicity have become taboo and, since 2001, are illegal if they are perceived as divisionist.

Despite laws and policies that have made explicit discrimination against members of ethnic groups illegal, some Tutsi genocide survivors, Batwa, and members of the Hutu majority complain that they are victims of discrimination in many aspects of government and society. Addressing these complaints of ethnic-based discrimination can be extremely difficult, as advocacy on behalf of any of these groups is often interpreted as promoting division within society and is thus illegal.

Despite the government's mission to erase ethnic antagonism through the national unity policy, ethnicity has resurfaced in a dangerous fashion since the 2003 elections. Hutu citizens feel targeted by the implementation of Gacaca, and divisions among Tutsi, based on language and other differences, have become apparent as the RPF and President Kagame have reduced the circle of elites who wield power. Genocide survivors feel as if the government does not protect their interests. In addition, because Gacaca jurisdictions do not have the authority to address crimes perpetrated by the RPF or the Rwandan Defense Forces (RDF, formerly known as the Rwandan Patriotic Army), many citizens feel as if Gacaca is one-sided, victors' justice.

The Batwa minority continues to face widespread poverty and discrimination. The government has acknowledged the impoverished status of the Batwa and has encouraged district governments to include Batwa and all poor citizens in housing and tuition assistance programs. In 2006, President Kagame appointed a member of the Batwa community to one of eight senate seats reserved for "representatives of historically marginalized communities."[37] Despite these positive steps, the government has not sufficiently protected Batwa rights. For instance, the government has opposed peaceful organization among Batwa on the grounds that such organizing violates the principle of national unity framed in the constitution.[38] Since June 2004, the Ministry of Justice has refused to grant legal status to the Community of Indigenous Peoples in Rwanda (CAURWA), which defends the rights of the Batwa minority, because the organization identified the Batwa as Abasagwabutuka, or the first inhabitants of the land.[39] Following external pressure, the government agreed to engage in talks with CAURWA in 2006. CAURWA agreed to stop using the term Abasagwabutuka but refused to drop the term Batwa.[40] This concession was not enough to satisfy the government, which threatened to stop any form of funding to the Batwa in April 2006 "if the community continues to consider itself a separate ethnic group."[41] While the organization has not received a certificate of registration from the government, it has been allowed to continue operating.[42]

The government has made progressive efforts to protect people with disabilities from discrimination. Under the 2003 constitution, one senate seat is designated for a representative of people with disabilities. This senator is appointed by an umbrella of organizations promoting the interests of or providing services to people with disabilities. Nonetheless, a lack of resources hampers the ability of people with disabilities to participate effectively in society or receive an education. Other marginalized groups, such as street children, sex workers, and the indigent, face social discrimination as well as government policies that infringe on their rights.

The 2003 constitution protects freedom of conscience and belief, and the government generally respected this right in practice between 2004 and 2007. Religious groups are required to register with the Ministry of Justice under the 2001 NGO law. In general, no group's activities were curtailed as a result of delays or difficulties in the registration process. However, the ministry continued the 2003 suspension of two local splinter organizations, the Eglise Methodiste Unie au Rwanda (the United Methodist Church of Rwanda) and the Communauté Methodiste Union Internationale (the International Union Methodist Community).[43]

The 2003 constitution recognizes freedom of association, but this right is restricted in practice. Rwandan law protects the right to form, join, and participate in trade unions; however, unions must follow the same onerous certification and registration process as other NGOs (see Accountability and Public Voice). Overall, trade unions are able to advocate for the interests of their members to a limited degree. In 2004, Imbaraga (Syndicate of Farmers and Ranchers of Rwanda) was named as one of the local NGOs promoting divisionism. While the union was not forced to stop all its activities, it faced a great deal of scrutiny from local, regional, and national governments.

Freedom of assembly is protected by law, but is not fully guaranteed in practice. Protests and demonstrations in line with RPF or government policies occur on a regular basis. To hold a demonstration, the sponsoring groups must apply for a permit. Between 2004 and 2007, demonstrations against government policies or critiquing the RPF have not taken place.

Recommendations

- Swift and thorough investigations into cases involving threats to, attacks on, or killings of genocide survivors or witnesses should be conducted by local and national police authorities. Instances of extrajudicial executions or the use of disproportionate force by the National Police or Rwandan Defense Forces should be investigated by the relevant internal review boards or investigation units and perpetrators held to account before criminal courts or military tribunals, as detailed in Rwandan law.
- The 2001 Law on Non-Profit Associations should be amended to reduce the administrative and bureaucratic hurdles for NGOs to become officially registered; the rules should be clear to avoid arbitrary abuses, and the government should not control project objectives or budgets.
- Government actions to root out genocidal ideology and divisionism should incorporate due process and human rights standards. The government should not publicly accuse individuals or organizations of these offenses without thorough investigation of facts and without giving them a chance to defend themselves.
- Historically marginalized groups, such as the Batwa, should be allowed to organize to advocate for their interests in accordance with the law.
- Prosecutions of military and civilian personnel accused of revenge killings or war crimes should take place as part of the Gacaca process or in the standard criminal justice courts.

RULE OF LAW

INDEPENDENT JUDICIARY:	1.20
PRIMACY OF RULE OF LAW IN CIVIL AND CRIMINAL MATTERS:	0.50
ACCOUNTABILITY OF SECURITY FORCES AND MILITARY TO CIVILIAN AUTHORITIES:	1.50
PROTECTION OF PROPERTY RIGHTS:	1.33
EQUAL TREATMENT UNDER THE LAW:	1.67
CATEGORY AVERAGE:	**1.24**

Thirteen years after the genocide, the Rwandan judiciary still faces nearly unparalleled challenges. Participation in the 1994 genocide occurred on an unprecedented scale, and the judiciary was decimated in its wake. In March 2005, the secretary general of the Justice Ministry stated that approximately 761,000 suspects had been identified in the investigation phase of Gacaca.[44] The judiciary is still struggling to rebuild itself and deal with the massive undertaking of holding accountable those responsible for genocide.

In 2005, the judicial reform process launched in 2003 was completed and most genocide cases were directed to the Gacaca courts. The regular courts began operating again following the reorganization, although cases still proceed slowly as courts in many areas lack judges or other judiciary staff due to a lack of qualified personnel. As part of the judicial reforms, certain minimum criteria for judges, such as age and years in practice, were lowered to increase the numbers of candidates eligible to serve. Some judges appointed under these new criteria may not have adequate legal training to fulfill their duties. The majority of cases before the regular courts have been criminal trials and land disputes.

The 2003 constitution guarantees judicial independence, yet in practice the judiciary is subject to influence by the executive and by members of the political, military, and economic elite. One prominent case that demonstrated the lack of judicial independence in the regular courts was that of former president Pasteur Bizimungu and former public works minister Charles Ntakirutinka. In February 2006, the Supreme Court upheld the convictions and sentences of Bizimungu and Ntakirutinka on counts of treason and embezzlement.[45] Human Rights

Watch noted many irregularities as well as weakness in the prosecution's case, most notably the many contradictions of the prosecution's star witness.[46] The government has made some efforts to increase the professionalism of employees of the justice system. In November 2005, prosecutors from around the country met to review national search warrant and arrest procedures to ensure that the relevant authorities followed the procedures.[47]

The 2003 constitution guarantees the right to independent counsel, a right that was not previously assured. However, in the regular courts handling criminal cases or more serious genocide crimes, defendants do not always have access to defense as there are few qualified lawyers in the country, and few Rwandans have the means to hire a lawyer. The Gacaca law (Organic Law No. 16/2004 of June 19, 2004) prohibits defendants from being assisted by counsel.

It is common for civil and criminal disputes to be handled outside the formal judicial system. Local officials often intervene in rape cases to encourage the parties involved to resolve the matter amicably, in part to protect victims from the social stigma of rape. The 2003 constitution established mediation committees to help resolve certain disputes at the local level before the parties go to court. However, the mediators are unpaid, which has led to fears of corruption.

Regular and military tribunals have tried few cases of war crimes and revenge killings committed against Hutu, and most of these resulted in only nominal penalties. The International Criminal Tribunal for Rwanda (ICTR) has also been accused of one-sided justice as it has declined to investigate allegations of war crimes by the RPF. Each time the ICTR prosecutor has initiated investigations of RPF war crimes, the Rwandan government ceases its cooperation with the ICTR, which makes prosecuting genocide cases impossible. While some RPF officials have faced judicial proceedings in standard courts, notably for corruption, they generally enjoy impunity until they are no longer useful to the akazu.

Gacaca jurisdictions began systematic investigations into genocide crimes in January 2005 and began trials throughout the country in March 2005. The national government has done a great deal to raise the awareness about Gacaca and to promote it as the best solution for genocide survivors and the families of those accused of participating in the genocide. Prior to 2001, 115,000 people accused of genocide crimes were in prison, kept in inhumane and degrading conditions with little prospect of facing trial due in the overburdened Courts of First Instance.[48] The Gacaca presented a real prospect for achieving closure: it was predicted that they would finish hearing cases in a matter of years, rather than the decades it would have taken the ordinary court system to do the same. In theory, the Gacaca promote restorative justice by reintegrating convicts, making use of community service sentences, and recognizing the role of women as key players in the reconciliation process. Their introduction was initially welcomed by the citizenry, and moreover, in April 2005 President Paul Kagame stated publicly that any member of the government summoned before the Gacaca courts must testify.[49]

However, despite early support, the Gacaca jurisdictions failed to gain the trust of the populace, increasing popular fears of political instability and decreasing their sense of security. In March and April 2005, thousands of Rwandans fled into exile in Burundi and Uganda because they feared unfair treatment by the Gacaca courts.[50] Following a mass repatriation in June 2005, thousands of Rwandans again crossed the border; these refugees numbered 19,000 in March 2006.[51] In 2005, a joint commission between the Burundian government and the UNHCR began evaluating individual asylum requests by Rwandans. Between April 12, 2006, and June 13, 2006, the Burundian government had repatriated 5,206 Rwandans, according to a UNHCR representative.[52]

In the wake of the mass prisoner releases, Ibuka, an umbrella organization of genocide survivor groups, protested that the released prisoners were a "security threat" and that "their release will only serve to weaken the Gacaca courts as survivors will find these courts irrelevant."[53] In some regions, there was evidence of efforts to sabotage Gacaca, and certain clandestine groups called *Ceceka* (Kinyarwanda for "be quiet") organized a code of silence in some communities.[54] Killings of potential witnesses in genocide cases as well as of Gacaca judges in 2004 and 2006 threatened to undermine the ability of the courts to carry out trials in certain communities. According to Ibuka, 177 survivors and witnesses of the genocide were murdered between 2000 and 2007.[55] As a consequence, witnesses prefer to keep silent and fewer and fewer citizens and judges participate in the process.[56]

Numerous actions by the courts made citizens doubt their impartiality. In 2006, the Gacaca courts jailed dozens of witnesses and defendants for refusing to speak completely or truthfully.[57] In other instances, the Gacaca courts refused to reduce the sentences of those who had admitted guilt, a promise that had been made in order to encourage people to confess. One of the primary fears of the populace was that the courts would be used to settle personal scores or ends other than justice. In one case, a panel of judges jailed a journalist for eleven months on false charges after he published an article on corruption in Gacaca jurisdictions.[58]

The independence of the Gacaca jurisdictions was brought into question in a very public way when Rwandan authorities arrested Belgian Catholic priest and journalist Guy Theunis, a strong critic of the RPF, as he passed through Kigali in early September 2005.[59] Witnesses before a Gacaca court accused him of publishing material that had incited people to participate in the 1994 genocide. In 1994, Theunis was editor of the French-language review *Dialogue*, which had translated and published excerpts from the extremist Kinyarwanda newspaper, Kangura, renowned for its anti-Tutsi rhetoric, which had inflamed anti-Tutsi hatred in the lead-up to the 1994 genocide. After considerable diplomatic pressure from Belgium, the Rwandan government agreed to transfer Theunis to Belgium, where the case would be tried.

The presumption of innocence is protected in the constitution but is essentially absent in many criminal cases, especially genocide cases. The government publishes a list of suspects accused of the most heinous genocide crimes. While the suspects have yet to be tried, many Rwandans view those named on the list as guilty. Appearance on the list can result in a loss of civil rights such as suffrage. There are also concerns about the broadcasting on radio of the names of some of those accused of divisionism.

Gacaca judges are elected by the local community; however, these elections were marred by the same problems as other local-level elections. In some jurisdictions, the judges were elected through a queuing system, rendering citizens' votes public instead of secret. In other jurisdictions, there were irregularities in the balloting. By the end of 2006, 45,000 Gacaca judges had been accused of genocide, further calling into question the impartiality of the Gacaca jurisdictions.[60] Moreover, Gacaca courts sometimes operate outside the parameters of the law, as some judges lack basic understanding of legal principles. In particular, judges have been rejecting confessions or refusing to reduce sentences without the necessary judicial justifications.[61] Gacaca judges have received very little training, and observers have found that what instruction they did receive has often been inconsistent from one training site to the next. Avocats Sans Frontieres highlights the challenges that Gacaca judges face in remaining impartial and objective in their duties, as they have little protection from reprisals from the local community.[62] In December 2006, a Gacaca judge was killed in Eastern province.[63]

Senior military officials continue to play an important role in the government and akazu. Security forces have continued to improve their professionalism since 2004, and the RDF are acknowledged as being among the best-disciplined troops in Africa. In December 2005, the RDF hosted and participated in a regional training session on international humanitarian law sponsored by the International Committee for the Red Cross.[64] Nonetheless, security forces continued to commit abuses, including arbitrary arrest and possible extrajudicial executions. In January 2007, Human Rights Watch reported on the killings of individuals in custody.[65] All criminal cases involving RDF or the police are referred to military tribunals for hearings, and these tribunals do not have any oversight by the judicial or legislative branches and limited oversight by the executive branch. Since national elections in 2003, the RDF no longer has deputies in the Parliament, but it continues to hold great influence within the executive branch of government.

The 2003 constitution guarantees the right to own private property individually or collectively. In a country where approximately 90 percent of the population subsists from agriculture, land is the most important form of private property. Land was one of the root causes of the genocide, and land access remains a volatile issue, as Rwanda is a densely populated country. In 1959, hundreds of thousands of Tutsi refugees fled to neighboring countries in the wake of ethnic violence, abandoning their land to those who remained. In the immediate aftermath of the 1994 genocide, a huge number of Hutu refugees fled the country just as the 1959 refugees returned to Rwanda. Many of the 1959 returnees occupied houses and land that had been left vacant by those who fled more recently. In an effort to find a solution for the 1959 refugees, who were not supposed to claim the homes or land they had left decades ago, and for genocide survivors whose homes had been destroyed, the government and donors built resettlement villages. With forced repatriation in 1996 and 1997 of more than 1 million mostly Hutu refugees, tensions over land and real estate property again flared. The government applied a national policy of villagization, which required all Rwandans to move to the villages, instead of to traditional, dispersed habitats. From 1998 to 2000, villagization was carried out on a large scale, sometimes by force or coercion. Villagization was a key element of the counter-insurgency campaigns in the Northwest. Many farmers lost their land in the process or had their houses destroyed, and many families were obligated to share their land with 1959 refugees.[66] The land law of 2005 reiterated the villagization policy after several years of government silence on the issue. These events have laid the foundation for extensive land disputes.

Given the growing land crisis, the government embarked on the development of a national land policy in 2000. Population growth, inheritance customs, and land scarcity have resulted in tiny dispersed plots where many families survive on less than one hectare. Given the mountainous terrain of the country and variations in soil types, intercropping and dispersed plots served as the best way for families to ensure enough food to survive. Yet an underlying assumption of the land policy process was that such use of land was irrational. Thus, the land policy attempted to "modernize agriculture" and encourage "rational" use of the land. On this basis, senior government and military officials and important businessmen assumed control of large plots of land to use as commercial farms, particularly marsh land, which had historically been provided to farming cooperatives or poor families by local government officials. Families who were displaced from the land rarely had access to due process or compensation for their loss.

In September 2005, the government published a law on land tenure. In accordance with the 2003 constitution, the land law guaranteed Rwandans (and foreign investors) the right to own land.[67] The final version of the land bill states that women have equal rights with men to inherit or own land. Despite these legal guarantees, the law also granted the government far-reaching powers over land use.[68] The law states that farmers who fail to follow the national plan for land use may see their land "requisitioned," with no compensation.[69] While a detailed implementation plan is still being developed, officials in some regions have begun to give directives to the population. For instance, in 2006 officials in two districts in Southern province ordered residents to cut down their banana plantations, a primary food crop, and replace them with ornamental trees or "more productive" cash crops.[70] Following public protest in one district, officials said that residents would not be forced but only "persuaded" to comply.[71]

In efforts to modernize the capital city, Kigali, many people living in noncadastral properties have had their property confiscated to make way for new, "modern" buildings under a new urban planning program known as PIGU (Urban Management and Infrastructure Project).[72] Many of the relocated people said that they were not compensated by the government as required by Rwandan law, or that compensation was insufficient to build a house elsewhere.[73]

Litigants seeking to enforce contracts face an extremely slow judicial process that discourages them from seeking government intervention.

Recommendations
- The Gacaca law should be amended to allow defendants and civilians to protect their rights through access to independent counsel.
- The Gacaca law should be amended to include jurisdiction over abuses perpetrated by the Rwandan Defense Forces (formerly known as the Rwandan Patriotic Army), as well as reprisal attacks committed by civilians against those suspected of genocide.
- The land law should be amended to protect private citizens' property rights by guaranteeing them compensation for the value of land requisitioned by the government as well as any improvements thereupon.
- The central government, particularly the ministries of agriculture and local governance, should clarify government policies vis-à-vis land use and decisions about appropriate crops for farmland.

ANTICORRUPTION AND TRANSPARENCY

ENVIRONMENT TO PROTECT AGAINST CORRUPTION:	2.80
EXISTENCE OF LAWS AND ETHICAL STANDARDS BETWEEN	
PRIVATE AND PUBLIC SECTORS:	2.75
ENFORCEMENT OF ANTICORRUPTION LAWS:	2.50
GOVERNMENTAL TRANSPARENCY:	1.86
CATEGORY AVERAGE:	**2.48**

The Rwandan government and bureaucratic infrastructure are widely recognized for their professionalism. As a result, Rwanda enjoys the reputation of having less corruption as compared to other African countries. Between 2004 and 2007, the government has continued reforms aimed at reducing corruption even further. Tough measures aimed at curbing public-sector corruption, such as asset disclosure and codes of conduct for public servants, were instituted in 2004, and beginning in 2005 certain prominent government officials were accused of corruption in both the media and the courts. In recognition of the government's success in controlling corruption, significant amounts of the country's national debt have been canceled.[74]

In general, the government is free from excessive bureaucratic controls and registration requirements. Nonetheless, private citizens face situations where they are required to "thank" local officials or bureaucrats with small monetary payments for handling their paperwork quickly.

Several institutions are involved in combating corruption. In 2004, the Ombudsman's Office was established to monitor transparency and compliance with regulation in all public sectors, among other duties. According to U4 Anti-Corruption Resource Centre, the Ombudsman's Office has embraced its mission, declaring that those who do not comply will face prosecution.[75]

The Office of the Auditor-General regulates financial management and adherence of public entities to financial accountability and transparency standards. The auditor-general is required to submit annual audit reports and findings to Parliament. The 2003 constitution mandates that the budget process be transparent and that the Parliament oversee the process. However, Parliament has yet to assert this power in practice.

The National Tender Board regulates public procurement and tender processes in a centralized system for large contracts. The Rwanda Utility Regulation Agency, the Auditor-General's Office, the Anticorruption Division in the Revenue Authority, and the National Bureau of Standards are all in place to enforce regulations as well. On numerous occasions the president has spoken out against corruption and declared that all public servants must make open declarations about possible conflicts of interest. In this vein, the government has decreed July 11 of each year as Public Accountability Day, when government officials will open up their offices to voters. Despite this rhetoric, it is yet to be determined whether this openness will result in genuine and rigorous financial accountability.

In state-sponsored educational institutions, the government has protected higher education from pervasive corruption. Students are not required to pay bribes for admission or for good grades. Given the lack of oversight of private universities, technical colleges, and secondary schools, however, it is unclear to what degree these institutions may be educationally deficient or corrupt.

Enforcement of anticorruption laws tends to occur in cycles. In 2004, a number of high government officials, including the attorney general and a former minister, as well as more than a hundred police officers, forty-seven district mayors, and five governors, resigned or were removed from office over allegations of corruption. Yet none of these high officials faced charges in court. In late 2006 and early 2007, another cycle of anticorruption enforcement began. In 2006, the National Tender Board halted a tender for a study of the social and economic integration of youth in the country by the Ministry of Youth, Culture, and Sports. The youth and culture minister said that he requested the criminal investigations department to intervene and investigate irregularities in the tender process, including the possibility of bribes paid to tender committee members.[76] In February 2007, former Public Service and Labor Ministry secretary general Charlotte Mukankusi was arrested in connection with abuse of public office after she allegedly awarded illegal tenders to RUMA, a local consultancy and auditing firm, in exchange for kickbacks.[77] The criminal investigations department also investigated the link between RUMA and the Ministry of Public Service, Skills Development and Labor (MIFOTRA). It was alleged that the ministry awarded numerous tenders to RUMA without following the normal tendering procedures.[78] It remains to be seen whether these officials will answer the allegations in court. In several other instances in 2006, the National Tender Board reminded various ministries of the need to follow tendering procedures for large contracts. In cases where upper-level government officials, such as ministers, deputy ministers, and secretaries of state, have been accused of corruption, the national news media have covered the stories in depth. However, the perception remains that many government officials have engaged in corruption but are protected as long as they remain in good stead with the akazu. There are no whistle-blower laws or other means to make citizens feel secure when reporting cases of corruption.

The positive NEPAD peer review outlined several areas in which the government needs to make changes in order to adhere to the Code of Good Practices on Transparency in Monetary and Financial Affairs.[79] The review lauded the government's achievements in sound public finance management, yet it also noted the lack of capacity in the parliament in performing its oversight functions in all areas of economic policy making and implementation.[80]

Government policies are lacking in transparency and accessibility to the general public. No law guarantees public access to government information. Since the release of the 2004 report of the Office of the Auditor-General, the office's annual reports have not been widely publicized and are not readily available to the general public. The government primarily imparts information to the public through national radio broadcasts, national television broadcasts, the state-owned newspaper, Imvaho-Nshya, and "sensitization" meetings organized by local officials. These meetings are sometimes billed as soliciting popular feedback, but most Rwandans view them as forums for the government to provide information without allowing the people to express differing points of view or provide input. In this way, the government is able to control the timing and content of public access to information.

Overall, the government is praised for its fair and legal administration and distribution of foreign assistance.

Recommendations

- Each year, the Office of the Auditor-General should publish and publicize the findings of its annual report to the Parliament.
- The Office of the Auditor-General should be granted the necessary resources and powers in order to thoroughly investigate allegations of corruption. When the Auditor-General uncovers evidence of corruption, he should turn all findings over to the police to conduct a criminal investigation. The judiciary should pursue vigorous prosecution of corruption charges against all government officials.
- The capacity and resources of the Parliament should be reinforced so that it is prepared to assume its duties as overseer of all areas of economic policymaking and implementation.
- The Parliament should pass legislation guaranteeing public access to government information.

NOTES

1 See for example, Filip Reyntjens, "Post-1994 Politics in Rwanda: Problematising 'Liberation' and 'Democratisation'," *Third World Quarterly* 27, no. 6 (2006).

2 Filip Reyntjens, "Chronique Politique Du Rwanda Et Du Burundi, 2003–2005," *L'Afriques des Grands Lacs, Annuaire 2004–2005* (2005): 13.

3 "Rwanda: Local Government Polls Begin," IRIN, 6 February 2006, http://www.irin news.org/report.asp?ReportID=51547&SelectRegion=Great_Lakes&SelectCountry= RWANDA., accessed 7 February 2007.

4 "Rwanda—Events of 2006" (New York: Human Rights Watch [HRW], 2007), http:// hrw.org/englishwr2k7/docs/2007/01/11/rwanda14782.htm, accessed 7 February 2007.

5 Ibid.

6 Ibid.

7 "Country Review Report of the Republic of Rwanda" (Midrand, South Africa: The New Partnership for Africa's Development [NEPAD], 2006), 135.

8 "Rwanda" (London: Amnesty International [AI], 2006), http://web.amnesty.org/report 2006/rwa-summary-eng, accessed 7 February 2007.

9 "Rwanda Country Report," in *Attacks on the Press in 2005* (New York: Committee to Protect Journalists [CPJ], 2006).

10 "Radio France Internationale Censored" (CPJ, 2006), http://www.cpj.org/cases06 /africa_cases_06/rwanda27nov06ca.html, accessed 19 December 2006.

11 "Police Confiscate Opposition Fortnightly, Hold Editor for 7 Hours" (Paris: Reporters Without Borders [RSF], 2005); available from http://www.rsf.org/article.php3?id _article=15064, accessed 19 December 2006.

12 "Rwanda: Newspaper Editor Goes into Hiding" (CPJ, 2006), http://www.cpj.org /news/2006/africa/rwanda09aug06na.html, accessed 19 December 2006.

13 "Rwandan Journalist Freed after 11 Months in Jail" (CPJ, 2006), http://www.cpj.org /news/2006/africa/rwanda31july06na.html, accessed 19 December 2006.

14 Ibid.

15 Ibid.

16 "High Court Upholds One-Year Suspended Sentence and Heavy Fine for Editor Who Published Political Analysis" (RSF, 2006), http://www.rsf.org/article.php3?id_article =12964, accessed 19 December 2006.

17 "Umuvugizi Editor Latest Target in Harassment of Independent Press" (RSF, 2006), http://www.rsf.org/article.php3?id_article=18505, 19 December 2006.

18 Eleneus Akanga, "Rwanda: Uncertainty as Journalists' Beatings Mount," *New Times* (Kigali), 17 February 2007.

19 "In Rwanda, Newspaper Director Jailed for Publishing Critical Letter" (CPJ, 16 January 2007), http://www.cpj.org/news/2007/africa/rwanda16jan07na.html, accessed 21 February 2007.

20 "President Kicks Off Verbal Onslaught on Journalists by Government Officials" (RSF, January 31, 2006), http://www.rsf.org/article.php3?id_article=16325, accessed 19 December 2006.

21 "Killings in Eastern Rwanda," (HRW, Backgrounder, no. 1 [2007], January 2007).

22 "Rwanda: Release of Thousands of Prisoners Begins," IRIN, 1 August 2005, http://www
.irinnews.org/report.asp?ReportID=48373&SelectRegion=Great_Lakes&SelectCountry
=RWANDA., accessed 9 February 2007.

23 Ibid.

24 "Rwanda—Events of 2006" (HRW).

25 Reyntjens, "Chronique Politique," 4–5.

26 Ibid., 5.

27 "Swept Away: Street Children Illegally Detained in Kigali, Rwanda," (HRW, Backgrounder, no. 2 [2006], May 2006, 9.

28 Ibid.

29 "Rwanda—Events of 2006" (HRW).

30 "Rwanda: Reports of Extrajudicial Executions in Mulindi Military Detention Centre
Must Be Independently Investigated" (AI, 16 March 2006), http://web.amnesty.org
/library/print/ENGAFR470042006, accessed 18 December 2006.

31 "Killings in Eastern Rwanda" (HRW).

32 Telephone interviews with family members of victims and personal communications
from victims, December 2006, March 2007, and May 2007.

33 "Rwanda—Events of 2006" (HRW).

34 Ibid.

35 Felly Kimenyi, "Rwanda: Makuza Tasked over 2003 Kaduha Killings," *New Times*, 7
February 2007.

36 Compiled from http://www.rwandaparliament.gov.rw/, accessed 2 November 2006.

37 "Rwanda: Funds for Batwa under Threat over Name Change," IRIN, 3 April 2006,
http://www.irinnews.org/Report.aspx?ReportId=58628, accessed 15 February 2007.

38 "Submission of the Forest Peoples Programme Concerning the Republic of Rwanda and
Its Compliance with the International Convention on Civil and Political Rights (Nether-
lands: Forest Peoples Programme, 5 October 2006), http://www.forestpeoples.org
/documents/africa/rwanda_hrc_rep_oct06_eng.pdf, accessed 15 February 2007.

39 "Rwanda: Funds for Batwa under Threat over Name Change," IRIN.

40 Ibid.

41 Ibid.

42 Telephone interview by author with human rights observer, 15 February 2007.

43 "Rwanda," in *International Religious Freedom Report 2006* (Washington, D.C.: U.S.
Department of State, Bureau of Democracy, Human Rights and Labor, 2006).

44 Reyntjens, "Chronique Politique," 13.

45 Felly Kimenyi, "Supreme Court Upholds 15-Year Sentence for Bizimungu" *New Times*
February 22, 2006 (Kigali: Rwanda Development Gateway, 2006), http://www.rwanda
gateway.org/article.php3?id_article=1614, accessed 7 February 2007.

46 "Historic Ruling Expected for Former President and Seven Others" (HRW, Backgrounder no. 1 [2006], January 2006..

47 "Rwanda: Prosecutors Meet on Search Warrant, Arrest Procedures," IRIN, 7 November
2005, http://www.irinnews.org/report.asp?ReportID=49955&SelectRegion=Great_Lakes
&SelectCountry=RWANDA, accessed 7 February 2007.

48 Amnesty International (AI) "Gacaca: A Question of Justice" 17 December 2002, http://web.amnesty.org/library/index/engafr470072002.

49 "Rwanda: Year in Brief 2005—a Chronology of Key Events," IRIN, 13 January 2006, http://www.irinnews.org/report.asp?ReportID=51100&SelectRegion=Great_Lakes& Select Country=RWANDA, accessed 9 February 2007.

50 Rwandans' Asylum Claims Must Be Heard (HRW, 2005), http://hrw.org/english /docs/2005/05/26/burund11030_txt.htm, accessed 18 December 2006.

51 "Burundi-Rwanda: Bujumbura Hands over 571 Rwandans," IRIN, 11 May 2006, http://www.irinnews.org/report.aspx?ReportID=58990, accessed 7 February 2007.

52 "Burundi-Rwanda: Thousands More Asylum Seekers Repatriated," IRIN, 13 June 2006, http://www.irinnews.org/report.asp?ReportID=53896&SelectRegion=Great_Lakes& SelectCountry=BURUNDI-RWANDA, accessed 7 February 2007.

53 "Rwanda: Release of Suspects in the 1994 Genocide Angers Survivors," IRIN, 9 August 2005, http://www.irinnews.org/report.asp?ReportID=48504&SelectRegion=Great _Lakes&SelectCountry=RWANDA, accessed 7 February 2007.

54 Reyntjens, "Chronique Politique," 13.

55 "Rwanda/Genocide—177 Survivors and Witnesses of the Genocide Murdered since 2000, Ibuka Reports," Hirondelle News Agency, 31 January 2007.

56 Ibid.

57 "Rwanda—Events of 2006" (HRW).

58 Ibid.

59 "Rwanda Country Report" (CPJ).

60 "Rwanda—Events of 2006" (HRW).

61 "Monitoring of the Gacaca Courts, Judgement Phase" (Brussels: Avocats Sans Frontieres, 2005).

62 Ibid.

63 "Killings in Eastern Rwanda" (HRW).

64 "Great Lakes: Junior Army Officers Learn Humanitarian Law," IRIN, 7 December 2005, http://www.irinnews.org/report.asp?ReportID=50527&SelectRegion=East_Africa, Great _Lakes&SelectCountry=GREAT LAKES, accessed 7 February 2007.

65 "Killings in Eastern Rwanda" (HRW).

66 "Uprooting the Rural Poor in Rwanda" (HRW, 2001).

67 "Rwanda—Human Rights Overview" (HRW).

68 Ibid.

69 Ibid.

70 "Rwanda—Events of 2006" (HRW).

71 Ibid.

72 "Rwanda: Counting the Cost of Modernisation," IRIN, 13 September 2006, http://www .irinnews.org/report.asp?ReportID=55529&SelectRegion=Great_Lakes&SelectCountry =RWANDA, accessed 7 February 2007.

73 Ibid.

74 "Rwanda: Year in Brief 2005—a Chronology of Key Events," IRIN.

75 "Corruption in Rwanda" (Norway: U4 Anti-Corruption Resource Centre, May 2005), http://www.u4.no/helpdesk/helpdesk/queries/query58.cfm, accessed 20 February 2007.

76 Ignatius Ssuuna and Godwin Agaba, "Rwanda: Youth Ministry Officials Quizzed over 60m Tender," *New Times*, 9 February 2007.

77 Ignatius Ssuuna, "Rwanda: Former Mifotra Sg Arrested," *New Times*, 12 February 2007.

78 Robert Mukombozi and Ignatius Ssuuna, "Rwanda: New Twist in Mifotra Saga as Probe Widens," *New Times*, 17 February 2007.

79 "Country Review Report of the Republic of Rwanda" (NEPAD), 60–61.

80 Ibid., 73.

SWAZILAND

CAPITAL: Mbabane
POPULATION: 1.1 million
GNI PER CAPITA: $2,430

SCORES	2005	2007
ACCOUNTABILITY AND PUBLIC VOICE:	1.85	1.88
CIVIL LIBERTIES:	2.98	3.18
RULE OF LAW:	1.45	2.10
ANTICORRUPTION AND TRANSPARENCY:	1.85	2.05

(scores are based on a scale of 0 to 7, with 0 representing weakest
and 7 representing strongest performance)

John Daniel

INTRODUCTION

There is no tradition of democracy in Swazi politics. Since Swaziland
emerged as a state in the early nineteenth century, Swazi political culture has been authoritarian, with power centralized in a hereditary
monarchy, and the nation's politics and economy dominated by the royal
lines of the Dlamini clans. The late colonial period and the first five years
of independence introduced some choice and party-political competitiveness into the polity, but this ended in 1973 with the suspension of
the independence constitution and the proscription of political parties.

Swaziland's political regime is a diarchic one, with two distinct but
interrelated sets of institutions: those of the Swazi nation (the monarchy and its key advisory institutions); and those of the Swazi government, comprising the cabinet, parliament, and judiciary. It was in the
latter that Britain vested constitutional authority at independence in
1968. However, then-King Sobhuza II was able to circumvent this dilu-
tion of his traditional authority by forming a political party, the

John Daniel is a former member of the political science department at the University
of Swaziland and retired Professor of Political Science at the University of Durban-
Westville, South Africa.

Imbokodvo National Movement, which won all parliamentary seats in elections leading up to independence in 1968. Thus, although not a member of the legislature himself, Sobhuza was able to ensure that the body enacted no legislation of which he did not approve. The king's domination of the postindependence power arrangement was articulated by then–prime minister Prince Makhosini Dlamini, who stated "It is the king, not I, who leads the people."[1] This is the central principle of Swazi political life, and to challenge it is regarded by the ruling elite as treasonable.

This period of postindependence one-party rule gave way to no-party rule in 1973, when Sobhuza responded to an opposition group winning three out of twenty-eight seats in the first elections held after independence and a successful high court challenge of controversial immigration legislation by abrogating the constitution. A state of emergency was declared (which de jure persists today, more than thirty-four years later), a detention-without-trial provision was introduced, Parliament was dissolved, and all political parties, even the royalist Imbokodvo Movement, were banned. In an address to the Swazi people, Sobhuza justified his actions by declaring that the independence constitution was incompatible with Swazi tradition as it had "permitted the imposition into our country of highly undesirable political practices, alien and incompatible with the way of life in our society, and designed to disrupt and destroy our own peaceful and constructive and essentially democratic method of peaceful political activity."[2]

What Sobhuza was targeting as "undesirable" and "alien" was the political party as an institution. His words remain salient today, as they essentially inform the view of his successor, Mswati III, and his advisers. This group regards political parties as un-Swazi and incompatible with their concept of tradition. Therefore, to concede to the Swazi people the right to freely organize themselves politically would involve an ideological paradigm shift on the part of the monarchy.

Since 1973, Swaziland has functioned as a near-absolute monarchy. In 1996, the king appointed a constitutional review commission that five years later reported, without supporting evidence, that the Swazi nation preferred no change to the political status quo. The king then appointed a group headed by one of his brothers to draft a new constitution. This was unveiled in 2004, proposing a continuation of the monarchy's supreme executive, legislative, and judicial powers as well as the ban on political parties. Despite representations from a number of individuals and organizations objecting to the draft, in June 2005 the Swazi parliament adopted, with only minor changes, the document as proposed by the review committee. King Mswati III signed the constitution into law on July 26, 2005, announcing it would come into force six months hence. It took effect on February 7, 2006. It was anticipated that the king would then promulgate the repeal of the emergency proclamation of April 12, 1973, but he did not. Thus, a nine-year review process costing several million dollars resulted in basically nothing changing politically and with the king retaining absolute powers.

Swaziland is confronted by a human disaster of alarming proportions in the form of one of the highest, if not the highest, HIV/AIDS infection rate in the world. According to a 2005 survey by the Swazi Ministry of Health, the proportion of sexually active adults between the ages of nineteen and forty-nine infected with HIV/AIDS was 42.6 percent in 2004, with the rate as high as 56 percent in the twenty-five to twenty-nine age category. A follow-up survey in 2006 found that the figure had dropped to 39.2 percent for those between nineteen and forty-nine years of age in 2005.[3]

With an economy performing weakly (growth in 2006 is estimated to have been at 2 percent, consistent with the rate over the past five years) while levels of corruption continued to rise along with government expenditure, food prices, and unemployment levels, prime minister Themba Dlamini admitted in his 2007 New Year's message that Swaziland had an "increasingly negative international image."[4]

ACCOUNTABILITY AND PUBLIC VOICE

FREE AND FAIR ELECTORAL LAWS AND ELECTIONS:	0.25
EFFECTIVE AND ACCOUNTABLE GOVERNMENT:	1.75
CIVIC ENGAGEMENT AND CIVIC MONITORING:	3.00
MEDIA INDEPENDENCE AND FREEDOM OF EXPRESSION:	2.50
CATEGORY AVERAGE:	**1.88**

Politically, Swaziland is an absolute monarchy with executive, legislative, and some judicial powers vested in the king, although there is a partially elected but thoroughly subordinated Parliament. As noted previously, a constitutional review process originally touted as reformist concluded with an affirmation of the political status quo. At the time of the draft's publication in 2004, the public was invited to comment on it, but only as private individuals and not as representatives of organized groups. Thus, local groups highly critical of the dispensation in Swaziland, like the Swazi Federation of Labor, the Swaziland Youth Congress (SWAYOCO) and human rights groups, were excluded from the process. Instead, four local groups coalesced as the National Constitutional Assembly and applied to the High Court for the draft to be set aside. While the court accepted the case, it eventually ruled against the group.

The promulgation of the constitution in July 2005 led to another round of critical comment from, among others, the British Trades Union Congress, the International Confederation of Free Trade Unions, the Congress of South African Trade Unions (COSATU), and the South African Communist Party. In early 2006, both the British High Commissioner to Swaziland and the Dutch ambassador strongly criticized the political system in Swaziland when presenting their diplomatic credentials to the king. Britain's Paul Boateng stated that "corruption, violence, intimidation and torture have no place in the new Africa of the twenty-first century. It is on issues such as these that the reputation of Swaziland rests."[5]

The draft constitution proposed no changes to the electoral system, but there seems to be some confusion around the status of political parties under the new charter. While the king has never repealed the 1973 emergency proclamation banning political parties, he is reported to have stated in April 2006 that the decree had lapsed when the constitution came into force in February. Days later, however, he told the international press that the country was "not ready for political parties." In May, the attorney general stated that the constitution did not "disallow political parties because it did not address the issue, but that the Swazi people were not yet ready for them."[6]

Parliamentary elections are held every five years. These are conducted in terms of a traditional *tinkundhla* system: candidates run only as individuals and not as representatives of any party or grouping. The number of candidates per constituency is limited to three, and their nomination is subject to a local screening process. This is conducted in public by a show of hands by the local chiefs in the area. The franchise is open to all adults over the age of eighteen, and votes are cast by secret ballot.

Despite the democratic form of this electoral process, Swazi elections do not conform fully to the now widely accepted "free and fair" criteria for democratic elections. The ban on party political activity limits the range of political choice. So does the local screening process, which inevitably results in a majority of candidates linked or sympathetic to the royalist structure. Finally, balloting is for only fifty-five of the ninety-five parliamentary seats. This means that 42 percent of legislative seats are non-elective and are the prerogative of the king himself. Thus, even in the unlikely case that a majority of elected members turned out to be reformists, their capacity for change would be neutralized by the nominated bloc of royalist-aligned members of Parliament. Under current circumstances, therefore, a lawful or constitutional change in power in Swaziland is unlikely, if not impossible. Given that the executive branch of government, in the form of the monarchy, conceptualizes itself as not subject to statutory laws, there are obvious limitations on the capacity of the judicial and legislative branches to oversee the executive branch.

Recruitment into the civil service is largely by merit, and a high proportion of public servants hold university degrees and appropriate technical qualifications. At entry level, female applicants appear not to be discriminated against, and significant numbers of women occupy upper-level civil service positions. On the other hand, this situation is offset by the fact that most senior posts in the civil service tend to be filled by males regarded by the traditional authorities as politically reliable. These are often princes of the dominant Dlamini clan, or individuals with close ties to the royal family.

Civil society in Swaziland is weak, though this is not because the government makes it especially difficult for the sector to operate. The Coordinating Assembly of Non-Governmental Organisations (CANGO) has some seventy affiliates that are concerned with a range of social issues including child abuse, population control, women's empowerment, youth and orphan care, and the like. These groups can attempt to influence policy and legislation although, as noted above, they were barred from commenting on the draft constitution. They are not subject to onerous registration requirements, nor is there evidence that their funders are subject to state pressure. The disabilities they face are twofold. One is the political apathy of the majority of Swazis and the continuing internalization of a political culture that demands unquestioning subservience to the wishes and whims of the traditional royalist and chieftaincy authorities. The second is government's distrust of the sector, which it does not regard as a partner in the fight against poverty and other ills. Many of the groups are in fact regarded by the royalist sector as the agents or partners of foreign forces. A royalist spokesman was recently quoted as saying "Who are these groups? Where do they come from? We know their financing comes from abroad . . . what is their agenda?"[7]

Suspicion and hostility characterizes the state's attitude toward the media. Freedom of speech and of the press in Swaziland is not legally protected, and the government has frequently acted against the media to discourage critical coverage of the royal family. This has included closing down newspapers and magazines as well as detaining and harassing journalists and broadcasters. There are two daily newspapers in Swaziland, one of which is government owned. The state has a monopoly over television and radio ownership. In 2003, a censorship policy for the state-owned Swaziland Broadcasting and Information Services was imposed to prohibit the dissemination of negative information about the government.

Libel laws and detention have been used by the government to intimidate journalists. For example, in 2004 Deputy Prime Minister Albert Shabangu sued the *Times of Swaziland* for defamation over an article in which the paper had noted Shabangu's past links to opposition groupings. In July 2005, he was awarded the equivalent of US$116,000 in damages by the High Court, a decision that was reversed in May 2006 by the Supreme Court, which also ordered Shabangu to pay the newspaper's legal costs.

In August 2006, Minister of Public Service and Information Themba Msibi warned the media against criticizing the king. This came after the state broadcaster had aired critical comments made by a local human rights lawyer following a visit to the kingdom by an African Union human rights group. Management of the radio station was told to "toe the line." In response, a senior journalist at the radio station told the Media Institute of Southern Africa that "censorship is an everyday occurrence here. As a government medium, there is very little we can do."[8] There is no censorship body, nor are there censorship laws, operative in Swaziland. Such censorship as exists then is self-censorship in response to direct threats from state authorities.

The telecommunications network is poor by comparison with neighboring South Africa but the mobile telephony network is growing rapidly. There are about 36,000 regular internet subscribers in Swaziland and there are seven Internet service providers operative in the country, access to which is not blocked or hindered by the government. Government ministries do not have their own websites but there is a central government site which reflects the work of each ministry (www.gov.sz).

Recommendations

- All political offices should be opened to free and competitive elections under an independent election commission.
- The ban on political parties should be lifted, and all candidates should have the opportunity to campaign openly.
- The government should take all necessary steps to bring the 2006 constitution into compliance with Swaziland's international and regional human rights treaty obligations, and a vigorous and independent legal reform process should be instituted to facilitate such incorporation into domestic law. Ongoing training should be provided to all state officials on the professional and other implications of these obligations.
- An enabling environment should be created for the vigorous expression of views and opinions by freeing the press and broadcast media from all forms of threat or censorship, as well as through the creation of an independent media authority to ensure a nonpartisan state media.

CIVIL LIBERTIES

PROTECTION FROM STATE TERROR, UNJUSTIFIED IMPRISONMENT, AND TORTURE:	2.57
GENDER EQUITY:	2.50
RIGHTS OF ETHNIC, RELIGIOUS, AND OTHER DISTINCT GROUPS:	2.75
FREEDOM OF CONSCIENCE AND BELIEF:	5.67
FREEDOM OF ASSOCIATION AND ASSEMBLY:	2.40
CATEGORY AVERAGE:	**3.18**

Swazi law does not prohibit the use of torture, and the increasing number of reports of torture and mistreatment of detainees suggest that such practice is becoming routine. While the Prison Act provides for the prosecution of officials suspected of torture or degrading treatment, there have been no reports of any such cases being mounted.

In September and October 2005, ten pipe and gasoline bomb attacks were directed at the offices of two important traditional institutions as well as at the homes of three police officers and two politicians close to the royal family. No one was killed in these attacks, but one police officer suffered severe injuries. In December police detained twenty sympathizers of two opposition groups, the People's United Democratic Movement (PUDEMO) and the Swaziland Youth Congress (SWAY-OCO). Of these, fifteen were charged with the destruction of government property, attempted murder, and treason. Among them was Mduduzi Mamba, whose wife, LaFakudze, was detained late in December and who died of abdominal trauma only hours after her release from custody.[9]

The fifteen accused of treason were released on bail in March 2006. Their freeing came after the acting chief justice of the High Court, Jacobus Allandale, stated that the prosecution had failed to make a convincing case of a link between the accused and the bombings. He also ordered an investigation into allegations that the accused had been beaten and tortured. No such investigation was conducted. A rally convened to welcome the release of the accused was dispersed by the police. In September, and in a further indication that there is little protection against arbitrary arrest, four of the accused were re-arrested on further charges of damage to property. As of February 2007, the accused were still awaiting trial amid indications that the state was having difficulty building its case.

Prison conditions in Swaziland are generally poor. A lack of basic hygiene and unsafe sexual practices contribute to the spread of HIV/AIDS within prisons. Moreover, pretrial detention facilities are overcrowded, a fact exacerbated by the introduction in the early 1990s of nonbailable provisions for a range of alleged criminal actions that include rape, murder, and public order and security offenses.

Although Swaziland has a functioning bail system, excessive pretrial detention is a problem. Apart from the courts, which are unpredictable, there are few effective redress mechanisms, like ombuds offices, available to ordinary citizens when their rights are violated.

In 2004, Swaziland acceded to four core international human rights treaties, including the UN Convention on the Elimination of all Forms of Discrimination Against Women (CEDAW). However, no attempt has been made to incorporate CEDAW's provisions into domestic law, as many of the convention's provisions would undermine key tenets of Swazi law and custom.

Men and women do not occupy an equal status in Swazi society. Women are subordinate in both civil and traditional marriages. The new constitution did grant certain new rights to Swazi women, notably in regard to property, inheritance, and financial issues. Thus, for example, married Swazi women will no longer lose their property and other inheritance rights upon the deaths of their husbands, nor will their spouses' permission be required to open bank accounts, acquire passports, travel abroad, purchase land, and undertake a host of other acts that men take for granted. Other legal discrepancies remain in force. In terms of customary law, Swazi men can practice polygamy, while women cannot. While not common, instances have occurred of young Swazi teenage girls—many of them still school-going—being forced into marriages with members of the royal family, the king included.

There is a long history of violence directed against women and girls in Swaziland. According to Amnesty International's 2006 report on Swaziland, incidents of rape and other forms of sexual abuse of women and girls, including the rape of minors twelve years of age and below, have been rising since 2002.[10] The government responded by tabling a draft Sexual Offenses and Domestic Violence Bill, which proposed a new and tougher definition of rape and sought to criminalize marital rape. It also proposed new civil law remedies for victims of domestic violence. The disproportionately high incidence of HIV/AIDS among Swazi women (in contrast to Swazi males) reflects their generally unequal status socially and their disempowered sexual status in particular.

In October 2006, police in Mpumalanga province in South Africa, adjacent to Swaziland and Mozambique, announced that they were investigating a child-trafficking racket involving a trade in girls aged between ten and sixteen from Swaziland and Mozambique. After being lured into South Africa, the girls were forced into prostitution. Police stated that they believed the racket had been operating for some six years. There is no evidence of the Swazi police having acted in an attempt to combat such trafficking.

In May 2005, the international nongovernmental organization Save the Children released the results of a survey that found that over a two-week period 59 percent of the 2,750 Swazi children surveyed revealed they had been subjected to corporal punishment at school.

Legislation and general practice in Swaziland are not sensitive to the needs of people with disabilities. While all new government buildings must provide ramps and easy-access facilities to disabled persons, no attempt has been made to equip existing public buildings for this purpose.

Given that Swaziland is largely homogeneous ethnically, issues of ethnic discrimination or disadvantage do not arise, nor is there any sustained record of religious discrimination. While there is no formal legal provision for religious freedom in Swaziland, the government generally respects freedom of religion in practice and respects the rights of non-believers and the beliefs of minority religious groups. The one exception is the Jehovah's Witnesses, against whom state action has from time to time been directed. New religious groups must register with the government, and state permission is required for the construction of religious buildings. There is no record of refusals in regard to these two requirements. On occasion, prayer meetings have been disrupted or banned because they were considered political gatherings.

Freedom of association is not guaranteed in Swaziland and is often actively restricted. Police permission is required and routinely refused for meetings and demonstrations of a political nature. Where such gatherings or marches do occur, they are invariably broken up by force with the use of tear gas, baton charges, rubber bullets, and water cannons. Despite this antipathy to gatherings of a political nature, the government does respect the right to form and join trade unions. This has, however, not protected trade unionists from state action; the detention and general harassment of pro-democracy trade union leaders is common.

Recommendations

- The provisions of the CEDAW treaty should be incorporated fully and without any qualifications into Swazi domestic law. In addition, the government should accede to the Optional Protocol to the

CEDAW so that Swazi women can lodge complaints with the UN treaty-monitoring body established under the Protocol.

• The state should institute effective measures to protect Swazi children from all forms of violence, including sexual violence and corporal punishment in schools and homes. Such measures could include a public campaign against domestic violence and an educational campaign aimed at school administrators and teachers.

• Laws requiring prior permission for meetings and protests should be repealed, and the use of force against peaceful demonstrators should be banned.

RULE OF LAW

INDEPENDENT JUDICIARY:	2.00
PRIMACY OF RULE OF LAW IN CIVIL AND CRIMINAL MATTERS:	2.17
ACCOUNTABILITY OF SECURITY FORCES AND MILITARY TO CIVILIAN AUTHORITIES:	1.00
PROTECTION OF PROPERTY RIGHTS:	2.33
EQUAL TREATMENT UNDER THE LAW:	3.00
CATEGORY AVERAGE:	**2.10**

Swaziland operates a dual court system comprising traditional courts, in which presiding chiefs apply customary law, and a Roman-Dutch system of magistrate courts, a High Court, and a Court of Appeals. The last is not a permanent body but one currently staffed mainly by retired southern African judges who convene in Swaziland two to three times per year. Their rulings are, however, based on Swazi law. All judges, including those for the Court of Appeals, are appointed by the king, and their appointments are not subject to parliamentary approval or scrutiny. In the late 1990s, then–prime minister Sibusiso Dlamini unilaterally scrapped the commission originally set up to make recommendations for judicial appointments and replaced it with a special committee on justice composed of certain cabinet ministers, the attorney general, the director of public prosecutions, the commissioner of police, heads of the security services, the chief justice, and palace advisers; all these officials are appointed by the king and are consequently subject to dismissal by him. Its brief went well beyond judicial appointments and involved a close scrutiny of the workings of the entire justice system.

With the promulgation of the new constitution, the king reinstated the Judicial Services Commission, comprising primarily representatives of the ministry of justice, the legal profession, the magistracy and serving judges. Their brief is to screen potential candidates for the bench and recommend suitable candidates to him. Since then, the king has appointed three acting judges supported by the commission.

Despite this advance, the coexistence of two legal traditions with fundamentally different conceptions of rights lies at the core of the political tensions that have afflicted Swaziland since the early 1970s. These tensions began with the declaration of the state of emergency in 1973, which was triggered in part by the fact that the High Court had acted to overturn the legislative will of Parliament, which functioned then as the handmaiden of the monarchy. A dramatic manifestation was the 2002 resignation en bloc of the appeals bench, stemming from the monarchy's refusal to implement decisions with which it did not concur.

The political and legal crises stemming from this action on the part of the monarchy severely compromised the independence of the judiciary and threw the administration of the judicial system into disarray. Throughout 2003 and 2004, Swaziland remained without a Court of Appeals. This resulted in a continued violation of the rights of those villagers who had been forcibly removed from their homes as well as those numerous individuals whose civil and criminal cases were at the appeal stage and therefore could be neither heard nor concluded.

What the last three decades of Swazi political life have revealed is that in any clash between the two legal systems, it is the view of the Swazi king and his advisers and the law of custom that prevails. What this means politically is that an unelected and unaccountable monarchical order refuses to accept any constitutional or legal limits to its rule. The casualties of this ideological worldview have been numerous: the Swazi democratization process, the rule of law, the administration of justice, and perhaps above all, the economic and social development of the people.

Despite political pressures and attempts at intimidation, the collective body of judges—local and expatriate—that has since 1968 served in the High Court and the Court of Appeals of Swaziland has developed a reputation as able and competent judicial officials. For the most part, the Swazi bench has attempted to apply the law fairly and consistently, and it has at times resisted attempts by the state and traditional authorities to influence decisions through various forms of interference. Some of the instances cited above in this report illustrate this fact.

According to the "saved provisions" of the 1968 independence constitution, a High Court judge can be removed from office only on grounds of an "inability to perform the functions of his office, whether arising from infirmity of body or mind or any other cause or for misbehavior." This provision is supposed to be invoked only after the chief justice has requested that the king investigate the conduct of the judge in question, which must occur through a tribunal appointed by the king. None of these requirements were met in 2003, when Justice Thomas Masuku was "transferred" from the high to the industrial court. This de facto removal from the bench was challenged successfully in the High Court by the Swazi Law Society.

The presumption of innocence until proven guilty is undermined in Swaziland through the Non-Bailable Offenses Order. According to this legislation, Swazi courts are prohibited from granting bail to persons charged with one or more so-called scheduled offenses. These include murder, rape, robbery, and offenses referred to in public order and antisubversion laws. In 2001, the Court of Appeals struck down the order, describing it as "draconian" and "inconsistent with the presumption of innocence and an . . . invasion of the liberty of the subject." In the face of this rejection, the government issued Decree Number 3 of 2001, reimposing the provisions of the 1993 order. Challenges to this decree were launched by two pretrial detainees denied bail, resulting in November 2002 in a second Court of Appeals ruling striking down the legislation. In response, the then–prime minister announced that the act would remain in force and that all government agencies had been instructed to ignore the court's ruling.

Citizens have the right to independent counsel of their choice. For most Swazis, however, this is nominal, given that approximately half of them are living below the poverty line and a huge percentage of the potential labor force is unemployed. There is no state system of legal aid for those unable to afford counsel.

Prosecutors rarely act independently, particularly in cases with political overtones. Likewise, the prosecution of public officials for wrongdoing is rare and nonexistent in the case of those officials related to, or with strong connections to, the royal family.

Any civilian state control of the security services by the judicial and legislative branches of government is ineffective, as the services essentially function as an enforcement arm of the traditional authorities in the executive branch. The services consequently do not refrain from interfering in the political process and there are no known cases of members being held accountable for any abuses of power. In their actions, the security services show scant respect for human rights. Thus, for example, the use of force to break up marches or demonstrations, even lawful ones, is routine.

The issue of property rights in Swaziland is complex. There is a dual land system with distinct freehold and leasehold sectors. This roughly corresponds with the urban–rural divide of the country. For those with freehold rights, all residents of the country have an equal right—though obviously not an equal capacity—to property ownership. This sector operates under normal market conditions, and the state adequately enforces and protects property rights and contracts. A very different situation prevails in the communal leasehold sector, in which the majority of Swazi citizens reside. In these areas, land cannot be bought and sold, and the tenure rights of the occupants are dependent on the good will of the chiefs who administer the land on behalf of the king. This situation can be manipulated for political and other reasons, and there is a long history in Swaziland of the precarious nature of tenure rights being used as a means to pressure or discipline commoners residing in the leasehold sector. In short, those who do not comply with their chiefs' orders can have their land taken from them, and forcible eviction of families or whole communities is not uncommon.

The most politically significant case in recent years involved 120 residents of the KaMkhweli and Macetjeni communities who were forcibly evicted from their homes by the police in October 2000, along with their chief, when they refused to accept the appointment of one of the king's brothers as their new chief. The evictees have on several occasions taken their case to court, and in all but one instance their right to return to their homes has been upheld. Finally, in November 2002, the Court of Appeals made such an order, and the government publicly stated it would not obey. This led to the resignation of the appeal bench. In its ruling the court also upheld an earlier High Court decision to jail the commissioner of police for contempt because he had not implemented earlier rulings allowing the residents to return to their homes. This order was never implemented. Even though the judges' strike was suspended in late 2004, their rulings on this land eviction case remain unimplemented, and the evictees in question have still not been allowed to return to their homes. In 2007, they remain displaced, without access to their traditional lands and homes.

Recommendations
- An urgent political will is required on the part of the executive to protect the independence of the judiciary by henceforth respecting and implementing the judgments of the courts.
- Steps need to be taken to restore the presumption of innocence to judicial and administrative practices by restoring to the courts the discretion to decide on matters of bail.
- The government must ensure in law and in practice that all residents of Swaziland are protected from forced evictions from their homes.
- The government should allow the immediate return to their homes of all members of the KaMkhweli and Macetjeni communities evicted in 2000 and an impartial body should be appointed to determine the level of financial reparations payable to the evictees.

ANTICORRUPTION AND TRANSPARENCY

ENVIRONMENT TO PROTECT AGAINST CORRUPTION:	1.80
EXISTENCE OF LAWS AND ETHICAL STANDARDS BETWEEN	
PRIVATE AND PUBLIC SECTORS:	2.75
ENFORCEMENT OF ANTICORRUPTION LAWS:	1.50
GOVERNMENTAL TRANSPARENCY:	2.14
CATEGORY AVERAGE:	**2.05**

According to the 2006 Country Report on Swaziland compiled by the Economist Intelligence Unit (EIU), "corruption is endemic in Swaziland."[11] This is especially true of the monarchy and the institutions of the Swazi nation, where expenditure is lavish and rarely accounted for. For example, in recent years the king has sought state funds to purchase an executive jet for his personal use and to construct new royal palaces for his fourteen wives, as well as supply each of them with expensive luxury vehicles. He himself is the owner of a Daimler Chrysler Maybach, reportedly one of the world's most expensive motor vehicles at about US$700,000. In April 2004, he spent US$600,000 on a party in the national stadium to celebrate his thirty-fourth birthday at a time of severe strain in the economy prompted by a fourth consecutive year of drought. Similar such lavish parties were staged to mark the king's thirty-fifth and thirty-sixth birthdays in 2005 and 2006.

Corruption in Swaziland is not a result of excessive bureaucratic regulations or registration requirements. It stems, rather, from the undemocratic nature of the political order and from a view within the Swazi political establishment that state resources are, as the EIU put it, "an entitlement . . . corruption in Swaziland is estimated to cost up to 40 million Euros (US$54.3 million) monthly."[12]

In response to criticism by various national and international groups and media reports of corruption, as well as threats of cuts in aid, Parliament in 2006 passed the Prevention of Corruption Order. The act established an Anticorruption Commission and an Anticorruption Unit as dedicated entities for the investigation of corrupt activities involving public officials, companies, and public enterprises. This unit replaces an earlier one, established in 1998, that never produced any indictments, as it lacked powers to investigate and charge suspects. The institutions started functioning in July 2006. In February 2007, police arrested eight individuals, including senior officials in the Ministry of Finance and directors of private companies, four days after the commission issued a report on the plundering of some 50 million euros (approximately US$68.2 million) from a fund set up for capacity building. There are no whistle-blower-type laws on the statute book.

The Swazi economy is capitalist. Foreign investment is sought and encouraged, and there are few controls on the repatriation of profit. There is a well-developed private banking system. There is, however, considerable state involvement in the economy in the form of royalist-controlled investment corporations. The largest of these is the Tibiyo Take Ngwane Fund. At independence, control over Swaziland's mineral rights and royalties was vested in the Swazi nation and not the government. To administer the concession, the king established Tibiyo. Headed by a board whose majority are princes (male relatives of the king) and answerable only to the monarchy, Tibiyo pays no taxes, is not required to publish an annual statement (although it has done so for the last ten years), and is not answerable to parliament. According to the EIU, "Tibiyo is a controversial institution that has some high-profile equity holdings in Swaziland, ostensibly made in the national interest, although some people have made accusations that its revenue is appropriated by the royal family."[13]

Over the years, Tibiyo has developed into a major corporation and a source of wealth for the royal family and those close to it. Funds were initially used to buy back freehold land from non-Swazis, much of which was developed into royally owned maize and dairy estates. Tibiyo then moved into the retail sector, establishing butcheries, liquor stores, and taxi routes. Ultimately, the fund generated sufficient capital to begin acquiring equity (usually in the range of 40 percent to 49 percent) in practically every foreign company active in the economy. These have included huge agro-industrials in the sugar, timber, citrus, and fruit processing industries, large wholesalers, and banks, as well as mining, manufacturing, and tourist companies. In this way, Tibiyo has spread its net into all sectors of the economy, establishing a solid partnership with foreign capital, the dividend payments from which have become Tibiyo's largest source of revenue. It has also been the means by which the Swazi aristocracy has acquired for itself a considerable material base in the modern economy, complementing their control of the traditional agrarian sector, which is achieved through its monopoly over the right to allocate and withdraw land tenure rights. In other words, the Swazi aristocracy—the royalist lines within the Dlamini clan—is not just a privileged elite but a modestly wealthy capitalist class for whom a regime change or even a significant democratization of the system could have negative consequences.

No asset register exists to record the business and other interests of, or gifts to, public officials. Tax collection is reasonably efficient and accountable in the formal (that is, outside the institutions of the Swazi nation) sector of the economy and in regard to ordinary citizens/commoners. Swaziland has no independent auditing office such as an auditor-general or ombudsman. Bribes are not necessary to gain admission to higher education, although in some cases pressure has been applied successfully on the authorities of the University of Swaziland to admit members of the royal family lacking the necessary admission standards.

In May 2006, the European Union (EU) Ambassador to Swaziland announced the suspension of all direct funding to the Swaziland Government. The EU has been one of the major donors in Swaziland in recent years, having provided aid to the value of 4.1 million euros in 2005. Announcing the decision, Ambassador Peter Beck said the action was being taken "due to the absence of adequate fiscal controls" and would be reviewed only when "government implements a solid accounting and auditing mechanism to monitor its coffers. . . . Swaziland is behind other African countries," he noted.[14]

The public has little access to state information, and no legal mechanisms facilitate it. The process of awarding government contracts and tenders is public, but it is susceptible to corruption. The executive budget-making process is not transparent and government does not publish for public consumption detailed accounts of its expenditure. Nor are such details provided of expenditures by the king. Parliament does exercise a watchdog role over the budget and government expenditure. It has at times undertaken this function to good effect by reining in, for example, reckless spending on the part of some government ministries.

Recommendations

- An independent auditing watchdog in the form of an auditor-general's office should be established, as well as an independent complaints directorate in the form of an ombudsman's office.
- Legislation should be enacted to guarantee the public's right to both official state information and their individual personal records held by the state.
- The Tibiyo Fund and other such royalist-controlled private corporations should be converted into public corporations and required to operate in terms of relevant company laws. This would include subjecting their financial records to public scrutiny as well as rendering them taxable.
- Whistle-blower-type legislation should be enacted to encourage the public to expose corruption while at the same time providing effective protection to whistle-blowers.

- Parliament should ensure that the Anticorruption Commission and the Anticorruption Unit have sufficient funds, human resources, and legal guarantees to pursue cases of official wrongdoing vigorously and without fear.

NOTES

[1]   See Johnson Vilane and John Daniel, "Swaziland: Political Crises, Regional Dilemma," *Review of African Political Economy* 35 (May 1986): 55.

[2]   Vilane and Daniel, 56.

[3]   International Monetary Fund, Statement by Peter Gakunu, Executive Director for the Kingdom of Swaziland and Bhadala T. Mamba, Adviser to the Executive Director, 31 January 2007, appendix to The Kingdom of Swaziland: Staff Report for the 2006 Article Consultation. Washington D.C., January 2007.

[4]   Southern African Contact (Denmark), Swaziland@Newsletter 45, 15 January 2007, 2, http://uk.groups.yahoo.com/group/SAK-Swazinewsletter.

[5]   Swaziland@Newsletter 30, 5 March 2006, 3.

[6]   *Country Profile 2006: Swaziland* (London: Economist Intelligence Unit [EIU], 2007), 7.

[7]   Swaziland@Newsletter 46. 30 January 2007, 2.

[8]   Swaziland@Newsletter 40, 11 September 2006, 1.

[9]   See John Daniel and Marisha Ramdeen, "Swaziland" in Andreas Mehler, Henning Melber and Klaas van Walraven (eds.) *Africa Yearbook 2: Politics, Economy and Society South of the Sahara in 2005* (Brill: Leiden, 2006).

[10] Amnesty International. Annual Report on Swaziland. Cited in Swaziland@Newsletter 37, 3 July 2006, 1–3.

[11] *Country Profile 2006: Swaziland* (London: EIU, 2007), 15.

[12] Ibid.

[13] *Country Profile 2004: Swaziland* (London: EIU, 2005), 6.

[14] Swaziland@Newsletter 35. 5 June 2006, 1–2.

SYRIA

CAPITAL: Damascus
POPULATION: 19.9 million
GNI PER CAPITA: $1,570

SCORES	2005	2007
ACCOUNTABILITY AND PUBLIC VOICE:	1.29	1.41
CIVIL LIBERTIES:	2.04	2.16
RULE OF LAW:	2.13	2.19
ANTICORRUPTION AND TRANSPARENCY:	1.70	1.93

(scores are based on a scale of 0 to 7, with 0 representing weakest and 7 representing strongest performance)

David W. Lesch

INTRODUCTION

Syria has been a stable authoritarian state since 1970, when Hafiz al-Asad assumed power and consolidated rule under the Ba'ath party. After his death in 2000, his son Bashar al-Asad took over as Syria's president.

The February 2005 assassination of former Lebanese prime minister Rafiq Hariri in Beirut presented a turning point for the Syrian regime. Regional and international pressure on Damascus had been building even prior to the assassination, with the passage of UN Security Council (UNSC) Resolution 1559 the previous fall in response to Syria's role in the extraconstitutional extension of pro-Syrian Lebanese President Emile Lahoud's tenure in office. The resolution called for the withdrawal of foreign troops from Lebanon as well as the disarmament

David W. Lesch is Professor of Middle East History at Trinity University in San Antonio, Texas. Among his publications are: *The Arab-Israeli Conflict: A History* (Oxford University Press, 2007); *The Middle East and the United States: A Historical and Political Reassessment* (Westview Press, 4th edition, 2007); *The New Lion of Damascus: Bashar al-Asad and Modern Syria* (Yale University Press, 2005); *1979: The Year that Shaped the Modern Middle East* (Westview Press, 2001); and *Syria and the United States: Eisenhower's Cold War in the Middle East* (Westview Press, 1992).

of all militias in the country, but it was widely understood to be aimed at Syria and the pro-Syrian Shiite Islamist movement Hezbollah. Following Hariri's death, calls for Damascus to change its behavior increased exponentially, as did its regional and international isolation. The tumult of the last two years has, if anything, made Syria's domestic political environment more restrictive.

The Syrian regime condemned Hariri's murder and vehemently denied any responsibility for it, but the mounting international pressure compelled Bashar to withdraw all Syrian forces from Lebanon. The last troops left in April 2005, ending an almost thirty-year presence. In October, Detlev Mehlis, the UN representative in charge of investigating the Hariri case, submitted his preliminary report to the UN Security Council, in effect concluding that the assassination could not have occurred without Syrian connivance. The report cited a trail of evidence that led to the heart of the regime in Damascus, implicating the powerful head of Syrian intelligence, Asef Shawkat (the president's brother-in-law), and Bashar's younger brother, Maher al-Asad. It remains unclear whether Bashar was directly involved in ordering the assassination.

While calls in the United States for regime change in Damascus intensified, press reports indicated that Israel was against this, preferring the status quo to the chaos that could follow any sudden intervention. Nonetheless, Bashar al-Asad's rule was extremely uncertain for a time, and he has been reconsolidating his domestic position since the international pressure peaked. He has tightened state control in the country and shifted his rhetoric to emphasize Syrian over Arab nationalism, though he has also resorted to anti-American and anti-Israeli slogans that are popular in the Arab street.

Bashar astutely utilized the nationalistic response to UN and U.S. pressure and shored up support for his regime, especially after the perceived victory of Hezbollah in its conflict with Israel in July and August 2006. In February 2006, he shuffled his cabinet and the top ranks of the military-security apparatus. The cabinet has been given more authority than any other in recent memory, suggesting that Bashar has confidence in the security of his own position. Whether this can be leveraged into fresh domestic reforms or renewed peace negotiations with Israel depends on a variety of factors, but the regime has repeatedly indicated that it would welcome a resumption of talks on a regional peace accord that had broken off in 1999 and 2000.

During his first years in power, Bashar was dismissed by some observers as an inexperienced leader who lacked the aptitude to rule Syria and navigate the politics of the wider region. However, his ability to survive subsequent crises has largely dispelled such assessments. Meanwhile, optimists inside and outside Syria seized on Bashar's relative youth, his training as an ophthalmologist, and his stated fondness for computer technology and modernization, hoping that he might lead the country away from the ossified political and economic system he inherited from his father. Indeed, during the first six months of his tenure, dubbed the Damascus Spring, an unprecedented political opening led to discussion salons, critical content in the newspapers, and releases of political prisoners. The period of retrenchment that followed has disappointed those who expected meaningful and lasting progress, but it is not surprising given the depth of the country's problems and the volatility of the region. There have been some significant reforms, particularly in government administration, banking, monetary structure, and education, but changes in the crucial political and judicial spheres have been largely cosmetic.

ACCOUNTABILITY AND PUBLIC VOICE

FREE AND FAIR ELECTORAL LAWS AND ELECTIONS:	1.25
EFFECTIVE AND ACCOUNTABLE GOVERNMENT:	2.00
CIVIC ENGAGEMENT AND CIVIC MONITORING:	1.00
MEDIA INDEPENDENCE AND FREEDOM OF EXPRESSION:	1.38
CATEGORY AVERAGE:	**1.41**

According to the 1973 constitution, Syria is a Socialist Popular Democratic Republic. The charter allows for a multiparty, pluralist system and states that "sovereignty is exercised by the people." However, in actuality Syria is governed by a one-party, authoritarian regime with only some of the trappings of democracy. The people have no practical ability to change their leaders, and candidates for election are vetted by the ruling party and government.

In the run-up to the 2007 elections the government altered the Election Law of 1973 to limit campaign expenditures to US$58,000 per person. While the official rationale was to combat corruption and level the playing field for candidates, commentators suggest that it was primarily intended to prevent opposition candidates from receiving financial support from outside sources, such as the U.S. government.[1]

The constitution establishes the executive, legislative, and judicial branches of government. The unicameral Parliament consists of 250 representatives elected by popular vote every four years. The Parliament proposes the candidacy of the president, proposes and votes on laws (which are generated by the executive branch or the Ba'ath party), discusses cabinet policy, and approves the budget. Moreover, the constitution guarantees that the Ba'ath party receives at least half of the parliamentary seats. Currently, the ruling National Progressive Front (NPF), a coalition dominated by the Ba'ath party that includes six other leftist parties, holds 167 seats. Non-NPF independents, all of whom are vetted by the government, hold the remaining 83 seats.

A new law on political parties was passed in March 2006, creating the surface features of a multiparty system. While it represents a small step toward true pluralism, the law contains a number of qualifications that appear to undermine its positive effect. For example, the legislation stipulates that the founder of any new party should be someone who "has not acted in behavior that is opposed to the 'Revolution of March 8'" (the March 8, 1963, revolution that brought the Ba'ath party to power in Syria). Article 17 of the new law states that it is "prohibited to relaunch any party that was disbanded before the year 1963," a provision that is clearly aimed at the outlawed Muslim Brotherhood. Therefore, the only parties operating before 1963 that are legally allowed to participate are the Ba'ath, the Syrian Social Nationalist Party (SSNP), and the Communist Party.

A coalition of Syrian exiles and opposition groups, including the Muslim Brotherhood and former Syrian vice president 'Abd al-Halim Khaddam, has come together in recent years with the goal—tacitly supported by the United States—of overthrowing the current Syrian regime. As a result, the government has imposed certain restrictions on expressing dissent both inside and outside the country, and has barred domestic groups from receiving funding from external sources. For example, Human Rights Watch documented the arrest of twenty-six democracy activists in Syria during the first three months of 2006.[2] In addition, Ammar Qurabi, former spokesman for the Arab Organization for Human Rights, and Samir Nashar, head of the Alliance of Free Nationalists and a member of the Provisional Committee for the Damascus Declaration, were arrested in March 2006 after attending conferences in the United States and Europe. Both were released quickly but still face potential charges.[3] In May 2006, a group of twelve Syrian activists were arrested for signing a petition on May 12 that called for Syria to recognize Lebanon's independence. Those arrested included prominent activists Michel Kilo and Anwar al-Bunni. Kilo was charged with "weakening national sentiment" and "spreading false or exaggerated news that can affect the standing of the state."[4]

The state has utilized other methods of suppressing dissent as well. A number of individuals have been prevented from leaving the country, according to Human Rights Watch. Among them are Radwan Ziadeh, director of the Damascus Center for Human Rights Studies, Suheir al-Atassi, head of the Jamal al-Atassi Forum for Democratic Dialogue (which was shut down in 2005), and Walid al-Bunni, a physician who was a founder of the Committees for the Revival of Civil Society.[5] As Joe Stork, the deputy director of the Middle East and North Africa division at Human Rights Watch, said in July 2006, "These travel bans are a crude attempt to prevent Syrian civil society activists from interacting with the outside world. Shy of putting these activists in jail, the Syrian government is instead putting them under a type of national house arrest."[6]

The president is elected to a renewable, seven-year term after nomination by the Regional Command of the Ba'ath party and the Parliament. The president, the party, and the cabinet can issue legislation whether or not the Parliament is in session. The late president Hafiz al-Asad was confirmed in office five times, standing unopposed in successive referendums and usually garnering 99 percent approval. Bashar ran unopposed following his father's death and received 97.29 percent of the vote in a national referendum. Political opposition to the president is not tolerated, except for that of the so-called loyal opposition within the Parliament, which provides no institutional check on the executive. The next presidential election is scheduled for the summer of 2007, and it appears that Bashar will run unopposed in a referendum format.

[UPDATE: On May 27, 2007, Bashar al-Asad was elected by referendum to a second seven-year term as president. Official results gave him a 97.62 percent vote on turnout of over 95 percent. The opposition and dissidents urged a boycott of the vote.]

The Ba'ath party, particularly the party's Regional Command, retains substantial decision-making authority over the cabinet and the ministries. Several members of the cabinet are also in the Regional Command, and Bashar is the party's secretary general. He has attempted to transform the Ba'ath party into an advisory body within the government rather than an entity that interferes with or dictates government policy, as has often been the case in the past. At the Ba'ath party congress in June 2005, the size of the Regional Command was reduced to sixteen members, and a number of the old guard, including longtime vice president 'Abd al-Halim Khaddam, were removed from their positions. This reinforced Bashar's attempts to strengthen the cabinet at the expense of the Regional Command. A further reshuffling in February 2006 resulted in Bashar's most loyal cabinet to date, filled mostly by technocrats with the ultimate goal of economic and administrative rather than political reform. It is also the most independent cabinet under Bashar, with individual ministers designing their own portfolios and reorganizing their particular ministries. However, the most important decisions, particularly in the foreign policy arena, still rest with the president, his small circle of advisers, and elements of the Regional Command and military-security apparatus.

There have been recent improvements in the selection of the civil service, with a 2003 purge taking place aimed at officials who had been accused of corruption. In general, however, selection for government positions is not entirely transparent or merit-based.[7]

Decree 39 of 1958, Syria's Law of Association, requires every civil organization to register with and obtain a license from the Ministry of Social Affairs. In the months following Bashar's assumption of the presidency, hundreds of civil society organizations, most operating from within the homes of the organizers, received licenses. Today, only those groups that suit the government's political interests receive licenses. Asma al-Asad, the president's wife, is very active in advocating the growth of nongovernmental organizations in Syria. In particular, she has taken a leading role in the Fund for the Integrated Rural Development of Syria (FIRDOS), a group that facilitates rural development primarily through microfinance. Nevertheless, the fact that she is the president's wife casts doubt on the organization's independence. Civil society activists have been able to maintain some pressure on the regime, but they have become more cautious in recent years, particularly since late 2005. On the whole, civil society has little opportunity to influence policy.

During the Damascus Spring, Bashar promoted freer and more pluralistic media in Syria. For the first time in forty years, private newspapers were licensed and public criticism of the regime was permitted, even from state-controlled entities. Although publications that criticized the government—including the hugely popular satirical weekly *al-Dumari* (the Lamplighter), which ceased publication in April 2003 due to government pressure—have since struggled against the restrictions of the regime, the fact that such criticism was permitted for some time indicates that there may be some cracks in the edifice of political repression. The media can criticize in general terms corruption, economic performance, and bureaucratic inefficiency because these themes coincide with regime discourse; however, the criticisms must not go so far as to implicate high-ranking officials by name. Similarly, criticism regarding religion or central political or foreign policy issues is usually off-limits.

The crackdown on journalism became evident with Decree 50 of 2001. This law enables privately owned newspapers, magazines, and other periodicals to seek licenses to publish, but they essentially do so at the discretion of the government. The prime minister's office can deny licenses for reasons "related to the public interest." In addition, the decree prohibits articles and reports about "national security, national unity, and details of secret trials." It also establishes harsh criminal penalties for publishing "falsehoods and fabricated reports."[8] In effect, editors express opposition to regime policies only when they have official instructions to do so. In recent years this crackdown has intensified, with a particular focus on online journalists (see below).

The state runs the Syrian media, but Lebanese newspapers and pan-Arab satellite news channels such as Al-Jazeera, both widely available in Syria, allow open political discussion and criticism of the government to continue. In addition, the Syrian government permitted more criticism of the Ba'ath party in 2003–2004; in fact, the editor of the party newspaper wrote a series of articles severely criticizing the party, and in October 2004, this editor became the new minister of information, a sign that Bashar wanted to revamp the party and its role. After the Hariri assassination, however, the government reversed the trend toward more open criticism, due both to real and perceived threats to the regime. Media outlets have since adopted a Syrian nationalist tone, echoing the position of the government, and both foreign and domestic newspapers are censored by the Ba'ath party before distribution.[9]

Although the state is the sole official internet provider and restricts access to politically sensitive material, Bashar's aggressive push to bring Syria into the computer and internet age has widened the flow of information from abroad. He has significantly increased the number of computers available at state universities, and many Syrians go online through Lebanese internet service providers and have unlimited access to the web. Unfortunately, the spread of the internet is hampered by most residents' inability to afford personal computers and internet service. The authorities have also reportedly intervened in a number of instances in recent months to suppress freedom of expression on the internet.[10] In addition to blocking access to opposition, and Israeli and Kurdish websites, there has been a crackdown on cyber-journalists who criticize the regime. Following arrests in 2005 and 2007 there are now four cyber-journalists in prison. The prisoners include a Kurdish blogger who was held in secret without access to a lawyer.[11]

Recommendations

- In cooperation with the United Nations or nongovernmental organizations outside the country, the government should offer workshops and training programs to prepare Syrians to run political campaigns and hold municipal and parliamentary elections.
- Media freedom needs to be restored and protected by law. Reforms should ensure freedom for independent private newspapers, an end to censorship, freedom of association for civil society forums and their allied publications, and freedom to travel to foreign conferences without fear of arrest on returning to Syria.
- Bashar must publicly guarantee the government's adherence to Article 38 of Syria's constitution, which states that "every citizen has the right to freely and openly express his views in words, in writing, and through all other means of expression." The authorities should also fulfill their obligations under the International Covenant on Civil and Political Rights.[12]

CIVIL LIBERTIES

PROTECTION FROM STATE TERROR, UNJUSTIFIED IMPRISONMENT, AND TORTURE:	1.43
GENDER EQUITY:	2.75
RIGHTS OF ETHNIC, RELIGIOUS, AND OTHER DISTINCT GROUPS:	2.00
FREEDOM OF CONSCIENCE AND BELIEF:	3.00
FREEDOM OF ASSOCIATION AND ASSEMBLY:	1.60
CATEGORY AVERAGE:	**2.16**

Bashar al-Asad's inaugural speech was, by Syrian standards, remarkably enlightened, and even criticized certain past policies. However, the new reformists in the government were more technocrats than democracy proponents; Bashar tasked them with modernizing Syria, implementing administrative reform in the ministries, and devising ways to improve the moribund economy. They did not introduce political reform to advance civil liberties.

One of the regime's prime weapons against internal dissent has been Decree 51, as amended and promulgated on March 9, 1963, one day after the Ba'ath party came to power in Syria. It declared a state of emergency that was ostensibly designed to deal with the Israeli military threat but has instead been used to stifle internal political challenges. The Syrian leadership considers the decree a fundamental right recognized in the International Covenant on Civil and Political Rights, which allows states to violate its main provisions "in time of public emergency which threatens the life of the nation and the existence of which is officially proclaimed."[13] Under Decree 51, the Martial Law Administrator (the prime minister) and his deputy (the interior minister) are empowered to issue wide-ranging orders restricting freedom in all areas of life.

Bashar has admitted that mistakes have been made with Decree 51 and that government officials have abused the law for their own purposes. While not committing himself to lifting the decree, he has told journalists and others that it should be used to genuinely protect the people and not to abuse them.[14] However, given the current international environment, Decree 51 is likely to remain in place for the foreseeable future.

Arbitrary arrests and violations of due process still occur, although most agree that the problem is not as severe as under Hafiz al-Asad. As detailed in the previous section, human rights activists report that government arrests and harassment of members of the political opposition have measurably increased in connection with the added international pressure over Lebanon. At the same time, there have been enhanced efforts by Syrian exile groups to unify, publish joint declarations, and combine their activities to overthrow the regime. As Deputy Prime Minister Abdullah Dardari stated in an interview, "The survival of this regime and the stability of this country was threatened out loud and openly. There were invitations for foreign armies to come and invade Syria. So you could expect sometimes an overreaction, or a reaction, to something that is really happening."[15] Accordingly, the authorities since early 2005 have prohibited civil society and democracy activists from traveling outside the country. For those who are detained by the regime, both criminals and dissidents, conditions are bleak: Syrian prisons are overcrowded and inmates are often denied food and basic medical treatment. Moreover, the Syrian government prohibits all independent monitoring of prisons, and torture is frequently inflicted upon detainees.

One of the hallmarks of the Damascus Spring was the November 2000 closing of the infamous Mezzeh prison and the release of some 600 political prisoners, reportedly the first time the Syrian government acknowledged holding prisoners for political reasons.[16] Over the next several years, a number of leading political activists, many of whom had been in and out of prison for two decades and some of whom had been released during the Damascus Spring, were again arrested in a sporadic fashion, including the parliamentarians Riyad Seif and Ma'mun al-Humsi. Most of the activists arrested were again sent to prison, although the sentences and conditions were less severe than on previous occasions. In January 2006, Seif and al-Humsi were released for a second time. In July 2004, Bashar decreed an amnesty for more than 250 political prisoners, who would be released in stages to mark the fourth anniversary of his presidency; 190 more were released in late 2006 during the Muslim Eid celebrations. Those released include cyber-dissident and journalist Ali Sayed al-Shihabi.[17] Despite these periodic gestures, political space has clearly been restricted by the regime due to perceived external threats operating through the domestic and exiled opposition.

Article 25 of the constitution stipulates that citizens are equal before the law, and various articles of the penal code prescribe penalties for discrimination. Syria supports women's rights to a greater degree than most Middle Eastern states, but civil society organizations regularly demand equal treatment of women in their statements and manifestos, suggesting that enforcement lags behind constitutional mandates.

Although unevenly applied, Labor Act 91 of 1959 enshrines gender equality in the workplace, and Legislative Decree 4 of 1972 confirms equal remuneration for men and women. The Electoral Law promulgated in Decree 26 of 1973 grants women the right to vote in public elections and to stand as candidates in elections to the Parliament, where they currently hold 10 percent of the seats. Women also hold ministerial positions, are represented in the cabinet, and in 2006 al-Asad appointed Syria's first female vice president, former culture minister Najah Al-Attar.[18] Nevertheless, a number of discriminatory laws and practices remain in place, especially on personal status issues, such as divorce and child custody, that fall under the jurisdiction of Sharia (Islamic law) courts. In 2004, Syrian mothers submitted a petition to the government to alter citizenship laws that prevent a mother from passing Syrian nationality onto her children even if they are born in Syria; however, the government delayed addressing the petition for "political reasons."[19] A similar lack of progress has been seen with new anti-trafficking legislation that was promised in 2005, with no new laws being drafted as of March 2007, despite Syria being one of the main destinations for trafficked women from Iraq.[20]

Syria's 1.5 million to 2 million ethnic Kurds for the most part do not seek an independent state. They demand the right to teach their language, which is denied by law, as well as full citizenship, which is required for state education and employment. A 1962 census rendered many Kurds stateless, leading to a current population of some 300,000 resident Kurds who lack Syrian citizenship.[21] Tensions between Arabs and Kurds have persisted. In March 2004, Kurds mounted riots and demonstrations, apparently inspired by events in the Kurdish areas of neighboring Iraq. The July 2004 amnesty included about 100 Kurds who had been arrested after clashes with security forces in which forty people were killed following a soccer match in Qamishli. An uneasy truce has prevailed since the 2004 violence, and the regime has attempted over the last year to implement agricultural improvements to benefit the rural population, particularly in the Kurdish areas of the northeast.

Syria is the only Arab country other than Lebanon whose constitution does not establish Islam as the state religion, although it does require the president to be a Muslim. As with women's rights, the secular philosophy of the ruling Ba'ath party and dominant role played by members of the minority Alawi Muslim sect ensure better protection of religious freedom than in most Arab countries. Generally, the country's Christian minority groups (about 10 percent of the population) and the small Jewish community have been free to practice their religions without government interference.

There is mounting concern over the spread of Islamist groups that oppose the regime and support jihadist insurgents in Iraq. It is difficult to assess the strength of Islamists in Syria because the state prevents most expressions of political dissent, such as demonstrations or protests. However, evidence of growing Islamism includes the appearance of more women wearing the veil, more muscular speeches by imams in mosques, and a few violent incidents. The regime appears to have been caught somewhat off-guard by these trends, and it has at least tolerated the Iraqi insurgency in the face of popular support, but the authorities are generally effective at repressing and infiltrating domestic Islamist opposition groups. Potential rebels are also deterred by the example of the 1982 Hama incident, in which government forces crushed that city's Islamist resistance, leaving between 10,000 and 20,000 people dead.

Through its control of the media, the state is able to promote a more quietist form of Islam. Moreover, the state-appointed *'ulama* (religious scholars) tend to promote ecumenism and interfaith dialogue, as advocated by the highly respected late mufti of Syria, Ahmad Kuftaro. The government has also been able to isolate its domestic Islamist opponents to some extent by supporting foreign, anti-Israeli Islamist groups like Hezbollah in Lebanon and Hamas in the Palestinian territories, both of which have opted to participate in the electoral process in recent years. Finally, roughly half of the population belongs to groups that would not welcome the creation of a radical Sunni Islamic republic in Syria, including non-Arab ethnic minorities, non-Muslim religious minorities, minority Muslim sects, popular and typically moderate Sufi Muslim organizations, and the secularized business class. These groups provide the regime with something of a buffer against Sunni extremists. On the other hand, the government's attempts to co-opt Islamist elements, in part by constructing more mosques and revising the religious education curriculum, may over the long term create an environment more conducive to the rise of an influential Islamist opposition, as happened in Egypt. This possibility is enhanced by the repression of secular prodemocracy reformists and the country's halting economic performance.[22]

On July 19, 2004, the president enacted a law to protect the rights of Syrians with disabilities and provide them with education, job training, and financial support. Currently, very few government buildings and public areas are accessible to people with disabilities, and the Ministry of Social Affairs has yet to issue detailed instructions on what sort of accommodations will be required under the law. In addition to the legislation, the government provides tax incentives for businesses to employ disabled people.[23] The Syrian government provides free medical care and social services to people with disabilities, and since the 2004 law, resources that were previously concentrated in Damascus have become more widely available, especially in provinces with a high concentration of land-mine victims. The government also operates dedicated rehabilitation facilities for these victims in the Syrian Golan, and in 2006, the government reenergized its land-mine education program in schools.[24]

In February 2001, the Ministry of Social Affairs announced that political forums (discussion groups, often with guest speakers) could not meet without its permission, which would only be granted if specific information was provided as to the location of the meeting and who was attending. Unauthorized demonstrations are prohibited, and protests or rallies for certain causes are often arranged by the government. There are no free trade unions, but there is a government-controlled labor union.

Any form of unofficial protest against the government is usually met with arrests or state-sponsored violence. In March 2006, the government organized a violent counterprotest to disrupt a peaceful demonstration against the Emergency Law. In the same month, tear gas was used and seventy-five Kurds were arrested in Aleppo during Kurdish New Year celebrations. The government also uses the law as a tool to curtail freedom of association. In 2006, the Supreme State Security

Court handed down several death sentences for membership in the Muslim Brotherhood, which has been a crime eligible for capital punishment since 1980.[25]

Recommendations

- It is imperative for the Syrian regime to declare an end to the state of emergency.
- The Syrian government should increase its efforts to eliminate human rights violations, including arbitrary arrests of political activists, torture, and inhumane prison conditions, in part by upholding the individual rights articulated in the constitution.
- The government should lift its restrictions on the formation of civil society organizations and political forums. This would create space for secular political discussion and check the growth of radical groups.
- The government must implement new and existing laws to protect freedom of association, freedom of speech, and the right to due process in accordance with the Syrian constitution and the International Covenant of Civil and Political Rights.

RULE OF LAW

INDEPENDENT JUDICIARY:	1.80
PRIMACY OF RULE OF LAW IN CIVIL AND CRIMINAL MATTERS:	2.83
ACCOUNTABILITY OF SECURITY FORCES AND MILITARY TO CIVILIAN AUTHORITIES:	1.00
PROTECTION OF PROPERTY RIGHTS:	3.00
EQUAL TREATMENT UNDER THE LAW:	2.33
CATEGORY AVERAGE:	**2.19**

The Syrian legal system is primarily based on civil law, and was heavily influenced by the period of French rule that stretched from 1920 to 1946. It is also drawn in part from Egyptian law—particularly as a result of Syria's temporary merger with Egypt to form the United Arab Republic (1958–1961)—and from Sharia. Syria has separate secular and religious courts. Civil and criminal cases are heard in secular courts, while the Sharia courts handle personal, family, and religious matters in cases between Muslims or between Muslims and non-Muslims. Doctrinal courts hear cases primarily involving members of the Druze sect, and spiritual courts settle personal status cases for Christians, Jews, and other non-Muslims.

Under the 1963 State of Emergency Act (Decree 51), Supreme State Security Courts were established in 1968 and in principle follow the procedures of the ordinary courts. The security courts consist of two divisions, each with a presiding panel of three judges, one of whom is a military judge. Their judgments are considered final but are not enforceable until they have been ratified by the president, who has the right to annul them, order retrials, or commute the sentences. Defendants appearing before the security courts (who are almost exclusively political prisoners) are guaranteed the same rights that they would enjoy before ordinary courts, but such rights are rarely observed by the authorities, especially because the trials are closed to the public. A number of activists' security court trials were opened to certain journalists and foreign diplomats between 2001 and 2004, but this practice seems to have been abandoned since that time. Many Kurds arrested in the March 2004 disturbances were secretly tried in the security courts and were reportedly not allowed to see their families; visits from lawyers were carefully monitored.

The executive branch continued to use the court system to crack down on political opponents in 2005 and 2006. The security courts were employed in March 2006 to suppress a Kurdish party, and in December 2006 five alleged Islamists were sentenced for membership in "a secret group aimed at changing the economic and social nature of the state." As part of the fallout from the Hariri assassination, former vice president 'Abd al-Halim Khaddam was charged in April 2006 with inciting a foreign attack against Syria and plotting to take power. In December 2005, Khaddam stated that Bashar had threatened Hariri before the assassination.

The judicial system is generally corrupt, inefficient, and rife with political influence. Guilt must be proven in the normal legal process, but not in the state security courts. Citizens have the right to counsel in all courts, but in practice they are often denied genuine legal assistance in the security courts and receive incompetent or corrupt counsel in the ordinary courts. The international community's calls to try the Syrians implicated in the Hariri assassination in an international criminal tribunal hint at widespread doubts about the impartiality of the Syrian courts.

Article 131 of the constitution stipulates that "the judiciary shall be independent, its independence being guaranteed by the President of the Republic with the assistance of the Higher Council of the Judiciary." The council is responsible for the administration of the judiciary, and has the authority to appoint, promote, and transfer judges. It is presided over by the minister of justice and includes the president. The highest constitutionally ordained judicial body in the country is the Supreme Constitutional Court, whose five justices are appointed by the president for four-year terms. This court rules on the constitutionality of laws and election disputes, and can try officials of the state, including the president, for criminal offenses.

In practice there is very little judicial independence, especially above the lower-court level. Particularly with Decree 51 in place, the executive branch wields far too much power over the judiciary, and judges' appointments and decisions at all levels are ultimately subject to the approval of the executive branch or martial-law representatives. In the lower courts, corruption is rampant, with the size of bribes dependent on the alleged offense. Proceedings for capital crimes, especially murder, are less susceptible to corruption, unless a powerful political or economic figure is involved. Business and government connections play a major role in the determination of guilt or innocence, or even whether charges are filed. Prosecutors have some independence at lower levels and in minor cases, but in the higher courts and in high-profile cases they can come under considerable pressure from the government or powerful families. Public officials and ruling-party actors are prosecuted for abuse of power and corruption, but these cases are almost always initiated by the executive for political reasons. The judiciary has been criticized by Amnesty International for using confessions and evidence obtained through torture. There are laws in place that outlaw torture and make evidence gained from it inadmissible; however, these are generally ignored and in practice, state actors involved in torture or inhuman and degrading treatment of prisoners are not held accountable for their actions.[26]

The educational system in Syria is extremely lacking in skills training, and lawyers and judges are for the most part ill-prepared. Judges are often chosen based on loyalty to the regime. Thus, the system generates a vicious circle of judicial incompetence and lethargy. The regime understands these shortcomings, and with the assistance of French consultants it has attempted to implement reforms. One manifestation of this effort was the government's removal in late 2005 of eighty-one judges, presumably for incompetence or corruption. The government also overhauled wages, taxes, and insurance for the judicial branch in order to improve judges' standard of living, attract more qualified personnel, and inhibit corrupt activities. Critics of the regime contend that the effort simply reinforced executive interference in judicial affairs.[27]

Since the government tends to exert its influence before court decisions are issued, there is seldom any cause for the authorities to waive or reverse judges' rulings. The case of Michel Kilo, mentioned above, demonstrated the persistence of the state in judicial matters; he was charged and imprisoned a second time after spending ten months in jail and winning release on bail following his initial arraignment.

The military-security apparatus has tremendous influence over the judicial and legislative branches and at times even over the executive branch, which it essentially serves. It has a kind of symbiotic relationship with private business interests in Syria, creating avenues of influence and enrichment that extend in both directions and discourage the emergence of an independent business class. The military is intimately involved in the political process, often vetting candidates both within and outside the Ba'ath party for elected and appointed positions.

The right to own property is guaranteed in the constitution. The state for the most part protects property rights and contracts once they are consummated; the process leading up to this point, however, is often fraught with corrupt practices. Under martial law, the state reserves the right to confiscate property and holdings for the public good. Individuals have the right to reasonable compensation, but many claim that the restitution is not fair and very few legal appeals have been successful.

Recommendations

- The state security courts must be abolished through revocation of the state of emergency. This would scale back the mechanisms of control emanating from the military-security apparatus, help decouple the executive from the judiciary, and begin to protect Syrian citizens from the arbitrary use of state power.

- Bashar al-Asad should reinforce the independence of the judiciary by encouraging legislation that removes the office of the president from the Higher Council of the Judiciary and makes his appointments to the council and the Supreme Constitutional Court subject to approval by an independent parliament.
- Syria needs to continue to improve its training of lawyers and judges, starting with educational reform in the universities that extends beyond technological modernization.
- The regime must continue to adopt the recommendations of outside consultants as part of its systematic reform of the judicial branch. The removal of the eighty-one judges in 2005, if done for the proper reasons, sends a powerful signal that incompetence and corruption will not be tolerated. On the other hand, the regime must be careful not to not overstep its bounds through undue meddling in the judicial arena.

ANTICORRUPTION AND TRANSPARENCY

ENVIRONMENT TO PROTECT AGAINST CORRUPTION:	1.20
EXISTENCE OF LAWS AND ETHICAL STANDARDS BETWEEN PRIVATE AND PUBLIC SECTORS:	2.50
ENFORCEMENT OF ANTICORRUPTION LAWS:	2.00
GOVERNMENTAL TRANSPARENCY:	2.00
CATEGORY AVERAGE:	**1.93**

Syria is well known for its corrupt business environment. Transparency International's 2006 Corruption Perceptions Index gave Syria a score of 2.9 on a 10-point scale, according the country a rank of 93 out of 163 countries surveyed.[28] As in most countries where the public sector plays a dominant role in the economy, the opportunities for corruption are numerous.

Syria is classified as a middle-income country by the World Bank, with a per capita income of US$1,570. Depending on the source, the economy was expected to expand in 2006–2007 by between 1.5 percent and 3 percent. The recent rise in global oil prices has compensated for Syria's dwindling production, now less than 400,000 barrels per day.

It is estimated that Syria, barring new discoveries, will become a net importer of oil in a few years, with domestic production running out in the 2020s. The country will be forced to diversify and modernize its economy before that deadline, moving away from oil and traditional agriculture and developing new products for export.

The government publicly embraced the transition to a market-oriented economy (or what it calls a "social market economy") at the Ba'ath party congress in June 2005, and it has instituted some measures to attract much-needed foreign investment, such as reducing tariffs on imports. The regime has also relaxed foreign currency rules with a view to establishing an inter-bank market; issued a decree on October 2, 2006, authorizing the establishment of the long-awaited stock market; worked toward reducing unemployment, currently estimated at about 20 percent; and implemented other reforms to move toward a normal monetary system.

The most common form of corruption is *wasta*, or the use of influence and personal connections to consummate business deals and other types of favors. It is almost an accepted form of doing business in Syria, but it restricts access to the Syrian economy and dampens any free-market tendencies. One cannot enter into a private or public-sector business agreement of any significance without local mediators (often called 5-percenters), who tend to multiply as the business relationship deepens. In reality, wasta is a form of control by the state, fragmenting bourgeois and upper-bourgeois classes who might otherwise coalesce into a recognizable pressure group. In addition, it spreads wealth to certain classes, supplements the income of government officials tied into the 5-percenter organizations, and gives more people an interest in maintaining the current regime.

The public sector in Syria, a creation of the Ba'athist socialist doctrine of the 1960s, is dominant in most industries and creates consistent opportunities for corruption. Licensing and bureaucratic regulations are oppressive, inefficiently applied, and subject to bribery. The black-market economy, especially the portions that have become intertwined with Lebanese business transactions (although those are more circumscribed since the withdrawal of Syrian troops from Lebanon), competes with the legal economy in terms of overall domestic product.

The state launched a program to promote integrity and honesty in Syrian society soon after Bashar came to power. There was little progress between 2000 and 2005, although further promises of reform came with the tenth five-year plan, which was announced in 2006. Legislative progress on the issue has been limited and there were further calls from the Ba'ath party to introduce stronger anticorruption mechanisms in 2005.[29] A number of ministries are now hiring based on merit rather than connections, though the process is far from being judged successful at this time. There have been a number of purges conducted by the government since 2003 aimed at combating corruption. These include the arrest of the head of the Court of Cassation and his deputy on corruption charges in 2005 and a purge of public employees from the civil service and military in late 2003.[30] However, anticorruption laws are applied selectively, either for political reasons or to punish cronies who behave in an irresponsible, abusive fashion. Individuals involved in high-profile corruption cases are ultimately at the mercy of the regime, the military-security apparatus, and the judicial mechanisms they control. Corruption allegations are often accompanied by media coverage, although the latter, as it is state controlled, is usually orchestrated by the government to legitimize its charges and reinforce its anticorruption credentials.

In theory, the constitution outlaws conflicts of interest by preventing members of the Council of Ministers from sitting on the board of directors of any private company or being involved in government contracts for services. Similarly, the constitution prohibits members of the Assembly using their positions to their advantage in any activity.[31] However, allegations of cronyism and nepotism abound in Syria. Under the regime of Hafiz al-Asad, senior officials who displayed unswerving loyalty to the president were allowed to enrich themselves through mostly corrupt methods. Wealth was funneled into the hands of powerful families who were either in or closely linked to the government. Ba'ath party members, the sons and daughters of high-level officials, and rich families have received preferential treatment in higher education, although the current regime is trying to incrementally raise the standards for Ba'ath party cadres before they are automatically accepted into universities.

Bashar al-Asad led a well-publicized anticorruption campaign shortly before ascending to the presidency, although his critics contend that this was designed in part to remove potential opponents of his pending succession. Most reports suggest that overt corruption has receded in Syria since Bashar came to power, but cronyism still exists at the highest levels. This centers primarily on the powerful Makhluf family, in particular Rami Makhluf, Bashar's first cousin, who runs the telecommunications firm SyriaTel.

Syrians have generally embraced government anticorruption campaigns, but Bashar's progress in this area has been hindered. He is apparently attempting to create a critical mass of support in the government and the party that will allow him to implement judicial reform and anticorruption policies. He has gone a long way toward accomplishing this, especially with actions taken at the Ba'ath party regional congress in 2005 and the cabinet shake-up in early 2006, but the hostile regional and international environment has compelled him to sacrifice reform for regime support and stability. It has been reported that a human rights activist was jailed for five years for criticizing SyriaTel, suggesting that those who identify corrupt practices may face repercussions from the state if the criticism lands too close to home.[32]

The tax administrator does not implement effective internal audits. Tax collection is inefficient and subject to political interference, and there is no auditing body outside the executive branch to address the problem. Some regulatory committees with supervisory capacities exist, but they are largely hamstrung by corruption and government pressure. While citizens can petition for information, their requests are often ignored or fall victim to the bloated and inefficient bureaucracy.

Transparency in the Syrian judicial and business environments is minimal. The current regime, with French and British assistance, has taken some steps in the judicial and financial sectors (such as the establishment of private banks and free-trade industrial zones) that will create more transparency and attract investment. The UN Program on Governance in the Arab Region has launched a number of projects in cooperation with the Syrian Government to promote good governance and combat corruption, including reform of the Customs Directorate and support in implementing the tenth five-year plan, which reiterated Bashar's intent to combat corruption.[33]

The budget-making process is officially subject to both parliamentary approval and the input of the Ba'ath party Regional Command, but in practice the Parliament acts as a rubber stamp for the party and the executive. The government does not publish accounting expenditures in a timely or coordinated fashion; however, expenditures are detailed periodically through the state-controlled media. The state's ostensibly open and competitive bidding process for contracts and procurement is hindered by the influence of political connections and under-the-table payments. Many terms for procurement bids are less than forty-five days, advantaging those who are already favored by the government and implying that outcomes are often predetermined.[34]

Syria does not receive much aid from international institutions; therefore, the state's performance in administering and distributing such funds legally receives very little scrutiny. Private assistance and grants from foreign countries to the government are more common, and the funds are distributed at the government's discretion. The money is generally put toward the most pressing needs at any given time, but sometimes they are funneled to projects run by well-placed individuals.

Recommendations

- The government should create an independent agency tasked with enforcing the conflict of interest regulations.
- The authorities should reform the bidding process for international contracts to increase transparency and regulatory oversight.
- The state should create appropriate mechanisms to enable citizens and journalists to effectively petition for and obtain government information.

NOTES

[1] David Schnecker, "Why Syrian Elections Matter" (Washington D.C.: Washington Institute for Near East Policy, 20 April 2007), http://www.washingtoninstitute.org/template C06.php?CID=1046

[2] Human Rights Watch (HRW), "Recent Arrests and Detentions of Syrian Activists," news release, 11 April 2006, http://hrw.org/english/docs/2006/04/11/syria13151_txt.htm.

[3] Ibid.

[4] HRW, "Syria: Free Activists Detained Over Petition," news release, 20 May 2006, http://hrw.org/english/docs/2006/05/20/syria13425_txt.htm.

[5] HRW, "Syria: Civil Society Activists Barred From Traveling," news release, 12 July 2006, http://hrw.org/english/docs/2006/07/12/syria13722_txt.htm.

[6] Ibid. See this site as well for the names of a number of other prominent Syrian activists who have been prevented from traveling outside of the country, including Riyad Seif, who was released from jail in January 2006 after five years in prison following the crackdown after the Damascus Spring.

[7] The Fund for Peace *Syria Country Profile 2006* (Washington D.C.: The Fund for Peace), http://www.fundforpeace.org/web/index.php?option=com_content&task=view&id=227 &Itemid=363.

8   Committee to Protect Journalists (CPJ), *Attacks on the Press in 2003* (New York: CPJ, March 2004), http://www.cpj.org/attacks03/mideast03/syria.html.

9   Reporters Without Borders, *Syria Country Report 2006* (Paris: Rapporteurs Sans Frontiers) http://www.rsf.org/article.php3?id_article=17220

10 For example, see the International Freedom of Expression Exchange's news releases for Syria from January through April 2007, available at http://www.ifex.org/en/content/view /full/230/.

11 Reporters Without Borders *Syria Country Report 2007* (Paris: Rapporteurs Sans Frontiers), http://www.rsf.org/article.php3?id_article=20777.

12 HRW, "Recent Arrests and Detentions of Syrian Activists."

13 Syrian Arab Republic, *International Covenant on Civil and Political Rights: Consideration of Reports Submitted by States Parties Under Article 40 of the Covenant; Second Periodic Report of States Parties Due in 1984—Syrian Arab Republic* (Geneva: United Nations Human Rights Committee, 19 January 2000), http://www.hri.ca/fortherecord2001 /documentation/tbodies/ccpr-c-syr-2000-2.htm.

14 Interview with President Bashar al-Asad, Damascus, Syria, 26 May 2004.

15 Michael Slackman, "Syria Imposing Stronger Curbs on Opposition," *New York Times*, 5 April 2006.

16 Congressional Research Service (CRS), *Syria: U.S. Relations and Bilateral Issues* (Washington, D.C.: CRS, 15 November 2002), 10.

17 "Syria: 190 Political Prisoners Released: Hundreds Remain," Amnesty International, 4 November 2005; *The Syria News Wire*, 18 January 2006, "Political Prisoners Released: Riyad Sayf and Mamun Homsi..

18 *Arab News*, 24 March 2006.

19 Women Living Under Muslim Laws, "Syria: Women's Rights Activists Face Resistance," 4 March 2006, http://www.wluml.org/english/newsfulltxt.shtml?cmd%5B157%5D =x-157-531283.

20 IRIN Humanitarian News and Analysis, "Sex Traffickers Target Women In War-Torn Iraq" (New York: UN Office for the Coordination of Humanitarian Affairs), http://www.irinnews.org/report.aspx?reportid=61903.

21 Maureen Lynch and Perveen Ali, "Buried Alive: Stateless Kurds in Syria" (Washington, D.C.: Refugees International), 14 February 2006.

22 For a cogent analysis of Islamist forces in Syria, see Stephen Ulph, *Jihadi After Action Report: Syria* (West Point, N.Y.: U.S. Military Academy, Combating Terrorism Center, November 2006).

23 "Learning to Live with Disability," *Syria-Today*, August 2006, http://www.syria-today.com/pkg05/index.php?page=view_article&dir=articles&ex=2&id=518&First=0& Last=9&CurrentPage=0&src=cat&cat_id=1.

24 Landmine Monitor, *Report 2006* (New York: International Campaign to Ban Landmines, 2006), http://www.icbl.org/lm/2006/syria.

25 "Learning to Live with Disability," *Syria-Today*, August 2006, http://www.syria-today.com/pkg05/index.php?page=view_article&dir=articles&ex=2&id=518&First=0& Last=9&CurrentPage=0&src=cat&cat_id=1.

[26] Amnesty International, "Unfair trial and sentencing of Muhammad Haydar Zammar" (London: Amnesty International), press release, 22 March 2007 http://web.amnesty.org/library/Index/ENGMDE240202007?open&of=ENG-SYR.

[27] Chris Buell, "Syria Sacks 81 Judges in Set of Judicial Reforms" (University of Pittsburgh: Jurist) http://jurist.law.pitt.edu/paperchase/2005/10/syria-sacks-81-judges-in-set-of.php, 5 October 2005.

[28] Transparency International, *Corruption Perceptions Index 2006* (Berlin: Transparency International, 2006), http://www.transparency.org/policy_research/surveys_indices/cpi/2006. In 2004, Syria ranked 71 out of 146 countries, with a score of 3.4. So while Syria's position relative to the total number of ranked countries remained about the same, the score—utilizing a variety of indices on corruption and the business environment—decreased in absolute terms. By comparison, the United States ranked 20 with a 7.3 score in 2006, Jordan at 40 with a 5.3 score, Lebanon at 63 with 3.6, Iran at 105 with 2.7, and Iraq at 160 with a 1.9 score. Tied for first were Finland, Iceland, and New Zealand with a 9.6 score.

[29] United Nations Development Project, http://www.undp.org.sy.

[30] United Nations Program on Governance in the Arab Region www.pogar.org/countries/anticorruption.asp?cid=19.

[31] Constitution of the Syrian Arab Republic articles 120 and 68(1), respectively.

[32] "Who's Who in Syria's Leadership," *BBC News*, 3 March 2005, http://news.bbc.co.uk/2/hi/middle_east/4314787.stm.

[33] UNDP-POGAR, http://www.undp.org.sy/practice_area_2.php.

[34] UNDP-POGAR, http://www.undp-pogar.org/countries/compare.asp.

TAJIKISTAN

CAPITAL: Dushanbe
POPULATION: 7.1 million
GNI PER CAPITA: $390

SCORES	2005	2007
ACCOUNTABILITY AND PUBLIC VOICE:	1.77	1.51
CIVIL LIBERTIES:	2.74	2.51
RULE OF LAW:	2.84	2.78
ANTICORRUPTION AND TRANSPARENCY:	1.40	1.62

(scores are based on a scale of 0 to 7, with 0 representing weakest and 7 representing strongest performance)

Lawrence P. Markowitz

INTRODUCTION

Tajikistan's civil war concluded in 1997 with a peace agreement between ex-Communists and the United Tajik Opposition (UTO). The conflict left a devastating imprint on the country's politics, society, and economy from which Tajikistan has yet to emerge. Installed in late 1992 as the head of an extremely weak government whose initial authority drew heavily upon Russian support, President Imomali Rahmon has successfully consolidated presidential power and edged out political rivals. Rahmon's institutionalization of authoritarian rule under the veil of postconflict stability and state building has ushered in a status quo style of politics that supersedes efforts at genuine political reform. The Tajik government has been able to legitimize stasis over change by invoking memories of the political turbulence that preceded the country's civil war. While this strategy has sustained Rahmon's rule, a growing economy, combined with a contracting circle of the regime's supporters, may generate new challenges in the future.

Lawrence P. Markowitz is Visiting Assistant Professor of Politics at Oberlin College.

Tajikistan's economy has experienced sustained growth at the rate of 7 to 10 percent annually since 2001—primarily driven by lucrative commodity exports and labor remittances from abroad.[1] At the same time, the country's exports have steadily increased and inflation has been brought under control. Between 1995 and 2005, Tajikistan's gross domestic product (GDP) nearly doubled from US$1.2 billion to US$2.3 billion.[2] The regime, however, has been unable to translate economic growth into democratic development, in part because political liberalization would threaten elites' ability to siphon off national wealth derived from cotton and aluminum exports. These profits and other spoils of public office have been crucial in securing elite allegiance to the Rahmon government.

Despite economic growth, Tajikistan's elections have consistently fallen short of the Organization for Security and Co-operation in Europe's (OSCE) norms, civil society organizations remain weak, and concentration of power in the executive (nationally and locally) has prevented land reform and privatization from achieving their intended effect. As a result, most people's economic situation remains dire. Poverty afflicts over half the population, 75 percent of whom are rural and suffer from the effects of undernourishment. The average annual income is approximately US$390 (GNI per capita)—well below the average even in low-income countries.

The Tajik civil war also fundamentally reordered the country's social structures, heightening the salience of regionalism (*mahallagaroie*) and local identities such as "clan." Rahmon's systematic and overt concentration of political power and national wealth among natives of his home region of Kulob (now part of Khatlon province) has exacerbated these divisions and raises the specter of renewed conflict. As Rahmon reneges on the 1997 power-sharing agreement between ex-Communists and UTO and asserts regional hegemony, grinding poverty and rising discontent in other parts of the country have fueled regional and local tensions within Tajikistan. In Soghd province, as well as in several localities directly subordinated to the national government, concentrations of ethnic Uzbeks (who constitute 16 percent of Tajikistan's population) remain a source of anxiety for the regime. Recently, resettlement policies have sought to assert an ethnic Tajik influence in Tursonzade district by relocating 1,000 Tajik families from Khatlon province. Tursonzade contains Tajikistan's leading source of export revenue—its massive aluminum smelter.[3] Similarly, the national government's control over the Rogun hydroelectric plant and other energy initiatives in eastern parts of the country are also tenuous, as these areas were opposition strongholds during the civil war. The central leadership has sought to increase foreign direct investment (entertaining proposals from Russia, the United States, and China) as a means of extending its influence over key resources based in these areas. Justified as government-sponsored development, such initiatives often use foreign investors to subsidize unwanted state presence.

Against this background, Tajikistan's domestic politics was dramatically affected by the forced abdication of President Askar Akaev of Kyrgyzstan in the wake of parliamentary elections in March 2005. Despite broad-based support, Rahmon stepped up efforts to solidify his dominance in national politics by undercutting and dividing the political opposition, driving out international nongovernmental organizations and tightly controlling local ones, harassing human rights organizations, marginalizing independent media, and strengthening his political party's majority in the legislature. As a result, Tajikistan has experienced setbacks in certain aspects of democratic development, raising doubt about the regime's commitment to genuine political change.

ACCOUNTABILITY AND PUBLIC VOICE

FREE AND FAIR ELECTORAL LAWS AND ELECTIONS:	1.25
EFFECTIVE AND ACCOUNTABLE GOVERNMENT:	1.50
CIVIC ENGAGEMENT AND CIVIC MONITORING:	1.67
MEDIA INDEPENDENCE AND FREEDOM OF EXPRESSION:	1.63
CATEGORY AVERAGE:	**1.51**

Although the Tajik government has reformed legislation concerning elections, in practice, elections have failed to meet many OSCE standards. Large-scale irregularities during the 2005 parliamentary elections and 2006 presidential election undermined several promising procedural and legal changes that were enacted in 2004. The changes—including amendments to the Constitutional Law on Elections—incorporated provisions for political party observers, improved candidates' access to mass media outlets, and provided for the immediate posting of election results at each polling station. If fully implemented, this revamped legislative framework has the potential to serve as a basis for democratic elections. However, the intimidation and arrest of leading opposition figures, glaring errors in tabulating ballots, and extensive interference by local authorities ensured that neither election held under the new system was open and competitive.

Tajikistan's electoral administration enjoys only limited public confidence; it lacks both transparency and political balance. Tajikistan has a three-tiered system of election commissions: a national-level Central Commission on Elections and Referenda (CCER), district election commissions (DECs), and polling state commissions (PSCs). A total of forty-one DECs and 2,953 PSCs administered the parliamentary elections, whereas sixty-eight DECs and 3,059 PSCs ran the presidential election. Members of the CCER are proposed by the president and elected by Parliament's lower house, the Majlisi Namoyandagon, although the dominance of the president's party, the People's Democratic Party of Tajikistan (PDPT), in the legislature ensured PDPT control over the body. Despite electoral law requirements for open meetings, the decision making and functioning of the CCER have not been transparent. Similarly, the staffing of local electoral commissions has been so compromised by local government interference that it was at times difficult to distinguish between the two.[4]

The legislative elections held on February 27, 2005, consolidated PDPT control over the legislative branch. The Majlisi has sixty-three seats, to which twenty-two members are elected from party lists and forty-one members from single-member constituencies. For three seats in the latter group, failure to reach a majority led to runoff elections on March 13. Of the six parties that entered candidates, the PDPT took an overwhelming fifty-two seats, whereas the progovernment Communist Party (CP) won three seats, the Islamic Renaissance Party (IRP) won two seats, and independent candidates took the remaining six seats.

Election observers from the OSCE's Office for Democratic Institutions and Human Rights (ODIHR) found major shortcomings in the conduct of the legislative election, noting widespread instances of multiple voting and unmonitored tabulation processes in district commissions, where many protocols were illegally altered. Moreover, restrictive registration criteria (including a newly imposed US$500 deposit, a higher education requirement, and the need to gather 500 signatures from eligible voters in the candidate's constituency) resulted in the exclusion of approximately 100 prospective candidates by DECs. In addition, just months before the election, criminal charges were brought against prominent candidates, including Mahmadruzi Iskandarov (head of the Democratic Party, DP) and Sulton Kuvatov (head of the unregistered Taraqqiyot Party), disqualifying them from electoral competition. Both the timing of the criminal charges and the disqualification of opposition candidates raised serious concerns about the openness of the election.

Immediately following the election, three opposition parties (IRP, DP, and the Social Democratic Party) declared that they would not recognize the election results, although their ability to contest the validity of the election was diluted when winning IRP and CP candidates accepted their seats. In addition, complaints filed with the CCER and in several district courts were either overruled or ignored.[5] Analysts have noted that while these developments indicate a willingness to challenge the government in court, the government response has been muted at best.[6]

In terms of Tajikistan's presidential election on November 6, 2006, changes to the constitution in 2003 gave President Rahmon the legal basis to run for two additional seven-year terms in office, possibly extending his tenure until 2020. The election returned Rahmon to office with a reported 79.3 percent of the vote, followed by Olimjon Boboev (6.3 percent), Amir Karakulov and Ismoil Talbakov (each with 5.2 percent), and Abduhalim Ghafarov (2.8 percent). None of the major opposition parties ran in the election, leaving Rahmon facing a field of unknown candidates.[7] Not suprisingly, the OSCE reported that the election campaign lacked real debate and competition. The weakness and rudderlessness of the opposition was partially due to the arrests of Iskandarov and Kuvatov and the death of IRP leader Said Abdullo Nuri in August 2006.[8] But it was also a result of limitations imposed on candidates' access to media outlets, basic security concerns when traveling, and the heavy involvement of local authorities in organizing local PDPT political machines.[9] While Rahmon did not officially campaign, his four challengers held no independent rallies and campaigned in joint gatherings organized by local government or the CCER.[10]

In one positive contrast to earlier elections, presidential candidates were allowed to use limited airtime on state-run television and radio stations and advertise in government newspapers. However, an OSCE report heavily criticized the presidential election for ad hoc voter registration methods, limitations imposed on candidates seeking enough signatures to reach the 5 percent threshold necessary to enter the competition, negative voting (in which voters strike out those candidates they do not want), the absence of female candidates, proxy (usually family) voting practices, failure to follow counting procedures, and significant discrepancies between official figures and local tallies at DECs.[11] In contrast to the parliamentary election a year earlier, no serious attempts were made to challenge the election results. Instead, opposition voices have raised concerns that Rakhmon's reelection will be used to further extend his personal power and divest the country of its resources.[12]

Presidential power in Tajikistan continues to be organized around local and regional affiliations and sustained through the distribution of patronage and the manipulation of institutional rules. Political elites from Khatlon province (especially those from Rahmon's home district of Dangara) have enjoyed favored access to key political and economic posts in the national government. Although the 1997 Moscow peace accord that ended the civil war allocated 30 percent of national government posts to the opposition, Rahmon has systematically excluded them from national politics in recent years. Systematic exclusion of elites from other areas of the country in favor of selected Khatlon elites has limited accountability in government and become a potentially destabilizing factor.

This predominance of executive authority is replicated at local levels as well. District governors and local economic elites—particularly in the cotton-growing regions—exercise undue power over production quotas, privatization, and land reform. As the International Crisis Group concluded, "[l]ocal administrators (*raises*) are appointed and have no accountability to those they govern."[13] As a result, in most parts of the country, the power of local administrators is unchecked by oversight by the legislature, judiciary, or other national institutions. Tajikistan's civil service is generally more effective than political offices and law enforcement bodies, although low salaries leave many government workers open to bribery and corruption.[14]

In addition to restrictions imposed on candidates in Tajikistan's elections, civil society groups and media outlets have also faced obstacles, compromising opportunities for public accountability. Since the end of the civil war, Tajikistan has seen a significant rise in the number of nongovernmental organizations (NGOs), many of which focus on post-conflict peacebuilding, socioeconomic development, and humanitarian projects.[15] From the start, these groups were limited in their capacity to testify against the government or influence policy, and recent actions by the government have placed further restrictions on NGOs' scope of action. In the spring of 2005, the government ordered financial audits of several international organizations in Tajikistan, and later that year authorities refused registration to a number of NGOs, including Freedom House and the National Democratic Institute for International Affairs. In March 2006, the government extended its restrictions by passing the Law on Public Associations, which requires NGOs to register annually.[16] Through these and other mechanisms, government authorities continue to pressure both local and international civic organizations.

Although freedom of speech is guaranteed by Tajikistan's constitution and the Law on the Mass Media, government authorities have used various methods to restrict access to information that is potentially of public interest. A new requirement that nonstate media outlets obtain licenses from the Ministry of Culture was only one of forty amendments to Tajikistan's media laws in 2005.[17] Since 2004, independent print newspapers have been forced out of circulation; *Nerui Sokhan, Ruzi Nav,* and *Odamu Olan* were all denied accreditation for failure to pay taxes or for technical violations.[18] The government has arrested and intimidated editors and reporters, including correspondents from the British Broadcasting Corporation (BBC), *Sardoi Mardum* (Tajikistan's parliamentary paper), and *Nerui Sokhan.*[19] The editor of the latter was convicted of theft (for siphoning electricity from street lights), sentenced to two years in prison, and stripped of 20 percent of his earnings during this time.[20]

In early August 2006, the BBC's application for a broadcasting license was refused by Tajikistan's licensing commission for failing to meet the 2005 law On Licensing Certain Types of Activities.[21] Since the shutdown of Tajikistan's last independent television station, Somonien, in 2005, the broadcast media has been dominated by three state-run television stations that have received a 25 percent increase in government funding.[22] In October 2006 (one month before the presidential election), the Ministry of Communications blocked domestic access to five news websites published abroad: *Centrasia, Ferghana, Arianastorm, Charogiruz,* and *Tajikistantimes.*[23] One positive development is that three independent provincial television stations in the cities of Isfara, Panjakent, and Istaravshan were allowed to operate after negotiations with government authorities. Nonetheless, public access to information is extremely limited, as evidenced by the absence of any daily newspapers (independent or state owned) published in the country.[24]

Posing a further challenge to media freedoms, the Tajik state has also intensified its use of onerous registration requirements, tax liabilities, and libel laws that impose fines and imprisonment on print and broadcast media outlets that attempt to scrutinize government policies. Alongside these tactics, state authorities have stifled press and broadcast media freedoms through the use of extralegal intimidation, arbitrary arrests, and detentions. In rare cases, journalists have successfully appealed their arrests and convictions in court, occasionally overturning previous court verdicts.[25] On balance, however, accusations against journalists are not investigated by authorities fairly or expeditiously. Cultural expression is monitored by the government and enjoys only limited autonomy; access to media is highly regulated, and music, art, and theater that diverge from progovernment themes are rarely, if ever, allowed.

Recommendations

- The government should make more genuine efforts to include and promote other regional voices and interests in its political structures and decision-making processes. Toward that end, the government should appoint a more balanced distribution of regional politicians to cabinet-level positions.
- All opposition parties should be permitted to hold public meetings, campaign for support, and have adequate opportunities to disseminate their message without fear of harassment, intimidation, and arrest.
- Elections should be carried out without interference from the ruling party or local government authorities. Specifically, district and local election commissions should be staffed by people from different political parties and from outside the locality in order to enhance transparency and political balance.
- Foreign and domestic NGOs, particularly those devoted to strengthening democracy and civil society, should be allowed to register and renew their activities. The Law on Public Associations, which requires NGOs to register annually, should be repealed and avenues for NGO input into policy making should be established.

- The Law on Licensing Certain Types of Activities should be rescinded and independent media—print, broadcast, and internet-based—should be allowed to register and operate without government intimidation or undue tax and regulatory inspections.

CIVIL LIBERTIES

PROTECTION FROM STATE TERROR, UNJUSTIFIED IMPRISONMENT, AND TORTURE:	1.71
GENDER EQUITY:	3.75
RIGHTS OF ETHNIC, RELIGIOUS, AND OTHER DISTINCT GROUPS:	2.50
FREEDOM OF CONSCIENCE AND BELIEF:	2.00
FREEDOM OF ASSOCIATION AND ASSEMBLY:	2.60
CATEGORY AVERAGE:	**2.51**

Tajikistan continued to be a focus of criticism, at home and abroad, for the execution of prisoners, for reports of torture and ill-treatment by police, and for a tradition of impunity for such violations. Procurators continue to rely on extracted confessions rather than thorough and impartial investigation as evidence against defendants. In cases in which inmates were mistreated by police or prison officials and complaints were filed with the General Procuracy, the latter rarely pressed charges.[26] On the positive side, police and procuracy officials have been actively participating in OSCE seminars promoting the protection of human rights during investigations and pretrial detention.[27] Without access to those detained by authorities, however, independent monitoring will yield little systematic evidence of whether a real change in attitudes among law enforcement personnel is occurring.

Prison conditions in Tajikistan are extremely poor, with overcrowding a major concern; there are 100 prisoners per cell in certain prisons.[28] After a jump from 6,000 inmates in 1996 to 11,000 in 2001, the prison population in Tajikistan stabilized and remains at 11,000 today.[29] The International Committee of the Red Cross, which had previously been able to visit and provide aid to inmates, has not been granted access to prisons by the Ministry of Interior since 2004.[30] In August 2005, a prison disturbance in Kurgan-Teppe—allegedly provoked by the appointment of Izzatullo Sharipov as head of the prison system—was primarily a result of the long-term deterioration of conditions and the use of torture in prisons. Government authorities responded to this incident by handing down harsh sentences to the ringleaders of the revolt but showed little zeal for prison reform.[31]

In the months leading up to the 2006 presidential election, various members of the political opposition were arrested and detained, revealing a clear pattern on the part of government authorities of using the state's law enforcement and judicial organs as a means of reining in the opposition. In December 2004, Mahmudi Iskandarov, leader of the Democratic Party and likely presidential candidate, was arrested in Moscow by Russian authorities at Tajikistan's request. Immediately after his release by Russian authorities in April 2005, he disappeared (allegedly abducted), and ultimately resurfaced in the custody of the Tajik government. On October 5, 2005, he was sentenced to twenty-three years in prison and fined 1.5 million Tajik somoni (US$470,000) for terrorism and unlawful possession of weapons.

Taraqqiyot Party Deputy Chair Rustam Faziev and Chair Sulton Kuvatov were both arrested and sent to prison on charges of insulting the president after publishing an open letter critical of President Rahmon. In mid-2005, Social Democratic Party parliamentary candidates Nizomiddin Begmatov and Nasimjon Shukurov were arrested and sentenced to a year and eighteen months, respectively, for hooliganism (allegedly for using foul language during a court hearing).[32] In early 2006, Islamic Renaissance Party member Tojiddin Abdurakhmonov—convicted of involvement in organized criminal activity, possession of weapons, and possession of forged documents—was sentenced to sixteen years' imprisonment.[33]

Public order and safety are poorly maintained by government and law enforcement, primarily because Tajikistan's law enforcement entities cannot provide adequate and immediate assistance to citizens in need. Limited manpower, low wages, few resources, and poor training contribute to the lack of professionalism and undermine a sense of public service.

Due to outdated legislation and prevailing legal norms in Tajikistan, women have limited legal protection in certain areas. The police, for example, have no special training in rape investigations, and few cases actually go to court. Moreover, the criminal code does not address domestic violence, which is typically viewed as private problem that is outside the state's responsibility. Moreover, women remain underrepresented in public positions in Tajikistan, though they have historically constituted a significant minority in parliament and other national offices.[34] Following the 2005 parliamentary election, women filled 17.5 percent (eleven seats) of the sixty-three seats in the lower house of Parliament and 23.5 percent (eight seats) of the thirty-five seats in the upper house.[35] However, no women serve in leadership posts within the executive branch at either the national or subnational level.

In February 2005, Tajikistan's Parliament approved a law on gender equality that is designed to address many of these shortcomings. The law establishes several enforcement mechanisms, including a unified national gender policy, the supervision of executive organs and city councils (*hukumats*) in selecting women for higher government posts, the supervision of the law by the general prosecutor, and the authority of juridical organs to adjudicate violations of the law.[36]

Conditions for women and youth in Tajikistan have been worsened by the country's civil war and a permeable border with Afghanistan. The former led to a problematic demographic outflow of men, forcing women to become second or even third wives; in major cotton-growing areas, women make up 85 percent to 90 percent of the rural work force. Extremely low pay scales for rural labor have forced some younger women to resort to prostitution. Cotton production has also led to the institutionalization of child labor in Tajikistan (as in other Central Asian countries).[37] Thus far, the state has made little effort to ameliorate these problems.

A permeable border with Afghanistan has fostered cross-border human trafficking. While Tajikistan does not fully meet standards for eliminating human trafficking, it has taken significant steps to implement a national plan aimed at improving its antitrafficking law enforcement capacity. The number of investigations into trafficking increased from fourteen in 2004 to eighty-one in 2005. In February 2006, the Ministry of Interior opened an Intelligence and Analytical Center for Counter-Narcotics and Trafficking in Persons, which trains border guards to screen better for human trafficking. Recent arrests, however, have implicated low-level law enforcement officials in the trafficking of underage girls for sexual exploitation.[38]

Freedoms of conscience and belief are guaranteed by the constitution. There is no official state religion, though the government recognizes two Islamic holy days, Eid Al-Fitr and Idi Qurbon (Eid al-Adha in Arabic), as state holidays.[39] Nonetheless, government authorities have attempted to curtail certain fundamental freedoms since 2005. In March 2006, the government prepared a single law on religion that would codify existing practices and add new restrictions on religious freedoms, including a 200-signature requirement to register religious associations, state control over religious education, a limit on the number of mosques in Tajikistan, and the imposition of state control over pilgrimages to Mecca. To date, this law has not been passed due to opposition from religious communities.[40] In March 2007, headscarves were banned in educational institutions, though women are allowed to wear a hijab when photographed for official documents.[41]

In addition, some local government bodies have displayed a bias against religious organizations. The State Committee on Religious Affairs (SCRA), under the Council of Ministers, is supposed to register religious groups of ten persons or more. In at least one case, however, local authorities in Tursonzade District refused registration to Jehovah's Witnesses despite national registration and pressure from SCRA.[42] As this case illustrates, the protection of religious, ethnic, and other minorities in practice is difficult to enforce and extends only as far as the government's writ.

Furthermore, state monitoring of Islam has steadily increased since the Islamic Movement of Uzbekistan (IMU) used Tajikistan to launch armed incursions into Uzbekistan. Under Article 187 (which bans the arousal of religious and ethnic dissension) and Article 307 (which bans calls to overthrow the government) of Tajikistan's criminal code, government authorities have arrested about 500 alleged members of the international Islamist party Hizb ut-Tahrir between 2000 and 2005. Although only 189 cases were brought to court, there are an estimated 150–200 Hizb ut-Tahrir members currently imprisoned.[43] The targeting of Hizb ut-Tahrir as a security threat, subsequent arrests, and the lack of transparency in court proceedings have raised serious concerns over the government's restriction of religious observance and affiliation.[44] Nevertheless, there have been no arrests of high-profile religious leaders, and SCRA has even loosened some of its institutional controls over the selection of imams.[45]

The government's monitoring and pressure on Islamist groups such as Hizb ut-Tahrir may carry ethnic overtones as many of the group's activities reportedly involve members of the Uzbek minority population in Tajikistan.[46] As a result, crackdowns on Islamists have fallen disproportionately on the Uzbek minority. Moreover, ethnic minorities, particularly Uzbeks and Russians, continue to be underrepresented in national government, despite the constitutional guarantees and government efforts to protect minorities—especially Uzbeks—against discrimination in public life.

Tajikistan's 1991 Law No. 459 calls for the social defense of individuals with disabilities, yet the disabled continue to experience widespread discrimination in everyday life. This problem is particularly acute in Tajikistan, where there has been a dramatic increase in the disabled population due to injuries sustained during the civil war and from landmines. Between 1990 and 2000, the number of disabled persons registered with Tajikistan's Ministry of Labor and Social Welfare rose from 67,832 to 104,272.[47] In addition to the inaccessibility of public transportation and most buildings, the disabled face a very low degree of public acceptance.

The constitutional right to assembly and association continues to be curtailed by the state. The law "On assemblies, meetings, demonstrations and rallies" stipulates broad restrictions on public rallies, though it also places some limitations on government and law enforcement agents seeking to ban demonstrations. In practice, though, the government has sought to prevent public gatherings through the use of force and through rhetoric associating demonstrations with the outbreak of civil war in 1992.

The government has interfered in the formation of free and independent trade unions; currently, such organizations are parastatal entities. Citizens are often compelled to join trade unions and, as a consequence, these organizations rarely address citizens' genuine concerns, even regarding the egregious labor violations among Tajik migrants in Russia and Kazakhstan.[48]

Recommendations

- The government should create more effective mechanisms—by setting up an oversight system of autonomous legislative and judicial organs and empowering an internal affairs office with monitoring and

investigative practices—to hold law enforcement agencies accountable for human rights violations.
- The government should devote more resources to genuine prison reform, beginning with the construction of new facilities and the provision of regular access to healthcare.
- Politically motivated arrests of members of the opposition should cease immediately, and those who have been imprisoned should be released.
- The government should increase enforcement of its national action plan against human trafficking, with a particular focus on addressing corruption among border patrol officers.
- New laws limiting freedoms of assembly and association should be repealed; groups espousing views different from those of the government should be allowed to meet without fear of arrest; and peaceful demonstrations should be permitted.

RULE OF LAW

INDEPENDENT JUDICIARY:	1.80
PRIMACY OF RULE OF LAW IN CIVIL AND CRIMINAL MATTERS:	2.67
ACCOUNTABILITY OF SECURITY FORCES AND MILITARY TO CIVILIAN AUTHORITIES:	2.75
PROTECTION OF PROPERTY RIGHTS:	3.00
EQUAL TREATMENT UNDER THE LAW:	3.67
CATEGORY AVERAGE:	**2.78**

Although the constitution provides for an independent judiciary, the justice system is heavily influenced by the executive branch and by criminal groups. The procurator's office, situated firmly within the executive, commands powers that effectively emasculate the judiciary. Procurators have the right to supervise the implementation of laws, launch criminal proceedings, conduct investigations, issue an arrest warrant, arrange prosecution on behalf of the state at trials, and protest a court ruling if the procurator finds the verdict unsubstantiated or too lenient to enforce. The ability to protest rulings is particularly influential since a judge whose decisions have been frequently protested is likely to be removed.

Constitutional guarantees of the right to an attorney and of a fair and immediate trial are often not met. According to Tajikistan's criminal code, pretrial detention by police without an arrest warrant can last for seventy-two hours, and procurators can extend detention for ten days. In rare cases, the procurator general can extend detention up to fifteen months without trial.[49] Generally, however, people are released if no charges were filed. This process is generally followed in practice, though state-appointed attorneys are not always available and often provide a substandard defense. Presumption of the defendants' guilt remains the norm. In addition, criminal groups and other informal networks permeate judicial and law enforcement organs (often through personal relationships established during the civil war) to such a degree that procurators are often intimately connected to Tajikistan's illegal economy.[50]

The judiciary primarily consists of the Constitutional Court, Supreme Court, Supreme Economic Court, Military Court, Court of Gorno Badakhshan Autonomous Oblast, courts of provinces, the city of Dushanbe, towns, and districts. Judges of the Constitutional Court, Supreme Court, and Economic Court are appointed by the president, and each lower court can issue appeals to the court above it (although appeals are rare due to an overriding mistrust of the judicial system). Judges at all levels are underpaid and thus susceptible to bribery. The volume of cases brought to court is relatively high: the Supreme Court considered a total of 885 criminal and 1,421 civil legal proceedings in 2005 and heard appeals in 536 criminal proceedings, resulting in 160 cases being remitted for further consideration and 151 sentences being changed.[51] Despite this activity, however, judicial oversight of other state institutions is severely lacking. Judges are, nonetheless, appropriately trained to carry out justice, particularly those trained during the Soviet period.

Modernization of Tajikistan's rule of law has concentrated on legal professional reform. Yet rather than undertaking reforms to enhance the autonomy of the country's legal professionals, the government has taken steps to subordinate them further to executive authorities. The 2004 Law on Licensing required advocates to register with the Ministry of Justice (MOJ), marking a clear departure from the 1995 Law on

Advocacy, which defined the legal profession as "an independent professional affiliation." As a result, advocates routinely ignore the registration requirement and base their authority on the previous Law of Advocacy, presenting an order from their collegium rather than a license from the MOJ to appear in court. Although the new law was intended to unify advocates and systematize the profession, advocates' resistance to implementing it has left its effects uncertain.[52] Moreover, the MOJ's decision to eliminate a qualification examination for licensing as an advocate removed a potential contribution that the law might have made.

Many advocates, despite their education, have inadequate access to legal resources and fair pay. With approximately 12,000 to 13,000 full-time students enrolled in law schools, the number of graduates far exceeds available positions—especially the more coveted posts in the procurator and security organs and in the court system. Most lower-level and less-connected graduates enter the remaining ranks as advocates, nonadvocate jurists, or notaries public.[53]

President Rahmon retains firm control over the Ministry of Defense and the Presidential Guard. The former has remained under Major-General Sherali Khayrulloyev since 1994, and the latter has been placed under one of Rahmon's relatives. Both served as a source of troops to man the Tajikistan-Afghanistan border after Russian troops were withdrawn.[54]

Torture and abuse of prisoners and impunity within the security forces remain common. Not only are police not held accountable to civilian authorities, they were at times used by the president and his inner circle to make politically motivated arrests. However, there are occasional cases where security forces are held accountable. In one case, for instance, three police officers were detained and investigated by procurators after an Islamic Renaissance Party activist died while in custody.[55]

While formal statistics demonstrate a gradual expansion of private property ownership in Tajikistan, the process is often carried out unfairly due to collusion among local officials. Many ordinary people with claims to private land cannot depend on either Tajikistan's ineffective legal professionals or on a judicial system largely under the control of local and central executive bodies. As a result, many people have few, if any, avenues for the defense of their property rights, and contracts are rarely enforced. In rare cases in which independent farmers and private entrepreneurs have challenged local government attempts to seize their property, they have been required to appeal their case through several levels of local and regional courts, where the influence of local authorities is greatest.

It is possible, in theory, for Tajik citizens to find some recourse from upper courts, such as the Supreme Economic Court, but this may take more than a year—as in the case of twenty-eight farmers in Rudaki district where a case, initiated in 2004, extended well into the next year. Generally, farmers and entrepreneurs lack a full knowledge of their legal rights and do not usually consider using the legal system to their advantage.[56]

Recommendations
- To establish a truly independent judiciary, the executive should be able to select judges only with a genuine legislative approval. Moreover, the institutional powers of the procurator's office should be limited.
- Prisoners should be able to receive guaranteed access to an attorney at the beginning of their detention, and if the state assigns counsel, the court should make the appointment rather than the procurator.
- The government should limit the interference of local authorities—including the procurator's office and the courts—to ensure that land reforms are carried out and that property rights are protected.

ANTICORRUPTION AND TRANSPARENCY

ENVIRONMENT TO PROTECT AGAINST CORRUPTION:	1.60
EXISTENCE OF LAWS AND ETHICAL STANDARDS BETWEEN	
PRIVATE AND PUBLIC SECTORS:	1.25
ENFORCEMENT OF ANTICORRUPTION LAWS:	1.50
GOVERNMENTAL TRANSPARENCY:	2.14
CATEGORY AVERAGE:	**1.62**

Deep-seated corruption, the criminalization of state structures, and close ties between the government and the informal economy have become entrenched in Tajikistan's politics. Ranked as one of the world's most corrupt countries in Transparency International's 2006 Corruption Perceptions Index, Tajikistan received a score of 2.2, tying with Nigeria,

Pakistan, and the Democratic Republic of Congo.[57] This score is marginally improved from the previous year.

In general, a culture of impunity prevails among government officials within the state apparatus. Public office is routinely viewed as a vehicle for personal enrichment, and the state rarely acts to establish an environment that discourages corruption. At times, however, high-level officials have been dismissed and arraigned on charges of corruption and embezzlement. In 2003, Tajikistan's aluminum plant director, Abduqodir Ermatov, was dismissed and about to be charged when he fled abroad. Ghaffor Mirzoev, the former commander of the Presidential Guard and head of the Drug Control Agency, was sentenced in August 2006 to life in prison for abuse of office, murder, and an attempted coup d'etat.[58] However, these dismissals were politically motivated and do not indicate a new era of enforcement of anticorruption laws.

The blurred line between the private and public spheres permeates Tajikistan's economy, particularly in professions where salaries are paid by the state; this issue has been particularly salient in the health and education sectors. Bribery is pervasive in higher education, involving students, instructors, deans, institute directors, and even the Ministry of Higher Education. Bribes range from small gifts to pass an exam to large fees for university entrance. As a result, an anticorruption department was set up within the procurator general's office in June 2004, with a specific mandate to review the education and health sectors.[59] These are minor efforts given the widespread nature of corruption in these areas.

Attempts to enforce anticorruption laws have led to new and expanded mandates within Tajikistan's law enforcement agencies. In 1999, Tajikistan passed several laws establishing anticorruption instruments: the Presidential Decree on Additional Measures to Step up the Struggle against Economic Crime and Corruption, the Law on the Fight against Corruption, the Law on Civil Service, as well as changes to the criminal code. Importantly, the Law on the Fight against Corruption addresses corruption by attempting to control conflicts of interest and mandating annual declarations of income and assets.[60] Despite these legislative changes, law enforcement agencies are themselves rarely subjected to external inspection, relying instead on internal controls—a significant problem, given that predatory and unfair tax collection has been found to impede the development of small and medium enterprises.[61]

Tajikistan ranks poorly among countries in Eastern Europe and Central Asia with respect to the ease of starting a business, obtaining credit, and negotiating tax and court regulations.[62] The various bureaucratic regulations constrict small business development, but they are permitted to continue since they enhance opportunities for corruption. The procurator's office monitors corruption through its own department, which can challenge any decision by any administrative body (private or public). While the number of investigations completed by the procurator general's anticorruption department increased from nineteen in 2003 to forty-five in 2005, the department remains heavily biased.[63] As a result, victims of corruption have no adequate mechanisms to assert their rights—particularly since there is no independent complaint mechanism outside the offices of the procurator or the Ministry of Justice. Anticorruption advocates and whistle-blowers, lacking a supportive legal environment, frequently find themselves targeted by state agencies that they have identified as corrupt.

Progress on budgetary reforms has been mixed. There have been some improvements: the government has taken steps to consolidate public funds, thus improving budget management, and has submitted the republican budget, local budgets, and the budget of the social protection fund for parliamentary review.[64] However, Tajikistan's major industries, including cotton and aluminum production, are not included in these disclosed budgets, making legislative review largely ceremonial. Expenditures in these areas remain a state secret.[65] Moreover, the system of government contract allocation in these critical areas is not transparent and is therefore susceptible to corruption.

Excessive state intervention continues to define Tajikistan's economy, particularly in cotton and aluminum production and water resource management. In addition, since 2004 Tajikistan has become highly dependent upon foreign aid, much of which is regulated through the Aid Coordination Unit (ACU) situated within the presidential administration (and established through presidential decree). ACU does provide some public reporting of international aid (e.g., grants and loans) through published annual reports.[66] However, this agency is not integrated into other government institutions, suggesting that it serves primarily as a show-piece for potential international donors.

While citizens do have a legal right to obtain information about government operations, with particular rights to information granted to journalists, a recent survey found that attempts to acquire basic information from government offices on the use of the death penalty, on economic growth, on how state funds were spent on social activities, or even on the amount of drugs confiscated by government agencies were refused. This information was designated classified or a state secret, leaving citizens no means to petition government agencies for it.[67] The state makes no effort to provide information about government services and decisions in formats and settings that are accessible to disabled people.

Recommendations

- To reduce officials' susceptibility to bribery, salaries of government employees, especially in the health and education sectors, should be raised.
- Government agencies responsible for enforcing anticorruption laws—the tax police and the procurator's office—should themselves be subject to external inspection and review by fact-finding committees that report to judicial and legislative branch offices.
- Recently enacted laws requiring public officials to disclose their financial assets or conflicts of interest should be systematically enforced by an independent prosecutor selected by the legislature. Sanctions for failure to comply should include criminal prosecution.
- Public disclosure of state revenues and expenditures in the national budget should also include information on key areas of agricultural and industrial production.

NOTES

[1] Labor remittances now constitute 12 percent of Tajikistan's GDP. See *Tajikistan—Policy note: Enhancing the development impact of remittances* (Washington, D.C.: World Bank, Report No. 35771TJ, June 2006), www-wds.worldbank.org/external/default/WDSContentServer/WDSP/IB/2006/08/22/000160016_20060822094201/Rendered/PDF/357710TJ.pdf.

[2] *Tajikistan at a Glance* (World Bank, 13 August 2006), http://devdata.worldbank.org/AAG/tjk_aag.pdf.

[3] Bruce Pannier, "Tajikistan: Officials Entice Ethnic Tajiks to Western Border Region," *Eurasia Insight* (New York: EurasiaNet.org), 18 November 2006, www.eurasianet.org/departments/insight/articles/pp111806.shtml.

[4] *OSCE/ODIHR Election Observation Mission Final Report, Republic of Tajikistan, Parliamentary Elections 27 February and 13 March 2005* (Warsaw: Organization for Security

and Co-operation in Europe [OSCE], Office of Democratic Institutions and Human Rights [ODIHR], 2005), 6, www.osce.org/documents/odihr/2005/05/14852_en.pdf; *OSCE/ODIHR Election Observation Mission Report, Republic of Tajikistan, Presidential Elections 6 November 2006* (OSCE, 2007), www.osce.org/documents/odihr/2007/04 /24067_en.pdf.

5 *OSCE/ODIHR Election Observation Mission Final Report, Republic of Tajikistan, Parliamentary Elections 27 February and 13 March 2005* (OSCE, 2005).

6 Pannier, "After Ruling Party Victory in Tajikistan, What Next?" (Prague and Washington, D.C.: Radio Free Liberty/Radio Liberty [RFE/RL]), 2 March 2005, www.rferl.org /reports/centralasia/2005/03/8-020305.asp.

7 Representatives of IRP claimed they were opting out of the presidential election not only because of the environment in which the election took place but also as a strategy that would limit a backlash against IRP due to fears of rising Islamism in Tajikistan. See Dadojan Azimov, "Islamists Shun Tajik Election with Eye to Future" (London: Institute for War and Peace Reporting [IWPR], RCA No. 467, 5 October 2006), www.iwpr.net/?p =rca&s=f&o=324364&apc_state=henirca2006.

8 "Tajikistan: Opposition Disorganized as Presidential Election Nears" (RFE/RL, 24 August 2006), www.rferl.org/featuresarticle/2006/8/CE926B40-A58F-4215-8171-025BD977EBCE.html.

9 OSCE/ODIHR Election Observation Mission Report, Republic of Tajikistan, Presidential Elections, 6 November 2006 (OSCE, 2007).

10 Pannier, "Tajikistan: Presidential Candidates Take to Campaign Trail—Together," *Eurasia Insight*, 28 October 2006, www.eurasianet.org/departments/insight/articles/pp102806 .shtml.

11 *OSCE/ODIHR Election Observation Mission Report, Republic of Tajikistan, Presidential Elections 6 November 2006* (OSCE, 2007).

12 "Rakhmoniston: kazhdy rodivshchisya v Tadzhikistane stanovitsya rabom ego prezidenta," *Charoghiruz* 1, 113 (2007): 11-14, http://charogiruz.ru/nomer/2007-01/2007-01.pdf.

13 "The Curse of Cotton: Central Asia's Destructive Monoculture" (Brussels: International Crisis Group [ICG], Asia Report No. 93, 28 February 2005), www.crisisgroup.org /library/documents/asia/central_asia/093_curse_of_cotton_central_asia_destructive_ monoculture.pdf.

14 "Tajikistan Country Profile" (The Fund for Peace, 2007), http://www.fundforpeace .org/web/index.php?option=com_content&task=view&id=183&Itemid=312.

15 One source estimated that over 1,200 NGOs registered in 2002 alone. See Sabine Freizer, "Neo-liberal and communal civil society in Tajikistan: merging or dividing in the post war period?," *Central Asian Survey* 24, 3 (September 2005): 227.

16 Ibid.

17 See the chapter on Tajikistan in *Media Sustainability Index 2005* (Washington, D.C.: International Research and Exchanges Board [IREX], 2005), www.irex.org/programs /MSI_EUR/2005/MSI05-Tajikistan.pdf.

[18] "Government controls on news compromise vote in Tajikistan" (New York: Committee to Protect Journalists [CPJ], 2006), www.cpj.org/news/2006/europe/tajik03nov06na .html; "Tajikistan's Beleaguered Media" (IWPR, RCA No. 429, 9 January 2006), www .iwpr.net/?p=rca&s=f&o=258905&apc_state=henirca2006.

[19] "Tajikistan—2006 Annual Report" (Paris: Reporters Without Borders [RSF], 2006), www.rsf.org/article.php3?id_article=17480.

[20] "Human Rights in the OSCE region," *IHF Report 2006* (OSCE, 2006), p. 425, www .ihf-hr.org/viewbinary/viewdocument.php?download=1&doc_id=6865.

[21] "Tajik Government 'Tightening the Screws' on Independent Media," *Eurasia Insight,* 25 August 2006, www.eurasianet.org/departments/insight/articles/eav082506a.shtml.

[22] "Attacks on the Press in 2006: Tajikistan" (CPJ, 2006), www.cpj.org/attacks06/europe06 /taj06.html.

[23] "Government controls on news compromise vote in Tajikistan" (CPJ, 2006).

[24] The three provincial stations were allowed to continue operating only after paying additional broadcast fees and agreeing to air a government program. "Attacks on the Press in 2006: Tajikistan" (CPJ, 2006).

[25] See, for instance, "Djumaboi Tolibov freed after seven months in custody" (Paris: Reporters Without Borders [RSF], 2005), 21 December 2005, http://www.rsf.org /article.php3?id_article=16008

[26] "Tajikistan: Report 2005" (Washington, D.C.: Amnesty International [AI], 2005), http://web.amnesty.org/report2005/tjk-summary-eng. "Tajikistan Report 2007," (Washington, D.C.: Amnesty International [AI], 2007), http://thereport.amnesty.org/eng /Regions/Europe-and-Central-Asia/Tajikistan.

[27] See "OSCE Centre in Dushanbe" (OSCE, 2007), http://www.osce.org/tajikistan /13488.html.

[28] Human Rights in the OSCE region," *IHF Report 2006* (OSCE, 2006), p. 427, www. ihf-hr.org/viewbinary/viewdocument.php?download=1&doc_id=6865.

[29] "World Prison Brief for Tajikistan" (London: Kings College London, International Centre for Prison Studies [ICPS], 20 April 2007), www.kcl.ac.uk/depsta/rel/icps/world brief/continental_asia_records.php?code=113.

[30] "Regional Delegation in Tashkent," *ICRC Annual Report 2005* (Geneva: International Committee of the Red Cross, 1 June 2006), www.icrc.org/Web/Eng/siteeng0.nsf /htmlall/6PNL7H/$FILE/icrc_ar_05_tashkent.pdf?OpenElement.

[31] "Tajik Prison Rioters Get Extended Jail Terms" (RFE/RL, 1 August 2006), www.rferl .org/featuresarticle/2006/8/10F24B5D-D211-4F2A-82FD-7C3BABDE5E21.html; "Tajikistan Report 2007," (Washington, D.C.: Amnesty International [AI], 2007), http: //thereport.amnesty.org/eng/Regions/Europe-and-Central-Asia/Tajikistan.

[32] "Tajikistan: Country Summary," *World Report 2006* (New York: Human Rights Watch [HRW], 2006), http://hrw.org/english/docs/2006/01/18/tajiki12243.htm.

[33] "Tajikistan: Country Summary," *World Report 2007* (HRW, 2007), http://hrw.org /englishwr2k7/docs/2007/01/11/tajiki14827.htm.

[34] For example, women constituted approximately 25 percent of the judges on Tajikistan's Peoples Courts. See SH. M. Ismoilov and M. H. Sa'diev, *Mahomoti Adliya va Sudhoi Tojikiston 75 sol* (Dushanbe: Qonuniyat, 1999).

35 "Women in National Parliaments" (Geneva: Inter-Parliamentary Union [IPU], 31 March 2007), www.ipu.org/wmn-e/classif.htm.

36 Analysis of the Law of the Republic of Tajikistan on State Guarantees of Equal Rights for Men and Women and Equal Opportunities in the Exercise of Such Rights (ABA/ CEELI, September 2005), http://www.untj.org/files/reports/analysis_of_tajik_gender _equality_law.pdf.

37 "The Curse of Cotton: Central Asia's Destructive Monoculture" (ICG), 16–17.

38 "Tajikistan" in *Trafficking in Persons Report* (Washington, D.C.: U.S. Department of State, 5 June 2006), www.state.gov/g/tip/rls/tiprpt/2006/65990.htm.

39 "Tajikistan" in *International Religious Freedom Report 2006* (U.S. Department of State, 15 September 2006), http://www.state.gov/g/drl/rls/irf/2006/71412.htm.

40 "Tajikistan: Country Summary," *World Report 2007* (HRW, 2007), http://hrw.org /englishwr2k7/docs/2007/01/11/tajiki14827.htm.

41 Farangis Najibullah, "Tajikistan: Authorities Exclude Miniskirt, Hejab on Campuses" *Eurasia Insight*, 25 April 2007, http://www.eurasianet.org/departments/insight/articles /pp041507.shtml.

42 "Tajikistan" in *International Religious Freedom Report 2005* (U.S. Department of State, 8 November 2005), www.state.gov/g/drl/rls/irf/2005/51585.htm.

43 Emmanuel Karagiannis, "The Challenge of Radical Islam in Tajikistan: Hizb ut-Tahrir al-Islami," *Nationalities Papers* 34, 1 (March 2006): 2.

44 Hizb ut-Tahrir calls for the establishment of an Islamic state, and thus violates Tajikistan's Constitution and criminal code. However, without transparency in court proceedings, there is no way to determine whether the basis of convictions is established intent to overthrow the state or merely alleged membership in the organization.

45 Ibid.

46 Gulnoza Saidazimova, "Central Asia: Radical Islamists Challenge Government Efforts at Control (Part 3)" (RFE/RL, 8 August 2005), http://www.rferl.org/specials/religion /archive/central-asia3.asp.

47 "Country Profile on Disabilities: Tajikistan" (Tokyo: Japan International Cooperation Agency [JICA], March 2002), 7, http://siteresources.worldbank.org/DISABILITY /Resources/Regions/ECA/JICA_Tajikistan.pdf.

48 K. Osipyan, "Trade unions of Tajikistan and Russia should deal with labor migration problems together," *Avesta/Tajikistan News* 15 February 2007, http://www.avesta.tj/en /articles/20/5870.html.

49 International Service for Human Rights, "Committee Against Torture: 37th Session 6–24 November 2006, Republic of Tajikistan (Initial Report)," 20 November 2006, http://www.ishr.ch/hrm/tmb/treaty/cat/reports/cat_37/cat_37_tajikistan.pdf.

50 For numerous examples of this, see Erica Marat, "The State-Crime Nexus in Central Asia: State Weakness, Organized Crime, and Corruption in Kyrgyzstan and Tajikistan," *Silk Road Paper* (October 2006): 1–137, www.silkroadstudies.org/new/docs/Silkroad papers/0610EMarat.pdf.

51 A highly active court does not necessarily indicate greater institutional capacity. Increased activity may reflect either the autonomy of the judiciary or the ability of procurators and criminal groups to use the court to their advantage. "Recent Legal Developments in

Tajikistan: February 2006" (Chicago: American Bar Association, Central European and Eurasian Law Initiative [ABA/CEELI]), www.abanet.org/ceeli/countries/tajikistan/feb 2006.html.

52   Legal Profession Reform Index [LPRI] for Tajikistan (ABA/CEELI, September 2005), www.abanet.org/ceeli/publications/lpri/lpri_tajikistan_2006.pdf.

53   Ibid.

54   Johan Engvall, "The State Under Siege: The Drug Trade and Organised Crime in Tajikistan," *Europe-Asia Studies* 58, 6 (September 2006): 827–854.

55   "Tajikistan Report 2007," (Washington, D.C.: Amnesty International [AI], 2007), http://thereport.amnesty.org/eng/Regions/Europe-and-Central-Asia/Tajikistan.

56   "The Curse of Cotton: Central Asia's Destructive Monoculture" (ICG), 14–15.

57   *Corruption Perceptions Index 2006* (Berlin: Transparency International [TI], 2006), http://www.transparency.org/news_room/in_focus/2006/cpi_2006__1/cpi_table.

58   Daniel Kimmage, "Tajikistan: No Surprises Expected in Presidential Election," *Eurasia Insight*, 5 November 2006, www.eurasianet.org/departments/insight/articles/pp100506 .shtml.

59   Akbar Sharifi, "Tajikistan's Lacklustre Anti-Corruption Effort" (IWPR, RCA No. 333, 10 December 2004), http://iwpr.net/?p=rca&s=f&o=162110&apc_state=henirca2004.

60   "Regional Anti-Corruption Action Plan: Tajikistan" (Paris: OECD Directorate for Financial, Fiscal and Enterprise Affairs, Anti-corruption Network for Transition Economies, 21 January 2004), 2–3, http://unpan1.un.org/intradoc/groups/public/documents /UNTC/UNPAN018019.pdf.

61   BISNIS, "Tajikistan's Investment Climate Report (Dushanbe: U.S. Embassy, 18 October 2003), www.fdi.net/documents/WorldBank/databases/tajikist/TAJ_Inv_climate_ by_BISNIS_US_2003.pdf.

62   "Doing Business Report 2007—Where Tajikistan Stands?" (World Bank, 2007), http:// web.worldbank.org/WBSITE/EXTERNAL/COUNTRIES/ECAEXT/TAJIKISTAN EXTN/0,,contentMDK:21119498~pagePK:141137~piPK:141127~theSitePK:2587 44,00.html.

63   "Tajikistan: Update on Action to Implement Recommendations" (OECD Directorate for Financial, Fiscal and Enterprise Affairs, Istanbul Anti-Corruption Plan, 13 December 2006), 6, www.oecd.org/dataoecd/11/3/38011697.pdf.

64   "Staff Assessment of Qualification for the Multilateral Debt Relief Initiative—Republic of Tajikistan" (Washington, D.C.: International Monetary Fund, 8 December 2005), 3, www.internationalmonetaryfund.com/external/np/pp/eng/2005/TJK.pdf.

65   Personal interview with Ilkhom Hakimov, Head of Economic Division, Ministry of Agriculture, Dushanbe, 16 December 2002. This data is also omitted from Ministry of Statistics publications.

66   Sabina-Margarita Dzalaeva, "Foreign Aid Management and the State Budget Cycle in Tajikistan," News 2007 xiv, 1 (Winter 2007), http://www.nispa.sk/_portal/files/publications /newsletter/NISPAceeNews_winter_2007.pdf.

67   "Legal Protections and Barriers on the Right to Information, State Secrets and the Protection of Sources in OSCE Participating States" (London: Privacy International, 2 May 2007), http://www.privacyinternational.org/foi/OSCE-access-analysis.pdf.

THAILAND

CAPITAL: Bangkok
POPULATION: 65.7 million
GNI PER CAPITA: $2,990

SCORES	2005	2007
ACCOUNTABILITY AND PUBLIC VOICE:	4.04	2.99
CIVIL LIBERTIES:	3.72	3.65
RULE OF LAW:	4.22	3.79
ANTICORRUPTION AND TRANSPARENCY:	3.48	3.43

(scores are based on a scale of 0 to 7, with 0 representing weakest and 7 representing strongest performance)

Duncan McCargo

INTRODUCTION

From September 1992 until September 2006, Thailand followed a troubled but broadly liberal political path. The country turned its back on a long history of military-dominated politics exemplified by the February 1991 coup d'etat, which had culminated in the deaths of dozens of unarmed protesters on the streets of Bangkok in May 1992. In 1997, Thailand promulgated a hard-won "people's constitution," the product of years of elite bargaining and an unprecedented exercise in popular consultation. The core agenda of the constitution-drafters was to create legal mechanisms that would help institutionalize a stable and relatively clean form of representative politics. These mechanisms centered on a set of independent institutions that were supposed to curtail abuses of power and reduce the well-established dominance of money in the country's electoral politics.

Duncan McCargo is Professor of Southeast Asian politics at the University of Leeds in the United Kingdom. His most recent books on Thailand are *The Thaksinization of Thailand* (with Ukrist Pathmanand) (NIAS, 2005) and *Rethinking Thailand's Southern Violence* (edited, Singapore University Press, 2007).

Instead, the new constitution ushered in the premiership of Thaksin Shinawatra, a wealthy telecommunications magnate backed by a large catch-all political party, Thai Rak Thai (TRT: Thais Love Thais). Without amending a word of the 1997 constitution, Thaksin proceeded systematically to subvert it. He bragged publicly that his landslide election victories in January 2001 and February 2005 gave him an unprecedented mandate, a legitimacy that trumped that of the Constitutional Court and other bodies. Thaksin actively re-politicized the military, installing his old friends, classmates, and relatives in key positions. Most important, he often appeared ready to challenge the prerogatives of the king—an unprecedented stance for a recent Thai prime minister.

By 2006, Thaksin's bold and assertive leadership style had divided the nation. He was still supported by tens of millions of Thais, especially by rural dwellers in the north and northeast, who admired his populist programs and saw him as a champion of the poor and the voiceless. Indeed, Thaksin had no serious political rivals, either inside or outside TRT. However, most of the Bangkok elite and middle classes, as well as residents of the south, became deeply alienated by his authoritarian leadership style and by growing allegations of corruption.

A turning point came in January 2006, when Thaksin sold his family's telecom holdings to Temasek, a Singaporean investment company. The deal raised serious questions about conflicts of interest and placed Thaksin under intense political pressure. He reacted by dissolving Parliament in the hope of securing a third landslide victory, but the tactic backfired when the opposition boycotted the election. The election degenerated into farce and was eventually annulled by the courts, following advice by the king. Thaksin promised to step down from the position of prime minister—even handing over day-to-day authority to one of his deputies for a time—but never actually resigned.[1]

For a time, many leading intellectuals were calling for the king to dismiss Thaksin and establish a royally appointed government, but the monarch declined to do so. A fresh election was eventually scheduled for October 15, 2006. However, on September 19, a military junta known as the Council for National Security (CNS) staged an anachronistic coup d'etat, overturning all the progress toward political liberalization that had taken place during the 1990s, apparently with the full blessing of the palace. In time-honored fashion, the coup-makers immediately abrogated the 1997 charter and announced that they would need a year to oversee the preparation of a new constitution and fresh elections. The CNS leadership cited several reasons for their putsch, including: Thaksin's divisiveness, his actions "bordering on lèse majesté," concerns about corruption, and his government's lack of respect for the 1997 constitution—a curious charge, given that the CNS themselves had summarily abolished this very constitution.[2] The CNS appointed Surayudh Chulanont, a former army commander and member of the Privy Council, to the post of prime minister. He proceeded to appoint a cabinet comprising mainly conservative ex-bureaucrats. The CNS also established a National Legislative Assembly—a non-elected Parliament— and a set of bodies charged with preparing a new constitution. A provisional constitution was announced as an interim measure. A national referendum on the draft constitution was promised.

Initially, the CNS won considerable popular support; leading Thai commentators hailed the coup as a necessary evil that had removed Thaksin from office without recourse to political violence. Yet the new government failed to act decisively against the former prime minister, and from his roving exile Thaksin was able to outmaneuver and disconcert Surayudh and the military. Thailand remained in a deep political crisis as Thaksin's allies regrouped, and the new government appeared to lack a clear vision for restoring representative democratic politics or managing the economy.

ACCOUNTABILITY AND PUBLIC VOICE

FREE AND FAIR ELECTORAL LAWS AND ELECTIONS:	2.25
EFFECTIVE AND ACCOUNTABLE GOVERNMENT:	2.75
CIVIC ENGAGEMENT AND CIVIC MONITORING:	4.33
MEDIA INDEPENDENCE AND FREEDOM OF EXPRESSION:	2.63
CATEGORY AVERAGE:	**2.99**

Prior to the 2006 coup, Thailand had a rather open political order, and power had rotated among a number of political parties during the previous fourteen years. Most parties, however, do not represent genuine ideological or policy alternatives but are little more than interest groups closely associated with powerful political faction bosses and cliques.

Given the merger of smaller parties with the ruling TRT, by the February 2005 elections political choice had been reduced to only three parties: TRT, the Democrats, and the small Muanchon Party. Parties were equally free to campaign, but the overwhelming dominance of TRT gave the incumbent considerable advantages. Major opposition parties boycotted a snap general election held in April 2006, arguing that Thaksin's dissolution of Parliament was an unjustified ploy to retain power.

Under the 1997 constitution, a powerful Election Commission (EC) was established, with extensive powers to manage, oversee, and regulate the electoral process. However, despite the existence of campaign finance laws and state support for political parties through the EC, much campaign spending went toward vote buying and other illegal activities that were never declared. Accordingly, candidates with strong financial backing possessed a considerable advantage.

The EC made little serious attempt to monitor spending by political parties. After May 2001, the original, highly interventionist team of five national election commissioners was completely replaced. Their successors were far less independent-minded and pursued very few complaints following the February 2005 elections. After the controversial April 2006 general election, allegations were widespread that the EC had favored TRT, and numerous calls were made for the commissioners to resign. Their resignations were only forthcoming in June, after they were arrested and briefly jailed on charges of mismanaging the election.

The EC was abolished following the September 19 coup. TRT (as well as the opposition Democrats) faced legal proceedings for electoral irregularities—primarily the hiring of fake opposition candidates in the April 2006 election—that had the potential to cause the party's dissolution. [UPDATE: TRT was eventually dissolved by the courts in May 2007, and all of the party's executive members, including Thaksin, were banned from political office for five years. Residual elements of TRT began scrambling to create a range of new parties.]

The 1997 constitutional arrangements were deliberately constructed to create a system of checks and balances, primarily through a nonpartisan Senate (whose members are barred from party affiliation) and a range of independent agencies, including the Election Commission, the Constitutional Court, the Administrative Court, and the National Counter-Corruption Commission. Unfortunately, the reality was rather different. The first Senate was full of the wives, children, and associates of politicians, as well as a large contingent of former government officials, many with close personal and financial ties to party leaders and cliques of members of parliament (MPs).[3] Only a handful of Thailand's senators, who served between 2000 and 2006, consistently performed the kind of monitoring role envisaged by the constitution. A second group of senators elected in April 2006 appeared even less independent, but the coup meant that the new Senate was never convened. At the time of writing, the future of an elected Senate under a new constitution looked highly uncertain.

Similar problems characterized many of the post-1997 independent agencies. The Thaksin government sought, often successfully, to politicize the process of appointments to these agencies. Given the weakness of the Senate and other bodies, dominant power interests such as the ruling TRT were exposed to limited critical scrutiny. Most civil service posts are gained through open appointment procedures, although some processes—notably for the police and the interior ministry—have been tainted by persistent reports of cheating. Immediately after the September 2006 coup, most of the independent agencies were summarily abolished, except for the auditor general.

Civic groups are able to comment relatively freely on policy issues and legislation, and many have been very influential. At the same time, formal mechanisms for consultation remain weak; despite a recent vogue for public hearings, the government has tended to rely on ad hoc consultation structures, which produce arbitrary outcomes. The longer Thaksin remained in office, the less attention his government paid to critical views from civil society bodies. For example, the outspoken Thailand Development Research Institute (TDRI), a technocratic think tank employing many of the country's top economists, was marginalized for refusing to accept the TRT line. In March 2005, Thaksin himself set up a high-powered National Reconciliation Commission (NRC) packed with the great and the good to propose policy alternatives to address the growing political violence in the country's Muslim-majority southern border provinces, which claimed hundreds of lives in the period following January 4, 2004. After the NRC submitted its report in June 2006, however, Thaksin apparently did not even read the document.[4] Privy Council president Prem Tinsulanond was critical of the NRC report, rejecting the proposal that Malay be adopted as a working language in the south.[5] In the period following the 2006 coup, civic organizations struggled to find a clear role; any statements that implied criticism of the Surayudh government tended to be construed as expressing opposition to the coup and closet support for Thaksin. This crude bifurcation of public discourse made open debate difficult.

The Thaksin government also put pressure on major funders of civic organizations, including the progressively inclined Thai Health Fund, which derives its income from a hypothecated excise tax on alcohol and tobacco products. Because there are demanding requirements for nongovernmental organization (NGO) registration under legislation dating from 1942, most NGOs are not formally registered with the interior ministry. In practice, legal registration is not required, and Thailand has one of the most vigorous NGO communities in Southeast Asia. Activists aligned with the NGO movement played a leading role in the 2005–2006 anti-Thaksin movement, which involved a series of mass rallies in Bangkok and other major cities. The government sought to intimidate anti-Thaksin demonstrators, sometimes resorting to crude forms of violence.[6] The post-September 2006 coup group has made extensive use of martial law provisions to curtail political gatherings, but the government recently permitted some demonstrations by organizations critical of the coup.

Electronic media are largely controlled by the state and have always been subject to considerable political interference. Radio frequencies remain dominated by the military, supposedly for reasons of national security, but in practice because they are a lucrative source of revenues. Attempts to reform control of the airwaves have so far failed. The CNS has persistently sought to curtail internet materials critical of the new government.

Thailand has a long tradition of vigorous and critical print media, with a parallel tradition of press manipulation and cooptation by power-holders. The Thaksin government was widely criticized for putting pressure on critical media voices—such as the English-language daily *The Nation* and the small but outspoken Thai-language daily *Thai Post*—and for using a combination of sticks and carrots to promote more favorable coverage.[7]

Print media are not directly funded by the state, but the Thaksin administration ensured that progovernment newspapers carried the bulk of state-funded advertising. Media ownership in Thailand is also a problematic issue; there are persistent rumors that prominent figures close to the government have acquired formal or informal ownership of elements in the print media. The CNS and the Surayudh government used a variety of measures to muzzle the media, including positioning tanks outside the offices of leading newspapers, and "advising" the press not to publicize the activities of Thaksin and his supporters after his deposal. The Surayudh government also blocked the popular website YouTube because of a controversial video clip that portrayed the Thai king in a negative light. The Ministry of Culture has recently become increasingly active in policing cultural expression in Thailand through a newly established Cultural Surveillance Center, which played a role in banning an English-language book about Thailand containing images deemed improper.[8] While Thaksin's government was adept at backdoor means of controlling and influencing media, Surayudh tended to revert to older forms of direct censorship.

Thai libel laws are deeply problematic: those charged with libel may face immediate imprisonment if they are unable to produce the large sums typically required for bail. Politicians and their associates have not hesitated to harass critics through use of these punitive laws. During the height of the 2005–2006 anti-Thaksin movement, politically motivated lawsuits flowed thick and fast. The king criticized such lawsuits in his December 2005 birthday speech, prompting Thaksin to drop six criminal and civil cases brought against leading critic Sondhi Limthongkul.[9]

Although there is considerable freedom of cultural and political expression in Thailand, a notable exception lies in lèse majesté laws, which outlaw all criticism of the royal family. These laws were increasingly politicized during the political unrest of 2005 and 2006. After Thaksin dropped regular lawsuits against Sondhi, Thaksin loyalists among the police proceeded to charge him with lèse majesté.[10] Later, in an ironic reversal, the September 19 coup-makers made Thaksin's alleged acts of lèse majesté one of their justifications for seizing power.[11] In October 2006, Surayudh's principal aide urged people to desist from criticizing the new cabinet lineup, as such criticisms could constitute lèse majesté.[12]

Recommendations

- A new constitution is urgently needed that retains most of the key provisions of the 1997 constitution. In particular, independent agencies must be restored to provide checks and balances and curtail future abuses of power.

- Free and fair elections should be held as quickly as possible, allowing the military to focus solely their professional role as the guardians of national security.
- Some form of national broadcasting commission to allocate radio frequencies should be established without further delay, and the commission should ensure that control of radio frequencies is completely removed from the military.
- Thailand's libel laws should be urgently overhauled so that those accused of libel do not face imprisonment and cannot be forced to pay disproportionate levels of damages.
- Thailand's lèse majesté laws should be amended to ensure that they cannot be exploited for political purposes.

CIVIL LIBERTIES

PROTECTION FROM STATE TERROR, UNJUSTIFIED IMPRISONMENT, AND TORTURE:	3.00
GENDER EQUITY:	3.75
RIGHTS OF ETHNIC, RELIGIOUS, AND OTHER DISTINCT GROUPS:	3.50
FREEDOM OF CONSCIENCE AND BELIEF:	4.00
FREEDOM OF ASSOCIATION AND ASSEMBLY:	4.00
CATEGORY AVERAGE:	**3.65**

Despite constitutional injunctions against it, torture and abuses of pretrial detainees by both police and military agencies continue, especially in relation to rural protest movements and alleged drug offenders. Punishment of state officials for such abuses is very rare. Pretrial detention for up to eighty-four days is widely used in criminal cases, and extensions may be requested for complex cases. Thai prisoners are kept in poor conditions: they sometimes have to pay for a space to sleep (even on the floor) and generally need money from outside in order to obtain reasonable food.[13] International monitors claim that prisoners are often shackled in leg irons, despite the fact that this is illegal, and trusted convicts are sometimes allowed to beat fellow prisoners.[14] No state officials have faced arrest, prosecution, or trial for acts of torture.

Murders of local politicians, journalists, and activists occur regularly in Thailand. Between February 2001 and the end of 2005, eighteen human rights defenders were murdered, yet Thaksin publicly urged human rights activists in Thailand not to "sink the boat" by reporting abuses to the international community.[15] The arbitrary arrest of demonstrators is a widespread practice. During the Thaksin period, citizens were at risk from nonstate actors using hired thugs to enforce land clearances and other actions.

The most serious assault on civil liberties in modern Thai history was the 2003 war on drugs, an apparently officially sanctioned policy of extrajudicial killing that involved some 2,500 deaths in its initial three months. While the authorities implausibly claimed that most of these killings resulted from drug dealers turning their weapons on each other, there was ample evidence of widespread official collusion in numerous murders.[16] To date, no proper investigation of the war on drugs has taken place, no list of its victims has been published, and no one has been brought to trial over the extrajudicial killings—though the Surayudh government has mooted such actions.

A further area of concern relates to the government's handling of political violence in the southern border provinces since January 2004. Around 80 percent of the populations of Pattani, Yala, and Narathiwat provinces are Malay Muslims, whose first language is not Thai. This region has been characterized by longstanding yet sporadic separatist violence. The Thaksin government dismantled the existing security command structure in May 2002, placing the police in charge of maintaining order. Tensions mounted following a large-scale attack on an army base on January 4, 2004, and a spate of shootings and small explosions followed. Martial law was subsequently imposed in these provinces. By February 2007, over 2,000 people had been killed in political violence; some had been murdered by the security forces or had disappeared, while many others apparently met their deaths at the hands of Muslim extremists.[17] Many others had been injured. Victims included Buddhist monks, Islamic teachers, government schoolteachers, village leaders, a judge, a deputy governor, and a prominent Muslim senator.

The National Human Rights Commission received complaints of beatings and abductions associated with heavy-handed raids on Muslim communities, including Islamic boarding schools, or *pondok*. Somchai

Neelaphaijit, an activist lawyer from the area, accused the police of torturing five suspects charged with involvement in the January army base raid, a claim that was verified by the Commission. On March 12, 2004, Somchai disappeared; although five police officers were charged with his abduction and one was sentenced to a three-year jail term in January 2006, the other four were acquitted for lack of evidence, and his murder remains unsolved.[18] In late 2006, however, the Department of Special Investigations seemed to be closer to resolving the case, and Army Commander Sonthi Boonyaratglin told reporters: "I have received information from investigators that some individuals close to former prime minister Thaksin were behind the disappearance of Somchai."[19] The authorities confirmed that Somchai had been murdered. Somchai's widow Angkhana was later appointed one of the charter drafters for the new constitution.

On April 28, 2004, 106 Muslim men and five security officers were killed when groups of lightly armed militants launched a coordinated attack on eleven security positions in the southern border provinces of Pattani, Yala, and Songkla. The day's events culminated in a siege of the historic Kru-Ze mosque in Pattani, where thirty-two Muslim men were killed by commandos, allegedly at point-blank range. Although an investigation found that the military had used excessive force, the prime minister refused to accept the resignation of General Pallop Pinmanee, the officer who ordered this attack.[20] Pallop responded by publishing a bestselling book defending his actions.[21] Matters worsened considerably when eighty-four Muslim protesters died in events arising from a demonstration on October 25, 2004, outside a police station in Tak Bai, Narathiwat province. The authorities claimed that seventy-eight of the deceased had died as a result of suffocation after they were arrested and piled into army trucks. An investigation was highly critical of the military commanders responsible but concluded that the deaths were unintentional.[22]

The Tak Bai events triggered an international outcry, partly because of Thaksin's inept handling of the issue and failure to apologize properly for the deaths. Surayudh made a full public apology in November 2006.[23] Human rights groups continued to highlight occasional suspicious disappearances and extrajudicial killings during 2005 and 2006, although such cases had apparently declined markedly. After Tak Bai, the security forces adopted a less confrontational approach to mass protests in the south, usually seeking to disperse demonstrators through negotiations.

Emergency legislation hastily introduced in August 2005 allowed suspects in security cases to be held for up to thirty days without charge; these provisions have been used extensively in the southern border provinces.[24] The law also allows for prisoners to be held in irregular places of detention and grants immunity from prosecution to enforcement officials accused of human rights violations. The emergency legislation was widely criticized by lawyers and human rights organizations both inside and beyond Thailand.[25] In principle, the emergency legislation could be implemented anywhere in the country, including Bangkok, and used to curtail public protest and gag the media.

The 1997 constitution gave citizens the right to petition the president of the Senate for the removal of national politicians or high-ranking officials accused of corruption or abuses of power (Article 304), but the procedure was never successfully invoked, partly because 50,000 signatures were required. Citizens may also bring complaints to independent agencies such as the Counter-Corruption or Human Rights commissions, both of which were overwhelmed by the number of cases referred to them. The credibility of the NCCC was seriously undermined in 2005, when the nine commissioners were given two-year suspended jail terms for illegally raising their own salaries.[26] The body ceased to function until it was reestablished by the Surayudh government, by which time a backlog of more than 10,000 cases had built up.

Under the 1997 constitution, the state was committed to promoting equal rights between men and women (Article 80) and to supporting individuals with disabilities and underprivileged people. Thailand has a very high level of female participation in the labor force—65 percent—but in 2005 around 10 percent of MPs and senators were female, and only two out of thirty-six cabinet ministers.[27] In the Surayudh government, only one ministry was headed by a woman.[28] While around two-thirds of civil servants are female, only 20.2 percent of those in the top three civil service grades (9, 10, and 11) were women, and only 9.7 percent in the top grade (11).[29] Some women are now serving as ambassadors (19 percent),[30] but the important positions of provincial governor (1.4 percent) and district officer (0.3 percent) remain overwhelmingly dominated by men.[31] Only ten of the one hundred members of the new constitution-drafting assembly were women.

A number of constitutional provisions support gender equality, but changes in both legislation and practice are needed in relation to issues such as rape and domestic violence, which are often not taken seriously or handled sensitively by the police. According to a Labor Ministry survey, women are paid around 17 percent less than men—a figure that compares favorably with those in many developed countries. Despite legislation forbidding trafficking in people, Thailand is a major nexus for human trafficking, notably from Burma, Cambodia, China, Laos, and to a lesser extent, Vietnam. Much of this trafficking involves placing women and children in the lucrative Thai sex industry, though some of those trafficked are employed in sweatshops, agriculture, construction, and fisheries. The state has made some efforts to tackle the problem by prosecuting offenders and protecting some victims, but there have been no recent prosecutions of police officers or other government officials, some of whom are believed to be implicated in the trade.

Racial discrimination was also prohibited by the 1997 constitution (Article 30), but there was no specific mention of ethnic minorities. This reflects the official view that all Thais are simply Thai and a persistent tendency to deny the significance of ethnic difference. Chapter III of the 1997 constitution was explicitly titled "Rights and liberties of the Thai people," thereby excluding all noncitizens from exercising those rights. As one informant told Amnesty International, "The Thai constitution does not apply to me, because I am an ethnic minority."[32]

Many ethnic minority peoples in the northern highland areas of Thailand are not Thai citizens and have been subject to persistent discrimination; similar problems apply in the case of Burmese refugees and illegal workers from Cambodia. The estimated half million Karen or other so-called hill tribe people lack Thai citizenship and are effectively stateless. Many are unable to prove that they were born in Thailand, while others are similarly unable to claim Burmese citizenship. Like Burmese migrants working illegally in Thailand, these groups are vulnerable to arbitrary arrest.[33] The predicament of such groups was highlighted by the arrest in Hong Kong of a stateless man from the Thai-Burmese border region; the Thai government refused to repatriate him.[34] Many Muslims, especially in the southern border provinces, have a poor command of the central Thai language, which further restricts their already limited economic opportunities. The Thai state has been slow to recognize the need to address issues of discrimination on racial and ethnic grounds; for many local government officials, minority groups are stereotyped as sources of insecurity, crime, and social problems, to be dealt with by forcible incorporation into Thai cultural norms.[35]

Discrimination against people with disabilities is illegal under the constitution but widespread in practice, and many public buildings lack proper access. In one widely publicized recent case, a law graduate who suffered some slight disabilities from childhood polio was barred from sitting for the examination to become a judge. The government has a poor record of making information available to people with disabilities through, for example, braille or audio versions of important documents. On the positive side, sign language is widely used to accompany television broadcasts. Overall, the government's record on enforcing equality issues is mixed.

In theory, Thais enjoy freedom of religion, and religious observance is not restricted. However, the Thai state exercises control over the *sangha* (Buddhist order) and has moved to exclude dissident religious groups from the officially sanctioned order. In other words, the state has arrogated to itself the right to determine what does and does not constitute true Buddhism.[36] During 2007, there was renewed debate about designating Buddhism as the national religion.

In 2006, a former minister assumed the supposedly independent role of secretary-general of the Islamic Council of Thailand, allegedly claiming in a television interview that Thaksin had assigned him to this position.[37] Since 2002, Islamic, Christian, and other religious groups have been overseen by the Department of Religion (part of the Ministry of Culture), while a National Office of Buddhism is located in the office of the prime minister. Registering a new Christian church in Thailand is virtually impossible, as the Department of Religion asks the existing registered churches whether new applicants should be regarded as genuine Christians, with predictable results.[38] As a result, many Christian and other religious organizations operate without formal registration.[39]

Freedom of association is broadly respected in Thailand, although levels of unionization remain low (at less than 2 percent of the total workforce) except in state enterprises, where more than half of employees are union members. Although people are free to join unions, there is evidence that some employers have dismissed union leaders or executive members. When such cases were brought to government-backed tribunals, the union activists received back pay but employers were not otherwise penalized. The Thaksin government failed to fulfill its 2001 election pledges to ratify International Labor Organization conventions 87 and 98 on freedom of association and collective bargaining.

There is no evidence of citizens being forced by the state to join particular associations. The right to peaceful organization and mobilization is generally widely practiced and respected, but the state has supported harsh repression of certain kinds of protest movements, particularly anti-development movements and those opposing the Thaksin government. In 2006, Thaksin supporters also mobilized pro-Thaksin demonstrations to counter political moves against him.

Recommendations

- A review of prison conditions should be made, and inhumane practices such as shackling prisoners in leg irons should be rooted out.
- Thailand should immediately hold a full public inquiry into the circumstances surrounding the war on drugs of 2003 and the extrajudicial killings associated with it.
- Firm action should be taken against state officials allegedly responsible for human rights abuses, torture, and disappearances in the south, including criminal trials where appropriate.
- The 2005 emergency legislation should be repealed.
- Full citizenship rights should be granted to all members of Karen and so-called hill tribe minority groups who are long-term residents of Thailand.

RULE OF LAW

INDEPENDENT JUDICIARY:	4.60
PRIMACY OF RULE OF LAW IN CIVIL AND CRIMINAL MATTERS:	4.67
ACCOUNTABILITY OF SECURITY FORCES AND MILITARY TO CIVILIAN AUTHORITIES:	2.00
PROTECTION OF PROPERTY RIGHTS:	4.33
EQUAL TREATMENT UNDER THE LAW:	3.33
CATEGORY AVERAGE:	**3.79**

Thailand's judiciary is generally independent but also sometimes corrupt. This skews the justice system based on the suspect's ability to pay bribes, leading to structural inequalities and often allowing the guilty to walk free. A national survey in 2000 found that a third of those who had been involved in court cases had been asked to pay bribes to secure a favorable outcome. Of the bribes, 47 percent were paid to public prosecutors, 15 percent directly to judges, and 29 percent to other court officials, some of whom may have been acting on behalf of judges.[40]

The Economist Intelligence Unit suggests that government interference in the judiciary is increasing. Despite a series of widely publicized fraud cases in the 1990s—such as the collapse of the Bangkok Bank of Commerce, in which a number of prominent politicians were implicated—not a single conviction had been achieved by the end of 2002.[41] Well-publicized criminal cases, such as the 2004 acquittal of a politician's son on charges of murdering a policeman, have undermined public confidence in the judicial system.[42] However, in several high-profile security cases, judges appeared to act independently and rejected political pressures to convict. In 2005, such cases included those against Dr. Waemahadi Wae-daoi, a Narathiwat doctor accused of terrorist offenses, and Najmuddin Ummar, a southern TRT MP who had been accused of treason.[43]

The Appeal Court—sometimes referred to as "the money court"[44]—has had a particularly problematic reputation. The Central Bankruptcy Court has also been criticized for making politicized decisions that undermined the confidence of foreign investors.[45] However, Thailand's strict contempt-of-court laws—which apply outside the courtroom—make open discussion of the judicial system very difficult. This, in turn, curtails critical reporting where abuses in the legal process may be widely suspected. Thaksin's lawyer was charged with contempt of court for his criticisms of some 2006 verdicts concerning the EC.[46] Successive Thai governments have always complied with judicial decisions.

All career judges must be qualified as barristers, have no less than two years of legal experience, and pass a difficult and competitive examination before being appointed as trainee judges for a trial period of one year. There is no jury system, and notes dictated by judges themselves constitute the only formal record of court proceedings, a practice that makes appeals difficult to substantiate. Judges are generally held in high regard in Thai society. In a major policy statement, the Surayudh government identified the "nonpolitical" professional judiciary (in contrast with judges of the Constitutional Court, whose appointments have been politicized) as the most dependable institution in Thailand.[47] Relative to other Thai institutions, the judiciary has a clean and positive image.

Article 33 of the constitution specifies that criminal suspects are presumed innocent until convicted. Citizens have the right to a fair trial with independent counsel. Despite these provisions, extrajudicial killings have taken place in recent years, notably in the southern border provinces. Those accused of serious crimes are provided with lawyers by the state if they cannot afford to pay for their own defense. However, these court-appointed lawyers are often recent graduates with little experience in conducting a defense.[48] Thammasat University runs an active legal aid and legal literacy program. There are persistent allegations that prosecutors are sometimes subject to political influence.

Leading politicians (including a former prime minister and the former secretary-general of the ruling Democrat Party) and senior officials have been tried on corruption-related charges by the Constitutional Court, although its judgments have been criticized as erratic,[49] especially the controversial acquittal of Prime Minister Thaksin on charges of asset concealment in 2001.[50] Full written judgments were sometimes not published for up to a year after Constitutional Court decisions, thereby undermining the court's credibility. The CNS abolished the Constitutional Court on September 19, 2006; it remains unclear whether a similar body will be established.

The Thai military (mainly the army) has attempted and successfully staged numerous coups since the end of the absolute monarchy in 1932. Until the violence of May 1992, the military was a prominent and outspoken participant in the political processes of the country. After 1992, the military returned reluctantly to the barracks, maintaining a low profile but retaining various economic and other privileges. In the face of rising discontent with the Thaksin government and a deteriorating security situation in the south, the military grew increasingly assertive during 2005 and 2006 and finally seized power in a bloodless coup d'état on the night of September 19, 2006.

Despite much talk of security sector reform, no substantive changes have been enacted. Civilian politicians have remained wary of interfering with the military's internal workings, despite general recognition that the armed forces are bloated (with an estimated 1,400 generals) and of doubtful professional competence. The Thaksin government pursued a policy of co-opting the military, and relatives and former classmates of the prime minister were appointed to numerous key positions.[51] In the process, however, he alienated rival military factions and destabilized the army, thereby helping create the conditions for the 2006 coup that toppled him.

As an ex-police officer himself, Thaksin enjoyed good relations with the police force, enlisting it in support of various government initiatives. Both the military and the police enjoy close relationships with a range of actors engaged in legal and illegal business activities. The Asian Human Rights Commission has claimed that making complaints against the police is virtually impossible: they cite the case of a Saraburi man trying to pursue serious charges of extortion, illegal detention, and other offenses against a group of police officers. Although he complained to more than nine different institutions and agencies, he was unable to obtain any redress.[52] The military coup of September 2006 has further eroded the accountability of the armed forces, since future elected politicians will be more wary of challenging military privileges and abuses.

The Surayudh government has mooted a complete restructuring of the police. Longstanding rivalries between the police and the military may have contributed to the deteriorating security situation in the south. Police and military officers have rarely been held accountable for abuses of power or violations of human rights, as illustrated by prominent recent cases relating to the south: Somchai, Krue Se, and Tak Bai.

Property rights are recognized in law, although in practice the system of land title deeds is complex, and many poor people do not have proper ownership of the land they farm. Many hold so-called Sor Tor Kor deeds, or usufructuary land licenses.[53] Abuse of land and contractual rights by local elites and corrupt officials is widespread in rural areas, and structural corruption in the legal system often disempowers the poor.

The Economist Intelligence Unit describes Thai courts as "generally competent and effective in enforcing property and contractual rights," but notes that "extra-legal means" may complicate cases involving wealthy or powerful individuals.[54] Problems are exacerbated by legal provisions that allow people to sell land provisionally yet retain the right to redeem it. Many sell their land in this way, only to discover that in practice their redemption rights are almost impossible to exercise.[55]

The Sor Pho Kho 4-01 land reform program in the 1990s resulted in many local elites improperly obtaining lands that were supposed to be allocated to poor farmers. Local traditions of common land usage have been widely overridden by the state; the Kho Jo Ko program of the 1980s and early 1990s saw many poor farming communities forcibly evicted from lands designated as reserve forest areas, despite their having lived on them for decades or even generations.[56]

For the most part, discrimination on grounds of gender, sexual orientation, or ethnic origin is not illegal in Thailand, and the 1997 constitution explicitly differentiated between the rights of nationals and non-nationals.

Recommendations

- A special investigative team should be created to identify corrupt judges and prosecutors, who should be swiftly suspended and then dismissed from office.
- A substantive program of security sector reform is needed, first concentrating on the core objective of reducing the number of generals— a problem that underpins a culture of military privilege.
- A new independent agency should be created to police the police, with an emphasis on identifying and removing officers deeply involved in the illegal economy.
- Land tenure needs to be reformed so that wherever possible those who actually farm the land own the land, and laws need to be rewritten to allow farmers to borrow money without having to hand over their land to predatory creditors and local elites.

ANTICORRUPTION AND TRANSPARENCY

ENVIRONMENT TO PROTECT AGAINST CORRUPTION:	3.00
EXISTENCE OF LAWS AND ETHICAL STANDARDS BETWEEN PRIVATE AND PUBLIC SECTORS:	4.00
ENFORCEMENT OF ANTICORRUPTION LAWS:	3.00
GOVERNMENTAL TRANSPARENCY:	3.71
CATEGORY AVERAGE:	**3.43**

Thailand is a legalistic and bureaucratic state in which opportunities for official corruption are legion. The state is extensively involved in the economy, notably through numerous state enterprises, including the Electricity Generating Authority of Thailand, the Petroleum Authority of Thailand, the State Railway, Thai Airways International, and the Thailand Tobacco Monopoly. Privatization of state enterprises has been much discussed, but progress has been slow. Given the current structure of the economy, it seems likely that greater privatization would simply allow privileged elites further opportunities for self-enrichment.

Under Article 110 of the 1997 constitution, MPs were not permitted to hold state concessions or contracts, but in practice such regulations are readily subverted. Thaksin nominally transferred most of his considerable business assets to his family and his servants.

Asset declarations are required from all cabinet members, MPs, senators, and other senior elected officials. Those made by ministers (including the prime minister) are open to public and media scrutiny, but the assets declaration system has so far failed to stop endemic conflicts of interest between politicians and the business sector. Concessions allocations in Thailand typically reflect a culture of benefit sharing rather than the public interest or the interests of individual consumers.

The award of government contracts has never been open and transparent in Thailand: whatever formal procedures are observed, these processes are widely seen as vitiated by structural corruption. Following the controversial sale of his family company Shin Corp. to Singapore's Temasek in January 2006, Thaksin was accused of abusing his powers as prime minister to further his business interests.[57] The Thaksin case has raised public awareness about the issue of conflicts of interest, but there is no culture of state intervention to regulate private sector interest conflicts.

Transparency International rates Thailand 63rd out of 163 countries assessed in its 2006 Corruption Perceptions Index, with 3.6 out of a possible 10 points.[58] In theory, victims of corruption could lodge complaints with the National Counter-Corruption Commission (NCCC), which has extensive powers to investigate corruption by state officials. However, the 2003 appointment of new commissioners widely seen as government-friendly meant that the NCCC was effectively neutralized.[59] The post-coup government has struggled to create effective new mechanisms to investigate corruption under the Thaksin administration, including allegations of massive irregularities surrounding the Suvarnabhumi Airport project. The new airport opened in September 2006 but by January 2007 was facing partial closure because of serious cracking on its runways. Access to higher education is generally open, although scandals concerning alleged abuses of the entrance examination system surface occasionally.[60]

Collection of income taxes is uneven. In 2004, there were 6.27 million taxpayers (including corporate and value-added taxpayers), a figure the Revenue Department hopes to increase to 20 million by 2009.[61] The Revenue Department has been encouraging taxpayers to pay online, as this reduces the scope for bribery. The Economist Intelligence Unit has suggested that up to 100 billion baht or US$3 billion (one-fifth of potential revenue) may be lost annually through tax evasion.[62]

The State Audit Commission and the auditor general have extensive authority to monitor the proper use of public funds, but in the past their effectiveness has been hampered by lack of timely cooperation on the part of the police, as well as lack of power to implement their findings. Auditor General Jaruvan Menthaka was ousted in controversial circumstances in 2004, allegedly because of her critical position concerning various mega-projects backed by leading ministers.[63] The Jaruvan case became an important touchstone for criticism of Thaksin's interference in the independent agencies, and she was restored to office in 2006, apparently following a royal intervention.[64]

Issues concerning corruption by politicians are widely aired in the print media, although the electronic media rarely offer critical perspectives on current power-holders. Whistle-blowers do not feel secure; as media activist Supinya Klangnarong told the *New York Times*, there is a hierarchy of punishment in Thailand: "If you act too much, you'll be killed. If you talk too much, you will be sued. If you're an academic, you might be discredited."[65] The Thaksin governments created a climate of fear and self-censorship among media practitioners.[66]

Thailand enacted the Official Information Act in 1997. In principle, this legislation affords extensive disclosure rights to citizens, but in practice its provisions have been extensively circumvented and thwarted by government agencies.[67] In theory, the national budget is open to scrutiny by the legislature—and dozens of senior officials attend annual parliamentary sessions for this purpose—but during the period of TRT party dominance in the House of Representatives, this scrutiny was necessarily limited. Foreign assistance can be freely distributed in Thailand, although the relatively high level of economic development means that apart from long-standing support from Japan and from the Asian Development Bank, Thailand is not a major aid-recipient country.

Recommendations

- New legislation to regulate potential conflicts of interest between politicians and business concerns is urgently needed.
- Current loopholes allowing serving MPs and ministers to transfer their business assets to relatives and servants should be closed.
- The Revenue Department should be strongly supported in its attempts to increase the tax base and curtail tax evasion.
- New legislation should be enacted to protect whistle-blowers from dismissal or harassment.

NOTES

[1] For a detailed account and analysis, see Kasian Tejapira, "Toppling Thaksin," *New Left Review* 39 (May–June 2006): 5–37.

[2] "Thai coup-leaders' statements," BBC News, 19 September 2006, http://news.bbc .co.uk/2/hi/asia-pacific/5361756.stm.

[3] Sombat Chantornvong, "The 1997 constitution," in Duncan McCargo (ed.), *Reforming Thai Politics* (Copenhagen: NIAS, 2002), 108.

[4] See *Overcoming Violence Through the Power of Reconciliation* (Bangkok: National Reconciliation Commission [NRC], 2006 [English version]).

[5] "Prem not happy with NRC's idea," *The Nation* (Bangkok), 26 June 2006.

[6] For example, authorities did little to prevent attacks on the leaders of the opposition Democrat Party in Chiang Mai on 31 March 2006. Worse still, Thaksin's own security staff assaulted members of the public at the Siam Paragon department store in Bangkok in August 2006. See "Six allege assault by Thaksin supporters," *The Nation*, 22 August 2006.

[7] See *Gagging the Thai Press* (Bangkok: Southeast Asia Press Alliance, n.d., but apparently published 2004), 23–67.

[8] See Michael K. Connors, "Ministering Culture: Hegemony and Politics of Culture and Identity in Thailand," *Critical Asian Studies* 37, 4 (December 2005): 523–551.

[9] See "Thailand: P.M. Suits Dropped, But Media Still Under Threat" (New York: Human Rights Watch [HRW], 8 December 2005), http://hrw.org.

[10] "Sondhi faces deluge of lèse majesté claims," *Bangkok Post*, 30 March 2006.

11 "The administration is usually bordering on 'lest majest' [*sic*] actions against the revered King" (initial statement by Thai coup leaders); "Frequently the dignity of the Thai people's king was affected" (first communiqué by Thai coup leaders). Translated by BBC News, 19 September 2006, http://news.bbc.co.uk.

12 Cited in "Thailand: Events of 2006" (HRW, 2006), http://hrw.org.

13 *Thailand Guide* (London: Prisoners Abroad, n.d.), 35–39, www.prisonersabroad.org.uk.

14 *Thailand: Widespread abuses in the administration of justice* (London: Amnesty International [AI], ASA 39/003/2002, 2002), 1.

15 "Thailand Human Rights Overview" (HRW, 2007), http://hrw.org.

16 "Not enough graves" (HRW, June 2004), 7–19.

17 Exact numbers of politically related deaths are difficult to establish, as Thailand has a high murder rate, and some of the killings may have been the outcome of nonpolitical business or personal conflicts.

18 "Disappearance of a human rights defender and disappearance of justice in Thailand" (Hong Kong: Asian Human Rights Commission [AHRC], 18 June 2004), www.ahrchk .net.

19 "Thaksin aide link to kidnap of Somchai," *The Nation*, 2 November 2006.

20 *Raingan khanakamakan isara taisuan kho thae jing karani hetkan masayit krue se (phakraek) [Report of the Independent Fact-finding Commission on the Kru-Ze mosque incident (Part I)]* (Bangkok: 26 July 2004).

21 Pallop Pinmanee, *Phom phit ru? thi yut Krue Se! [Was I wrong to storm Krue Se?]* (Bangkok: Good Morning Publishing, 2004). The book is completely unapologetic, arguing that any military in the world would have responded similarly. Pallop explains how he ordered twelve commandos to throw eight hand grenades into the mosque before opening fire through the windows (39–41).

22 *Raingan khong khanakamaka nisara sop kho thaejing karani phu sia chiwit nai hetkan amphoe tak bai jangwat narathiwat mua wan thi 25 tulakhom 2547 [Report of the independent commission to investigate the deaths in the Tak Bai incident, 25 October 2004]* (Bangkok: 2004).

23 "Surayud apologises for govt's abuses in South," *The Nation*, 3 November 2006.

24 See *Thailand's Emergency Decree: No Solution* (Brussels: International Crisis Group [ICG], 18 November 2005), 1–4, www.crisisgroup.org.

25 For example, "More power, less accountability: Thailand's new emergency decree" (Geneva: International Commission of Jurists [ICJ], August 2005), www.icj.org.

26 See "Court finds Thai anticorruption commission corrupt," Reuters, 26 May 2005. www .abc.net.au/news/newsitems/200505/s1378107.htm.

27 *Women's right to a political voice in Thailand* (Bangkok: Women for Democratic Development Foundation and UNDP, 2006), 22, www.undp.or.th/mdg/publication-MDG3.html.

28 The postcoup Thai cabinet was sworn in 9 October 2006. The only ministry headed by a woman was the tiny Ministry of Culture; another woman occupied a junior post as the PM's office minister.

29 *Women's right*, 14.

30 Ibid., 16.

31 Ibid., 18.

32 *Thailand: Grave Developments: Killings and Other Abuses* (London: AI, ASA 39/008/03, November 2003), 11.

33 Ibid., 23.

34 "The tale of a man with no country," *The Standard*, 10 July 2006.

35 Pinkaew Laungaramsri, "Constructing marginality: The 'hill tribe' Karen and their shifting locations within Thai state and public perspectives," in Claudio Delang (ed.), *Living at the Edge of Thai Society: The Karen in the highlands of Northern Thailand* (London: Routledge, 2003), 31. Pinkaew points out that the term "hill tribe" is pejorative and inaccurate with respect to the Karen.

36 Duncan McCargo, "Buddhism, democracy and identity in Thailand," *Democratization* 11, 4 (2004): 164–167.

37 "Ja kert arai khun mua nayok saeksaeng kitchakan sasana islam [What will happen when the prime minister intervenes in Islamic affairs?]," *Muslim Thai Newspaper*, 15 April–14 May 2006.

38 The registered churches comprise the Catholic Church and four "subgroups" including the Baptist and Seventh Day Adventist churches. For example, see "Protestant 'cult' triggers concern," *The Nation*, 21 January 1999.

39 "Thailand" in *International Religious Freedom Report 2006* (Washington, D.C.: U.S. Department of State, 2006), www.state.gov/g/drl/rls/irf/2006/71359.htm.

40 Pasuk Phongpaichit, Nualnoi Treerat, Yongyuth Chaiyapong, and Chris Baker, *Corruption in the Public Sector in Thailand: Perceptions and Experience of Households* (Bangkok: Chulalongkorn University, Political Economy Centre, 2000), 58?–59.

41 Siriporn Chanjindamanee, "White collar crime: Ten years on, not one conviction," *The Nation*, 12 December 2002.

42 "Insufficient, contradictory evidence clears Duang," *The Nation*, 27 March 2004.

43 Michael Connors, "On Trial: Competing Interpretations of Violence in the South of Thailand," *Asian Analysis* (November 2005), www.aseanfocus.com/asiananalysis/article.cfm?articleID=896.

44 *Thailand* (Prisoners Abroad), 26.

45 Shawn W. Crispin, "Courts under the spotlight," *Far Eastern Economic Review*, 4 September 2003.

46 "Thaksin lawyer faces charge of contempt of court," *Xinhua News*, 14 February 2007.

47 "Text of Government's Statement on Administrative Reform," *The Nation*, Thai Press Reports, 28 November 2006 [unofficial translation].

48 *Thailand* (Prisoners Abroad), 20.

49 For detailed discussion, see James R. Klein, "The battle for the rule of law in Thailand: the role of the Constitutional Court," in Amara Raksataya and James R. Klein, *The Constitutional Court of Thailand: The Provisions and Workings of the Court* (Bangkok: Constitution for the People Society, 2003), 76–78.

50 "Retiring president warns court's impartiality at risk," *The Nation*, 4 October 2002.

51 Duncan McCargo and Ukrist Pathmanand, *The Thaksinization of Thailand* (Copenhagen: NIAS Press, 2005), 121–157.

52 "Thailand: The impossibility of complaint against the police" (Hong Kong: Asian Human Rights Commission, 18 July 2006), http://www.ahrchk.net/statements/mainfile.php /2006statements/645.

53 Philip Hirsch, *Political Economy of the Environment in Thailand* (Manila: Journal of Contemporary Asia, 1993), 60–61.

54 "Thailand risk: legal and regulatory risk country briefing," *RiskWire* (London: Economist Intelligence Unit [EIU]), 7 October 2004.

55 Vitit Muntarbhorn and Charles Taylor, *Roads to Democracy: Human Rights and Democratic Development in Thailand* (Bangkok and Montreal: International Centre for Human Rights and Democratic Development, 1994), 37.

56 Somchai Phatarathaananunth, *Civil Society in Northeast Thailand: The Struggle of the Small Scale Farmers' Assembly of Isan* (Leeds: University of Leeds, unpublished PhD thesis, 2001), 85–86.

57 The many questions raised by the Shin Corp. sale were summarized in Manok and Denokkrop [pseudo.], *25 Khamtham bunglang dun tek over Shin Corp [25 Questions Behind the Shin Corp Takeover]* (Bangkok: Open Books, 2006).

58 "Corruption Perceptions Index" (Berlin: Transparency International, 2006), www.transparency.org. The Thai data were based on nine surveys.

59 Pasuk and Baker, *Thaksin*, 175.

60 See, for example, "Exam test scandal—Adisai distorted report: Sumet," *The Nation*, 5 June 2004.

61 "Thailand Tax Regulations Country Briefing," *ViewsWire* (EIU), 10 February 2004.

62 Ibid.

63 "Senate votes to seek Jaruvan's replacement," *Bangkok Post*, 2 November 2004.

64 "Committee agrees to reinstate Jaruvan as auditor general," *The Nation*, 16 February 2006.

65 Jane Perlez (*New York Times*), "Thai Activist is sued by Thaksin, and can't wait for court," *Cambodia Daily*, 9 July 2004.

66 See Ubonrat Siriyuvasak, ed., *Pit hu, pit ta, pit pak: sithi seriphap nai mu turakitkanmuang sua [Close your ears, close your eyes, close your mouth: Rights and freedoms in the clutches of a politicized media business]* (Bangkok: Khop Fai, 2005).

67 See the detailed discussion in *Gagging the Thai Press*, 68–77.

TUNISIA

CAPITAL: Tunis
POPULATION: 10.2 million
GNI PER CAPITA: $2,970

SCORES	2005	2007
ACCOUNTABILITY AND PUBLIC VOICE:	1.65	1.74
CIVIL LIBERTIES:	3.08	3.11
RULE OF LAW:	2.79	2.92
ANTICORRUPTION AND TRANSPARENCY:	3.53	3.08

(scores are based on a scale of 0 to 7, with 0 representing weakest
and 7 representing strongest performance)

Stephen J. King

INTRODUCTION

Tunisia is a small, semiarid Mediterranean country on the northern coast
of Africa. Villages and rain-fed agriculture supplemented by groundwa-
ter irrigation dominate the rural landscape. Land distribution is typically skewed toward large landholders, and agricultural production varies
enormously with rainfall.

The largely homogeneous population of approximately 10 million
is primarily Arab and Sunni Muslim. Like Algeria and Morocco, Tunisia
was subjected to French colonial rule. Since independence in 1956,
Tunisian politics have featured a hegemonic, authoritarian political party
whose name has changed over time. Currently the party is known as the
Rassemblement Constitutionelle Democratique (Constitutional Democratic Rally, or RCD). Borrowing key cadres from the party to fill bureaucratic and government posts, Tunisia's first postindependence president,
Habib Bourguiba, built a new institutional order that replaced the
French colonial system. To consolidate its rule, the single-party state utilized ancillary corporatist organizations to pull various social forces
under the state-party umbrella. These included labor, peasant, business,

Stephen J. King is Associate Professor of Government at Georgetown University.

student, and professional associations. Atop the system stood the Tunisian president, who was both head of the ruling party and head of state.

Since independence, Tunisian leaders have achieved substantial progress in modernizing their society and, more recently, bringing it into the global economy. Partly due to their choice of development strategy, current challenges in Tunisia include fostering the private sector and carrying out the privatization of state-owned enterprises. The government must implement these policies while simultaneously providing adequate social safety nets; tackling the critical issue of unemployment, mainly among the young; reforming the civil service; increasing transparency; and decentralizing decision making. In addition, Tunisian leaders have been forced to rethink politics in order to give a voice to a more educated populace and a growing middle class, while dealing with political dissent inspired by a literalist understanding of Islam similar to that in other parts of the Muslim world.

There are a number of signs of success in the economic and social spheres. The country has relatively low rates of poverty, and literacy and education levels that are high for the developing world. Furthermore, social policies stretching back to the early years of independence have been progressive in terms of women's rights.

Unfortunately, political conditions stand in jarring contrast to such achievements. President Zine el-Abidine Ben Ali, who replaced the aged Bourguiba in a bloodless coup in 1987, spearheaded a timid democratic opening in the late 1980s and early 1990s. However, since then the regime has systematically asserted control over all institutions that could constitute a countervailing power—parliament, the judiciary, the press, political parties, universities, professional associations, and other such entities.[1] Ben Ali's legalization of multiple parties and introduction of electoral competition between them in 1989 has settled, for the moment, into a striking example of the institutionalization of the forms of democracy without any of the substance.

With democratic institutions providing little legitimacy in recent years, the regime has sought to secure social compliance with its rule through progress in economic development, success in combating Islamic extremists, and a willingness to utilize the state's coercive and intelligence organizations against any perceived threat. Still, Tunisian society has a number of traits, such as high levels of literacy and urbanization and a large middle class, that typically produce pressure for accountability and public voice and, over time, an unwillingness to accept anything less.[2]

ACCOUNTABILITY AND PUBLIC VOICE

FREE AND FAIR ELECTORAL LAWS AND ELECTIONS:	1.25
EFFECTIVE AND ACCOUNTABLE GOVERNMENT:	3.00
CIVIC ENGAGEMENT AND CIVIC MONITORING:	1.33
MEDIA INDEPENDENCE AND FREEDOM OF EXPRESSION:	1.38
CATEGORY AVERAGE:	**1.74**

Despite having the opportunity to vote in regular, nominally competitive elections for the legislature and the presidency, Tunisian citizens do not have sufficient rights to be able to change their government. The ruling party still has a monopoly on public life in the country. It dominates the cabinet, the legislature, and regional and local government. There is no true opportunity for the effective rotation of power among a range of different political parties representing competing interests and policy options.

Tunisia held presidential and parliamentary elections on October 24, 2004. Zine el-Abidine Ben Ali retained the presidency with 94.48 percent of the vote, while his party, the RCD, won 87.7 percent of the votes for the Chamber of Deputies. Tunisian law requires that 20 percent of the seats in the chamber be distributed to the legal opposition parties in proportion to their relative success in the national vote; otherwise, the RCD would have swept the Parliament. It was instead awarded 152 seats. Of the 37 seats distributed to opposition parties, 14 went to the Movement of Democratic Socialists (MDS), 11 to the Party of People's Unity (PUP), 7 to the Unionist Democratic Union (UDU), 3 to the Renewal Movement, and 2 to the Social Liberal Party (PSL); the remaining legal party, the Progressive Democratic Party (PDP), did not win a seat.[3] The ruling party is committed to ensuring that at least 25 percent of its candidates are women. Overall, 43 percent of the 189 deputies elected in 2004 were women.[4]

Some political variation among the legal opposition parties emerged in the elections, partly in reaction to constitutional amendments in 2002 that allowed the president to seek a fourth term in office, and to a 2003 electoral law amendment that imposed a fine of 5,000 dinars (US$4,000) for violation of a new ban on using privately owned or foreign television and radio stations to campaign. Four members of the "loyal opposition"— the MDS, UDU, PSL, and PUP—supported the constitutional amendments and took a favorable view of the 2004 legislative and presidential elections. However, a second camp of legally established parties has grown more critical of the president and the RCD. For example, the left-wing PDP called for a boycott of the presidential election. Its leader, Ahmed Nejib Chebbi, claimed that "the poll would reproduce one-man rule monopolizing all power."[5] The Renewal Movement, a group of independent figures and small left-wing parties, had launched a democratic initiative, calling on Ben Ali to release political prisoners prior to the elections and fielding its own candidate for the presidency, Mohamed Ali Halouani. However, the PDP and the Renewal Movement performed worse in the 2004 elections than in the 1999 elections.[6] The outcome led Suheir Ben Hassan of the Tunisian League of Human Rights to assert that the authorities had rewarded loyal parties and punished insubordinate ones.[7] The lone opposition group with substantial public support, the illegal Islamist party Al-Nahda, called for a boycott of the elections.

Majoritarian electoral rules continue to facilitate the RCD's domination of the Chamber of Deputies. While many democracies employ winner-take-all (WTA) rules, WTA legislative elections offer particular advantages to incumbents in countries emerging from single-party rule.[8] In Tunisia, WTA elections prevent opposition parties from gradually building up membership in the legislature, since a party can garner a substantial portion of the national vote without winning in a single constituency. In 2006, five opposition parties led by the PDP called on the government to amend the constitution to abolish the de facto one-party system and revise press, political party, and electoral legislation.[9]

In addition to enforcing electoral rules that favored the ruling party, the government denied equal campaigning opportunities for all parties in the Chamber of Deputies elections. The Tunisian League of Human Rights report on the 2004 elections declared that Article 8 of the constitution, which guarantees protection of the media and freedom of expression, was not being observed by state officials. Journalists received instructions to cover opposition activities only on the request of the government. Opposition campaign advertisements on radio and television were easily outnumbered by RCD ads, and on state television the opposition ads ran when the fewest viewers would be watching.[10] During the campaign, 77 percent of the print media coverage and 92 percent of the electronic media coverage focused on the activities of President Ben Ali and the ruling party.[11] Campaign financing in Tunisia is carried out according to Law Number 97-48, promulgated on July 21, 1997, and usually consists of state subsidies or loans.

It is highly unlikely that legislative tallies in 2004 reflected the will of the people. Ayachi Hamammi, a lawyer for the opposition democratic initiative, declared that the elections were rigged through ballot stuffing, complete media blackouts of candidate activities, media misinformation, and censorship.[12] The government also influenced election monitoring by vetting domestic and international members of the National Electoral Observatory. The selected international observers came from countries with their own electoral shortcomings, including members of the League of Arab States, the African Union, and the International Organization of la Francophonie.[13] Representatives of more credible international organizations were passed over by the National Electoral Observatory.

The RCD won a landslide victory in the 2005 municipal elections, continuing its pattern of employing rural notables and state patronage to deliver the vote of the peasantry, lock them into clientelistic relationships, and alienate them from formal institutions such as the national agricultural union, in which they were central participants during the first decades after independence.[14] State privatization and credit policies that have favored rural and urban economic elites in recent years have helped create a new base of support for the authoritarian regime. Partly counterbalancing these trends are programs like 2626, a fund under presidential auspices that is designed to aid poorer areas. For some elite supporters of the regime this amounts to a form of coerced charity, as there is significant state pressure to contribute to the fund.[15]

The 2004 presidential elections in Tunisia were equally noncompetitive. According to the constitution and electoral code, only the leaders of parties holding seats in Parliament are eligible to run for president. The loyal opposition ran three candidates: Mohamed Bouchia, secretary general of the PUP; Mounir Beji, president of the PSL; and Halouani of the Renewal Movement. As noted, Halouani and his party became more critical of the regime over time, and they paid for it at the ballot box.[16] The other two candidates ran symbolic races in which they essentially endorsed Ben Ali's reelection. The incumbent won 94.48 percent of the vote, while Halouani, who received 0.95 percent, publicly decried the results.[17] There are concerns that the 2002 constitutional amendments eliminating the three-term limit for presidents will allow Ben Ali to attain an overwhelming victory in the 2009 election as well.[18] Recent studies of political regimes with both democratic and authoritarian traits have established a benchmark of 75 percent of the vote for victorious incumbent presidential candidates as the key indication that the regime may be considered authoritarian rather than democratic.[19]

The 2002 constitutional amendment that ended the three-term limit for presidents also created a second parliamentary chamber, the Chamber of Advisors. One-third of its members are chosen by an electoral college representing local officials, another third are elected by trade unions and other sociopolitical organizations, and the remaining third are chosen by the president.[20] The creation of the second chamber allows the government to mitigate any unfavorable votes in the lower house, a strategy utilized effectively by the regime in Morocco.[21] In July 2005, the government conducted elections for the new chamber. The General Union of Tunisian Workers (UGTT) refused to name candidates for what it viewed as an undemocratic initiative.[22]

The Tunisian president has nearly absolute powers. Both houses of Parliament operate under the control of the ruling party, which he dominates. The president selects the prime minister and cabinet ministers, and appoints the governors of Tunisia's twenty-three provinces. The executive initiates legislation, and the president rules by decree when the legislature is not in session. The president is commander in chief of the armed forces and enjoys judicial immunity while in office.[23]

The president's control of the legislative process is reinforced by the judiciary's inability to serve as a balancing power. Despite the existence of constitutional and legal guarantees of judicial independence, the executive dominates the judicial domain. The president appoints members of the Constitutional Council and exercises indirect authority over it through powers of assignment, tenure, and transfer.[24] The Tunisian civil service, while qualified and efficient, is also subject to presidential control due to its hierarchical, centralized structure and its strong links to the ruling party.[25]

Associational life in Tunisia is stifled by various governmental measures. In recent years the government has effectively repressed human rights organizations that had been at the forefront of efforts to increase public accountability. Among other tactics, the authorities used supporters to infiltrate and undermine organizations. Counterterrorism legislation passed on December 10, 2003, has become a tool to restrict the freedom to establish organizations and political parties.[26] The law, which aimed to support international efforts against terrorism and money laundering, erodes defendants' rights and contains a broad definition of terrorism that could be used to prosecute peaceful dissent. During a World Summit on the Information Society (WSIS) that took place in Tunisia in 2005, opposition figures held a hunger strike to draw attention to political prisoners. The government clamped down on nongovernmental organizations (NGOs) during the run-up to the conference, and members of human rights groups in particular faced arrest, imprisonment, and even physical attacks in the street.[27] Domestic donors to civic organizations and public policy institutes remain subject to state pressure.

The media is tightly controlled in Tunisia, the internet is monitored, and freedom of political expression is extremely limited even by regional standards.[28] According to the Tunisian League of Human Rights, the Association of Women Democrats, and the National Council for Freedom in Tunisia, the public did not have access to fair and balanced media coverage during the 2004 legislative and presidential elections.[29] The Tunisian media include a set of private and state-owned newspapers as well as state-sponsored television and radio. Both public and private media outlets produce material favorable to the government in most instances. There are 245 privately owned magazines, but most are owned by figures close to the president. Self-censorship is significant, and repressive measures are taken against any outlets that offer oppositional viewpoints; for example, most online publications, such as *Kalimat* and *Tunizine*, are accessible only from abroad. The authorities frequently tell journalists whom to cover and how.

The 2003 counterterrorism legislation further restricted freedom of the media and freedom of expression. Tactics used against the press include publishing delays, newspaper seizures at vending points by the Ministry of the Interior, restriction of mail service, and banning of foreign newspapers when unfavorable articles appear. The latter measure has affected publications including *Le Monde*, *Al-Hayat*, and *Le Canard*

Enchaine. Independent websites are banned or censored, and journalists run the risk of being jailed, tortured, fired, or exiled. In May 2004, 160 journalists who had been arbitrarily fired created an association to defend the rights of their profession. The Ministry of the Interior declared their action illegal even though union activities are permitted under Tunisian law.

In May 2005, the authorities abolished the legal depot, a measure that required all media to be vetted by the Ministry of the Interior before publication. This positive step is tempered, however, by the regime's ongoing commitment to controlling information flow at every possible level. Separately, in February 2005, Tunisia's first private satellite television channel was launched, with a second following soon after.

Despite the adoption of the Tunis Commitment and the Tunis Agenda for the Information Society at WSIS to ensure freedom of the press and cultural expression, the Tunisian government continues to ignore the provisions or apply its own interpretations. A play that indirectly criticized the government's treatment of human rights organizations, trade unions, and other civic associations was staged in Tunisia in early 2007, but only after numerous delays and editing to satisfy the Ministry of Culture. The play also criticized radicalism and extremist Islamist groups.

Recommendations

- Elections should be administered by a neutral authority that is insulated from the ruling party, the RCD.
- The electoral administration should be sufficiently competent and resourceful to take specific precautions against fraud in the voting and vote counting. This could be achieved, in part, by improving the training for members of the electoral administration.
- The police, military, and courts should treat competing candidates and parties impartially throughout the electoral process.
- Participating parties should have equal access to the public media. This could largely be attained by the enforcement of current laws.
- Voting and vote counting at all locations should be independently monitored, the secrecy of the ballot should be protected, and procedures for organizing and counting the votes should be transparent. International observers should not be handpicked by the regime.

CIVIL LIBERTIES

PROTECTION FROM STATE TERROR, UNJUSTIFIED IMPRISONMENT, AND TORTURE:	2.43
GENDER EQUITY:	4.25
RIGHTS OF ETHNIC, RELIGIOUS, AND OTHER DISTINCT GROUPS:	4.00
FREEDOM OF CONSCIENCE AND BELIEF:	2.67
FREEDOM OF ASSOCIATION AND ASSEMBLY:	2.20
CATEGORY AVERAGE:	**3.11**

In Tunisia, the state often violates the civil liberties of its citizens. It is not uncommon for opponents of the regime to be harassed and arbitrarily detained. The government frequently justifies crackdowns on peaceful dissent by citing the threat of terrorism and religious extremism. There are widespread and credible reports of the use of torture to obtain incriminating statements.[30]

Since the implementation of the 2003 counterterrorism legislation, violations of civil liberties have increased. Abuses in prison are widespread, and appeals to the authorities from family members of the victims usually go unheeded.[31] At the end of 2006, a large number of people were seized by the police, kept in custody without specific charges, and denied family contact and medical attention, all of which are illegal under Tunisian criminal law.[32] Even after their release, authorities monitored the dissidents, denied them passports and most jobs, and warned them against speaking out about politics and human rights. Citizens can register complaints about torture and abuses of civil liberties at the Ministry of Justice and Human Rights and the Ministry of the Interior. However, these ministries do not respond effectively to such petitions.

In March and November 2006, President Ben Ali pardoned or conditionally released about 1,800 political prisoners. Some were members of Al-Nahda who had been incarcerated after mass trials in 1992, in which they had been accused—dubiously, in many cases—of plotting to topple the government. The number of political prisoners remains above 350. In another positive step toward strengthening civil liberties, the government now permits the International Committee of the Red Cross to inspect prisons.[33]

Prison conditions in Tunisia fall short of minimum standards. Prisoners suffer long-term solitary confinement, violence, and sexual and physical abuse by guards and fellow inmates, generally sponsored by the guards. Hygiene is extremely poor, and prisoners rarely have access to showers and washing facilities. Cells are overcrowded, with most prisoners forced to share beds or sleep on the floor. Contagious diseases, particularly scabies, are widespread, and prisoners lack adequate medical care. Additional discriminatory and arbitrary measures worsen the conditions of detention. Several political prisoners and prisoners of conscience have been kept in solitary confinement for more than a decade, and prisoners have faced legal obstructions when they have sought redress in the courts. Human rights defenders, including lawyers who call on the authorities to protect prisoners' rights, face intimidation and harassment.[34]

Tunisia faces a significant terrorist threat, especially along the border with Algeria. The population is under heavy surveillance in these areas. Security forces attacked Islamist militants at the end of 2006 and the beginning of 2007 south of Tunis, near the Algerian border. The large-scale operation, carried out by police with support from army units, led to the killing of twelve and the arrest of fifteen alleged Islamist militants, who were said to be members of the Algeria-based Salafist Group for Call and Combat (GSPC).[35]

The state in Tunisia has continued to be a regional leader in ensuring that women enjoy the same civil and political rights as men. The government systematically promotes the participation of women in Parliament, leading to a ratio of female lawmakers that is high by global standards.[36] For the 2004 legislative elections, President Ben Ali ordered that at least one in four of the ruling party's candidates be women, and set the same figure as a goal for women in government service. Although Tunisia is at the forefront among Arab countries in providing opportunities for women, patriarchal cultural norms have some lingering effects. The number of women and girls wearing the *hijab*, or headscarf, has increased in recent years. The Tunisian authorities have responded by banning the *hijab* as a form of sectarian dress that acts as a cover for dangerous political extremism. The government does not acknowledge the wearing of the *hijab* as a religious right, personal choice, or cultural symbol, associating it only with deleterious political motives.[37]

Tunisia is a largely homogeneous Sunni Arab country. Ninety-eight percent of the population is Muslim. The indigenous Berber population has long been Arabized, as has the small nomadic population of the south. Just as women are not permitted to wear the *hijab*, men may not wear beards. However, the government generally respects freedom of worship, and other signs of Islamic religiosity are allowed. The small number of Christians, Jews, and Baha'i members benefit from government measures that guarantee their religious freedom. Still, bias in the media, especially against Jews, does occur. The international terrorist group al-Qaeda claimed responsibility for an unusual April 2002 attack on the most famous synagogue in Tunisia, the El Ghriba synagogue in Djerba, but the bombing has not been followed by similar incidents, likely due to state vigilance. The government attempts to control the appointments of religious leaders, for instance by paying the salary of the grand rabbi of the Jewish community.[38]

The security apparatus actively constrains what it views as signs of Islamist extremism. Most political prisoners are Islamists, and some have been confined for a decade or more without receiving a fair trial. Religious political parties, including Al-Nahda, are banned. Al-Nahda has claimed support for democracy and nonviolence, and has a genuine popular following, making the ban a serious obstacle to truly representative multiparty elections. The battle between violent Islamist extremists and state security forces has been utilized as a cover to justify repression of peaceful dissidents of various political stripes.

The Tunisian state has taken progressive measures to modify existing laws and practices that constitute discrimination against people with disabilities. The Nobel Prize–winning organization Handicap International has been working in Tunisia since 1992. Services and best practices for disabled people are strong in coastal areas but weaker in the country's interior. Those living in the interior often lack access to basic health centers and rehabilitation units.[39]

The Tunisian state does not guarantee rights of association and assembly. Sociopolitical organizations are tightly controlled by the government, and public demonstrations, whether peaceful or not, are rarely allowed. Since 2004, the authorities have banned numerous demonstrations called by opposition parties, human rights organizations, unions, and student groups. The police disperse protesters by force when demonstrations do occur.[40]

In recent years, human rights groups and lawyers have been the foremost victims of the state's violation of association and assembly rights. The Tunisian League of Human Rights has faced systematic repression and subversion, including the replacement of its leadership. According to Human Rights Watch, human rights dissidents "are subject to heavy surveillance, arbitrary travel bans, dismissal from work, interruptions in phone service, physical assaults, harassment of relatives, suspicious acts of vandalism and theft, and slander campaigns in the press."[41] Similar steps have been taken against the lawyers' syndicate.

Recommendations

- The government should cease using antiterrorist laws against peaceful dissidents.
- The state should improve transparency and oversight in the trial and detention system.
- The new laws, institutions, and actions that limit the associational rights and independence of human rights groups and the lawyers' syndicate should be rescinded.
- The government should guarantee the right of peaceful Islamists to assemble and participate in politics.

RULE OF LAW

INDEPENDENT JUDICIARY:	2.20
PRIMACY OF RULE OF LAW IN CIVIL AND CRIMINAL MATTERS:	2.67
ACCOUNTABILITY OF SECURITY FORCES AND MILITARY TO CIVILIAN AUTHORITIES:	1.75
PROTECTION OF PROPERTY RIGHTS:	4.00
EQUAL TREATMENT UNDER THE LAW:	4.00
CATEGORY AVERAGE:	**2.92**

The Tunisian judiciary is not independent of the executive branch. The president nominates judges and magistrates and heads the Supreme Judicial Council, which oversees judicial matters. Tunisia introduced a Constitutional Council system in 1987 by presidential decree. The council rules on the constitutionality of legislation referred to it by the president, who appoints its members. The president also dominates the Ministry of Justice and Human Rights.

The executive branch has recently increased its interference in judicial matters. In 2005, the authorities removed the elected leadership of the Tunisian Association of Magistrates after it called for more judicial independence, installing a progovernment leadership in its place.[42] In May 2006, a new law created a state-run academy for the training of lawyers, giving broad authority to the Ministry of Justice and Human Rights to decide who may enter the academy and go on to practice law.[43] The legal academy law, along with a strategy of using regime supporters to infiltrate and undermine the lawyers' syndicate, removed one of the few centers of opposition and independence from the Tunisian political scene.

Islamists and political dissidents suffer from discrimination in the administration of justice. Civilians suspected of terrorism are tried in military courts without the right of appeal, and the number of cases of this sort has increased since the implementation of the antiterrorism law in 2003. Aside from the problems created by the new legal training law, lawyers for defendants in political cases face obstacles to effective representation, including denial of access to their clients and relevant government files.[44] Prosecutors report to the Ministry of Justice, but the Ministry of the Interior also plays a role and prevents prosecutorial independence.

In theory, every defendant is presumed innocent until proven guilty; however, in practice, this is not always the case. Defendants have a right to legal counsel during trial and arraignment, but not during pre-arraignment detention.

Once known for its civilian rule, the Tunisian state has become increasingly dominated by the military and security services since President Ben Ali, a general and former director general of national security at the Ministry of the Interior, came to power in 1987. Today, the RCD's monopoly on power is bolstered by the military, security, intelligence, and national police services. The coercive apparatus of the state actively intimidates dissenters during elections, openly keeping a watchful eye on the proceedings. The security services subject suspected dissidents to heavy surveillance, physical assaults, arbitrary arrests, and glaring violations of their human rights. Military tribunals try cases involving military personnel and civilians accused of crimes affecting national security.[45] The state's definitions of "national security" and "crimes" have been quite broad, leading to violations of human rights and complaints by relatives of dissidents and numerous human rights organizations.[46] Members of the security forces are not held accountable for the abuses they commit.

The government has made extensive progress in the protection of property rights in the last two decades as it has worked to liberalize the economy. All citizens have the right to own property. However, small-scale farmers tend to lose disputes over land ownership. In the 1990s, Tunisia began the final stages of the privatization of state-owned land that had been reclaimed from the French and turned into agricultural cooperatives. The peasants working on these cooperatives were often descendants of the land's occupants before French colonization, but state privatization policy favored large landowners over these peasants.[47] There is also controversy concerning the settlement of property rights and titles for collective land. Political power and corruption played an important role during the privatization of customary land tenure.[48] While contracts in Tunisia are enforceable, conflicts have arisen due to the political nature of privatization policies.

Recommendations
- Urgent steps should be taken to strengthen the power and independence of the judicial branch, especially with respect to politically sensitive cases.
- Military courts should no longer be used to try civilians, and the scope of "national security" in criminal law should be clearly and narrowly defined.
- Detained suspects should be promptly charged and processed, or cleared and released. The common practice of detaining suspects for long periods without charges should be abolished.
- The government needs to institute mechanisms to improve justice and transparency in the distribution of remaining collective land.

ANTICORRUPTION AND TRANSPARENCY

ENVIRONMENT TO PROTECT AGAINST CORRUPTION:	3.20
EXISTENCE OF LAWS AND ETHICAL STANDARDS BETWEEN	
PRIVATE AND PUBLIC SECTORS:	4.00
ENFORCEMENT OF ANTICORRUPTION LAWS:	2.25
GOVERNMENTAL TRANSPARENCY:	2.86
CATEGORY AVERAGE:	**3.08**

As in other countries, economic liberalization in Tunisia has reorganized opportunities for corruption and rent-seeking.[49] The process, which accelerated in the 1990s, has been guided by patronage networks that intertwine public office and personal interest, particularly at the upper echelons of the state. State-owned assets have been privatized in an uncompetitive manner, and monopolies have been transferred intact to the private sector without an adequate regulatory framework.[50] Furthermore, financial disclosures and asset declarations of public officials are not open to public and media scrutiny. These shortcomings point to a genuine need for effective auditing mechanisms and other controls as Tunisia makes the transition to a market economy.

The family of the president's wife and other well-placed families have been implicated in improper business deals. Having started with few if any economic holdings, the Trabelsi clan—brothers and sisters of the president's wife Leila—has been accused of improperly accumulating assets since her marriage to the president, including the only private radio station in the country, Radio Mosaique; the country's most important airline and hotel company, Carthago Airlines; and important stakes in the wholesale, service, and agribusiness sectors. Similar dynamics exist in rural areas, where a rent-seeking elite has taken advantage of the privatization of state land. More productive small- and medium-scale farmers have been denied access to these resources amid the new policy focus on privatization, a market economy, and exports.

Tunisia's score on Transparency International's Corruption Perceptions Index has worsened over the past two years, dropping from 5 to 4.8 on a 10-point scale, with 10 representing the lowest level of perceived corruption. Countries with a score of 5 or below are deemed to have a serious corruption problem.

Indices of economic freedom give Tunisia average grades and show some progress in recent years. The Heritage Foundation's 2007 Index of Economic Freedom ranked Tunisia above the regional average, at six out of seventeen countries, as well as 1.8 percentage points higher than in 2006. The index did note complex trade regulations and opaque bureaucratic practices that increase opportunities for corruption, but Tunisia received relatively high marks for freedom from government intervention in the economy. It is also comparatively easy to start, operate, and close a business in Tunisia.[51]

Two public institutions are centrally involved in the enforcement of anticorruption laws. The Cour des Comptes (National Audit Office) is charged with auditing public sector accounts, while the Disciplinary Financial Court is responsible for punishing violations of financial laws and regulations by public authorities. However, these institutions are likely rendered ineffective by the reality of patronage-based privatization in Tunisia and the involvement of the president's family and high government officials in much of the malfeasance. People who denounce official corruption risk persecution or imprisonment. In this environment, whistle-blowers, anticorruption activists, and investigators do not feel secure about reporting cases of bribery and graft.

Historically, corruption has not been pervasive in higher education in Tunisia, but there are growing signs that well-connected officials influence the outcome of exams, appointments, and staff transfers.[52] The state continues to make efforts and progress in tax collection, administration, and auditing, in part by gradually enacting legislation that draws on internationally accepted standards.[53] The administration and distribution of foreign assistance appears to be devoid of corruption, although the government maintains control of any funding for civil society organizations.

According to the International Monetary Fund (IMF), Tunisia has made substantial progress in some aspects of governmental transparency since the state initiated market reforms in the 1980s. Public access to government information has been improved through the posting of more data on the internet. Since 2002, Tunisia has participated in the IMF's Special Data Dissemination Standard in order to implement international best practices with respect to economic and financial statistics. Tunisia has also participated in World Bank and IMF programs on financial policy transparency, fiscal transparency, banking supervision, securities regulation, and insurance supervision.[54] This transparency drive has obviously not included the introduction of regulatory structures to prevent privatization that encourages rent-seeking.

The executive branch controls the budgetary process in Tunisia, and it keeps areas that it deems politically sensitive out of public view. The budget is not subject to meaningful legislative scrutiny. The state does not ensure transparency, open bidding, or effective competition in the awarding of government contracts; instead, contracts often go to government cronies.

Recommendations

- A regulatory framework needs to be established to prevent any remaining state assets from being transferred to private monopolies.
- Tunisia should continue adopting auditing mechanisms that are consistent with international standards.
- The government should make public financial disclosures and asset declarations of all high-level officials. An independent body should be established to enforce compliance and verify submitted information.
- Tunisia should strengthen critical institutions such as the central bank, the finance ministry, the legal code, the judicial system, regulatory bodies, and revenue authorities so as to maintain macroeconomic stability, protect property rights, and guarantee contracts.

NOTES

[1] Reporters sans Frontieres (RSF), *Silence, On Reprime* (Paris: RSF, Rapports Moyen-Orient, 1999).

[2] Many have argued that socioeconomic development fosters democracy. For an early formulation see Seymour Martin Lipset, "Some Social Prerequisites of Democracy: Economic Development and Political Legitimacy," *American Political Science Review* 53 (March 1959).

[3] Aysha Ramadan, "Foregone Conclusion," *Al Ahram Weekly*, 28 October–3 November 2004.

[4] John P. Entelis, "The Sad State of Political Reform in Tunisia," *Arab Reform Bulletin* 2, no. 10 (November 2004).

[5] "Q&A: Tunisia Votes," BBC News, October 23, 2004. http://news.bbc.co.uk/1/hi/world/middle_east/3754410.stm.

[6] Ibid.

[7] Ibid.

8   Marsha Pripstein Posusney, "Multiparty Elections in the Arab World," in *Authoritarianism in the Middle East and North Africa: Regimes and Resistance*, ed. Posusney and Michele Penner Angrist (Boulder: Lynne Rienner Press, 2005), 98.

9   Michelle Dunn, "Tunisia: Crackdown on Activists," *Arab Reform Bulletin* 4, no. 3 (April 2006).

10 Tunisian League of Human Rights, Democratic Association of Tunisian Women, and National Council for Tunisian Liberty, *Report on the Presidential and Legislative Elections in Tunisia of October 2004.*

11 Ibid.

12 Ibid.

13 Ramadan, "Foregone Conclusion."

14 Stephen J. King, *Liberalization Against Democracy: The Local Politics of Economic Reform in Tunisia* (Bloomington: Indiana University Press, 2003).

15 Stephen J. King, "Failed Democratization in Egypt, Tunisia, Algeria, and Syria," *Political Science Quarterly* (forthcoming).

16 Ramadan, "Foregone Conclusion."

17 Entelis, "The Sad State . . . "

18 "Ben Ali's Dictatorship Is Creating More Islamists," *Daily Star*, 26 January 2007.

19 Larry Diamond, "Elections Without Democracy: Thinking about Hybrid Regimes," *Journal of Democracy* 13, no. 2 (April 2002).

20 Information obtained from the Tunisian government website, http://www.tunisiaonline.com/government/government1.html.

21 Mohamed Charfi, *Reforming Public Management and Development: The Case of Tunisia*, (Beirut: International Centre for Prison Studies [ICPS]–Lebanon, 2004).

22 Senate of France, "Senates of the World: Tunisia," http://senat.fr/senatsdumonde/english/tunisie.html.

23 Carnegie Endowment for International Peace, "Arab Political Systems: Baseline Information and Reforms—Tunisia," Carnegie Endowment for International Peace, September 2, 2005, http://www.carnegieendowment.org/files/Tunisia_APS.doc.

24 Programme on Governance in the Arab World (POGAR), "Democratic Governance: Judiciary—Tunisia," United Nations Development Programme (UNDP), http://www.undp-pogar.org/countries/judiciary.asp?cid=20.

25 Commission of the European Communities, *Country Report Tunisia, 2004* (Brussels: Commission of the European Communities, 12 May 2004), http://ec.europa.eu/world/enp/pdf/country/tunisia_enp_country_report_2004_en.pdf.

26 Bassam Bounenni, "Tunisia: Closing Off Avenues for Dissent," *Arab Reform Bulletin* 4, no. 6 (July 2006).

27 "Hunger for Change," Tunezine, 11 October 2005, www.tunezine.com/article.php3?idarticle=977. See also Amnesty International (AI), "Tunisia: Government Repression "Making a Mockery" of World Summit on Information Society," news release, 16 November 2005.

28 Entelis, "The Sad State . . ."

29 Tunisian League of Human Rights, *Report on the Presidential and Parliamentary Elections* . . . ; see also RSF, "Tunisia: Annual Report 2005," http://www.rsf.org/article.php3?id article=13302.

30 Human Rights Watch (HRW), *World Report 2007* (New York: HRW, 2007).

31 "Scandale a Borj Erroumi, l'Abou Ghraib tunisien," *Tunisnews*, 28 April 2004, http://www.tunisnews.net/scandal.htm.

32 AI, "Incommunicado Detention/Fear of Torture," news release, 18 January 2007.

33 HRW, *World Report 2007.*

34 AI, *Report 2006* (New York: AI, 2006)

35 Riccardo Fabiani, "Terrorism Risk Remains in North Africa," World Security Network, 14 February 2007.

36 Entelis, "The Sad State . . . "

37 "Hijab Ban Debate Heats Up in Tunisia," Islam Online, 7 October 2006, http://www.islamicawakening.com/viewnews.php?newsID=8210.

38 Ibn Khaldun Center for Development Studies, *Civil Society and Democratization in the Arab World, Annual Report 2004* (Cairo: Ibn Khaldun Center for Development Studies, July 2005).

39 Handicap International, "Tunisia," Handicap International, http://www.handicap-international.org.uk/page_212.php, accessed 22 June 2007.

40 HRW, "Tunisia: Protests Ahead of Global Information Summit," news release, 16 March 2005.

41 HRW, *World Report 2007.*

42 Ibid.

43 Bounenni, "Tunisia: Closing Off Avenues . . . "

44 HRW, "Human Rights Overview: Tunisia," HRW, http://hrw.org/english/docs/2006 /01/18/tunisi12232.htm.

45 Carnegie Endowment, "Arab Political Systems . . . "

46 HRW, "Human Rights Overview: Tunisia."

47 King, *Liberalization.*

48 Ibid.

49 Steven Heydemann, ed., *Networks of Privilege in the Middle East* (New York: Macmillan, 2004), 6.

50 Hector Schamis, *Re-Forming the State: The Politics of Privatization in Latin America and Europe* (Ann Arbor: University of Michigan Press, 2002), 4.

51 Heritage Foundation, *2007 Index of Economic Freedom* (Washington, D.C.: Heritage Foundation, 2007).

52 Neziha Rejiba, "No Respect for the Rules of Democracy: Ben Ali's Young Sharks," *Le Monde Diplomatique*, March 2006.

53 International Monetary Fund, "IMF Executive Board Concludes 2006 Article IV Consultation with Tunisia," news release, 8 June 2006.

54 POGAR, "Democratic Governance: Financial Transparency—Tunisia," UNDP, http://www.pogar.org/countries/finances.asp?cid=20.

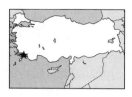

TURKEY

CAPITAL: Ankara
POPULATION: 74.0 million
GNI PER CAPITA: $5,400

SCORES	2005	2007
ACCOUNTABILITY AND PUBLIC VOICE:	4.35	4.40
CIVIL LIBERTIES:	3.98	3.82
RULE OF LAW:	4.18	3.97
ANTICORRUPTION AND TRANSPARENCY:	3.43	3.64

(scores are based on a scale of 0 to 7, with 0 representing weakest and 7 representing strongest performance)

Sarah Repucci

INTRODUCTION

Turkey presents an ever-shifting dichotomy between democratic progress and resistance to reform. Although the ruling party has pushed through a host of legal and real improvements in areas such as freedom of expression, Kurdish and women's rights, and reduction of torture in police detention, setbacks have followed advancements. Media freedom, judicial independence, and civilian control of the military have not yet been fully consolidated in the Turkish system, with periodic ebbs and flows in recent years.

The prospect of European Union (EU) membership was the major driving force behind Turkey's reforms, both as an incentive for the government and as a justification to the public for sometimes painful change. Although the EU began membership negotiations with Turkey in June 2006, talks on some items were frozen the following December because of EU insistence that Turkey open its ports to Cypriot ships and

Sarah Repucci is a senior research coordinator at Transparency International in Berlin. She is a governance and democracy specialist and an analyst of Turkish politics.

planes (something Turkey refuses to do until the EU ends Northern Cyprus's economic isolation). As cautious and even anti-Turkish rhetoric has increased from the EU and its member states, support for EU membership in Turkey has cooled dramatically. Meanwhile, previously strong relations between Turkey and the United States have been strained due to disagreements linked to the war in Iraq, which borders Turkey.

The modern Turkish republic was founded by Kemal Mustafa Ataturk in 1923. Ataturk was a visionary who wanted to make Turkey a modern nation. He separated Islam from the state and banned such external signs of religion as the fez and the headscarf. He also created a Turkish identity and a nationalism that had not existed previously, under the Ottoman Empire. Although his party ruled uninterrupted for more than twenty-five years, he helped put in place a number of democratic institutions, which became an important legacy of his rule.

In 1980, Turkey experienced the most recent of three military coups that temporarily took power from the elected civilian government. The military-led government wrote a new constitution that Turkey's citizens approved in a 1982 referendum. This constitution—an adapted version of which is in use today—strengthened the role of the military and restricted many fundamental freedoms. Soon afterward, fighting began in the southeast that ultimately developed into a fifteen-year guerrilla war between Turkish forces and Kurdish separatists.

Three subsequent events combined to spark a new era of rights and reforms in Turkey. A ceasefire was declared with the separatists after the capture of their leader, Abdullah Ocalan, in 1999. In the same year, the EU accepted Turkey as an official candidate for membership in response to Turkey's initial application in 1987. As a final turning point, Turkey's financial system collapsed in 2001, and the International Monetary Fund (IMF) stepped in to help with restructuring and large financial aid.

In November 2002 elections, the new Justice and Development Party (AKP) came to power. The AKP had grown out of the remnants of the Welfare Party—an Islamic-oriented party that had been banned after it was pressured out of power in 1997 by the military in a soft coup (the military did not subsequently assume power). Before being elected, however, the AKP had publicly renounced any intentions to change Turkey's secular orientation, and many of its supporters in 2002 voted for change, not religion. Because Recep Tayyip Erdogan, the AKP's leader, had been banned from politics due to a prior conviction for reading an allegedly Islamic poem in public, he was not immediately permitted to become a member of parliament. After the AKP won a majority of parliamentary seats (a rare event in a country that has almost always been led by fragile coalitions), Abdullah Gul served as prime minister until the party used its majority to change the constitution and pave the way for Erdogan's leadership.

After he became prime minister in March 2003, Erdogan's government pursued a vigorous, pro-EU reform agenda, passing a string of constitutional amendments and legal packages and taking serious steps toward ensuring their implementation. Turkey's rapid progress in terms of rights and freedoms was widely acknowledged in the first years of Erdogan's rule. However, with mixed messages coming from various EU quarters on whether Turkish membership is realistic and with elections for Turkey's president and prime minister due in 2007, movement toward reform has slowed dramatically. Meanwhile, Turkey's own internal security situation has deteriorated again as fighting in the southeast has resumed.

Moreover, despite the recent changes, Turkey's military-drafted constitution fundamentally lacks the inclusiveness, the clearly defined rights, and the limitations on state power that are crucial for democracy in a multicultural society such as this. While Turkey's population has generally supported the reforms, they were broadly imposed from the outside. This is symptomatic of the lack of public engagement in politics in the country; in its place is a great faith among the public in the state's ability to serve their best interests. The culture of freedom and democracy advocated by government rhetoric has yet to pervade the general population. The education system is still weak, with insufficient opportunities for the poor. Today, those who use claims of Turkish nationalism to justify infringement of others' rights and security are more of a threat to open democracy than any traditional authoritarian tendencies.

Nevertheless, progress has not stopped altogether. For example, in 2005–2006 a new penal code went into effect, an ombudsman office was established, and implementation of earlier reforms was systematically improved. Turkey continues on its path, if more slowly than before, toward increased democratic governance.

ACCOUNTABILITY AND PUBLIC VOICE

FREE AND FAIR ELECTORAL LAWS AND ELECTIONS:	5.25
EFFECTIVE AND ACCOUNTABLE GOVERNMENT:	4.00
CIVIC ENGAGEMENT AND CIVIC MONITORING:	4.33
MEDIA INDEPENDENCE AND FREEDOM OF EXPRESSION:	4.00
CATEGORY AVERAGE:	**4.40**

Turkey is a parliamentary democracy. A president, elected by parliament (the Turkish Grand National Assembly), is head of state but is not formally involved in policy making. The current president, Ahmet Necdet Sezer, was elected in 2000 for a nonrenewable seven-year term. Presidential elections are scheduled for May 2007. The National Assembly is composed of 550 deputies elected by universal suffrage to five-year terms. The prime minister is technically chosen by the president, although in practice he/she is the leader of the party in power. Parliamentary elections are scheduled for November 2007.

[Update: In April 2007, Erdogan nominated Gul for the presidency despite opposition from the army and the Republican People's Party (CHP), who considered Gul a threat to Turkey's secularism. The nomination sparked massive protests in Turkey, and the army posted on its website a thinly veiled threat to intervene should Gul be elected. Parliament failed to reach a quorum in the presidential vote in April due to an opposition boycott, and on these grounds the pro-secular constitutional court ruled the vote invalid. As a result, Gul withdrew his candidacy on May 6, and Erdogan called parliamentary elections for July 2007. The presidential vote was postponed.]

Turkish laws establish a framework for democratic elections generally in line with international standards, although with certain restrictions. A party can be shut down if its program is not in agreement with the constitution, and this can be widely interpreted to include support for Kurdish insurgents and opposition to state pillars such as secularism and the military. Restrictions are used to target certain groups. While even small gatherings can face difficulties, the most extreme example is the Kurdish Democratic People's Party (DEHAP), which is accused of being the political arm of the Kurdistan Workers' Party (PKK)—recently renamed Kongra-Gel and considered a terrorist organization by the Turkish government as well as by the EU and the United States. DEHAP has faced continual legal battles and arrests. Still, DEHAP does not represent the interests of most Kurds, who, when living outside the southeast, are generally more integrated and participate in mainstream politics.

A so-called double barrier impedes entry to the National Assembly. In order to win seats a party must be organized in at least half of the Turkish provinces and one-third of their districts, and it must also obtain at least 10 percent of the votes cast nationwide. As a result of this provision, many parties with considerable support are not represented in the National Assembly, particularly if their base is regional. Limits on campaign donations are not enforced, and party financing is not transparent.[1]

The last National Assembly elections, in November 2002, were widely judged both domestically and internationally as free and fair. A large number and variety of parties participated in active campaigning, the ruling parties lost, and opposition parties won seats in the National Assembly, thus attesting to the ability of the electorate to effect change. In fact, the old guard saw a sharp drop in support amid widespread public discontent with official corruption and inept handling of the economy (manifested in particular by the 2001 financial crisis). Only two parties passed the 10 percent threshold—the AKP and the Republican People's Party (CHP). The AKP won just 35 percent of the total vote but ended up with more than 70 percent of the seats, a stark demonstration of the limitations of the election rules.

Eight parties now hold seats in parliament due to changes in party affiliation. Nevertheless, opposition parties continue to lack the power to truly challenge government policy. The AKP holds about 350 seats and the CHP holds about 150. The Motherland Party, which was voted out in the last election, holds more than 20 seats; no other party holds more than 10 seats.

Observers continue to debate the extent to which the AKP has abandoned its former Islamist aspirations. Although the party has supported some loosening of restrictions on religious activity, such as the bans on headscarves and on the admission of students from religious schools to secular universities, it has not made any serious attempt to undermine Turkey's secular underpinnings. The party comprises both conservative

Muslims and more moderate yet religious Turks who favor reform. AKP policies sometimes seem aimed at one or the other, and nationalist rhetoric has increased as the 2007 elections approach. The risk of EU disapproval seems still to be a check on extreme policies.

Although no parliamentary system has complete separation of powers, legislative oversight of Turkey's executive branch is especially weak. Very little legislation actually originates in the National Assembly; instead, it is drafted by the government for review by parliamentarians. The party leader wields great power, and most decisions are made by the prime minister and a small group of advisers. Civil servants in Turkey are officially hired on the basis of examinations, but patronage undeniably plays a large role in practice.[2]

Civic groups have grown in strength and number since the 1980s, when they were mistrusted and tightly controlled. State–societal relations have improved, and civic groups have become more engaged in public policy. However, political groups still suffer from a lack of capacity and public support.[3] Recent reforms have eased restrictions on the establishment of associations; the impact of the Law on Associations, adopted in November 2004 and ending many outdated limitations, has been especially positive. Still, associations cannot form if they have "prohibited objectives" (Article 30 of Law on Associations) or are "in contravention of law and morality" (Article 56); these vague terms leave room for interpretation, allowing judges and prosecutors to target those whose activities they disagree with.[4] In addition, while the most severe restrictions on nongovernmental organizations (NGOs) funding have been lifted, limits on foreign funding remain. NGOs are often taken to court, and although most cases end in acquittal or fines, they make work difficult and at times economically unfeasible for such groups. Some human rights defenders have been intimidated, tortured, and imprisoned.[5] Those who refer to Kurdish rights are particular targets. NGOs and others are consulted on draft laws, but critics complain that public consultation is perfunctory and input not taken seriously.[6]

Turkey's constitution establishes freedom of the media (Articles 28–31), and EU harmonization reforms have included many measures to reduce political pressure on the media—including an improved Press Law in 2004. Nevertheless, major impediments remain. Turkey's Supreme Council of Radio and Television (RTUK) has the authority to sanction broadcasters if they are not in compliance with the law or its expansive broadcasting principles; fines and cancellation of programs or licenses occur. In February 2007, television station Kanal Turk reported attempts by officials to intimidate it into curtailing reporting critical of the ruling party.[7]

Implementation of the 2005 penal code (see Rule of Law) was delayed after large public protests; media groups criticized the fact that it would have made sentences longer in cases in which the law was violated by the media. The code was implemented in June 2005 after relevant changes were made. However, some crimes under the new penal code can still be punished with imprisonment, in violation of the new Press Law. Nobel Prize winner Orhan Pamuk—who was charged with "insulting Turkishness" as a result of his comments to a Swiss newspaper regarding the 1915 mass killings (which many call genocide) of Armenians by Turks and the deaths more recently of Kurds at the hands of Turkish security forces—is one of many journalists and writers tried under the now infamous Article 301 of the 2005 penal code, which makes illegal the ill-defined act of insulting the state and state institutions. As of December 2006, International PEN was monitoring more than eighty cases of writers and journalists on trial in Turkey.[8] Charges are dropped more often than not, but trials are time-consuming and expensive, constituting a deterrent to free speech. The prime minister launched a number of libel cases against writers and cartoonists in 2005.

Journalist Hrant Dink was shot dead outside his Istanbul office in January 2007. He had complained to the police of receiving death threats for some time before. His confessed, Turkish assailant did not act as part of any group with political aims but disapproved of Dink's position on the Armenian killings. Dink had been convicted with a suspended sentence under Article 301 for comments he had made on the same subject. He was Turkish of Armenian descent but did not support either the Turkish government or nationalist Armenian diaspora views on the issue.

Cultural expression is also limited by the effects of the restrictive laws, although the Turkish Publishers Association has reported that publication of books related to sensitive topics has become easier.[9] Novelist Elif Shafak, for example, was charged with but acquitted of denigrating Turkish national identity as a result of comments made by her fictional characters in one of her best-selling books. Internet freedom can also be affected; a court ordered Turkey's main internet provider to ban access to video-sharing website YouTube in March as a result of a video making fun of Ataturk. A draft bill on internet crimes would ban access to Turkish websites with content related to crimes defined under the new anti-terror law (see Rule of Law).

Censorship is not explicit, but censorship and self-censorship occur among both editors and journalists, who are concerned about violating the many restrictions.[9] Furthermore, media organizations are nearly all owned by giant holding companies with interests in many sectors beyond media, and they therefore influence news to serve their own business interests, in addition to allegedly trading positive coverage for political favors. The quality of the Turkish media is low.

Some very positive steps have been taken to expand media freedom. Perhaps most significantly, a series of recent laws have increasingly allowed broadcasts in minority languages, including Kurdish. The first broadcasts took place in 2004, and in 2006 a ban on local broadcasts as well as limitations on the length of cultural (though not political) programs was lifted. A taboo on discussing the 1915 Armenian killings was broken in 2005, when Bilgi University hosted a conference on the topic; the conference is indicative of a more blunt and critical public discussion of previously sensitive subjects, which has gradually increased in Turkey over the past ten years. Still, more dramatic steps need to be taken to ensure full freedom of expression.

Recommendations
- To reduce voter disfranchisement and produce more political pluralism in the National Assembly, the 10 percent threshold should be lowered to a level that allows for greater representation of the popular vote.
- The grounds for sanctions of political parties should be restricted to only those expressions that provoke violence, and dissolution of political parties should be a last resort.
- Press offenses should not be punishable by imprisonment and need to be unambiguously defined to preclude varying interpretations across courts. Article 301 should be abolished.
- The RTUK should be restructured to include members chosen by civil society in addition to those chosen by the government, and the broadcasting principles should be changed to give it more limited authority.

CIVIL LIBERTIES

PROTECTION FROM STATE TERROR, UNJUSTIFIED IMPRISONMENT, AND TORTURE:	3.71
GENDER EQUITY:	3.75
RIGHTS OF ETHNIC, RELIGIOUS, AND OTHER DISTINCT GROUPS:	3.75
FREEDOM OF CONSCIENCE AND BELIEF:	3.67
FREEDOM OF ASSOCIATION AND ASSEMBLY:	4.20
CATEGORY AVERAGE:	**3.82**

Many of the EU harmonization reforms that Turkey has passed since 2001 have been specifically geared toward protection of civil liberties, including increased minority and women's rights, broadened freedom of association and religion, stronger measures to protect against and prosecute torture, and a more democratic penal code. Moreover, the government is watching implementation closely. It has set up rights-monitoring boards to receive complaints and conduct independent monitoring of police stations to help prevent torture. A Parliamentary Human Rights Investigation Committee now investigates abuses, and police, judges, and public prosecutors receive human rights training. Long-term detention has been effectively curbed by reforms.[11] Turkey ratified a European Convention protocol abolishing the death penalty in February 2006. Nevertheless, problems remain, particularly (although not entirely) with implementation.

Torture and ill-treatment by officials continue to be an issue in Turkey. Although the Council of Europe in 2006 reported a continued decline in ill-treatment by law enforcement personnel, cases are still reported.[12] The 2005 penal code increases the punishment for those convicted of torture, and the legal framework is widely considered comprehensive, but mixed results on implementation have been reported.[13] In addition, trials are excessively long and often drag on beyond the statute of limitations. Although a number of cases have been brought against security forces, convictions are rare and appropriate sanctions are rarer.[14] The situation continues to improve, but slowly.

Prison conditions are harsh in some facilities, including treatment such as solitary confinement and medical neglect. Most controversial are the so-called F-type prisons, which isolate their prisoners. A Turkish lawyer ended a ten month hunger strike in January 2007 after the Ministry of Justice issued a decree doubling the amount of time these prisoners can socialize. An especially contentious imprisonment is that of Abdullah Ocalan, former leader of the Kurdish guerrilla movement, who is serving a life sentence in solitary confinement on a Turkish island and allegedly has not had adequate access to his lawyer or to visitors.[15] Ocalan's trial was ruled unfair by the European Court of Human Rights (ECHR) in May 2005, but he has not yet been retried.

The government is unable to prevent nonstate violence. Traditionally, such violence has come from Kurdish separatists in the southeast. Their organization, the PKK, ended its five-year ceasefire with the government in 2004, initiating a surge in attacks on civilians. Many recent attacks have been claimed by the Kurdistan Freedom Falcons, whose connection to the PKK is unclear. Violent clashes with security forces have increased as well, particularly in 2006; observers have blamed both separatism and general discontent with social and economic conditions. The PKK renewed the ceasefire in 2006, but the government did not recognize it, and attacks on both sides continued. Riots took place in southeastern cities after some PKK funerals in March 2006; ten civilians were killed.

In November 2005, a bomb in a bookstore in a southeastern city sparked protests and violent clashes with police throughout the region. Detained protesters alleged ill-treatment in custody and lack of access to lawyers.[16] Two Turkish security officials were convicted in connection with the bombing. However, evidence of government pressure, and especially the dismissal of the prosecutor involved, led critics to allege a lack of independence and thoroughness in the final, inconclusive investigation.[17]

Women's rights in Turkey are not fully realized in the cities and are observed even less in rural districts. Although the legal framework is strong, women still face discriminatory practices. NGOs and the Ministry for Women and Families report that about a third of women in Turkey are victims of violence.[18] A 2004 report by Amnesty International also documented forced marriages, deprivation, and lack of access to justice, which, it said, were tolerated and even endorsed by community leaders and government officials.[19] Women are also discriminated against in certain professions. Only about 28 percent of women participate in the formal workforce, and just 7 percent outside agriculture. Although women have had the right to vote and run for office since 1934, only 4 percent of parliamentarians are female. Education rates for girls are generally high, but in some rural provinces more than 50 percent of girls between the ages of six and fourteen are out of school. The World Economic Forum ranked Turkey 105th out of 115 countries surveyed in terms of its gender gap.[20]

Honor crimes, including killings—in which family members punish women who are considered to have brought dishonor on their family through situations such as pregnancy while unmarried or having been raped—continue to occur among traditional families. The 2005 penal code includes more severe punishment for these crimes among its other provisions designed to improve women's rights. A Turkish parliamentary delegation visited the southeast in December 2005 to raise public awareness about honor killings, and implementation of the new law has indeed had some effect.[21] In contrast, women's groups have reported rising suicide rates among women; some claim the stricter laws are provoking this as families pressure women in an attempt to circumvent the law.[22]

Turkey is a destination and transit country for trafficking in women and children for prostitution and forced labor. The government has been making serious efforts to curb human trafficking, including a hotline number for victims and numerous arrests.[23] The 2005 penal code includes an article mandating prison terms for traffickers.

Most of Turkey's population is Muslim, and many citizens are devout. While the constitution protects freedom of religion, the Turkish republic was set up on the premise of secularism, in which state and religious affairs are separated. In practice, this has meant considerable government control of religion; most prominently, the Directorate of Religious Affairs regulates the country's mosques and employs their imams, who are civil servants and are occasionally instructed on what to say by the government. Perhaps most contentiously, external signs of piety are banned in public institutions, which means that women are not allowed to wear headscarves in public universities and government offices, and observant men are reportedly dismissed from the military.[24] There are periodic protests against the headscarf ban, although the European Court of Human Rights ruled in June 2004 that it is legal. The AKP dropped its attempt to introduce an easing of the ban in the 2005 penal code.

Under the 2005 penal code, discrimination on the basis of personal characteristics is illegal. Minorities in Turkey are defined by religion, and only Jews (about 25,000 of whom live in Turkey), Greek Orthodox Christians (3,000), and Armenian Orthodox Christians (50,000) are recognized.[25] These groups are not integrated into the Turkish establishment. Although their rights are generally respected, freedom of religion is difficult for non-Muslims. Moreover, there are many other groups that likewise do not belong to the dominant Sunni Muslim sect and that have less protection. Other Christian and Muslim sects—including Alevis, who practice a combination of Islam and pre-Islamic religion—as well as mystical religious-social orders, have no legal status, and some of their activities are banned. Priests and churches were targeted violently on a few occasions in 2005–2006, in some cases resulting in deaths.

The Kurds are the largest group of non-ethnic Turks in Turkey, estimated at about 12 to 15 million people.[26] Many are well integrated and suffer no problems. However, the legacy of the fifteen-year guerrilla war in the southeast, in which more than 35,000 people were killed,[27] as well as Ataturk's emphasis on Turkishness over multiculturalism, has left the Kurds facing restrictions on their language, their culture, and their freedom of expression. The situation has improved with recent reforms, especially the start of Kurdish-language broadcasts (see Accountability and Public Voice). However, 2003 regulations allowing for classes in Kurdish permitted only private courses, and bureaucratic obstacles and financial problems led the last five Kurdish schools to close in 2005. Kurds voicing support for improved rights are targets for arrest.

Kurds suffered severe human rights abuses and institutionalized discrimination during the 1990s insurgency. About 35,000 compensation claims have been processed so far,[28] and Kurds have clearly benefited from broader human rights reforms. But village guards—a civil defense force first put in place by the central government in the southeast during the insurgency—continue to be insufficiently accountable, and compensation is reportedly lacking (see Rule of Law).

In July 2005, a new law on people with disabilities was passed, which added "disability" to the list of characteristics against which discrimination is punishable under the penal code. The law also promises better access for disabled persons to public areas and services but lacks the sanctioning power that may be required for enforcement. The interests of people with disabilities are addressed by the High Council of Disabilities, which brings public officials together with nongovernmental groups. Although the council has admirable aims, the needs of such people continue to exceed the limited services provided. Employers are required to reserve 3 percent of their workforce for employees with disabilities, but discrimination persists. Information about government services and regulations is not readily available in formats accessible to people with disabilities. No enforceable laws protect people with mental illnesses from arbitrary detention. A September 2005 report exposed severe abuses of patients in psychiatric hospitals, including inappropriate use of electric shocks.[29]

The constitution protects freedom of assembly, and reforms have decreased the number of restrictions. However, broad language in laws leaves room for interpretation. Despite an official end to bans on demonstrations, the International Helsinki Federation for Human Rights reported thirty-four meetings and demonstrations prohibited by authorities in 2005. Moreover, police regularly disperse peaceful public gatherings and continue to use excessive force in some cases.[30] In March 2005, police violently dispersed an unauthorized demonstration in Istanbul marking International Women's Day. Witnesses saw police beating and kicking demonstrators. The government investigated and punished those involved.

Employees have the right to join trade unions and cannot be discriminated against for doing so, although fines for discrimination are too small to act as a deterrent. Unions face restrictions on assembly similar to those of civic groups, and public employees do not have the right to strike. Many unions report harassment; Turkey's largest union, representing teachers, has faced difficult legal battles threatening closure and police interference in its peaceful demonstrations due to its support for mother-tongue (i.e., Kurdish) education.[31] While the constitution protects citizens from being forced to join an organization (Article 33), certain fields have professional organizations in which membership is compulsory.

Recommendations

- Visits to monitor and ensure respect for human rights in police stations and gendarmeries should be countrywide and independent and include members of respected human rights organizations; findings should be reported to the government and the public.
- All human rights violations must be promptly and thoroughly investigated and prosecuted by civilians, and officials under investigation should be suspended from duty.
- The principle of multiculturalism needs to be embraced, perhaps through constitutional amendment, to ensure that all religious, ethnic, and cultural groups are treated equally.
- Female education rates need to be improved, particularly in the southeast, to increase women's possibilities for labor market and political participation.[32]

RULE OF LAW

INDEPENDENT JUDICIARY:	3.60
PRIMACY OF RULE OF LAW IN CIVIL AND CRIMINAL MATTERS:	3.83
ACCOUNTABILITY OF SECURITY FORCES AND MILITARY TO CIVILIAN AUTHORITIES:	3.75
PROTECTION OF PROPERTY RIGHTS:	4.33
EQUAL TREATMENT UNDER THE LAW:	4.33
CATEGORY AVERAGE:	**3.97**

Two opposing forces operate in Turkey's judicial system: the enlightened reforms and their supporters, who promote the rule of law and increased civil liberties, versus more restrictive legal interpretations by those in the system, who see the reforms as a threat to the fundamental nature of the Turkish Republic. The recent reforms seriously curbed the role of the military in the justice system, and fundamentally revised the penal code. However, pre-reform ideas about defending national integrity, governmental institutions, and Turkish identity continue to persist among judges, prosecutors, and the officials of the Ministry of Justice. It is not yet certain which side will prove stronger over the long term.

According to the constitution (Article 15), everyone has a right to be presumed innocent until proven guilty. Recent reforms give all detainees the right to see a lawyer immediately, free of charge; enjoyment of this right has improved, including through a considerable increase in free legal aid.[33] In order to improve implementation of new reforms, judges and prosecutors have received training in human rights principles and the new penal code. However, access to counsel is sometimes delayed, compromised by police supervision, or not granted throughout an interrogation. Perhaps most worryingly, a request for legal counsel sometimes sparks ill-treatment.[34] Trials can drag on excessively.

The Turkish constitution provides for an independent judiciary, but in fact the executive sometimes interferes in the court system.[35] Through its links to the High Council of Judges and public prosecutors, the executive can influence judicial training, appointment, promotion, and financing, as well as bias placement of judges and prosecutors in sensitive trials. A 2005 law authorizing the Justice Ministry to be more involved in judicial appointments caused vocal protests from the judicial sector as well as opposition members. Training of judges is inadequate, and because there is no proper review of cases, many of those that end up in the courts result in acquittal due to lack of merit. Public prosecutors in Turkey have a status very close to that of judges, both functionally and symbolically, thus placing the defense in an inferior position. Increasing numbers of cases have been reported of judges and prosecutors taking bribes to affect decisions.[36]

A gunman shot five judges, killing one, in a courtroom in May 2006. The court was known for its strict secular principles, and the attacker allegedly said his motive was to protest the judges' ruling in favor of the headscarf ban.[37]

The constitution grants immunity to all legislators and cabinet ministers, and the AKP has reneged on a preelection promise to end immunity. Furthermore, permission is required from the superiors of public officials (or the National Assembly, in the case of ministers) to open investigations against them. Some officials have been tried after leaving office, but often the statute of limitations has expired before a case can legally be brought against them.

In September 2004, the National Assembly approved the first major overhaul of the penal code since it was written seventy-eight years earlier. The fundamental changes in the new code include explicit guidelines on what constitutes a crime, accompanied by a statement that no other acts are punishable, and institutionalization of the concept that punishment should be in proportion to the crime committed. The revisions fill many of the gaps in the system. There are accusations, however, that residual ambiguities still allow judges to interpret some laws at will, despite dozens of circulars sent to prosecutors for clarification. More generally, unequal treatment under the law remains a problem, as discrimination against the poor in the administration of justice is common.

A 2006 antiterrorism law, which makes many criminal offenses punishable more harshly if they are committed in support of terrorism, has provoked fears that some of the advances will be reversed, given the broad definition of terrorism used. Despite protests by human rights and other groups, the government considered the bill necessary to address the rising violence in the southeast. Among other things, access to a lawyer can be denied for twenty-four hours under the new law.

State security courts, which had been accused of human rights abuses and an absence of due process, were abolished in 2004. Cases against the integrity of the state, which were formerly under their jurisdiction, have been passed to new heavy penal courts. The latter have been criticized, however, as not representing an improvement; they may even use the same judges and prosecutors formerly accused of abuses, and there is no impartial reexamination of evidence in retrials.[38]

The military holds a special place in the Turkish republic. Since Turkey's first military coup, in 1960, it has acted as the guarantor of Turkey's secularism, territorial integrity, and government functioning. While it has never stayed in power long, it used the first coup, and subsequent ones in 1971 and 1980, to increase its autonomy and enhance its role during civilian rule. Turkish generals have expressed opinions on everything from judicial decisions to draft bills in the National Assembly to EU membership, and those opinions have seldom been ignored altogether. After the Welfare Party came to dominate the ruling coalition in 1996, leading to increased fundamentalism, the military forced its removal.

The EU continues to criticize Turkey for lack of civilian control of the military. Turkey's EU-inspired reforms have confined the once-powerful National Security Council (NSC) to an advisory role with a civilian at its head, removed military members from political bodies such as the higher education council and RTUK, and increased transparency and parliamentary oversight of military expenditures. Moreover, the reforms have been accompanied by increased space for open public critique of the military. However, the military is still not entirely subservient to the civilian ministry of defense, and it maintains autonomy in its strategic decision making. High-ranking military officers continue to voice opinions on domestic and foreign policy issues; in October 2006 the chief of staff accused the government of encouraging Islamic fundamentalism. Meanwhile, public trust in the military is strong, and military schools are among the best in the country, which contribute to the continued power and prestige of this institution.

Property rights are generally respected in Turkey, although in some areas societal biases impede women from owning property. The most significant property rights problem in Turkey continues to relate to the hundreds of thousands of people driven from their homes in the southeast by government forces in the 1990s.[39] The government has initiated a project to compensate these people and return them to their villages. Official and unofficial sources agree that more than 110,000 have returned so far,[40] and 2006 saw the first victims to receive financial compensation under a 2004 law sparked by an ECHR decision. However, critics claim the commission dealing with claims is biased, depriving victims of fair compensation, and village guards have allegedly used intimidation and violence to prevent others from returning to their homes.[41] The ECHR ruled in January 2006 that the compensation law provides adequate redress, but Human Rights Watch has argued that implementation has subsequently deteriorated.[42]

Recommendations

- Governmental immunity must end so that official wrongdoing can be prosecuted properly.
- Executive influence over judges and public prosecutors must be eliminated in structure and in practice, beginning with an end to executive authority over judicial appointments and other judicial matters.
- The government must abolish the village guard system, beginning with immediate disarmament and followed by the provision of alternative employment for current guards, to ease the return of displaced people and build trust between the government and the people in the southeast.

- The military should be clearly separated from civilian matters. It should not make public statements on or otherwise be involved in issues beyond military, defense, and security, and any involvement it attempts should be resisted by the civilian government.

ANTICORRUPTION AND TRANSPARENCY

ENVIRONMENT TO PROTECT AGAINST CORRUPTION:	3.20
LAWS AND ETHICAL STANDARDS BETWEEN PRIVATE AND PUBLIC SECTORS:	4.00
ENFORCEMENT OF ANTICORRUPTION LAWS:	3.50
GOVERNMENTAL TRANSPARENCY:	3.86
CATEGORY AVERAGE:	**3.64**

Turkey continues to struggle with substantial corruption in government and in daily life. The AKP rose to power, despite (or perhaps because of) being relatively unknown, in part due to the corruption and economic mismanagement of previous governments. Turkey has signed a series of international corruption conventions; the UN Convention against Corruption entered into force in June 2006. However, the AKP's commitment to fighting corruption has been cast in doubt by lack of follow-through. Perhaps even more so than with other reforms, the anticorruption framework has not translated into individuals changing their behavior, although with time it may have more significant effects.

Upon taking office, the AKP instituted an urgent action plan that included anticorruption measures. However, although it formed a ministerial committee closely connected to the government, it never established a single, independent anticorruption committee, nor has the draft anticorruption law been passed.

Bureaucracy pervades the system. The government made efforts to streamline regulations after the 2001 financial crisis, including a considerable privatization program to reduce the number of state-owned enterprises; several state-owned companies were sold in 2005–2006. Nevertheless, businesses continue to face more complexity than in other OECD countries;[43] business leaders surveyed by the World Economic Forum in 2006 listed "inefficient government bureaucracy" as the most problematic factor for doing business in Turkey.[44] Many government officials have business interests that conflict with their public service duties.[45] All must file asset-disclosure forms, but these forms are inaccessible to the public and are not generally used for investigative purposes. Nevertheless, Erdogan declared his assets quite publicly in February 2006. The government adopted an ethics code for the public sector in April 2005 and proposed a political ethics law in January 2007.

Conflicts of interest in the private sector are regulated by laws in each sector, not by a single piece of legislation, although draft revisions to the commercial code would extend audit and governance standards to all companies. The 2001 financial crisis sparked the disclosure of the huge conflicts of interest that existed in the financial sector. Conversely, corruption in the education sector is not a serious problem.

The new penal code punishes corruption-related crimes more severely, and the statute of limitations was extended. However, many of those cases that make it to court result in acquittal or light sentences.[46] Civil society has criticized the government for not investigating and prosecuting corruption effectively, a charge that the government denies.[47] All legislators and ministers have immunity from prosecution (see Rule of Law), despite significant allegations of legislative corruption. Charges that former prime minister Mesut Yilmaz and former economy minister Gunes Taner interfered in the privatization of Turkbank were withdrawn in June 2006 after a judge ruled the charges could not be verified.

The media report widely on such cases and have also revealed lower-level corruption. Reporting is hampered, however, as journalists risk imprisonment for investigations of those still in office as well as censorship by the business interests that own their outlets.[48] Although public officials have a legal obligation to report offenses, whistle-blowers do not have significant protection.[49]

A 2006 law establishing an ombudsman linked to the National Assembly was passed over a presidential veto. A court of accounts conducts annual audits of revenues and expenditures of public bodies on behalf of the National Assembly, but overlapping responsibilities for inspection and investigation mean that irregularities are not consistently investigated.[50] Tax auditing currently is performed by several different units of the ministry of finance at the national and local level and is largely ineffective; corruption in the tax system is a problem.[51] A new law ensuring budget transparency went into effect in 2004–2005, although it has although it has not been fully implemented.[52] In terms of foreign aid, a National Authorizing Officer audits EU funds, but effective antifraud provisions and implementing legislation for financial management and control are lacking.[53]

The government launched a reform of the public procurement system in the aftermath of the financial crisis to ensure transparency and accountability, culminating in a new law adopted in 2002. However, the AKP overturned certain provisions, leaving room for corruption once again. An investigation launched into tender fraud in public agencies in fall 2006 led to the arrests of many suspects. A law on freedom of information went into effect in April 2004. While this greatly increased public distribution of information, the law is not consistently followed, and vague provisions exempting state and trade secrets have led to allegedly overly conservative interpretations.[54]

Recommendations

- A specialized agency should be empowered to investigate corruption and work with law enforcement on preventive measures, thus coordinating the anticorruption effort. The government must repeal government officials' immunity and prosecute governmental corruption.
- A legal mechanism should be passed to prevent and punish conflicts of interest among government officials.
- Public awareness of the impact of corruption must be increased, including through the education system to target citizens at an early age.
- Access to information should be improved through clear guidelines on implementation of the law and strengthened independence for the board that reviews decisions under the law.

NOTES

[1] Yilmaz Esmer, "Turkey," *Global Integrity Report* (Washington, D.C.: Center for Public Integrity, 10 September 2004), http://www.globalintegrity.org/reports/2004/2004/country20e1.html?cc=tr; "Response of Toplumsal Saydamlik Hareketi Dernegi to EC's Questions about Corruption and Transparency in Turkey" (Istanbul: Toplumsal Saydamlik Hareketi Dernegi [TSHD-TI Turkey], 5 July 2004), www.saydamlik.org/haber.html [in Turkish]; "Turkey: 2006 Progress Report" (Brussels: European Commission [EC], 8 November 2006).

[2] Esmer, "Turkey."

3 I?il Sariyüce and Kristen Stevens, "Turkish human rights spring forth," *Turkish Daily News*, 13 December 2006.

4 "Turkey: 2006 Progress Report" (EC).

5 "Human Rights Defenders in Turkey" (Vienna: International Helsinki Federation for Human Rights, 3 April 2006).

6 See "Freedom of Expression in the New Turkish Penal Code" (Ankara: Human Rights Agenda Association, 2006).

7 "Authorities harass critical television station, probe finances of staff and programme guests" (Washington, D.C.: Freedom House, 27 February 2007).

8 "Turkey: Author Ipek Calislar acquitted in Turkey; Trials against others continue" (London: International PEN, 21 December 2006).

9 "Turkey: 2006 Progress Report" (EC).

10 Esmer, "Turkey"; author interview, 15 November 2006.

11 "Turkey: First Steps Toward Independent Monitoring of Police Stations and Gendarmeries" (Brussels: Human Rights Watch [HRW], Briefing Paper, 6 March 2006).

12 "Report to the Turkish Government on the Visit to Turkey Carried out by the European Committee for the Prevention of Torture and Inhuman or Degrading Treatment or Punishment (CPT) from 7 to 14 December 2005" (Strasbourg: Council of Europe, 6 September 2006).

13 "Report to the Turkish Government on the Visit to Turkey Carried out by the European Committee for the Prevention of Torture and Inhuman or Degrading Treatment or Punishment (CPT) from 7 to 14 December 2005" (Strasbourg: Council of Europe, 6 September 2006); "Turkey: Abdulkadir Bartan" (London: Amnesty International [AI], AI Index EUR 44/020/2005, 25 May 2005).

14 "Turkey: Insufficient and Inadequate: Judicial Remedies against Torturers and Killers" (AI, Public Statement, AI index EUR 44/037/2004, 16 November 2004); "Turkey: Protecting the Torturers? Grave concerns at trial proceedings in Iskenderun" (AI, Press Release, AI Index EUR 44/015/2005, 21 April 2005); "Turkey: 2006 Progress Report" (Brussels: European Commission [EC], 8 November 2006).

15 "Report to the Turkish Government . . . by the CPT" (Council of Europe).

16 "Turkey: Recent human rights violations must be investigated" (AI, Public Statement, EUR 44/005/2006, 12 April 2006).

17 "Turkey: No impunity for State Officials Who Violate Human Rights" (AI, EUR 44/006/2006, May 2006).

18 "Parliament Leaves Women Unprotected," *Turkish Daily News*, 13 January 2007.

19 "Turkey: Women Confronting Family Violence" (New York: AI, Stop Violence against Women series, June 2004).

20 "Haydi Kızlar Okula! [Off to School, Girls!]—the Girls' Education Campaign in Turkey" (New York: UNICEF,[no date]), http://www.unicef.org/turkey/pdf/ge47.pdf; "Gender Gap Index 2006" (London: World Economic Forum, 2006).

21 "Turkey: 2006 Progress Report" (EC).

22 See Filiz Kardam, *The Dynamics of Honor Killings in Turkey: Prospects for Action* (Ankara: UNDP and UNPF, November 2005), http://europeandcis.undp.org/?menu=p_cms /show&content_id=3E9AC2FE-F203-1EE9-BF415971B62D7FE0.

23 *Trafficking in Persons Report* (Washington, D.C.: U.S. Dept of State, June 2006); "687 people tried for human trafficking last year," *Turkish Daily News*, 10 August 2006.

24 Levent Korkut, "Country Report: Turkey," *Report on Measures to Combat Discrimination in the 13 Candidate Countries* (Brussels: Migration Policy Group, May 2003).

25 Senem Aydin and E. Fuat Keyman, "European Integration and the Transformation of Turkish Democracy" (Brussels: Centre for European Policy Studies, EU–Turkey Working Papers No 2, August 2004).

26 "Third Report on Turkey" (Strasbourg: European Commission against Racism and Intolerance, 15 February 2005).

27 Aydin and Keyman, "European Integration . . ."

28 "Turkey: 2006 Progress Report" (EC).

29 "Behind Closed Doors: Human Rights Abuses in the Psychiatric Facilities, Orphanages and Rehabilitation Centers of Turkey" (Washington, D.C.: Mental Disability Rights International, 28 September 2005).

30 "Human Rights in the OSCE Region: Europe, Central Asia and North America: Report 2006" (Vienna: International Helsinki Federation for Human Rights, 8 June 2006).

31 "Turkey: Annual Survey of Violations of Trade Union Rights" (Brussels: International Confederation of Free Trade Unions, 2006).

32 For more details see for example, "Improving Educational Opportunities for Girls: Lessons from the Past Decade" (Ankara: Unicef Turkey, 2003).

33 "Turkey: 2006 Progress Report" (EC).

34 "Turkey: First Steps . . ." (HRW).

35 See, for example, "Turkey: 2006 Progress Report" (Brussels: European Commission [EC], 8 November 2006).

36 "Judiciary in Turkey: Rooting out Corruption," in *Global Corruption Report* (Cambridge: Cambridge University Press, forthcoming).

37 "Prime Council of State attack suspect comes clean," *Turkish Daily News*, 12 August 2006.

38 "Turkey: Unfair trials—failed justice under new courts" (AI, press release 44/014/2006, 6 September 2006).

39 While the government places the number at about 370,000, a respected study by Hacettepe University put the number between 950,000 and 1.2 million. "Turkey migration and internally displaced population survey" (Ankara: Hacettepe University Institute of Population Studies, press release, 6 December 2006); see also, "Unjust, Restrictive, and Inconsistent: The Impact of Turkey's Compensation Law with Respect to Internally Displaced People" (HRW, December 2006).

40 "Gov't takes step to combat sad legacy of PKK conflict: internally displaced persons," *Turkish Daily News*, 1 October 2006.

41 "Third Report on Turkey" (European Commission against Racism and Intolerance); "Unjust, Restrictive, and Inconsistent . . ." (HRW).

42 "Unjust, Restrictive, and Inconsistent . . ." (HRW).

43 "Economic Survey of Turkey, 2006" (Paris: Organisation for Economic Co-operation and Development [OECD], Policy Brief, October 2006).

44 Augusto Lopez-Claros, ed., *The Global Competitiveness Report 2006–2007* (Geneva: World Economic Forum, 2006).

45 "Response . . ." (TSHD-TI Turkey), www.saydamlik.org/haber.html [in Turkish, translation provided to author].

46 Ibid.

47 "Joint First and Second Evaluation Round: Evaluation Report on Turkey" (Strasbourg: Group of States against Corruption, 10 March 2006).

48 "Response . . ." (TSHD-TI), www.saydamlik.org/haber.html; author interview, 15 November 2006.

49 "Joint First . . ." (Group of States against Corruption).

50 Ibid.

51 "Global Corruption Barometer 2006" (Berlin: Transparency International, 7 December 2006); James H. Anderson and Cheryl W. Gray, "Anticorruption in Transition: Who is Succeeding and Why" (Washington, D.C.: World Bank, 2006).

52 "Economic Survey of Turkey, 2006" (OECD).

53 "Turkey: 2006 Progress Report" (EC).

54 Anderson and Gray, "Anticorruption in Transition . . ." (World Bank); David Banisar, "Freedom of Information around the World 2006" (Washington, D.C.: Freedominfo.org, July 2006); "Joint First . . ." (Group of States against Corruption).

ZAMBIA

CAPITAL: Lusaka
POPULATION: 11.5 million
GNI PER CAPITA: $630

SCORES	2005	2007
ACCOUNTABILITY AND PUBLIC VOICE:	3.85	4.08
CIVIL LIBERTIES:	4.57	4.65
RULE OF LAW:	4.26	4.15
ANTICORRUPTION AND TRANSPARENCY:	3.39	3.46

(scores are based on a scale of 0 to 7, with 0 representing weakest and 7 representing strongest performance)

David Simon

INTRODUCTION

Just as Zambia's transition to multiparty democracy in 1991 heralded a moment of great optimism for democracy across Africa, its apparent lapse into old authoritarian habits during the administration of President Frederick Chiluba (1991–2001) was seen as emblematic of the dashed hopes that democratic transitions might revolutionize African governance. Now, more than fifteen years after the return of multiparty politics to Zambia, a more nuanced story is developing, calling for moderation of both the excessive optimism of the era's early years and the pessimism that set in later.

From Zambia's independence in 1964 until 1991, the country was ruled by Kenneth Kaunda and his United National Independence Party (UNIP). Although multiparty competition existed at independence (and had, indeed, featured prominently in the process of decolonization), Kaunda banned opposition parties within a decade of coming to power. By the late 1980s, opponents of Kaunda's regime found common cause

---

David J. Simon is a lecturer in political science at Yale University.

in their challenge to the single-party nature of the state. Forming a coalition known as the Movement for Multiparty Democracy (MMD), they forced Kaunda to legalize opposition parties. After becoming a party bearing the same name, the MMD resoundingly defeated Kaunda and UNIP in an election in October 1991.

Succeeding Kaunda, Chiluba embraced the rhetoric of both political and economic liberalization but often backpedaled in terms of substance. Chiluba twice declared states of emergency, during which he imprisoned political opponents. In 1996, the MMD regime wrote changes into the constitution that barred several leading opponents— including Kaunda—from running for president. Toward the end of his term, only widespread objections from civil society and some members of the MMD itself, supplemented by pressure from donor countries and organizations, kept Chiluba from seeking to extend his tenure beyond the constitutionally mandated limit of two terms.

Chiluba's hand-picked successor, one-time vice president Levy Mwanawasa, won the presidential election in 2001, prevailing by the slimmest of margins over a sharply divided opposition. Mwanawasa garnered just 29 percent of the vote, a mere 2 percentage points more than his nearest rival. Upon assuming office, Mwanawasa unveiled what he called a "New Deal" for Zambia, emphasizing his intention not only to reinvigorate the economy but also to commit to better governance. He surprised many by launching an anticorruption drive that began by targeting his predecessor. The strategy appeared to be tantamount to political suicide—Mwanawasa had relied on the support of staunch Chiluba backers for his narrow win in 2001, and the opposition had vowed not to repeat its fateful fractionalization in the next electoral cycle. Yet Mwanawasa returned to office for a second term in elections held in September 2006. He apparently benefited from the untimely (but not suspicious) death of his main rival, 2001 runner-up Anderson Mazoka, in May 2006. Mwanawasa's willingness to go after his one-time sponsors also paid political dividends, as he won over many of his former opponents.

On economic matters, which necessarily establish the context in which trends in liberty and freedom play themselves out, Zambia has also been paradigmatic for much of Africa. After a promising postindependence performance, during which per capita gross domestic product (GDP) growth averaged 2.2 percent per year from 1964 to 1969, per capita GDP declined by an average of 2.0 percent per year over the course of the 1970s, 1980s, and 1990s. Mirroring broader continental trends, per capita GDP growth returned in the 2000s, averaging 2.5 percent per year from 2000 through 2005.[1] A wide range of factors contributed to the improved performance, including improved trading terms with the United States, debt relief, increased foreign exchange earnings from tourism displaced from Zimbabwe, and a mid-decade boom in the price of copper. Beyond macroeconomic figures, however, poverty is widespread in Zambia. According to the most recent available World Bank data, 87 percent of the population lives below the US$2-per-day poverty line.[2]

It is in this context—democratic consolidation efforts led by an apparently sincere but politically vulnerable president, ongoing partisan realignment, and improving economic performance amid widespread poverty—that the recent trends in accountability, civil liberties, rule of law, and anticorruption efforts must be considered.

ACCOUNTABILITY AND PUBLIC VOICE

FREE AND FAIR ELECTORAL LAWS AND ELECTIONS:	4.25
EFFECTIVE AND ACCOUNTABLE GOVERNMENT:	4.00
CIVIC ENGAGEMENT AND CIVIC MONITORING:	4.33
MEDIA INDEPENDENCE AND FREEDOM OF EXPRESSION:	3.75
CATEGORY AVERAGE:	**4.08**

The September 2006 elections tested the ruling party's ability to stay in power, particularly in light of President Mwanawasa's efforts to prosecute his predecessor, Frederick Chiluba, on charges of corruption. The elections also challenged the Mwanawasa regime's commitment to improved governance, revealing whether the principles underlying the "New Deal" could force a break with the legacy of heavily incumbent-biased elections in Zambia.[3]

Substantively, the elections produced a narrow but solid victory for the ruling MMD. Mwanawasa secured a presidential victory with 44 percent of the vote, versus 29 percent and 25 percent for his nearest rivals, the Patriotic Front's Michael Sata and the United Democratic Alliance's Hakainde Hichilema, respectively. Meanwhile, the MMD won

72 out of the 150 National Assembly seats, with the constitutional provision that the president may appoint up to 8 additional lawmakers further guaranteeing MMD control over parliament. Procedurally, the elections were relatively smooth, with few reports of mishandled ballots or ballot boxes. A 2006 Electoral Act had introduced transparent ballot boxes and voter identification cards bearing the holders' photographs. Voter registration, previously conducted only before elections, was reformed to allow continuous updates of the voter rolls. Although there were scattered allegations of fraud, none cast the essential results of the elections in doubt.

Several problems, each of which had plagued earlier elections, remain unresolved. The most contentious is the constitutional framework under which elections take place. The draft constitution produced by the Mung'omba Constitutional Review Commission, which Mwanawasa had appointed to consider revising or replacing the constitution, had recommended a new requirement that the winner of a presidential election garner more than 50 percent of the votes—in contrast to the prevailing single-round, first-past-the-post system. Yet despite having pledged to sponsor a new constitution, Mwanawasa delayed making any changes until after the electoral cycle.

Also unchanged is the political status of the Electoral Commission. Critics have called for more institutional independence for the commission with respect to both its composition and its funding. In the absence of constitutional changes, the commission remains composed of presidential appointees, with its funding dependent on annual budgetary allocations and, in many recent years, donor contributions.

The new Electoral Act also called on the Electoral Commission to produce a new set of ground rules for campaigning in light of recurrent concerns over vote buying and the abuse of state resources for political purposes in past elections. The resulting document, the Electoral Code of Conduct, mandated equal access to the state-owned media. Indeed, the Zambia National Broadcasting Company (ZNBC) apparently complied with these rules with respect to programming. However, a study by the Media Institute of Southern Africa found that thirty-six out of forty-eight news radio stories pertaining to political parties featured the incumbent MMD.[4] The code also instituted enforceable penalties for coercive or intimidating behavior over the course of the campaign, which helped to realize a largely peaceful and quiet electoral period. Violence, generally nonlethal, and confrontations did greet the announcement of the results, as supporters of the Patriotic Front initially refused to accept Mwanawasa's reelection.[5] Within days, however, reports of postelection violence subsided, and the legitimacy of Mwanawasa's term was accepted almost universally.

Although the 2006 elections resulted in a fourth consecutive term for what is, historically, one of only two ruling parties in Zambian history, they inspired confidence in the electoral mechanism as a means of providing accountability. The ruling party defeated its rivals on a relatively level playing field. In fact, other than the constitutional issues noted above, the only factor instrumental to the MMD's success outside of its popularity and that of its candidates was probably the death of Mazoka, then the presumptive candidate of the United Democratic Alliance, in May 2006. Compared with Mazoka, Hichilema was relatively unknown and probably had less nationwide appeal. Taking into account the institutional ground rules, the Mwanawasa victory represents the most legitimate reflection of the will of the people that the system could provide.

No rules regulate campaign finance in Zambia. A controversy arose during the 2006 campaign when it was reported that Sata, who had criticized Chinese investors, was being bankrolled by Taiwanese business interests. There was no public mechanism to confirm or refute the allegations, and the episode served to shed light on the need for better accounting of campaign revenues and expenditures. The lack of campaign finance regulation presents economically powerful actors with an opportunity to exert undue influence on Zambian politics. Innuendo aside, however, there is little direct evidence that any such actors have done so in recent elections.

Electoral participation continued an upward trend that began in 2001, following years of low and falling participation. Almost 2.8 million Zambians voted in the 2006 contest, over a million more than in the previous set of elections. In addition to a higher rate of voter registration, the turnout rate also reached a record level of 71 percent. The advent of rolling voter registration did much to facilitate political participation, although a concerted registration drive in advance of the 2006 elections was still necessary. The 2006 elections also witnessed a large increase in the number of ballot boxes within existing polling stations, as well as a small increase in the number of polling stations, vastly reducing the time spent in queues and thereby lowering the economic opportunity cost of voting.

The narrow margin of the MMD's National Assembly victory has strengthened the parliament's role in the legislative process, as the government cannot afford to ignore potential defections. This differs from the Kaunda years, when the legislature was subordinate to the UNIP apparatus, and the Chiluba years, when overwhelming MMD majorities allowed the administration to use the parliament as a rubber stamp for policies formulated within the cabinet. During Mwanawasa's first term, when the MMD also held a narrow majority, the government was forced to make deals with the opposition and even bring non-MMD members into the cabinet, at times throwing the opposition into disarray over whether or not to cooperate.

Meanwhile, the judiciary remains structurally subservient to the executive branch, with its members essentially serving at the pleasure of the president. While Mwanawasa has not noticeably abused or even used the power to fire judges and magistrates, long-planned constitutional revisions would do well to strengthen the independence of the judiciary.

Notwithstanding the noteworthy improvement in the meaning and conduct of elections in Zambia, the level of accountability must be viewed in the context of how government works on a daily basis. Members of parliament continue to lack the means or incentives to serve their constituencies in specific ways, particularly outside of the campaigning season. At least in the MMD, the party's national executive committee retains the right to determine who will stand for election in a given constituency, meaning that for sitting members of parliament, loyalty to the party leadership is often more important than service to constituents. Meanwhile, too few opportunities exist for most citizens to contact their political representatives, and lawmakers rarely make themselves available to constituents. Local government remains underfunded and thus unable to respond to constituent needs, rendering its greater proximity to the public an unexploited resource for improved governance.

The government has espoused decentralization with respect to decision making, but it is not yet clear whether the financial resources to make it effective from a governance perspective will be allocated. For many rural Zambians, traditional rulers remain the usual recourse for addressing public grievances and needs. Despite the institutionalization of the House of Chiefs—a body of twenty-seven traditional rulers limited to advisory powers—traditional leadership is, at best, awkwardly integrated with the other elements of constitutional government in Zambia. The formal state is unwilling and politically unable to actively provide incentives for good government by traditional rulers. For their part, citizens may be wary of further institutionalizing traditional leaders, since for many the cost of doing so—potentially forgoing accountability with respect to private matters (i.e., dispute resolution)—is seen as greater than the benefit of increased accountability on public matters. Thus, the quality of local leadership in terms of responsiveness and the provision of public goods is uneven.

The most noteworthy hindrance to the Zambian bureaucracy has traditionally been the informal system of tribal preferences by which many posts were allocated. To some extent, the conditions that created the fragile political position of the Mwanawasa regime—primarily the fracturing of the MMD coalition, which was perceived to have been strongly dominated by Bemba speakers, and the subsequent necessity to forge coalitions with former rivals—have reduced the hold of the politically driven, ethnicity-based patronage complex. Although bureaucratic decisions, including those pertaining to human resources, remain open to decision-makers' and supervisors' biases, the more competitive political environment has led to fewer publicly confirmed instances of blatant patronage, and increases the likelihood that such abuses would come to light.

The Zambian state has engaged in the rhetoric of protecting and advancing the interests of historically disadvantaged groups, including women and people with disabilities. The constitution bars many forms of discrimination, although the protected categories do not include sexual preference or orientation. In 2006, the government created a Ministry of Gender and Women in Development with the objective of promoting women's interests at the cabinet level. It is unclear, after only a year of operations, what effect the ministry will have on budgetary allocations and policy making.

The state generally respects the right of interest groups to organize, so long as they adhere to a set of fairly straightforward registration procedures. The state does not, however, necessarily feel compelled to listen to them and does not provide regular opportunities to engage with them. For example, the National Assembly is less dedicated to committee hearings and meetings than to its sometimes raucous floor debates.

As a result, nongovernmental organizations (NGOs), whether organized around specific issues or identity groups, often feel marginalized in the political sphere. The experiences of the Oasis Forum, an umbrella organization that has lobbied for a new constitution and broad-based participation in its creation, are somewhat emblematic. While the Mung'omba Commission's draft constitution was congruent with the proposals of the Oasis Forum in many respects, the government's decision to postpone responding to the commission's recommendations until after the 2006 elections left the group feeling stymied and impotent. Many NGOs receive a substantial portion of their funding from foreign donors. The Mwanawasa administration has not been as critical of such funding arrangements as its predecessor but has occasionally attacked NGOs' foreign links as a means of questioning their activities.[6]

Media freedom remains a contested subject in Zambia. The *Post*, an opposition newspaper, has served as a lightning rod for government criticism of the press. The *Post*'s editor, Fred M'membe, was arrested on defamation charges in November 2005 following an editorial in which he wrote that Mwanawasa was a man of "foolishness, stupidity, and lack of humility."[7] Mwanawasa had specifically criticized the *Post* the day before. The incident was somewhat extraordinary, however, in that over the past three years, the government has generally eschewed formal legal proceedings against media outlets with which it disagrees. Indeed, in early 2006, the government decided against prosecuting M'membe for the "foolishness" incident. The decision conformed to a well-established pattern of harassment of the media in Zambia, whereby threats of prosecution for defamation and libel are far more frequent than actual prosecutions. Such apparent restraint speaks to the relative independence of the judiciary.

More frequently, the government and others have preferred informal intimidation. M'membe himself had been questioned by police, and *Post* vendors had been harassed by MMD supporters, under similar circumstances in June 2005.[8] The host of a call-in program on a privately owned station, Radio Phoenix, received similar treatment in June 2005 when he read a fax he said he had received that was critical of the government. After the police questioned the host, the radio station's owners dismissed him, undoubtedly in an effort to avoid the type and consequences of disfavor that the *Post* had faced.[9]

Supporters of the ruling party were not alone in attacking the *Post*'s operations: at the time of the 2006 elections, supporters of the Patriotic Front political party attacked the *Post*'s office after the paper projected that the MMD would win. In other incidents, Patriotic Front supporters intimidated a cameraman from the government-owned ZNBC, and supporters of another opposition party, the United Party for National Development, barred a reporter with the government-owned *Times of Zambia* from a press briefing.[10] The perpetrators of these acts of intimidation were apparently not pursued by the authorities.

In recent years, the domination of the private media by the public media has diminished somewhat. Private and community radio stations have proliferated, leaving the ZNBC with a declining share of the radio market. The government still owns two of the three major newspapers, the *Times of Zambia* and the *Zambia Daily Mail*, although the *Post* is widely available as well. Only in the realm of broadcast television are the state media unchallenged, with the ZNBC still alone on the airwaves. Cable offers some alternative local programming but is not widely available. Most private media outlets are not dependent on the government for advertising revenue. While the state owns and operates one of the two major internet service providers, it does not censor or limit access to external websites. Similarly, the state has refrained from interference in more traditional, cultural media, such as literature and music.

The creation of space for the media to operate is a structural matter subject to ongoing debate. The constitution grants conditional freedom of expression to the media; the concept is enshrined in Article 20, but is diluted with exceptions and language found elsewhere in the constitution and the penal code that protects the president and the National Assembly from criticism. Although the incidents cited above reflect continued sensitivity to criticism on the part of the government, there are signs of increased tolerance. On at least two occasions, the speaker of the National Assembly, Amusaa Mwanamwambwa, refused to initiate defamation proceedings against journalists who had criticized the body, despite requests to do so from MMD lawmakers. It is worth noting that actors outside the government have also availed themselves of defamation suits against the press. Presidential candidate Michael Sata in August 2006 successfully sued for an injunction on the *Zambia Daily Mail* against publishing further "defamatory stories," after the paper ran two critical articles, "PLOT 1: Where does Sata stand?" and "Michael Sata Scares Investors."[11]

Three pieces of legislation under consideration would increase the protection and support for the media. A Freedom of Information bill, composed but not yet before the parliament, would provide greater access to government information. After the elections, Mwanawasa's new minister of information, Vernon Mwaanga, declined to move on the bill, which had been withdrawn in 2002 after it was ruled that the creation of the bureaucracy to implement it would require budgetary authorization.

The other two bills—the Independent Broadcasting Authority (IBA) Act and the ZNBC (Amendment) Act—provide for independent boards to govern the state-owned media. Both bills became law but have not been implemented by the government. The High Court handed down a contempt-of-parliament ruling against the government for its failure to submit an ad hoc committee's nominees for the independent boards to lawmakers for final approval. However, in 2007 the Supreme Court of Zambia overturned that decision, upholding the government's right to block the nominations.[12]

The freedom of the media is also limited by codes of conduct. All major outlets except the *Post* adhere to a voluntary code, the Media Ethics Code of Zambia (MECOZ). Subscribers to the code are subject to a fine for violating its standards. The *Post*'s refusal to join MECOZ reflects a justifiable suspicion that pro-government subscribers might try to use it to punish or prevent the publication of critical coverage, even as the government avoids the taint of formal involvement in media suppression. The Electoral Commission, as authorized in a separate bill, also passed a code of conduct that applies to various participants in political campaigns, including the media. The code puts limits on projecting the winner before a formal announcement by the commission, a provision prompted by disparate and generally inaccurate polls prior to the 2001 elections.

Recommendations

- The National Assembly should enact a law that regulates campaign financing by requiring transparent and timely disclosure of all sources of campaign funds.

- The Assembly should regularly engage with civil society and private individuals through open parliamentary hearings at which the testimony of civil society groups and private citizens is solicited.
- The director of public prosecutions should make an explicit commitment to prosecute those who impede or intimidate journalists and the media.
- The government should comply with the IBA and ZNBC reform laws and submit nominees for the independent boards to the parliament for ratification.

CIVIL LIBERTIES

PROTECTION FROM STATE TERROR, UNJUSTIFIED IMPRISONMENT, AND TORTURE:	4.00
GENDER EQUITY:	3.50
RIGHTS OF ETHNIC, RELIGIOUS, AND OTHER DISTINCT GROUPS:	4.75
FREEDOM OF CONSCIENCE AND BELIEF:	6.00
FREEDOM OF ASSOCIATION AND ASSEMBLY:	5.00
CATEGORY AVERAGE:	**4.65**

Notwithstanding the high-level rhetorical support for various freedoms as exercised in the public and private spheres, numerous constraints continue to impede the full realization of Zambians' civil liberties.

The constitution bars torture, and there were no cases of public figures alleging such abuse between late 2004 and early 2007. In fact, torture claims were notably absent from two recent cases involving government opponents. In July 2005, Michael Sata, one of Mwanawasa's two emergent political rivals, was arrested on arguably politically motivated charges of sedition and espionage for his support of a mineworkers' strike. On his release on bail two weeks later, Sata did not allege that torture had taken place while he was incarcerated. Likewise, an aide loyal to former president Frederick Chiluba, Richard Sakala, spent five years in prison on corruption charges and did not report having been tortured.

Nonetheless, torture remains common at the less visible level of the local police precinct. The most extreme cases have resulted in death, such as when a man named Kennedy Zulu died from wounds he suffered while in police custody in Lusaka in 2005.[13] Working only from cases in which it was approached by complainants, the nongovernmental Legal Resources Foundation (LRF) reported many other instances of nonfatal torture. Most involved police officers trying to extract confessions from suspects in custody, overzealous apprehension methods, or abuse of authority motivated by apparent malice.[14]

Prisons in Zambia are appallingly overcrowded. The Zambia Central Prison, reportedly constructed in 1926, was designed to handle no more than a few hundred inmates. It has never been expanded and, as of April 2006, housed approximately 3,000 inmates.[15] Countrywide, more than 14,000 prisoners languish in a system designed for a maximum capacity of approximately 5,500.[16] Overcrowding results in the spread of epidemic diseases such as tuberculosis and AIDS, as well as malnourishment. Prison staffs have additional difficulty maintaining control—and protecting prisoners from other prisoners—in such conditions.[17]

A lack of resources throughout the criminal justice system exacerbates prison congestion, creating a disturbing pattern of detention without trial as legal proceedings are delayed amid shortages of attorneys, magistrates, and courtroom workers.

Citizens of Zambia do have the means to seek redress for the violation of their rights, although it is not clear how widely this is appreciated. The Permanent Human Rights Commission accepts petitions alleging the abrogation of human rights, and the LRF assists citizens with complaints against the police or other government bodies. Many of the cases the LRF takes on involve complainants who had previously tried without success to gain access to the local judicial process, suggesting that the ordinary means of pursuing the redress of human rights violations are often insufficient. Indeed, particularly with respect to cases of undue detention without trial, the same constraints and shortages that led to the original violation may affect the handling of the complaint as well.

Extended pretrial detentions weaken the force of the constitutional protection against arbitrary arrest. Political critics and opponents of the government are occasionally subject to detention, as in the case of Fred M'membe noted above. On a more routine basis, the state can employ defamation investigations without ever bringing charges, or it can bring charges that it has little intention of seeing through in court. A defamation investigation involves police questioning of suspects about their political views to determine whether they have violated restrictions on criticizing public officials, effectively allowing the authorities to detain and intimidate opponents. For example, Guy Scott, a former minister and an official in Sata's Patriotic Front, was questioned by police for two hours over statements he made at a Patriotic Front demonstration during President Mwanawasa's opening of parliament in 2006.[18]

An excessive caseload—and, at times, indifference—leads to inconsistent results when private citizens ask the police to investigate instances of abuse by private actors. Following a rash of mining-related deaths in 2004 and 2005, the perceived hesitancy of the MMD to put pressure on foreign investors who mistreated their employees or neglected worker safety became a campaign issue, although evidence of systematic abuse by foreign mine owners has not surfaced.

The status of women in Zambia is influenced both by formal, legal declarations and cultural practice. Article 23 of the constitution prohibits discrimination against women in matters to which the state is a party. However, in the fourth clause of the article, an exception is made "with respect to adoption, marriage, divorce, burial, devolution of property on death or other matters of personal law," thereby undermining the principle of equal treatment in a range of fundamentally important areas. While Article 23 protections directly apply to the government and its employment decisions, they do not clearly cover private actors, and there is little legal precedent for gender discrimination claims against private entities.

Domestic abuse is widespread in Zambia. One report found that over half of all Zambian women had experienced physical abuse.[19] Under customary law, women may be subject to physical abuse and the deprivation of property. The practice of "cleansing," in which a widower "cleanses" himself by having sex with a member of his deceased wife's family (ideally, under the practice, a virgin), or in which a widow is forced to have sex with a brother-in-law, continues in many parts of the country. In addition to frequently being nonconsensual, the practice contributes to the spread of AIDS. Although a 2005 amendment to the penal code increased the penalties for rape and domestic abuse, it did not address marital rape or nonphysical forms of abuse. Moreover, progress depends on more consistent and vigorous prosecution of abusers. The Victim Support Unit of the Zambian police is gaining more recognition but is still ill-equipped to handle a caseload that would reflect the true level of need in the country.

Human trafficking is also reported in Zambia, albeit more frequently in general terms than in specifics. An April 2006 UN report on patterns of human trafficking rated Zambia's role as a point of origin as "moderate," but called the frequency of its use as a transit point and destination "very low."[20] One notable case involved a Congolese woman who was caught bringing more than a dozen children into Zambia en route to Zimbabwe. The incident, for which the smuggler could only be fined in the absence of a legal framework on human trafficking, prompted the criminalization of the practice in the penal code.[21] As of the end of 2006, the state had not yet applied the new penalties to a criminal case. Zambia also acceded to the UN's Protocol to Prevent, Suppress and Punish Trafficking in Persons, Especially Women and Children, in April 2005.

In addition to women, Article 23 of the constitution protects ethnic, religious, and other distinct groups. Zambia is home to dozens of ethnic groups based on a variety of linguistic- or lineage-based affinities. Members of a given ethnic group may often expect and receive preferential treatment from their fellow members in private interactions, but discrimination in the public sector is rare, or at least rarely commented upon. Ethnic discrimination emerged as a point of debate during the 2006 election campaigns. While some observers perceived a split between the Tonga and Lozi ethnic groups in the selection of Hakainde Hichilema as the United Democratic Alliance (UDA) candidate, and Patriotic Front candidate Michael Sata alleged that both the UDA and the MMD were biased against the Bemba, the press and most observers bristled at the reintroduction of tribalist language in Zambian politics. The ruling party and President Mwanawasa generally avoided engaging in the debate.

Criticism of foreign nationals is less taboo than internal ethnic division, and it has mounted in recent years as Chinese investors, firms, and laborers have increased their presence in Zambia. A surge of anti-Chinese sentiment was reported at the time of Chinese president Hu

Jintao's visit to Zambia in February 2007.[22] Similarly, university students chanted anti-Chinese slogans in demonstrations following the funeral of forty-six workers who died in an explosion at a Chinese-owned mine in April 2005.[23]

Zambia remains a "Christian Nation" according to the constitution, although the Mung'omba Commission's draft constitution calls for the repeal of that clause. It has had minimal effect in any event, as state and society have been broadly tolerant of all religions practiced in Zambia. The state has generally refrained from interfering with the operation and leadership of religious bodies and from placing restrictions on religious observance, ceremonies, and education.

The government has increasingly taken the concerns and issues of people with disabilities seriously. The Electoral Act of 2006 gave the Electoral Commission the responsibility of ensuring that disabled Zambians could vote. Monitors of that year's elections reported only a few problems in this regard.[24]

Zambia has few limitations on the right of association, but authorities are somewhat restrictive of the right to assembly. The government does not limit membership in trade unions, although some private investors have reportedly taken stronger stances against union organization of late than the government traditionally has. The government also does not compel membership in any groups. The practice of card checks, whereby political party activists roam neighborhoods to ensure—by threat of force, if necessary—that residents hold a membership card for the party to which the activists belong, was reported less frequently in the 2006 election period than it had been in previous electoral cycles.

Zambians are generally free to organize and mobilize on behalf of their chosen causes. Under the Public Order Act, however, the state requires organizers to obtain police permission seven days before staging a demonstration. The act has drawn criticism for being both unduly restrictive and impractical, since it prevents protesters from responding quickly to unforeseen events. The authorities sometimes turn down requests to hold demonstrations. For example, police in Kasama denied the Patriotic Front permission to hold a rally in March 2006. The Oasis Forum, which advocates the repeal of the Public Order Act, has faced attempts to dissuade its members from holding demonstrations, but has not been denied a permit when it has applied. At least since 2001, Zambian protests have been predominantly peaceful affairs.

Recommendations

- The government should mobilize public prosecutors to pursue cases against police officers suspected of torture and brutality, and launch a public awareness campaign focusing on the rights of citizens with respect to detention and criminal charges.
- The government should construct new prisons and rehabilitate existing facilities to accommodate the surging inmate population, while employing alternatives to imprisonment for nonviolent offenders.
- The government should modify the constitution to ban all forms of discrimination against women, including in matters of divorce, custody, and inheritance.
- The police should increase the funding of Victim Support Units. The number of the units should be increased, and more resources should be devoted to publicizing their role.
- The National Assembly should modify or repeal the Public Order Act to allow spontaneous demonstrations.

RULE OF LAW

INDEPENDENT JUDICIARY:	5.00
PRIMACY OF RULE OF LAW IN CIVIL AND CRIMINAL MATTERS:	3.33
ACCOUNTABILITY OF SECURITY FORCES AND MILITARY TO CIVILIAN AUTHORITIES:	4.75
PROTECTION OF PROPERTY RIGHTS:	3.33
EQUAL TREATMENT UNDER THE LAW:	4.33
CATEGORY AVERAGE:	**4.15**

The independence of the judiciary remains fairly strong in Zambia. Although the constitution endows the president with the power to appoint and dismiss judges, the judiciary is relatively free of political, religious, and ethnic influence. The Mwanawasa administration did not exercise its authority to dismiss sitting judges in the 2005–2006 period, and the government generally complies even with unfavorable judicial decisions.

The judiciary is constrained by economics, however. The country's poverty and lack of budgetary resources cause absenteeism among court officials (including judges) due to outsized caseloads, moonlighting and sickness leaves; these factors result in extended trials, detentions, and an overall slowdown of the legal process. The economic conditions of the judiciary were brought into sharp relief when magistrates went on strike in 2006, citing low pay and benefits.[25] Although the University of Zambia and Evelyn Hone Technical College both offer degree programs in legal and paralegal studies, more specific job-related training within the judiciary tends to rely on donor funding, which can be sporadic. Moreover, many lawyers trained in Zambia end up working in South Africa or Botswana, where professional remuneration is higher.

Although the courts have demonstrated a tendency to treat people of all ethnicities, religions, and nationalities equally, economic differences have created the conditions for unequal treatment. High-profile cases involving wealthy defendants are likely to get swifter attention than others. Economic disparities in society, paired with an overburdened judiciary, provide ample opportunities for undue financial influence on judicial rulings, although no such instances have been reported since the resignation of Chief Justice Matthew Ngulube for allegedly accepting bribes in 2003.

Under the constitution, defendants are considered to be innocent until proven guilty in court. Defendants have a right to legal aid when they cannot afford representation, but are often constrained by the scarcity of available counsel. The constitution explicitly declares that the government is not responsible for paying state-provided counsel. The activity of NGOs has partially filled the void left by the inadequacy of the government's legal aid office, and in the past two years the Ministry of Justice has worked to expand the traditionally government-staffed legal aid program to incorporate greater participation by professionals in private practice.[26]

The military and police do not exert political control over the judiciary. Indeed, the military has tended to stay out of politics more generally in Zambia, which has not experienced a coup in its forty-three years of independence. Officers of the law have exhibited poor levels of respect for human rights, however, as noted above. Police are at best infrequently prosecuted for illegal or unduly violent acts committed in the course of duty. Police officers are also regularly cited in news reports for pursuing personal agendas in violent and intimidating ways.[27] Still, the police and military remained admirably impartial during the political campaigns and elections of 2006, contributing to the smooth execution of the balloting itself. One report was filed with the Legal Resources Foundation of a military officer claiming harassment by superior officers for his failure to support a particular political party.[28]

The state has placed an increased emphasis on property rights in recent years, and the judiciary is generally adequate in its enforcement of such rights. Conflicts have arisen between traditional authorities and the state over the allocation of land to foreigners, including immigrant farmers from South Africa and Zimbabwe, and in one case the government of Libya.[29] In March 2007, in an action not seen since the Kaunda era, the government moved to demolish untitled (and therefore "illegal") settlements around the country, starting in Lusaka.[30] No compensation was provided to residents. Insofar as many of the targeted areas are slums on the outskirts of cities, where opposition to Mwanawasa and support for the Patriotic Front's Michael Sata is high, the demolition campaign has at least the appearance of political motivation and is likely to stoke political tensions.

Recommendations

- Article 96 of the constitution, which allows the president to revoke judicial appointments without justification, should be amended to permit only narrow and specific grounds for dismissal, such as proven corruption, criminal conviction, or incapacitation.
- The government should take concrete measures to reduce judicial absenteeism, including incentive-based remuneration for all court employees.
- The government should provide more state funding for the legal representation of indigent defendants who face possible jail time.
- The authorities should halt slum demolitions and instead pursue a program to grant legal property titles to residents.

ANTICORRUPTION AND TRANSPARENCY

ENVIRONMENT TO PROTECT AGAINST CORRUPTION:	3.20
EXISTENCE OF LAWS AND ETHICAL STANDARDS BETWEEN	
PRIVATE AND PUBLIC SECTORS:	3.75
ENFORCEMENT OF ANTICORRUPTION LAWS:	3.75
GOVERNMENTAL TRANSPARENCY:	3.14
CATEGORY AVERAGE:	**3.46**

President Mwanawasa has placed anticorruption efforts at the center of his administration's agenda, beginning with his politically costly pursuit of his predecessor, Frederick Chiluba. The primary vehicle for this effort has been the Task Force on Economic Plunder, an ad hoc body comprising members of standing organs such as the Anticorruption Commission and the Drug Enforcement Commission. The task force has drawn criticism for failing to produce convictions of high-profile officials (including Chiluba, whose trial appears to be on hiatus due to health issues) and for being vulnerable to political pressure from the president.

In 2005, a case involving a former Health Ministry permanent secretary accused of misusing public funds provided the task force with an opportunity to assert its independence. The official had recently voiced his support for Mwanawasa, who in turn ordered the chief prosecutor of the task force to drop the case. The prosecutor refused and ultimately secured a conviction.[31] The incident served to raise the credibility of the body among those who suspected it might be a mere vehicle for political vendettas, although it also highlighted the uncertainty over the task force's legal grounding. Without addressing its legal status, Mwanawasa extended the mandate of the task force indefinitely in January 2007.[32] To date, most of the task force's attention has been focused on Chiluba-era activities. However, in a move signaling that the current administration is not immune from scrutiny, Mwanawasa fired his minister of lands in February 2007 after discovering that she had distributed state property to members of her family.[33] The dismissal sends a strong message that the use of public office for private gain will not be tolerated.

Zambia also has asset-declaration measures for public officials. These apply to the president (via the constitution) and to government ministers and deputy ministers (via the parliamentary and ministerial code of conduct). Nonministers, permanent secretaries, and members of the judiciary are not required to disclose their assets, liabilities, and incomes. While compliance with the procedures is a matter of public record, the asset-declaration provisions are weakened by the difficulty members of the public face in obtaining copies, and by the absence of a verification mechanism.[34]

The administration has had less success extending its anticorruption message to lower levels of the government. Indeed, while the focus on grand corruption is laudable, it runs the risk—in a world of limited resources—of succeeding at the expense of efforts to control petty corruption. Even though the state holds fewer economic assets than it did during the Kaunda years, the legacy of several decades of state domination of the economy is a veritable culture of regulation. With it comes an expectation that virtually any public act requires advance permission or approval by the government. The World Bank's International Finance Corporation found that it would take 6 procedures and 35 days to start a business in Zambia, and 16 procedures and 196 days to legally begin to construct a warehouse.[35] Although corruption was not formally accounted for in these calculations, each step represents a potential opportunity for bribery demands. Private individuals are affected as well: a 2005 survey by Transparency International (TI) Zambia found that 79 percent of Lusaka residents believed "a service could be provided only if one paid something for it."[36] Although legal recourse for victims of corruption exists, many judge the hassle of pursuing it to be too great, particularly without any guarantee that additional layers of corruption will not impede their efforts. The same TI survey found that the courts themselves were perceived as moderately corrupt.[37]

A 2006 TI report suggested that petty corruption had increased over the course of the Mwanawasa administration.[38] In the 2005 survey, respondents rated the police and the Roads Office as the most corrupt government services. Over half of the respondents reported having been asked for a bribe at a police roadblock.[39] In that context, an April 2005 decision by the Lusaka police to cease most roadblocks in the city is notably positive.[40] Schools were rated as significantly less corrupt, although respondents did cite the need to make informal payments to headmasters to reserve a school placement.

Mwanawasa's intention to make fighting corruption a priority has created something of a paradox for the Task Force on Economic Plunder and the more conventional institutional tools to be employed in the effort. Mwanawasa has sought to exert presidential control over officials and institutions such as the director of public prosecutions, the auditor general, the Anticorruption Commission, the Drug Enforcement Commission, and the investigator general. While the multiplicity of actors may suggest an expansive effort to fight corruption, it also makes possible the politicization of the effort, in that Mwanawasa can focus on the body or bodies that he feels will support his agenda. Thus the Drug Enforcement Commission has played an increasingly large role in anticorruption efforts, while the investigator general's Commission on Investigations, which serves an ombudsman's role in Zambia, has been largely absent from the fight. Insufficiently funded and decentralized, the investigator general's office is an ineffective tool for civil society to hold the government accountable. Whistle-blowers in Zambia are not protected by law, a situation that may also detract from ground-up efforts to combat corruption.

Finally, citizens generally lack access to information about government officials and spending policies. As noted earlier, the government has considered a Freedom of Information bill for several years, but in late 2006 the government decided against putting the bill before parliament.[41] The public has, in theory, access to information about the government's budget and the bidding process for government contracts. The budgeting process is primarily controlled by the government—that is, the president and his cabinet—and parliamentary input is relatively scant. Press reports on budgetary presentations suggest little alteration between the president's budget proposal and the final version approved by the National Assembly. Information about revenues and spending is difficult to obtain, particularly in a timely manner. A significant portion of government funds come from outside aid, which is treated as off-budget and is therefore less transparent than normal spending. As most dissemination of budget information is carried out via the internet, access is limited to relatively wealthy citizens with computers and internet connections. Oral dissemination of the type of fiscal information described above (or, indeed, of almost any element of government's workings) would serve the blind, illiterate, and those without internet access, but no such effort has been undertaken.

Recommendations

- Asset, liability, and income declaration requirements should be expanded to include all members of parliament, permanent secretaries, judges, and magistrates. Anticorruption Commission resources should be employed to publicize and verify those declarations.
- The police should reduce the number of roadblocks and checkpoints nationwide, maintaining only those for which there is an active need to detect smuggling.
- The National Assembly should enact legislation to protect whistle-blowers.
- The government should elevate the profile of the investigator general and the Commission on Investigation through a publicity campaign that gives citizens a greater awareness of their roles, their responsibilities, and the tools available to them in fighting corruption.
- The National Assembly should debate the Freedom of Information bill and clear a robust version for the president's signature.

NOTES

[1] Source: author's calculation using World Development Indicators Online Edition, http://ddp-ext.worldbank.org/ext/DDPQQ/member.do?method=getMembers, accessed 15 May 2007.

[2] Data for 2004. Source: author's calculation using World Development Indicators Online Edition, http://ddp-ext.worldbank.org/ext/DDPQQ/member.do?method=getMembers, accessed 15 May 2007.

[3] The exception, of course, is 1991, when the MMD unseated UNIP in Zambia's return to multiparty politics. Since then, however, the MMD used its rule-making abilities and access to state resources to its advantage in 1996 and 2001. Prior to 1991, UNIP's prohibition on opposition parties represented the ultimate in incumbency bias.

[4] Media Institute of Southern Africa, "MISA Highlights Bias in News Coverage Ahead of Local Elections," news release, 27 September 2006, http://www.ifex.org/en/content/view/full/77378/.

[5] Bivan Saluseki, Nomusa Michelo, and Kwenda Paipi, "PF cadres and police clash over election results," *Post of Zambia*, 1 October 2006.

[6] For example, see Isabel Chimangeni, "State blows lid off Coalition 2005 Plot," *Times of Zambia*, 31 December 2004; "Silavwe slams NGO's dependency syndrome," *Times of Zambia*, 12 December 2004.

7   See Reporters Without Borders, "Police Launch Manhunt before Finally Arresting Editor Who Criticized President," news release, 10 November 2005.

8   See Committee to Protect Journalists (CPJ), "The Post Censored," 15 June 2005; CPJ, "Fred M'membe, the Post Harassed," June 29, 2005, http://www.cpj.org/cases05/africa_cases05/zambia.html.

9   See Media Institute of Southern Africa, "Police Question 'Radio Phoenix' Talk Show Host," news release, June 2005; Bivan Saluseki, "CPJ doubts Zambia's commitment to freedom of expression," *Post of Zambia*, 29 June 2005.

10 See Media Institute of Southern Africa, "Television Crew from State-Owned Broadcaster Harassed by Crowd at Opposition Rally," news release, September 13, 2006, www.ifex.org/en/content/view/full/77019/; Media Institute of Southern Africa, "Photojournalist Harassed at Press Conference by Opposition Party Supporters," news release, 29 May 2006, www.ifex.org/en/content/view/full/74727/.

11 Noel Sichawe, "Court awards Sata injunction against Zambia Daily Mail," *Post of Zambia*, 30 August 2006.

12 "State wins media case," *Times of Zambia*, 16 March 2007.

13 See Amnesty International, "Zambia Overview," *Report 2006* (London: Amnesty International, 2006), http://web.amnesty.org/report2006/zmb-summary-eng.

14 The Legal Resources Foundation's online newsletter, back issues of which are available at www.lrf.org.zm/newsarchives.htm, features many examples of each of these. For an example of torture, see "Ndola Police Officers Torture Suspect," *LRF Newsletter*, August 2005, www.lrf.org.zm/Newsletter/august2005/ndolapolice.html. For an example of overzealous apprehension methods, see "Chisamba Cops Shot Man in the Arm," *LRF Newsletter*, October 2005, www.lrf.org.zm/Newsletter/october2005/chisambacops.html. For an example of malicious abuse of authority by police, see "L/stone Cops Batter Woman Over Brother's Case," *LRF Newsletter*, June 2005, www.lrf.org.zm/Newsletter/june2005/lstone.html.

15 See Bivan Saluseki, "Mumbuwa bemoans overcrowding in prisons," *Post of Zambia*, 16 April 2006.

16 Speedwell Mupuchi, "Prisons commissioner urges judiciary to review prisons' sentencing policy," *Post of Zambia*, 18 January 2006.

17 See, for example, "Juveniles Sodomised at Kamfinsa," *LRF Newsletter*, December 2004, http://www.lrf.org.zm/Newsletter/december2004/juveniles.html.

18 See McDonald Chipenzi, "Police charge Dr. Scott," *Post of Zambia*, 19 January 2006.

19 See "ZAMBIA: More Than 10 Girls Raped Every Week," *IRIN Reports* (Nairobi: UN Office for the Coordination of Humanitarian Affairs, 27 November 2006), www.irinnews.org/report.aspx?reportid=61665.

20 *Trafficking in Persons: Global Patterns* (New York: United Nations Office on Drugs and Crime, April 2006), www.unodc.org/pdf/traffickinginpersons_report_2006ver2.pdf.

21 See "Permsec condemns K2m fine on human trafficker," *Times of Zambia*, 15 June 2005.

22 See Dickson Jere, "Anti-Chinese sentiment high in Zambia," *Independent Online* (IOL), 1 February 2007, www.iol.co.za/index.php?set_id=1&click_id=68&art_id=qw117031716 0274B252.

23 See Brighton Phiri, "Bishop O'regan blames govt for Chambishi deaths," *Post of Zambia*, 25 April 2005.

24 See *Zambia: Tripartite Elections, September 2006* (Oslo: University of Oslo, Norwegian Centre for Human Rights, Norwegian Resource Bank for Democracy and Human Rights, Report 17/2006, December 2006).

25 Mwala Kaluka, "Saki urges govt to be proactive in resolving workers' grievances," *Post of Zambia*, 6 October 2006.

26 See "State to provide free legal services to needy citizens," *Times of Zambia*, 10 March 2007.

27 See, for example, Monica Kunda, "Mansa Cop Beats Man Over Ex-Girl Friend," *LRF Newsletter*, January 2006, www.lrf.org.zm/Newsletter/january2006/mansacopbeatsman .html; Madube Pasi Siyauya, "Kalomo Cop Rapes Woman," *LRF Newsletter*, May 2005, www.lrf.org.zm/Newsletter/may2005/kalomo.html.

28 Madube Pasi Siyauya, "Army Harasses Soldiers For Supporting Opposition," *LRF Newsletter*, October 2006, www.lrf.org.zm/Newsletter/october2006/army.html.

29 Alfarson Sinalungu, "Allocation of land to Libya is questionable—Miyanda," *Post of Zambia*, 25 May 2005.

30 See "Zambia Demolition Campaign Begins," *BBC News Online*, 10 March 2007, http: //news.bbc.co.uk/2/hi/africa/6438339.stm.

31 "Former health secretary jailed for corruption," *Times of Zambia*, 22 February 2007.

32 "Task force on corruption mandate extended," *Times of Zambia*, 10 January 2007.

33 Chris Mfula, "Zambia Investigates Suspect Land Deals," *IOL/Reuters*, 2 March 2007, http://www.iol.co.za/index.php?click_id=68&set_id=1&art_id=nw20070302120658546 C929711.

34 Alfred Chanda, "Position Paper on Disclosure Laws in Zambia" (Lusaka: Transparency International [TI]–Zambia, February 2005), www.tizambia.org.zm/download/uploads /POSITION_PAPER_ON_DISCLOSURE_LAWS_IN_ZAMBIA.pdf, accessed 1 March 2007; alternative web location: http://209.85.165.104/search?q=cache:Z-5amaaaz C0J:www.tizambia.org.zm/download/uploads/POSITION_PAPER_ON_DISCLO SURE_LAWS_IN_ZAMBIA.pdf+disclosure+zambia+chanda&hl=en&ct=clnk&cd=4 gl=us, accessed 18 May 2007.

35 International Finance Corporation, "Doing Business: Explore Economies: Zambia," www.doingbusiness.org/ExploreEconomies/Default.aspx?economyid=207, accessed 18 May 18 2007. Zambia rates more favorably than the average of its Sub-Saharan African peers but well below that of the OECD countries.

36 Musonda Lemba, "Opinion Poll on Lusaka Residents' Perception of Corruption" (TI-Zambia, January 2005), 12, http://www.tizambia.org.zm/download/uploads/OPINION _POLL_ON_LUSAKA_RESIDENTS_PERCEPTIONS_OF_CORRUPTION.pdf.

37 Lemba, "Opinion Poll," 10.

38 Darlington Mwendabai, "TIZ findings show increase in petty corruption," *Times of Zambia*, 4 May 2006.

39 Lemba, "Opinion Poll," 11.

40 "Lusaka police halt roadblocks," *Times of Zambia*, 18 April 2005.

41 McDonald Chipenzi, "Freedom of information bill won't be tabled soon, says Mwaanga," *Post of Zambia*, 16 February 2006.

SURVEY METHODOLOGY

Countries at the Crossroads is an annual survey of government performance in sixty strategically important countries worldwide that are at a critical crossroads in determining their political future. The in-depth comparative analyses and quantitative ratings—examining government accountability, civil liberties, rule of law, and anticorruption efforts and transparency—are intended to help international policy makers identify areas of progress, as well as to highlight areas of concern that could be addressed in diplomatic efforts and reform assistance. A new edition of *Crossroads* is published each year, with one set of thirty countries analyzed in odd-numbered years and the other thirty in even-numbered years.

The 2007 edition is the fourth in the *Countries at the Crossroads* series. It evaluates the countries last examined in the 2005 edition, providing an opportunity for a year-on-year analysis and assessment of the extent to which this group of countries is backsliding, stalling, or improving in terms of democratic governance. The time frame for events covered is November 1, 2004, through March 31, 2007.

In cooperation with a team of methodology experts, Freedom House designed a methodology that includes a questionnaire used both to prepare analytical narratives and for numerical ratings for each government. The survey methodology provides authors with a transparent and consistent guide to scoring and analyzing the countries under review, and uses identical benchmarks for both narratives and ratings, rendering the two indicators mutually reinforcing. The final result is a system of comparative ratings accompanied by narratives that reflect governments' commitment to passing good laws and also their records in upholding them.

Freedom House enlisted the participation of prominent scholars and analysts to author the survey's country reports. In preparing the survey's written analyses with accompanying comparative ratings, Freedom House undertook a systematic gathering of data. Each country narrative report is approximately 7,000 words long. Expert regional advisers reviewed the draft reports, providing written comments and requests for revisions, additions, or clarifications. Authors were asked to respond as fully as possible to all of the questions posed when composing the analytical narratives.

For all countries in the survey, Freedom House, in consultation with the report authors and academic advisers, has provided detailed numerical ratings. Authors produced a first round of ratings by assigning scores on a scale of 0–7 for each of the eighty-three methodology questions, where 0 represents weakest performance and 7 represents strongest performance. The scores were then aggregated into eighteen subcategories and four main thematic areas. The regional advisers and Freedom House staff systematically reviewed all country ratings on a comparative basis to ensure accuracy and fairness. All final ratings decisions rest with Freedom House.

In devising a framework for evaluating government performance, Freedom House sought to develop a scale broad enough to capture degrees of variation so that comparisons could be made between countries in the current year, and so that future time-series comparisons might be made to assess a country's progress in these areas relative to past performance. These scales achieve an effective balance between a scoring system that is too broad—which may make it difficult for analysts to make fine distinctions between different scores—and one that is too narrow—which may make it difficult to capture degrees of variation between countries and therefore more difficult to recognize how much a given government's performance has improved or eroded over time.

Narrative essays and scoring were applied to the following main areas of performance, which Freedom House considers to be key to evaluating the state of democratic governance within a country:

ACCOUNTABILITY AND PUBLIC VOICE

- Free and fair electoral laws and elections
- Effective and accountable government
- Civic engagement and civic monitoring
- Media independence and freedom of expression

CIVIL LIBERTIES

- Protection from state terror, unjustified imprisonment, and torture
- Gender equity

- Rights of ethnic, religious, and other distinct groups
- Freedom of conscience and belief
- Freedom of association and assembly

RULE OF LAW

- Independent judiciary
- Primacy of rule of law in civil and criminal matters
- Accountability of security forces and military to civilian authorities
- Protection of property rights
- Equal treatment under the law

ANTICORRUPTION AND TRANSPARENCY

- Environment to protect against corruption
- Existence of laws, ethical standards, and boundaries between private and public sectors
- Enforcement of anticorruption laws
- Governmental transparency

Scoring Range

The survey rates countries' performance on each methodology question on a scale of 0–7, with 0 representing the weakest performance and 7 the strongest. The scoring scale is as follows:

Score of 0–2: Countries that receive a score of 0, 1, or 2 ensure no or very few adequate protections, legal standards, or rights in the rated category. Laws protecting the rights of citizens or the justice of the political process are minimal, rarely enforced, or routinely abused by the authorities.

Score of 3–4: Countries that receive a score of 3 or 4 provide some adequate protections, legal standards, or rights in the rated category. Legal protections are weak, and enforcement of the law is inconsistent or corrupt.

Score of 5: Countries that receive a score of 5 provide many adequate protections, legal standards or rights in the rated category. Rights and political standards are protected, but enforcement may be unreliable and some abuses may occur. A score of 5 is considered to be the basic standard of democratic performance.

Score of 6–7: Countries that receive a score of 6 or 7 ensure all or nearly all adequate protections, legal standards, or rights in the rated category. Legal protections are strong and enforced fairly. Citizens have access to legal redress when their rights are violated, and the political system functions smoothly.

METHODOLOGY QUESTIONS

1. **Accountability and Public Voice**
   a. *Free and fair electoral laws and elections*
      i. Is the authority of government based upon the will of the people as expressed by regular, free, and fair elections under fair electoral laws, with universal and equal suffrage, open to multiple parties, conducted by secret ballot, monitored by independent electoral authorities, with honest tabulation of ballots, and free of fraud and intimidation?
      ii. Are there equal campaigning opportunities for all parties?
      iii. Is there the opportunity for the effective rotation of power among a range of different political parties representing competing interests and policy options?
      iv. Are there adequate regulations to prevent undue influence of economically privileged interests (e.g., effective campaign finance laws), and are they enforced?
   b. *Effective and accountable government*
      i. Are the executive, legislative, and judicial branches of government able to oversee the actions of one another and hold each other accountable for any excessive exercise of power?
      ii. Does the state system ensure that people's political choices are free from domination by the specific interests of power groups (e.g., the military, foreign powers, totalitarian parties, regional hierarchies, and/or economic oligarchies)?
      iii. Is the civil service selected, promoted, and dismissed on the basis of open competition and by merit?
      iv. Is the state engaged in issues reflecting the interests of women; ethnic, religious, and other distinct groups; and disabled people?
   c. *Civic engagement and civic monitoring*
      i. Are civic groups able to testify, comment on, and influence pending government policy or legislation?

    ii. Are nongovernmental organizations free from legal imped-
iments from the state and from onerous requirements for
registration?

   iii. Are donors and funders of civic organizations and public
policy institutes free of state pressures?

  d. *Media independence and freedom of expression*

     i. Does the state support constitutional or other legal protec-
tions for freedom of expression and an environment conducive to media freedom?

    ii. Does the state oppose the use of onerous libel, security, or
other laws to punish through either excessive fines or imprisonment those who scrutinize government officials and
policies?

   iii. Does the government protect journalists from extralegal
intimidation, arbitrary arrest and detention, or physical violence at the hands of state authorities or any other actor,
including through fair and expeditious investigation and
prosecution when cases do occur?

   iv. Does the state refrain from direct and indirect censorship of
print or broadcast media?

    v. Does the state hinder access to the internet as an informa-
tion source?

   vi. Does the state refrain from funding the media in order to
propagandize, primarily provide official points of view,
and/or limit access by opposition parties and civic critics?

   vii. Does the government otherwise refrain from attempting to
influence media content (e.g., through direct ownership
of distribution networks or printing facilities, prohibitive
tariffs, onerous registration requirements, selective distribution of advertising, or bribery)?

  viii. Does the state protect the freedom of cultural expression
(e.g., in fictional works, art, music, theater, etc.)?

2. Civil Liberties

  a. *Protection from state terror, unjustified imprisonment, and torture*

     i. Is there protection against torture by officers of the state,
including through effective punishment in cases where torture is found to have occurred?

    ii. Are prison conditions respectful of the human dignity of inmates?

    iii. Does the state effectively protect against or respond to attacks on political opponents or other peaceful activists?

    iv. Are there effective protections against arbitrary arrest, including of political opponents or other peaceful activists?

    v. Is there effective protection against long-term detention without trial?

    vi. Does the state protect citizens from abuse by private/non-state actors?

    vii. Do citizens have means of effective petition and redress when their rights are violated by state authorities?

b. *Gender equity*

    i. Does the state ensure that both men and women are entitled to the full enjoyment of all civil and political rights?

    ii. Does the state take measures, including legislation, to modify or abolish existing laws, regulations, customs, and practices that constitute discrimination against women?

    iii. Does the state take measures to prevent trafficking in women?

    iv. Does the state make reasonable efforts to protect against gender discrimination in employment and occupation?

c. *Rights of ethnic, religious, and other distinct groups*

    i. Does the state ensure that persons belonging to ethnic, religious, and other distinct groups exercise fully and effectively all their human rights and fundamental freedoms (including ethnic, cultural, and linguistic rights) without discrimination and with full equality before the law?

    ii. Does the state take measures, including legislation, to modify or abolish existing laws, regulations, customs, and practices that constitute discrimination against ethnic, religious, and other distinct groups?

    iii. Does the state make a progressive effort to modify or abolish existing laws, regulations, customs, and practices that constitute discrimination against people with disabilities?

    iv. Does the state make reasonable efforts to protect against discrimination against ethnic, religious, and other distinct groups in employment and occupation?

    d. Freedom of conscience and belief
- i. Does the state accept the right of its citizens to hold religious beliefs of their choice and practice their religion as they deem appropriate, within reasonable constraints?
- ii. Does the state refrain from involvement in the appointment of religious or spiritual leaders and in the internal organizational activities of faith-related organizations?
- iii. Does the state refrain from placing restrictions on religious observance, religious ceremony, and religious education?

    e. Freedom of association and assembly
- i. Does the state recognize every person's right to freedom of association and assembly?
- ii. Does the state respect the right to form, join, and participate in free and independent trade unions?
- iii. Are citizens protected from being compelled by the state to belong to an association, either directly or indirectly (e.g., because certain indispensable benefits are conferred on members)?
- iv. Does the state effectively protect and recognize the rights of civic associations, business organizations, and political organizations to organize, mobilize, and advocate for peaceful purposes?
- v. Does the state permit demonstrations and public protests and refrain from using excessive force against them?

3. Rule of Law
    a. Independent judiciary
- i. Is there independence, impartiality, and nondiscrimination in the administration of justice, including from economic, political, or religious influences?
- ii. Are judges and magistrates protected from interference by the executive and/or legislative branches?
- iii. Do legislative, executive, and other governmental authorities comply with judicial decisions, which are not subject to change except through established procedures for judicial review?
- iv. Are judges appointed, promoted, and dismissed in a fair and unbiased manner?

     v. Are judges appropriately trained in order to carry out justice in a fair and unbiased manner?

b. *Primacy of rule of law in civil and criminal matters*

     i. According to the legal system, is everyone charged with a criminal offense presumed innocent until proven guilty?

     ii. Are citizens given a fair, public, and timely hearing by a competent, independent, and impartial tribunal?

     iii. Do citizens have the right and access to independent counsel?

     iv. Does the state provide citizens charged with serious felonies with access to independent counsel when it is beyond their means?

     v. Are prosecutors independent of political direction and control?

     vi. Are public officials and ruling party actors prosecuted for the abuse of power and other wrongdoing?

c. *Accountability of security forces and the military to civilian authorities*

     i. Is there effective and democratic civilian state control of the police, military, and internal security forces through the judicial, legislative, and executive branches?

     ii. Do police, military, and internal security services refrain from interference and/or involvement in the political process?

     iii. Are the police, military, and internal security services held accountable for any abuses of power for personal gain?

     iv. Do members of the police, military, and internal security services respect human rights?

d. *Protection of property rights*

     i. Does the state give everyone the right to own property alone as well as in association with others?

     ii. Does the state adequately enforce property rights and contracts, including through adequate provisions for indigenous populations?

     iii. Does the state protect citizens from the arbitrary and/or unjust deprivation of their property (e.g., Does the state unjustly revoke property titles for governmental use or to pursue a political agenda)?

e. *Equal treatment under the law*

     i. Are all persons entitled to equal protection under the law?

     ii. Are all persons equal before the courts and tribunals?

    iii. Is discrimination on grounds of gender, ethnic origin, nationality, and sexual orientation prohibited and prosecuted by the state?

4. Anticorruption and Transparency

  a. Environment to protect against corruption

    i. Is the government free from excessive bureaucratic regulations, registration requirements, and/or other controls that increase opportunities for corruption?

    ii. Does the state refrain from excessive involvement in the economy?

    iii. Does the state enforce the separation of public office from the personal interests of public officeholders?

    iv. Are there adequate financial disclosure procedures that prevent conflicts of interest among public officials (e.g., Are the assets declarations of public officials open to public and media scrutiny and verification)?

    v. Does the state adequately protect against conflicts of interest in the private sector?

  b. Existence of laws, ethical standards, and boundaries between private and public sectors

    i. Does the state enforce an effective legislative or administrative process designed to promote integrity and to prevent, detect, and punish the corruption of public officials?

    ii. Does the state provide victims of corruption with adequate mechanisms to pursue their rights?

    iii. Does the state protect higher education from pervasive corruption and graft (e.g., Are bribes necessary to gain admission or good grades)?

    iv. Does the tax administrator implement effective internal audit systems to ensure the accountability of tax collection?

  c. Enforcement of anticorruption laws

    i. Are there effective and independent investigative and auditing bodies created by the government (e.g., an auditor general or ombudsman), and do they function without impediment or political pressure?

  ii. Are allegations of corruption by government officials at the national and local levels thoroughly investigated and prosecuted without prejudice?

  iii. Are allegations of corruption given wide and unbiased airing in the news media?

  iv. Do whistle-blowers, anticorruption activists, and investigators have a legal environment that protects them, so they feel secure about reporting cases of bribery and corruption?

d. *Governmental transparency*

  i. Is there significant legal, regulatory, and judicial transparency as manifested through public access to government information?

  ii. Do citizens have a legal right to obtain information about government operations, and means to petition government agencies for it?

  iii. Does the state make a progressive effort to provide information about government services and decisions in formats and settings that are accessible to disabled people?

  iv. Is the executive budget-making process comprehensive and transparent and subject to meaningful legislative review and scrutiny?

  v. Does the government publish detailed and accurate accounting of expenditures in a timely fashion?

  vi. Does the state ensure transparency, open bidding, and effective competition in the awarding of government contracts?

  vii. Does the government enable the fair and legal administration and distribution of foreign assistance?

771

ABOUT FREEDOM HOUSE

**Freedom House is an independent private organization
supporting the expansion of freedom throughout the world.**

Freedom is possible only in democratic political systems in which governments are accountable to their own people, the rule of law prevails, and freedoms of expression, association, and belief are guaranteed. Working directly with courageous men and women around the world to support nonviolent civic initiatives in societies where freedom is threatened, Freedom House functions as a catalyst for change through its unique mix of analysis, advocacy, and action.

- **Analysis.** Freedom House's rigorous research methodology has earned the organization a reputation as the leading source of information on the state of freedom around the globe. Since 1972, Freedom House has published *Freedom in the World*, an annual survey of political rights and civil liberties experienced in every country of the world. The survey is complemented by an annual review of press freedom, an analysis of transitions in the post-Communist world, and other publications.

- **Advocacy.** Freedom House seeks to encourage American policy makers, as well as other governments and international institutions, to adopt policies that advance human rights and democracy around the world. Freedom House has been instrumental in the founding of the worldwide Community of Democracies, has actively campaigned for a reformed Human Rights Council at the United Nations, and presses the Millennium Challenge Corporation to adhere to high standards of eligibility for recipient countries.

- **Action.** Through exchanges, grants, and technical assistance, Freedom House provides training and support to human rights defenders, civil society organizations, and members of the media in order to strengthen indigenous reform efforts in countries around the globe.

Founded in 1941 by Eleanor Roosevelt, Wendell Willkie, and other Americans concerned with mounting threats to peace and democracy, Freedom House has long been a vigorous proponent of democratic values and a steadfast opponent of dictatorships of the far left and the far right. The organization's diverse Board of Trustees is composed of a bipartisan mix of business and labor leaders, former senior government officials, scholars, and journalists who agree that the promotion of democracy and human rights abroad is vital to America's interests abroad.